D0078495

· THE ·
WARREN
COURT

· THE · WARREN COURT

A Retrospective

EDITED BY
BERNARD SCHWARTZ

New York Oxford
Oxford University Press
1996

Oxford University Press

Oxford New York
Athens Auckland Bangkok Bogota Bombay
Buenos Aires Calcutta Cape Town Dar es Salaam
Delhi Florence Hong Kong Istanbul Karachi
Kuala Lumpur Madras Madrid Melbourne
Mexico City Nairobi Paris Singapore
Taipei Tokyo Toronto

and associated companies in
Berlin Ibadan

Published by Oxford University Press, Inc.
198 Madison Avenue, New York, New York 10016

Library of Congress Cataloging-in-Publication Data
The Warren Court : a retrospective / Bernard Schwartz, editor.
p. cm.
Papers presented to a Warren Court conference in 1994.
Includes index.
ISBN 0-19-510439-0
1. United States. Supreme Court—History. 2. Warren, Earl
1891–1974. I. Schwartz, Bernard, 1923–
KF8742.A5W367 1994
347.73'26—dc20 95-26376
[347.30735]

1 3 5 7 9 8 6 4 2
Printed in the United States of America
on acid-free paper

PREFACE

A judge-made revolution? The very term seems an oxymoron. Yet it cannot be denied that the Warren Court brought about what Justice Abe Fortas once termed "the most profound and pervasive revolution ever achieved by substantially peaceful means." More than that, it was the rarest of all political animals: a judicially inspired and led revolution. Without the Warren Court decisions giving ever-wider effect to individual rights, most of the movements that have so transformed American society would never have gotten off the ground. In terms of creative impact, the tenure of Earl Warren can only be compared with that of John Marshall.

Now that the Warren Court belongs to history, it is time for a retrospective look at its accomplishments. That was the purpose of a major conference in 1994 at the University of Tulsa College of Law. This volume is based upon the papers presented at the conference. It examines the Warren Court's jurisprudence, the Justices, and the Court's impact upon the nation. This commemorative volume should be a notable reminder of the Court that so transformed the law and the society.

Tulsa, Oklahoma
June 1996

B. S.

CONTENTS

II. THE JUSTICES

III. A BROADER PERSPECTIVE

CONTRIBUTORS

Richard S. Arnold, Chief Judge, Eighth Circuit United States Court of Appeals.

William J. Brennan, Jr., Associate Justice (Retired), United States Supreme Court.

Tyrone Brown, Law Clerk to Chief Justice Warren, 1967–1968; Federal Communications Commissioner, 1977–1981; Telecommunications Attorney.

George E. Bushnell, Jr., President, American Bar Association, 1994–1995.

Louis D. Bilionis, Associate Professor of Law, University of North Carolina.

Julius L. Chambers, Chancellor, North Carolina Central University; Former Director-Counsel, NAACP Legal Defense Fund.

Norman Dorsen, Stokes Professor, New York University Law School; Chairman, Lawyers Committee for Human Rights; Former President, American Civil Liberties Union.

Richard A. Epstein, James Parker Hall Distinguished Service Professor of Law, University of Chicago Law School; Editor, *Journal of Law and Economics*.

James G. Exum, Jr., Chief Justice (Retired), North Carolina Supreme Court.

Stephen M. Feldman, Professor, University of Tulsa College of Law.

David J. Garrow, Distinguished Historian in Residence, American University; Author, *Bearing the Cross; Liberty and Sexuality*.

David Halberstam, Author, *The Fifties*.

Kermit L. Hall, Dean, College of Humanities, and Professor of History and Law, Ohio State University.

Yale Kamisar, Clarence Darrow Distinguished University Professor, University of Michigan Law School; Coauthor of all eight editions of *Constitutional Law: Cases–Comments–Questions*.

Alex Kozinski, Judge, Ninth Circuit United States Court of Appeals.

Philip B. Kurland, Late William R. Kenan Distinguished Service Professor Emeritus, University of Chicago Law School.

Anthony Lewis, Columnist, *The New York Times*; Author, *Gideon's Trumpet; Make No Law: The Sullivan Case and the First Amendment.*

Richard Neely, Justice (Retired), West Virginia Supreme Court.

James B. O'Hara, Special Assistant for Executive Programs, Sellinger School of Business and Management, Loyola College, Maryland.

Ronald D. Rotunda, Albert E. Jenner, Jr., Professor of Law, University of Illinois.

Bernard Schwartz, Chapman Distinguished Professor, University of Tulsa College of Law.

John Sexton, Dean, New York University Law School.

James F. Simon, Martin Professor, New York Law School; Author, *Independent Journey: The Life of William O. Douglas.*

Nadine Strossen, Professor, New York Law School; President; American Civil Liberties Union.

Lord Woolf, Master of the Rolls, Britain.

· THE · WARREN COURT

• 1 •

INTRODUCTION

JAMES B. O'HARA

This volume commemorates the tenure of Earl Warren as Chief Justice of the United States. The contributors stress the almost revolutionary significance of the Supreme Court's role in extending the jurisprudence of civil rights, equal protection, and freedom of speech during Warren's sixteen years of leadership.

The volume begins with a remembrance by Justice William J. Brennan, Jr. This is a rare personal statement by the most important member of the Warren Court, after the Super Chief himself (the sobriquet is Brennan's).

David Halberstam then places Earl Warren in the historical context of his era. With the deftness for which he is noted, Halberstam tells Warren's story, concluding that he was "the least abstract of men," optimistic by nature, not flashy, something of a "square," and thus easy to underestimate. Yet Warren was the right man for his place and time, who gave his country a "beginning" in some of the most complex problems of the era.

The remaining chapters are grouped in three parts: (1) "The Constitutional Corpus," an in-depth analysis of the substantive contributions of the Warren Court in key legal areas; (2) "The Justices," analytical appraisals of six of the towering figures of that Court; and (3) "A Broader Perspective," an effort to see the Warren Court in an appropriate historical and legal focus.

The first great theme of the volume—the constitutional corpus—deals with substantive jurisprudence of the Warren Court in seven key areas: equal protection, freedom of speech, freedom of the press, church and state, criminal law, economic rights, and federalism.

The essays—all by distinguished lawyers, judges, and academics—are balanced in their approaches. At times the Warren Court is praised; at times it is sharply criticized.

Julius L. Chambers, writing on equal protection, has warm praise for the work of the Warren Court, which saw the Fourteenth Amendment as more than a

This introduction is based on O'Hara, "The Warren Court Revisited: The Tulsa Conference," 15 *The Supreme Court Historical Society Quarterly* 8 (Number 4, 1994).

last resort. *Brown v. Board of Education* was the high point of the Warren era equal-protection jurisprudence, but there were other major milestones as well: *McLaughlin v. Florida*, which established that racial classifications are always constitutionally dubious and require the Court's careful attention; *Loving v. Virginia*, which struck down state miscegenation laws; *Evans v. Newton*, which forbade the city of Macon, Georgia, to maintain a segregated park; *Swain v. Alabama*, forbidding peremptory challenges based on race in selecting juries; and finally *Baker v. Carr*, the "one man, one vote" decision. Chambers personally argued many cases before the Burger and Rehnquist Courts, but he is sharply critical of the more restrictive approach of the post-Warren era, although he cautions that all is not suddenly bleak. The Warren influence and the Warren precedents continue to have a major impact on current decisions.

Nadine Strossen lauds the Warren Court as "the most speech-protective Court that we have seen," which brought a refreshing attitude toward speech cases. But she notes a downside in the Warren era jurisprudence: There was no specific doctrinal rationale to provide a guideline to future Courts.

Ronald Rotunda writes on freedom of the press. His paper notes the difficulty the Court had in distinguishing "press" free speech from "ordinary" free speech; but he applauds Warren and his colleagues for the significant change in attitude they brought to speech and press issues.

John Sexton admits that the Warren Court added little to church-state jurisprudence. In Warren's sixteen years as Chief Justice, the Court only addressed ten cases on this topic. Sexton complains that the work of the Warren Court on the religion clauses was not pathmaking, since it lacked "substantive majesty".

Yale Kamisar deals with the Warren Court and criminal law, with a careful analysis of four cases of continuing importance: *Mapp v. Ohio*, which established the exclusionary rule in state cases; *Escobedo v. Illinois*, on the right to consult one's lawyer; *Miranda v. Arizona*, requiring that a suspect must be advised of rights before questioning begins; and *Gideon v. Wainwright*, which guaranteed legal representation to indigents if the charges against them could lead to imprisonment. Kamisar notes that, for the most part, the Warren Court was not as revolutionary as its critics charged. *Escobedo* seemed to say more than it really did, and *Miranda*, while later somewhat watered down, has never been overruled.

Richard Epstein writes about economic rights. Professor Epstein's paper is a brilliant, closely researched, and sometimes humorous critique, noting that the Warren Court practiced a jurisprudence of avoidance on economic rights, resulting in a glorification of mishmash in its approach to water rights, lien rights, and takings.

Richard Neely concludes the part of the volume on the *constitutional corpus*. Neely has acquired a reputation as a challenging, salty, humorous writer—an intellectual gadfly whose colorful regional manner of expression forces the reader to look at legal problems in a new light. He does not disappoint, calling for "bright-line" rules that can only come from the Supreme Court. Neely asserts that product liability law is now in the same crisis that criminal law was in Earl Warren's day. Plaintiff-based judges in state courts tend to follow the latest and most irresponsible decision from other state courts in a "race to the bottom." Justice Neely, writing in the context of federalism, reminds the reader that the common law in England was "common" because it was everywhere observed, while in the United States there are fifty-four bodies of law: federal law, the laws of fifty states, and the laws of the District of Columbia, Puerto Rico, Guam, and the Virgin Islands. At least in the area of product liability, the fragmentation of law has become critical, and Neely challenges the Supreme Court to address product liability issues with the same pragmatic insight that characterized the Warren era.

The second portion of the volume, "The Justices," is fascinating and often deeply moving. The authors are biographers or former law clerks to the six greatest Justices of the Warren era: Justices Brennan, Douglas, Black, Frankfurter, and Harlan and Chief Justice Warren himself. Richard Arnold calls his year clerking for Justice Brennan "probably the best job I ever had." Judge Arnold traces Brennan's prudent use of history in his approach to issues like capital punishment, school prayer, tax exemption for church property, and state promotion or display of religious symbols. But the real highlight of the judge's comments is the appreciation he so obviously feels for the warm and attractive presence of William J. Brennan, Jr.

James Simon, in his chapter, begins by noting that his task is difficult, because his subject, William O. Douglas, was "not nice." Simon, author of the standard Douglas biography, traces the career of the always larger-than-life Justice, beginning with his sickly childhood through his days as an outstanding law professor, chairman of the Securities and Exchange Commission, and, finally, his thirty-six years on the Court as an "injudicious" judge who flouted conventional norms both personally and professionally. Justice Douglas's original and often brilliant mind made it possible for him to realize his own philosophy that he would rather make a precedent than follow one.

Gerald T. Dunne, author of an important biography of Hugo L. Black, was unable to submit his planned essay because of illness. Instead, Bernard Schwartz, the volume's editor, unwilling to neglect the contribution of Justice Black, writes on the Justice, noting Black's "inner firmness," his literal interpretation of the constitutional text, his efforts to extend the Bill of Rights to the states, and finally his greatest contribution: changing the way Americans think about law.

Philip B. Kurland, former law clerk to Felix Frankfurter and an admitted stalwart Frankfurter partisan, remembers the Justice as humane and erudite. A high point of his chapter is its quotation from previously unpublished letters to and from Frankfurter and correspondents as varied as Dean Acheson, Groucho Marx, and Judge Learned Hand.

Norman Dorsen writes warmly of John Marshall Harlan, for whom he had clerked. Contrasting Harlan with Frankfurter, Dorsen makes clear that the latter was energetic—a ball of fire, while the former was staid, reserved, and in his way, boring. There are no anecdotes for Harlan, he notes. But for all his self-effacement, Justice Harlan was an indispensable part of the Warren Court—"intelligent, determined professionally skillful, and above all principled." For most of his time on the Court, Harlan moved against the tide. He was not a reactionary; indeed, he avoided extremes. He was deeply committed to the principles of federalism and judicial restraint, deference to lower courts, and to the legislative will. He looked for justice in procedure, and was no friend of egalitarianism. Prior to 1967, Justice Harlan dissented an average of sixty-seven times a year! But in his last two years, 1969 to

1971, as President Nixon's appointments joined the Court, Harlan found himself leading rather than attacking, and his dissents dropped to a trickle. All in all, Dorsen's portrait of Harlan shows a Justice committed to balance, who wanted to "keep things on an even keel."

Bernard Schwartz also writes about Earl Warren, whom he calls a "character out of Sinclair Lewis," a Middle-American believer in the sanctity of motherhood, flag, and family. Tracing Warren's career, Schwartz finds that Warren's earlier political offices, particularly as governor of California, gave him experienced executive competence. He was a real leader who knew how to run things.

The Warren jurisprudence was pragmatic: he saw law as an instrument to obtain the right result; indeed, he was the paradigm of the result-oriented judge—a sort of modern-day chancellor, dispensing equity and searching for fairness. But Schwartz notes that Warren's jurisprudence worked best when the political institutions had defaulted on their responsibility to try to address problems such as segregation and reapportionment and cases where the constitutional rights of defendants were abused. For the matching of his human qualities to the legal requirements of the day, Warren was second only to the great John Marshall in his impact on American law.

Perhaps the most moving of all the presentations is the essay "Clerking for the Chief Justice," by Tyrone Brown. Calling Warren "a priest at the altar of equal justice," Brown recounts the story of his own mother's meeting with the Chief Justice. He tells of the time when Warren was outraged at the Court's initial refusal to hear a case involving prison inmates who had been mistreated in a Florida jail. The Chief Justice expressed great moral indignation over the attitude of his brethren—"Put it in the books and let *posterity* decide who was right." Refusing to let the matter stand, Warren eventually led the other Justices, one by one, to change their votes.

The volume's last segment, "A Broader Perspective," presents the insights of judges, practitioners, and scholars who evaluate the Warren Court's place in history. George Bushnell, Jr., praises the Warren Court for its boldness in settling issues left unsolved by the political process, but decries the present-day temptation to use litigation and the justice system as a "black box" into which social problems can be placed for judicial solution. The judicial system has become the first rather than the last resort, and that, Bushnell asserts, tarnishes the legacy of Warren. He calls on the profession to defend the justice system from the politicians and the demagogues who would abuse it.

Kermit Hall contrasts the received wisdom about the Warren era with a series of revisionist theories, with obvious admiration for the courage of the Warren majority for the constructive dialogue it initiated with the country and with earlier Courts.

James G. Exum, Jr., and Louis D. Bilionis examine the development of state constitutional law, noting that many of the states had a bill of rights before the federal Constitution was even written, and that state courts have often gone beyond the Supreme Court in safeguarding the rights of citizens.

Stephen M. Feldman offers a masterly analysis of the Warren Court's impact on jurisprudence. Feldman argues that the Warren Court helped terminate one era of legal thought and ushered in a new one.

Lord Woolf, whose position in the House of Lords is roughly the equivalent of an American Supreme Court Justice, contrasts the purpose and methodology of the high courts of Britain and the United States. Noting that the Warren Court did have an impact on legislation in Great Britain, Lord Woolf explains that fundamental differences in the structure and purposes of the courts in the two countries made direct influences by the Court on the House of Lords improbable.

Judge Alex Kozinski was asked to critique the Warren Court. While praising the vision and courage behind *Brown v. Board of Education*, Kozinski notes that the Court seemed to reason that if judicial power could reverse the pattern of segregation, judicial power could be a force for justice in other areas also. *Baker v. Carr* and *Reynolds v. Sims*, the reapportionment cases, overturned over a hundred years of constitutional history with the slogan "One man, one vote." Judge Kozinski argues that equally weighted votes might even impede real equality, and that in actuality slogans usually make for bad law. Similarly, he urges, the Warren Court protections for those accused of crime are often artificial, masking the real problems with police procedures and behavior. And since the Warren Court decisions in this area often lacked substantial jurisprudential underpinnings, later Courts have chipped away at the Warren results.

Judge Kozinski is also critical of the Warren Court's work in other areas. The Court neglected copyright and trademark law and was quiescent in economic areas, except for labor and antitrust law, where it evidenced a strong antibusiness bias. Judge Kozinski complains that the Warren Court was only selectively activist, and finally predicts that history will ultimately judge the Court as a kind of legal Icarus, flying too close to the sun to have any permanent life.

David Garrow summarizes the contributions of the Warren Court under four headings: racial equality (*Brown*); political equality (*Baker v. Carr*); sexual liberty and gender equality (*Griswold v. Connecticut*); judicial courage and judicial authority (*Cooper v. Aaron*). Treating each to careful analysis, Garrow offers especially interesting insights into the background of the *Griswold* case, where powerful religious forces had pressed to keep an antiquated Connecticut anti–birth control law in place, thereby forcing the test case that not only overturned the law but that provided the legal basis for *Roe v. Wade*.

Anthony Lewis sums up the Warren legacy. Taking issue with Judge Kozinski, Lewis enumerates what were, in his estimation, the greatest contributions of the Warren Court: *Baker*, *Brown*, *New York Times v. Sullivan*, *Griswold*, *Gideon*, *Mapp*, and *Miranda*. It was "the age of judicial heroism," he asserts. Lewis's words are a fitting culmination of this major retrospective on the Chief Justice and the Court that, in the words of the title of a Warren biography, "changed America." No study of Earl Warren and his era will ever be complete without consulting this volume.

• 2 •

A PERSONAL REMEMBRANCE

WILLIAM J. BRENNAN, JR.

I am delighted to have been asked to join this retrospective assessment of the Supreme Court during the tenure of Chief Justice Earl Warren. In a 1970 tribute to the Chief Justice, Senator Edward Kennedy observed that when Earl Warren took his seat on the Court in 1953, our nation stood at a crossroads in its history. The great struggle to define ourselves in the rapidly changing postwar world was beginning in earnest, as was the struggle to keep our founding fathers' promises of freedom and equality. Any thorough study of this period of our nation's history must include some consideration of the cases decided by the Supreme Court in those years.

In recent years, I have been tempted to write or speak about some of the more familiar cases decided by the Supreme Court during Earl Warren's sixteen-year tenure. I also have thought it might be useful to attempt some comparative study between that period and the remainder of the two-hundred-year history of the Court. After some consideration, however, I have decided that this is a task best left to others. To my chagrin, I have found that my role as a participant on the Court has made it impossible for me to maintain the objectivity that is required for meaningful discourse. In any event, I have few doubts that there is little I could add to the rather exhaustive treatment that has already been given these matters in this volume. Accordingly, I thought I might just add a few words about the human side of some of the members of the Warren Court, including the Chief Justice himself.

The Supreme Court I joined in 1956 was a Court of giants. Consider this: When I joined the Court, Bill Douglas had already been on the Court for seventeen years. This was, at that time, longer than half of the seventy-eight Justices who had come before him. Yet even after my appointment to the Court, Bill Douglas did not have the seniority to assign a majority opinion. By tradition at the Supreme Court, the power of assignment goes either to the Chief Justice or to the senior Associate Justice in any majority. With the Chief Justice, Hugo Black, Stanley Reed, and Felix Frankfurter on the Court at that time, it was certain that in any configuration of at least five Justices, there would be someone with more seniority than Bill Douglas.

Even the relatively newer Justices on the Court were quite distinguished.

Harold Burton had served with distinction on the Court for eleven years before I arrived, and for six years in the United States Senate before that. Tom Clark, the spindly Texan, was a relative newcomer to the Court, but, of course, he had received a great deal of attention as the attorney general. And John Marshall Harlan, the Court's freshman before I joined, had developed quite a reputation as one of the finest practicing lawyers in the nation.

My first meeting with these giants came in 1956, a few days after President Eisenhower told me that he was going to nominate me to the Court. Earl Warren brought me to one of the rooms in the Supreme Court building where the Justices all were assembled, and I remember that the lights were turned off. As I was introduced around the room, it became clear that my new colleagues were becoming increasingly agitated. Finally, one of them—I do not remember who—told me to get out of the way because I was blocking the television set on which they were all watching the first game of the World Series.

It became clear to me on that day that no one was more pleased by my appointment than John Harlan. He too had been appointed by President Eisenhower, but one year earlier. My arrival at the Court meant that he would no longer be required to assume a few of the thankless administerial duties traditionally assigned to the Junior Justice. (As an aside, I should disclose that my tenure as Junior Justice was rendered mercifully short by the arrival of Charles Whittaker to the Court one year later.) John and I formed what would become a fast friendship on that first day when I visited the Court. During a break in the baseball game, John asked if I smoked. When I said I did, which was the case in those days, he invited me to his office for a smoke, relieved to finally have an ally.

John Harlan was a true scholar, perhaps more than anyone else with whom I've served, even Felix Frankfurter. He had a very proper, patrician bearing, and every so often I'd greet him as "Johnny," and you could just see the color drain from his face.

Of course, he and I disagreed more often than we agreed on important matters. That began, I recall, with my very first opinion. There was and still is a tradition on the Court that a new Justice tries to select as a first case one that may produce a unanimous court, and that everyone else tries hard to join that first opinion. I will never forget how anguished he was when he came in to see me to tell me that he would have to dissent in my first decision, *Putnam v. Commissioner*, a tax case. Sure enough the opinion came down, eight to one.

Perhaps the strongest disagreements on the Warren Court were the personal clashes of wills between Felix Frankfurter and Bill Douglas. Felix would engage in these long monologues, discussing cases at the Court's conferences—it is often said you could set your watch to them, they lasted precisely as long as lectures at Harvard Law School, where he had been a professor. He would sometimes get up and pace about the room, pulling cases out to cite passages. From time to time, Bill Douglas would announce that he could take no more, would get up and leave, and vow to return only when Felix was finished. To his credit, Earl Warren would never get in the middle, but would just lean back, smile, and continue pushing us through our business.

As I began to develop a stronger relationship with the Chief, Felix became more determined to bring me under his wing. He always enjoyed attempting to persuade his colleagues about important matters, and since I had been a student of his at Harvard, I suppose he saw me as a special project. In those days, I took all of my clerks from Harvard, where Felix Frankfurter was a revered name. He would routinely visit my chambers to try to persuade me about a case, making sure to stop in to see the "boys" from Harvard in the back room first, trying to win them over, as well. But after a while, he just gave up on me. At a dinner one night, after I had been on the Court for several years, he finally proclaimed that while he had always encouraged his students to think for themselves, "Brennan goes too far."

Bill Douglas was, perhaps, one of the most interesting characters the Court has ever known. When I arrived at the Court, Bill had so many diverse interests that his attention was never fully focused on the Court. Occasionally, this made it difficult for the Court to resolve its business as the end of a term drew near and he left for his home in Goose Prairie, Washington. I recall many occasions when he would leave me with a list of votes and I would cast them for him at conference in his absence. Once, I cast his vote to affirm in a case, and, without ever discussing the matter with me or anyone else, he later mailed in a vote to reverse, complete with a dissent.

Bill had a rather strong personality and was not afraid of confrontation. It was not unusual for his law clerks to wander over to my chambers to seek shelter after discussing a case, or some other matter, with him. But despite his ways, his staunch defense of individual rights and his love for the environment have left a lasting legacy.

The biggest giant of them all, of course, was Hugo Black. His dissent in *Adamson v. California*, which proposed total incorporation of the Bill of Rights within the Fourteenth Amendment to be applied to the states, moved him to the forefront of constitutional innovation and debate. Hugo Black, more than anyone, provided the Warren Court with the early vision that carried it through the 1960s.

This brings me at last to Earl Warren himself, or, as I have come to refer to him since 1969, "Super Chief." I have often remarked that the term "the Warren Court" is a fitting tribute to his effective leadership during a period that brought to the Court some of the most troublesome and controversial questions in its history. His great gift was his sensitivity to the diverse and conflicting opinions held by his brethren. He had about him a grace and courtesy that we all respected deeply, and he set a tone that ensured that even the most heated discussions would be conducted with decorum and consideration. Thanks to him, our decisions always were the product of robust debate; rarely did any of the great Justices with whom I served during Earl Warren's tenure, whether they were in the majority, the dissent, or somewhere in between, feel slighted.

He was a man of integrity and fairness, and no one ever brought more of a sense of humanity and quiet wisdom to the Court than he did. His great opinions, from *Brown v. Board of Education* to *Miranda v. Arizona*, display his greatest gift to our nation's jurisprudence: his belief that human dignity is perhaps the primary value fostered by the Constitution. He expressed his great vision on the occasion of his retirement thus: "Where there is injustice, we should correct it; where there is poverty, we should eliminate it, where there is corruption, we should stamp it out; where there is violence, we should punish it; where there is neglect, we should provide care; where there is war, we should restore peace; and wherever corrections are achieved, we should add them permanently to our storehouse of treasure."

Earl Warren was a great friend to me, and I shall treasure his friendship always. But the greatest gift he has given me is a gift he has given to all of you as well; he made our country a better place. I am certain of the way that history will remember Earl Warren. He was one of the greatest judges and men our nation has ever known.

· 3 ·

EARL WARREN AND HIS AMERICA

DAVID HALBERSTAM

We are all shaped by many things: our genes, the values of our family, our good (or bad) personal fortune, and of course, the era we live in. The last is particularly important in dealing with Earl Warren, a man of innate inner optimism who came to political power at the height of what Henry Luce of *Time-Life* called the American Century. Let me give the historical setting.

Earl Warren saw an America going from sleepy isolationist nation to superpower status—under the press of modern technology, much of it American-driven, and the press of terrifying, indeed cataclysmic events in Europe, and the coming of a new modern mass production economy.

By the end of World War II, when Earl Warren was governor of California and fifty-one years old, America existed almost apart from the rest of the world in its affluence. It was now rich in a world that was poor. Europe had inflicted suicidal war twice on itself within a space of barely twenty-five years. Ally and adversary alike were in ashes after the war. The colonial age, though not everyone realized it, was over—a victim of the decline of the European powers (ever weaker because of the losses suffered during those two wars) and the growing power, as yet unrealized in the developed world, of modern communications among those who lived in the colonized world.

England was a victor, but it was exhausted spiritually and financially, and it was about to get rid of its colonies. France was also a victor, but it had been humiliated by its experience during World War II, and in order to show that it was still a great nation and to regain its lost glory, it was about to fight two pyrrhic colonial wars. Germany was defeated, ravaged physically and psychically by its wartime experiences. It had lost some twenty million people and it was cut in half by its victorious opponents. The Soviet Union was also a victor; but it had also lost twenty million people, it was governed by one of the worst tyrants of the modern age, and it had an economic system that demonstrably did not work. Japan had been, to quote Winston Churchill, ground to powder, and its defeat in the war was not merely physical, it was spiritual—as if a certain treasured self-definition of Japan had been destroyed as well.

Yet in America the opposite was true. World War II had brought us, just as our own economy was taking off anyway, to the zenith of our power. Our manufacturing capability, already awesome on the eve of the war, was infinitely greater—we had muscles now in places where in the past we had been underdeveloped. Not a bomb had been dropped on American soil or on an American factory. The economy had boomed during the war—many ordinary families had two incomes, and ordinary Americans, their loved ones overseas, had doubled up at home, which meant they had considerable disposable income when the war was over. America was poised to be the greatest consumer nation in the history of mankind. All American industry had to do was throw a switch to go from a military economy to a civilian one, to produce cars instead of tanks.

As the distinguished British historian Robert Payne wrote after coming to America in 1949: "There never was a country more fabulous than America. She sits bestride the world like a colossus; no other power at any time in the world's history has possessed so varied or so great an influence on other nations. . . . Half of the wealth of the world, more than half the productivity, nearly two-thirds of the world's machines are concentrated in American hands; the rest of the world lies in the shadow of American industry."

Never was there a nation so rich, but even more important—for there are nations that are rich, like Saudi Arabia, for example, where the wealth does not touch the tissue of life for ordinary people—never had the wealth of a nation been so equitably distributed among so many ordinary people. Millions of average Americans were moving into the middle class in that period every year.

Some called it the American Century. A brilliant colleague of mine in Japan, Naohiro Amaya, called it the Oil Century, in contrast to the Coal Century, which had preceded it, and in which only a handful of people—the owners themselves—were beneficiaries of the work of the many. I have taken to calling this age, instead, the Century of the Common Man, a time in which ordinary people came to live in the middle-class and began to enjoy the fruits and dignity of middle-class life, a type of existence in the past reserved only for the wealthy. It had begun even before the end of World War II, and even before the Depression, for its roots were in the changeover from coal as the prime fuel of an industrial economy to oil, and the coming of new mass production lines in this oil age.

The principal architects of it were an unlikely pair—since they despised each other—Henry Ford and Franklin D. Roosevelt. Ford, because he created the modern assembly line, had become arguably, and in spite of himself, the century's great revolutionary: with his assembly line he turned the worker into a consumer. Ford liked to say of his mass production line—quite accurately—that "every time I bring the price of a car down one dollar, I can sell one thousand more." For the first time in any real sense the ordinary worker benefited from his own labor.

FDR is important because, with the coming of the New Deal, he created a political-social balance in the workplace, adjudicating deftly the different rights of owners, managers, and workers. He helped create in this explosive new time a fairer place to work and a desperately needed element of economic democracy in the workplace.

In terms of economic progress for ordinary citizens, that period was the most expansive one imaginable. Daniel Yergin, in his excellent book on the coming of the oil economy, calls the worker in this new economy Hydrocarbon Man. The ordinary worker became a beneficiary of his labor—he has soon in this magical era, a car, a house, and then two cars, all sorts of modern new toys for the kitchen of the new house, and sometimes perhaps, even a second house. Amaya has pointed out that Marx was the last great philosopher of the Coal Age, and that if he had lived until the Oil Age, he might have written differently. Simply stated, coal as a fuel produced far less fruit from one man's labor, and workers still lived in abject conditions, working endless hours in Dickensian poverty.

In America, that era, immediately after World War II, was not surprisingly a time of great optimism and confidence. More and more people were living better than ever before and moving into the middle class. People whose parents had lived in cold-water flats were buying brand new houses in instant suburbs from builders like William Levitt, who was the lineal descendant of Henry Ford. Levitt turned housing into a mass production with only a hundred dollars down. Since houses were too large to come down a production line, Levitt shrewdly brought the assembly line to the site—he bulldozed an area and then brought his different production teams out to the site to build there.

Nor was this merely a moment of economic optimism; there was a parallel social optimism, too. Not only was World War II considered a *good* war, a worthy democratic cause waged against the forces of darkness and totalitarianism, thereby greatly enhancing the spirit of the nation, but there was a new, greatly enhanced social optimism at work as well. World War II had brought us the G.I. Bill and with it a new sense of social fluidity—the coming of America as a true meritocracy. In small town after small town, local boys who had once lived below the salt—no matter what their native talent—and who in most cases would not have been able to go to college, had learned during the war that they could go beyond both the geographical and social limits of their small towns. Returning after the war, they were not willing to return to being soda jerks. They had often commanded men who by birth were more privileged than they. Now they had come home, and they could go virtually free to the nation's best colleges. We had started this century with political democracy, and now the psychological boost of winning the war, plus the G.I. Bill, had given us social democracy as well.

We were optimistic and confident. The economy was booming—nowhere, I might add, as magically as in California; everyone's income in those first twenty years after the war, seemed to go up ten percent a year. Everyone was moving up to bigger cars, bigger houses, better vacations, and above all better dreams of the future. The American dream, in the truest sense, seemed finally to have arrived for the most ordinary of people. Ten years after the war, only African Americans, then still called Negroes, particularly those in the South, seemed to be denied full participation in this amazing new boom society.

This then was the nation at the moment when Earl Warren became Chief Justice of the United States in 1953, after presiding for so long over the remarkable smaller miracle taking place within the larger miracle, the coming of California as the great new American nation state: a new land where almost magically houses were built, factories opened, schools created—the golden place in the golden era.

To contrast that time of optimism with today's very different society with its very different social problems and its vastly diminished optimism, one only need take Pat Brown, Earl Warren's lineal descendant—it was in any true sense one administration, a Warren-Brown one with a shared optimistic vision of American affluence and what government could do (in education, in services supplied)—and contrast it to the difficulties of Kathleen Brown Rice Sauter in her race for governor in 1994. Kathleen, the Brown family member most like her father, ran for governor in a much more difficult, much more pessimistic era, one where people are nervous and defensive on crime and immigration. Above all, today's America is significantly less generous. If Earl Warren had been born, say, in 1944, rather than 1894, he might have been very different in his political outlook.

He was born in California in the previous century, of Norwegian ancestry. He was part of the westward movement, a good midwesterner of Scandinavian ancestry, part of a family restlessly moving ever westward in its journey. The name was originally Varran, and was later Americanized to Warren. He was acutely aware of the pain that poverty could bring—he had his father's own life to teach him. Years later, Earl Warren could say that when he read Dickens's *Oliver Twist*, the first thing he thought of was his father's life. Matt Warren was a railroad car repairman. That was in an age of bitter labor divisions, and Matt Warren was a labor man, often unemployable because of his union activities. The difficulties faced by his father made the son immensely sensitive to the hardships inflicted on ordinary people by big impersonal companies; some of the roots of his liberalism are in his father's labor struggles. Earl Warren was in many ways the perfect twentieth-century American liberal hybrid, in his roots, his personal experiences, and his optimism. Conservative and thrifty and cautious by instinct and training, he came of age in an ever-expanding California, and he was more liberal when he was older than when he was younger—he became the moderate-liberal Republican, a benign populist, distrusted by his own party and elected by Democratic votes.

He was, befitting his ethnic roots and the hard times he lived through, a great square, and a thrifty man. His father had taught him to save part of everything he made. He went to Berkeley, a beneficiary of public education, on money saved from an endless series of petty jobs, delivering ice and groceries among them. His education was a good one, it had cost very little, and it had unlocked a rich future; he was able with surprising ease to rise quickly above his origins and above his own expectations. As the American dream worked for him because of his *education*, he believed—more firmly than in anything else—in the obligation of the state to make the same kind of educational opportunity available for every young person in the nation.

He grew in office. Somewhat narrow in his earlier years as a prosecutor, he broadened his political outlook in succeeding jobs, always aware—and this was what set him apart from men with greater abstract intellectual ability—of the impact of every issue on ordinary citizens. Warren was the least abstract of men: he was in no way a man of theory. He did not quote Hobbes or Locke. But he knew how people lived, what their fears were, what their hopes were, and what great human potential might be locked up in the simplest and least prepossessing of homes. The government, he came to believe, had a mandate to expedite the most elemental hopes of ordinary people—to give each American, particularly young Americans, one good shot to reach their full potential and to play on a level playing field. Not surprisingly the key to this was education, and not surprisingly it is this that we principally remember him for. One law clerk thought there were three things that mattered most to Earl Warren: the first was the concept of equality, the second was education, and the third was the right of young people to a decent life. Not surprisingly his enduring legacy is *Brown v. Board of Education*. He was an optimist and activist, and he was an optimist and an activist when America was optimistic itself and ready for activism.

It was easy to underestimate him, and a good many people did who normally might have been expected to know better. He took pleasure in being a square. He did not mind it when people underrated his abilities—if anything, it tended to work towards his advantage. He was a better listener than a talker. He was a member of the Moose and the Masons. To Judge Learned Hand, he was just a big dumb Swede. John Gunther, arguably the greatest American journalist of that era, wrote of him in 1947: "Earl Warren is honest, likeable and clean; he will never set the world on fire or even make it smoke; he has the limitations of all Americans of his type with little intellectual background, little genuine depth or coherent political philosophy; a man who has probably never bothered with abstract thought twice in his life; a kindly man with the best social instincts, stable and well balanced."

That was both true and untrue—he ran deeper than he liked to appear. But it was also his strength—he was so ordinary, so much *of* the people, that he had a sure sense of how Americans responded to political change and challenge, and what they were capable of because it was the way he responded himself. He knew how they felt because it was the way he himself felt. In many ways his life and his roots were not unlike those of the man who had appointed him, Dwight Eisenhower, and his strength and his innate decency were not, in theory at least, that different from Ike's. But thirty years in the military had removed Ike from contemporary society and made him wary and distrustful of politics, and turned him (covertly) into an extremely conservative man, while if anything, those same thirty years had made Warren ever more optimistic about the possibilities of ordinary men (the Eisenhower whom Warren most resembled was Milton, Ike's brother). Ike had moved further from his roots as he became president, and he hung out with the wealthiest of CEOs; Warren by contrast remained as he was, ever the square, unaffected by the change in his personal fortune. "His great strength," Justice Potter Stewart said years later of him, "was his simple belief in all the things we now laugh at—motherhood, marriage, family and the flag."

He was the right man at the right place at the right time. That was a generous, confident America he was called to serve in 1953. More than any other member of the Court at that time, Warren had been immersed in the daily life of America, and not only did he have a feel for the possibilities of what ordinary Americans could do if they had the chance at a decent education, but he had, of all his colleagues, the truest sense of how they felt about themselves, a knowledge of their own self-portrait. He was, in that time at least, the Norman Rockwell of our judicial system. He knew how they would feel about giving those long denied equal opportunity a fair chance at the American Dream they themselves cherished.

Because he was so ordinary and so low key it was easy to underestimate the intensity of his purpose—what would today be called his agenda. Anthony Lewis has written of him, "Earl Warren was the closest thing the United States has had to a Platonic Guardian, dispensing law from a throne without any sensed limits of power except what was seen as the good of the society. Fortunately he was a decent, humane, honorable, democratic guardian."

I am glad to participate in this volume to acknowledge my particular personal debt to Chief Justice Warren. There are two places where I feel particularly obligated to him. The first is that because of the change in our libel laws to the realistic fair ones which were achieved in his tenure I was able to write my signature books, most particularly *The Best and The Brightest*. The second is that, as someone who was a reporter in Mississippi in 1955, I never have to explain to my young daughter, as we travel together through the American South, what signs which say "white only" mean and why they could still exist in this country. Very simply, he allowed a generation of us who love freedom, to love our country that much more.

· I ·

THE CONSTITUTIONAL CORPUS

• 4 •

RACE AND EQUALITY
The Still Unfinished Business of the Warren Court

JULIUS L. CHAMBERS

> Where there is injustice, we should correct it; where there is poverty, we should eliminate it; where there is corruption, we should stamp it out; where there is violence, we should punish it; where there is neglect, we should provide care; where there is war, we should restore peace; and wherever corrections are achieved we should add them permanently to our storehouse of treasures.[1]

This passage, authored by Earl Warren and engraved on his tombstone, captures, in essence, the direction of his efforts as Chief Justice of the United States.[2] Constitutional recognition of an individual's right to privacy,[3] formulation of broad protections of the rights of criminal defendants,[4] and the discernible extension of the equal protection guarantee to racial minorities[5]—the focus of this essay—are all hallmarks of the Warren era. These contributions of Chief Justice Warren and the legacy of the Court era that bears his name have been subject to meticulous scrutiny (some of which will be addressed below) since the end of his tenure on the Court in 1969.[6] It simply cannot be denied, however, that the decisions of the Warren Court[7] in the area of race revolutionized our society by beginning in earnest the ongoing challenge to eliminate, root and branch, the ugly vestiges of American slavery.

As the title of this article—borrowed from a piece written almost twenty-five years ago[8]—indicates, I believe that the job of the Warren Court remains incomplete. In a series of opinions, beginning with *Brown v. Board of Education*,[9] the Warren Court paved the way for the application of the ideals of liberty, equality, and justice, embodied in the founding documents of our nation, to Americans of African descent. Subsequent developments in the Supreme Court,[10] however, have jarred the foundation upon which the promise of the Warren era was built, and today threaten to dismantle completely the constitutional cornerstone on which racial equality rests. Thus, "[t]he most urgent particular item in the unfinished business of the Warren Court," as Professor Charles Black argued years ago, "is [still] the work of eradicating racism in the United States—to opening full citizenship to black people."[11]

I do not suggest that the central holding of *Brown*—that separate-but-equal is constitutionally intolerable—is in jeopardy. To do so would be hyperbolic and would discount the real and substantial progress that has been made in the lives of African Americans and all Americans over the past four decades.[12] But to appreciate fully the gravity of what I perceive to be a mounting judicial retreat from the equality principles announced in the opinions of the Warren Court, one first must comprehend fully the scope of the promise inherent in the constitutional amendments to which the Warren Court gave life.

An examination of the decisions of the Supreme Court in the area of civil rights over the past thirty years exposes a steady and unsettling trend to contain, if not eliminate, the availability of judicial relief to victims of racial discrimination. This trend—facilitated by ingenious perversions of *Brown* and its progeny—is based in part upon a misconception, I believe, of the purpose and intent of the Civil War amendments, a niggardly conception of the judicial role, and an erroneous set of assumptions about the lingering effects of prior discrimination in today's society. It is this trend, both manifest and subtle, that "force[s] us to refocus on a question presented time and time again, before and after *Dred Scott:* whether meaningful equality can be obtained for African Americans through law."[13]

Section I of this essay briefly chronicles the defining decisions of the Warren era that at long last extended constitutional relief to blacks through the Equal Protection Clause and aided in inspiring presidential and congressional action. Also examined are those cases in which opportunities to refine the antidiscrimination principles and to construct a coherent design by which they should be implemented were missed or not fully appreciated. Finally, this survey also includes key reapportionment cases decided during the Warren era. Ultimately, I conclude that the Warren Court's decisions, despite some shortcomings, were, in essence, consistent with the central purpose of the Civil War amendments.[14]

Section II examines the Burger Court's[15] contributions—pro and con—in the area of race and equality. In large part, the Burger Court left intact both the egalitarian principles enunciated by the Warren Court and the two-tier mode of equal protection analysis that emerged during that era.[16] Indeed, the Burger Court broadened the classes of persons encompassed by the suspect classification strand of equal protection doctrine.[17] Important developments during the Burger years, however, bear testament to a mixed legacy on the issue of race. On the one hand, the Burger Court wrestled with the question of remedies for victims of racial discrimination and began to devise standards for relief left undeveloped by the Warren Court. Yet it was the Burger Court that erected the ominous barrier of discriminatory intent as an absolute prerequisite for relief under the Constitution. The intent requirement implicitly reflects a misunderstanding of, or a skepticism in, the lingering effects of racism. This skepticism has manifested itself in the Rehnquist era in the form of virulent opposition to race-conscious remedies.

Section III anticipates the legacy of the Rehnquist Court[18] in the area of racial equality by examining significant doctrinal shifts that have heightened burdens of proof for putative victims of racial discrimination, restricted the scope of available remedies, and tenaciously discounted the significance, if not the existence, of racial discrimination—past and present—or the relevance of gross statistical disparities as evidence of such. In short, to date, the decisions of the Rehnquist Court signal an arrested development in the evolution of Fourteenth Amendment jurisprudence as envisioned by the Reconstruction Congress and as pursued by the Warren Court.

Finally, section IV addresses select criticisms of the Warren Court's equality jurisprudence. Two of those criticisms, one concerning the legitimate parameters of the judicial function and the other, the appropriate methodology to interpret constitutional text, complement one another to the detriment of minority interests, and also underlie many of the decisions of the Rehnquist Court. If these criticisms are sufficient to cast irreparable doubt on the validity of the Warren era decisions—a proposition that I reject—then one must reevaluate seriously the role of law and the courts in a pluralistic democracy.

I

Prior to the Warren era, the Civil War amendments, and particularly the Fourteenth, had lain dormant in the protection of the very citizens whose treatment in this country had induced their enactment. Notwithstanding the Supreme Court's seemingly resounding declaration in the *Slaughter-House Cases*,[19] that "the one pervading purpose" of the amendments was "[t]he freedom of the slave race, the security and firm establishment of that freedom, and the protection of the newly-made freeman and citizen from the oppressions of those who had formerly exercised unlimited dominion over him,"[20] subsequent narrow judicial interpretations[21] of those amendments for decades stymied their potential effectiveness collectively to secure basic civil rights for African Americans.[22] The Warren Court's willingness to articulate and embrace an antidiscrimination principle brought blacks—who had endured on the periphery of the protective capacity of the law[23]—squarely within the purview of the Constitution and its fundamental guarantee of individual equality, and hence, personal dignity. As a result of the Warren Court's transformation of constitutional interpretation from empty ideals to tangible principles, the Equal Protection Clause of the Fourteenth Amendment is no longer the "last resort of constitutional arguments,"[24] but rather a "significant force in shaping the American response to the continuing challenge of a pluralistic society."[25]

The litany of cases in which the Warren Court forged new directions in the area of equal protection for racial minorities needs no lengthy explication. Beginning with *Brown*,[26] the Warren Court formulated an antidiscrimination principle, which was designed to undo the legacy of white supremacy and domination that had been sanctioned judicially in *Plessy v. Ferguson*.[27] But it was not until 1964 that the Warren Court expressly enunciated a rule that racial classifications, standing alone, were presumptively suspect.

In *McLaughlin v. Florida*,[28] the Court struck down a state law criminalizing cohabitation by unmarried interracial couples. Unlike state regulations that made prohibitions of certain activity or the imposition of increased penalties applicable only to blacks, the statute challenged in *McLaughlin* imposed identical sanctions on those violating the statute regardless of race.[29] In reviewing the statute, the Warren Court refused to endorse what was at root a reversion to the *Plessy* conception of equality—a conception that was built on the premise that race was a perfectly appropriate basis upon which invidious legislative choices could be made. Instead, it found that racial classifications "[bear] a heavy burden of justification [and] w[ould] be upheld only if [necessary] and not merely rationally related to the accomplishment of a permissible state policy."[30] Still, the Warren Court—as vehemently argued by the concurrence[31]—left open the possibility that conduct could justifiably be deemed criminal solely because of the color of one's skin.

In *Loving v. Virginia*,[32] the Court partially closed the gap left open in *McLaughlin*. Building upon the reasoning in *McLaughlin*, the Court applied "rigid"[33] judicial scrutiny to legislation criminalizing interracial marriage only between blacks and whites and required a stronger state interest than it had in the past.[34] Irrelevant was the fact that the legislation similarly "burdened" both races: "[T]he mere 'equal application' of a statute containing racial classifications," according to the Court, "[wa]s [not] enough to remove the classifications from the Fourteenth Amendment's proscription of all invidious racial discriminations."[35] Because the legislation enjoined behavior purely on the basis of race, the state was required to demonstrate that the legislation was "necessary to the accomplishment of some permissible state objective, independent of the racial discrimination which it was the object of the Fourteenth Amendment to eliminate."[36] This it could not do. "There [wa]s patently no legitimate overriding purpose independent of invidious racial discrimination which justifie[d] th[e] classification."[37]

McLaughlin and *Loving* make clear that *Brown* was more than a superficial rejection of separate-but-equal doctrine. Efforts to perpetuate racial domination through the law would no longer be condoned. Together with *Brown*'s antidiscrimination principle, the articulation of a judicial commitment to strict scrutiny of all invidious legislation containing racial classifications in the *McLaughlin/Loving* line of cases, disemboweled *Plessy*'s separate-but-equal fiction.

The Warren Court also supplied the theory for softening the effect of the "state action" requirement that had been engrafted onto the Fourteenth Amendment in the *Civil Rights Cases*.[38] The *Civil Rights Cases* considered the constitutionality of the Civil Rights Act of 1875, which proscribed racial discrimination in public accommodations. According to the Court, Congress had exceeded its powers under Section 5 of the Fourteenth Amendment, which did not "authorize Congress to create a code of municipal law for the regulation of private rights; but [only] to provide modes of redress against the operation of state laws, and the action of state officers."[39] In theory and in practice, the "state action" requirement limited Congress's role in giving force to the Fourteenth Amendment's broad provisions.[40]

In *Evans v. Newton*,[41] however, the Warren Court significantly altered the manner of thinking about state-sponsored discrimination. *Evans* considered a challenge to the continued segregation of a park on the basis of race. The park land, located in Macon, Georgia, had been held in trust by the city pursuant to the will of state senator Augustus O. Bacon. Senator Bacon's will had provided that the park be used solely for the benefit and enjoyment of whites. From 1911, when the park was established, until 1954, when the decision in *Brown* was rendered, the city had provided maintenance for the park, during which time the park enjoyed tax-exempt status. After *Brown*, the city resigned as trustee, and title was transferred to a group of private trustees. The Court held that notwithstanding the title transfer and the appointment of private trustees, the park could not remain segregated consistent with the Equal Protection Clause of the Fourteenth Amendment. Although the Court noted the continued connection between the city and the park—the city continued to provide some maintenance services—the opinion implied that the performance of certain "public functions" could not, under these circumstances, be delegated to private persons in contravention of the equal protection guarantee.[42]

In *Reitman v. Mulkey*[43] the Warren Court further refined its approach to "state action," holding that an article of the California Constitution prohibiting the state from interfering with the absolute discretion of a property owner to sell, lease, or rent his real property, or to refuse to do so, would impermissibly involve the state in private racial discrimination. Relying on the highest state court's finding that the amendment would increase the incidence of racial discrimination in the alienation of property, the Warren Court held that the state would be an impermissible actor in an unrestrained scheme of racial discrimination. *Reitman* was extremely important because it deterred states from engineering elusive statutory schemes that would obfuscate the Fourteenth Amendment's command—even as narrowly construed in the *Civil Rights Cases*—to eliminate discrimination by the state.[44]

Thus, under the Warren Court decisions that sought to define the state action concept, nominal private action could not operate as a subterfuge where there existed public authority for and participation in racial discrimination.[45] The utility of the Fourteenth Amendment's equal protection guarantee—concededly limited to prohibitions of state-sponsored discrimination—accordingly was revitalized by an expansive reading of the limitation.[46] In other words, the Court looked beneath the surface to ensure that governmental support—direct or indirect—of racially discriminatory conduct was unconstitutional.

Where challenged activity was indisputably state action, the Warren Court's decisions measuring compliance with the equal protection guarantee pursued two different tracks. The first, typified by *Swain v. Alabama*,[47] unhappily did not manifest the level of insight prevalent in *Reitman*. *Swain* involved a challenge to the state's exercise of peremptory challenges deliberately to remove blacks from the jury. While recognizing the right of black defendants to be tried before juries from which members of their race had not been systematically excluded, the Court nonetheless rejected the equal protection challenge to the consistent prosecution practice of striking potential black jurors. Both the majority and the dissenters maintained that only "systematic exclusion" gave rise to a constitutional infraction.[48] On its facts, the *Swain* Court was unconvinced that "purposeful discrimination based on race alone [wa]s satisfactorily"[49] sustainable on a showing of minimal disparity in the level of underrepresentation of blacks from the venire list.[50] The Warren Court's 1968 decision in *Green v. County School Board*,[51] however, signified a judicial willingness to hold government responsible for racial disparities not necessarily traceable to direct government action. In *Green*, the Court examined the impact of a "freedom of choice" desegregation plan adopted by the New Kent County school board under which formerly de jure segregated public schools remained predominantly of one race. Writing for the Court, Justice Brennan explained that the board had an affirmative duty to adopt appropriate measures to convert a dual-school system into a "unitary system in which racial discrimination would be eliminated root and branch."[52] The Court found that the challenged "freedom of choice" plan fell short of this obligation.[53]

The significance of *Green* to the development of equal protection doctrine was twofold: First, *Green* marked the beginning of the Court's serious examination of the issue of remedies for established practices of discrimination.[54] Secondly, *Green* hinted that the Court considered the *impact* of a governmental practice relevant to the determination whether the practice violated equal protection.[55] But *Green* was decided in the twilight of the Warren years. Fourteen years had elapsed since the Court's rejection of racial segregation in *Brown*. Yet little had been done actually to advance enforcement of blacks' equal protection rights. Indeed, the travesty of *Brown* came one year later in the 1955 *Brown II* "all deliberate speed" formula.[56]

> That formula was wrong for four reasons. First, it had no affirmative justification. . . . Secondly, there was on no view any need for the Court sanctioning delay. . . . Thirdly, on its face the formula invited white dissent and obstruction. . . . Fourthly, and most fundamentally, there was asked of the laity . . . an understanding that something could be unlawful, while it was nevertheless lawful to continue it for an indefinite time. Invocation of respect for law, the strongest weapon we could have had, became nothing but an invitation to dispute on this paradox.[57]

In 1958 the Court, in *Cooper v. Aaron*,[58] "condemn[ed] open resistance with firm resolve."[59] There, the Court rejected a petition by the Little Rock, Arkansas, school board requesting a stay of its integration plan due to public hostility and threatened violence. Notwithstanding the national attention that had been given to the Arkansas governor's decision to dispatch the National Guard to prevent integration, a fact that supported the board's asserted fear of violence, the Court, in a unanimous opinion, found that "the constitutional rights of [black children could] not be sacrificed or yielded to . . . violence and disorder." "[L]aw and order," the Court stated, "are not . . . to be preserved by depriving the Negro children of their constitutional rights."[60]

Despite this apparent unbending commitment to prompt desegregation, the Court's resolve soon weakened. In the interim between *Cooper* and *Green*, the Court had countenanced delay and failed to impose clear criteria with respect to the remedial obligations of the states to eradicate discrimination.[61] In the closing years of the Warren era, this pattern was perhaps simply too much for *Green* to overcome.

One other area in which the Warren Court made significant strides in the protection of minority interests under the Equal Protection Clause deserves mention—namely, reapportionment. The first major case to reach the Supreme Court challenging congressional districting was *Colegrove v. Green*.[62] The plaintiffs in *Colegrove* argued that the districting plan lacked the appropriate geographical compactness as well as approximate equality of population. A majority of the Court dismissed the action; however, the Justices could not reach agreement on the basis for dismissal. It was in *Colegrove*, however, that Justice Frankfurter coined the classic phrase: the "Court[ ] ought not enter into this political thicket."[63]

Following *Colegrove*, the first key reapportionment case to reach the Warren

Court was *Gomillion v. Lightfoot.*[64] In *Gomillion* black voters in Tuskegee, Alabama, challenged a districting plan devised by the Alabama legislature under which the City of Tuskegee was transformed from a square to a "strangely irregular" twenty-eight-sided polygon. The district court dismissed the claim. Observing that "[t]he essential inevitable effect of this redefinition of Tuskegee's boundaries [was] to remove from the city all save only four or five of its 400 Negro voters while not removing a single white voter or resident,"[65] the Warren Court found that plaintiffs had stated a justiciable claim of race discrimination. The basis of the Court's conclusion, however, stemmed, not from the Equal Protection Clause of the Fourteenth Amendment, but rather, from the Fifteenth Amendment.[66]

Two years later in *Baker v. Carr,*[67] the Warren Court broke new ground when it squarely found a reapportionment challenge justiciable under the Fourteenth Amendment.[68] The *Baker* Court's distinction between nonjusticiable reapportionment challenges, based on the Republican Form of Government Clause of the Constitution,[69] and justiciable claims, based upon the integrity of an individual's vote, set the stage for the "one person, one vote" principle ratified by Chief Justice Earl Warren in *Reynolds v. Sims.*[70]

Reynolds challenged the failure of the Alabama legislature—in contravention of the state constitution's mandate to do so—to reapportion decennially on the basis of population. The Warren Court found that to account for population shifts, states were required by the Fourteenth Amendment periodically to reapportion to ensure that districts remained approximately equal in size.[71] In other words, *Reynolds* rooted the state's obligation in the Fourteenth Amendment and opposed and precluded individual vote dilution by malapportioned districting practices.[72] The one person, one vote principle eventually was extended by the Warren Court to encompass, in addition to statewide apportionment plans, those of all local representative bodies with "general governmental powers."[73]

Baker and *Reynolds* supplied the groundwork for future developments in the voting rights area. The potential of the one person–one vote principle to provide effective constitutional protection against the vote dilution of racial minorities, however, was not fully appreciated during the era in which it was established.[74] Developments in this area, which have proved erratic, were left to future judicial administrations.[75]

Since *Brown,* much has been written about the antidiscrimination principle and the moral and legal force of the "equality" read into the Equal Protection Clause of the Fourteenth Amendment during the Warren years.[76] Indeed, "the very idea of equality as a constitutional norm"[77] has been sharply challenged. But if the enactment of the Fourteenth Amendment accomplished anything it was to incorporate into the Constitution "not the abstraction that likes should be treated alike, but the principle of equal citizenship."[78]

The first Justice Harlan, dissenting in *Plessy v. Ferguson,*[79] understood the nature of the citizenship afforded blacks under a complete reading of the Civil War amendments.[80] Harlan's dissent poignantly captures what was wrong with American society, and consequently, what the Civil War amendments were designed to correct. "[I]n view of the Constitution," Harlan argued, "in the eye of the law, there is in this country no superior, dominant ruling class of citizens. There is no caste here. Our Constitution is color-blind, and neither knows nor tolerates classes among citizens. In respect of civil rights, all citizens are equal before the law."[81]

Warren, like the first Justice Harlan, recognized a fundamental character of citizenship. During his tenure, a comprehensive, if not coherent definition of citizenship emerged—one that was not merely abstract and doctrinal, but concrete and practical. "First, citizenship is the right to be heard and counted on public affairs, the right to vote on equal terms, to speak, and to hold office when legitimately chosen."[82] "Secondly, citizenship means the right to be treated fairly when one is the object of action by that government of which one is also a part."[83] "Thirdly, citizenship is the broad right to lead a *private* life—for without this all dignity and happiness are impossible, and public rights mere futilities."[84] Finally, "to this triad, defining as it does the good political life, the Warren Court . . . added one more thing—a thing our history made it sadly necessary to add. It . . . affirmed, as no Court before [and since] . . . ever did, that this three-fold citizenship is to be enjoyed in all its parts without respect to race."[85]

The Warren Court, successfully resurrected Harlan's dissent in the sense that it too, beginning with *Brown*, endorsed an expansive view of citizenship. As a young man coming of age in the era of *Brown*, I can remember distinctly the doors and, more important, the minds, that opened as a result of the High Court's decision. Having attended segregated schools, I personally understood the import of the equal citizenship endorsed by *Brown*. That ideal released in numerous black children aspirations that previously had been unrealistic. Some tangible changes in the access to and provision of basic services also were evident. Without *Brown*'s liberating construction of the Equal Protection Clause, society's progress both within and without the realm of race relations is unimaginable. Nonetheless, the Warren Court failed completely to insulate itself, and more important, the antidiscrimination principle from persistent attack.[86] Once it had imposed the nondiscrimination requirement, the Warren Court spent the rest of its era in a doctrinal holding pattern.

To be certain, post-*Brown* cases of the Warren era extended and defended application of the principle,[87] but they did little to refine the principle or fashion remedial standards for redress. In the end, then, the Warren Court, while substantially advancing equal protection jurisdiction by giving content to the guarantee, failed to take adequate measures to ensure the longevity of the principle through proper enforcement or to articulate a coherent theory justifying its standards.

The threshold challenge, however, that the race decisions of the Warren Court were unprincipled infusions of the judicial will into the otherwise barren Equal Protection Clause[88] is unfounded. In each aspect of equal protection doctrine to which the Warren Court gave renewed life,[89] there existed sound judicial precedent.[90] The Warren Court boldly advanced the growth of these doctrines, but it did not, simply on a whim or in response to the politics of the day,[91] create law from whole cloth. Long before 1954, the Supreme Court had begun to recognize, if only sporadically, the hypocrisy of its racial jurisprudence under the Constitution. For example, as early as 1879, the Court held in *Strauder v. West Virginia*,[92] that a state statute excluding blacks from jury duty violated the Fourteenth Amendment. Explaining the content of the equal protection guarantee, the Court said, "[t]he words of the amendment, it is true, are prohibitory, but they contain a necessary implication of a positive immunity, or right, most valuable to the colored race,—the right to exemption from unfriendly legislation against them distinctively as colored. . . ."[93]

Almost sixty years later, the Supreme Court introduced the notion that heightened scrutiny of legislation classifying persons on the basis of race may be both appropriate and necessary to ensure effective protection of constitutional rights. In the otherwise unremarkable case of *United States v. Carolene Products Co.*,[94] Justice Stone, in the now famous footnote 4, emphasized the distinction between general legislation and that imposing restrictions affecting fundamental rights or minority interests, and pondered the proper judicial role within each category.[95] Justice Stone suggested that there may be "narrower scope" for the presumption of constitutionality of legislation affecting rights explicitly protected by the Constitution. He left open the questions whether legislation restricting the political process should be "subjected to more exacting judicial scrutiny" under Fourteenth Amendment challenge and "whether prejudice against discrete and insular minorities may be a special condition . . . which may call for a correspondingly more searching judicial inquiry."[96]

In *Shelley v. Kraemer*,[97] the Court considered whether judicial enforcement of racially restrictive covenants constituted discriminatory state action, and thus was prohibited by the Fourteenth Amendment. The Court ruled in the affirmative, expressing "no doubt" that the challenged conduct fell within the "full and complete" meaning of state action.[98] "[B]ut for the active intervention of the state courts, supported by the full panoply of state powers," the Court continued, "the petitioners would have been free to occupy the properties in question without restraint."[99] The Court, in effect, refused to tolerate state-sanctioned discrimination masquerading as purely private activity.[100]

Turning to the Warren Court's one person–one vote principle, one finds ample support in the case law implicating the values that Warren brought to the fore in *Reynolds v. Sims*. As early as 1886, the Supreme Court observed, "The . . . political franchise of voting is . . . a fundamental political right, because [it is] preservative of all rights."[101] Moreover, in the early part of the twentieth century the Court consistently reviewed—with some measure of success for minority interests—challenges under the Equal Protection Clause to procedures designed to prevent or deter blacks' exercise of the right to vote conferred by the Fifteenth Amendment.[102]

The contributions of the Warren Court to equal protection interpretation in the area of race were significant. The shortcomings of the Warren Court jurisprudence, however, left several unanswered questions. The responsibility to develop doctrinal standards thus passed on to the next Court under Chief Justice Warren Burger.

II

In 1969, when Warren Burger[103] assumed the position of Chief Justice of the United States, significant legislative advancements in the race discrimination area had occurred in Congress. A full array of civil rights legislation had been passed with the support and encouragement of President Lyndon B. Johnson.[104] Although the constitutionality of much of the Civil Rights era legislation already had been upheld by the Warren Court,[105] the Burger Court inherited the task of developing and articulating the appropriate standards that would govern its enforcement. Legitimate fears[106] that the Burger Court would eviscerate the protections afforded by the judicial current of the prior decades were both assuaged and realized. For although it is probably true that the Burger Court, on the whole, left intact, and in some instances broadened,[107] the core principles established during the Warren era, isolated examination of its contributions in select race cases reveals an irresolute body of equal protection law.

Perhaps most unfriendly to the equality principle of the Warren era was the Burger Court's near universal infusion of a constitutional standard of intent for claims of racial discrimination under the Civil War amendments.[108] Prior to 1976 it was not clear whether intent to discriminate was required to establish a constitutional violation where there was a disparate impact on a suspect class.[109] The *Green* majority during the Warren era had implied that adverse impact on racial minorities was at least relevant to the question whether the constitutional obligation under the Equal Protection Clause to desegregate had been satisfied, or conversely stated, whether equal protection had been violated.[110] Left unclarified, however, was whether the state's obligation to desegregate was identical to that not to discriminate initially, and, thus, subject to the same standard, or whether it was an independent, remedial obligation subject to a different standard under the Fourteenth Amendment. Finally, what the standard was and what would constitute proof thereof, similarly was imprecisely stated. The Burger Court added to the enigma in *Palmer v. Thompson*.[111]

Palmer v. Thompson addressed the decision of the city council of Jackson, Mississippi, to close all public swimming pools in defiance of court-ordered integration. As justification for its decision, the city argued that maintenance of the pools was no longer safe or economically feasible. In a sharply divided opinion, the Burger Court found that no rights protected by the Equal Protection Clause had been violated.[112] Although the state action requirement clearly was satisfied, the majority could discern no illicit motive of the Mississippi legislature, which, in its view was, in any event, irrelevant. The majority reasoned that if legislative motive were the linchpin on which the constitutionality of a legislative enactment turned, the legislature could simply reenact the challenged law on different grounds.[113] Conversely, the dissenters found a close nexus between the legislative motive and the timing of the decision to close the pools. In their view, closing the pools *after* an order to desegregate constituted an illegal contravention of the Fourteenth Amendment, which could not be cured by the post hoc advancement of nonracial reasons.[114] In short, the dissenters believed that the plaintiffs had satisfied their evidentiary burden, and further, that the improper legislative motive went far toward establishing invidious purpose.

In addition to rejecting improper legislative motive as probative evidence of a constitutional violation, the majority also maintained, albeit quite disingenuously, that the impact of the city's decision would be shared by both races.[115] Because both whites and blacks would be deprived of swimming facilities, there could be no claim that the city's action was taken with impermissible racial animus. In combination, the *Palmer* Court's views on the relevance of motive and impact seemed to suggest that, while motive was patently irrelevant, proof of disproportionate impact might give rise to a constitutional claim.[116] Specifically, the Court acknowledged that "[i]t is true there is language in some of our cases interpreting the Fourteenth and Fifteenth Amendments which may suggest that the motive or purpose behind a law is relevant to its constitutionality. But the focus in those cases was on the *actual effect* of the enactments, not upon the motivation which led the States to behave as they did."[117] Thus, *Palmer* represented an unhappy paradox for advocates of racial equality. On the one hand, the result of the decision was deplorable, for the clear effect was to deprive blacks access to swimming facilities. Moreover, parallel claims of safety and financial hardship had been dismissed by the Warren Court in *Cooper v. Aaron*.[118] On the other hand, however, the doctrinal implications of the Court's rejection of the probative force of discriminatory motive were, in retrospect, promising.

Any hopes aroused by *Palmer* were shattered by the Court's decision in *Washington v. Davis*.[119] *Davis* considered the claim by unsuccessful black applicants for positions on the police force in the predominately black District of Columbia, that the administration of a test assessing communication skills disproportionately operated to deprive blacks of employment in contravention of the Equal Protection Clause. Selectively citing prior case law,[120] the Burger Court declared that "our cases have not embraced the proposition that a law or other official act, without regard to whether it reflects a racially discriminatory purpose, is unconstitutional *solely* because it has a racially disproportionate impact."[121] Thus, the Court held that "[d]isproportionate impact is not irrelevant, but it is not the sole touchstone of an invidious racial discrimination forbidden by the Constitution. Standing alone, it does not trigger . . . strict[ ] scrutiny."[122]

Davis made clear that where state action produced a disparate effect on a suspect class equal protection was not violated ipso facto. Instead, in order to establish that an impermissible racial classification exists, thereby triggering strict scrutiny, plaintiffs must demonstrate that any disproportionate impact was by design, not by chance.[123] Only then will the state be subjected to a high burden of justification for its actions. After *Davis*, subjective motivation or intent generally is insufficient, if not irrelevant, to prove impermissible discriminatory purpose, and statistical evidence of disproportionate impact rarely will satisfy the intent requirement.

The Burger Court extended the reach of the intent requirement to voting rights claims under the Fifteenth Amendment in *City of Mobile v. Bolden*.[124] In *Bolden*, the Court refused to invalidate Mobile's at-large voting scheme for the election of all three of the city's commissioners. Notwithstanding proof that no black had ever been elected under the scheme, according to the Court, absent proof of a racially discriminatory purpose in the city's adoption of the procedure, no equal protection violation existed. The Burger Court's imposition of the intent requirement as the basis for liability in *Bolden* practically ensured that vote dilution claims against at-large election systems would be unsuccessful because it always would be virtually impossible to meet the evidentiary burden of proving the intent of such a large body.[125] To ease the ominous burden imposed in *Bolden*, Congress, two years later, amended Section 2 of the Voting Rights Act expressly to permit consideration of "[t]he extent to which members of a protected class have been elected to office in the State or political subdivision" as evidence of a violation.[126]

The Burger Court further heightened the threshold burden of those seeking relief from racially discriminatory practices in its rather provincial and unimaginative reading of the state action requirement. In a case arising out of the controversy underlying *Evans v. Newton*, the Burger Court significantly undercut the Warren Court's earlier decision prohibiting state involvement in private discrimination. In *Evans v. Abney*,[127] the Burger Court affirmed the holding of the Georgia courts that Senator Bacon's property reverted to his heirs for failure of testamentary purpose.[128] The Court reasoned that "[t]he construction of wills is essentially a state-law question, and in this case the Georgia Supreme Court, as we read its opinion, interpreted Senator Bacon's will as embodying a preference for termination of the park rather than its integration. Given this the Georgia court had no alternative under its relevant trust laws, which [we]re longstanding and neutral with regard to race, but to end the Baconsfield trust and return the property to the Senator's heirs."[129] The Court found that because "the Constitution impose[d] no requirement upon the Georgia court to approach Bacon's will any differently than it would approach any will creating any charitable trust of any kind,"[130] no equal protection guarantee was breached by impermissible state action.

In dissent, Justice Brennan's incisive rejoinder exposed the practical flaw in the majority's reasoning. When the senator's land had operated as a public park for almost half a century, Justice Brennan observed, and "would remain open but for the constitutional command that it be operated on a nonsegregated basis, the closing of the facility conveys an unambiguous message of community involvement in racial discrimination."[131] Moreover, Justice Brennan concluded, contrary to the majority, that "th[e] discriminatory closing [wa]s permeated with state action."[132]

Although not breaking new doctrinal ground, the Court's decision in *Moose Lodge No. 1 v. Irvis*[133] signaled a further retreat from Warren Court decisions considering whether proof of state action had been established. In *Moose Lodge* the privately owned lodge refused to provide service to blacks. Although the state granted the lodge its liquor license and closely monitored it on that basis, the Court refused to find sufficient nexus between the state and the overtly private discriminatory conduct.

Even in a series of cases involving court-ordered measures designed to remedy *established* violations of the Fourteenth Amendment, the Burger Court adopted a restrictive approach. In *Milliken v. Bradley*,[134] the Burger Court held that the district court lacked authority to order an interdistrict remedy after a finding of unlawful discrimination only within the city of Detroit. Despite the finding of the district court, affirmed by the court of appeals, that a Detroit-only remedy would be ineffective because, as a result of deliberate segregation, the school system in the city was 70 percent black, the Supreme Court held, in effect, that the district court's remedial powers did not extend beyond the geographic area of the violation.[135]

Similarly, in *Pasadena City Board of Education v. Spangler*,[136] the Court again rejected district court authority to order broad remedial relief in response to unlawful school segregation. After finding that the Pasadena school system had operated a dual system of education, the district court ordered annual adjustments of school district boundaries to guard against resegregation. In overruling the district court's decision, the Burger Court concluded that absent proof that disturbances in the racial balance of the school system were caused by "segregative acts" of the board in drawing district lines, the district court exceeded both its authority and responsibility to redress the initial charge of segregation. In short, *Milliken I*[137] and *Spangler* limited the scope of judicial power to remedy the intentional conduct from which liability arose, whether or not the remedy thus narrowed would redress the constitutional harm.

Perhaps the most troublesome (and troubling) aspect of race law during the Burger years arose in the context of race-conscious remedies for constitutional violations—affirmative action. Indeed, the Burger Court's internal discomfort with affirmative action is evident in its persistent inability to command a majority opinion. The Court first addressed the specific issue "whether government may use race-conscious programs to redress the continuing effects of past discrimination" in *Regents of the University of California v. Bakke.*[138] In perhaps its most famous decision[139] in the area of race, on facts now well known, the Court found the Davis Medical School special admissions plan—which "involve[d] the use of an explicit racial classification"[140] and quotas—repugnant to the Fourteenth Amendment. The Court refused, however, to bar all uses of race in fashioning remedies for past discrimination. Instead, the Court recognized that "the State has a substantial interest that legitimately may be served by a properly devised . . . program involving the competitive consideration of race and ethnic origin."[141]

The competing views of the opinion of Justice Powell and the separate concurrence and dissent authored by Justice Brennan on the influence of race in American society sounded a theme that would resonate in the Court's subsequent decisions on affirmative action. Specifically, the Powell opinion stated:

> The clock of our liberties . . . cannot be turned back to 1868. . . . [I]t is far too late to argue that the guarantee of equal protection to *all* persons permits the recognition of special wards entitled to a degree of protection greater than that others. . . . The concepts of "majority" and "minority" necessarily reflect temporary arrangements and political judgments. . . . There is no principled basis for deciding which groups would merit "heightened judicial solicitude" and which would not.[142]

Justice Brennan, on the other hand, urged candid recognition of American racial history:

> Our Nation was founded on the principle that "all Men are created equal." Yet candor requires acknowledgment that the Framers of our Constitution, to forge the 13 Colonies into one Nation, openly compromised this principle of equality with its antithesis: slavery. . . . Against this background, claims that law must be "color-blind" or that the datum of race is no longer relevant to public policy must be seen as aspiration rather than as description of reality.[143]

After *Bakke*, the Burger Court considered five additional direct challenges to affirmative action programs in distinct contexts.[144] The first of these *Fullilove v. Klutznick*[145] involved a challenge to congressional power to enact affirmative action relief for racial minorities. Although the plan, which set aside 10 percent of certain government contracts for minority businesses, was upheld, the question whether the equal protection guarantee—applicable to the federal government through the Due Process Clause of the Fifth Amendment—imposed any limits on the government's benign use of race-conscious criteria in awarding contracts was not resolved completely. Chief Justice Burger, without articulating the applicable standard, found that Congress possessed the power to eliminate racial discrimination in federal contracting. Justice Powell separately indicated that the set-aside was justified by a compelling governmental interest. Justice Marshall, joined by Justices Brennan and Blackmun, argued that a federal set-aside program should survive constitutional muster where the racial classification was substantially related to an important governmental interest.[146]

In the remaining four cases, *United Steelworkers of America v. Weber*,[147] *Wygant v. Jackson Board of Education*,[148] *Local 28, Sheetmetal Workers v. EEOC*,[149] and *Local No. 93, International Association of Firefighters v. Cleveland*,[150] the Court did little to advance understanding of the constitutionality of the benign use of race, whether voluntary or remedial. In *Weber*, the Court upheld a voluntary affirmative action plan of a private employer as consistent with Title VII. The Court emphasized, however, that because no state action was involved in adoption or maintenance of the plan no constitutional issue was presented. *Wygant*, on the other hand, invalidated a voluntary, race-based layoff policy implemented by the Jackson school board to maintain racial integration on its faculty. The Court indicated that "societal discrimination, without more, is too amorphous a basis for imposing a racially classified remedy."[151] There was some indication, however, that a similar *hiring* policy designed to promote diversity would be constitutionally permissible. The *Sheetmetal* case upheld a district court remedial order, which, in part, mandated a certain percentage of nonwhite membership to cure proven discrimination against prior nonwhite applicants. Finally, the *Firefighters* case upheld, under Title VII, a district court–sanctioned consent decree that required a race-conscious promotion plan to integrate blacks and Hispanics into the department.[152] None of the opinions commanded a majority of the Justices, however, or they were decided solely on statutory grounds; therefore, no coherent theory of the constitutionality of affirmative action plans or the standards by which they were to be judged emerged.

Notwithstanding these developments, not all was bleak for claimants of racial discrimination before the Burger Court. Indeed, ironically, one of the Court's landmark decisions, in which I was involved as lead counsel, sanctioning broad and comprehensive remedial measures to redress the effects of deliberate segregation was cited in support of the restrictive decisions in *Milliken I* and *Spangler*.[153] In an opinion authored by Chief Justice Burger, *Swann v. Charlotte-Mecklenburg Board of Education*[154] considered both the affirmative obligation of a school board "to eliminate . . . all vestiges of state-imposed segregation," and the scope of the judicial authority to act in the absence of school board compliance with the edict of *Brown*. Approved as appropriate remedial measures were (1) the requirement of a specified mathematical ratio as "a starting point in the process of shaping a remedy"; (2) retention of one-race schools only if the school board demonstrated the absence of present or past discriminatory action as causative of that status; (3) the rearrangement of school districts; and (4) busing. *Swann*, a then-modern-day *Cooper v. Aaron*, was a monumental decision, for it represented an uncompromising and continued commitment to *Brown* in the face of staunch public opposition to many of the sanctioned remedies.[155] The Court recognized that judicial relief must meet the violation; federal courts were not only empowered, but obligated, to tailor relief responsive to the illegal conduct. Thus, despite the subsequent decisions in *Milliken I* and *Spangler*, *Swann* represents a comprehensive approach to the scope both of the obligation to desegregate and the power of the judiciary to effectuate integration in the face of noncompliance.

The Burger Court also made positive contributions to racial equality in the field of criminal law. In *Furman v. Georgia*,[156] the Court invalidated Georgia's death penalty statute, which effectively stayed executions in all fifty states whose statutes were similarly drafted. Although the plurality's opinion, which invalidated the statute on due process grounds, failed to recognize the invidious influence of race on the operation of the death penalty, a Warren Court holdover, Justice Douglas explicitly made the connection in his concurrence. Justice Douglas maintained that the capital punishment statute was invalid under the Eighth Amendment, which barred imposition of the death penalty on the basis of "race, religion, wealth, social position, or class, or . . . under a procedure that gives room for the play of such prejudices."[157] Douglas suspected that "the death sentence is disproportionately imposed and carried out on the poor, the Negro, and members of unpopular groups," and hence violative of the Eighth Amendment.[158] Thus, regardless of the constitutional basis relied upon by the majority, Justice Douglas's concurrence suggested that the racial disparities in the imposition of the death penalty had not escaped the attention of the Burger Court in its deliberations.

Finally, in a somewhat curious twist of history, it was the Burger Court that overruled the Warren Court's ruling in *Swain v. Alabama*. In *Swain*, the Warren Court held that in order to establish a prima facie case of impermissible use of peremptory challenges to exclude blacks from petit juries, the plaintiff must demonstrate that the prosecutors consistently excluded blacks from service on juries in the relevant jurisdiction. In *Batson v. Kentucky*,[159] however, in an opinion authored by Justice Marshall, the Burger Court recognized an equal protection challenge to the state's exercise of peremptory challenges, and, rejecting the rigid evidentiary requirements of *Swain*, held that a prima facie case of intentional discrimination in violation of equal protection is established solely by reference to the prosecutor's exercise of peremptories in the particular trial.[160]

Notwithstanding its mixed legacy, the Burger Court paved new ground in a variety of contexts: *First*, the Court differentiated between discrimination based upon disparate treatment and that alleged on the ground of statistical disparities or disparate impact on minorities. The disparate treatment theory of governmental discrimination, which presupposes intentionally adverse action because of the claimant's race, violates both the equal protection guarantee and congressional civil rights statutes designed to implement that guarantee. Moreover, although the Burger Court refused in *Washington v. Davis* to give constitutional status to claims based solely upon evidence of disparate impact, proof of such disparities was not totally discounted. Adhering to the requirement that claimants of racial discrimination violative of the Constitution must offer proof of invidious discriminatory purpose, the Burger Court nonetheless in *Village of Arlington Heights v. Metropolitan Housing Dev. Corp.*,[161] agreed that "[s]ometimes a clear pattern, unexplainable on grounds other than race, emerges from the effect of the state action even when the governing legislation appears neutral on its face."[162] Similarly, it was the Burger Court that in *Griggs v. Duke Power*[163] sanctioned a lesser standard of proof to establish a statutory claim of race discrimination.[164] Specifically, statistical evidence of racial imbalance in the workplace alone could be sufficient to make out a prima facie case of racial discrimination under the civil rights statute. In short, proof of discriminatory intent was unnecessary to a successful statutory challenge.

Second, the Burger Court imposed the requirement that judicial remedies be tailored to the established harm. This principle, endorsed and applied in *Swann*, possessed dynamic potential effectively to redress the pernicious effects of past wrongs. The Burger Court's subsequent desegregation decisions[165] may be understood as narrow constructions of the proven violation as opposed to a retreat from the general principle that the remedy fit the violation.

Third, the Court began to tackle the issue of remedies—albeit with mixed results—particularly with respect to race-conscious measures.[166] Still, the legacy of the Burger Court, in constitutional terms, in the provision of remedial relief to victims of racial discrimination is inconclusive. Beyond consensus on the constitutional status of intent in initial claims of discrimination, the Burger Court was deeply divided on the constitutionality of race-conscious remedies. Where presented with the opportunity, the Court either avoided or failed to enunciate majority-supported principles for determining the constitutionality of such measures. Finally, although the Court consistently indicated that both the constitutional duty to eliminate racial discrimination and any remedies imposed for that purpose were time-bound, the Court failed to provide clear and consistent guidance on the appropriate duration of the remedy as well as the point at which the affirmative duty to eliminate past discrimination should cease. Like the Warren Court before it, the Burger Court bequeathed its own set of un- or underdeveloped issues to its successor.

III

Justice William Rehnquist became Chief Justice in 1986 after Justice Burger announced his retirement from the Court to oversee the nation's preparation for the celebration of the Bicentennial of the United States Constitution. Justice Rehnquist's nomination and ultimate assumption of the role of Chief was met by the civil rights community with even greater apprehension than that of his predecessor.[167] Since his initial appointment to the bench by President Richard Nixon in 1972, Justice Rehnquist had earned the reputation as the most conservative member of the Court. In that capacity, "he championed a confined Constitution and a smaller role for judges."[168] Thus, questions regarding what his leadership would portend for civil rights were inevitable. Within the first five years of the new Rehnquist era,[169] the Court repeatedly seemed to confirm the fears of the civil rights bar and community.

By one count, the Rehnquist Court entertained and issued decisions in twenty-nine race cases in its first five years.[170] From these and later cases emerge three disturbing patterns. First, in one category of cases consisting of *Richmond v. J. A. Croson Co.*,[171] *McCleskey v. Kemp*,[172] and the Court's more recent decision in *Shaw v. Reno*,[173] a disconcerting view of the current Court's understanding of the legacy of racial discrimination in this country and its continuing effects rises to the surface. A second category, including *Spallone v. United States*,[174] *Freeman v. Pitts*,[175] and *Board of Education of Oklahoma City Pub. Sch. v. Dowell*,[176] reveals the Court's restrictive interpretations of the propriety and scope of measures designed to remedy proven discrimination. Finally, a third category—while not directly constitutional in character—consisting of a series of employment decisions[177] under the civil rights statutes, unveils a disquieting trend towards blurring the standards of proof applicable to statutory claims of discrimination and those applicable to claims of racial discrimination violative of equal protection. Although the personality of the Rehnquist Court has not yet jelled (due in large part to the successive resignations of Justices Brennan, Marshall, Blackmun, and White), the decisions of the Court thus far evince an injudicious impatience with race discrimination claims and a stingy construction of the laws and constitutional provisions on which they are based.

Richmond v. J. A. Croson Co.[178] was the first affirmative action case to reach the Rehnquist Court. At issue in *Croson* was a minority set-aside program adopted by the City of Richmond, Virginia, and fashioned to increase representation of minority-owned businesses in city-awarded construction contracts. Writing for the Court, Justice Sandra Day O'Connor characterized the Court's dilemma as a "confront[ation] once again [concerning] the tension between the Fourteenth Amendment's guarantee of equal treatment to all citizens, and the use of race-based measures to ameliorate the effects of past discrimination on the opportunities enjoyed by members of the minority groups in our society."[179] So stated, the tone, if not the language, of the Court's opinion implied that the identified interests were incompatible and yet identical in constitutional and historical stature. The majority went on to hold squarely that the use of racial classifications by state and local entities for whatever purpose was subject, without exception, to strict judicial scrutiny.[180]

In *Fullilove v. Klutznick*,[181] the Burger Court, although divided in theory, sanctioned the federal set-aside program at issue. The *Fullilove* plurality was particularly persuaded by the flexibility permitted under the minority business enterprise (MBE) provision of the Public Works Employment Act of 1977,[182] and heavily relied upon its operation in concluding that it was constitutional.[183] The *Croson* majority found that the Richmond program departed from the "fine tuning to remedial purpose, [without which] the statute [challenged in *Fullilove*] would not have 'pass[ed] muster.'"[184] In the *Croson* Court's view, the record was barren of proof that the Richmond set-aside program was narrowly tailored to remedy the effects of demonstrable past discrimination in which the specific governmental entity had participated. General claims of discrimination, the Court explained, were insufficient to justify affirmative efforts to benefit minorities. The Court further distinguished between the authority of Congress versus that of state and local entities to implement programs designed to rectify racial imbalances in government enterprises. "That Congress may identify and redress the effects of society-wide discrimination," the majority stated, "does not mean that . . . the States and their political subdivisions are free to decide that such remedies are appropriate."[185]

Conversely, in a particularly passionate dissent, Justice Marshall, joined by Justices Brennan and Blackmun, applauded as "a welcome symbol of racial progress" the efforts of "the former capital of the Confederacy . . . to confront the effects of racial discrimination in its midst."[186] Moreover, Justice Marshall found especially distressful the majority's apparent equation of the historically state sanctioned animus against racial minorities—particularly African Americans—and the standard by which such discrimination must be judged, with contemporary attempts to rectify the adverse effects of past discrimination:

> A profound difference separates governmental actions that themselves are racist, and governmental actions that seek to remedy the effects of prior racism or to prevent neutral governmental activity from perpetuating the effects of such racism. . . . *In concluding that remedial classifications warrant no different standard of review under the Constitution than the most brutal and repugnant forms of state-sponsored racism, the majority of this Court signals that it regards racial discrimination as largely a phenomenon of the past*, and that government bodies need no longer preoccupy themselves with rectifying racial injustice. I, however, do not believe this Nation is anywhere close to eradicating racial discrimination or its vestiges. In constitutionalizing its wishful thinking, the majority today does a grave disservice not only to those victims of past and present racial discrimination in this Nation whom government has sought to assist, but also to this Court's long tradition of approaching issues of race with the utmost sensitivity.[187]

The difference in the approach and conclusions of the majority and dissenting opinions in *Croson* is explained in part by their respective interpretations of Supreme Court precedent, but more so by the underlying assumptions about race, racial discrimination, and the present significance of both in modern society.[188] In short, the Rehnquist Court majority is unwilling to accept illicit discrimination as an explanation for racial divisions in twentieth-century America. Those differences were most manifest in perhaps the most significant Fourteenth Amendment decision issued in the early stages of the Rehnquist Court, *McCleskey v. Kemp.*[189]

Warren McCleskey, a black man, had been convicted and sentenced to death for the murder of a white person. McCleskey challenged the constitutionality of Georgia's death penalty statute under the Eighth and Fourteenth Amendments. Under both amendments, the Rehnquist Court rejected the constitutional significance of racial disparities in the imposition of the death sentence compiled in a study—the Baldus study[190]—presented by McCleskey in support of his claims. Specifically, with stakes as high as life or death, the Court upheld Georgia's death penalty statute in the face of damning statistics that indicated that defendants charged with killing white victims were 4.3 times more likely to receive the death penalty than were those charged with killing blacks.[191] The Rehnquist Court rejected McCleskey's equal protection challenge holding that the statistics alone were insufficient to show purposeful discrimination in the adoption, maintenance, or administration of the death penalty statute.[192] Similarly, the Court found the force of McCleskey's statistical evidence irrelevant to his Eighth Amendment claim.[193]

Dissenting in *McCleskey*, Justice Brennan, joined by Justices Marshall, Blackmun, and Stevens, focused on McCleskey's Eighth Amendment challenge, emphasizing the force of history undergirding McCleskey's claim of arbitrary racial disparity in the administration of capital punishment. "History and its continuing legacy . . . buttress the probative force of McCleskey's statistics. Formal dual criminal laws may no longer be in effect, and intentional discrimination may no longer be prominent. Nonetheless, . . . 'subtle, less consciously held racial attitudes' continue to be of concern."[194] Justice Brennan further noted that "we remain imprisoned by the past as long as we deny its influence in the present."[195] Airing the dissenters' intense sense of frustration, Justice Brennan warned that "the way in which we choose those who will die reveals the depth of moral commitment among the living."[196]

The refusal or failure of the Rehnquist Court to take seriously the history of racial discrimination and its painful legacy is generally coupled by and reinforced with references to the limited role of the judiciary in American society. In *McCleskey*, the Court continued this custom. Specifically, the Court concluded that "McCleskey's arguments are best presented to the legislative bodies."[197] Again, however, Justice Brennan poignantly refuted the majority's reliance on role definition to avoid its responsibility:

> The Court is, of course, correct to emphasize the gravity of constitutional intervention and the importance that it be sparingly employed. . . . The judiciary's role in this society counts for little[, however,] if the use of governmental power to extinguish life does not elicit close scrutiny. . . . Those whom we would banish from society or from the human community itself often speak in too faint a voice to be heard above society's demand for punishment. It is the particular role of courts to hear these voices, for the Constitution declares that the majoritarian chorus may not alone dictate the conditions of social life. The Court thus fulfills, rather than disrupts, the scheme of separation of powers by closely scrutinizing the imposition of the death penalty, for no decision of a society is more deserving of "sober second thought."[198]

In the third and final case that I have identified as illustrative of my perception of a disturbing and, perhaps cynical, understanding of historic racial discrimination, the Court's purportedly mandated deference to the legislature was not as forthcoming. In *Shaw v. Reno*,[199] the Rehnquist Court recognized an equal protection challenge of white voters to a "bizarrely shaped" majority-minority district in my home state of North Carolina.[200] The white voters did not allege that the challenged district in any way diluted their voting strength as a racial group. "Rather, [they] . . . alleged that the deliberate segregation of voters into separate districts on the basis of race violated their constitutional right to participate in a 'color-blind' electoral process."[201] Responding to Justice Souter's dissent in which he found no cognizable constitutional harm, the majority identified the potential harm caused by race-conscious districting as follows: "[Reapportionment legislation that cannot be understood as anything other than an effort to classify and separate voters by race . . . reinforces racial stereotypes and threatens to undermine our system of representative democracy by signaling to elected officials that they represent a particular racial group rather than their constituency as a whole."[202] Unpersuasive, or unimportant, to the Court was that the legislature's plan was designed actually to effectuate "representative democracy." Justice Blackmun noted the irony in dissent, emphasizing that the novel constitutional claim recognized by the Rehnquist Court was "a challenge by white voters to the plan under which North Carolina . . . sent black representatives to Congress for the first time since Reconstruction."[203]

The Rehnquist Court also has moved incrementally toward eliminating or frustrating the obligation of governmental actors to eradicate discrimination in American society. More specifically, the Rehnquist Court has simultaneously removed barriers for potentially recalcitrant state actors while erecting barriers in the path of district courts seeking to provide complete and effective relief for victims of discrimination. For example, in *Spallone v. United States*,[204] contempt sanctions imposed on members of the city council of Yonkers, New York were reversed by the Supreme Court.[205] The district court leveled the monetary fines following successful litigation by the United States against the City of Yonkers in which the city was found in violation of the Fourteenth Amendment and Title VIII of the Civil Rights Act of 1968 for intentionally reinforcing segregation in housing. The district court ordered the city to take affirmative steps to distribute public housing throughout the city to remedy the violation. As part of a consent decree entered in the case, the city agreed to implement the remedial command, in part, by enacting an ordinance that would condition construction of multifamily housing on the inclusion of a specified percentage of subsidized units. When the ordinance was proposed, however, several council members—whose votes were necessary for passage—refused to favor its adoption. The district court found the city and its council members in contempt and imposed hefty daily sanctions to compel compliance with the consent decree. Recognizing that "[t]here can be no question about the liability of the city of Yonkers for racial discrimination,"[206] the Rehnquist Court nonetheless reversed, stressing that the judiciary must undertake those measures that are least likely to disrupt the orderly operation of "the normal legislative process."[207]

Similar themes resounded in *Freeman v. Pitts*[208] and *Board of Educ. of Oklahoma City Pub. Sch. v. Dowell*.[209] In *Freeman*, a previously adjudicated de jure school system was again before the district court pursuant to its supervisory authority.[210] In 1983, the plaintiffs challenged as violative of the school system's affirmative obligation to desegregate a plan to construct an additional school site to alleviate overcrowding in a predominantly white high school.[211] The district court twice found that racial imbalances in student assignments were attributable to demographic forces beyond the control and responsibility of the school system. In the first round of litigation, the district court concluded that the challenged construction could be enjoined only upon proof of discriminatory intent. After reversal and remand with instructions to determine first whether the school system had achieved unitary status, the district court again essentially found no obligation of the school system to redress racial disparities in student assignments. Although the district court did find vestiges of the prior de jure system in two other aspects of the system,[212] and therefore, concluded that the school system had not achieved unitary status, it nonetheless held that no further relief or judicial supervision was warranted in those categories in which unitary status had been achieved, including student assignments.[213] On appeal, the Eleventh Circuit upheld the ultimate finding of non-unitariness, but overruled the trial court's abandonment of its supervisory role until unitary status was achieved in all relevant categories of operation.[214]

The Supreme Court granted certiorari to consider whether unitary status may be properly obtained in piecemeal fashion and whether demographic changes operate to discharge the obligation of a former de jure school system to desegregate. On both counts, the Rehnquist Court responded affirmatively. Emphasizing the "end purpose" of restoring state and local control over adjudicated de jure school systems, the Rehnquist Court upheld the incremental withdrawal of judicial supervision, thereby acquiescing in, if not encouraging, fragmented efforts to provide nondiscriminatory education to our children. Ironically, in a case initiated by black children and their parents, the Rehnquist Court indicated that the school system's demonstrated good faith commitment to the plaintiffs to the fulfillment of the goals of the entire decree should be a factor in the district court's determination whether judicial supervision should be incrementally withdrawn.[215] The Court also upheld as "credible" the district court's finding that the resegregation of the student population was not traceable to any unlawful conduct of the school system.[216]

In *Dowell*,[217] the Rehnquist Court again addressed questions concerning the proper scope, extent, and duration of judicial supervision of a prior de jure school system. After five years of active judicial supervision, the Oklahoma school system, in 1977, was declared unitary.[218] In 1984, however, the school board adopted a student reassignment plan under which the Oklahoma schools would essentially return to their previous one-race status.[219] The reassignment plan was adopted for the asserted purpose of alleviating unequal busing burdens imposed on black children as the result of demographic changes in the state. Just as in *Freeman*, parents of black students in *Dowell* charged that the new initiative would result in or exacerbate segregation. The *Dowell* plaintiffs, therefore, sought to revive the previously entered desegregation decree. The district court refused to reopen the case, however, adhering to the 1977 finding of unitariness.[220] On appeal, the court of appeals held that the plaintiffs could challenge the plan because the 1977 holding had not terminated the prior desegregation decree. As such, the school system remained under the supervision of the district court. On remand, the district court held that the school district's "good faith" compliance with the desegregation decree for over a decade justified dissolution of the decree. In addition, the district court found that the original plan was no longer workable, and that the new plan, notwithstanding the plaintiffs' contention that it would result in resegregation, was not adopted with discriminatory intent. The Tenth Circuit again reversed the district court, holding that the school district remained subject to the desegregation decree, until it could demonstrate "'grievous wrong evoked by new and unforeseen conditions.'"[221]

The Rehnquist Court rejected what it described as a "Draconian result" stemming from the stringent standard for dissolution of an injunction adopted and applied by court of appeals, and therefore reversed.[222] In its view, "[t]he test [for dissolution of a desegregation decree] espoused by the Court of Appeals would condemn a school district . . . to judicial tutelage for the indefinite future."[223] Instead, the Court reasoned that "federal supervision of local school systems [has always been] . . . intended as a temporary measure to remedy past discrimination."[224] "Considerations based on the allocation of powers within our federal system," the majority maintained, "support[ed] [the] view [that] injunctions entered in school desegregation cases . . . [we]re not intended to operate in perpetuity."[225]

Although it upheld the right of the plaintiffs to challenge the dissolution order, the Rehnquist Court remanded the case to the district court to determine whether the school board was, at the time the challenged plan was adopted, in sufficient compliance with the desegregation decree. If so, the Court indicated that it would be entitled to have the desegregation decree dissolved, and further, that any challenge to the present plan "should then . . . [be] evaluate[d] . . . under appropriate equal protection principles."[226] In other words, proof of intentional discrimination in the adoption of the challenged plan would be necessary following a determination that dissolution of the desegregation decree was warranted in 1985.

As to the question whether demographic changes would constitute constitutionally sufficient justification for the school board's adoption and implementation of the plan, the *Dowell* majority "hint[ed] that the District Court could ignore the effect of residential segregation in perpetuating racially identifiable schools if the court finds residential segregation to be 'the result of private decisionmaking and economics.'"[227] In dissent, Justice Marshall detailed the role of the Oklahoma school system in contributing to and exploiting residential segregation and renounced the majority's "equivocation" "on the effect to be given to the reemergence of racially identifiable schools."[228] Indeed, as indicated by the dissent, "that school segregation 'may have a profound reciprocal effect on the racial composition of residential neighborhoods'" is well established.[229] Moreover, "the roles of the State, local officials, and the Board in creating . . . self-perpetuating patterns of residential segregation . . . [and] negative 'personal preferences' . . . should not absolve a school district that played a role in creating such 'preferences' from its obligation to desegregate the schools to the maximum extent possible."[230] In light of the lessons of history, both generally and on the record of *Dowell*, the Rehnquist Court's failure to acknowledge directly residential segregation as a probable vestige of a de jure school system "is completely unsatisfying."[231]

In a perfect world, perhaps the decisions of the Rehnquist Court in *Freeman* and *Dowell* might be imminently prudent. Both decisions, however, are, in my view, grounded on the faulty or fanciful premise that all segments of American society are voluntarily marching, lockstep, towards the elimination of racial prejudice and discrimination. Yet they are in keeping with the Rehnquist Court's intransigent efforts to ascribe innocent explanations to even glaring indicia of racial discrimination, and, consequently to relieve nonminorities of the shared burden of achieving racial equality.

The Rehnquist Court's disturbing approach to race litigation is punctuated by five employment cases,[232] which prompted corrective congressional action, in which the Court practically eviscerated decades of civil rights precedent that had afforded significant relief to victims of discrimination. *Patterson v. McLean Credit Union*,[233] considered whether a Reconstruction statute[234] guaranteeing the right of all individuals "to make and enforce contracts" on equal grounds, included the right to be free from racial harassment and discriminatory treatment in the terms and conditions of employment. Employing a formalistic construction of Section 1981, the Court held that "the conduct which petitioner labels as actionable racial harassment is postformation conduct by the employer relating to the terms and conditions of continuing employment."[235] As such, it did not implicate the threshold rights protected by Section 1981, namely, to enter into the contract free of discrimination. In short, employers may not discriminate in their initial hiring practices; they may, however, without running afoul of Section 1981, impose unbearable and discriminatory conditions of employment on members of protected classes.[236]

In *Lorrance v. AT&T Technologies*,[237] the Court undercut the ability of employees to challenge successfully the harmful effects of discriminatory seniority plans. There the Court held that the statute of limitations applicable to such challenges commenced to run at the time the seniority plan was adopted as opposed to the time at which the harmful effects were realized. In *Price Waterhouse v. Hopkins*,[238] the Court heightened the burden on employees to establish liability in mixed motivation cases—that is, where the challenged conduct of the employer was based on a combination of legitimate and discriminatory factors.[239] *Martin v. Wilks*,[240] effectively made uncertain the rights of minorities pursuant to judicially approved consent decrees. In *Wilks*, white firefighters sued the City of Birmingham arguing that less-qualified blacks were promoted by the city on the basis of race. Black firefighters had sued the city successfully in 1974 for violation of Title VII in its hiring practices. A second trial challenging the city's promotional practices was aborted by two consent decrees entered prior to the judge's decision. The white firefighters had failed to intervene in either proceeding. The consent decrees developed an extensive remedial scheme that included hiring and promotion goals for black applicants and employees, respectively. Affirming the decision of the Eleventh Circuit, the Rehnquist Court recognized a broad right of the white firefighters to challenge the previously entered consent decrees.[241] The probable effect of *Wilks* was to invite litigation whenever an employer complied with a consent decree, thereby both discouraging settlement on the part of the employer and rendering reliance on judicially approved remedies imprudent for the intended beneficiaries of the consent decree.

Wards Cove Packing Co. v. Atonio,[242] perhaps more than any other case in this series, struck a potentially devastating blow to decades of civil rights law. The claim in *Wards Cove* was that a cannery company maintained a segregated workforce in violation of Title VII. Statistics indicated that white workers were concentrated in the skilled positions whereas nonwhite workers (Alaskan natives) were clustered in its unskilled positions. The Supreme Court "granted certiorari for the purpose of addressing . . . disputed questions of the proper application of Title VII's disparate-impact theory of liability."[243] On this question the Rehnquist Court reasoned that "[r]acial imbalance in one segment of an employer's work force does not, without more, establish a prima facie case of disparate impact with respect to the selection of workers for the employer's other positions, even where workers for the different positions may have somewhat fungible skills. . . ."[244] The something more that was needed, in the Court's opinion, could consist of proof that nonwhites were prevented or discouraged from applying for certain positions or that they actually were hired in those positions at a significantly lower rate than whites.[245]

In addition to rejecting the relevance of significant statistical disparities, the *Wards Cove* majority also shifted the evidentiary burden of explaining such disparities away from employers onto employees. Specifically, the Court found that employment programs or policies producing racially imbalanced workforces may be justified if they serve "legitimate employment goals" of the employer.[246] Despite the disparate impact caused by such practices, they need not be either "'essential' or 'indispensable'" to the business. Moreover, "[t]he burden of persuasion [that the practices are unjustified] . . . remains with the disparate-impact plaintiff."[247] The reasoning in *Wards Cove* ran completely counter to that relied upon by the Burger Court in *Griggs*. "While *Griggs* followed *Brown*'s aspiration to a society free of racial distinctions, *Wards Cove* reject[ed] such aspirations as meddlesome to employers and tainted with the possibility of racial parity."[248]

On November 21, 1991, the Civil Rights Act of 1991 was signed into law. The chief objective of the legislation—like that of an earlier version vetoed by President Bush in 1990—was to nullify the harmful effects of the Supreme Court's 1989 term employment discrimination decisions. Indeed, the act as ultimately passed endeavored to do more. In addition to restoring many of the principles that had previously effectively and fairly governed employment discrimination lawsuits, Congress provided for compensatory and punitive damages for successful civil rights claimants.[249] Also permitted in certain circumstances under the provisions of the 1991 act are jury trials in intentional discrimination cases.[250]

Notwithstanding the swift and forceful legislative response from Congress, the Rehnquist Court has already issued decisions narrowing the reach of the 1991 Civil Rights Act. In *Landgraf v. USI Film Products*,[251] the Court held that the provisions for compensatory and punitive damages, and trial by jury, should such damages be claimed, do not apply retroactively to cases pending on appeal at the time the statute was passed. Similarly, in *Rivers v. Roadway Express*,[252] the Court rejected retroactive application of the legislative reversal of *Patterson v. McLean Credit Union*. What may be expected for the future of race law under the leadership of Chief Justice Rehnquist is unpredictable. Indeed, there have been scattered successes for minority interests before the Court since the start of his tenure as Chief.[253] Yet the tone and effect—intended or not—of the bulk of Rehnquist Court decisions considering traditional charges of discrimination by racial minorities or the constitutionality of race-conscious remedies for violations of the civil rights laws or the equal protection guarantee[254] have persistently questioned, challenged, or totally discounted the relevance of race and racial discrimination to the current condition of racial minorities, most notably, African Americans. While the race decisions of the Rehnquist Court denounce any presumption that statistical disparities are indicative of invidious barriers to minority access to and participation in the challenged activity, they all too eagerly embrace the converse presumption that the condition of racial minorities is solely of their own choosing. In my estimation, unless this Court begins to appreciate and enforce the broad, reformative purpose and potential of the Civil War amendments, it cannot and will not treat with the requisite sensitivity the complex racial dynamic in contemporary American society.

IV

Perhaps with the exception of the right to privacy encompassing a woman's choice to terminate a pregnancy,[255] much of the Supreme Court's jurisprudence expanding the scope of substantive rights has not evoked the intense reaction and condemnation—either from the public or the legal community—that exists in the area of race. This fact alone suggests that we have not overcome the dilemma of race in American society. The consequence of our failure as a nation to confront squarely the issue of race has obvious long-term social effects. But the notion that law is not equipped to address effectively some of the racial problems that continue to plague us is ultimately destructive: "Racism *is* a special subject in the United States, whether in or outside the law; it is *the* special subject in the United States. A system of law which is self-disabled from seeing it as such, and so from fashioning concepts and remedies to fit racism, if need be, uniquely, would be a law that could not be of any use as the legal system of the United States."[256]

The Warren Court's courageous and, to a significant degree, successful efforts to effect positive social change defy arguments to the contrary. Criticisms of those efforts have exaggerated the message of and distorted the actual role played by the Warren Court. In *Earl Warren: A Public Life* by Edward White, for example, White argues that Warren "invited the public to think that 'every major social ill . . . can find its cure in some constitutional principle.'"[257] Others have suggested that the Warren Court's activism was counter to our time-honored principles of democracy. Raoul Berger posed the question "whether the people may govern themselves or whether they have surrendered self-government to a nonelected, life-tenured, self-constituted set of Platonic Guardians."[258] The notion that activism always results in judicial fiat, usurpations, or counter-majoritarian policy-making, however, is neither obvious nor inevitable. Instead, activism may indeed "alert the remainder of the political system to legitimate problems that elected officials have failed to handle adequately."[259] Stubborn insistence that liberating initiatives come from the legislatures or not at all is simply irresponsible. "[I]ndividual rights adjudication under the constitution exists primarily to ensure an open political process and to protect powerless minorities against abuses of that process."[260]

Such protection includes judicial recognition and definition of individual rights. Moreover, contrary to the jaded argument that "courts simply are not equipped to make 'wise policy,' and therefore judicial policy-making can *never* effectively meet pressing societal needs,"[261] judges are as equipped as legislators to entertain intelligently questions of general social policy. The more germane inquiry is whether the law and the judges who interpret it are capable of fully extending to the least advantaged in our society those precious benefits and protections that for too long have been the exclusive possession of the dominant culture. This question is ultimately one of values. Neither structural nor process-oriented concerns dictate a different conclusion.

Conclusion

In concluding, I quote heavily from the article from which the title of my essay is paraphrased. The well-known charges against the so-called illicit judicial activism of the Warren Court are not merely academic. They undergird current thinking on the Supreme Court concerning the proper scope of the judicial role. Yet it seems to me that these concerns are either disingenuous, misguided, or both. Disingenuous because elements of activism have and do attach to even the most conservative of courts. And appropriately so. Misguided for precisely that reason. "Activism," in my opinion, is only inappropriate when it reflects the underlying fears that urge restraint. Thus, if judicial activism results in patently antidemocratic results—as measured by society's response through its elected representatives—then, the Court may be rightly indicted for usurping the democratic function. Even here, however, judgment must be tempered by the reality that our legal and political system has never purported to sanction the tyrannical reign of popular prejudices.

Far from undermining democracy, the Warren Court side-tracked the absolute political, social, and economic domination of African Americans, and in so doing, made real the democratic pledge of the Constitution. "The law of the Warren Court is on the whole a law of political health and wisdom, worth the most earnest sustaining advocacy, and sustainable if that advocacy is forthcoming."[262] That the racial jurisprudence of the Warren Court was and is consistent with the structural framework of our political system is confirmed by the receptive responses of the coordinate branches of government. When Congress or the Executive acts to implement both the letter and spirit of decisions of the Supreme Court, as it did during the Warren era, I believe that democracy has worked well. When, conversely, Congress is called upon to invalidate the judicial will as expressed in Supreme Court decisions, as has been the case in recent administrations, the process has broken down. In other words, charges of illicit judicial activism ring hollow where coordinate branches of the federal government act to confirm the courageous actions of another. Thus, on one view "[t]he genius of the Warren Court was not that it created rights . . . but rather, that it rejected the apologetic pluralism of its age . . . and placed into its jurisprudence a critical pluralist interpretation of politics."[263]

Professor Charles Black's examination of the work of the Warren Court one year after Warren's resignation retains vitality today. Black observed that "any legal system contains, intellectually, the means of frustrating itself, of bringing its most solemnly enunciated commands to nothing, just as any healthy human being carries with him always the means of bringing about his own disgrace or death."[264] Mechanistic applications of the law in ways that undermine the principle of *Brown* arguably may not be "technically wrong." But, as Black warned, the question then, as now, is whether "our legal system has the will to stand by *Brown*, and to make *Brown* stick, no matter what evasive scheme is devised? . . . [T]he answer to this question answers the question whether our legal system has in it enough honesty to deserve to live."[265]

In his classic commentary on the nature of constitutional decision making, Black continued:

> The intellectual soundness of a constitutional system may . . . be shown in its differentiating one kind of discrimination from another—or in its evidentiary or remedial rules which are applicable to one but not to the other—as by its lumping them together. If the life of the law has been experience, then experience teaches that tolerable solutions to the problems of law are rarely attainable by the utterance and Procrustean application of huge generalizations. Tolerable solutions, moreover, are not attainable, never have been attainable, and never will be attainable if justice must wait until answers are given to every question intellectual curiosity can suggest as to the reaches and connection of every rule.[266]

In the field of race relations in American society, the first Justice Harlan dissenting in *Plessy* admonished us long ago: "[T]he destinies of the two races, in this country, are indissolubly linked together, and the interests of both require that the common government of all shall not permit the seeds of race hate to be planted under the sanction of law."[267] The legacy of the Warren Court was one of racial equality and equal citizenship. The Warren Court decisions assisted in unifying the nation during turbulent times, and bore witness to the fact that racial harmony and racial equality are not incompatible goals. As incremental assaults on the groundwork of the Warren Court persist, "what might be the right question to put to ourselves about [its legacy,] . . . [t]he question with meaning, the realistic question, the answerable question, is not whether the Warren Court succeeded. . . . The answerable question, the question that hard realism asks, is whether we want to make it succeed."[268] I believe that with a concerted reaffirmation of and commitment to the promise of racial equality made over a century ago with the enactment of the Civil War amendments, that we, as a nation can make it succeed.

Notes

1. See Levy, Karst, and Mahoney, eds. *American Constitutional History* 292 (Macmillan, 1989).

2. It further exemplifies, in my view, the guiding principles that should inform the current Court in its treatment of the continuing effects of past racial discrimination in comtemporary society. That such effects continue to plague us should be beyond dispute. I do not suggest, however, that all wrongs or problems of this society can be addressed by the Constitution or court proceedings. Nor do I suggest that all of the disparities that exist between the African American and majority communities stem directly from racial discrimination or that none are influenced or caused by other factors: "To be sure, values are important, and a weakened value system is a factor in the unstable family life, crime, and a host of other problems faced by the black community. That is why a renewed and strengthened value system for our young people is central to self-development efforts. But so, too, are public policies that are supportive of those efforts." *The State of Black America 1994* (National Urban League, Inc., Jan. 1994).

3. See Griswold v. Connecticut, 381 U.S. 479 (1965).

4. See, e.g., Mapp v. Ohio, 367 U.S. 643 (1961) (giving birth to the exclusionary rule).

5. See Brown v. Board of Education, 347 U.S. 483 (1954).

6. One critic of the Warren era has suggested that the individual accomplishments of Earl Warren have been overstated and that "the ideas of the Court that set fires in the minds of men and women during the period came not from Warren but first from Hugo Black and then quickly, and for the balance of Warren's tenure, from William J. Brennan." Hutchinson, 1983 Survey of Books, "Hail to the Chief: Earl Warren and the Supreme Court," 81 *Mich. L. Rev.* 922 (1983) (reviewing Schwartz, *Super Chief: Earl Warren and His Supreme Court—A Judicial Biography* (1983). Hutchinson continues: "To the extent that the Court over which Warren presided has any intellectual legacy that is accessible to those trained in doctrine and not in ethics, it is Brennan who is responsible." Id. at 924. I do not attempt to access the accuracy of Hutchinson's observations. Nor do I deem them particularly relevant. There is no doubt that each jurist made substantial contributions to the principles of equality and justice for which they are justly applauded.

7. The composition of the Warren Court, like all others, changed during the years Earl Warren served as Chief Justice. The Justices who served on the Court, their terms of

office and the president who appointed them are as follows: Chief Justice Earl Warren, 1954–69 (Eisenhower); Hugo Black, 1937–71 (Franklin Roosevelt); Stanley E. Reed, 1938–57 (Roosevelt); Felix Frankfurter, 1939–62 (Roosevelt); William O. Douglas, 1939–75 (Roosevelt); Robert H. Jackson, 1941–54 (Roosevelt); Harold H. Burton, 1945–58 (Truman); Sherman Minton, 1949–56 (Truman); Tom C. Clark, 1949–67 (Truman); John M. Harlan, 1955–71 (Eisenhower); William J. Brennan, 1956–90 (Eisenhower); Charles Whittaker, 1957–62 (Eisenhower); Potter Stewart, 1958–81 (Eisenhower); Byron White, 1962–92 (Kennedy); Arthur Goldberg, 1962–65 (Kennedy); Abe Fortas, 1965–69 (Johnson); and Thurgood Marshall, 1967–91 (Johnson). The first nine constituted the original makeup of the Warren Court.

8. See Black, "The Unfinished Business of the Warren Court," 46 *Wash. L. Rev.* 3 (1970).

9. 347 U.S. 483 (1954) (*Brown I* or *Brown*). See also Bolling v. Sharpe, 347 U.S. 497 (1954), supplemented at 349 U.S. 294 (1955) (invalidating segregation of public schools in the District of Columbia). Decided on the same day as Brown, Bolling considered whether racial segregation in the public schools of the District of Columbia, a federal territory, violated the Due Process Clause of the Fifth Amendment. Responding in the affirmative, the Warren Court provided the foundation for directly importing into the Fifth Amendment Due Process Clause an equal protection guarantee.

10. My focus here is principally on pronouncements of the United States Supreme Court because, until recently, it was the High Court that properly assumed primary responsibility for definitive interpretation of the constitutional guarantee of equal protection. The current Court, however, by its inaction in a broad variety of contexts, has shifted a significant burden of definitive interpretation to the courts of appeals. Indeed, it did not go unnoticed that the Court has recently agreed to hear an unprecedented small number of cases. See Greenhouse, "Fierce Combat on Fewer Battlefields," N.Y. *Times*, July 3, 1994, sec. 4 (*Week in Review*), at 1, col. 2 ("The Supreme Court term that ended Thursday was a struggle: While the Justices decided fewer cases than in any term since 1955, many of the decisions they produced revealed deep divisions and some bore the marks of raw ideological combat."). For commentary on the ideological and methodological inclinations of Chief Justice Rehnquist's Court, see Biskupic, "The Mysterious Mr. Rehnquist: Where Is the Chief Justice Going and Who Will Follow?," *Wash. Post*, Sept. 25, 1994, § C (Outlook), at 1, col. 4.

In addition to this general trend on the Court, at least two other factors may further limit the role of the Supreme Court in the area of race. First, the perceived hostility within the Supreme Court and the lower federal courts to claims of putative victims of racial discrimination has seemingly stimulated greater interest in increasing activity in the state courts as well as in the legislatures, both federal and state. Cf. Chemerinsky, "The Supreme Court and the Fourteenth Amendment: The Unfulfilled Promise," 25 *Loy. L.A. L. Rev.* 1143 (1992) (suggesting in response to the "composition of the current Court . . . [a] shift . . . away from the Court and toward legislative action"). Of course, resort to the legislatures is not tantamount to judicial bypass. But to the extent that state legislative efforts are successful, state courts increasingly may be viewed as more attractive forums for the enforcement of race claims. The second factor potentially limiting adjudication of race claims before the Supreme Court is more grave. That is, the effect of Rule 11 of the Federal Rules of Civil Procedure has likely discouraged adjudication of race claims altogether.

11. Black, supra note 8, at 16–17.

12. Still, many disparities, arguably unexplainable on grounds other than race continue to haunt us. Two academics—one black, see Bell, *Faces at the Bottom of the Well:*

The Permanence of Racism (1992), and one white, see Hacker, *Two Nations: Black and White, Separate, Hostile, Unequal* (1992)—have commented on these disparities and concluded that race and racial subjugation continue to permeate American society.

13. Greene, "Race in the 21st Century: Equality Through Law?," 64 *Tul. L. Rev.* 1515, 1517 (1990). Of course, "[t]he infamy of the Dred Scott opinion was precisely this: its bland assumptions of racial superiority, its shameful equation of citizenship as whiteness." Karst, "Why Equality Matters," 17 *Ga. L. Rev.* 245, 271 (1983) (hereinafter cited as Karst, "Equality"). See also Dred Scott v. Sandford, 60 U.S. (19 How.) 393 (1857).

14. See, e.g., Carr, *Federal Protection of Civil Rights: Quest for a Sword* 36 (1947).

15. The Burger Court consisted of the following Justices: Chief Justice Warren Burger, 1969–86 (Nixon); Hugo Black, 1937–71 (Roosevelt); William O. Douglas, 1939–75 (Roosevelt); John M. Harlan, 1955–71 (Eisenhower); William Brennan, 1956–90 (Eisenhower); Potter Stewart, 1958–81 (Eisenhower); Byron White, 1962–92 (Kennedy); Abe Fortas, 1965–69 (Johnson); Thurgood Marshall, 1967–91 (Johnson); Harry Blackmun, 1970–94 (Nixon); Lewis Powell, 1971–87 (Nixon); William H. Rehnquist, 1971–present (Nixon); John Paul Stevens, 1975–present (Ford); and Sandra Day O'Connor, 1981–present (Reagan).

16. Under the two-tier structural framework, racial classifications were considered suspect and subject to a heightened standard of judicial review. Legislation that did not contain suspect classifications or that did not implicate fundamental rights was subject to mere rationality review. Although easy to state, the two-tier test created knotty issues of interpretation, not directly relevant here, that continue to plague the courts. What groups qualify as suspect classes and what criteria govern that determination, for example, cannot be stated with precision. Similarly, what qualifies as a "fundamental" right and how that determination is to be made continue to evoke intense debate on the Court. These determinations are not merely academic; once legislation is deemed to implicate either a suspect class or a fundamental right, a compelling governmental interest must support the enactment. Moreover, the means must be narrowly tailored to advance that interest.

17. See infra sec. II.

18. The Justices of the Rehnquist Court include Chief Justice William H. Rehnquist, 1971–present (Nixon); William Brennan, 1956–90 (Eisenhower); Byron White, 1962–92 (Kennedy); Thurgood Marshall, 1967–91 (Johnson); Harry Blackmun, 1970–94 (Nixon); Lewis Powell, 1971–87 (Nixon); John Paul Stevens, 1975–present (Ford); Sandra Day O'Connor, 1981–present (Reagan); Antonin Scalia, 1986–present (Reagan); Anthony M. Kennedy, 1988–present (Reagan); David H. Souter, 1990–present (Bush); Clarence Thomas, 1991–present (Bush); Ruth Bader Ginsburg, 1992–present (Clinton); and Steven Breyer, 1994–present (Clinton). The Rehnquist Court currently consists of Chief Justice Rehnquist, Justices Stevens, O'Connor, Scalia, Kennedy, Souter, Thomas, Ginsburg, and Breyer.

19. 16 Wall. 36 (U.S. 1873).

20. Id. at 71. See also Strauder v. West Virginia, 100 U.S. 303, 306 (1879) (holding that the Fourteenth Amendment was designed to secure to blacks "all the civil rights that the superior race may enjoy").

21. There were notable exceptions. See Shelley v. Kraemer, 334 U.S. 1 (1948); United States v. Carolene Products Co., 304 U.S. 144 (1938); Strauder v. West Virginia, 100 U.S. 303 (1879). These cases are discussed infra text accompanying notes 92–100.

22. In the first challenge to the Fourteenth Amendment after ratification, the Supreme Court in the Slaughter-House Cases, 16 Wall. 36 (U.S. 1873), practically disabled the amendment from realizing its broad, liberating potential. Writing for the majority, Justice Miller effectively eviscerated the Privileges or Immunities Clause, which has since

failed to counter in any meaningful way abusive exercises of state power. Similarly, though later transformed, the Due Process Clause was construed to impose no independent, substantive limitations on the exercise of state power. The Equal Protection Clause was admittedly, and in fact, according to Justice Miller, *only* applicable to racially discriminatory state action. The Court "[doubted] very much whether any action of a State not directed by way of discrimination against the negroes as a class, or on account of their race, w[ould] ever be held to come within the purview of this provision." Id. at 81. The sad truth of the matter, however, is that "[t]he fourteenth amendment has proven more useful in addressing interests unrelated to race than in effectuating its central purpose." Lively, "Equal Protection and Moral Circumstance: Accounting for Constitutional Basics," 59 *Fordham L. Rev.* 485, 488–89 (1991).

23. But cf. *Cong. Globe*, 39th Cong., 2d Sess. 101 (1867) ("The first duty of the Government is to afford protection to its citizens.") (remarks of Rep. Farnsworth, debating Reconstruction Act of 1867).

24. Buck v. Bell, 274 U.S. 200, 208 (1927).

25. Sherry, "Selective Judicial Activism in the Equal Protection Context: Democracy, Distrust, and Deconstruction," 73 *Geo. L.J.* 89 (1984).

26. 347 U.S. 483 (1954). In *Brown*, the Warren Court framed the issue for resolution as whether the "segregation of children in public schools solely on the basis of race, even though the physical facilities and other 'tangible' factors may be equal, deprive[s] the children of the minority group of equal educational opportunities?" Id. at 493.

27. 163 U.S. 537 (1896). The Brown Court held that the separation of black children "from others of similar age and qualifications solely because of their race generates a feeling of inferiority as to their status in the community that may affect their hearts and minds in a way unlikely ever to be undone." 347 U.S. at 494.

28. 379 U.S. 184 (1964).

29. Similar provisions previously had been sanctioned by the Court. See, e.g., Pace v. Alabama, 106 U.S. 583 (1882). In *Pace*, the Supreme Court upheld an Alabama statute that consisted of graduated penalties on the basis of race. Under the statute, interracial violators of the proscription against adultery or fornication were subject to stiffer penalties than were violators of the same race. The Court reasoned that racial discrimination was not at issue. Within each offense, members of each race were treated similarly. Thus, any discrimination in penalties was between offenses, not races.

30. 379 U.S. at 196.

31. Id. at 198 ("[T]he Court implies that a criminal law of the kind here involved might be constitutionally valid if a State could show 'some overriding statutory purpose.' This is an implication in which I cannot join, because I cannot conceive of a valid legislative purpose under our Constitution for a state law which makes the color of a person's skin the test of whether his conduct is a criminal offense. . . . I think it is simply not possible for a state law to be valid under our Constitution which makes the criminality of an act depend upon the race of the actor. Discrimination of that kind is invidious *per se*.") (Stewart, J., dissenting).

32. 388 U.S. 1 (1967).

33. Relying on Korematsu v. United States, 323 U.S. 214 (1944), the *Loving* Court declared that "[a]t the very least, the Equal Protection Clause demands that racial classifications . . . be subjected to the 'most rigid scrutiny.'" *Loving*, 388 U.S. at 11 (quoting *Korematsu*, 323 U.S. at 216).

34. "[W]e do not accept the State's contention that these statutes should be upheld if there is any possible basis for concluding that they serve a rational purpose." *Loving*, 388 U.S. at 8.

35. Id.

36. Id. at 11.

37. Id.

38. 109 U.S. 3 (1883). In the first challenge to legislation enacted pursuant to the Civil War amendments, the Supreme Court narrowly defined the powers of Congress to remedy violations of the Thirteenth and Fourteenth Amendments. In the Court's view, the Thirteenth Amendment was not a weapon against most private acts of discrimination. Similarly, the Fourteenth Amendment was violated only by state action. Thus, Congress's power under Section 5 of the Fourteenth Amendment could be exercised only to abolish state-sponsored discrimination. Distinguishing the powers of Congress under the two amendments, the Court stated: "Under the thirteenth amendment, the legislation, so far as necessary or proper to eradicate all forms and incidents of slavery and involuntary servitude, may be direct and primary, operating upon the acts of individuals, whether sanctioned by State legislation or not; under the fourteenth . . . it must necessarily be, and can only be, corrective in its character, addressed to counteract and afford relief against state regulations or proceedings." Id. at 23.

39. Id. at 11.

40. The Court in the *Civil Rights Cases* stated that "civil rights, such as are guaranteed by the Constitution against state aggression, cannot be impaired by the wrongful acts of individuals, unsupported by state authority in the shape of laws, customs, or judicial or executive proceedings." 109 U.S. at 17.

41. 382 U.S. 296 (1966).

42. In a continuation of the dispute underlying *Evans v. Newton*, the Burger Court undercut the earlier decision when it affirmed the Georgia court's holding that Senator Bacon's property reverted to his heirs for failure of testamentary purpose. Evans v. Abney, 396 U.S. 435 (1970). See infra text accompanying notes 126–31.

43. 387 U.S. 369 (167). Thurgood Marshall represented the United States as solicitor general.

44. See also Burton v. Wilmington Parking Auth., 365 U.S. 715 (1961) (holding that a privately owned restaurant could not discriminate on the basis of race where it leased space in a government-owned parking lot).

45. The Warren Court began to erode "the fiction of 'privateness,' and hence of immunity from constitutional control, in cases where the 'private' action is really supported by public authority and communal partication." Black, supra note 8, at 17.

46. In addition to its construction of the requisite "state action" under the Constitution, it was the Warren Court that finally recognized the authority of Congress to reach private action under Section 5 of the Fourteenth Amendment. See Katzenbach v. Morgan, 384 U.S. 641 (1966). The Court had already recognized broad congressional authority to reach private discrimination under the Commerce Clause. See Heart of Atlanta Motel v. United States, 379 U.S. 241 (1964) (reaching conduct similar to that sanctioned in the Civil Rights Cases, 109 U.S. 3 (1883) on the ground that Congress may permissibly impose reasonable regulations on private activity affecting interstate commerce). Thus, its interpretation of the scope of congressional power in *Katzenbach* added to the arsenal of civil rights litigants in the war against racial discrimination. Similar inroads were made with respect to congressional authority to enforce the provisions of the Thirteenth Amendment abolishing slavery. See Jones v. Alfred H. Mayer Co., 392 U.S. 409 (1968).

47. 380 U.S. 202 (1965).

48. Distinguishing between the selection process for service as jurors and the process of exercising peremptory challenges of persons called for jury service, the majority held that to establish a prima facie case of racial discrimination in the latter instance, "the

defendant must, to pose the issue, show the prosecutor's systematic use of peremptory challenges against Negroes over a period of time." *Swain*, 380 U.S. at 227. The dissent did not disagree that systematic exclusion need be proved; rather, the dissent maintained that "the petitioner . . . made out a prima facie case of unlawful jury exclusion" by proving that "no Negro ha[d] ever served on any petit jury in the history of Talladega County." Id. at 238 (Goldberg, J., dissenting).

49. 380 U.S. at 208–09.

50. In fairness to the Court's record, it did, two years later, find sufficient statistical disparity to set aside a murder conviction on the ground that the jury selection procedure had been infected with impermissible discrimination. See Whitus v. Georgia, 385 U.S. 545 (1967). See also Jones v. Georgia, 398 U.S. 23 (1967).

51. 391 U.S. 430 (1968).

52. Id. at 438.

53. The Court did not invalidate all "freedom of choice" plans. Instead, it recognized that some flexibility in fashioning remedial plans was warranted. Justice Brennan insisted, however, that inherent in the obligation to desegregate was the duty to adopt responsible plans that "promise realistically to work *now*." *Green*, 391 U.S. at 439 (emphasis in original).

54. The Court had five years earlier considered a similar question. In Goss v. Board of Education, 373 U.S. 683 (1963), the Court invalidated a procedure that permitted students to transfer from schools in which they were a racial minority to schools in which their race was in the majority. In invalidating the plan, the Court observed: "It is readily apparent that the transfer system proposed lends itself to perpetuation of segregation. Indeed, the provisions can work only toward that end." Id.

55. This feature of *Green* was an important and potentially progressive development regarding the sufficiency of evidentiary proof of discrimination. As later developments make clear, however, the Burger Court's imposition of intent as the standard for constitutional liability foreclosed the dynamic potential of *Green*. See infra text accompanying notes 107–22.

56. Brown v. Board of Educ., 349 U.S. 294, 301 (1955) (*Brown II*).

57. Black, supra note 8, at 22. Professor Black further explained why the asserted reasons for the Court's "all deliberate speed" formulation were wrong. First, "[t]here was just exactly no reason, in 1953, for thinking [that formulation] would work better than an order to desegregate at once." Id. Moreover, closely related to the first reason, "[d]elay would have been present in any event, for many specious evasive schemes . . . had to go through litigation." Id. And finally, "[w]hatever the Court said, it was clear that *feasible* speed, once delay of any kind had been sanctioned by law, would be an inverse function of community acquiescence." Id.

58. 358 U.S. 1 (1958). *Cooper* was the first school decision rendered by the Supreme Court after *Brown*.

59. Bell, *Race, Racism and American Law* 548 (3d ed., 1992) (hereinafter cited as Bell, *Race, Racism*).

60. 358 U.S. at 16.

61. Reviewing the works of Judge Robert Carter, former general counsel to the National Association for the Advancement of Colored People, Derrick Bell criticizes the Warren Court for "condon[ing] the application of procedural requirements and pupil placement laws which it knew were designed to delay or evade substantial compliance with the principles enunciated in *Brown I*." Bell, *Race, Racism*, at 549.

62. 328 U.S. 549 (1946).

63. Id. at 556.

64. 364 U.S. 339 (1960).

65. Id. at 341.

66. Id. at 341–43. But see Gomillion v. Lightfoot, 364 U.S. 339, 349 (1960) (Whittaker, J., concurring) ("It seems to me that the 'right . . . to vote' that is guaranteed by the Fifteenth Amendment is but the same right to vote as is enjoyed by all others within the same . . . political division. . . . But . . . 'fencing Negro citizens out of' Division A and into Division B is an unlawful segregation of races of citizens, in violation of the Equal Protection Clause of the Fourteenth Amendment.").

67. 369 U.S. 186 (1962). For competing views on the Warren Court's reapportionment decisions, see Berger, "Against an Activist Court," 31 *Cath. U. L. Rev.* 173 (1982), and Lamb, "Judicial Restraint Reappraised," 31 *Cath. U. L. Rev.* 181 (1982).

68. According to the Court, when a person's vote is debased by a reapportionment scheme the equal protection guarantee is violated. Such a challenge was distinguishable from those—like the ones asserted in *Colegrove*—based upon the Republican Form of Government Clause of Article IV of the Constitution.

69. U.S. Const. art. IV, § 4.

70. 377 U.S. 533 (1964) (considering challenge to apportionment scheme of the Alabama state legislature). *Reynolds* was preceded by two other apportionment cases in which the one person–one vote principle was forecast. See Wesberry v. Sanders, 376 U.S. 1 (1964) (invalidating on art. 1, § 2, grounds apportionment of Atlanta, Georgia, in a manner that limited Atlanta, which constituted 20 % of the state population, to electing 10 % of the state's congressional representatives); Gray v. Sanders, 372 U.S. 368 (1963) (invalidating Georgia's county unit method of tallying votes in Democratic Party primary elections for statewide office under the Equal Protection Clause). Indeed, the terminology has its origins in Justice Douglas's majority opinion in *Gray*: "The conception of political equality from the Declaration of Independence, to Lincoln's Gettysburg Address, to the Fifteenth, Seventeenth, and Nineteenth Amendments can mean only one thing—one person, one vote." 372 U.S. at 381. Cf. Justice Stewart's concurrence in Gray: "Within a given constituency, there can be room for but a single constitutional rule—one voter, one vote." 372 U.S. at 382.

71. The facts of *Reynolds* revealed that the Alabama legislature had not implemented any reapportionment since 1901. The result was rural domination in the legislature, notwithstanding the existence of more heavily populated urban areas. See *Reynolds*, 377 U.S. at 583–84.

72. The Court stated: "Since the achieving of fair and effective representation for all citizens is concededly the basic aim of legislative apportionment, we conclude that the Equal Protection Clause guarantees the opportunity for equal participation by all voters in the election of state legislators. Diluting the weight of votes because of place of residence impairs basic constitutional rights under the Fourteenth Amendment just as much as invidious discriminations based upon factors such as race, or economic status." 377 U.S. at 565–66 (citations omitted).

73. See Avery v. Midland County, 390 U.S. 474, 480 (1968).

74. See, e.g., Burns v. Richardson, 384 U.S. 73 (1966) (vacating the district court judgment that Hawaii's proposal for multimember senatorial districts on one of its islands failed to account for a variety of relevant factors, including race, on the ground that mathematical equality of districts ordinarily guards racial discrimination); Fortson v. Dorsey, 379 U.S. 433 (1965) (rejecting the contention of black voters that a countywide voting scheme prevented the election of a single candidate of their choice on the ground that population equality of the multimember district satisfied the Constitution).

In 1965, Congress enacted the Voting Rights Act, which, as amended, today serves as the key guardian of minority voting rights. The Civil Rights Act of 1957, the first such legislation since Reconstruction, had been enacted to enforce voting rights secured by the Fifteenth Amendment. Subsequent civil rights legislation also contained voting rights provisions designed to strengthen or fill gaps in the earlier acts. When these measures failed to contain the numerous and ingenious evasive devices that continued to undermine blacks' right to vote, the urgency of a more comprehensive statute became apparent. As Derrick Bell explains, "As the inadequacies of the 1957, 1960, and 1964 Acts became more apparent, and the often violent response to peaceful voting rights marches and protests first embarrassed, then alarmed the nation, political pressure increased for what was to become the Voting Rights Act of 1965." See Bell, *Race, Racism* at 202. The constitutionality of the Voting Rights Act of 1965 was upheld by the Warren Court in South Carolina v. Katzenbach, 383 U.S. 301 (1966).

75. See generally Blacksher and Menefee, "From *Reynolds v. Sims* to *City of Mobile v. Bolden:* Have the White Suburbs Commandeered the Fifteenth Amendment?," 34 *Hastings L.J.* 1 (1982).

76. For a description of the dominant attacks on the "egalitarian decisions" of the Warren era, see, e.g., Karst, "Equality," supra note 13, at 246 and nn.3–5.

Recent scholarship adds the observation that "[d]octrinal innovations by the Warren Court in the area of equal protection of the law led to decisions that provided formal access to governmental institutions—when formal access was denied. However, the Warren Court did not look at deeper structural, social, economic, and political inequalities." Kahn, "The Supreme Court as a (Counter) Majoritarian Institution: Misperceptions of the Warren, Burger, and Rehnquist Courts," 1994 *Det. C. L. Rev.* 1, 29 (1994). Kahn offers as an explanation for this failure, the influence of "polity principles"—the "justices' deeply held ideas about where decision-making power should be located when deciding questions of constitutional significance," id. at 3,—and "rights principles"—"beliefs held by justices . . . about establishing legally enforceable claims for individual powers, privileges, or immunities guaranteed under the Constitution, statutes, and common law," id. at 5, on the decisional processes of the Warren Court.

By focusing analysis on the role of these principles in the fundamental rights decisions of the Warren era, Kahn suggests that "[t]he Warren Court was no more pure in its vision of equality than the Burger or Rehnquist Courts from the point of view of the ideologies of its members. The vision of purity attributed to the Warren Court understates the degree to which polity concerns informed Warren Court equal protection jurisprudence." Id. at 29.

77. See Karst, "Equality," supra note 13, at 246.

78. Id. at 272. Construed in this manner, hostile attacks on affirmative action as a legitimate measure to remedy past discrimination ring hollow. See infra sec. III.

79. 163 U.S. 537 (1896).

80. "The dissent is not about the Equal Protection Clause, but rather about the meaning of freedom embodied in the Thirteenth Amendment and the nature and scope of rights inhering in national citizenship as embodied in the Fourteenth Amendment." Aleinikoff, "Re-Reading Justice Harlan's Dissent in *Plessy v. Ferguson:* Freedom, Antiracism, and Citizenship," 1992 *U. Ill. L. Rev.* 961, 963–64.

81. 163 U.S. at 559.

82. Black, supra note 8, at 8.

83. Id. at 9.

84. Id. (emphasis in original).

85. Id. at 9. Professor Black characterizes this last addition to the nature of citizenship as fulfillment of "the long-unhonored promise of the *Slaughter-House Cases.*" Id.

86. My subsequent role in Swann v. Charlotte-Mecklenburg Board of Education, 402 U.S. 1 (1971), is illustrative of the continuing and necessary struggle to make real the principles enunciated in *Brown*. See infra text accompanying notes 153–54.

87. See, e.g., Schiro v. Bynum, 375 U.S. 395 (1964) (affirming a district court order invalidating segregation in a public auditorium); Gayle v. Browder, 352 U.S. 903 (1956) (affirming a district court order invalidating the segregation of public buses); Mayor of Baltimore v. Dawson, 350 U.S. 877 (1955) (affirming a court of appeals order invalidating segregation of public beaches).

88. See, e.g., Berger, "Against an Activist Court," supra note 67, at 180.

89. Namely, the content of the equality guaranteed by the Fourteenth Amendment, the level of judicial scrutiny to be applied to challenges thereunder, and the scope of the state action prohibited by the amendment's first section.

90. One author recently has argued that "by 1940 the Court possessed a theory capable of justifying a presumptive rule against racial classifications." Klarman, "An Interpretive History of Modern Equal Protection," 90 *Mich. L. Rev.* 213, 226 (1991).

91. Indeed, the politics of the day—as the ensuing Civil Rights movement confirmed—ran counter to the judgments of the Court in the area of race.

92. 100 U.S. 303 (1879).

93. Id. at 307. The Court continued: "—exemption from legal discriminations, implying inferiority in civil society, lessening the security of their enjoyment of the rights which others enjoy, and discriminations which are steps towards reducing them to the condition of a subject race." Id.

94. 304 U.S. 144 (1938). The *Carolene Products* case involved a due process challenge to congressional legislation prohibiting the interstate shipment of filled milk.

95. For a comprehensive interpretation of the role of the *Carolene Products* footnote in racial jurisprudence, see Cover, "The Origins of Judicial Activism in the Protection of Minorities," 91 *Yale L.J.* 1287 (1982).

96. 304 U.S. at 152, n.4.

97. 334 U.S. 1 (1948).

98. Id. at 18. The Court stated: "The short of the matter is that from the time of the adoption of the Fourteenth Amendment until the present, it has been the consistent ruling of this Court that the action of the States to which the amendment has reference, includes action of state courts and state judicial officials." Id.

99. Id. On the facts of *Shelley*, both the black potential purchaser and the white seller were willing to enter into a contract of sale. Thus, the state courts' involvement in the enforcement of the racial covenant was particularly odious. Still, the underlying sentiment of the Court in *Shelley*, and that promoted by the Warren Court's state action decisions, was that states not become entangled with private activity that, if practiced directly by the states, would violate the Fourteenth Amendment.

100. See also Barrows v. Jackson, 346 U.S. 249 (1953) (rejecting action for damages against a white property owner who sold in violation of racially discriminatory covenant on the theory that award of such damages would constitute punishment for refusal to discriminate).

101. Yick Wo v. Hopkins, 118 U.S. 356, 370 (1886).

102. See, e.g., Nixon v. Condon, 286 U.S. 73, 89 (1932) (holding that a general reliance on Fourteenth Amendment bars racial discrimination in primary elections); Nixon v. Herndon, 273 U.S. 536, 541 (1927) (invalidating on equal protection grounds racial classification attached to the right to vote in an election primary). See generally Bell, *Race, Racism*, supra note 59, at 190–96.

103. While this essay was awaiting publication, former Chief Justice Warren Burger died of heart failure on June 25, 1995. He was eighty-seven years old.

104. See Bell, *Race, Racism*, at 894–95 (citing 2 *Public Papers of the Presidents, Lyndon B. Johnson* 635–40 (Washington, 1965)).

105. See, e.g., South Carolina v. Katzenbach, 383 U.S. 301 (1966) (upholding the constitutionality of the voting rights provisions of the Civil Rights Act of 1964 under the Fifteenth Amendment); Heart of Atlanta Motel, Inc. v. United States, 379 U.S. 241 (1964) (sustaining, on Commerce Clause grounds, the validity of public accommodations provisions of the Civil Rights Act of 1964). The Court artfully avoided constitutional questions that arose in a number of other cases after passage of the Civil Rights Act of 1964. See Schwartz, *Super Chief: Earl Warren and His Supreme Court—A Judicial Biography* 552–59 (1983).

106. Richard M. Nixon, in the 1968 presidential campaign, openly compaigned against what was perceived as overreaching by the Supreme Court. Nixon vowed to stem the tide of constitutional policy-making by appointing to the high bench justices committed to the philosophy of judicial restraint. See Kohlmeier, *God Save This Honorable Court* 114 (1972). The appointment, in 1969, of the relatively undistinguished, but politically conservative Burger as Chief Justice of the Supreme Court, perhaps added to the fears of Warren Court supporters. For a brief sketch of Burger's career prior to his ascension to the Supreme Court, see Schwartz, *The Unpublished Opinions of the Burger Court* 4–5 (1988).

107. For example, the Burger Court extended the protections afforded under the equal protection "suspect classifications" strand of jurisprudence to include gender, see Craig v. Boren, 429 U.S. 190 (1976) (applying an intermediate level of scrutiny to statutory classifications that distinguish persons on the basis of gender); alienage, see Sugarman v. Dougall, 413 U.S. 634 (1973) (considering a constitutional challenge to New York statute that excluded aliens from government service requiring competitive examinations); and illegitimacy, see Weber v. Aetna Casualty & Surety Co., 406 U.S. 164 (1974) (invalidating a statute depriving illegitimate children of worker's compensation benefits upon the death of their natural father). Cf. Plyler v. Doe, 457 U.S. 202 (1982) (invalidating the denial of public schooling to children of illegally present alien parents); City of Cleburne v. Cleburne Living Center, 473 U.S. 432 (1985) (invalidating, on rational basis grounds, a zoning ordinance preventing construction of housing for the mentally disabled).

108. Cf. General Building Contractors Ass'n, Inc. v. Pennsylvania, 458 U.S. 375 (1982) (finding that proof of discriminatory purpose is a predicate for action under 42 U.S.C. § 1981, which was enacted pursuant to the Thirteenth Amendment); Memphis v. Greene, 451 U.S. 100 (1981) (implying that proof of discriminatory intent is required to make out a claim of racial discrimination under 42 U.S.C. § 1982, where a street connecting white and black neighborhoods was closed by city).

109. After *Brown*, the more difficult cases confronting the Supreme Court involved facially neutral government action that had a significant disparate effect on blacks. In such cases, proof of a constitutional violation invariably consisted of evidence, in varying degrees, both of racial animus and disparate impact. Whether overwhelming evidence of either alone was sufficient to establish a constitutional violation, however, was left unresolved. See Klarman, supra note 90, at 296 (explaining that cases brought prior to 1976 "invariably involved both a decisionmaking process consciously motivated by hostility towards blacks or geared to the assumption (explicit or implicit) of black inferiority and a result harmful to blacks," and that therefore, "these decisions did not require the Court to decide whether the Equal Protection Clause was concerned principally with barring race-

conscious decisionmaking or the cumulative disadvantaging (regardless of intention) of historically oppressed minorities.").

110. For a similar reading of *Green*, see Landsberg, *Race and the Rehnquist Court*, 66 *Tul. L. Rev.* 1267, 1279 (1992).

111. 403 U.S. 217 (1971). See also Klarman, supra note 90, at 296–97 (discussing the relevance of *Palmer* to the subsequent development of the intent standard).

112. But see Griffin v. Prince Edward County School Board, 377 U.S. 218 (1964) (deeming the closure of a local school system in response to an order to integrate to be racially discriminatory and subject to judicial order to reopen).

113. The Court stated: "[N]o case in this Court has held that a legislative act may violate equal protection solely because of the motivations of the men who voted for it. . . . It is difficult or impossible for any court to determine the 'sole' or 'dominant' motivation behind the choices of a group of legislators. Furthermore, there is an element of futility in a judicial attempt to invalidate a law because of the bad motives of its supporters. If the law is struck down for this reason, rather than because of its facial content or effect, it would presumably be valid as soon as the legislature or relevant governing body repassed it for different reasons." 403 U.S. at 224. Discriminatory motive is distinct from discriminatory purpose. See generally Bickel, *The Least Dangerous Branch* 209 (1962). While the former may be evidence of the latter, standing alone, it is insufficient to sustain a constitutional challenge under the Equal Protection Clause. See infra text accompanying notes 117–20.

114. *Palmer*, 403 U.S. at 231 (Douglas, J., dissenting) (noting that the city's decision was in response to a court order to desegregate); id. at 239 ("I conclude that though a State may discontinue any of its municipal services—such as schools, parks, pools, athletic fields, and the like—it may not do so for the purpose of perpetuating or installing apartheid or because it finds life in a multi-racial community difficult or unpleasant. If that is its reason, then abolition of a designated public service becomes a device for perpetuating a segregated way of life. That a State may not do."); id. at 240 (White, J., dissenting) ("I had thought official policies forbidding or discouraging joint use of public facilities by Negroes and whites were at war with the Equal Protection Clause. . . . It is also my view, but apparently not that of the majority, that a State may not have an official stance against desegregating public facilities and implement it by closing those facilities in response to a desegregation order.").

115. Of course, this was pure fiction. As the plaintiffs argued, the obvious impact of the city's action would be disproportionately visited upon blacks, who, unlike whites had no access to private swimming facilities. Moreover, as Justice White noted in dissent: "It is evident that closing a public facility after a court has ordered its desegregation has an unfortunate impact on the minority considering initiation of further suits or filing complaints with the Attorney General. As Judge Wisdom said [in dissent in the proceedings below], '[T]he price of protest is high. Negroes . . . now know that they risk losing even segregated public facilities if they dare to protest . . . segregated public parks, segregated public libraries, or other segregated facilities. They must first decide whether they wish to risk living without the facility altogether.'" 403 U.S. at 269. See also Brest, "*Palmer v. Thompson:* An Approach to the Problem of Unconstitutional Legislative Motive," 1971 *Sup. Ct. Rev.* 95 (providing contemporaneous critique of the Court's decision).

116. In the same year that *Palmer* was decided, the Court sanctioned the use of the disparate impact theory as a basis for recovery under Title VII of the Civil Rights Act of 1964, 42 U.S.C. § 2000e et seq., see Griggs v. Duke Power, 401 U.S. 424 (1971).

117. *Palmer*, 403 U.S. at 224 (citations omitted) (emphasis added).

118. See supra text accompanying notes 58–60. Citing *Cooper*, the Court conceded "that a city's possible motivations to ensure safety and save money cannot validate an otherwise impermissible state action. . . . Citizens may not be compelled to forgo their constitutional rights because officials fear public hostility or desire to save money." 403 U.S. at 226. According to the Court, however, "[T]he issue . . . [wa]s whether black citizens in Jackson [we]re being denied their constitutional rights when the city . . . closed the public pools to black and white alike." Id. The issue thus cast, the Court concluded that "[n]othing in the history or the language of the Fourteenth Amendment nor in any of our prior cases persuades us that the closing of the Jackson swimming pools to all its citizens constitutes a denial of 'the equal protection of the laws.'" Id.

119. 426 U.S. 229 (1976).

120. One of the cases cited by the Court in *Davis* was Keyes v. School District No. 1, 413 U.S. 189 (1973). *Keyes* was the first school case considered by the Supreme Court challenging segregation in the North. The petitioners in the case "concede[d] . . . that . . . where no statutory dual system has ever existed, plaintiffs must prove not only that segregated schooling exists but also that it was brought about or maintained by intentional state action." Id. at 198.

121. *Davis*, 426 U.S. at 239.

122. Id.

123. Professor Charles Lawrence argues that "requiring proof of conscious or intentional motivation as a prerequisite to constitutional recognition that a decision is race-dependent ignores much of what we understand about how the human mind works. . . . Therefore, equal protection doctrine must find a way to come to grips with unconscious racism." Lawrence, "The Id, the Ego, and Equal Protection: Reckoning with Unconscious Racism," 39 *Stan. L. Rev.* 317, 323 (1987).

124. 446 U.S. 55 (1980).

125. One commentator has suggested that "[t]he Court's use of intent as the standard for constitutional liability is perfectly consonant with a substantive view of American society as not responsible for the affirmative advancement of blacks and other disadvantaged minorities, a view that ignores the institutional legacies of historical discrimination." Issacharoff, "Making the Violation Fit the Remedy: The Intent Standard and Equal Protection Law," 92 *Yale L. J.* 328, 349–50 (1982). In *Bolden*, the problem of proving discriminatory intent was particularly acute given the Court's rejection of legislative motive as indicative of unconstitutional activity. Moreover, the motive of a legislative body—as the Court previously had acknowledged in *Palmer*, cannot be established adequately by evidence of the impermissible motivations of some of its members. See supra note 111. For methods of meeting the evidentiary burden of establishing discriminatory intent, see Arlington Heights v. Metropolitan Hous. Dev. Corp., 429 U.S. 252 (1977).

126. 42 U.S.C. § 1973(b) as amended by Pub.L. 97–205, sec. 3, June 29, 1982, 96 Stat. 134. See also Thornburg v. Gingles, 478 U.S. 30 (1986) (delineating standards applicable to a claim of racial vote dilution under amendments to Section 2 of the Voting Rights Act).

127. 396 U.S. 435 (1970).

128. "*Abney* apparently was the first decision since 1935 in which the Court dismissed on state action grounds an equal protection challenge to purposeful race discrimination." Klarman, supra note 90, at 291.

129. 396 U.S. at 444. The Court explained: "[T]here is not the slightest indication that any of the Georgia judges involved were motivated by racial animus or discriminatory intent of any sort in construing and enforcing Senator Bacon's will. Nor is there any

indication that Senator Bacon in drawing up his will was persuaded or induced to include racial restrictions by the fact that such restrictions were permitted by the Georgia trust statutes." Id. at 445.

130. Id. at 446.

131. Id.

132. Id. at 454.

133. 407 U.S. 163 (1972).

134. 418 U.S. 717 (1974).

135. But see Hills v. Gatreaux, 425 U.S. 284 (1976), characterizing the Court's decision in *Milliken I* as invalidating the district court's order "not because it envisioned relief against a wrongdoer extending beyond the city in which the violation occurred but because it contemplated a judicial decree restructuring the operation of local governmental entities that were not implicated in any constitutional violation." Id. at 296. In *Gatreaux* the Court unanimously affirmed the authority of the district court to order selection of sites for public housing outside the City of Chicago although discriminatory site selection had only been established within the city limits.

136. 427 U.S. 424 (1976).

137. In what became *Milliken II*, the district court on remand revised its decree to require broadsweeping educational reform within the city of Detroit. Included in the district court's educational reform package were counseling services, remedial education and career guidance. This order was affirmed by the Supreme Court as an appropriate response to remedy the deliberate segregation within the Detroit school system. Milliken v. Bradley, 433 U.S. 267 (1977) (*Milliken II*).

138. 438 U.S. 265, 324 (1978) (Brennan, J., concurring in part and dissenting in part).

139. Rivaled only perhaps by the seminal decision in Roe v. Wade, 410 U.S. 113 (1973) (recognizing the Fourteenth Amendment right of women to choose to terminate an unwanted pregnancy).

140. 438 U.S. at 319.

141. Id. at 330.

142. Id. at 295.

143. Id. at 326–27.

144. Cf. Firefighters Local Union No. 1784 v. Stotts, 467 U.S. 561 (1984), in which the Supreme Court invalidated a district court order requiring the lay-off of more senior white workers before black workers who were recent hires in order to maintain racial balance in the workforce. *Stotts* was not an affirmative action case. Although the city of Memphis had earlier entered into a court-sanctioned consent decree to settle a Title VII suit by blacks charging discrimination in hiring and promotions, the city has never achieved the goals of the decree.

145. 448 U.S. 448 (1980).

146. The dissenters—Justice Stevens, Joined by Chief Justice Burger and Justices Stewart and Rehnquist—rejected the use of race as an appropriate basis upon which to distribute government benefits.

147. 443 U.S. 193 (1979).

148. 476 U.S. 267 (1986).

149. 478 U.S. 421 (1986).

150. 478 U.S. 501 (1986).

151. 476 U.S. at 276.

152. According to the Court, "[T]he question presented in this case is whether . . . Title VII . . . precludes the entry of a consent decree which provides

relief that may benefit individuals who were not the actual victims of the defendant's discriminatory practices." 478 U.S. at 504.

153. In apparent tension, Chief Justice Burger in Swann alternatively stated that "[o]nce a right and a violation have been shown, the scope of a district court's equitable powers to remedy past wrongs is broad, for breadth and flexibility are inherent in equitable remedies," and further that "the nature of the violation determines the scope of the remedy." 402 U.S. at 15–16. It was the latter statement that the Burger Court seized upon in limiting the district court's powers in *Milliken I* and *Spangler*.

154. 402 U.S. 1 (1971).

155. For a chronicle of the internal debates on the Court in *Swann*, see generally Schwartz, *Swann's Way* 111–85 (1986). Chief Justice Burger reportedly was unwilling initially to sanction the broad relief ultimately approved in *Swann*. See Klarman, supra note 90, at 299–300.

156. 408 U.S. 238 (1972).

157. Id. at 249.

158. Id. at 249–50.

159. 476 U.S. 79 (1986).

160. The *Batson* rule was extended by the Rehnquist Court to bar the racially discriminatory exercise of peremptory challenges in civil litigation in Edmonson v. Leesville Concrete Co., 500 U.S. 614 (1991).

161. 429 U.S. 252 (1977).

162. Id. at 266. The Court continued, however: "The evidentiary inquiry is . . . relatively easy. But such cases are rare. Absent a [stark] pattern [of discriminatory disparity], . . . impact alone is not determinative, and the Court must look to other evidence." Id.

163. 401 U.S. 424 (1971).

164. The plaintiff class in *Griggs* challenged the imposition of educational requirements as a condition of employment and transfer at a power-generating facility in North Carolina as racially discriminatory. Endorsing the disparate impact theory of liability, the Court held that "practices, procedures, or tests neutral on their face, and even neutral in terms of intent, cannot be maintained if they operate to 'freeze' the status quo of prior discriminatory employment practices." 401 U.S. at 429.

165. See supra text accompanying notes 133–36.

166. See generally Landsberg, supra note 110.

167. Although perhaps predictable, Justice Rehnquist's nomination by President Ronald Reagan, whose views on individual rights and liberties independently raised concern, caused further dismay within the civil rights community.

168. See Biskupic, supra note 10, at C4, col. 1.

169. At the time of Justice Rehnquist's elevation, the Court consisted of Justices Brennan, White, Marshall, Blackmun, Powell, Stevens, and O'Connor. Justice Antonin Scalia was confirmed to fill the vacancy left as a result of Justice Rehnquist's designation as Chief.

170. See Landsberg, supra note 110, at 1276 and nn.39, 40.

171. 488 U.S. 469 (1989).

172. 481 U.S. 279 (1987).

173. ——U.S.——; 113 S.Ct. 2816 (1993).

174. 493 U.S. 265 (1990).

175. 503 U.S. 467 (1992).

176. 498 U.S. 237 (1991).

177. Patterson v. McLean Credit Union, 491 U.S. 164 (1989) (holding that discrimi-

natory treatment in the terms and conditions of employment are not actionable under 42 U.S.C. § 1981); Lorrance v. AT&T Technologies, 490 U.S. 900 (1989) (rejecting a Title VII challenge to a facially neutral seniority system producing disparate impact absent proof of discriminatory intent and assertion of claim at the time the seniority system was adopted); Martin v. Wilks, 490 U.S. 755 (1989) (rejecting a procedural bar to a white firefighter's challenge of employment decisions of the city of Birmingham pursuant to a consent decree in a previous Title VII proceeding in which white firefighters failed to intervene); Wards Cove Packing Co. v. Atonio, 490 U.S. 642 (1989) (rejecting statistical evidence of a segregated workforce as satisfying the plaintiff's burden of presenting a prima facie case of disparate impact under Title VII); Price Waterhouse v. Hopkins, 490 U.S. 228 (1989) (implying a lesser burden on an employer in a Title VII challenge after the plaintiff has demonstrated consideration of an impermissible factor—gender—in adverse employment action).

178. 448 U.S. 469 (1989).

179. Id. at 476. Reference to the underlying purpose of the Fourteenth Amendment, I believe, would resolve the current controversy surrounding the legality of affirmative action plans: "From the closing days of the Civil War until the end of civilian reconstruction some five years later, Congress adopted a series of social welfare programs whose benefits were expressly limited to blacks. . . . The race-conscious Reconstruction programs were enacted concurrently with the fourteenth amendment and were supported by the same legislators who favored the constitutional guarantee of equal protection. This history strongly suggests that the framers of the amendment could not have intended it generally to prohibit affirmative action for blacks or other disadvantaged groups." Schnapper, "Affirmative Action and the Legislative History of the Fourteenth Amendment," 71 *Va. L. Rev.* 753, 754 (1985).

180. Justice Scalia practically would ban the use of racial criteria by state and local governments altogether. In Justice Scalia's view, "[T]here is only one circumstance in which the states may act by race to 'undo the effects of past discrimination': where that is necessary to eliminate their own maintenance of a system of unlawful racial classification." 488 U.S. at 524 (Scalia, J., concurring in judgment). Citing school desegregation as an appropriate example, Justice Scalia continued to emphasize that generally, state efforts to redress past harms may and must be based upon classifications other than race: "Racial preferences appear to 'even the score' . . . only if one embraces the proposition that our society is appropriately viewed as divided into races, making it right that an injustice rendered in the past to a black man should be compensated for by disciminating against a white. Nothing is worth that embrace. Since blacks have been disproportionately disadvantaged by racial discrimination, any race neutral remedial program aimed at the disadvantaged as such will have a disproportionately beneficial impact on blacks. Only such a program, and not one that operates on the basis of race, is in accord with the letter and spirit of our Constitution." Id. at 528.

181. See supra text accompanying notes 144–45.

182. 42 U.S.C. § 6705(f)(2) (Supp. 1988).

183. The *Fullilove* Court rejected the argument that undeserving businesses or minorities would be the beneficiaries of the program. Instead, the Court found that "[t]he MBE provision . . . , with due account for its administrative program, . . . provides a reasonable assurance that application of racial or ethnic criteria will be [narrowly] limited to accomplishing Congress' remedial objectives and that misapplications of the program will be promptly and adequately remedied administratively." 448 U.S. at 487.

184. *Croson*, 488 U.S. at 489.

185. Id. at 490. The majority concluded: "The dream of a Nation of equal citizens in

a society where race is irrelevant to personal opportunity and achievement would be lost in a mosaic of shifting preferences based on inherently unmeasurable claims of past wrongs. . . . We think such a result would be contrary to both the letter and spirit of a constitutional provision whose central command is equality." Id. at 505–06.

186. Id. at 528 (Marshall, J., dissenting).

187. Id. at 551–53 (emphasis added). The outrage expressed by Justice Marshall in *Croson* is reminiscent of his separate opinion in *Bakke*: "It is unnecessary in 20th century America to have individual Negroes demonstrate that they have been victims of racial discrimination; the racism of our society has been so pervasive that none, regardless of wealth or position, has managed to escape its impact. The experience of Negroes in America has been different in kind, not just in degree, from that of other ethnic groups. It is not merely the history of slavery alone but also that a whole people were marked as inferior by the law. And that mark has endured. The dream of America as the great melting pot has not been realized for the Negro; because of his skin color he never even made it into the pot. . . . It is because of a legacy of unequal treatment that we now must permit the institutions of this society to give consideration to race in making decisions about who will hold the positions of influence, affluence and prestige in America. For far too long the doors to those positions have been shut to Negroes. If we are ever to become a fully integrated society, one in which the color of a person's skin will not determine the opportunities available to him or her, we must be willing to take steps to open those doors. I do not believe that anyone can truly look into America's past and still find that a remedy for the effects of that past is impermissible." *Bakke*, 438 U.S. at 400–01 (Marshall, J., concurring in part and dissenting in part).

188. Two years after *Croson*, the Court revisited the issue of congressional power to employ race-conscious criteria in meting out governmental benefits. In Metro Broadcasting, Inc. v. FCC, 497 U.S. 547 (1990), the Rehnquist Court held that "benign race-conscious measures mandated by Congress—even if those measures are not 'remedial' in the sense of being designed to compensate victims of past governmental or societal discrimination—are constitutionally permissible to the extent that they serve important governmental objectives within the power of Congress and are substantially related to the achievement of those objectives." Id. at 564–65. The Court continued to refuse to subject such congressional efforts to strict scrutiny, employing instead a more deferential, mid-level scrutiny. The Rehnquist Court, however, is poised during the 1994 term to revisit the congressional authority to adopt and implement race-conscious plans to benefit racial minorities. See Adarand v. Pena, 16 F.3d 1537 (10th Cir. 1994), *cert. granted*, 115 S.Ct. 41 (1994). See 63 *U.S. Law Week* 3048 (1994): "Questions presented: (1) Does congressional race-based set aside program for awarding highway construction contracts survive as applied constitutional challenge when that program seeks to remedy alleged broad-based societal discrimination, rather than clearly identifiable discrimination perpetuated by governmental entity seeking to remedy discrimination? (2) Is "strict scrutiny," as opposed to "lenient standard, resembling intermediate scrutiny," proper standard of review for determining constitutionality of race-based program adopted by Congress? (3) Does Fifth Amendment require federal agency, in implementing federal race-based set aside program and when exceeding goals adopted by Congress, to conduct inquiry set forth in *Richmond, Va., v. J.A. Croson Co.* . . . ?" While this article was awaiting publication, the Supreme Court, on June 12, 1995, issued its decision in *Adarand*. By a vote of five to four, the Court concluded that congressional affirmative action measures must survive strict scrutiny review. Justice Clarence Thomas, the Court's only black member, joined the majority, questioning the foundations of *Brown*. Justice Stevens, who was in dissent in *Fullilove*, see supra note 146, authored a passionate defense of governmental re-

sponsibility to distinguish invidious discrimination and race-conscious efforts to confront it.

189. 481 U.S. 279 (1987).

190. McCleskey's evidence consisted of a statistical study conducted by three law professors. The study was named for Professor David C. Baldus, the project's leader.

191. 481 U.S. at 287. This result obtained "even after taking account of 39 nonracial variables." Id. Moreover, the raw data indicated that "[w]hite-victim cases are nearly 11 times more likely to yield a death sentence than are black-victim cases." Id. at 353 (Blackmun, J., dissenting). Finally, as the majority conceded, "the Baldus study indicate[d] that black defendants, such as McCleskey, who kill white victims have the greatest likelihood of receiving the death penalty." Id. at 287.

192. Distinguishing away the relevance of judicial precedent recognizing the validity of statistics as proof of discriminatory intent, the majority found that the nature of McCleskey's claim, which struck at the heart of the criminal justice process "demand[s] exceptionally clear proof," id. at 297, before a claim under the Constitution is made. Justice Blackmun identifies the perversion of the majority's reasoning: "In *Brown v. Board of Education*, this Court held that, despite the fact that the legislative history of the Fourteenth Amendment indicated that Congress did not view racial discrimination in public education as a specific target, the Amendment nevertheless prohibited such discrimination. The Court today holds that even though the Fourteenth Amendment was aimed specifically at eradicating discrimination in the enforcement of criminal sanctions, allegations of such discrimination supported by substantial evidence are not constitutionally cognizable." 481 U.S. at 347 (Blackmun, J., dissenting) (citations omitted).

193. The Court stated, "At most, the [statistical] study indicates a discrepancy that appears to correlate with race. Apparent disparities in sentencing are an inevitable part of our criminal justice system." 481 U.S. at 311.

194. Id. at 334 (Brennan, J., dissenting). Justice Brennan further observed, at length, the pervasiveness of racial discrimination in America: "At the time our Constitution was framed 200 years ago this year, blacks 'had for more than a century before been regarded as being of an inferior order, and altogether unfit to associate with the white race, either in social or political relations; and so far inferior, that they had no rights which the white man was bound to respect.' Only 130 years ago, this Court relied on these observations to deny American citizenship to blacks. A mere three generations ago, this Court sanctioned racial segregation, stating that 'if one race be inferior to the other socially, the Constitution of the United States cannot put them upon the same plane.' In more recent times, we have sought to free ourselves from the burden of this history. Yet it has been scarcely a generation since this Court's first decision striking down racial segregation, and barely two decades since the legislative prohibition of racial discrimination in major domains of national life. These have been honorable steps, but we cannot pretend that in three decades we have completely escaped the grip of a historical legacy spanning centuries." Id. at 344.

195. Id.

196. Id.

197. 481 U.S. at 319.

198. Id. at 342–43.

199. 113 S.Ct. 2816 (1993).

200. "The *Shaw* decision . . . carefully refused to hold that the deliberate creation of a black-majority district was actionable, narrowly recognizing a Constitutional question only in the case of those rare districts that were especially bizarre." Jones, "In Peril: Black Lawmakers," N.Y. *Times*, Sept. 11, 1994 § 4, at 19 (Op-Ed Sunday), col. 4.

201. 113 S.Ct. at 2524.

202. Id. at 2828.

203. Id. at 2843.

204. 493 U.S. 265 (1990).

205. As characterized by the Court, "The issue here is whether it was a proper exercise of judicial power for the District Court to hold petitioners, four Yonkers city council members, in contempt for refusing to vote in favor of legislation implementing a consent decree earlier approved by the city." 493 U.S. at 267.

206. Id. at 273.

207. Id. at 280 ("This sort of individual sanction effects a much greater perversion of the normal legislative process than does the imposition of sanctions on the city for the failure of these same legislators to enact an ordinance."). Quoting from the contempt order, however, the dissent pointed out that the district court had not imposed the sanctions precipitously: "The issues transcend Yonkers. They go to the very foundation of the system of constitutional government. If Yonkers can defy the orders of a federal court in any case, but especially a civil rights case, because compliance is unpopular, and if that situation is tolerated, then our constitutional system of government fails." 493 U.S. at 281 (Brennan, J., dissenting).

208. 503 U.S. 467 (1992).

209. 498 U.S. 237 (1991).

210. The school system was first brought under district court supervision pursuant to a 1969 desegregation order. See Pitts v. Freeman, 755 F.2d 1423, 1424 (11th Cir. 1985) (recounting history of prior proceedings).

211. Specifically, the plaintiffs charged that the plan "avoided reassignment of those white students to nearby undercapacity high schools that were predominantly black." Pitts v. Freeman, 755 F.2d 1423, 1424 (11th Cir. 1985).

212. On remand from the first appeal, the district court ruled that the school system had obtained unitary status with respect to student assignments, transportation, physical facilities, and extracurricular activities, but had failed to do so with respect to faculty assignments and resource allocation. The district court continued to attribute disparities in student composition solely to demographic changes over which the defendant school system had no control, and consequently, no responsibility to address.

213. Based upon this finding, the district court imposed upon the plaintiffs the burden of demonstrating discriminatory intent in the school system's plan to construct the challenged facility. See Pitts v. Freeman, 755 F.2d 1423, 1424–25 (11th Cir. 1985) (recounting proceedings in district court).

214. Rejecting the argument that unitary status may be achieved incrementally, the Eleventh Circuit held that "[a] school system achieves unitary status or it does not." Pitts v. Freeman, 887 F.2d 1438, 1446 (11th Cir. 1989). To determine unitariness, the court of appeals instructed district courts to evaluate the six factors set forth in *Green v. County School Board:* student assignment, faculty, staff, transportation, extracurricular activities, and facilities. See Green v. County School Board, 391 U.S. 430, 435 (1968). "If the school system fulfills all six factors at the same time for several years, the court should declare that the school system has achieved unitary status. If the school system fails to fulfill all six factors at the same time for several years, the district court should retain jurisdiction." *Pitts*, 887 F.2d at 1446.

The Eleventh Circuit also rejected the district court's determination that independent demographic changes relieved the school system of any further obligation in the area of student assignments. The court stated: "We also reject the district court's refusal to require the DCSS to eradicate segregation caused by demographic changes. As the former

Fifth Circuit stated in Lee v. Macon County Board of Education, 616 f.2d 805, 810 (5th Cir. 1980): 'Not until all vestiges of dual system are eradicated can demographic changes constitute legal cause for racial imbalance in the schools. . . . Notwithstanding the school authorities' apparent good faith attempt to desegregate in 1970, the system has never achieved unitary status. . . . Consequently, the school board in Tuscaloosa is still under an affirmative duty to dismantle the dual system, regardless of current housing patterns.'" (Citing Flax v. Potts, 464 F.2d 865, 868–69 (5th Cir.), *cert. denied*, 409 U.S. 1007 [93 S.Ct. 433, 34 L.Ed.2d 299] (1972)). Id. at 1449.

215. See *Freeman*, 503 U.S. at 491–92.

216. Id. at 494–97.

217. 498 U.S. 237 (1991). The litigation in *Dowell* was conducted by the NAACP Legal Defense Fund during my tenure as director-counsel.

218. The plaintiffs did not appeal this finding. The order of the district court conferring unitary status on the Oklahoma public schools did not, however, expressly dissolve the desegregation decree entered in 1972. See *Dowell*, 498 U.S. at 244–45.

219. "Under the [Student Reassignment Plan] SRP, 11 of 64 elementary schools would be greater than 90 % black, 22 would be greater than 90% white plus other minorities, and 31 would be racially mixed." *Dowell*, 498 U.S. at 242.

220. See Dowell v. Board of Educ. of Oklahoma City Public Schools, 606 F. Supp. 1548 (WD Okla. 1985).

221. 890 F.2d at 1490 (10th Cir. 1989) (quoting Jost, "From *Swift* to *Stotts* and Beyond: Modification of Injunctions in the Federal Courts," 64 *Texas L. Rev.* 1101, 1110 (1986)) (analyzing United States v. Swift & Co., 286 U.S. 106 (1932)).

222. 498 U.S. at 249.

223. Id. Justice Marshall, joined in dissent by Justices Blackmun and Stevens, also advanced the application of a different standard than that applied by the Tenth Circuit. Justice Marshall argued that "the standard for dissolution of a school desegregation decree must reflect the central aim of our school desegregation precedents. . . . [Thus,] a desegregation decree cannot be lifted so long as conditions likely to inflict the stigmatic injury condemned in *Brown I* persist and there remain feasible methods of eliminating such conditions." 498 U.S. at 251–52 (Marshall, J., dissenting). The dissent made clear, however, its disagreement with the majority's characterization of both the standard applied by the court of appeals as well as its likely effect: "In its concern to spare local school boards the 'Draconian' fate of 'indefinite' 'judicial tutelage,' the majority risks subordination of the constitutional rights of Afro-American children to the interest of school board autonomy. . . . Retaining the decree does not require a return to active supervision. It may be that a modification of the decree which will improve its effectiveness and give the school district more flexibility . . . is appropriate. . . . But retaining the decree seems a slight burden on the school district compared with the risk of not delivering a full remedy to the Afro-American children in the school system." Id. at 267–68 (citations omitted).

224. 498 U.S. at 247.

225. Id. at 248.

226. Id. at 250.

227. 498 U.S. at 264.

228. Id. at 263.

229. Id. at 264 (citing Keyes v. School Dist. No. 1, 413 U.S. 189, 202 (1973); see also Columbus Bd. of Educ. v. Penick, 443 U.S. 449, 467 n.13 (1979) (acknowledging the evidence that "school segregation is a contributing cause of housing segregation"). Quote is in footnote 13 of page 467 of the opinion.

230. Id. at 265.

231. Id. at 264.

232. In addition to the five cases briefly treated in the text, Congress also nullified the effects of Rehnquist Court decisions in EEOC v. Arabian Am. Oil Co., 499 U.S. 244 (1991) (rejecting coverage of Title VII to American citizens employed abroad by United States corporations), and West Virginia Univ. Hosp. Inc. v. Casey, 499 U.S. 83 (1991) (limiting the amount and nature of expert fees recoverable for prevailing parties in § 1983 actions). See also Crawford Fitting Co. v. J.T. Gibbons, Inc., 482 U.S. 437 (1987) (imposing identical limitations under Title VII).

233. 491 U.S. 164 (1989).

234. 42 U.S.C. § 1981 (1988).

235. 491 U.S. at 179.

236. The dissent, authored by Justice Brennan, emphasized the legislative history of § 1981 and the facts on which it was based. The Reconstruction Congress that enacted the act "realized that, in the former Confederate States, employers were attempting to 'adher[e], *as to the treatment of the laborers,* as much as possible to the traditions of the old system, *even where the relations between employers had been fixed by contract.*'" Id. at 206 (emphasis in original).

237. 490 U.S. 900 (1989).

238. 490 U.S. 228 (1989).

239. Writing for the Court, Justice Brennan, joined by Justices Marshall, Blackmun, and Stevens, rejected the district and appellate courts' application of a clear and convincing standard of proving that the same decision would have been made absent the discriminatory conduct. 490 U.S. 239–58.

240. 490 U.s. 755 (1989).

241. Justices Stevens, Brennan, Marshall, and Blackmun, in dissent, acknowledged a limited right in the white firefighters to lodge a collateral attack against the consent decrees. The dissenters further observed, however, that "[remedial measures for minorities] will necessarily have an adverse impact on whites, who must now share their job and promotion opportunities with blacks. Just as white employees in the past were innocent beneficiaries of illegal discriminatory practices, so is it inevitable that some of the same white employees will be innocent victims who must share some of the burdens resulting from the redress of the past wrongs." Id. at 791–92. (Stevens, J., dissenting).

242. 490 U.S. 642 (1989).

243. Id. at 650 (citations omitted).

244. Id. at 653.

245. Exhibiting, I believe, an unfounded apprehension of quotas, the Court explained further, "any employer who had a segment of his work force that was—for some reason—racially imbalanced, could be haled into court and forced to engage in the expensive and time-consuming task of defending the 'business necessity' of the methods used to select the other members of his work force. The only practicable option for many employers will be to adopt racial quotas, insuring that no portion of his work force deviates in racial composition from other portions thereof . . . ." Id. at 652.

246. Id. at 661.

247. Id. at 659. "[Plaintiffs] . . . also have to demonstrate that the disparity they complain of is the result of one or more of the employment practices that they are attacking . . . , specifically showing that each challenged practice has a significantly disparate impact on employment opportunities for whites and nonwhites. To hold otherwise would result in employers being potentially liable for 'the myriad of innocent causes that may lead to statistical imbalances in the composition of their work forces.'" Id. at 657.

248. *Greene*, supra note 13, at 1522.

249. See Civil Rights Act of 1991, Pub. L. No. 102-166, § 1977A 105 Stat. 1071 (codified as amended in scattered sections of 42 U.S.C.). The Supreme Court had suggested that Title VII's provision of equitable relief did not encompass "general or punitive damages." Great Am. Fed. Sav. & Loan Ass'n v. Novotny, 442 U.S. 366, 374–75 (1979).

250. Civil Rights Act of 1991, Pub. L. No. 102-166 § 1977A(c) 105 Stat. 1071 (codified as amended in scattered sections of 42 U.S.C.).

251. ——U.S.——; 114 S.Ct. 1483 (1994).

252. 114 S.Ct. 1510 (1994). In *Rivers*, black garage mechanics who were subject to retaliatory discharge after successfully pursuing grievances against their employer brought suit under both Title VII and § 1981. The § 1981 claim was dismissed on the authority of *Patterson*, which was decided before the trial on the mechanics claims.

253. See, e.g., Landsberg, supra note 109, at 1275 n.40 (collecting cases).

254. The Rehnquist Court's overt "[h]ostility to affirmative action is especially puzzling given the Court's allowance of legislative favoritism outside the racial context." Lively, supra note 22, at 507–08 (1991) (citing Personnel Adm'r v. Feeney, 442 U.S. 256, 280–81 (1979) (upholding state hiring schemes granting preference to veterans against a gender-based equal protection challenge)). Of course, the legislation involved in *Feeney* was gender-neutral. But that distinction as compared to race-conscious affirmative action plans is artificial. The clear impact of the legislation upheld in *Feeney* was to exclude women. The Court held, however, that proof of discriminatory intent was required. Moreover, proof of intent required a showing that the challenged plan was "selected or reaffirmed . . . at least in part 'because of,' not merely 'in spite of,' its adverse effects upon an identifiable group." *Feeney*, 422 U.S. at 279.

255. See Roe v. Wade, 410 U.S. 113 (1973).

256. *Black*, supra note 8, at 25.

257. See Boudin, "Book Review: The Last Liberal Chief Justice of the Twentieth Century," 36 *Stan. L. Rev.* 863, 868 (1984).

258. Berger, supra note 67, at 180.

259. Lamb, supra note 67, at 184.

260. Lupu, "Untangling the Strands of the Fourteenth Amendment," 77 *Mich. L. Rev.* 981, 1041 (1979).

261. Lamb, supra note 67, at 186 (emphasis added).

262. Black, supra note 8, at 14.

263. See Kahn, supra note 76, at 25–26. "The Warren Court could not accept America as a normative phenomenon. Chief Justice Warren and a majority of the Warren Court represented the view that the polity was not operating as the pluralist equilibrium model had said it would." Id. at 25.

264. Black, supra note 8, at 28.

265. Id.

266. Id. at 15.

267. 163 U.S. at 560.

268. Black, supra note 8, at 13.

• 5 •

FREEDOM OF SPEECH IN THE WARREN COURT

NADINE STROSSEN

Preparing this essay on the Warren Court's free speech jurisprudence has been a great educational and inspirational experience. Of course, like everyone who has studied First Amendment issues, I had a general impression that free speech advocates are beholden to that Court. But I never appreciated quite how true this was until I specifically took stock for this essay.

I should say, by way of disclaimer, that the American Civil Liberties Union played an active role in many of the great free speech cases of the Warren years, either by directly representing the party pressing a First Amendment claim[1] or as amicus. No wonder that in Samuel Walker's history of the ACLU, the chapter covering the Warren era is called "The Great Years"![2]

Conversely, steeping myself in the Warren Court's free speech rulings sadly underscored for me how much slippage we have seen since then in many critical areas. Certainly there are exceptions, but on the whole, the Warren Court was the most speech-protective Court that we have yet seen, leaving us a lasting legacy of protective precedents and principles. As Gerald Gunther stated, in the First Amendment area, "[t]he Warren Court . . . [was] almost as prolific in its doctrinal innovations as in its speech-protective results."[3]

I. Speech-Protective Doctrines Pioneered by Warren Court

One can quickly appreciate the Warren Court's singularly significant role in protecting free speech by considering the number of speech-protecting doctrines or concepts that this Court essentially pioneered—either by being the first Court to formulate the doctrine or concept, or by being the first to meaningfully develop and implement it.

Let me list some of the essential entries in our First Amendment lexicon, derived from the Warren Court:

Freedom of association—the idea that the First Amendment guarantees the right to join with others to advocate ideas[4]

Academic freedom—the view that the First Amendment provides a special haven for free and independent inquiry by individuals and institutions in the academic arena[5]

The right to receive information and ideas—the notion that the First Amendment extends rights to those at whom expression is aimed, as well as to those engaging in the expression[6]

Public forum—the vision of public property[7]—and, indeed, some private property[8] too—as a sanctuary for the exercise of First Amendment rights

Chilling effect and self-censorship—the understanding that First Amendment rights can be as endangered by measures that indirectly deter their exercise as by measures that directly prevent or punish their exercise[9]

Vagueness[10] *and overbreadth*[11]—two doctrines recognizing that any speech regulation must be fine-tuned so as not to threaten expression that should be protected

Less restrictive alternatives—yet another concept arising from the Court's appreciation of the fragility of free speech rights, and the importance of protecting them against indirect, as well as direct, assaults.[12] Consistent with this concept, the Court would not condone any speech-abridging measure if the government purpose that it promoted could be effectively served by some other measure posing less danger to free speech.

So, many key terms in our current First Amendment vocabulary were placed there—given meaning—by the Warren Court.

II. Broadening the Concept of First Amendment "Speech"

The Warren Court also brought whole categories of expression within the ambit of the Free Speech Clause for the first time—expression that had historically been assumed to be beyond the pale of constitutional protection. With visionary boldness, the Warren Court looked beyond these long-standing, unexamined assumptions.

In *New York Times v. Sullivan,* the Court declared that, despite the common law pigeonhole, "libel [laws] can claim no talismanic immunity from constitutional limitations."[13] Just as the Warren Court lifted the "talismanic immunity" that all defamation actions had enjoyed prior to *Sullivan,* so too it lifted the talismanic immunity that other kinds of speech-limiting measures had enjoyed, for various reasons: because of the subject or content of the speech; because of the place where the speech occurred; or because of the status of the speaker.

Accordingly, along with *Sullivan*'s holding that defamatory expression was not beyond the First Amendment pale, the Warren Court held likewise concerning other kinds of speech whose content also had traditionally immunized it from First Amendment protection. For example, the Court looked beyond the label "obscenity" and innovatively recognized that it simply obscured what was in fact First Amendment speech—sexual speech.[14]

Additionally, the Warren Court first gave meaningful constitutional protection to the type of speech that had been the preeminent target of suppression throughout our history, not only by other government officials, but also by the Court itself—namely, "subversive advocacy," or speech that allegedly undermines national security or personal safety. In *Brandenburg v. Ohio*[15] in 1969, the Warren Court wove together all the speech-protective strands of prior judicial opinions concerning such speech.[16] Drawing upon opinions by Louis D. Brandeis, Oliver Wendell Holmes, and Learned Hand, the *Brandenburg* Court made it extremely difficult—indeed, usually impossible—to suppress speech because of any danger feared to flow from the ideas it conveys.

Likewise, the Warren Court lifted long-standing presumptions that expression was ipso facto unprotected just because it took place in certain settings—including various kinds of public property other than the streets, parks, and sidewalks that had been deemed "traditional public forums" or special sanctuaries for expressive activity. Thus, the Warren Court upheld First Amendment rights in settings such as a state capitol,[17] a courthouse,[18] and a public library.[19] Further, the Warren Court upheld First Amendment rights of picketers even on private property—specifically, a privately owned shopping mall.[20]

In the same vein, the Warren Court was unwilling to perpetuate long-lived assumptions that certain speech could be restricted because of the identity or status of the speakers. For example, in the landmark case of *Tinker v. Des Moines School District*,[21] the Court shattered a time-honored shibboleth when it ruled that students do not shed their First Amendment rights at the schoolhouse gate. In the same spirit, the Warren Court dispelled previous assumptions that individuals such as public school teachers[22] and other government employees,[23] lack First Amendment rights just by virtue of their occupations.

In short, the Warren Court eliminated artificial categories and classifications among speech—treating all speech as presumptively protected and considering differences among various types of speech only in evaluating whether particular restrictions were justified.

In contrast, subsequent Courts have reerected categories and classifications not only among types of speech but also among types of restrictions.[24] Therefore, the Rehnquist Court now applies a searching First Amendment scrutiny only to certain types of regulations on certain types of speech, in certain places, and by certain kinds of speakers. Under this complex compartmentalization, most speech is not presumed to be entitled to full-fledged First Amendment protection, and most restrictions are not presumed to be unconstitutional. This has been a sad reversal of the Warren Court approach.

III. Win-Loss Record of Free Speech Claimants

Another indication of the Warren Court's outstanding role in the free speech arena is the unusually high success rate it dealt to litigants who pressed speech claims. Consider, for example, one comparative study of free expression cases before the Warren and Burger Courts.[25] This 1987 study by F. Dennis Hale showed that parties invoking free speech rights won almost three-fourths of their cases before the Warren Court, whereas such parties won less than half their cases before the Burger Court.[26] The study by Hale shows that from 1931 to 1981, the overall success rate of Supreme Court free expression cases was 58 percent.[27] So the Burger Court was less supportive of free speech than previous Courts, and the Warren Court was significantly more supportive.

This same disparity persists if we examine particular types of cases that both Courts frequently entertained. In obscenity cases, parties asserting free speech rights had a 63 percent success rate before the Warren Court, but only 39 percent before the Burger Court. In libel cases, the free speech victory rates were 87 percent in the Warren Court compared to 47 percent in the Burger Court. And in cases involving access to government information, the free speech success ratio under Warren was 67 percent and under Burger only 29 percent.[28]

IV. An Expansive Vision of Free Speech and the First Amendment

Now I'd like to try to convey some sense of the Warren Court's unique devotion to free speech values from a very different perspective—one that focuses on attitudes and words, rather than on numbers. Harry Kalven, whose mature scholarly life essentially coincided with the Warren Court, and who was the foremost contemporary analyst of that Court's First Amendment jurisprudence, once wrote that the Court's preeminent contribution was not so much a series of specific decisions, noteworthy as those were. Rather, he suggested, the Court's overriding contribution to free expression was the general spirit or attitude with which it approached all free speech issues, and the broad vision of the First Amendment that informed and infused all its specific holdings.[29]

More consistently than other Courts either before or since, the Warren Court approached free speech questions from the perspective that freedom of expression is a preferred constitutional value. Therefore, even though the Warren Court did not automatically protect speech—to the consternation of Justice Hugo Black, who castigated his brethren's "balancing" approach to speech issues[30]—still, the Warren Court undertook its balancing with a "thumb on the scales" in favor of speech. In that significant sense, the Warren Court's version of First Amendment balancing was far more protective than the versions practiced by later Courts.

The Warren Court's comparative weighing of free speech and countervailing goals was also much more speech-protective than the weighing process practiced by other Courts for another major reason: The Warren Court had a realistic, pragmatic appreciation of the actual adverse impact that various measures had on speech.[31] The Court's concern was always to shelter expression, which it saw as fragile, from any measure that, as a practical matter, would burden or deter it.

Thus, the Court held that the First Amendment was violated not only by direct criminal sanctions, specifically and intentionally targeting speech, but also by a wide range of measures that were likely to have any substantial adverse impact on speech, even if indirect or incidental, and even if subtle. For example, in *Bates v. City of Little Rock*, the Court declared that First Amendment freedoms "are protected not only against heavy-handed frontal attack, but also from being stifled by more subtle governmental interference."[32] Hence, the Warren Court's willingness to extend First Amendment protection to a wide range of expression, as previously noted—including expression that had not traditionally triggered First Amendment scrutiny—was matched by its willingness to find the First Amendment violated by a wide range of government measures—including measures that had not traditionally triggered First Amendment scrutiny.

Later Courts have not shown a similar understanding or concern for the actual impact of government measures or of their own rulings. As Thomas Emerson commented in a 1983 book about the Burger Court: "The Burger Court has lost that feeling for the dynamics of the system of freedom of expression which was the hallmark of the Warren Court."[33] Likewise, Justice Potter Stewart said that, in contrast to the Warren Court, the Burger Court took "a crabbed view" of the First Amendment and showed a "disturbing insensitivity" to free expression concerns.[34]

To be sure, there was a downside to the Warren Court's positive stance toward free speech values. As the saying goes, this approach had the defect of its virtues. For just as the Court's speech-protective rulings often flowed from a general, positive outlook toward expression, correspondingly, those rulings often did not articulate specific doctrinal analyses, and therefore did not provide firm guidance for future Courts. As Professor Emerson observed: "In general, the Warren Court protected expression to an unprecedented degree. But this resulted more from a strongly favorable attitude toward First Amendment values than from a well-developed theory of the First Amendment. As a result, Warren Court decisions contained many ambiguities, loopholes, and loosely formulated rules."[35]

Because the Warren Court's speech-affirming decisions often did not lay out precise doctrinal or analytical guidelines, the Burger and Rehnquist Courts, which lack the earlier Court's enthusiastic commitment to free speech, have often reached results that are at variance with the Warren Court's ethos, but without having to expressly overrule Warren Court precedents. In this way, the substantial erosion in free speech protection since the Warren era has no doubt escaped the full measure of comment and criticism it would otherwise provoke.[36]

V. Eloquent Additions to the Free Speech Tradition

The Warren Court's overarching legacy of an expansive, enthusiastic stance toward the First Amendment is conveyed by some eloquent, quotable statements in that Court's opinions. The importance of these declarations transcends the key parts they played in framing particular speech-protective results. Even beyond that, these words shape our perception of free speech and the First Amendment more generally. They become part of what Harry Kalven called our "free speech tradition":[37] the ideas and words and history that, along with particular judicial decisions, give actual meaning to freedom of expression in America. Our devotion to and our actual exercise of free speech rights depend on not only the *law*, but also the *lore* of the First Amendment, and further on its *allure*. This idea was well captured by Jamie Kalven, Harry Kalven's son and the editor of his posthumous book; the younger Kalven said, "The tradition of protecting words lives by words."[38]

Harry Kalven's own favorite Warren Court words-about-protecting-words were from the Court's landmark 1964 case, *New York Times v. Sullivan*,[39] which granted First Amendment protection for statements defaming public officials. Like many memorable declarations about free speech, these were written by Justice William Brennan: "[W]e consider this case against the background of a profound national commitment to the principle that debate on public issues should be uninhibited, robust, and wide-open, and that it may well include vehement, caustic, and sometimes unpleasantly sharp attacks on government and public officials."[40] These powerful words could be taken as the Warren Court's First Amendment motto more broadly. They embody the Court's overall philosophy about all free speech and free press issues. Here is Kalven's commentary on them:

> What catches the eye is the daring, unconventional selection of adjectives. These words capture the special quality of the Court's stance toward first amendment issues. They indicate an awareness that heresy is robust; that counterstatement on public issues, if it is to be vital and perform its function, may not always be polite. And, most significantly, they express a desire to make a fresh statement about the principles of free speech rather than simply repeat the classic phrases of Holmes . . . and Brandeis. . . . The Court is interested enough to be minting contemporary epigrams. . . .[41]

One of my favorite Warren Court encomiums to free expression comes from another constitutional libel case, also decided in 1964, and also authored by Justice Brennan: *Garrison v. Louisiana*. The Court there proclaimed: "Speech concerning public affairs is more than self-expression; it is the essence of self-government."[42]

Another example of the Warren Court's eloquent free speech epigrams that Kalven singled out comes from Justice Stewart's 1959 opinion in *Kingsley Pictures Corp. v. Regents*,[43] which overturned a decision that had allowed New York State to ban the movie version of *Lady Chatterley's Lover* because of its sympathetic treatment of adultery. Rejecting the argument that expression could be banned because of inconsistency with prevailing moral, religious, or legal standards, Stewart wrote: "[T]he Constitution['s] [free speech] guarantee is not confined to the expression of ideas that are conventional or shared by a majority. It protects advocacy of the opinion that adultery may sometimes be proper no less than advocacy of socialism or the single tax. And in the realm of ideas it protects expression which is eloquent no less than that which is unconvincing."[44] Here is Kalven's insightful commentary on this passage: "Again what strikes the special note is not just the firm grasp of the basic principle but the gallantry . . . of its restatement. It is easier to champion freedom for the thought we hate than for the thought that embarrasses."[45]

VI. Numerical Indicia of Ongoing Importance

The Warren Court's ongoing impact on free speech law is indicated by some numbers. Justices Holmes and Brandeis, widely perceived as the "architects" of First Amendment doctrine, participated in some thirty-four free speech cases; in contrast, even by the time of Earl Warren's resignation, Justice Brennan had participated in over three-hundred such cases—and that was more than twenty years before his own resignation.

In 1920, when Zechariah Chafee wrote the first edition of his influential book *Free Speech in the United States*, the Supreme Court had decided about twenty free speech cases. In 1949, when Alexander Meiklejohn wrote his *Free Speech and Its Relation to Self-Government*, there were about one hundred such cases. By the end of the Warren era, when Harry Kalven was working on his free speech book, which was published posthumously, there were well over four hundred such cases—more than half of which had been decided by the Warren Court.[46]

The Warren Court's enduring free speech legacy is marked not only in quantity, but also in quality, or importance. To this day, the free speech sections of leading constitutional law casebooks and treatises are dominated by Warren Court decisions. I teach from Gerald Gunther's constitutional law casebook.[47] Of the forty-three major free speech cases it includes, almost 40 percent are Warren Court cases.

A comprehensive or detailed discussion of such an extensive body of law cannot possibly be presented here. Rather, I will have to continue to paint in broad brush-strokes, giving only a "Big Picture" perspective on the Warren Court's free speech rulings, instead of attending to the fine points, qualifications, nuances, and exceptions that would appear in a more microscopic examination. Just as the Warren Court itself had a bold and generous approach to the Free Speech Clause, it is especially appropriate to take a broad view of those Warren Court rulings.

Accordingly, the remainder of this essay will describe one important general pattern or theme that emerges from these hundreds of decisions. Of the many broad themes that cut across the Warren Court's free speech cases, one is of particular current, ongoing interest.

As a free speech advocate, I am especially eager to draw lessons that not only shed light on where we have been, but that also point the way toward where we can and should go in forging a firm freedom for speech. To me, that's the most promising aspect of this volume: It should serve not only as a retrospective celebration of a great Court, but also as a source of guidance and inspiration for future work by all of us in all of our capacities—scholars, teachers, lawyers, activists, judges and other public officials, and citizens.

VII. The Positive Interrelationship Between Free Speech and Equality Values: A Broad Theme Emerging from Warren Court Cases

The general theme that I will emphasize, in this forward-looking spirit, is closely tied to the Warren Court's equal protection jurisprudence. For the Court's support for equality rights and racial justice was achieved not only through its Equal Protection Clause rulings, but also through its Free Speech Clause rulings.

Thus, the Warren Court record roundly rebuffs some views that recently have become influential—namely, that equality and free speech values are at war with each other, and that we can effectively advance equality only by cutting back on free speech. To the contrary, the Warren Court record dramatically demonstrates the mutually reinforcing relationship between free speech and equality, and the critically important role that broad First Amendment rights played in the Civil Rights movement. Having thus summarized my thesis, I will elaborate on it in the remainder of this essay.

In the recent past, it has become increasingly fashionable to argue that free speech and equality values are inevitably, inherently in tension with each other. This idea has been advanced by some prominent law professors and has had significant impact on academic and public policies, and on some judicial rulings as well.

This notion has fueled, for example, the mounting arguments for suppressing so-called hate speech—namely, speech expressing racist, sexist, and other biased ideas. For instance, in a 1993 book entitled *Words That Wound*,[48] several prominent law professors argue that we should cut back on First Amendment protection for hate speech in order to advance racial equality and curtail racial discrimination. They maintain that our robust free speech concept has protected racist expression and has undermined the fight for racial equality.

These arguments have prompted many colleges and universities all over the country to adopt codes that proscribe and punish hate speech.[49] They have also prompted various governments to target hate speech. So far, the courts have found such measures unconstitutional, but there are some troubling qualifications and exceptions in their rulings.[50]

The same contention that speech and equality rights are at odds with each other also underlies the arguments that have been made by some influential feminists, including law professor Catharine MacKinnon and writer Andrea Dworkin, that certain sexual speech should be banned in the service of women's rights. They argue that this expression, which they label "pornography," leads to—or even *is*—discrimination and violence against women.[51] As MacKinnon wrote in her 1993 book *Only Words*: "The law of free speech and the law of equality are on a collision course in this country."[52]

These arguments have had a profound impact on our public policy and law recently, leading to widespread suppression of sexual expression.[53] Again, as in the hate speech situation, while the courts have not directly upheld what may be called the "MacDworkinite" arguments, they have not completely rejected them either. Moreover, some courts have in fact upheld these arguments in the context of sexual harassment cases.

I will not elaborate further on the many other disturbing ways that this notion of a purported opposition between speech and equality rights recently has shaped our law and culture. For purposes of this essay, I want to stress how the Warren Court provides a resounding refutation of this now-prevalent and insidious notion—namely, that the First Amendment is at best irrelevant, and at worst adverse, to the crucial causes of advancing equality and reducing discrimination. For the Warren Court's firm enforcement of the First Amendment played an absolutely critical role in the Civil Rights movement.

Important as the Court's equal protection rulings were, those rulings could not even have been achieved, let alone effectively implemented, without the organizing and litigating efforts of the NAACP, without the speeches and demonstrations of Martin Luther King and other civil rights leaders and activists, and without the press coverage that mobilized the support of the American public and of the national government. And all of these essential foundations for advances in civil rights depended upon the Warren Court's broad, vigorous conception of free speech—a conception sufficiently broad and vigorous that it necessarily also encompasses hate speech and other forms of speech that now are said to undermine equality.

Case after case in the Warren Court's First Amendment corpus arose from the Civil Rights movement and was as important for facilitating that movement's equality goals as it was for fostering free expression more generally. Only a few examples will be cited.

New York Times v. Sullivan[54] not only created new protection for expression criticizing public officials in general; it also deprived Southern officials of a powerful weapon against the Civil Rights movement and made it possible for the national press to bring that struggle to the forefront of national attention.

NAACP v. Alabama[55] and its progeny not only recognized an implied First Amendment right of association, but also made it possible for the NAACP to survive the onslaughts of hostile local and state officials and to continue its law reform activities.

NAACP v. Button[56] not only recognized that solicitation of legal clients and litigation are protected First Amendment activities—in one historian's words, "a virtual charter of freedom for litigation as an agent of social change"[57]—but it also made possible the lawsuits that were necessary to bring about desegregation.[58]

Brown v. Louisiana,[59] *Cox v. Louisiana,*[60] *Edwards v. South Carolina,*[61] and many similar cases not only extended First Amendment protection to novel forms of expression and protest—including sit-ins and other types of demonstrations—but also allowed civil rights activists to capture the attention of their local communities and to capture the conscience of the nation.

Bond v. Floyd[62] not only established the free speech rights of politicians and government officials, but also ordered the seating of one of the few black legislators in the South at the time, and sent an important message about racial politics around the country.

Gibson v. Florida Legislative Investigating Commission[63] not only imposed significant limits on the power of legislative investigating committees to inquire into political beliefs and associations, but also specifically freed the Civil Rights movement from the McCarthyite tactics that Southern states had launched against it.

Talley v. California[64] not only recognized the important First Amendment right to distribute anonymous handbills, but also facilitated a boycott on behalf of an organization protesting denial of "equal employment opportunities to Negroes, Mexicans, and Orientals" in a hard-fought struggle to end discrimination by certain merchants and businessmen.

And the list could go on and on. As I reread the Warren Court's free expression cases, I was repeatedly struck by how many cases that we generally think of in terms of their First Amendment legal holdings arose in the factual context of the struggle for racial justice, and thus had a direct positive impact on equality rights as well as free speech rights.

In light of these many decisions, I cannot understand the skeptical view of those who advocate hate speech restrictions, questioning whether the First Amendment did indeed play a positive role in the civil rights cause.[65] The Warren Court record conclusively shows that, in the words of historian Samuel Walker, "The . . . civil rights movement . . . depended on the First Amendment."[66]

The Warren Court record further shows that it is impossible to erect free speech principles that will protect pro–civil rights expression without also protecting the expression of all other political messages, no matter how controversial or unpopular—including Communist and anti–civil rights messages. Indeed, during the Warren era, pro–civil rights messages were often equated with Communist ones—not only because many believed the Communist Party to be a mainstay of the Civil Rights movement—but also more generally, insofar as both causes were seen as subversive, threatening widely held and deeply cherished views about "our way of life."

Professor Kalven explored this connection in his 1965 book entitled *The Negro and the First Amendment*. He noted that, from a Southern standpoint, the NAACP, along with the Communist Party, was also a "domestic conspiracy aiming at a revolution."[67] In most Southern communities, the NAACP was the only organized voice of the Civil Rights movement. Therefore, it served as the lightning rod for segregationist fears.

Just as the Southern states saw the NAACP as posing the same kind of threat as the Communist Party, they responded to the NAACP through the same legal weapons—contrary to First Amendment rights—that our national, state, and local governments had aimed against Communism during the Cold War. Throughout the South, government officials mounted inquisitions against the NAACP.[68] They passed laws requiring the NAACP to disclose the names and addresses of its members and contributors, thereby exposing them to retaliation by their employers and to Klan violence. Arkansas barred NAACP members from all government jobs; a non-NAACP membership affidavit was required as a condition of public employment. Many states sought to disqualify the NAACP from seeking and representing clients in desegregation cases. Southern legislatures also undertook harassing investigations of NAACP activists.[69]

The notorious House Un-American Activities Committee, HUAC, itself conducted witch-hunts not only against suspected Communists, but also against civil rights activists—who, by definition, they equated with suspected Communists. The Communist bogeyman was systematically used to harass civil rights activists. As Justice Hugo Black said in a 1961 dissent: "If the House Un-American Activities Committee is to have the power to interrogate everyone who is called a Communist, there is one thing certain beyond the peradventure of a doubt—no legislative committee, state or federal, will have trouble finding cause to subpoena all persons anywhere who take a public stand . . . against segregation."[70]

In a series of decisions sheltering the NAACP against this campaign of harassment and intimidation, the Warren Court recognized and developed a new constitutional right, implicit in the First Amendment: the freedom of association.[71] In the first such case, *NAACP v. Alabama*[72] in 1958, the Court recognized that "effective advocacy of public . . . points of view, particularly controversial ones, is undeniably enhanced by group association."[73] In *NAACP v. Alabama*, the Court held that the right of association was violated by the state's requirement that the NAACP disclose its members' names and addresses. The Court recognized that such compelled disclosure would in effect discourage people from joining this group, which was then so hated in Alabama. Writing for a unanimous Court, Justice Harlan explained that "privacy in group association may in many circumstances be indispensable to preservation of freedom of association, particularly where a group espouses dissident beliefs."[74] In the words of historian Samuel Walker: "The NAACP could not have survived in the South, and the civil rights movement would have been set back for years, without the new freedom of association protections."[75]

How sad that, recently, the NAACP itself refused to support this identical, crucially important principle. In 1993, in Texas, the Ku Klux Klan was apparently as controversial, hated, and feared as the NAACP was in Alabama in 1948. Accordingly, when the State of Texas ordered the Klan to disclose its membership lists in 1993, the ACLU agreed to defend the Klan's First Amendment right to refuse, citing *NAACP v. Alabama* and other Warren Court precedents.[76] Not only did the NAACP oppose this (ultimately successful) argument but, even worse, the Texas NAACP dismissed its volunteer general counsel, Galveston lawyer Anthony Griffin, who was also a volunteer ACLU lawyer and in that capacity was handling the Klan membership disclosure case.[77] This shows, sadly, historic myopia.

It is the same historic myopia that distorts the views of those who claim we have to choose between free speech and equality rights. The prominent law professors and others who now argue that because racism is an evil and dangerous ideology, government should protect listeners from racist ideas that they find wrong and offensive, should recall the historical context in which the Warren Court sheltered antiracist speech. For that speech carried messages that, in their time and place, were passionately believed to be false and dangerous. If public acceptance or non-offensiveness would have been the touchstones, the Warren Court could not have protected the pro–civil rights expressions that were repeatedly suppressed precisely because they were heard as so wrong and so threatening.

This point was powerfully made in Justice Black's 1961 dissent in *Braden v. United States.*[78] In that case, and its companion case *Wilkinson v. United States,*[79] by five-to-four votes, the Warren Court failed to protect two white civil right activists from harassment by the House Un-American Activities Committee. Black used this dissent to underscore the indivisibility of First Amendment rights for all speech—not only speech by Communists as well as civil rights activists but also speech by civil rights opponents as well as civil rights supporters. Black did this by criticizing a pre–Warren Court ruling, *Beauharnais v. Illinois,*[80] in which a five-to-four majority had upheld the state's law barring group defamation, as enforced against a white, pro-segregation speaker. Although the Court has never expressly overturned *Beauharnais*, the consensus among scholars and judges is that it was in effect overturned by several subsequent Warren Court rulings, including *New York Times v. Sullivan.*[81]

In his *Braden* and *Wilkinson* dissents, Justice Black noted that the majority decisions in those cases could have been based on *Beauharnais*, because there, too, according to Black, the Court had deviated from the Free Speech Clause's absolute, neutral guarantee. Commenting further about *Beauharnais*, Black said:

> Ironically, the need there . . . accepted by . . . this Court as sufficiently compelling to warrant abridgment of the [First Amendment] right . . . was the need to protect Negroes against . . . "libel . . . of a racial group. . . ." Thus, the decision in *Beauharnais* had all the outward appearance of being one which would aid the underprivileged Negro minority. [The *Braden*] decision, however, is a dramatic illustration of the shortsightedness of such an interpretation of that case. For the very constitutional philosophy that gave birth to

> *Beauharnais* today gives birth to a decision which may well strip the Negro of the aid of many of the white people who have been willing to speak up in his behalf. . . . The lesson to be learned from these . . . cases is . . . clear. Liberty, to be secure for any, must be secure for all—even for the most miserable merchants of hated and unpopular ideas.[82]

As the *Braden* and *Wilkinson* cases indicate, the Warren Court certainly did not have a perfect record in upholding free speech rights of actual or suspected Communists—although, in fairness to the Court, it must be remembered that it was sufficiently protective of those rights to earn the vicious attacks of anti-Communists,[83] and even to be accused of being subject to Communist influence.[84]

Some critics have charged that the Warren Court enforced a double standard toward Communists and toward civil rights activists, interpreting the First Amendment more generously where the latter were concerned. In Harry Kalven's words: "It is tempting to join the [legal] 'realist' and state the operative principle bluntly: The Communists cannot win; the NAACP cannot lose."[85] The ACLU's legal director at the time, Mel Wulf, said even more colorfully: "There are red cases and [there are] black cases."[86]

While there is some basis for this charge, it is also true that, over time, the Warren Court moved toward increasingly protective rulings in the free speech area. This development came well after the height of Cold War hysteria and right at the height of the Civil Rights movement. Thus, it's hard to sort out to what extent the Civil Rights movement was the beneficiary of the Court's ideological evolution in the First Amendment area, and to what extent this ideological evolution was the beneficiary of the Civil Rights movement.

In any event, the prospeech rulings that the Warren Court issued in the civil rights context have since inured to the benefit of all speakers and associations, including those of a Communist stripe. By 1963, in *NAACP v. Button*,[87] Justice Black's views on this point had apparently prevailed. The majority took pains to stress that free speech should neutrally protect all ideas, no matter how sympathetic or unsympathetic they might be to their audience or to the Court itself. Explaining its ruling upholding the NAACP's First Amendment rights, the Court said:

> That the [NAACP] happens to be engaged in . . . expression and association on behalf of the rights of Negro children to equal opportunity is constitutionally irrelevant to . . . our decision. [The First Amendment's] protections would apply as fully to those who would arouse our society against the objectives of the petitioner. . . . For the Constitution protects expression and association without regard to the race, creed, or political or religious affiliation of the . . . group which invokes its shield, or to the truth, popularity, or social utility of the ideas and beliefs which are offered.[88]

By the Warren Court's last year, it issued a decision that vividly demonstrated the indivisibility of free speech for advocates of all viewpoints—including Communism, and pro– and anti–civil rights groups. The Court's landmark 1969 decision in *Brandenburg v. Ohio*,[89] as already noted, formulated a new, and still enduring, test for judging speech whose ideas are feared to lead to dangerous consequences. Under that very speech-protective test, such speech cannot be punished unless it is an intentional incitement to imminent unlawful conduct and is likely to produce such conduct.

Many recall that the *Brandenburg* case involved a Ku Klux Klan rally, so that the immediate beneficiary was a Klan leader who voiced racist and anti-Semitic ideas. Less well-known is the fact that the particular law under which this Klan leader had been convicted, and which the Warren Court struck down, was Ohio's so-called Criminal Syndicalism Law. Laws of this type, which made it a crime to advocate violence to bring about political change, had been the principal weapon against Communists and other radicals since World War I, all over the United States. Thus, *Brandenburg* immediately redounded to the benefit of Communists, giving their expression protection it had never achieved in the many cases directly involving their own members.[90]

Moreover, in a 1982 case, the Court relied on *Brandenburg* to uphold the rights of NAACP officials to advocate violent reprisals against individuals who violated an NAACP-organized boycott of white merchants who had allegedly engaged in racial discrimination. After these inflammatory speeches, some violence was subsequently committed against blacks who patronized white merchants, but it occurred weeks or months later. The lower court had declared the boycott illegal and held the NAACP responsible for the large financial losses that white merchants suffered from it. But, applying the *Brandenburg* test, the Supreme Court overturned that ruling, in a major victory for the civil rights cause as well as free speech.[91] Thus, the Warren Court's legacy of protecting speech and civil rights simultaneously was carried forward by a later Court, through the vehicle of a Warren Court case that had protected racist rantings.

In 1965, Professor Kalven predicted that when we look back at the Warren Court's free speech decisions, "we may come to see the Negro as winning back for us the freedoms the Communists seem to have lost for us."[92] Only strong principles of free speech and association could—and did—protect the drive for desegregation. Martin Luther King wrote his historic letter from a Birmingham jail,[93] but the Warren Court later struck down the Birmingham parade ordinance that King and other demonstrators had violated, holding that it had violated their First Amendment rights.[94]

The more disruptive, militant forms of protest, which Charles Lawrence and other current free speech skeptics credit with having been more effective[95]—such as marches, sit-ins, and kneel-ins—were especially dependent on the Warren Court's generous constructions of the First Amendment.[96] Notably, many of these protective interpretations initially had been formulated in cases brought on behalf of anti–civil rights demonstrators. Similarly, the insulting and often racist language that more militant black activists hurled at police officers and other government officials also was protected under the same principles and precedents.[97]

The foregoing history does not prove conclusively that free speech is an essential precondition for equality, as some respected political philosophers have argued.[98] But it does belie the central contention of Professor Lawrence and others who claim an incompatibility between free speech and equality—namely, their argument that equality is an essential precondition for free speech. And this history also shows the positive, symbiotic interrelationship between free speech and equality. As Eleanor

Holmes Norton put it, reflecting back on the Civil Rights movement: "There was always the First."[99]

I'll conclude by embellishing on Ms. Norton's apt observation. While the First Amendment *has* always been there on paper since 1791, it did not become a vital force for protecting free speech or equality until the Warren Court breathed life into it. Therefore, I would like to end by thanking the Warren Court for—in Justice Brennan's vivid words—making the First Amendment "leap off the page and into people's lives."[100]

Notes

For research assistance with this essay, Professor Strossen thanks Stephen Hendricks, Thomas Hilbink, Jaci Pickens, Karen Shelton, and Raafat S. Toss.

1. See, e.g., Spence v. Washington, 418 U.S. 405 (1974); Parker v. Levy, 417 U.S. 733 (1974); Street v. New York, 394 U.S. 576 (1969); Tinker v. Des Moines School District, 393 U.S. 503 (1969); United States v. O'Brien, 391 U.S. 367 (1968); Bond v. Floyd, 385 U.S. 116 (1966); Wilkinson v. U.S., 365 U.S. 399 (1961); Barenblatt v. United States, 360 U.S. 109 (1959); Schware v. Board of Bar Examiners of New Mexico, 353 U.S. 232 (1957).
2. Walker, *In Defense of American Liberties: A History of the ACLU* 217 (1990).
3. Gunther, *Constitutional Law* 1222 (12th ed. 1991).
4. See, e.g., NAACP v. Alabama, 357 U.S. 449 (1958).
5. See Keyishian v. Board of Regents, 385 U.S. 589 (1967); Sweezy v. New Hampshire, 354 U.S. 234 (1957).
6. See Lamont v. Postmaster General, 381 U.S. 301 (1965).
7. See Cox v. Louisiana, 379 U.S. 536 (1965); Edwards v. South Carolina, 372 U.S. 229 (1963).
8. See Amalgamated Food Employees v. Logan Valley Plaza, 391 U.S. 308 (1968), overruled by Hudgens v. NLRB, 424 U.S. 507 (1976) and Lloyd Corp. v. Tanner, 407 U.S. 551 (1972).
9. See New York Times v. Sullivan, 376 U.S. 254 (1964).
10. See Baggett v. Bullitt, 377 U.S. 360 (1964).
11. See United States v. Robel, 389 U.S. 258 (1967); Keyishian v. Board of Regents, 385 U.S. 589 (1967); Aptheker v. Secretary of State, 378 U.S. 500 (1964); Shelton v. Tucker, 364 U.S. 479 (1960).
12. See Shelton v. Tucker, 364 U.S. 479 (1960).
13. 376 U.S. 254, 269 (1964).
14. See Roth v. United States, 352 U.S. 964 (1957).
15. 395 U.S. 444 (1969).
16. See Gunther, "Learned Hand and the Origins of Modern First Amendment Doctrine: Some Fragments of History," 27 *Stan. L. Rev.* 719 (1975); Gunther, *Learned Hand: The Man and the Judge* 603 (1994).
17. Edwards v. South Carolina, 372 U.S. 229 (1963).
18. Cox v. Louisiana, 379 U.S. 536 (1965).
19. Brown v. Louisiana, 383 U.S. 131 (1966).
20. Amalgamated Food Employees v. Logan Valley Plaza, 391 U.S. 308 (1968),

overruled by Hudgens v. NLRB, 424 U.S. 507 (1976) and Lloyd Corp. v. Tanner, 407 U.S. 551 (1972).

21. 393 U.S. 503 (1969).

22. Pickering v. Board of Education, 391 U.S. 563 (1968).

23. Keyishian v. Board of Regents, 385 U.S. 589 (1967) (librarian at state university).

24. See, e.g., Werhan, "The Liberalization of Freedom of Speech on a Conservative Court," 80 *Iowa L. Rev.* 51, 57 (1994) (noting that the post–Warren Court's categorization approach to free speech extended even to "subcategorization," whereby categories of protected speech are subdivided and receive differing levels of protection).

25. Hale, "Freedom of Expression: The Warren and Burger Courts," 9 *Comm. & L.* 3 (1987).

26. Id. at 10.

27. Id.

28. Id. at 11.

29. Kalven, "Uninhibited, Robust, and Wide-Open—A Note on Free Speech and the Warren Court," 67 *Mich. L. Rev.* 289 (1968).

30. See Konigsberg v. State Bar of California, 366 U.S. 36, 61–80 (1961) (Black, J., dissenting).

31. See Emerson, "First Amendment Doctrine and the Burger Court," 68 *Cal. L. Rev.* 422, 467 (1980).

32. 361 U.S. 516, 523 (1960).

33. Emerson, "Freedom of the Press Under the Burger Court," in *The Burger Court: The Counter-Revolution That Wasn't* 26 (Blasi ed., 1983).

34. Branzburg v. Hayes, 408 U.S. 665, 725 (1972) (Stewart, J., dissenting).

35. Emerson, supra note 31, at 440.

36. See Strossen, "The Free Speech Jurisprudence of the Rehniquist Court," 29 *Free Speech Yearbook: The Meaning of the First Amendment* 83 (1991).

37. Kalven, *A Worthy Tradition: Freedom of Speech in America* xiii (Kalven ed., 1988).

38. Id. at xxvi.

39. 376 U.S. 254 (1964).

40. Id. at 270.

41. Kalven, supra note 29, at 289.

42. Garrison v. Louisiana, 379 U.S. 64, 74–75 (1964).

43. 360 U.S. 684 (1959).

44. Id. at 688–89.

45. Kalven, supra note 29, at 290.

46. See Kalven, supra note 37, at xv.

47. Gunther, supra note 3.

48. Matsuda, Lawrence, Delgado, and Crenshaw, *Words That Wound: Critical Race Theory, Assaultive Speech, and the First Amendment* (1993).

49. See Thomas S. McGuire, "Note, 23" *Seton Hall L. Rev.* 1067, 1069 (1993) (stating that "[c]urrently, speech codes are in effect at about 350 colleges and universities," citing Innerst, "Senate Silence Expected on Proposal Defending Free Speech on Campus," *Washington Times*, September 11, 1992, p. A10).

50. See R.A.V. v. City of St. Paul, 112 S.Ct. 2538 (1992); Dambrot v. Central Michigan University, 839 F. Supp. 477 (E.D. Mich. 1993); U.W.M. Post, Inc. v. Board of Regents of the University of Wisconsin System, 774 F. Supp. 1163 (E.D. Wis. 1991); Doe v. University of Michigan, 721 F. Supp. 852 (E.D. Mich. 1989).

51. For this analysis by Dworkin, see her *Men Possessing Women* (1979); "Against the Male Flood: Censorship, Pornography, and Equality," 8 *Harv. Women's L.J.* 1 (1985); "Pornography's Exquisite Volunteers," *Ms. Mag.*, March 1981; "Pornography: The New Terrorism," 8 *N.Y.U. Rev. of L. & Soc. Change* 215 (1978–79); "Pornography's Part in Sexual Violence," *Los Angeles Times*, May 26, 1981. For similar analysis by Catharine MacKinnon, see her *Only Words* (1993); "Not a Moral Issue: Pornography, Civil Rights and Free Speech," 20 *Harv. C.R.-C.L. L. Rev.* 1 (1985).

52. MacKinnon, *Only Words*, supra note 51, at 71.

53. See Strossen, *Defending Pornography, Free Speech, Sex, and the Fight for Women's Rights* (1994).

54. 376 U.S. 254 (1964).

55. 357 U.S. 449 (1958).

56. 371 U.S. 415 (1963).

57. Walker, *Hate Speech: The History of an American Controversy* 117 (1994).

58. As the Court said, "In the context of NAACP objectives, litigation is . . . a means for achieving the lawful objectives of equality of treatment by all government . . . for the . . . Negro community in this country. It is thus a form of political expression. Groups which find themselves unable to achieve their objectives through the ballot frequently turn to the courts. . . . And under the conditions of modern government, litigation may well be the sole practicable avenue open to a minority to petition for redress of grievances."

59. 383 U.S. 131 (1966).

60. 379 U.S. 536 (1965).

61. 372 U.S. 229 (1963).

62. 385 U.S. 116 (1966).

63. 372 U.S. 539 (1963).

64. 362 U.S. 60 (1960).

65. See Lawrence, "If He Hollers Let Him Go: Regulating Racist Speech on Campus," 1990 *Duke L.J.* 431, 466 (1990) ("Most blacks . . . do not have faith in free speech as the most important vehicle for liberation.") (citing Bell, *Race, Racism and American Law* 283–87, 287–330 (2nd ed. 1980)).

66. Walker, supra note 2, at 241.

67. Kalven, *The Negro and the First Amendment*, 66 (1965).

68. See Branch, *Parting the Waters: America in the King Years*, 1954–1963, 181–82, 468–69 (1988). See also O'Reilly, *"Racial Matters": The FBI's Secret File on Black America*, 1960–72, 125–55 (1989) (describing the FBI's attempt to link Martin Luther King, Jr. and other leaders of the Civil Rights movement with Communism).

69. See Kalven, supra note 67, at 66–70; Walker, supra note 57, at 116; Walker, supra note 2, at 240–42.

70. Braden v. United States, 365 U.S. 431, 442 (1961) (Black, J., dissenting).

71. See NAACP v. Flowers, 377 U.S. 288 (1964); NAACP v. Button, 371 U.S. 415 (1963); Louisiana *ex rel.* Gremillion v. NAACP, 366 U.S. 293 (1961); Bates v. Little Rock, 361 U.S. 516 (1960); NAACP v. Alabama, 357 U.S. 449 (1958).

72. 357 U.S. 449 (1958).

73. Id. at 460.

74. Id. at 462.

75. Walker, supra note 2, at 241.

76. *Ex Parte Lowe*, 887 S.W. 2d 1 (Tex. 1994).

77. Verhovek, "A Klansman's Black Lawyer, and a Principle," *N.Y. Times*, September 10, 1993, p. B9; Moran, "Black Lawyer Lauded for KKK Support," *Houston Chroni-*

cle, October 25, 1994, p. A20. For Griffin's own account of the situation, see Griffin, "The First Amendment and the Art of Storytelling," in Gates et al., *Speaking of Race, Speaking of Sex: Hate Speech, Civil Rights, and Civil Liberties*, 1995.

78. 365 U.S. 431 (1960).

79. 365 U.S. 399 (1961).

80. 343 U.S. 250 (1952).

81. See, e.g., Collin v. Smith, 578 F.2d. 1197, 1205 (7th Cir.), *cert. denied*, 439 U.S. 916 (1978) (citing cases expressing "doubt, which we share, that *Beauharnais* remains good law at all after the constitutional libel cases"). See also Tribe, *American Constitutional Law*, 926–27 (2d ed. 1988) (noting that "New York Times v. Sullivan seemed to some to eclipse *Beauharnais*' sensitivity to . . . group defamation claims . . . because *New York Times* required public officials bringing libel suits to prove that a defamatory statement was directed at the official personally, and not simply at a unit of government").

82. 343 U.S. 250, 263 (1952) (Black, J., dissenting).

83. See Walker, supra note 2, at 243.

84. See Schwartz, *Super Chief: Earl Warren and His Supreme Court—A Judicial Biography* 249–50 (1983).

85. Kalven, supra note 37, at 259.

86. Walker, supra note 2, at 240.

87. 371 U.S. 415 (1963).

88. Id. at 444–45.

89. 395 U.S. 444 (1969).

90. See Walker, supra note 57, at 114–15. Walker comments: "There was no small irony in the fact that through most of its history the Communist party had been a vigorous advocate of restricting the rights of the Klan and other racist groups—as in its national campaign to deny speaking permits to Gerald L. K. Smith in the 1940s." Id. at 115.

91. NAACP v. Claiborne Hardware, 458 U.S. 886 (1982).

92. Kalven, supra note 67, at 6.

93. Martin Luther King, "Letter From Birmingham Jail," in *Why We Can't Wait* 72 (1964).

94. Shuttlesworth v. Birmingham, 394 U.S. 147 (1969).

95. See Lawrence, supra note 65, at 466 and n.129.

96. See Walker, supra note 2, at 241.

97. See Lewis v. New Orleans, 415 U.S. 130 (1974); Brown v. Oklahoma, 408 U.S. 914 (1972); Gooding v. Wilson, 405 U.S. 518, 523 (1972).

98. See, e.g., Beck, "Liberty and Equality," 10 *Idealistic Studies* 24, 36 (1980); Machan, "Equality's Dependence on Liberty," 2 *Equality & Freedom* 663, 664–65 (G. Dorsey ed., 1977).

99. Walker, supra note 2, at 241.

100. Hentoff, "The Constitutionalist," *New Yorker*, March 12, 1990, at 45, 70.

· 6 ·

THE WARREN COURT AND FREEDOM OF THE PRESS

RONALD D. ROTUNDA

Historians like to name, organize, and categorize events. The actual events may not fit neatly into the categories, but historians have learned to accept that problem. Thus, the Hundred Years War did not last a century but from 1377 to 1453. Years ago, when studying American history, I learned that the twentieth century began in 1897, not 1901 as the calendar might suggest.

Legal historians often divide the history of the U.S. Supreme Court into segments that are titled after the person who happens to be Chief Justice at the time, even if the historical divisions do not neatly match the name of the Chief. The Chief Justice, after all, is only the first among equals. He has a slightly larger salary and office, and a longer title, but no substantial power over his colleagues. His vote counts for no more than any of the other eight. If he is in the majority, he can assign the majority opinion to another Justice who is in the majority, but, even then, the other Justices each decide for themselves whether to sign on to the draft opinion tentatively designated as majority. When we carefully look at the Chief Justice's main authority, we find that he mainly has only the power to persuade.[1]

Not all Chief Justices were really influential enough to have a slice of history named after them. Earl Warren does deserve the title. There really was a Warren Court. And its influence has lasted beyond the time that Warren graced the office of Chief Justice.

Later events have showed that the appointment of Warren as Chief was a significant milestone in the history of the U.S. Supreme Court, although his appointment was not considered pivotal at the time it was made.[2] Earl Warren was simply not the kind of person whom many people might predict would make a great Chief Justice. But, as Justice Brennan later said, "Earl Warren will always be the Super Chief."[3] The California politician who interned Japanese Americans during World War II[4] became the great civil libertarian. The successful politician became the nation's chief jurist.

In Washington, D.C., a town of no small egos, he remained a humble man. Once, during a great state dinner hosted by the president, the tourists and sightseers witnessed the long parade of fancy cars and chauffeured limousines that made their way up the White House circular drive. Then came an old station wagon, and driving it was Earl Warren, the head of the third branch of the federal government.

Years later, on his deathbed, he spoke, not about himself, but about a then-current proposal for a national court of appeals. He worried that the proposal "threatened to shut the door of the Supreme Court to the poor, the friendless, the little man."[5] This incident speaks volumes. Think about it. The man is on his deathbed. Imminent death serves to concentrate one's focus, to force one to think about the most important things of life. And at that crucial moment, Warren thought of others, not himself.

This volume has divided up the work of the Warren Court into various categories. My essay will focus on the Warren Court and the free press. In approaching this topic, the first question to ask is whether the Warren Court itself distinguished the Speech Clause from the Press Clause. Or, is this another case of mistitled categories, of taking a war that lasted seventy-six years and calling it the Hundred Years War?

The First Amendment provides that Congress shall make no law "abridging the freedom of speech, or of the press . . . ."[6] Did the framers intend to distinguish or differentiate between speech and press, thereby giving more (or fewer) rights to the press? Should the First Amendment be read to guarantee *everyone* freedom of "speech" and grant further, special protections only to "the press"? And if the First Amendment means that, what are those special protections? And how do the courts decide what is "the press"?

The Court has told us for two centuries that we should never assume that any part of our pithy Constitution should be regarded as redundant.[7] If the "Press" Clause does not give any special rights to the press, why did the framers of the Bill of Rights put it in there?

Of course, if "the press" has special rights, then the Court must tell us what is, or who is, "the press." The Court would have to demarcate and distinguish "the press" from "speech." If "the press" means "the institutional press," we have to admit that the adjective, "institutional," does not define the word "press" in any meaningful way. Even in the days when our country was young, it did not take much to print up some handbills and circulate them to the public. Nowadays, it takes only a fairly small amount of money and a small computer to create your own publications, more professional looking than any that Ben Franklin ever devised. If you do not know what to do, just go to the local news rack and pick up a copy of one of the various magazines that feature desktop publishing. Or cruise the Internet, and be your own publisher by joining an electronic bulletin board. You will have an audience larger in size than any who attended *Hamlet* in Shakespeare's days.

The question of whether "speech" is really different from "the press," has been much mooted in the literature,[8] and I do not wish to repeat that debate, nor review the historical arguments. What is important is that the Warren Court acted as if it is most logical to treat the phrase "speech, or of the press" simply as a way to make sure that the framers covered all bases. Whatever the framers may have thought, the Warren Court did not distinguish between "speech" and "the press."

Those of us old enough to remember the television game shows of the 1950s will recall that a typical question was whether something was bigger than a bread box. The next question that followed was "Is it animal, vegetable, or mineral?" The phrase "animal, vegetable, or mineral" was intended to include everything. Everything was expected to fall into one of these three categories, none of which were overlapping. No one conceived of something that was neither animal, nor vegetable, nor mineral, or part animal and part mineral. In this simpler era, before *Star Trek*, we did not think of silicone-based life forms that would be neither truly "animal" nor really "mineral."

That is how the Warren Court saw the Speech and Press Clauses. The Court acted as if the framers intended the clauses to cover all forms of communication, whether spoken or written. The framers obviously did not think about movies, or digitized videos, or e-mail, because they were not prophets. But they were wise enough—they foresaw enough—to realize that there might be forms of communication that they would not foresee, but that they still wanted to protect. Because they did not intend to exclude any particular form of communication, they certainly did not intend to exclude modern ways of communication we now find ordinary, any more than we would now intend to exclude future methods of communicating that the framers could not predict, or we even now foretell.

This bequest of the Warren Court—granting the institutional press and mass media no fewer rights than the rest of us, and granting all of us the same rights as the *New York Times* or the *National Enquirer*—is one of that Court's most important legacies. It recognizes that there is no principled way of distinguishing between speech and the press.[9] The press has an informing function, but so do "lecturers, political pollsters, novelists, academic researchers, and dramatists."[10] The lonely pamphleteer has all the free speech rights of the *Washington Post*, or the Cable News Network.

This principle means, for example, that when the Court has guaranteed a First Amendment right of access, such as the right it now recognizes in granting a right of access to criminal and civil trials, that right is granted to all. It is not limited to the institutional press.[11] And because the press is not singled out for special treatment, it is not subject to separate burdens or disabilities.[12]

Years after Chief Justice Warren left the Court, the Justices considered the constitutionality of a state law that made a newspaper civilly liable for publishing the name of a rape victim, even though the newspaper had lawfully obtained it through a publicly released police report. The purpose of this law was said to be to protect the privacy of the victim, who may not want others to know that she had been raped. In *Florida Star v. B.J.F.*,[13] the Court protected the newspaper in question, and invalidated the state law as a violation of the First Amendment.[14]

Justice Scalia's concurring opinion made the valid and crucial point that this law was not really drafted to prevent speech or gossip about the unfortunate rape victim, who may be embarrassed by the crime. It only prevented such speech when the institutional press engaged in it. The rape victim's hurt and mortification when news of her misfortune was circulated among, and by, her friends, associates, and acquaintances, should be

> at least as great as her discomfort at its publication by the media to people to whom she is only a name. *Yet the law in question does not prohibit the former in*

> either oral or written form. Nor is it at all clear, as I think it must be to validate this statute, that Florida's general privacy law would prohibit such gossip. Nor, finally, is it credible that the interest meant to be served by the statute is the protection of the victim against a rapist still at large—an interest that arguably would extend only to mass publication. *There would be little reason to limit a statute with that objective to rape alone; or to extend it to all rapes, whether or not the felon has been apprehended and confined. In any case, the instructions here did not require the jury to find that the rapist was at large.*
>
> *This law has every appearance of a prohibition that society is prepared to impose on the press but not upon itself.* Such a prohibition does not protect an interest "of the highest order."[15]

Free press is not preferred over free speech, but it surely should not be treated worse, and, under the Warren Court, it was not. Justice Scalia's opinion in *Florida Star* is within the intellectual legacy of the Warren Court.

Chief Justice Warren Earl Burger not only has a name similar to Earl Warren, but he also followed in Warren's footsteps when he wrote his concurring opinion in *First National Bank v. Bellotti.*[16] In that opinion, Burger specifically rejected the notion that "the press," whatever that means, should have different First Amendment rights than "free speech."

Bellotti invalidated a state law that prevented corporations from spending money to influence the vote on a referendum question submitted to the voters. The law covered situations where the referendum did not directly affect the corporation's business, property, or assets. The speaker in that case was a commercial bank that wanted to publicize its view against a proposed state constitutional amendment. The amendment would have allowed the legislature to impose a graduated personal income tax, and the Massachusetts bank (domiciled in a state nicknamed "Taxachusetts") argued that the increased tax was bad for business because it would make it harder to keep and retain employees, who would be more likely to move to, or stay in, a lower-taxing state.

Some people might argue that the bank does not have the same free speech rights of flesh and blood humans. The Court rejected these arguments, and thereby avoided the problem of trying to create some way to distinguish the free speech rights of the *New York Times* (a major, vertically integrated, profit-motivated corporation, whose stock is publicly traded). Instead, the majority maintained that the "inherent worth of the speech in terms of its capacity for informing the public does not depend upon the identity of its source, whether corporation, association, union, or individual."[17]

The post-Warren Court has never formally adopted the notion that the First Amendment distinguishes between speech and press. Yet in spite of Chief Justice Burger's separate opinion in *Bellotti,* the post-Warren Court has certainly flirted with the idea, an idea that the Warren Court never embraced.

Take, for example, the question of libel. In *New York Times v. Sullivan,*[18] the Warren Court constitutionalized the state law of libel and offered new protections to those who criticize (or defame) public officials. Sometimes people refer to this decision as an example of how the Warren Court protected "the press." But we should remember that the defendants were not limited to the *New York Times.* As

Justice Brennan, speaking for the Court,[19] carefully explained, Mr. L. B. Sullivan, one of the elected commissioners of Montgomery, Alabama, "brought this civil libel action against the four individual petitioners, who are Negroes and Alabama clergymen, and against petitioner the New York Times Company."[20] The defendants included individuals as well as the newspaper. All were sued because the former had published in the latter an advertisement asking for funds to fight racial discrimination. The Court made no distinction between the individual defendants and the *New York Times*.

The Court freely acknowledged that it was "uncontroverted" that the advertisement contained some false statements. For example, the advertisement said that black students in a particular protest sang "My Country 'Tis of Thee." In reality, they had sung the national anthem. The advertisement also said that Martin Luther King had been arrested seven times, but in fact he had only been arrested four times. For misstatements such as these, the jury awarded Sullivan $500,000, and the state supreme court affirmed. The U.S. Supreme Court overturned the award.

This $500,000 award was real money back in 1964, before three decades of inflation.[21] To give you some idea of what $500,000 was worth then, consider this: In 1964, a Rolls-Royce Silver Cloud cost under $14,000, delivered in the United States.[22] Nowadays, it is easy to spend over $200,000 for a Rolls.

If the Court, in 1964, had allowed a verdict in the magnitude of half a million dollars, the individuals and the newspaper would certainly have been chilled in the exercise of their free speech. Such a verdict would also serve as an object lesson to all others who thought of criticizing public officials for their support of racist policies.

In *Sullivan*, the Warren Court responded to this threat by holding that the defamation defendants could not be liable unless they *lied* about the plaintiff. More specifically, the Court said that none of the defendants would be liable unless they defamed the plaintiff with what is called "*New York Times* malice." The Court then defined "malice" to mean "scienter," that is, "with knowledge that it was false or with reckless disregard of whether it was false or not."[23] As an aside, I should point out that years later, Justice Stewart regretted that the *Sullivan* opinion (which he had joined) used the phrase "actual malice." "In common understanding, malice means ill will or hostility, [but *New York Times* malice] has nothing to do with hostility or ill will."[24] It means scienter, which is the term that I will generally use.

People have criticized *Sullivan* over the years as being insufficiently protective of libel defendants. Perhaps. But one thing is clear, it protected libel defendants without regard as to whether they were individuals or media defendants.

Sullivan specifically applied the same requirement of "actual malice" or "scienter" to the individual defendants, the nonmedia defendants, and held that it was unconstitutional to hold them liable. The Court did not regard the issue as a difficult one: "The case of the individual petitioners requires little discussion," said the Court.[25]

Then, the Court turned to the *Times*, applied the *same* test, and "similarly conclude[d] that the facts do not support a finding of actual malice."[26]

The Court admitted that there "is evidence that the *Times* published the advertisement without checking its accuracy against the news stories in the *Times*' own files."[27] The *Times*, in a sense, "knew" that some of the allegations in the advertisement were incorrect, because the newspaper's own "morgue"—the collection of old *Times* stories buried somewhere in the bowels of the incorporeal entity known as the *New York Times*—indicated what the correct facts were. But, said the Court, "the mere presence of the stories in the files does not, of course, establish that the *Times* 'knew' the advertisement was false, since the state of mind required for actual malice would have *to be brought home* to the persons in the *Times* organization having responsibility for the publication of the advertisement." Instead, the most that could be said was that the *Times* was negligent in failing to discover the misstatements, but that is "constitutionally insufficient to show the recklessness that is required for a finding of actual malice."[28]

Mere negligence is not enough; plaintiffs have the burden to prove "scienter," and they must meet that burden by "convincing clarity."[29] Later the Court used the term "clear and convincing,"[30] a term signifying a burden that is somewhere between "beyond a reasonable doubt"—the standard used in criminal cases—and "preponderance of the evidence"—the standard used in most civil cases.

New York Times v. Sullivan has been enormously important in protecting the institutional press as well as all of us. There are those who decry and disparage this protection against defamation suits, because it belongs to the irresponsible press as well as the *New York Times*. Perhaps the libel protection should be stronger for all, but the Court cannot pick and choose among those libel defendants who have the protection of the First Amendment. The purpose of the Free Speech and Press Clauses is to protect unpopular speech; popular speech has no need of protection.

The protection that *Sullivan* and its progeny offer has benefited all of us, from those who exercise political speech, to those who exercise the more prosaic speech of commerce. Once, while I was in London, I read a local newspaper story that said, in essence, that one member of parliament accused another British M.P. of something. The second M.P. challenged the first one to repeat the words outside Parliament, where there would be no immunity. The first M.P. repeated the words while in Parliament, but did not repeat them outside.

That was all the newspaper told us. We never knew what the first or second M.P. said. If the newspaper had printed that, it could have been liable for defamation, for repeating the libel. How is the citizenry to judge its politicians if we cannot know what the charges are? Granted, either the first or the second M.P. may have been in error, or even been a demagogue. And the recent trend in politics to flyspeck everyone's career may not be for the best. But ultimately, the basic assumption of a democracy is that the people should know, so that the people can decide. Know the truth, and the truth will set you free.

Let us now turn to an example from the world of commerce. After the death of Robert Maxwell, the British media king, his empire quickly collapsed, and his financial misdeeds came to light. The British press, we then learned, was unwilling or unable to publish relevant allegations earlier because Maxwell had used Britain's tough libel laws to silence his critics.[31] In America, the competitors of a business tycoon like Maxwell would have been bolder, less reluctant to be the sources for stories of financial misconduct. In addition, the American institutional press would not have been prevented from reporting these charges and investigating them, because the First Amendment would have protected them from defamation suits unless they deliberately lied.

The Warren Court knew better than to try to protect media defendants in libel cases more than nonmedia defendants in libel cases. As *Sullivan* should have made clear, all are subject to, and protected by, the same standard. "The press" is treated like "speech." The Warren Court, in cases after *Sullivan*, continued to give the same protections to all libel defendants and did not offer more rights to the media defendants.[32]

The same has not been true of the post-Warren era. Consider the 1985 decision, *Dun & Bradstreet, Inc. v. Greenmoss Builders, Inc.*,[33] an opinion with no majority. The plaintiff was a construction contractor who discovered that Dun & Bradstreet, a credit reporting agency, had sent a statement to five of its subscribers. This credit report mistakenly stated that the contractor had filed a petition for voluntary bankruptcy. The contractor learned of the error on the same day that the report was sent to these five people and called Dun & Bradstreet's regional office. Dun & Bradstreet promised to look into the matter, did so, and issued a correction about seven or eight days later. The new report explained that it was one of the contractor's former employees and not the contractor who had filed for bankruptcy, and that the contractor continued in business as usual.

The contractor then sued for defamation. The state trial judge had instructed the jury that the plaintiff was not required to prove actual damages "since damage and loss [are] conclusively presumed."[34] The court also instructed the jury to award punitive damages without the plaintiff having to prove scienter or "*New York Times* malice." The plaintiff won $50,000 in so-called presumed damages and $300,000 in punitive damages. A splintered U.S. Supreme Court affirmed.

Justice Powell's plurality claimed that all of the previous cases where the Court found constitutional limits to state libel laws were cases where the speech involved expression "on a matter of public concern" or "*public speech*."[35] Powell, joined by Justices Rehnquist and O'Connor, announced that speech on matters of "purely private" concern has less First Amendment protection, and therefore the state law may allow awards of presumed and punitive damages, "even absent a showing of 'actual malice.'"[36] The plurality allowed juries to presume damages because, Powell said, proof of actual damages is often impossible. As for punitive damages, the plurality allowed that as well, even if the libel defendant did not act with "malice" or scienter.

The Warren Court would not allow defamation juries to simply presume damages, because that would not be consistent with the free, uninhibited, robust debate that the First Amendment envisioned. Free speech needs "breathing space."[37] The Powell plurality, in contrast, allowed presumed damages because it might be difficult or impossible for the plaintiff to prove actual damages. While the Warren Court was worried about breathing space for the First Amendment, the Powell plurality was worried that plaintiffs might not win enough cases if they were forced to prove actual damages.

The Warren Court never really considered the question of punitive damages in *Sullivan*. As to public officials, it required scienter merely for an award of actual damages. Perhaps the Warren Court might not have allowed any punitive damages, because if you need something more than scienter just to obtain actual damages, there is really nothing more than that. In 1974, the Court held that when the libel plaintiff is a private figure (not a public official or public figure), then the plaintiff cannot collect actual damages unless the plaintiff can prove at least negligence. Such a plaintiff can collect punitive damages or presumed damages only if the plaintiff can go beyond prove of negligence and also prove scienter.[38] Logically, one would expect the Court to hold that any punitive damages for libels against public officials or public figures will interfere with the "breathing space" that the First Amendment requires.[39] But the Court, even the Warren Court, did not always follow the logic of Boolian algebra.

The *Dun & Bradstreet* plurality did not discuss whether the plaintiff could collect presumed and punitive damages even in the absence of any proof of the defendant's negligence. In an earlier case, *Gertz v. Robert Welch, Inc.*,[40] the Court had held that the Constitution required proof of negligence before a *private* libel plaintiff (as opposed to a libel plaintiff who was a public official or public figure) could collect any damages for defamation. *Gertz* even required proof of scienter before the private plaintiff could collect punitive damages. But now the Powell plurality reinterpreted that case and said explicitly that *Gertz* only "involved expression on a matter of undoubted public concern."[41] In *Gertz*, a magazine published by the John Birch Society falsely accused Gertz, a reputable Chicago lawyer, of being involved in a Communist frame-up that led to a murder conviction of a third party.

That accusation, Powell announced in *Dun & Bradstreet*, was "a matter of undoubted public concern." But other than asserting this conclusion, the Powell plurality did not bother to explain why the false charges against a *private* Chicago lawyer were of "undoubted public concern."

In my experience, if someone cannot prove something, we often find that they make the assertion and then use a word such as "obviously" or "undoubted." Those words are usually signals that there is no support for what follows. And so it was in *Dun & Bradstreet*, because the Justices give us no real explanation of why false charges against a private Chicago lawyer were of "undoubted public concern." Remember that the term "matter of public concern" is hardly self-defining. One does not solve the definition problem by using the adjective "undoubted."

In an even greater blow to free speech and press, the Powell plurality appeared to suggest that if the allegedly defamatory speech does not involve a matter of public concern, then plaintiff could collect presumed and even *punitive* damages without proof of any kind of fault or negligence on the part of the defendant. Justice White read the Powell opinion in this manner, and his separate opinion concurring in the judgment in *Dun & Bradstreet* so concluded.[42]

Even more important, there is nothing in the Powell plurality that would limit its application to cases where the plaintiff is a private person rather than a public official or a public figure. For Justices Powell, O'Connor, and Rehnquist, it may well be the case that a public official (like the president), or a public figure (like O. J. Simpson)[43] could also collect presumed or *punitive* damages without even a showing of negligence on the part of the defendant, *if* the alleged defamation did not involve that amorphous, undefined, and nebulous concept, a "matter of public concern."

Even if the trial or appellate court eventually makes the ad hoc judgment that the alleged defamation did not involve a "matter of public concern," the Powell plurality has given a plaintiff the opportunity to involve a defendant in possibly lengthy litigation with a settlement value. As long as the alleged defamation *might* not involve "public concern," then the plaintiff has the right to go to the jury and involve the defendant in costly litigation. This post-Warren ruling, if it attracts a majority of the present-day Court, will greatly deflate protection for all of us, including the news media.

After embracing this hazy test, "a matter of public concern," the *Dun & Bradstreet* plurality then tried to apply it. Is the incorrect credit report regarding the bankruptcy of a local contractor a matter of public concern? The Justices told us that it was not, because it did not involve a public issue. "It was speech solely in the individual interest of the speaker and its specific business audience."[44]

From this brief explanation, as well as the reference to the commercial motive of the libel defendant, one might be tempted to conclude that all credit reports, or all types of commercial speech, fall in the category of speech that is given reduced protection as involving matters not of "public concern." But the Justices in the plurality specifically rejected that conclusion.

Some credit reports, we are told, are of public concern, and some are not. How do we find out which is which? That's easy, just ask the Justices and they will tell you, case by case. The test they offer is simple enough to state but vague to apply: "The protection to be accorded a particular credit report depends on whether the report's 'content, form, and context' indicate that it concerns a public matter."[45] The "public concern" test is like a raft, and the Justices refuse to supply any rudder to guide its use.

In applying its test, the Powell plurality relied on the fact that the credit report was made available to only five subscribers. Dun & Bradstreet made these subscribers promise that they would not disseminate it further. Dun & Bradstreet placed this term in their contract to safeguard the property value of the information that it was collecting. Otherwise, a subscriber could resell the information to a third party, depriving Dun & Bradstreet of any royalties for its intellectual property. The Powell plurality turned this fact against Dun & Bradstreet. The confidential nature of the information collected was evidence, said the Justices, that the material did not involve a matter of public concern.

Dun & Bradstreet resurrects two important fallacies that the Warren Court had already discovered and buried. But phoenix-like, these fallacies rose again, in the post-Warren era.

The first Warren Court principle is that any rule trying to grant more rights to the institutional press or the mass media to engage in libel is bad policy. Justice Powell's ruling created an anomaly: If the defendant takes care not to publish the libel too widely, it is *less likely* to be protected by *New York Times v. Sullivan*. To the extent that the defendant takes care to widely publicize and spread the alleged defamatory falsehoods, he or she is *more likely* to be protected. Dun & Bradstreet's problem was that it treated the information too confidentially! If it had widely broadcast the error, it would have had greater protection from libel suits. The Warren Court, in *New York Times v. Sullivan*, knew better than to rely on such a perverse doctrine. It subjected the individual defendants and the mass media to the same test.

Second, any rule attempting to define a matter of "public concern" is unprincipled. The Powell plurality rejected that wisdom from the Warren Court. In trying to define "public concern," the Powell plurality required judges to look at the content of the speech, after it was made, in order to determine if the Justices should bestow protection on it. In a 1971 case, decided shortly after Warren retired from the Supreme Court, Justices Marshall, Stewart, and Harlan—all Justices tempered in the Warren era—warned that courts are ill-equipped for such an ill-defined task, which inevitably involves ad hoc, after-the-fact balancing.[46]

The Warren Court taught that the state should not discriminate in its regulation of expression on the basis of the content of that expression.[47] The state may regulate some expression in some circumstances. For example, the state may prohibit libel, subject to the restrictions in the case law, such as in *New York Times v. Sullivan*. But even then, the state may not regulate libel based on its content. The state may not constitutionally regulate libel against Democrats but permit libel against Republicans, or prohibit libel that falsely attacked the government but exempt libel that falsely praised the government.[48]

Judges are not able to determine what is "public concern" without examining the content of that speech and then applying their subjective judgment to that content.[49] The Warren Court knew better than to give such broad, unprincipled discretion to the thousands of state and federal judges in our country. The Warren Court categorized speech, and applied different standards to the various categories, but it did not give judges the power to look at the content within those categories, and then engage in ad hoc balancing.[50]

Another important area in which the post-Warren Court has flirted with distinguishing the news media or the institutional press from the rest of us is the area of campaign financing. Money talks, both literally and figuratively, and the power to regulate and control campaign financing can be the power to regulate and control the election. The Court should make sure that government officials do not improperly control the processes by which they and other government officials are engendered.

We should all be concerned when the government regulates campaign financing, because the regulators will not be "the government" in any abstract, institutional sense, but rather fallible, self-interested individuals, politicians who are seeking to be elected to higher office or reelected to their present offices. We should not be surprised if sometimes the incumbents have a bipartisan interest to remain incumbents.[51] It can be politically incestuous when the government regulates "the day-to-day procedures by which the Government is selected," because the government should not "control the machinery by which the public expresses the range of its desires, demands, and dissent."[52] There is a risk when elections become yet another regulated industry, because the regulators are the incumbents.

The post-Warren Courts flirted with a press/speech distinction in a campaign financing context in *Austin v. Michigan Chamber of Commerce.*[53] The Court upheld provisions of the Michigan Campaign Finance Act that prohibited corporations—except for media corporations and labor unions—from using corporate funds for independent expenditures in support of, or in opposition to, any candidate in election for a state office. The Michigan Chamber of Commerce sued.

The Supreme Court had already held that it is unconstitutional for the government to limit individuals from using their funds for *independent* expenditures on behalf of political candidates.[54] And it reaffirmed that ruling when it held that the independent expenditures by a political committee in support of a candidate cannot constitutionally be limited by statute, because such expenditures "produce speech at the core of the First Amendment."[55] The Michigan law forbade the chamber to make any independent expenditures relating to a specific candidate.

The Michigan Chamber of Commerce challenged the law. The chamber's bylaws provide that it is a nonprofit corporation with both political and nonpolitical purposes. It funds its activities through annual dues from its members, seventy-five percent of whom are for-profit corporations. The chamber wanted to run an advertisement in a local newspaper to support a particular candidate for state office. The U.S. Supreme Court ruled that the Michigan statute forbidding this expenditure was valid.

The Court argued that the chamber, although a voluntary association with political interests, does not have the narrow focus of a voluntary association supporting a single issue.[56] The Court expressed concern that if any of the chamber's members disagreed with the chamber's politics, they could disassociate themselves from the chamber only if they were willing to accept the disincentives that would accompany a complete separation. Many of the chamber's activities are "politically neutral," and focus on economic and business issues. The chamber, for example, provides its members with group insurance and educational seminars. Membership also provides networking. Those who disassociate themselves from the chamber lose those advantages.

The Court was, in addition, concerned that the chamber of commerce accepted dues from for-profit corporations. Thus, the chamber's use of the dues to support candidates might undercut the state's general prohibition against for-profit corporations using their money to support particular candidates.

Finally—and this portion of the majority opinion is particularly troubling—the Court ruled that the state's decision to regulate only corporations (but not unincorporated labor unions and not media corporations) did not violate any free speech or equal protection rights. The state law explicitly exempted newspapers, magazines, and broadcasting stations in the "regular course of publication or broadcasting." The majority claimed that the Michigan law was "precisely tailored to serve the compelling state interest of eliminating from the political process the corrosive effect of political 'war chests' amassed with the aid of the legal advantages given to corporations."[57]

Justice Kennedy, joined by Justices O'Connor and Scalia, dissented, objecting to Michigan's two forms of censorship. First, Michigan enacted a content-based law that makes it a crime for a nonprofit corporate speaker to endorse or oppose a candidate for Michigan public office. Second, Justice Kennedy objected to what he called the "value-laden, content-based" speech suppression that allows some non-profit corporations to engage in political speech but not others.[58]

Justice Scalia wrote a separate dissent, which focused on the speech/press distinction found in the Michigan law and uncritically accepted by the majority. The majority, he said, was "Orwellian." What Michigan has done is to restrict speech on the ground that too much speech is an evil. It was as if the state had said: "Attention all citizens. To assure the fairness of elections by preventing disproportionate expression of the view of any single powerful group, your Government has decided that the following associations of persons shall be prohibited from speaking in support of any candidate: _____."[59] In the blank, one merely fills in the disfavored groups of the moment.

This particular Michigan law exempted mass media and labor unions from its prohibitions. Future laws may exempt different groups, in an effort to balance what the appropriate amount of speech is, in the view of the government. All this troubled Justice Scalia, and it should have.

The *Austin* majority only concluded that Michigan's exemption for media corporations was constitutional, not that the exemption was constitutionally required. Justice Marshall, for the Court, made that point quite clear when he carefully said: "Although the press' unique society role may not entitle the press to greater protection under the Constitution, it does provide a compelling reason for the State to exempt media corporations from the scope of the political expenditure limitations."[60]

What if the state changed its mind, and decided to forbid newspapers or broadcasters from making candidate endorsements? Michigan or another state might decide that media corporations should be regulated or prohibited from making candidate endorsements. If Justice Marshall's caveat and distinction are valid, a state or the federal government may regulate speech that is at the core of the First Amendment, speech that endorses or opposes candidates for political office.

Michigan might decide that its wealthy media corporations should be regulated. Indeed, Michigan could decide that it makes more sense to regulate the mass media than to regulate nonmedia corporations on the plausible theory that "[a]massed corporate wealth that regularly sits astride the ordinary channels of information is much more likely to produce the New Corruption (too much of one point of view) than amassed corporate wealth that is busy making money elsewhere."[61]

I think that the *Austin* decision does not have to mean as much as the majority, or Justice Scalia, indicated that it might, though I offer no guarantees of what a future Court will do. The issue before the Court in *Austin* was only the constitutionality of the state's ban on corporations making independent expenditures in connection with state candidate elections. The law did not prohibit corporations from endorsing candidates or issues, only from making independent expenditures on behalf of a candidate.

If a newspaper published an editorial in favor of a candidate, the marginal cost to the newspaper in publishing that editorial would be zero. If the newspaper did not write an editorial on that particular subject, it would write it on another. Similarly, if a chamber of commerce published a weekly or monthly newsletter, it should be able to say what it wants. The marginal cost to the chamber, in endorsing a candidate or an issue in its weekly newsletter would be zero. Corporations (even a chamber of commerce) have free speech too, as the *Bellotti* Court earlier held.[62] What the chamber cannot do is republish its editorial and then hire people to distribute it to the general public. That would be an independent expenditure, and its marginal cost to the chamber would be greater than zero. Similarly, this distinction would mean that a state could forbid a corporation that is a newspaper from engaging in an independent expenditure by reprinting its editorials endorsing a candidate and then hiring people to distribute them to the public at large, or renting billboards that reprint its editorials endorsing particular candidates.

Thus, the fact that the Court in *Austin* approved the Michigan state law does not mean that it would approve a state law that prohibited newspapers from endorsing or opposing candidates, because when a newspaper endorses a candidate in its editorial, it is making no independent expenditure. That is, it is making no expenditure with a marginal cost greater than zero. Thus the chamber could publish its endorsement in its own newsletter, but it could not pay a local newspaper to run an advertisement supporting a particular candidate. Unfortunately, the majority's language and analysis in *Austin* could have been written to provide more comfort to newspapers and other members of the institutional press.

I do not mean to suggest that the Warren Court was always a strong supporter of free speech. We know now, thanks to the excellent historical work of Professor Bernard Schwartz, that Earl Warren himself would have upheld the government's power to prohibit the burning of the American flag,[63] while the modern Court has ruled otherwise,[64] using the symbolic speech analysis that Chief Justice Warren had earlier developed in *United States v. O'Brien*.[65]

In the area of obscenity, the Warren Court meandered about in a series of rulings that gave little guidance to the lower courts as to what was or was not "obscene" in a constitutional sense.[66] Courts, from each trial court all the way up to the Supreme Court, were forced to watch the movies themselves in order to make the decision on obscenity. And when the Supreme Court did make a decision, the Justices often issued *per curiam* reversals, with no opinion, so lower courts were kept in the dark as to how to apply the test on obscenity.[67] At one point, Justice Stewart seemed to throw up his hands in despair in attempting to define obscenity. Some people think that he said, "I can't define it, but I know what I like." What he really said was "I shall not today attempt to further define the kinds of material that I understand to be embraced within that shorthand description [of hardcore pornography]; and perhaps I could never succeed in intelligibly doing so. But I know it when I see it, and the motion picture involved in this case is not that."[68]

However, this volume is not the place to bury the Warren Court in criticism, but to praise it. If, in the quarter of a century that has passed, we now look back at some of the cases of that era and find that the Warren Court was insufficiently attentive to the needs of free speech and free press, it is only because we have learned, in the fullness of time, to place even greater value on the First Amendment. If we see further than those who have gone before us, it is because we stand on the shoulders of these legal giants. As the Greek Xenophanes once said:

> The gods did not reveal, from the beginning,
> All things to us; but in the course of time,
> Through seeking, we may learn, and know things better.[69]

Of the many basic principles that we can learn from the legal titans who served on the Warren Court, one of the most important is that the Court should not engage in the fruitless task of trying to draw a distinction between speech and press. Both are part of the same amendment that has made our country a shining beacon for freedom around the world. To distinguish between the two clauses only results in unprincipled decision making and perverse results. Together, they give us more free speech; separated, they limit our freedom. Both clauses should be interpreted broadly, to protect and foster free speech and press.

If ancient scholars sat around a table and discussed how society should be organized, the people who proposed a free speech guarantee as broad as ours might be laughed out of the room. Such a society could not exist, we would be told. America is the experiment that showed the world that a nation with a strong free speech and free press guarantee not only can survive, but thrive.

Notes

1. I say "he," because all the Chief Justices have been male.

2. A story illustrates the significance of changing leaders. A widow complained to the funeral director that her late husband was not dressed properly for the wake. "Look at him," she cried, when she saw the body laid out just before the wake was to begin. "He has a Kelly green suit and a garish tie, and a contrasting plaid vest and jacket. You got the instructions all wrong!" "Don't worry," said the funeral director. "I'll take care of the problem. I'm sorry about the mistake." "But," stressed the widow, "the funeral is about to begin, in just fifteen minutes. The people are almost here. How can you do anything in time?" "Trust me," said the funeral director. "It's no big undertaking." The distraught woman left, and when the funeral started, less than a quarter hour later, the deceased was dressed in a beautiful silk suit, with a white-on-white shirt, splendid tie, matching pocket handkerchief, and so on. A few months later, when the widow collected herself, she asked the funeral director, "How did you do that? I was really impressed." "Easy," he replied. "I just changed heads." And so you see, changing heads can make a big difference. When Earl Warren became Chief, that little change made quite a difference.

3. Schwartz, *Super Chief: Earl Warren and His Supreme Court—A Judicial Biography* 771 (1983).

4. See id. at 15–17. Warren's memoirs acknowledged that he "deeply regretted the removal order and my own testimony advocating it . . . ." Warren, *Memoirs* 149 (1977). The memoirs were published posthumously, Warren having died in 1974. Schwartz, supra note 3, at 771–72.

5. Brennan, "Chief Justice Warren," 88 *Harv. L. Rev.* 1, 4 (1974). A discussion and criticism of this proposal may be found at 1 Rotunda and Nowak, *Treatise on Constitutional Law: Substance and Procedure,* § 2.6 (2d ed. 1992).

6. U.S. Const. amend. 1.

7. E.g., Hurtado v. California, 110 U.S. 516, 534–35 (1884): "According to a recognized canon of interpretation, especially applicable to formal and solemn instruments of constitutional law, we are forbidden to assume, without clear reason to the contrary, that any part of this most important amendment is superfluous." See also

McCulloch v. Maryland, 17 U.S. (4 Wheat.) 316, 413 (1819); Knowlton v. Moore, 178 U.S. 41, 87 (1900); Wright v. United States, 302 U.S. 583 (1938); Richardson v. Ramirez, 418 U.S. 24, 55 (1974). Note that in later cases, the Court has said that the Tenth Amendment "states but a truism that all is retained which has not been surrendered." United States v. Darby, 312 U.S. 100, 117 (1941).

8. See generally Nimmer, "Introduction—Is Freedom of the Press a Redundancy: What Does It Add to Freedom of Speech?," 26 *Hastings L.J.* 631 (1975); Stewart, "Or of the Press," 26 *Hastings L.J.* 631 (1975); Lange, "The Speech and Press Clauses," 23 *U.C.L.A. L. Rev.* 77 (1975); Nimmer, "Speech and Press : A Brief Reply," 23 *U.C.L.A. L. Rev.* 120 (1975); Bezanson, "The New Free Speech Guarantee," 63 *Va. L. Rev.* 731 (1977); Abrams, "The Press Is Different: Reflections on Justice and the Autonomous Press," 7 *Hofstra L. Rev.* 563 (1979); Lewis, "A Preferred Position for Journalism?," 7 *Hofstra L. Rev.* 595 (1979); Sack, "Reflections of the Wrong Question: Special Constitutional Privilege for the Institutional Press," 7 *Hofstra L. Rev.* 629 (1979); Van Alstyne, "The First Amendment and the Free Press: A Comment on Some New Trends and Some Old Theories," 9 *Hofstra L. Rev.* 1 (1980); Anderson, "The Origins of the Press Clause," 30 *U.C.L.A. L. Rev.* 455 (1983); Levy, *Emergence of a Free Press* (1985); Levy, "On the Origins of the Free Press Clause," 32 *U.C.L.A. L. Rev.* 177 (1984); Van Alstyne, "Congressional Power and Free Speech: Levy's Legacy Revisited," 99 *Harv. L. Rev.* 1089 (1986); Nowak, "Using the Press Clause to Limit Government Speech," 30 *Ariz. L. Rev.* 1 (1988).

9. See, Zurcher v. Stanford Daily, 436 U.S. 547 (1978). The Court refused to create any special protections for newspapers that might be searched by government authorities pursuant to a valid search warrant that was based on probable cause. In the facts of this case, the warrant was used to look for and seize photographic evidence of a crime (assault of police during a sit-in demonstration). These newspaper photographs were thought to be stored in the office of the *Stanford University Daily* newspaper.

While the majority clearly rejected any claim based on the First Amendment that would require the use of subpoenas rather than the more intrusive search warrant procedure, when the premises to be searched are a newspaper's offices, the Court did emphasize that if "the materials sought to be seized may be protected by the First Amendment, the requirements of the Fourth Amendment must be applied with 'scrupulous exactitude.'" Id. at 564, citing Stanford v. Texas, 379 U.S. 476, 485 (1965). This special protection of the First Amendment applies to everyone, not just the institutional press.

In this case the majority was obviously concerned about creating, out of whole cloth, a constitutional definition of "press." Congress responded to Zurcher by creating the Privacy Protection Act of 1980, codified at 42 U.S.C.A. §§ 2000aa–2000aa-12. This law offers special protection from a search warrant for any work product (including mental impressions) prepared in anticipation of communicating such materials to the public. Excluded are materials that are the fruits or instrumentalities of a crime. The protection extends to newspapers, books, or broadcasts in or affecting interstate or foreign commerce.

The protection is subject to various exceptions. For example, it does not cover border searches. It also allows a search warrant instead of a subpoena if giving notice via subpoena would result in destruction, alteration, or concealment of the materials. Ironically, this last exception would have meant that the Privacy Protection Act would not have protected the *Stanford Daily*, because it had announced that it would destroy the photographs rather than give them to the police.

Congress can limit search warrants by statute, and, if it does, it can define the group protected. While the Court has no principled way of creating a definition of "the press," Congress has extensive power to create certain rights not required by the Constitution and then extend those rights to some groups and not others, to nonborder searches, for example.

10. Branzburg v. Hayes, 408 U.S. 665, 704–05 (1972).

11. E.g., Richmond Newspapers, Inc. v. Virginia, 448 U.S. 555 (1980). The plurality opinion of Burger, C.J., joined by White and Stevens, JJ., emphasized: "[W]e note that historically both civil and criminal trials have been presumptively open." 448 U.S. at 581 n.17. If the courtroom has limited capacity, so that not all who wish to attend in person are able to do so, the court may impose reasonable restrictions on general access, and, as part of these restrictions, may grant preferential seating for representatives of the media. Richmond Newspapers, Inc. v. Virginia, 448 U.S. at 581 n.18 (Burger, C.J., joined by White and Stevens, JJ.).

12. See, Van Alstyne, "The Hazards to the Press of Claiming a 'Preferred Position,'" 28 *Hastings L.J.* 761 (1977).

13. Florida Star v. B.J.F., 491 U.S. 524 (1989).

14. Supporters of the Florida law justified it as a means of protecting women victims. It is interesting that, after *Florida Star,* the editor of the *Des Moines Register,* Geneva Overholser, published an essay in her paper arguing that newspapers who do not routinely publish the names of rape victims actually harmed them. She explained that when newspapers refuse to publish the names of rape victims, but systematically print the names of burglary victims, robbery victims, etc., the newspapers attach a stigma to rape victims that will not go away until the names are published as a matter of routine. Failure to publish the names suggests that the rape victim was somehow to blame for the crime done to her.

Ms. Overholser's essay persuaded an Iowa rape victim to discuss her story in a five-part series that led to many letters to the editor from women and men applauding her decision to go public, so that the rape victim will lose the stigma that somehow she did something wrong and, somehow, she should be shunned because she had been raped. See, Gartner, "The Scarlet Letter of Rape: A Courageous Victim Fights Back," *Wall Street Journal,* Mar. 15, 1990, at p. A15, col. 3–6 (Midwest ed.).

15. Florida Star v. B.J.F., 491 U.S. at 542 (emphasis added) (Scalia, J., concurring in part and concurring in the judgment). See, Rotunda, "Eschewing Bright Lines," *Trial Magazine* 52, 54–55 (Dec. 1989), discussing *Florida Star.*

16. 435 U.S. 765, 795 (1978) (Burger, J., concurring).

17. Id. at 777 (Powell, J., for the majority). See generally, Rotunda, "The Commercial Speech Doctrine in the Supreme Court," 1976 *U. Ill. L. Forum* 1080 (1976); Prentice, "Consolidated Edison and Bellotti: First Amendment Protection of Corporate Political Speech," 16 *Tulsa L.J.* 599 (1981); "Note, The Corporation and the Constitution: Economic Due Process and Corporate Speech," 90 *Yale L.J.* 1833 (1981); Brundy, "Business Corporations and Stockholders' Rights Under the First Amendment," 91 *Yale L.J.* 325 (1981).

18. 376 U.S. 254 (1964).

19. The phrase, "speaking for the Court," is standard boilerplate. But note that when the decisions are formally announced, the Justices seldom read (or speak) their opinions any more, and when they do, they seldom read more than a summary or extract. But the Court today treats "speaking" and "writing" as interchangeable, the "speech" or "press." Similarly, the framers and their contemporary commentators used "freedom of speech" interchangeably and synonymously with "freedom of the press." Levy, *Legacy of Suppression: Freedom of Speech and Press in Early American History* 174 (1960), reprinting comments by an eighteenth-century journalist who treated "speech" and "press" synonymously.

20. 376 U.S. at 256.

21. For many of us, thanks to the inflation, our last car cost more than our first house.

22. A Rolls-Royce Silver Cloud III, with air conditioning, cost approximately £4,750 in 1964, converting to $13,140. See Robson, *Rolls-Royce Silver Cloud* 73–84, 126–27 (Motorbooks International, 1980); Clarke, *Rolls-Royce Silver Cloud*, 1955–1965 (Brooklands, 1978).

23. 376 U.S. at 279–80.

24. Herbert v. Lando, 441 U.S. 153, 199 (1979) (Stewart, J., dissenting).

25. 376 U.S. at 286.

26. Id. at 286.

27. Id. at 287. The *Times* "knew" what was in its files only in the sense that someone in the corporation may have known what was in the *Times* old newspaper files, or could have accessed these files. However, for "malice," that is, for "scienter," the plaintiffs would have had to demonstrate that there was actual knowledge by the particular persons in charge of publishing the advertisement. Id. at 287.

28. Id. at 288 (emphasis added).

29. Id. at 285–86.

30. Gertz v. Robert Welch, Inc., 418 U.S. 323, 331–32 (1974).

31. Hayes, "Britain's Libel Laws Helped Maxwell Keep Charges of Misdeeds from Public," *Wall Street Journal*, Dec. 9, 1991, at B2, col. 3–4 (Midwest ed.).

32. See also Henry v. Collins, 380 U.S. 356 (1965).

33. 472 U.S. 749 (1985).

34. Id. at 755.

35. Id. at 757 and n.4 (emphasis in original).

36. Id. at 760 (footnote omitted).

37. 376 U.S. at 270.

38. Gertz v. Robert Welch, Inc., 418 U.S. 323, 350 (1974).

39. See, "Comment, Punitive Damages and Libel Law," 98 *Harv. L. Rev.* 847 (1985).

40. 418 U.S. 323 (1974).

41. 472 U.S. at 756.

42. Id. at 773 (White, J., concurring in the judgment): "Although Justice Powell speaks only of the inapplicability of the Gertz rule with respect to presumed and punitive damages, it must be that the Gertz requirement of some kind of fault on the part of the defendant is also inapplicable in cases such as this."

43. The famous and retired football player, charged, in the spring of 1994, with the murder of his former wife.

44. 472 U.S. at 762 (footnote omitted).

45. Id. at 762, n.8.

46. Rosenbloom v. Metromedia, Inc., 403 U.S. 29, 78–81 (Marshall, J., dissenting, joined by Stewart, J.) (1971). Harlan's separate dissent agreed with this analysis. 403 U.S. at 62.

47. See, e.g., United States v. O'Brien, 391 U.S. 367, 377 (1968) (Warren, C.J., for the Court). See generally, 4 Rotunda and Nowak, *Treatise on Constitutional Law: Substance and Procedure*, §§ 20.47(a), (b), (c); 20.48; 20.49 (2d ed. 1992). In *O'Brien*, Chief Justice Warren upheld a federal law that banned knowing destruction of a selective service certificate. This law "did not bar only *contemptuous* destruction; if the act had been written in the those terms, it would have indicated that its purpose was to punish the publication of certain opinions, in violation of part three of the O'Brien test." Id. at § 20.49 at 339 (emphasis in original; footnote omitted).

48. See Rotunda, "A Brief Comment on Politically Incorrect Speech in the Wake of R.A.V.," 47 *So. Meth. U. L. Rev.* 9 (1993) for a discussion of these issues.

49. See the line of cases from Marsh v. Alabama, 326 U.S. 501 (1948), to the Warren Court decision in Amalgamated Food Employees Union v. Logan Valley Plaza, Inc., 326 U.S. 501 (1968), to Lloyd Corp., Ltd. v. Tanner, 407 U.S. 551 (1972), a post-Warren era case that limited free speech protest rights based on the content of the speech, to Hudgens v. N.L.R.B., 424 U.S. 507 (1976), which realized the error of trying to limit protest speech based on its content.

As Justice Stewart said in *Hudgens*, "[W]hile a municipality may constitutionally impose reasonable time, place, and manner regulations on the use of its streets and sidewalks for First Amendment purposes, and may even forbid altogether such use of some of its facilities, what a municipality may *not* do under the First and Fourteenth Amendments is to discriminate in the regulation of expression on the basis of the content of that expression." 424 U.S. at 520 (emphasis in original). See generally, Rotunda and Nowak, 2 *Treatise on Constitutional Law: Substance and Procedure*, § 16.2.

50. In cases like Connick v. Meyers, 461 U.S. 138 (1983), the modern Court distinguishes between the types of speech that protect a public employee from discharge (where the Court must relate the type of speech in which the employee engaged to the effective functioning of the office). It is quite another thing for the Court to engage in the much more open-ended task of trying to decide what is a "matter of public concern" in the *Dun & Bradstreet* sense. In the *Connick* sense, the Court at least has a hook on which to hang its analysis, because the Court decides what is relevant to the effective functioning of a particular job. Such a test is not open-ended because it is connected to a particular job.

51. Cf. Rotunda, "A Commentary on the Constitutionality of Term Limits," in Crane and Pilon, eds., *The Politics and Law of Term Limits* 141 (Cato Institute, 1994) (discussing incumbent self-protection).

52. Burger, C.J., concurring in part and dissenting in part, in Buckley v. Valeo, 424 U.S. 1, 248 (1976), quoting Senator Howard Baker, in 120 *Cong. Rec.* 8202 (1974).

53. 494 U.S. 652 (1990).

54. Buckley v. Valeo, 424 U.S. at 45–48 (1976) (per curiam). It is interesting that Buckley, 424 U.S. at 48, cited and relied on New York Times v. Sullivan, 376 U.S. at 269.

55. Federal Election Committee v. National Conservative Political Action Committee, 470 U.S. 480, 493 (1985).

56. The *Austin* Court distinguished Federal Election Commission v. Massachusetts Citizens for Life, Inc. [MCFL], 479 U.S. 238 (1986), as a single-issue voluntary association. *MCFL* had invalidated, as applied, a federal law that prohibited corporations from using treasury funds to make an expenditure "in connection with any election to any public office." MCFL, the Court emphasized, was not a business corporation. It was formed for an express political purpose, a narrowly focused purpose, supporting respect for human life, "born and unborn." It cannot engage in business activities; it has no shareholders with a claim to its assets; and it accepts no contributions from any business corporations or labor unions, so that it could not be their conduit.

57. 494 U.S. at 666.

58. Id. at 695–96 (Kennedy, J., dissenting).

59. Id. at 679 (Scalia, J., dissenting).

60. Id. at 668.

61. Id. at 691 (Scalia, J., dissenting).

62. First National Bank v. Bellotti, 435 U.S. 765 (1978), invalidating a Massachusetts law that prohibited corporate expenditures for the purpose of influencing the vote

on any referendum, other than a referendum materially affecting the property, business, of assets of the corporation.

63. Schwartz, supra note 3, at 733, pointing out that at the October 25, 1968, conference on Street v. New York, 394 U.S. 576 (1969), Warren said: "The only question is whether New York can punish public burning of the flag. I think the state can do so to prevent riots and the like. It's conduct and not speech or symbolic speech."

During Warren's tenure on the Court, the Justices did overturn a flag desecration conviction, but only on narrow grounds, after finding that the conviction might have been rested solely on speech divorced from the conduct or action of desecrating the flag. Thus, the Court managed to avoid the free speech issue directly. E.g., Street v. New York, 394 U.S. 576 (1969), on remand, 250 N.E. 2d 250 (N.Y. 1969). In this case, Street burned a flag that he personally owned on a New York street corner while talking to a group of about thirty onlookers. The arresting officer testified that he heard Street say, "We don't need no damn flag." Street was convicted of violating a statute that made it a misdemeanor to "cast contempt" on any flag of the United States "by words or act." Because it was possible that Street's words alone were the basis of his conviction, the Court overturned the conviction.

64. Texas v. Johnson, 491 U.S. 397 (1989); United States v. Eichman, 496 U.S. 310 (1990). See generally, Rotunda and Nowak, supra note 47, at § 20.49, at 347–51.

65. 391 U.S. 367 (1968). Cf. Rotunda, *The Politics of Language* (1986), on the importance and significance of political symbols.

66. The issues and history of this period, from Roth v. United States, 354 U.S. 476 (1957), to the Burger Court era, are discussed in Rotunda and Nowak, supra note 47, at §§ 20.57–20.60. See also, Strossen, *Defending Pornography: Free Speech, Sex, and the Fight for Women's Rights* (1994) for a careful analysis of free speech issues in the context of pornography.

67. This tactic was called the *Redrup* approach, after the first case to use it. Redrup v. New York, 386 U.S. 767 (1967) (per curiam). See, Paris Adult Theater I v. Slaton, 413 U.S. 49, 82–83 (1973) (Brennan, J., dissenting, discussing the *Redrup* approach).

68. Jacobellis v. Ohio. 378 U.S. 184, 197 (1964) (Stewart, J., concurring).

69. Quoted in Popper, *In Search of a Better World* 188 (1992).

· 7 ·

THE WARREN COURT AND THE RELIGION CLAUSES OF THE FIRST AMENDMENT

JOHN SEXTON

I do not doubt for a moment the general statement that without the Warren Court, most of the movements that have so transformed American society would never have gotten off the ground. Indeed it is probably right that in terms of creative impact, the tenure of Earl Warren can only be compared with that of John Marshall himself. The veracity of that statement does not, however, turn on the Court's work on church and state.

This is not to say that the Warren Court's decisions in this area did not have broad political and social impact. Certainly, when the Court proclaimed in *Engel v. Vitale*[1] and *Abington Township v. Schempp*[2] that prayer or Bible reading in the public schools violated the Constitution, it was a political and social event. And the Court's broad interpretation of the rights of conscientious objectors in *United States v. Seeger*[3] was equally significant politically and socially.

But, as matters of constitutional law, the results in those cases were uncontroversial and unremarkable. Only Justice Stewart dissented in the school prayer cases; and only Justice Clark dissented in *Seeger*. Quite simply, the Warren Court cases on church and state that were noteworthy political and social events added little to the jurisprudence of the First Amendment's Religion Clauses.

The Corpus of Cases

The Warren Court's Religion Clause jurisprudence began with the 1961 quartet of cases upholding Sunday closing laws;[4] and it ended in 1969 with the *Presbyterian Church* case,[5] in which the Court unanimously invalidated a Georgia law allowing juries to determine church property disputes by examining whether the mother church's leaders had departed from the tenets of their faith.

The corpus of the cases involving the Religion Clauses of the First Amendment decided by the Warren Court is small. If one counts the Sunday closing cases, which the Court decided simultaneously, as a single case, there are only ten cases in all.

And one of the ten is *Flast v. Cohen*,[6] the case that established general taxpayer standing to invoke the Establishment Clause; in truth, *Flast* is more a federal courts case than a Religion Clause case.

Moreover, the results in most of the cases in the corpus were viewed by the Court as relatively uncontroversial. Four of the ten cases were unanimous; no decision drew more than three dissenting votes; and, only three of the ten drew more than one dissenting vote.

In addition to the cases already mentioned, the Warren Court decided two clear cases. In *Torcaso v. Watkins*,[7] the Justices unanimously invalidated a provision in the Maryland Constitution requiring officeholders to declare a belief in God; and, in *Epperson v. Arkansas*,[8] they unanimously found unconstitutional an Arkansas statute forbidding the teaching of evolution.

The remaining two decisions of the Court were close constitutional cases, and each drew vigorous dissents. The Court's decision validating New York's practice of providing textbooks to students in parochial schools, *Board of Education v. Allen*,[9] drew dissent from Justices Black, Douglas, and Fortas. And *Sherbert v. Verner*,[10] which held that South Carolina could not apply the eligibility provisions of its unemployment compensation statute so as to deny benefits to a claimant who had refused work on religious grounds, did so over dissents from Justices Harlan and White.

As indicated, the work of the Warren Court on the Religion Clauses of the First Amendment cannot be described as pathbreaking. Only *Sherbert* can be viewed as a seminal case, and then only if one shares my view that the Supreme Court's earlier decisions in *Schneider v. New Jersey*,[11] *Cantwell v. Connecticut*,[12] and *Murdock v. Pennsylvania*[13] did not establish a right of free exercise with sufficient doctrinal clarity. Moreover, even if one does view *Sherbert* as seminal, its doctrinal power and ultimate influence are open to serious question.

The Establishment Clause decisions of the Warren Court did little to advance either constitutional doctrine or the ways in which it is analyzed and developed. Instead, they repeated and relied upon the work of the Court in the decade before Earl Warren became Chief Justice, and that repetition served only to reinforce the approaches—some of which were problematic—taken in the earlier cases.

In general, it may be said that the work of the Warren Court on the Religion Clauses lacks substantive majesty. This is partly a product of the questions that came to the Court—in most cases, first-generation questions with relatively clearcut answers that could be derived easily from the broad principles that had been enumerated by prior Courts. Thus, the heavy doctrinal lifting had been done earlier, and the difficult applications of doctrine were left to the Burger Court.

But the lack of substantive majesty also is partly the result of some doctrinal problems, which the Warren Court either perpetuated or generated itself. Three such doctrinal problems will be discussed. Two suggest themselves: they are, respectively, the Warren Court's free exercise jurisprudence and its Establishment Clause jurisprudence. The third, which implicates what in my view is the most original work done by the Warren Court on these clauses, involves the Court's efforts to provide a workable definition of the word "religion" in the constitutional text.

Free Exercise

The Warren Court's seminal free exercise decision was *Sherbert v. Verner*.[14] It would be inappropriate, however, to discuss *Sherbert* without first discussing the Warren Court's decisions two years earlier in the Sunday Closing cases—specifically its decision in *Braunfeld v. Brown*,[15] the Free Exercise challenge to the Blue Laws.

In *Braunfeld*, a four-Justice plurality found that Sunday closing laws were the least burdensome way that the state could provide a weekly respite from labor for its citizens, a goal the Justices found important. The plurality opinion made two somewhat conflicting points. First, the Justices emphasized that the statute only indirectly burdened Orthodox Jews who could not work on Saturday because of their faith, and who could not work on Sunday because of the statute. The closing law, in the view of the Justices, did not make any religious practices unlawful; it simply made the practice of religious belief more expensive. The plurality implied that such statutes, creating indirect burdens, were constitutionally "unassailable."

The plurality's second point, however, contradicted that implication, and instead reaffirmed the principle (laid down twenty years earlier in *Murdock*, *Schneider*, and *Cantwell*) that even indirect burdens are constitutionally forbidden if "the State may accomplish its purposes by means which do not impose such a burden."[16] On this view, it was the Justices' conclusion that no such burdenless alternative was available to achieve the state's goal, a conclusion that was critical to upholding the laws.

Two years after *Braunfeld*, the Court decided *Sherbert*. A Seventh Day Adventist, who had been discharged because she would not work on Saturday, filed a claim for unemployment compensation benefits under the South Carolina Unemployment Compensation Act. The act provided that claimants were ineligible for benefits if they failed, without good cause, to accept suitable work that had been offered. The Unemployment Commission denied Sherbert's claim on the ground that she would not accept suitable work, but the Supreme Court held that this denial abridged Sherbert's free exercise right.

Sherbert rejected *Braunfeld*'s distinction between direct and indirect burdens and held that free exercise protection applied not only where government imposed a direct cost, but also where government withheld an economic benefit. As Justice Brennan put it, the emergence of an increasingly pervasive, affirmative state had blurred the distinction between benefits and burdens too thoroughly to make it a tolerable dividing line in constitutional adjudication.

Sherbert also advanced the development of doctrine by adopting formally the least-restrictive-alternative / compelling-state-interest mode of analysis in a free exercise context. *Schneider*, *Cantwell*, and *Murdock* had pointed toward those two requirements. *Braunfeld* had applied the least-restrictive-alternative requirement but not the compelling-state-interest one, and the *Braunfeld* plurality's focus on the dichotomy between direct and indirect burdens had muddied the issue.

Since *Sherbert*, the Court consistently has held that the state cannot force a person to choose between conscience and material advantage unless the state's reasons for doing so are weighty. To use a phase from the vernacular, the Court has talked the *Sherbert* talk. But, over the thirty years since *Sherbert*, the Court actually has acted on that principle in only one case other than *Sherbert*'s direct unemployment benefits progeny: in *Wisconsin v. Yoder,*[17] it held that Wisconsin's stake in requiring all children to pursue a recognized program of education until the age of sixteen was not sufficient to justify the state's interference with the religiously motivated commitment of the Amish to integrate children into their working society at the age of fourteen. In every other free exercise case, the Court has failed to honor the broad dictum of *Sherbert.*

Here, a broader view might help. In a nineteenth-century case, *Reynolds v. United States,*[18] the Supreme Court rejected not only the claim of Mormons to a free exercise right to practice polygamy; it also rejected as unthinkable the idea that each religious believer could create a microenvironment of law molded to his separate beliefs. In this regard, *Reynolds,* which to this day is cited favorably by the Court, stands as a challenge to the constitutional model announced in *Sherbert.*

Over the last three decades, the *Sherbert* line and *Yoder* emerge as exceptions rather than the rule. The Court seems, in fact, to be more sympathetic to the spirit of *Reynolds* than that of *Sherbert.* In some cases since *Yoder* and outside the unemployment benefits area, the Court has paid lip service to the *Sherbert* rule, but in each of these cases it has found the compelling state interest test of *Sherbert* satisfied. The result is that, while in other constitutional areas the compelling state interest is fairly characterized as "strict in theory and fatal in fact," in the religion cases the test is (in the words of Ira Lupu) "strict in theory but feeble in fact."[19]

Lawrence Sager and Christopher Eisgruber argue that *Sherbert* was doomed to be limited in this way because of an analytical flaw.[20] They argue that what is needed is a fresh start. Whether one agrees with them or not, an analysis of their argument sheds interesting light on *Sherbert.*

Sherbert, they say, is based upon the idea that it is the unique value of religious practices that sometimes entitles them to constitutional attention. They call this the "privileging view" of religious liberty. The underlying logic of the privileging view of religious exemptions is this: It is a matter of constitutional regret whenever government prevents or discourages persons from honoring their religious commitments; accordingly, government should act so as to avoid placing religious believers at a substantial disadvantage by virtue of their efforts to conform their conduct to their beliefs. This is the principle of unimpaired flourishing.

Unimpaired flourishing is sometimes offered as a principle of equity, as though it functions merely to make those who respond to the strong demands of their religious beliefs no worse off than others. But in truth unimpaired flourishing is more than a principle of equity: it privileges religious commitments over other deep commitments that persons have.

As a conception of religious freedom, unimpaired flourishing presents a striking normative difficulty. Religious belief need not be founded in reason, guided by reason, or governed in any way by the reasonable. Accordingly, the demands that religions place on the faithful, and the demands that the faithful can in turn place on society in the name of unimpaired flourishing, are potentially extravagant.

But, of course, the *Sherbert* Court did not mean to take us into this ungainly world. And even the strongest proponent of the principle of unimpaired flourishing would wish collective authority to remain pretty much as it is; but, if that is so, then

Sherbert simply created a haven for religiously motivated conduct at the margins of state authority. And, this produces incoherence of a much more immediate and troubling sort, as *Sherbert* doctrine is reduced to offering an unexplainably selective, comparatively modest, practical agenda for reform, all based on a sweeping and deeply radical principle of political justice. The result is an analytical scramble.

Beset by these difficulties, those who must apply *Sherbert* take refuge in the compelling-state-interest test. The compelling-state-interest test is normally applied in constitutional contexts where practically all instances of collective behavior with the triggering feature are expected to be unconstitutional, but extraordinary cases can be imagined that would pass constitutional scrutiny.

But in many religious exemption cases, the presumptive invalidity implicit in the compelling-state-interest test is misplaced. There is a substantial range of religiously motivated conduct—readily observable in contemporary national experience—that quite clearly must yield to conflicting secular laws. This has been recognized tacitly by the all-but-total failure of *Sherbert*'s dictum to travel outside the unemployment benefits situation. To be sure, the Supreme Court has paid lip service to that standard in some non-*Sherbert* exemption cases, but it has found the test satisfied in all except *Yoder*. That experience could reflect merely the distortions of a small sample, of course, were it not for the fact that the courts of appeals have similarly applied the test in words only, and so found a diverse set of garden-variety legislative interests powerful enough to overwhelm the claims of religious exemption. Under these circumstances, the compelling-state-interest test becomes just another balancing test, obscuring rather than clarifying analysis.

These flaws in the analysis used in *Sherbert* certainly have limited its impact and, given the Supreme Court's 1990 decision in *Employment Division v. Smith*,[21] may have caused its demise. For the *Smith* majority, the distinct constitutional status of religion rather mysteriously runs out once the state frames its laws in terms of general application. Under the majority approach, even the *Sherbert* line seems imperiled, or at very best relegated to an exceptional category more or less hand-tailored to unemployment insurance cases.

There are answers: Sager and Eisgruber would view the Free Exercise Clause as a protective (antidiscrimination) device designed, in conjunction with the Establishment Clause, to ensure fair and equal treatment of religious adherents. Such theories deserve exploration elsewhere. For the moment, it is sufficient to note that the Warren Court did not travel that road, and that the course it took is problematic.

Establishment Clause

Let us turn now to the Warren Court's Establishment Clause cases. On no account could these be considered seminal. The 1947 decision of the Court in *Everson v. Board of Education*[22] had announced in the strongest terms the modern doctrine of separation of church and state, and its principles were easily applied to the cases faced by the Warren Court, with the possible exception of *Allen* (the textbook case).[23]

It should be noted that, in the course of deciding *Abington*,[24] the Court enunciated a test, drawn from its summary of previous cases, that foreshadowed the three-part test announced by Chief Justice Burger in *Lemon v. Kurtzman*,[25] the test that now has been used by courts for two decades to decide Establishment Clause cases.

It also should be noted that several Establishment Clause opinions written by the Warren Court—most notably Justice Brennan's magnificent concurring opinion in *Abington*—added considerably to the Court's historical analysis of the Establishment Clause. But, and this is the significant point, as erudite as these additional historical analyses were, they maintained the essential heuristic construct adopted by the *Everson* Court. Since, in my view, that construct was seriously flawed, the fact that the Warren Court perpetuated and solidified it is no virtue. To make my points let me begin with *Everson*.

Though Justice Wiley Rutledge voiced his assertion that "[n]o provision of the Constitution is more closely tied to its generating history than the religious clause of the First Amendment"[26] while dissenting from the Court's decision in *Everson*, he and Justice Hugo Black (who wrote for the Court) shared the view that the "generating history" of the Religion Clauses was the key to understanding their meaning. Moreover, though they came to opposite conclusions about the case before them, the two Justices based their opinions upon virtually identical historical accounts.

In the three decades after *Everson*, the Warren Court reiterated the view that understanding the period of formulation was the key to understanding the Religion Clauses, and various Justices repeated the history of that period provided by Justices Black and Rutledge. Whether it was right or wrong, the *Everson* Court's "history" of the Religion Clauses became the orthodox view. What is that orthodoxy?

Justice Black's opinion for the Court in *Everson* began by noting that European history to the time of the American Revolution was marked by rampant religious persecution and that the nasty habits "of the old world were transplanted to and began to thrive in the soil of the new America."[27] This brought him to a pivotal point in his argument: he identified Virginia as the principal battleground over church-state relations during the period of the constitution's formulation.

Once he had made that critical move, his historical argument flowed smoothly: if the Virginian experience was the key, then the landmarks of that experience became the critical materials from which to derive the meaning of the constitutional text. Three documents became the "legislative history" of the First Amendment's religious clauses: the Virginia Declaration of Rights of 1776 (written by George Mason with important amendments by James Madison), Madison's 1785 "Memorial and Remonstrance against Religious Assessments," and the 1786 Virginia Statute for Religious Freedom (drafted by Thomas Jefferson in 1779).

In the end, Justice Black derived from these subtexts one succinct passage[28] that married his understanding of the clauses and Jefferson's metaphorical "wall of separation," thereby generating a theory (strict separation) that would dominate the Court's thinking about church-state relations for decades to come. Justice Rutledge, the author of the principal dissent, embraced the essence of Black's history and metaphor.

Even in its own time, the *Everson* Court's account of the generative history of the Religion Clauses did not go unchallenged. One year after *Everson* was decided, Justice Stanley Reed, dissenting in the very next religion case to come to the Court, argued that the framers may have intended the establishment clause "to be aimed only at a state church."[29] And Justice Reed was not the only Justice to challenge the orthodox view that the Religion Clauses were designed to implement a doctrine of strict separation of church and state. In *Zorach v. Clauson*[30] (the "released time" case), Justice Douglas described our American tradition in terms strangely at odds with Justice Black's invocation of Jefferson's wall of separation: "We are a religious people whose institutions presuppose a Supreme Being,"[31] Justice Douglas proclaimed.

These counterorthodox views were not without support in academe. Even as Justice Reed wrote his dissent in *McCollum*, a few scholars were suggesting that the Religion Clauses required only that government treat religions even-handedly, not that government separate itself altogether from them. To support their position, they advanced an account of the generative history of the Religion Clauses sharply at odds with the one offered by the *Everson* Court. This alternative history made two points: first, the Virginia disestablishment struggle was not typical of church-state relations in colonial and revolutionary America; second, even in Virginia, the strict separationists did not win the total victory portrayed by Justices Black and Rutledge (indeed, they contended that not even Jefferson and Madison favored the kind of strict separation embraced by the *Everson* Court).

The dispute over the history of the First Amendment's Religion Clauses is more than an academic squabble. As posited, it is a war to determine which camp wins the right to call the past to the bar as a "trump" witness—for both camps see the "correct" understanding of the period of formulation as determining the "correct" application of the Religion Clauses to given church-state controversies.

No single case better illustrates the stakes in the debate than the Supreme Court's 1983 decision in *Marsh v. Chambers.*[32] For years, the Nebraska legislature had retained a minister to open its sessions with prayer; indeed, the legislature had used public funds to compile and publish the minister's prayers as a book. Finally, a taxpayer sued to have these payments declared unconstitutional.

Nebraska's practice seemed clearly to violate the well-settled doctrine of strict separation; yet a historical argument, based upon facts drawn from the period of formulation, seemed to indicate that hiring legislative chaplains did not violate the Religion Clauses. The argument proceeded as follows: Justices Black and Rutledge identify Madison as the principal author of the First Amendment; Madison was a member of the committee in the First Congress that successfully recommended hiring chaplains for the House and Senate; therefore, the framers clearly did *not* understand the Religion Clauses to bar paying legislative chaplains from public funds.

In *Marsh*, the Justices faced a dilemma. The doctrines generated by *Everson* commanded one result; the historiography unleashed by the case commanded another. Six Justices, led by Chief Justice Burger, decided that history could "trump" doctrine. Thus, while emphasizing that a "historical trump" of doctrine would be appropriate only in a case where the "original intent" of the framers was clear, they upheld Nebraska's legislative chaplain scheme. Not since *Everson* had the Justices focused so intently and exclusively on the period of formulation in order to decide a case. And their commitment to a historiography that viewed the framing period as dispositive led them to disregard thirty years of doctrinal development in reaching their result.

Marsh illustrates the heuristic problem with the approach the Supreme Court took to the history of the Religion Clauses in *Everson*—an approach that became embedded in the Court's jurisprudence as a result of the opinions of the Warren Court.

Good historians deal with currents and crosscurrents as they build pictures of the past. Good lawyers are zealous advocates in service of a cause (with the desirable result always set *ex ante*), and to that end, they seize upon data favorable to their argument, exaggerate its importance, and extrapolate the conclusions they seek from the distorted picture they have created. Given this reality, it is not surprising that good lawyers often make bad historians—or that when lawyers use history to make arguments, they often use it one-sidedly.

Even the brief account of the Religion Clauses debate I have offered reveals that there is conflicting data from the period of formulation. The results have been what you would expect from lawyer-historians. Each advocate charges that the other fails to account for "crucial" evidence, yet each ignores equally "crucial" evidence against its own position. And neither produces a balanced picture of the period of formulation.

A second, and more fundamental, flaw flows from the shared premise that the key to interpreting the Religion Clauses is understanding the history of the period of formulation. By obsessively focusing on the period of formulation, both sides of the present debate engage in a profoundly antihistorical exercise: They fail to acknowledge the evolution of both religion and American society, and they fail to credit the concomitant changes in the relationship of religion and other institutions in American life.

History is the story of change over time. True, historians write histories of "periods"—indeed, as suggested above, we might write a better history of the period of formulation. But, even if it were available, the "perfect" history of the period of formulation would not alone provide the "perfect" interpretation of the Religion Clauses—for, in the interpretation of a constitutional text, it is not appropriate to "freeze" the moving picture of history at one frame, treating the snapshot thus produced as though it captured the whole story.

Moreover, freeze-frame history is singularly inappropriate when the constitutional text being interpreted is the Religion Clauses. In no area of constitutional law has there been such dramatic evolution—evolution that, in some ways, has completely transformed the terms of discussion and the institutions to which they apply.

The Warren Court embraced the freeze-frame approach to history taken by the *Everson* Court. It may have chosen a frame that is popular with law professors. But, it took an approach that was bound ultimately to lead to the now famous debate on constitutional interpretation between Justice Brennan and Edwin Meese[33]—a debate that will not be resolved satisfactorily until a more sophisticated approach to constitutional history is embraced.

The Definition of Religion

Our third topic is the Warren Court's considerable contribution to the effort to define the word "religion" in the constitutional text: "Congress shall make no law respecting an establishment of religion, or prohibiting the free exercise thereof."

While helpful in ascertaining the purposes of the Religion Clauses, the views of the framers offer little guidance in fixing the meaning of the word "religion." There is no doubt that, to the framers, religion entailed a relationship of man to some Supreme Being. Nonetheless, while they were theists themselves, there is no clear evidence that they wished to protect only theism. More importantly, the relationship between religion and government expressed by the First Amendment, like all constitutionally described relationships, can evolve as society and its needs change. And nobody can doubt that there has been a remarkable diversification of religious experience in the last two hundred years: there are far more blossoms in the theological garden than there were at the time of the adoption of the Constitution.

Despite this process of diversification, until fairly recently the predominant judicial definition of religion stressed traditional elements like theologies, sacraments, and, above all, worship of a deity. In 1890, the Supreme Court in *Davis v. Beason* stated: "[T]he term religion has reference to one's views of his relations to his Creator, and to the obligations they impose of reverence for his being and character, and of obedience to his will."[34] And, as late as 1931, Chief Justice Hughes concluded that "[t]he essence of religion is belief in a relation to God involving duties superior to those arising from any human relation."[35]

In its 1961 decision in *Torcaso v. Watkins*,[36] the Warren Court struck down a provision of the Maryland Constitution that had been used to deny a secular humanist appointment as a notary public because he refused to declare belief in God. The Court reasoned that, under the Establishment Clause, government cannot force a person to profess either belief or disbelief in any religion, and cannot aid theistic religions against nontheistic ones. Among the beliefs the Court explicitly identified as religious were Buddhism, Taoism, Ethical Culture, and secular humanism.

The Court shortly made it clear that *Torcaso* was not an eccentric ruling. In *Seeger*,[37] it offered one of the most detailed discussions of the definition of religion ever given by the Supreme Court. Construing the Universal Military Training and Service Act of 1948 requirement that those requesting conscientious objector status believe they live by "a relation to a Supreme Being," the Court characterized the question as "whether a given belief . . . occupies a place in the life of its possessor parallel to that filled by the orthodox belief in God."[38]

Although the *Seeger* Court couched the issue narrowly as one of statutory construction, its holding clearly implicated the meaning of the word "religion" in the constitutional text. Certainly, the Court strained the plain meaning of words and disregarded the evident intention of Congress to exclude nontheists from exemption. The Court presumably found such a distortion necessary because a literal construction, discriminating between theists and followers of other traditions, would have, as Justice Douglas noted in his concurrence, rendered the provision constitutionally vulnerable.

Seeger is not unambiguous. It purports to push the definition to a deeper level by placing within the ambit of religious belief all sincere beliefs "based upon a power or being, or a faith, 'to which all else is subordinate or upon which all else is ultimately dependent.'"[39] While these notions of subordination and dependence have some of the same indeterminacy as the parallel position standard, they do make clear that the Supreme Court had come substantially to accept protecting atheists and agnostics as well as members of traditional religions.

In 1970, in *Welsh v. United States*,[40] the Burger Court returned to the same section of the Selective Service Act that had been at issue in *Seeger*, and it extended *Seeger*. First, by holding that purely ethical and moral considerations were religious, it further blurred the distinction between religion and morality, at least when the conviction with which the latter is entertained approximates the intensity usually associated with more conventional religious belief. Second, it held that sincere petitioners might be denied the exemption only if their system of beliefs does "not rest at all upon moral, ethical, or religious principle but instead rests *solely* upon considerations of policy, pragmatism, or expediency."[41] *Seeger* had denied exemption to those whose views were "essentially" nonreligious, suggesting that a petitioner could have been denied an exemption even though his or her views had a substantial moral-religious component if the secular component were more substantial. *Welsh* foreclosed this interpretation.

Torcaso, *Seeger*, and *Welsh* suggest a willingness, in contexts raising free exercise questions, to adopt an expansive definition of religion. In my view, that willingness comports both with the Free Exercise Clause's concern for inviolability of conscience and with the diversity of contemporary religious experience. But, herein the problem with the Warren Court's work in the area. As Justice Rutledge put it:

> "Religion" appears only once in the [First] Amendment. But the word governs two prohibitions and governs them alike. It does not have two meanings, one narrow to forbid "an establishment" and another, much broader, for securing "the free exercise thereof." "Thereof" brings down "religion" with its entire and exact content, no more and no less, from the first into the second guaranty, so that Congress and now the states are as broadly restricted concerning the one as they are regarding the other.[42]

At present, the Court invalidates under the Establishment Clause those government programs that are undertaken for religious purposes, have effects that are primarily religious, or lead to impermissible governmental entanglement in the affairs of religion. To borrow the *Seeger-Welsh* test from the free exercise context and use it with present Establishment Clause doctrines would be to invite attack on all programs that further the ultimate concerns of individuals or entangle the government with such concerns. Doctrinal chaos might well result, and with it might come the wholesale invalidation of programs that, if analyzed in light of the values underlying the Establishment Clause, would be found benign. For example, the secularization movement in contemporary Christianity is unquestionably deserving of protection under the Free Exercise Clause. Yet the conclusion that secularization theology is a religion for Establishment Clause purposes might lead some to conclude that numerous humanitarian government programs should be regarded as unconstitutional.

Conclusion

A fourth and final point brings together the three already mentioned to highlight what might be the fundamental weakness of the Warren Court's work on the Religion Clauses.

Frequently it happens that a body of law develops, as if in a vacuum, with no regard of apparent awareness of cognate bodies of law with which it inevitably must connect. Such was the case with the Warren Court's work in each of the three areas that have been discussed.

Sherbert, which commanded a free exercise exemption for religious citizens whose privilege activity was burdened, never addressed the reconciliation of that command with the Court's doctrine on the Establishment Clause. The Establishment Clause cases never addressed the implications of the aggressive doctrine of separation they announced for a society committed, by the Free Exercise Clause, to a thinking religious sector. And the Court's attempt to define the constitutional concept "Religion" proceeded apparently without regard either for the free exercise or establishment implication of what was done.

The independent efforts of the Warren Court in each of the highlighted areas could not and did not remain independent forever. It is fair to say that the Burger Court, for at least a decade, continued to address the issues raised in a vacuum. Ultimately, the Court began to acknowledge the existing tensions, and began to speak of doctrinal disarray. And, in large measure, that is where we are.

The state of doctrine in this area is not good. The Warren Court built upon the work begun by the Court in the forties to help launch the enterprise of understanding the Religion Clauses. Its essential doctrinal instincts were rudimentary, but in the right direction. But, as with many new enterprises, mistakes were made. Now, informed by those mistakes, we must, in some sense, begin again.

Notes

1. 370 U.S. 421 (1962).
2. 374 U.S. 203 (1963).
3. 380 U.S. 163 (1965).
4. 366 U.S. 420 (1961); Two Guys from Harrison v. McGinley, 366 U.S. 582 (1961); Braunfeld v. Brown, 366 U.S. 599 (1961); Gallagher v. Crown Kosher Super Market, 366 U.S. 617 (1961).
5. Presbyterian Church v. Mary Elizabeth Hall Presbyterian Church, 393 U.S. 440 (1969).
6. 392 U.S. 83 (1968).
7. 367 U.S. 488 (1961).
8. 393 U.S. 97 (1968).
9. 392 U.S. 236 (1968).
10. 374 U.S. 398 (1963).
11. 319 U.S. 105 (1943).
12. 310 U.S. 296 (1940).
13. 308 U.S. 147 (1939).
14. 374 U.S. 398 (1963).
15. 366 U.S. 420 (1961).

16. 366 U.S. at 607.
17. 406 U.S. 205 (1972).
18. 98 U.S. 145 (1879).
19. Eisgruber and Sager, "The Vulnerability of Conscience: The Constitutional Basis for Protecting Religious Conduct," 61 *U. Chi. L. Rev.* 1245, 1247 (1994). See also Lupu, "The Trouble with Accommodation," 60 *Geo. Wash. L. Rev.* 743, 756 (1992).
20. Eisgruber and Sager, supra note 19.
21. 494 U.S. 872 (1990).
22. 330 U.S. 1 (1947).
23. 392 U.S. 236 (1968).
24. 374 U.S. 203 (1963).
25. 403 U.S. 602 (1971).
26. 330 U.S. at 33.
27. Id. at 9.
28. Id. at 15–16.
29. McCollum v. Board of Education, 333 U.S. 203, 244 (1948).
30. 343 U.S. 306 (1952).
31. Id. at 313.
32. 463 U.S. 783 (1983).
33. See *The Great Debate: Interpreting Our Written Constitution* (1986).
34. 133 U.S. 333, 342 (1890).
35. United States v. Macintosh, 283 U.S. 605, 633–34 (1931).
36. 367 U.S. 488 (1961).
37. United States v. Seeger, 380 U.S. 163 (1965).
38. Id. at 166.
39. Id. at 174.
40. 398 U.S. 333 (1970).
41. Id. at 342–43. Emphasis added.
42. Everson v. New Jersey, 330 U.S. at 32.

· 8 ·

THE WARREN COURT AND CRIMINAL JUSTICE

YALE KAMISAR

Many commentators have observed that when we speak of "the Warren Court," we mean the Warren Court that lasted from 1962 (when Arthur Goldberg replaced Felix Frankfurter) to 1969 (when Earl Warren retired).[1] But when we speak of the Warren Court's "revolution" in American criminal procedure we mean the Warren Court that lasted from 1961 (when the landmark case of *Mapp v. Ohio*[2] was decided) to 1966 or 1967.[3] In its final years, the Warren Court was *not* the same Court that had handed down *Mapp* or *Miranda*.[4]

The Closing Years of the Warren Era

The last years of the Warren Court constituted a period of social upheaval marked by urban riots, disorders on college campuses, ever-soaring crime statistics, ever-spreading fears of the breakdown of public order, and assassinations and near-assassinations of public figures.[5] Moreover, the strong criticism of the Court by many members of Congress and by presidential candidate Richard Nixon and the obviously retaliatory provisions of the Crime Control Act of 1968 contributed further to an atmosphere that was unfavorable to the continued vitality of the Warren Court's mission in criminal cases.[6]

In the closing years of the Warren era, the Court upheld the so-called informer's privilege (allowing the government to withhold the identity of its informant at a suppression hearing);[7] rejected the general assumption that errors of constitutional magnitude were not subject to the harmless error rule;[8] emphatically reaffirmed the doctrine that a defendant lacked "standing" to challenge evidence seized in violation of a third party's constitutional rights[9] (although such a requirement seemed inconsistent with the deterrence theory of the exclusionary rule, which had gained ascendancy, and most commentators had urged abolition of the "standing" requirement)[10] and repudiated the "mere evidence" rule, the rule banning the seizure of objects of "evidentiary value" only,[11] thus clearing the way for a system of court-ordered electronic surveillance that could satisfy Fourth Amendment standards.[12] (The following year, Congress granted law enforcement authorities broad powers to conduct continuing electronic surveillance for up to thirty days, with extensions possible).[13]

The Warren Court's performance in the field of criminal procedure does not fall into neat categories. Criminal defense lawyers did win some victories in the late 1960s,[14] but then they had lost some important cases earlier,[15] when the revolution in criminal procedure was supposed to be at its peak. Nevertheless, I think that in the main the revolution ended a couple of years *before* Earl Warren stepped down as Chief Justice.[16]

The Chief Justice's majority opinion in *Terry v. Ohio*[17] an important 1968 "stop and frisk" case, is a dramatic demonstration of the Warren Court's change in tone and attitude. Seven years earlier, of course, the Warren Court had imposed the Fourth Amendment exclusionary rule on the states as a matter of constitutional law.[18] But the Court was a good deal less exuberant about the exclusionary rule in 1968, when it upheld the police practice of "stopping" and "frisking" persons on less than probable cause to believe they were engaged in criminal activity. It recognized, almost poignantly, that "[t]he exclusionary rule has its limitations . . . as a tool of judicial control."[19]

I truly believe that if, say, in 1971 the Burger Court had written the same opinion in the "stop and frisk" cases that the Warren Court wrote in 1968, the Burger Court would have caught heavy fire for leaving the lower courts without adequate guidance concerning a widespread police practice and that its opinion would have been considered solid evidence of the emerging counterrevolution in criminal procedure.[20]

The Warren Court's approach in the 1968 stop-and-frisk cases contrasts sharply with the approach it had taken only two years earlier in *Miranda*.[21] There, greatly troubled by the lower courts' persistence in utilizing the ambiguity of the "voluntariness"–"totality of the circumstances" test to uphold confessions of doubtful constitutionality, the Court sought to replace the unruly traditional test with a relatively concrete and easily administered rule. But the stop-and-frisk cases established such a spongy test, one that allowed the police so much room to maneuver and furnished the courts so few bases for meaningful review, that the opinion must have been cause for celebration in a goodly number of police stations.[22] (At one point, for example, the Court said that an officer could frisk when he observes "unusual conduct" which leads him to conclude that "criminal activity may be afoot" and that the suspect may be armed and dangerous.)[23]

The Relevance of the Struggle for Civil Rights

As the late A. Kenneth Pye observed in the closing years of the Warren Court era, "The Court's concern with criminal procedure can be understood only in the context of the struggle for civil rights."[24] Continued Dean Pye:

> It is hard to conceive of a Court that would accept the challenge of guaranteeing the rights of Negroes and other disadvantaged groups to equality before the law and at the same time do nothing to ameliorate the invidious discrimination between rich and poor which existed in the criminal process. It would have been equally anomalous for such a Court to ignore the clear evidence that mem-

> bers of disadvantaged groups generally bore the brunt of most unlawful police activity.
>
> If the Court's espousal of equality before the law was to be credible, it required not only that the poor Negro be permitted to vote and to attend a school with whites, but also that he and other disadvantaged individuals be able to exercise, as well as possess, the same rights as the affluent white when suspected of crime.[25]

Moreover, as another commentator pointed out, writing at a time when the African American's struggle for civil rights and the response to that struggle by law enforcement officials were still vivid memories:

> What we have seen in the South is the perversion of the criminal process into an instrument of official oppression. The discretion which, we are reminded so often, is essential to the healthy operation of law enforcement agencies has been repeatedly abused in the South: by police, by prosecutors, by judges and juries. . . . We have had many reminders from abroad that law enforcement may be used for evil as well as for beneficent purposes; but the experience in the South during the last decade has driven home the lesson that law enforcement unchecked by law is tyrannous.[26]

When one thinks of "equal justice" the famous *Gideon* case[27] comes first to mind, but *Miranda* should not be overlooked. Especially when viewed against the background of *Escobedo v. Illinois*[28] (decided two years earlier), *Miranda*, too, may be regarded as an "equal justice" case.

Escobedo extended the role of counsel to the preindictment stage, but it was unclear whether the right to counsel came into play "when the process shifts from investigatory to accusatory—when its focus is on the accused and its purpose is to elicit a confession"[29] *or when* the process so shifts and one or more of the limiting facts in *Escobedo* are also present.[30] Mr. Escobedo had hired a lawyer (indeed, the lawyer had arrived in the station house and had tried unsuccessfully to meet with his client). Moreover, although not advised of his right to counsel, Mr. Escobedo had requested an opportunity to meet with his lawyer, but that request had been denied.

Although *Escobedo* grew out of a set of unusual facts, and arguably could be limited to these facts, the opinion had broad implications and at some places contained sweeping language. How grudgingly or expansively would the Court read this case? Would one who, unlike Mr. Escobedo, could not afford to hire a lawyer,[31] get the benefit of *Escobedo?* Would the person who, unlike Mr. Escobedo, was not smart enough or alert enough to ask for a lawyer on his own initiative fall under the protection of *Escobedo?*

Unhappy with *Escobedo* and its potential for expansion, many in the "legal establishment" maintained that the case should be read narrowly or limited to its special facts. In short, on the eve of *Miranda*, many were trying to use the inability to afford a lawyer and the ignorance of one's rights as convenient valves to limit the impact of a precedent they did not like.[32]

As we all know, this attempt failed. As Judge Henry J. Friendly, perhaps the most formidable critic of the Warren Court's criminal procedure cases, has noted, the equal protection argument is "a ground bass that resounds throughout the

Miranda opinion."[33] To quote Judge Friendly, as the *Miranda* Court saw it, "Equality [in the interrogation room] could be established only by advancing the point at which the privilege became applicable and surrounding the poor man with safeguards in the way of warning and counsel that would put him more nearly on a par with the rich man and the professional criminal."[34]

At her confirmation hearings, it is worth noting, Justice Ruth Bader Ginsburg defended *Miranda* largely on "equal protection" grounds:

> [The *Miranda* warnings provide information about] constitutional rights that should be brought home to every defendant.
>
> Now, sophisticated defendants will know them without being told, but the unsophisticated won't. . . .
>
> . . . [The *Miranda* rules] provide an assurance that people know their rights. It is an assurance that the law is going to be administered even-handedly because, as I said, sophisticated defendants who have counsel ordinarily will know about their rights. . . .[35]

Criticism of *Miranda*—From Opposite Directions

In *Gideon*, twenty-two state attorneys general filed an amicus brief on behalf of the defendant. But in *Miranda* and its companion cases twenty-six state attorneys general joined in an amicus brief urging the Supreme Court to "go slow" and to allow changes in the police-interrogation-confessions area to develop in nonconstitutional terms.[36] This led one observer to say that "the states had made a U-turn since *Gideon*."[37] I think not.

The twenty-two attorneys general who sided with Mr. Gideon did so on the understanding, inter alia, that the new constitutional right to appointed counsel in noncapital cases would not "attach" until the judicial process had begun.[38] The amicus brief concluded by urging the Court to "require that all persons *tried* for a felony in state court" be afforded the right to counsel.[39] In *Miranda*, however, the attorneys general were afraid that the Court would carry the "equality principle" to the point where it really bites—the police station.

That is why *Gideon* was a case that received much applause, but *Miranda* was the case that galvanized opposition to the Warren Court into a potent political force.[40] It cannot be denied that *Miranda* is a much-maligned case,[41] but it is also a much misunderstood one.

One source of confusion may have been that the *Miranda* Court led a goodly number to believe that it was "building on" and expanding *Escobedo* when it was actually making a "fresh start."[42]

As already indicated, at some places the majority opinion in *Escobedo* launched such a broad attack on the government's reliance on confessions that it threatened (or promised) to eliminate virtually all police interrogation of suspects. At one point, for example, in the course of rejecting the argument that if a suspect were entitled to a lawyer prior to indictment or formal charge, the number of confessions obtained by the police would be greatly reduced, the *Escobedo* Court retorted: "The fact that many confessions are obtained during this period points up its critical nature as a 'stage when legal aid and advice' are surely needed. The right to counsel would indeed be hollow if it began at a period when few confessions were obtained."[43]

At another point, the Court observed:

> We have learned the lesson of history . . . that a system of criminal law enforcement which comes to depend on the "confession" will, in the long run, be less reliable and more subject to abuses than a system which depends on extrinsic evidence independently secured through skillful investigation. . . .
>
> . . . No system worth preserving should have to *fear* that if an accused is permitted to consult with a lawyer, he will become aware of, and exercise these rights. If the exercise of constitutional rights will thwart the effectiveness of a system of law enforcement, then there is something very wrong with that system.[44]

The sweeping language and broad implications of *Escobedo* greatly troubled, one might even say alarmed, most law enforcement officials and many members of the bench and bar. Thus, on the eve of *Miranda*, a case that was to reexamine *Escobedo* and to clarify its meaning and scope, the nation's most respected lower-court judges (Charles Breitel, Henry Friendly, Walter Schaefer, and Roger Traynor) spoke publicly *in anticipation* of the Court's ruling and urged the Court to turn back or at least to reconsider where it was going.[45] Justice Schaefer, for example, voiced fear that "the doctrines converging upon the institution of police interrogation are threatening to push on to their logical conclusion—to the point where no questioning of suspects will be permitted."[46] And Judge Friendly warned that "condition[ing] questioning *on the presence of counsel* is . . . really saying that there may be no effective, immediate questioning by the police" and "that is not a rule that society will long endure."[47]

The Warren Court did not turn back, but *neither* did it hand down a ruling that these distinguished judges had anticipated and feared. The Court did not flatly prohibit police questioning of suspects. Nor did it condition such questioning *on the presence of counsel.* Nor did it require that suspects be advised of their rights by a defense lawyer or by a disinterested magistrate.

The Court continued to move in the same general direction as it had in *Escobedo*, but it "switched tracks"—it switched from a right-to-counsel rationale (which threatened to culminate in a right not to confess except with the tactical assistance of counsel) to a self-incrimination rationale (which gave the police more room to maneuver). A right-to-counsel rationale had almost no stopping point, but a self-incrimination rationale did—it required governmental compulsion.

But many members of the media and the public did not realize this. To them the important point was that the Court had *not* turned back.

At the time of the decision, many overlooked what has become increasingly clear in recent years—*Miranda* was very much a "compromise" between the old "totality of circumstances" test for admitting confessions and extreme proposals that—as the fear (or hope) was expressed at the time—would, in effect, have eliminated police interrogation of suspects. As the Court, per Justice O'Connor, pointed out twenty years after the *Miranda* case, *Miranda* "attempted to reconcile" two "competing concerns"—the need for police questioning as an effective law enforcement tool and the need to protect custodial suspects from impermissible coercion.[48]

Miranda left the police free to conduct general on-the-scene questioning even though the person being questioned was neither informed nor aware of his or her rights. And even when the suspect was in the station house and police interrogators were bent on eliciting confessions, it allowed them to obtain waivers of the right to remain silent and the right to the assistance of counsel (a) *without* the advice or presence of counsel, (b) *without* the advice or presence of a judicial officer, and (c) *without* any objective recording of the waiver transaction or the subsequent interrogation.[49]

At first *Miranda* was criticized for going too far. To a considerable extent, this was a result of the confusion over what the Court actually did. Many thought that because it had not read *Escobedo* narrowly, because it had not turned back, the Court had put additional restraints on the police. In short, to a considerable extent the Warren Court was criticized for what its critics had *anticipated* it would do (but what, it turned out, the Court did not really do).

In recent years, ironically, *Miranda* has been increasingly criticized for *not going far enough*—for example, for *not* requiring the advice of counsel before a suspect can effectively waive her rights or for not requiring a tape recording of how the warnings are delivered and how the suspect responds and, if the suspect does effectively waive her rights, for *not* tape recording the police questioning that follows.[50]

There is a good deal to be said for this criticism, but these commentators do not seem to appreciate the fact that in 1966 the Court was barely able to go as far as it did—that at the time it was probably not possible to persuade a majority of the Court to go one inch further than it did.[51] Moreover, the liberal critics of *Miranda* do not seem to realize that if, for example, the Court had explicitly required the police to make a tape recording, or even a verbatim stenographic recording, of the crucial events, it would have added much fuel to the criticism that it was exercising undue control over police practices—that it was "legislating."

How Did *Miranda* Fare in the Post-Warren Era?

Because *Miranda* was the centerpiece of the Warren Court's "revolution" in American criminal procedure and the prime target of those who thought the courts had become "soft" on criminals, almost all Court watchers expected the so-called Burger Court to treat *Miranda* unkindly. They did not have to wait very long.

The Impeachment Cases

The first blows the Burger Court struck *Miranda* were the rulings in two impeachment cases, *Harris v. New York*[52] and *Oregon v. Hass*.[53] The *Harris* case held that statements preceded by defective warnings, and thus inadmissible to establish the government's case-in-chief, could nevertheless be used to impeach the defendant's credibility if the defendant chose to take the stand in his or her own defense.[54] The Court noted, but seemed unperturbed by the fact, that some language in the

Miranda opinion could be read as barring the use of statements obtained in violation of *Miranda* for any purpose.

The Court went a step beyond *Harris* in the second impeachment case, *Hass*. In this case, after being advised of his rights, the suspect *asserted* his right to counsel. Nevertheless, the police refused to honor the request for a lawyer and continued to question the suspect. The Court ruled that here, too, the resulting incriminating statements could be used for impeachment purposes. Since many suspects make incriminating statements even after the receipt of complete *Miranda* warnings, *Harris* might have been explained—and contained—on the ground that permitting impeachment use of statements required without complete warnings would not greatly encourage the police to violate *Miranda*. But in light of the *Hass* ruling, when suspects assert their rights, the police seem to have very little to lose and much to gain by *continuing* to question them in violation of *Miranda*.[55]

The police need not advise suspects of their rights unless they are about to subject them to "custodial interrogation." The Burger Court construed the key concepts "custody" and "*custodial* interrogation" rather narrowly. If a suspect goes to the police station alone after an officer requests that he or she meet the officer there at a convenient time or even if a suspect "voluntarily" agrees to accompany the police to that site, *police station* questioning may not be "custodial interrogation" within the meaning of *Miranda*.[56]

What Is "Interrogation" Within the Meaning of Miranda?

Another frequently litigated issue is what constitutes "interrogation" within the meaning of *Miranda*. Considering the alternatives, the Burger Court gave this key term a fairly generous reading in *Rhode Island v. Innis*.[57] The Court might have taken a mechanical approach to *Miranda* and limited "interrogation," as some lower courts had, to instances where the police directly address a suspect. Or it might have limited interrogation to situations where the record establishes that the police *intended* to elicit a response, a difficult test for the defense to satisfy. The Court did neither. Instead, it held that *Miranda*'s safeguards are triggered whenever a person in custody is subjected either to express questioning or its "functional equivalent"—"interrogation" includes "any words or actions on the part of the police [other than those normally attendant to arrest and custody] that the police should know are reasonably likely to elicit an incriminating response from the suspect."[58]

The meaning of "interrogation" arose in an interesting setting in *Illinois v. Perkins*:[59] Suppose a secret government agent, posing as a fellow prisoner, is placed in the same cell or cell block with an incarcerated suspect and the secret agent induces the suspect to discuss the crime for which he has been arrested. Does this constitute "custodial *interrogation*" within the meaning of *Miranda?* No, answered the *Perkins* Court; "*Miranda* warnings are not required when the suspect is unaware that he is speaking to a law enforcement officer and gives a voluntary statement."[60]

Although *Perkins* has been sharply criticized for giving *Miranda* an unduly narrow reading and encouraging the police to use deception in order to obtain "uninformed confessions,"[61] I think the case was correctly decided. It is the impact on the suspect's mind of the *interplay* between police interrogation and police custody—each condition *reinforcing* the pressures and anxieties produced by the other—that makes custodial police interrogation inherently coercive. But in the "jail plant" situation, there is no interplay between the two conditions where it counts—in the mind of the suspect.

Miranda was designed to counter the inherent coercion generated by a police-dominated environment. But how can it be said that suspects are enveloped in a police-dominated atmosphere when they have no idea that the person with whom they are talking is a police officer or an agent of the police?[62] That is why, I believe, the Court reached the right result when it concluded that if it is not custodial police interrogation in the mind of the suspect it is not such interrogation within the meaning of *Miranda*.[63]

The Edwards Case: A Victory for Miranda in the Post-Warren Era

Although in the main the Burger Court interpreted and applied *Miranda* begrudgingly, the 1981 case of *Edwards v. Arizona*[64] is a notable exception. Unlike most *Miranda* cases, which deal with the need for, or the adequacy of, the warnings or the effectiveness of the suspect's alleged waiver of rights in immediate response to the warnings, *Edwards* involved what have been called "second-level" *Miranda* safeguards—those procedures *Miranda* tells us should be followed when suspects do assert their rights.[65]

In *Edwards*, the Burger Court gladdened the hearts of *Miranda* supporters by invigorating that case in an important respect. It held that when a suspect effectively asserts the right to a lawyer (as opposed to the right to remain silent)[66] he may not be subjected to further police interrogation "*until* counsel has been made available to him, *unless* [he] himself *initiates* further communication, exchanges, or conversations with the police."[67] In other words, once a suspect effectively exercises the right to counsel, the police cannot try to change the suspect's mind; they must wait to see whether she changes her mind on her own initiative. A valid waiver of the right to counsel cannot be established by showing only that the suspect responded further to police-initiated custodial interrogation even though she was given a fresh set of *Miranda* warnings at a subsequent interrogation session.

Edwards has been called "the Burger Court's first clear-cut victory for *Miranda*."[68] Indeed, *Edwards* (and its progeny) may be called the *only* clear-cut victory for *Miranda* since the Warren Court disbanded. It is a formidable rule, one that must worry every experienced interrogator, and in recent years it has become still more formidable—in some respects.

The rule applies even when the police want to question a suspect about a crime *unrelated* to the subject of their initial interrogation.[69] Moreover, as the Court recently held in *Minnick v. Mississippi*,[70] once a suspect invokes the right to counsel the police may not reinitiate interrogation in the absence of counsel *even if the suspect has been allowed to consult with an attorney in the interim*.[71]

The Weaknesses in the Edwards Rule

The post-Warren Supreme Court gave us *Edwards*, but the Court giveth and the Court taketh away. The Court has created two significant weaknesses in the *Edwards* rule (or, if one prefers to state it another way, allowed two good-sized weaknesses in the rule to develop).

The Court has told us that even though a suspect had earlier invoked the right to counsel and at no time had explicitly "invited" or "initiated" conversation about the subject matter of the case, she may furnish the police an opportunity to recommence interrogation simply by asking an officer, "What's going to happen to me now?" or presumably, "What comes next?"[72] Such comments strike me as expressions of concern, anxiety, or confusion *normally attendant* to arrest, removal from the scene of arrest, or transportation to the station house—*not* evidence of a generalized desire or willingness to discuss the subject matter of the investigation. Nevertheless, according to the Court, these simple and understandable questions dismantle the safeguards established by *Edwards*.

The other substantial gap in the *Edwards* rule created by the Court (or at least not filled by it) is the very recent decision in *Davis v. United States*.[73] In this case the Court drew a sharp line between those suspects who "*clearly*" assert their right to counsel (thereby triggering *Edwards*) and those who only make an ambiguous or equivocal reference to an attorney that might or might not be an assertion of the right to counsel. (E.g., "Maybe I should talk to a lawyer" or "Do you think I need an attorney here?") In the latter situation the police may immediately begin interrogating the suspect without asking any questions designed to clarify whether the suspect really meant to invoke the right to counsel.

I believe the approach adopted by the *Davis* Court is unsound. An ambiguous reference to counsel should not be totally ignored because it fails to satisfy a certain level of clarity. The police should be required to respond to such references by asking narrow clarifying questions designed to ascertain whether the suspect actually wishes to assert his or her right to a lawyer. Otherwise, the right to counsel turns not on the suspect's choice, but on the clarity with which he or she expresses that choice.[74]

Sociolinguistic research indicates that certain discrete segments of the population (women and a number of minority racial and ethnic groups) are far more likely than other groups to avoid strong, assertive means of expression and to use indirect and hedged speech patterns that give the impression of uncertainty or equivocality.[75] Moreover, since the custodial police interrogation setting involves an imbalance of power between the suspect and his or her interrogator(s), such a setting increases the likelihood that a suspect will adopt an indirect or hedged—and thus ambiguous—means of expression. Even within speech communities whose members do not ordinarily use indirect modes of expression, one who is situationally powerless, that is, aware of the dominant power of the person he or she is addressing, may also adopt a hedging speech register.

To borrow a phrase from Justice Souter's concurring opinion in *Davis* (really a dissent on this issue), a custodial suspect, one who will usually be experiencing considerable stress and anxiety, should not be expected or required to "speak with the discrimination of an Oxford don."[76]

Edwards is a formidable rule—if a suspect is lucky enough not to ask an officer what is going to happen next or careful enough to assert the right to counsel with sufficient precision and directness. The trouble with the rule is that its application turns on very fine, subtle distinctions—too fine and too subtle for the real world.

Those suspects who fall under the rule of *Edwards* will be well protected by its thick armor. But many similarly situated suspects will fall outside the rule because it has a soft underbelly.

I am fairly confident that the Court that decided *Miranda* would have rejected the exceptions to the *Edwards* rule that have developed in recent years. On the other hand, I have to say (and I never thought I would say this about a *Miranda* case in the post-Warren Court era), that I think *Minnick* may go *too far* in favor of criminal suspects.[77] To put it another way, I believe at least some members of the *Miranda* majority would have balked at the application of the *Edwards* rule to the *Minnick* fact situation.

If a suspect requests a lawyer and, unlike the situation in *Edwards* and other cases, the police do as the suspect asks—actually permit or bring about a meeting between the suspect and his lawyer—why can't the police approach the suspect a second time and give him a fresh set of warnings? Under these circumstances a suspect has more reason to believe than most suspects do that if he asserts his right to counsel at the second session the police will honor that right. They already did so once before. Why would they not do so again?

What Does It Mean to Say That the Miranda Rules Are Merely "Prophylactic"?

Although supporters of *Miranda* were troubled by the "impeachment" cases and by decisions giving "custody" and "custodial interrogation" a narrow reading, they were troubled still more by Justice Rehnquist's opinion for the Court in *Michigan v. Tucker*.[78]

Tucker was a mild case of police misconduct—a very attractive case from the prosecution's point of view. First of all, the police questioning occurred before *Miranda* was decided, although the defendant's trial took place afterward. Thus, *Miranda* was just barely applicable.[79] Second, *Tucker* dealt with the admissibility not of the defendant's own statements—they had been excluded—but only with the testimony of a witness whose identity had been discovered by questioning the suspect without giving him a complete set of *Miranda* warnings.

Under the circumstances, the Court held that the witness's testimony was admissible. *Tucker* can be read very narrowly, but the majority opinion contains a good deal of mischievous broad language.

The *Tucker* majority seemed to equate the "compulsion" barred by the privilege against self-incrimination with "coercion" or "involuntariness" under the pre-*Miranda* "totality of circumstances" test.[80] This is quite misleading. Much harsher police methods were needed to render a confession "coerced" or "involuntary" under the pre-*Miranda* test than are necessary to make a confession "compelled" within the meaning of the self-incrimination clause. That, at least, is the premise of *Miranda*.

That was why the old "voluntariness" test for the admissibility of confessions was abandoned in favor of *Miranda*. That is why law enforcement officials so fiercely resisted the application of the self-incrimination clause to custodial police interrogation. And that is why, although his questioning had been mild compared to the oppressive and offensive police methods that had rendered statements inadmissible in the older confession cases, Ernesto Miranda's confession was held inadmissible.[81]

By lumping together self-incrimination "compulsion" and pre-*Miranda* "involuntariness" or "coercion" and then declaring that a *Miranda* violation is not necessarily a violation of the self-incrimination clause—it only is if the confession was "involuntary" under traditional standards[82]—the *Tucker* majority rejected the core premise of *Miranda.*[83] If this view of *Miranda* were correct, then it is hard to see what that landmark case would have accomplished by applying the privilege against self-incrimination to the proceedings in the police station.

There is another troubling aspect to *Tucker.* In the course of holding that under the circumstances of the case the witness's testimony was admissible, the Court "recognized" that the *Miranda* warnings "were not themselves rights protected by the Constitution," but only "prophylactic standards" designed to "safeguard" or to "provide practical reinforcement" for the privilege against self-incrimination.[84] No, not quite.

The *Miranda* Court did observe that the Constitution does not "require adherence to *any particular solution* for the inherent compulsions of the interrogation process as it is presently conducted,"[85] but it quickly added: "However, unless we are shown other procedures which are *at least as effective* in apprising accused persons of their [rights] and in assuring a continuous opportunity to exercise [them], the following safeguards [the *Miranda* warnings] must be observed."[86] Moreover, later in the opinion, the *Miranda* Court reiterated: "The warnings required and the waiver necessary in accordance with our opinion today are, *in the absence of a fully effective equivalent*, prerequisites to the admissibility of any statements made by a defendant."[87]

A decade after *Tucker* was decided, first in *New York v. Quarles*[88] and then in *Oregon v. Elstad,*[89] the Court reiterated *Tucker*'s way of looking at, and thinking about, *Miranda.* In both *Quarles* and *Elstad* the Court underscored the distinction between *actual* coercion by physical violence or threats of violence and *inherent* or *irrebuttably presumed* coercion (the basis for the *Miranda* rules); between statements that are *actually* "coerced" or "compelled" and those obtained *merely* in violation of *Miranda*'s "procedural safeguards" or "prophylactic rules."

Is it not proper for the Court to assure that any confession is not *actually* compelled in violation of the privilege against self-incrimination by establishing conclusive presumptions and related forms of prophylactic rules to "implement" or to "reinforce" constitutional protections—in order to guard against *actual* constitutional violations?

No, maintains Joseph Grano; *Miranda,* as the Court *now* characterizes what it did in that case, is an "illegitimate" decision.[90] "To permit federal courts to impose prophylactic rules [rules that may be violated without violating the Constitution] on the states," he contends, is "to say in essence that federal courts have supervisory power over state courts."[91] According to Grano, the Court lacks constitutional authority to overturn state convictions when the Constitution has not actually been violated.

Stephen Schulhofer and David Strauss strongly disagree. "A conclusive presumption of compulsion," maintains Schulhofer, "is in fact a responsible reaction to the problems of the voluntariness test, to the rarity of cases in which compelling pressures are truly absent, and to the adjudicatory costs of case-by-case decisions in this area."[92]

Supporting Schulhofer, Professor Strauss maintains that prophylactic rules are "a central and necessary feature of constitutional law."[93] "Under any plausible approach to constitutional interpretation," continues Strauss, "the courts must be authorized—indeed, required—to consider their own and the other branches' limitations and propensities when they construct doctrines to govern future cases."[94] According to Strauss, "[I]t makes much more sense to read into the Constitution a general requirement that its various provisions be interpreted in light of institutional realities than to insist that these realities be ignored."[95]

I agree with Professors Schulhofer and Strauss that it is not inherently improper for a court to use conclusive presumptions or other kinds of prophylactic rules. I agree, too, that such rules are a pervasive form of constitutional decision making.

Suppose *Miranda* had established a *rebuttable* presumption that any incriminating statements obtained in a custodial setting in the absence of *Miranda* safeguards (or equally effective procedures) is compelled, but that this presumption could be overcome if the suspect were a police officer, lawyer, or law student. Such a presumption would produce the same result a *conclusive* presumption would in at least 95 percent of the cases. But so far as I know everybody agrees that a court's responsibility to achieve accurate fact finding permits it to assign burdens of proof and to adopt rebuttable presumptions.

As Professor Strauss argues, if it is legitimate for a court to decide that evidence of voluntariness is legally immaterial in some cases (where the evidence is insufficient to overcome a rebuttable presumption), why should it be—how can it be—improper for a court to extend that approach to all cases?[96]

Miranda is based on the realization that case-by-case determination and review of the "voluntariness" of a confession in light of the totality of the circumstances was severely testing the capacity of the judiciary and that institutional realities warranted a conclusive presumption that a confession obtained under certain conditions and in the absence of certain safeguards was compelled. As Schulhofer and Strauss maintain, under any plausible approach to constitutional interpretation, the courts must be allowed to take into account their fact-finding limitations.

Another word about "prophylactic rules." A few years ago, in *Withrow v. Williams*,[97] it is worth recalling, the Court rejected the government's argument that since *Miranda*'s safeguards "are not constitutional in character, but merely 'prophylactic,'" federal habeas review should not extend to claims based on violations of these safeguards.[98] The Court, per Justice Souter, accepted the government's characterization of the *Miranda* safeguards, for purposes of the case, but not its conclusion.

As I read the opinion of the Court in *Withrow*, it said in effect: Yes, we have sometimes called the *Miranda* rules "prophylactic" (because, explained the Court, violation of these rules might lead to exclusions of a confession "that we would not condemn as 'involuntary in traditional terms'"),[99] but so what?

The Court went on to say that "'[p]rophylactic' though it may be, . . . *Miranda* safeguards 'a fundamental *trial* right'. . . . By bracing against 'the possibility of unreliable statements in every instance of in-custody interrogation,' [it] serves to guard against 'the use of unreliable statements at trial.'"[100]

A final word about establishing conclusive presumptions and promulgating other kinds of prophylactic rules. If, as has been charged, the Warren Court exceeded its constitutional authority in *Miranda*, then so did the Burger Court (in *Edwards*) and the Rehnquist Court (in *Roberson* and *Minnick*).

Edwards held, in effect, that when custodial suspects invoke their right to counsel, thereby expressing their belief that they are incapable of undergoing police questioning without legal assistance, there is a *conclusive presumption* that any subsequent waiver of rights that comes at police instigation, not at the suspects' own behest, is compelled.[101] In *Roberson*, which reaffirmed and extended the *Edwards* rule,[102] the Court spoke *approvingly* of "the bright-line, prophylactic *Edwards* rule,"[103] pointing out that "[w]e have repeatedly emphasized the virtues of a bright-line rule in cases following *Edwards* as well as *Miranda*."[104]

Minnick made the *Edwards* rule more formidable still.[105] In the course of his majority opinion in *Minnick*, Justice Kennedy made a comment about the *Edwards* rule that applies to *Miranda* as well: "The rule ensures that any statement made in subsequent interrogation is not the result of coercive pressures. *Edwards* conserves judicial resources which would otherwise be expended in making difficult determinations of voluntariness. . . ."[106]

Dissenting in *Minnick*, Justice Scalia (joined by the Chief Justice), protested that the Court's ruling "is the latest stage of prophylaxes built on prophylaxes."[107] As Justice Scalia described the *Miranda-Edwards* line of cases: *Minnick* was a prophylactic rule needed to protect *Edwards*, which was a prophylactic rule needed to protect *Miranda*, which was a prophylactic rule needed to protect "the right against *compelled self-incrimination* found (at last!) in the Constitution."[108]

Justice Scalia left no doubt that he was unhappy about the Court building prophylaxis upon prophylaxis, but I think his description of what the Court did in *Edwards*, *Roberson*, and *Minnick* is accurate. If the Warren Court went wrong in *Miranda* by establishing "prophylactic rules," the Courts that succeeded it have been repeat offenders.

Why the Initial Hostility to Miranda Has Dissipated

Overruling *Miranda* seems to be an idea whose time has come and gone. Why is this?

A major reason why *Miranda* evoked much anger and caused much concern *at first* is that many feared—as the *Miranda* dissenters led us to believe—that the landmark decision would strike law enforcement a grievous blow. Few press accounts of the case failed to quote from Justice White's bitter dissent, in the course of which he asserted that "the rule announced today will measurably weaken the ability of the criminal law to perform [its] tasks" and result in "a good many criminal defendants . . . either not [being] tried at all or [being] acquitted if the State's evidence, minus the confession, is put to the test of litigation."[109]

Moreover, by giving *Miranda* limited retroactive effect, by applying the new doctrine to all cases *tried* after the date of the decision—even though the police interrogation had taken place and the confessions had been obtained *before Miranda* had been decided[110]—the Court "gave the impression that *Miranda* had affected police interrogation far more than it actually had."[111] In the weeks immediately following *Miranda*, a number of self-confessed killers walked free. Although these cases were widely publicized,[112] what was rarely made clear to the public was that the confessions being tossed out "were only a relatively tiny, special group that were reached retroactively by the *Miranda* decision."[113]

By the early 1970s, "the view that *Miranda* posed no barrier to effective law enforcement had become widely accepted, not only by academics but also [by] prominent law officials."[114] More recently, a special committee of the American Bar Association's Criminal Justice Section reached the same conclusion. It reported that "[a] very strong majority of those surveyed—prosecutors, judges, and police officers—agree that compliance with *Miranda* does not present serious problems for law enforcement."[115] Still more recently, the Court, per Justice Souter, observed: "[In the 27 years since *Miranda* was decided] law enforcement has grown in constitutional as well as technological sophistication, and there is little reason to believe that the police today are unable, or even generally unwilling, to satisfy *Miranda*'s requirements."[116]

The initial hostility to *Miranda* has faded away for another reason. In its early years, the case generated a considerable amount of confusion and uncertainty. For example, did it extend to questioning "on the street"?[117] Did it apply to a person interviewed in her own home by an IRS agent?[118] Two years after *Miranda*, Judge Friendly voiced concern that "the Court may be moving toward a position that compulsion exists *whenever* an officer makes an inquiry, so that warnings *must always* be given."[119]

But a quarter-century after *Miranda*, much of the uncertainty it once generated has largely been dispelled. It is now fairly clear that absent special circumstances (such as arresting a suspect at gunpoint or forcibly subduing him) police questioning "on the street" or in a person's home or office is *not* "custodial." Nor is "roadside questioning" of a motorist detained pursuant to a traffic stop. As a general matter, the *Miranda* doctrine has been limited, as Judge Friendly hoped it would be, to the police station or an equivalent setting.[120]

Some of *Miranda*'s harshest critics make no secret of the fact that they are determined to topple the decision because of its "symbolic status as the epitome of Warren Court activism in the criminal law area."[121] The *Miranda* case *is* a symbol. But *which way* does that cut?

As Stephen Schulhofer has pointed out, symbols are important, especially "the symbolic effects of criminal procedural guarantees," for they "underscore our societal commitment to restraint in an area in which emotions easily run uncontrolled."[122] Even Gerald Caplan, one of *Miranda*'s strongest critics, recognizes that the case may be seen as "a gesture of government's willingness to treat the lowliest antagonist as worthy of respect and consideration."[123]

Should the "Fruits" of Miranda *Violations Be Admissible?*

Although it is highly unlikely that *Miranda* will be overruled, the Rehnquist Court may yet strike *Miranda* a heavy blow—by ruling that all the clues and physical evidence obtained as a result of a *Miranda* violation are admissible. The Court has not quite said this yet, but it came close to doing so in *Oregon v. Elstad* (1985).[124] In that case, in the course of ruling that the fact that the police had earlier obtained a statement from the defendant in violation of his *Miranda* rights did not bar the use of a second confession obtained when the police did comply with *Miranda*, the Court indicated that the "fruits" of *Miranda* violations should be admissible whether they are a second confession, a witness, or "an article of evidence."[125]

Nietzche once observed that the commonest stupidity consists in forgetting what one is trying to do.[126] *What was* the *Miranda* Court trying to do? It was trying to take away the police's incentive to exploit a suspect's anxiety and confusion by implying that they have a right to an answer and that it will be worse for the suspect if she does not answer.[127] How could we expect the police to comply with *Miranda* if we were to prohibit *only* confessions obtained in violation of that doctrine, but allow the use of everything these confessions brought to light?[128]

As one commentator recently noted: "Expert interrogators have long recognized, and continue to instruct, that a confession is a primary source for determining the existence and whereabouts of the fruits of a crime such as documents or weapons."[129]

The Lineup Cases: The Warren Court Decisions That Suffered the Cruelest Fate

Unlike the Warren Court's most publicized criminal procedure rulings, *Mapp* and *Miranda*, the lineup cases were explicitly designed to protect the innocent from wrongful conviction. Ironically, these were the Warren Court decisions that suffered the worst treatment at the hands of the Burger Court.

Although mistaken identification has probably been the single greatest cause of conviction of the innocent,[130] surprisingly the Supreme Court did not come to grips with this problem until the closing years of the Warren tenure. Then the Court seemed to make up for lost time.

In a 1967 trilogy of cases, *United States v. Wade, Gilbert v. California*, and *Stovall v. Denno*,[131] the Court leapfrogged case-by-case analysis of various pretrial identification situations and applied the right to counsel to identification in one dramatic move. "Since it appears that there is grave potential for prejudice [in] the pretrial lineup, which [absent counsel's presence] may not be capable of reconstruction of trial," the Court deemed counsel's presence essential to "avert prejudice and assure a meaningful confrontation at trial."[132]

Although the pretrial identification in *Wade* and *Gilbert* occurred after the defendants had been indicted, nothing in the Court's reasoning suggested that an identification that takes place before a defendant is formally charged is less riddled with dangers or less difficult for a suspect to reconstruct without the presence of counsel than one occurring after that point. Nevertheless, in *Kirby v. Illinois*[133] the Burger Court announced a "post-indictment" rule, one that enables law enforcement officials to avoid the impact of the *Wade-Gilbert* rule by conducting identification procedures before formal charges are filed.

Nor is that all. A year after *Kirby*, the Burger Court struck the *Wade-Gilbert* rule another heavy blow. Although the defendant made a forceful argument that the availability of the photographs at trial furnished no protection against the suggestive manner in which they may have been originally shown to the witness or the comments of gestures that may have accompanied the display, the Court held in *United States v. Ash*[134] that the *Wade-Gilbert* right to counsel did not apply to a pretrial photo-identification procedure—even though the procedure was conducted after the suspect had been indicted and even though the suspect could have appeared in person at a lineup.

Taken together, *Kirby* and *Ash* virtually demolished the original lineup decisions. Nevertheless, *in-theory* abuses in photographic displays and in preindictment lineups are not beyond the reach of the Constitution: a defendant may still convince a court that the circumstances surrounding his identification present so "substantial" a "likelihood of misidentification" as to violate due process.[135] But the Burger Court made this quite difficult to achieve.

Although it ought to suffice, an "unnecessarily suggestive" identification is not enough—the "totality of circumstances" may still permit the use of identification evidence if, despite the unnecessary "suggestiveness," "the out-of-court identification possesses certain features of reliability."[136] This is an elusive, unpredictable case-by-case test that, as might be expected, has not turned out to be any more manageable for the courts or any more illuminating for law enforcement officers than the pre-*Miranda* "totality of the circumstances"–"voluntariness" test.[137]

The Burger Court's decisions concerning pretrial identification may well be the saddest chapter in modern American criminal procedure. The Burger Court was "far more impressed than its predecessor with the importance of the defendant's guilt,"[138] but its harsh treatment of the 1967 lineup cases indicates its willingness to subordinate even the reliability of the guilt-determining process to the demands for speed and finality.

Search and Seizure in the Post-Warren Era: A Prolonged Campaign of "Guerilla Warfare"

When the Burger Court handed down the *Kirby* and *Ash* decisions it demonstrated how quickly and effectively it could cripple a disfavored Warren Court precedent (without flatly overruling it), but this development constituted an exception to the Burger Court's general approach in criminal procedure. In the main, in place of the counterrevolution in criminal procedure that many expected, "the Burger Court waged a prolonged and rather bloody campaign of guerrilla warfare."[139] This observation applies with special force to the law of search and seizure.

There are two principal ways to reduce the impact of *Mapp v. Ohio:* (1) by narrowing the thrust of the exclusionary rule, that is, by restricting the circumstances in which evidence obtained in violation of the Fourth Amendment must be excluded, and (2) by shrinking the scope of the amendment itself (e.g., diluting what amounts to "probable cause," making it easy for the police to establish "consent" to what would otherwise be an illegal search, and taking a grudging view of what constitutes a "search" or "seizure"), thereby giving the police more leeway to investigate crime and the defense fewer opportunities to invoke the exclusionary rule. On a few occasions the post-*Miranda* Court did decide some search-and-seizure cases in favor of the defense,[140] but in the main it substantially reduced the impact of the exclusionary rule *both* by cutting back on the application of the rule itself *and by* downsizing the scope of the protection against unreasonable search and seizure.

The "Deterrence" Rationale Comes to the Fore

For much of its life, the "federal" or "Fourth Amendment" exclusionary rule, first promulgated in the famous 1914 *Weeks* case,[141] rested not on the *empirical* proposition that it *actually deterred* illegal searches, but on what might be called a "principled basis." That principle was to avoid "sanctioning" or "ratifying" the police lawlessness that produced the proffered evidence, to keep the judicial process from being contaminated by partnership in police misconduct and, ultimately, to remind the police and assure the public that the Court took constitutional rights seriously.[142] That view—what might be called the "original understanding" of the exclusionary rule—is the dominant theme of *Mapp v. Ohio*.[143]

But in the post-Warren Court era, ways of thinking about the exclusionary rule changed. The "deterrence" rationale, and its concomitant "interest balancing," bloomed. Thus, whether the exclusionary rule should be applied was said to present a question "not of rights but of remedies"—a question to be answered by weighing the "likely 'costs'" of the rule against its "likely 'benefits.'"[144] By "deconstitutionalizing" the rule—by shifting the nature of the debate from arguments about constitutional law and judicial integrity to arguments about "deterrence" and empirical data—the critics of the exclusionary rule won some important victories.[145]

This is hardly surprising. The "costs" of the exclusionary rule are immediately apparent—the "freeing" of a "plainly guilty" drug dealer—but the "benefits" of the rule are much less concrete. As Professor Schulhofer has observed, "[The benefits] involve safeguarding a zone of dignity and privacy for every citizen, controlling abuses of power, preserving checks and balances. One could view these as pretty weighty benefits, perhaps even invaluable ones. But the Court has viewed them as abstract, speculative."[146]

It is difficult to read the post-Warren Court's search-and-seizure cases without coming away with the feeling that it did its "balancing" in an empirical fog and that its cost-benefit analysis—although it sounds objective, even scientific—simply gave back the values and assumptions the Court fed into it. Thus, if one takes the position that "no empirical researcher . . . has yet been able to establish with any assurance whether the [exclusionary] rule has a deterrent effect even in the situations in which it is now applied,"[147] as the post-Warren Court does, and one characterizes the rule's social costs as "substantial," "well known," and "long-recognized,"[148] as the post-Warren Court also did,[149] the outcome is quite predictable.

Yet is not all the talk about the "substantial costs of *the exclusionary* rule" misleading? Is it not *the Fourth Amendment itself*, rather than the exclusionary rule, that imposes these costs? The "substantial costs" said to be exacted by the exclusionary rule would also be exacted by *any other* means of enforcing the Fourth Amendment *that worked*. A society whose police obey the Fourth Amendment *in the first place* "pays the same price" as the society whose police cannot use the evidence they obtained because they violated the Fourth Amendment: *both societies* convict fewer criminals.

If a society relies on the exclusionary rule to enforce the Fourth Amendment, some "guilty" defendants will not be convicted. If a society relies on a viable alternative means of enforcing the Fourth Amendment, however (and critics of the exclusionary rule have often assured us that the alternatives they have in mind would be at least equally effective), then "guilty" defendants will not be set free—but *only because* they will not be searched unlawfully in the first place.[150] *The only time* the Fourth Amendment would not impose the "substantial societal costs" that critics of the exclusionary rule complain about would be if the Amendment were converted into "an unenforced honor code that the police could follow in their discretion."[151]

The Leon Case: The Court Adopts a So-Called Good Faith Exception

The "deterrence" rationale and its concomitant "cost-benefit" or "balancing approach" to the exclusionary rule reached a high point in *United States v. Leon* (1984),[152] the case that adopted a so-called good faith (actually a "reasonable mistake") exception to the exclusionary rule. In *Leon* the Court held that what it called the "marginal or nonexistent" benefits produced by suppressing evidence obtained in objectively reasonable but mistaken reliance on a subsequently invalidated search warrant "cannot justify the substantial costs of exclusion."[153]

Although *Leon* may appear to be little more than a routine application of the "cost-benefit" approach utilized in earlier cases, it is not. The earlier cases[154] were based on the assumption that the exclusionary rule—fully applicable in a criminal prosecution against the direct victim of a Fourth Amendment violation—need not also be applied in certain "collateral" or "peripheral" contexts because "no significant *additional* increment of deterrence [was] deemed likely."[155]

Leon was a search warrant case, and there is a good deal to be said for confining the "good faith" exception to the warrant setting.[156] But the case must be read in light of the Burger Court's general hostility to the exclusionary rule, and the Court's doubts that "the extreme sanction of exclusion," as the Court called it in *Leon*,[157] can "pay its way" in any setting, let alone a setting where the Fourth Amendment violations are neither deliberate nor "substantial." In the future, I fear, the Rehnquist Court may say that the same cost balancing that led to the admissibility of the evidence in *Leon* supports a "good faith" exception across the board. It is hard to believe that the Court adopted such an exception in *Leon* only to limit it to the tiny percentage of police searches conducted pursuant to warrants.

The *Leon* decision is especially hard to defend in light of a decision the Court rendered only a year earlier, *Illinois v. Gates*,[158] a case that dismantled the existing probable cause structure in favor of a mushy "totality of the circumstances" test. The *Gates* Court made it fairly clear that "probable cause" is *something less* than "more probable than not" (although how much less is anything but clear). At one point, the *Gates* Court told us that "probable cause requires only a probability or *substantial chance* of criminal activity."[159]

What Is a "Search" or "Seizure"? The Court Takes a Grudging View

"Probable cause" is the heart of the Fourth Amendment. But diluting the standard of probable cause is only one way that the post-Warren Court has reduced the protection against unreasonable search and seizure. "Search" and "seizure" are key words—and key concepts. For police practices need not be based on individualized suspicion or conducted pursuant to search warrants—indeed, are not regulated by the Fourth Amendment at all—unless they are classified as "searches" or "seizures." Thus another way to diminish the security against unreasonable search and seizure is to take a narrow, stingy view of what amounts to a "search" or "seizure." The Burger and Rehnquist Courts have done just that.

Thus, because, according to the Court, a depositor who reveals her affairs to a bank "assumes the risk" that this information will be conveyed to the government, she has no legitimate expectation of privacy as to the checks and deposit slips she exposes to bank employees in the ordinary course of business.[160] Similarly, because, we are told, one who uses the phone "assumes the risk" that the telephone company will reveal to the police the numbers she dialed, the government's use of a pen register (a device that records all numbers dialed from a given phone and the time they were dialed, but does not overhear oral communications) is not a search or seizure either.[161] Thus, so far as the Fourth Amendment is concerned, the police need neither a warrant nor probable cause nor, presumably, any cause, to use such a device.

Asks Tracey Maclin: "Does the Court really believe that we have no sense of privacy in the telephone numbers we dial from our homes or in the financial records we deposit in the bank? . . . How would you feel if, during your drive to work, the radio station began broadcasting the telephone numbers you had dialed over the last month? Or if, while reading the morning newspaper, you saw copies of all the checks you had written during the past year?"[162]

What makes the "assumption of risk" in these cases voluntary? If you want to participate in modern American life at all, do you not have to assume these risks?[163]

Although one takes sufficient precautions (for example, erects a fence and posts warning signs) to render entry on one's private land a criminal trespass under state law, police entry on and examination of that land is beyond the curtilage and thus unprotected by the Fourth Amendment.[164] Moreover, even land admittedly within the curtilage (for example, a fenced-in backyard) may not come within the protection of the Fourth Amendment. Thus, the Court informed a marijuana-growing defendant that the Constitution failed to protect him against police aerial surveillance because, even though he had completely enclosed his backyard with two high fences, he had "knowingly exposed" it to the public.[165] Evidently he should have placed an opaque dome over his backyard.

An examination of a person's trash bags can reveal intimate details about that person's business dealings, political activities and associations, consumption of alcohol, and sexual practices. (Archaeologists tell us that if we want to find out what is really going on in a community, we should look at its garbage.) Nevertheless, the Rehnquist Court held that the police may rip open the sealed opaque trash bags one leaves at the curb for garbage pick-up and rummage through their contents for evidence of crime without engaging in a "search."[166] Thus this police investigatory technique, too, is completely uncontrolled by the Constitution.

The Rehnquist Court has also given the crucial term "seizure" a narrow reading. In 1991, for example, the Court told us that if armed police board an interstate bus at a scheduled intermediate stop, announce their mission is to detect drug traffickers, *randomly* approach a passenger, ask to see his bus ticket and driver's license, and then ask permission to search his luggage—a police practice that some lower courts "have compared to the tactics employed by fascist and totalitarian regimes of a bygone era"[167]—no "seizure" takes place. Under these circumstances, the Court told us, a reasonable person would feel free to terminate the encounter or to ignore the police presence and go about his or her business.[168] In other words, we are supposed to believe that with a police officer towering over him and at least partially blocking the narrow bus aisle, a reasonable bus passenger would feel free to *just say no*. We are supposed to believe that with a police officer "in his face," a reasonable passenger would feel free to tell the officer that he wanted to finish reading a *Sports Illustrated* article or return to the crossword puzzle he was working on—or just go to sleep.

What Constitutes a "Consent" to an Otherwise Illegal Search or Seizure? The Court Takes a Relaxed View

Although the post-Warren Courts have taken a grudging view of what constitutes a "search" or "seizure" within the meaning of the Fourth Amendment, they have taken a relaxed view of what constitutes a consent to an otherwise illegal search or seizure. "Consent" is law enforcement's trump card. It is the easiest and most propitious way for the police to avoid the problems presented by the Fourth Amendment. Thus, the protection afforded by the Amendment will vary greatly depending on how difficult or easy it is for the police to establish consent. *Schneckloth v. Bustamonte*[169] made it all too easy.

If an officer lacks authority to conduct a search, he may request permission to search, but he cannot *demand* it. To many people who confront the police, however, the distinction is very thin—or nonexistent. "[W]hat on their face are merely words of request take on color from the officer's uniform, badge, gun and demeanor."[170]

All the police have to do to make the distinction between "request" and "demand" meaningful is to advise a person that he has a right to refuse an officer's "request" and that such a refusal will be respected. But the *Schneckloth* Court dismissed such a requirement as "thoroughly impractical."[171] That such a warning would undermine what the Court called "the legitimate need for [consent] searches"[172] is quite clear; that such a warning would be "impractical" (as that word is normally defined) is not at all clear.

After *Schneckloth*, a person may effectively consent to a search even though he was never informed—and the government has failed to demonstrate that he was ever aware—that he had the right to refuse the officer's "request" to search his person, automobile, or home. After *Schneckloth*, the criminal justice system, in one important respect a least, can (to borrow a phrase from *Escobedo*) "depend for its continued effectiveness on the citizens' abdication through unawareness of their constitutional rights."[173]

More recently, in *Illinois v. Rodriguez*,[174] the Rehnquist Court held that a warrantless entry of one's home is valid when the police reasonably, but mistakenly, believe that a third party (in this case, a girlfriend who had in fact moved out of the apartment) possesses common authority over the premises. Thus, even though (a) no magistrate has authorized the search, (b) no probable cause supports the search, and (c) no exigency requires prompt action, the police may invade a person's home on the basis of the "seeming consent" of a third party.

The *Rodriguez* dissenters forcefully argued that when confronted with the choice of relying on the consent of a third party or obtaining a warrant, the police "should secure a warrant and must therefore accept the risk of error should they instead choose to rely on consent."[175] But the majority was not impressed: "What [a person] is assured by the Fourth Amendment . . . is not that no government search of his house will occur unless he consents; but that no such search will occur that is 'unreasonable'"[176]—and a search is not unreasonable when the police "reasonably (though erroneously) believe that the person who has consented to their entry is a resident of the premises."[177]

Is the Exclusionary Rule the Enemy of the Fourth Amendment?

A critic of the exclusionary rule might take all the search-and-seizure cases I have discussed (as well as others I have not) and throw them back at me. All that I have demonstrated, she might say, is that the exclusionary rule is *the enemy* of the Fourth Amendment. For the rule puts tremendous pressure on the courts to avoid "freeing a guilty defendant" and the courts respond by watering down the rules governing search and seizure. If the exclusionary rule had not been imposed on the states, she might argue, the Fourth Amendment would never have been construed as narrowly as it has been.

But a meaningful tort remedy or *any other effective alternative* to the exclusionary rule would also put strong pressure on the courts to water down the rules governing search and seizure. As Monrad Paulsen pointed out shortly before the *Mapp* case was decided, "*Whenever* the rules are enforced by meaningful sanctions, our attention is drawn to their content. The comfort of Freedom's words spoken in the abstract is always disturbed by their application to a contested instance. *Any* rule of police regulation *enforced in fact* will generate pressures to weaken the rule."[178]

Disparaging the exclusionary rule, Judge (later Justice) Benjamin Cardozo once said of it: "The criminal is to go free because the constable has blundered."[179] This is the most famous criticism of the rule and surely the best one-sentence argument ever made against it. Cardozo made this statement some seven decades ago, but it would make a snappy ten-second "sound bite" today.

In the post-Warren Court era, however, the criminal has "gone free" *less and less* because the exclusionary rule has been greatly narrowed by a "good faith" exception and other restrictions and because, as I have tried to show, the scope of the Fourth Amendment *itself* has shrunk quite significantly.

Seven decades ago, when Cardozo delivered his famous one-liner (and, I am willing to concede, even three decades ago, when the Warren Court imposed the exclusionary rule on the states), the law of search and seizure probably did unduly restrict the police—*on paper*. But *Mapp v. Ohio* has had a large impact. Whether or not the Warren Court intended this result or foresaw it, *Mapp* and its progeny have brought about a great clarification and simplification of the law of search and seizure—almost always *in favor* of the police.

This is probably the price we have had to pay for the exclusionary rule—or the price we would have had to pay for any remedy that *actually worked*. But that price *has been* paid.

Cardozo's famous epigram is outdated. The time has come to revise it. And, as revised, that epigram becomes a powerful argument *in favor* of the exclusionary rule: *Nowadays*, the criminal does not "go free" because the constable has made an honest blunder or a technical one. The post-*Mapp* cases have provided the police with so much room to operate without fear of the exclusionary rule that *nowadays* the criminal *only* "goes free" if and when the constable has *flouted* the Fourth Amendment—if and when he has blundered *badly*.

The "Selective Incorporation" Doctrine—And Its Impact on the Fourth Amendment Exclusionary Rule

The "total incorporation" doctrine—the view, advocated most notably by Justice Hugo Black,[180] that the Fourteenth Amendment "incorporates" all of the guarantees found in the Bill of Rights and applies them to the states in the same manner that they apply to the federal government—has never commanded a majority.[181] But during the Warren Court era the "selective incorporation" doctrine came to the fore, and, as a practical matter, produced the same results the "total incorporation" doctrine would have brought about.[182]

Under the "selective incorporation" approach, "[o]nce the Court had determined, upon analysis of the whole of a [Bill of Rights] guarantee, that the guarantee protected a fundamental right, that guarantee 'would be enforced against the States under the Fourteenth Amendment according to the same standards [that apply] against federal encroachment.'"[183] In less than a decade, in a series of cases beginning with *Mapp*, "the Court's conception of what was fundamental was expanded to include all the significant provisions of the Bill of Rights."[184]

In *Malloy v. Hogan*,[185] holding that the privilege against self-incrimination was a fundamental right and thus safeguarded against state action under the applicable federal standard of the Fifth Amendment, the Warren Court "undisputably established that selective incorporation had become the majority view."[186] As Professors LaFave and Israel have observed:

> A series of cases decided during the remainder of the decade reaffirmed the position taken in *Malloy*. Those cases held applicable to the states, under the

> same standards applied to the federal government, the Sixth Amendment rights to a speedy trial, to a trial by jury, to confront opposing witnesses, and to compulsory process for obtaining witnesses, and the Fifth Amendment prohibition against double jeopardy. In each case, the Court relied squarely upon a selective incorporation analysis. Moreover, in *Duncan v. Louisiana*, the Court noted that . . . the crucial issue was not whether a particular guarantee was fundamental to every "fair and equitable" criminal justice system "that might be imagined," but whether it was fundamental "in the context of the criminal processes maintained by the American states."[187]

The fact that the "incorporated" Bill of Rights guarantee applied to the states to the same extent that it applied to the federal government had an unfortunate side effect—one that Justice John Harlan, a formidable critic of "selective incorporation," was quick to flag. The only way to "temper" the "incorporated" Bill of Rights provision in order to "allow the States more elbow room," Harlan pointed out, was to dilute the federal guarantee itself.[188] Thus the many Supreme Court cases arising from state courts that narrowly and grudgingly interpret the scope of the protection against unreasonable search and seizure *apply to federal*, as well as state, prosecutions. Nor is that all.

Although Justice Tom Clark, the author of the *Mapp* opinion, presented as many reasons for the exclusionary rule as he could possibly muster,[189] his essential position, as Francis Allen observed at the time, was that "the exclusionary rule is part of the Fourth Amendment; the Fourth Amendment is part of the Fourteenth; therefore the exclusionary rule is part of the Fourteenth."[190] As a result, critics of *Mapp* had to direct their fire at the efficacy, validity, and constitutional basis of the "federal" or "Fourth Amendment" exclusionary rule itself, that is, the long-established rule excluding illegally seized evidence in *federal* prosecutions. This they have done with great force and considerable success.

At the time of *Mapp*, the "federal exclusionary rule" seemed quite secure.[191] But the "storm of controversy" over *Mapp* engulfed the "federal exclusionary rule" as well.[192] Thus the future of the 1914 federal rule, which had seemed so bright *before* the Warren's Court's revolution in criminal procedure got under way, is now rather clouded.

Another word about the exclusionary rule—both the Fourth Amendment kind and the Fourteenth Amendment variety. The reasoning the post-Warren Court has employed in the search-and-seizure cases outruns the results that have been reached to date. If, as the Court has told us, any search-and-seizure exclusionary rule must "pay its way" by deterring official misconduct[193] and if, as it has also told us, the deterrent effect of the exclusionary rule has never been established (to the satisfaction of the post-Warren Court at any rate),[194] why stop with only a narrowing of the exclusionary rule? Why not abolish the rule altogether?

Fortunately, law is not a syllogism. I very much doubt that the current Court will carry the way it talks about, and thinks about, the search-and-seizure exclusionary rule to its logical conclusion. I believe rather that a majority of the Justices are prepared to "live with" what they would probably call a "pruned" exclusionary rule and a "workable" Fourth Amendment (or what I would call a "battered" exclusionary rule and a "shrunken" Fourth Amendment).

The principal danger lies elsewhere. Now that the search-and-seizure exclusionary rule rests on an "empirical proposition" rather than a "principled basis"—now that application of the exclusionary rule presents a question not of "rights" but of "remedies"—the rule is almost defenseless against congressional efforts to repeal it (most likely by a statute that would purport to replace the rule with what we shall be assured is an "effective" tort remedy).

Why Was Gideon Warmly Applauded, But *Mapp* and *Miranda* Widely Criticized?

So far, I have said nothing about the famous *Gideon* case,[195] the *only* Warren Court criminal procedure decision in favor of criminal defendants that was greeted by widespread applause. What accounts for *Gideon*'s popularity?

An untrained, unrepresented, and often uneducated person trying to defend himself as best he can in a public courtroom makes a highly visible and most disconcerting spectacle. But few of us have ever seen or thought much about the plight of an individual who is being searched illegally in a poor neighborhood or "grilled" vigorously in the backroom of a police station.

Many of the people who accepted the *Gideon* principle "in principle" soon qualified their support or withdrew it completely when the Warren Court applied the principle to the point where it really bites—to custodial interrogation. Thurman Arnold may have provided as good an explanation as any for why *Gideon* received a warm reception but *Mapp* and *Miranda* evoked a hostile reaction. And Arnold made the point long before the Warren Court ever assembled. Too many people, he commented, are roused by any violation of "the symbol of a ceremonial trial," but "left unmoved by an ordinary nonceremonial injustice."[196]

Is Any Decision Restricting Police Powers Likely to be Criticized?

It was not the Warren Court's efforts to strengthen the rights of the accused *in the courtroom*, but its "activism" in the pre-trial "police practices" area that led many to believe that it was "too soft" on crime. It was the Court's search-and-seizure and confession cases that made it a major political issue in the 1968 presidential campaign.

It is hard to think of a single significant ruling against the police by *any* Supreme Court that has not evoked strong criticism. And the criticism has come from *opposite* directions. Either we are told that the ruling turns too heavily on the particular facts of the case and thus fails to provide clear-cut guidance for the future *or* we are told that the ruling is too broad and inflexible and thus demonstrates that the Court is acting like a legislature rather than a court. Almost every Supreme Court decision that has imposed some restraints on law enforcement can be, and I believe has been, criticized on one of these grounds or the other.

Is it any wonder that one gets the uncomfortable feeling that the police just want the Court to go away? That they resent and resist *any* external control—whether it comes from a civil rights commission or a civilian review board or a court?

When *Escobedo* was decided in 1964, it was severely criticized for being much too fuzzy—although it contained some sweeping language it also contained very narrow language that arguably limited the case to its special facts.[197] Then came *Miranda*. The *Miranda* Court seemed to be responding to the criticism of *Escobedo*. *This time* it seemed to be striving hard to provide the guidance it had failed to furnish in *Escobedo*. But *this time* the Justices caught heavy fire for *not* handling the cases before them on an individualized basis, but providing too much guidance in the abstract; for deciding too many things in "one gulp"; and for promulgating rules that were *too* specific, too rigid, and too inflexible.

The requirement that the police issue the now-familiar warnings and obtain valid waivers before subjecting a custodial suspect to interrogation is probably the feature of the *Miranda* case that has caught the heaviest fire. But this aspect of the case should have disturbed law enforcement officials the least.

As Professor Schulhofer has pointed out, three distinct steps were involved in *Miranda:* (1) informal pressure to speak (i.e., pressure *not* backed by legal process or any formal sanction) can constitute "compulsion" within the meaning of the Fifth Amendment; (2) this element of informal compulsion is present, indeed inherent, in custodial interrogation; and (3) the specified warnings or some equally effective alternative device is needed to dispel the pressure of custodial interrogation.[198]

The *first two* steps constitute "the core of *Miranda*."[199] If it had *stopped* with the first two steps and left law enforcement officials *to guess* at what countermeasures were needed to dispel the pressure of custodial interrogation, the Court would have incurred *far more* criticism.[200]

The required warnings may be *too feeble* a means of dispelling the pressure but it is hard to criticize the warnings on the ground that they "handcuff" the police. It would be more accurate to say that they serve to *liberate* the police. They enable the police to question a custodial suspect *without* running afoul of the Fifth Amendment.[201]

Did the Warren Court's Reform Effort Come at a Bad Time? Could It Have Come at a Better Time?

In his lively book, *The Self-Inflicted Wound* (an account of the Warren Court's revolution in criminal procedure), former *New York Times* Supreme Court reporter Fred Graham observes: "History has played cruel jokes before, but few can compare with the coincidence in timing between the rise in crime, violence and racial tensions [and] the Supreme Court's campaign to strengthen the rights of criminal suspects against the state. . . . The Court's reform effort could have come at almost any time in the recent past . . . [at a time] when it could have taken root before crime became the problem that it has become."[202]

When was that? According to the media, the claims of law enforcement officials, and the statements of politicians, we have *always* been experiencing a "crime crisis"—*at no time* in our recent, or not-so-recent, past has there *been a time* when "society" *could afford* a strengthening or expansion of the rights of the accused.[203]

In 1943 the Court held in *McNabb v. United States,*[204] in the exercise of its supervisory authority over the administration of federal criminal justice, that voluntary confessions should be excluded from evidence if they were obtained while the suspect was being held in violation of federal requirements that arrestees be promptly taken before a committing magistrate. The *McNabb* Court tried to do for the federal courts what, a quarter-century later, *Miranda* was designed to do for state, as well as federal, courts: bypass the frustrating "swearing contests" over the nature of the secret interrogation and reduce, if not eliminate, both police temptation and opportunity to coerce incriminating statements. The *McNabb* doctrine sought to do so by focusing on a relatively objective factor—the length of time a suspect was held by the police before being brought to a judicial officer to be advised of his rights.

Although it placed lesser restrictions on federal police than *Miranda* was to place on all police a quarter-century later, the *McNabb* rule was severely criticized by many law enforcement authorities and many members of Congress for barring the use of voluntary confessions. For example, in his testimony before a House subcommittee, the then head of the District of Columbia Police Department called *McNabb* "one of the greatest handicaps that has ever confronted law enforcement officers."[205]

Police officials and politicians were not the only ones unhappy with the *McNabb* decision. Most of the judges of the lower federal courts "were unsympathetic, if not openly hostile, toward a rule which suppressed evidence not only relevant but also cogent and often crucial in order to effectuate what seemed to them to be an exaggerated concern for individual rights."[206]

A year after the *McNabb* decision, at a time when a bill to repudiate it was gathering much support, the Court took another look at the doctrine in the *Mitchell* case.[207] With one eye on Congress, and stung by strong criticism from the bench and bar, as well as from police and prosecutors, the Court backed off; it wrote an opinion that could be read as limiting *McNabb* to its particular facts.[208]

As James Hogan and Joseph Snee, coauthors of the leading article on the *McNabb* doctrine, have noted: "The Supreme Court's decision in the *Mitchell* case sent the *McNabb* rule into eclipse. To the judges of the lower federal courts, who had viewed the earlier decision with ill-concealed astonishment and apprehension, the *Mitchell* case signaled a face-saving retreat by the Court from the untenable position which it had occupied the year before."[209]

Some years later, the Court revived and reaffirmed *McNabb*, first in *Upshaw v. United States*[210] and then *in Mallory v. United States*[211] (from 1957 on, the rule was often called the *McNabb-Mallory* rule or simply the *Mallory* rule), but the storm of controversy over the rule never subsided:

> The *Mallory* decision was greeted by law enforcement officials of the District of Columbia (where its impact was greatest) with something bordering on panic. The Chief of the Metropolitan Police Department declared (hyperbolically, it is hoped) that the decision renders the Police Department "almost totally ineffective." There were loud demands for a legislative re-examination of the law of arrest, and in the Congress bills were introduced either to expand the period of allowable detention or to abolish the *McNabb* rule itself.[212]

More bills were introduced to repeal, or at least soften, the doctrine, and in 1968 a law was finally enacted that badly crippled it.[213] (Because the *McNabb-Mallory* doctrine was a rule of evidence formulated in the exercise of the Court's supervisory authority over the administration of federal criminal justice, it was subject to repeal or revision by the Congress.)

The experience with the *McNabb-Mallory* rule is strong evidence that the 1940s and 1950s were hardly auspicious times for the Court to do what it was to do in *Miranda*—deem custodial interrogation by state police, as well as federal, "inherently coercive." Indeed, when, in the 1944 case of *Ashcraft v. Tennessee*,[214] a majority of the Court called *thirty-six hours of continuous relay interrogation* "inherently coercive," it evoked a powerful dissent by three Justices who severely criticized the majority for departing from the traditional "voluntariness" test.[215]

In another coerced confession case, one decided in 1949 (*Watts v. Indiana*), concurring Justice Robert Jackson warned that our Bill of Rights, as interpreted by the Court up to that time, imposed "the maximum restrictions upon the power of organized society over the individual that are compatible with the maintenance of organized society itself"—good reason for not indulging in any further expansion of them.[216]

Were the 1950s a good time to impose the search-and-seizure exclusionary rule on the states? When the California Supreme Court adopted the exclusionary rule on its own initiative in 1955,[217] the cries of protest were almost deafening. Prominent law enforcement officials called the exclusionary rule "the 'Magna Carta' for the criminals" and "catastrophic as far as efficient law enforcement is concerned" and warned that it had "broken the very backbone of narcotics enforcement."[218]

What of the 1930s? In 1935 Governor Herbert Lehman opened a conference on crime by warning: "There is no question that in recent years there has come a substantial increase in organized crime. The professional criminal has become bolder. . . . We must take steps to increase the certainty of punishment following crime. . . . We must have fewer legal technical loopholes in trials and appeals."[219]

The New York gathering on crime was not a unique event in those troubled times. The U.S. attorney general also called a conference on crime, and similar conferences were held in various states.[220] The public was so alarmed by the apparent increase in crime that a U.S. Senate investigating committee, chaired by Royal Copeland of New York, scoured the country for information and advice that could lead to a national legislative solution.[221] At these 1933 congressional hearings, witnesses attacked virtually every procedural safeguard found in the Bill of Rights.[222]

Going back still further, in 1931 the famous criminologist Harry Elmer Barnes voiced fear that the repeal of prohibition would trigger "an avalanche of crime"—as thousands of crooks, chased out of the booze business, would return to their old rackets.[223] He warned that "the only effective check we can think of . . . would be to turn our cities over for the time being to the United States Army and Marines."[224] Transferring the Marines from Central America to the streets of Chicago, added Barnes, "might not only promote the checking of the crime menace but also solve at one and the same time our diplomatic relations with Central America."[225]

"Every generation supposes that its own problems are new, unknown to its forefathers."[226] To most of those who lived during that period, the 1930s (as usual) was *not* a time for strengthening the rights of the accused. Rather it seemed to be a period when (as usual) criminal procedural safeguards had already been stretched to the breaking point.

Legislative Rulemaking vs. Constitutional Decision Making

I am sometimes asked if I would still be in favor of the search-and-seizure exclusionary rule or *Miranda* if the legislature were to provide more effective, or at least equally effective, protection for criminal suspects. My answer is the same one Charles Black gave when asked whether he would still be against capital punishment if he were sure it were being administered with perfect fairness, with divinely scrupulous and infallible fairness. Professor Black replied that that was like asking him, "Would you take trains if the earth were made flat, or would you fear they would run off the edge?"[227]

In 1968 the Congress dealt with the confession problem. How? By "repealing" both *Escobedo* and *Miranda* and offering nothing plausible in its place—nothing but the old elusive, unruly, and largely unworkable "totality of the circumstances"–"voluntariness" test.[228]

Judge Henry Friendly, the most powerful critic of the Warren Court's criminal procedure cases, warned that "the situation with which the Court was confronted in *Miranda* was sufficiently disturbing that those of us [who criticize the case] ought to search hard for alternatives rather than take the easy course of returning simply to the rule that statements to the police are admissible unless 'involuntary.'"[229] But Congress did take that easy course.

One might say that Congress pretended that *Miranda* never happened because it believed that violations of that case rarely if ever produced an untrustworthy confession. But the 1968 Congress also legislated in another area—lineups.

As discussed earlier,[230] a year after *Miranda* the Court at long last turned its attention to the problem of misidentification—a matter of serious concern in the administration of justice. "The problem here is not that of releasing an obviously guilty defendant because of the system's failure to respect his rights . . . [but] one of convicting the innocent."[231]

Although the Court dealt with the problem of misidentification by applying the right to counsel to lineups, this may not have been the best way to deal with the problem. It certainly is not the only way to do so. For example, in order to ensure that lineups are fairly conducted, a legislature might require that they be photographed and videotaped and that these records be produced in court. Or a legislature might remove identification procedures entirely from the police and place them in the hands of an expert and neutral administrative agency.

What alternative device did the Congress choose? None. It simply enacted a law purporting to repeal the lineup decisions.[232] I share Francis Allen's view that the congressional response (or lack of response) to this critical problem was "deplorable."[233]

It is sometimes said that the Warren Court's activism in the criminal procedure area removed both the incentive and opportunity to deal with these matters by legislative reform. Indeed, Chief Justice Warren Burger once said that "the continued existence of [the exclusionary rule] inhibits the development of rational alternatives."[234] But it is hard to take this argument seriously.

For many decades a large number of states had no exclusionary rule, yet *none of them* developed any meaningful alternative to the rule. Some forty-seven years passed between the time the federal courts adopted the exclusionary rule and the time the Court finally imposed the rule on the states, but in all that time none of the twenty-four states that still admitted illegally seized evidence on the eve of *Mapp*[235] had developed an effective alternative to the rule.

In short, a half-century of post-*Weeks* "freedom to experiment" with various ways to discourage police misconduct did not produce any meaningful alternative to the exclusionary rule *anywhere*.

One critic of the exclusionary rule has maintained that no alternative to the exclusionary rule will emerge until the rule is abolished because "[s]o long as we keep the rule, the police are not going to investigate and discipline their men, and thus sabotage prosecutions by invalidating the admissibility of vital evidence."[236] But this argument is not persuasive. How does the fear of "sabotaging" prosecutions inhibit law enforcement administrators from disciplining officers for committing the many unlawful searches that turn up nothing incriminating, in which no arrest is made, and about which the criminal courts do nothing?

To be sure, there is no shortage of *theoretically possible* ways, aside from the exclusion of evidence, to make the Fourth Amendment viable. But various commentators have called attention to the need for an effective alternative to the exclusionary rule and underscored the inadequacies of existing tort remedies or criminal sanctions against transgressing police since the 1930s.[237] The problem is not a lack of imagination or intellectual capacity. Rather it is a lack of political will.

Is there any reason to believe that today's or tomorrow's politicians are, or will be, any less fearful of crime and any more concerned about protecting people under investigation by the police than the politicians of any other era? Is there any reason to think that the lawmakers of our day are any more willing than their predecessors to invigorate tort and criminal remedies against law enforcement officials who commit excesses in their overzealous efforts to contend with "criminals" and "suspected criminals"?

Was the Warren Court's Revolution in American Criminal Procedure Bound to Fail?

Craig Bradley has forcefully argued that the Warren Court's revolution in criminal procedure has failed and that, given the inherent limitations of the judicial process, was bound to fail—"no Supreme Court, no matter how competent and regardless of its political leanings, could have done much better."[238] Observes Bradley:

> [I]n the area of criminal procedure, unlike any other field of Supreme Court endeavor, the doctrine must be clear, it must be complete, and it must be stable. It is in these respects that criminal procedure law has failed. The usual leisurely manner of constitutional decision making where the Supreme Court announces

> a rule one year and then answers the questions to which that rule gives rise over the next fifteen or twenty years is inappropriate in this field, where the police need clear guidance and where the penalty for police mistakes is high. . . .
>
> . . . .
>
> . . . The Court is never, by its nature, able to sit back and decide, apart from the cases before it, what the entire body of confession or search law should be like or to examine comprehensively what police behavior, in terms of arrest, booking, interrogation, identification procedures, and so on, is reasonable and what is not. A case-specific system necessarily leads to a patchwork system and to resulting confusion on the part of everyone involved in the process. . . .
>
> . . . .
>
> . . . The worst problem with the case method . . . is that it is not forward looking. It does not allow that Court, as an ordinary rulemaking body would, to anticipate future cases and to craft its rules, and the exceptions to those rules, with such cases in mind. Thus the Court is invariably left in the position of declaring a partial rule, such as the rule [about] when questioning must cease upon a suspect's invocation of the right to silence, that fails to deal adequately with the majority of subsequent cases that present related issues. . . . [239]

Few, if any, would deny that in the field of criminal procedure legislative rulemaking has advantages over constitutional decision making. But are the courts supposed to do nothing in the absence of legislative rulemaking? A legislature never *has* to act, but a court does; it must decide the case at hand.

I think there is much truth in Anthony Amsterdam's observation that "[t]he judicial 'activism' that [the Court's conservative critics deplored a generation ago], usually citing the Court's 'handcuffing' of the police, has been the almost inevitable consequence of the failure of other agencies of law to assume responsibility for regulating police practices."[240] As the late Herbert Packer said of the Warren Court's revolution in criminal procedure at a time when it was still taking place, "it is naive or disingenuous to expect the Court to hold its hand when its hand is the only one raised or raisable."[241]

Professor Packer called the Warren Court's landmark decisions "moves of desperation"—there was a law-making vacuum into which the Court felt it had to rush. Nobody else was policing the police, so the Justices felt they had to do so.[242]

It is easy enough to poke holes in this development, observed Packer, but what is the alternative? "If we can look nowhere else but to the courts," wrote Packer, "it is silly to ask whether the courts are doing an optimal job. One might as well ask whether surgery is optimally undertaken with a carving knife without revealing that on the particular occasion the surgeon has no other instruments at his disposal."[243]

The Warren Court did not accomplish nearly as much as its supporters hoped and its many critics in and out of law enforcement circles feared. But I for one am grateful that for a time the Supreme Court used its judicial resources in a determined effort "to alter significantly the nature of American criminal justice in the interest of a larger realization of the constitutional ideal of liberty under the law."[244]

Some day, perhaps (but not, I am afraid, in the lifetime of anyone now reading this book), the Court will be able to put down its carving knife in favor of the legislature's scalpel. In the meantime, it is comforting to know that, although battered and bruised, most of the Warren Court's famous precedents remain in place—waiting for a future Court to reclaim the torch.[245]

There is a distinct possibility, of course, that another Supreme Court will not reclaim the torch (at least not for a long time). Even so—"[b]y reason of what the Warren Court said and did, we now perceive as problems what too often were not seen as problems before. This is the dynamic of change, and that fact may well be more significant than many of the solutions proposed by the Warren Court."[246]

Notes

This essay is a revised and expanded version of the paper I presented at the University of Tulsa College of Law on October 10, 1994. At several places I have drawn freely on chapters I contributed to two collections of essays on the Burger Court—*The Burger Court: The Counter-Revolution That Wasn't* 62 (Blasi ed., 1983) and *The Burger Years* 141 (H. Schwartz ed., 1987).

1. See, e.g., Tushnet, "The Warren Court as History: An Interpretation," in *The Warren Court in Historical and Political Perspective* 1, 7 (Tushnet ed., 1993).
2. 367 U.S. 643 (1961).
3. See, e.g., Schulhofer, "The Constitution and the Police: Individual Rights and Law Enforcement," 66 *Wash. U. L.Q.* 11, 12 (1988), observing that in the field of criminal procedure "the 'real Warren Court'" emerged with the decision in Mapp v. Ohio, 367 U.S. 643 (1961). Some might argue that the Warren Court's revolution in criminal procedure commenced with Griffin v. Illinois, 351 U.S. 12 (1956), establishing an indigent criminal defendant's right to a free transcript on appeal, at least under certain circumstances. *Griffin* did foreshadow some of the cases handed down by the later Warren Court, but "it was only some years after [this] decision that a majority of the Court consistently took positions now regarded as characteristics of the Warren Court." Allen, "The Judicial Quest for Penal Justice: The Warren Court and the Criminal Cases," 1975 *U. Ill. L.F.* 518, 519 n.4.
4. Miranda v. Arizona, 384 U.S. 436 (1966).
5. See Graham, *The Self-Inflicted Wound* 14–16 (1970); Allen, supra note 3, at 539.
6. See note 5 supra. See also Bradley, *The Failure of the Criminal Procedure Revolution* 29–30 (1993); B. Schwartz, *Super Chief: Earl Warren and His Supreme Court—A Judicial Biography* 762–63 (1983).
7. McCray v. Illinois, 386 U.S. 300 (1967). The Court allowed the government to withhold the identity of its informant even when, as in *McCray*, the police act without a warrant. Where, apart from police testimony as to information supplied by an unidentified informer, there is insufficient evidence to establish probable cause, there is much to be said for utilizing an in-camera hearing, thus protecting the government from any impairment of necessary secrecy, yet still protecting the defendant from what could have been serious police misconduct. But the *McCray* Court did not suggest such a procedure. See generally 1 LaFave, *Search and Seizure: A Treatise on the Fourth Amendment* § 3.3(g) (2d ed. 1987).
8. Chapman v. California, 386 U.S. 18 (1967). See generally 3 LaFave and Israel, *Criminal Procedure* §§ 26(c), (d), and (e) (1984).
9. Alderman v. United States, 394 U.S. 165 (1969).
10. See generally 4 LaFave, supra note 7, at § 11.3; Kamisar, "Does (Did) (Should)

the Exclusionary Rule Rest on a 'Principled Basis' Rather Than an 'Empirical Proposition'?," 16 *Creighton L. Rev.* 565, 633–38 (1983).

11. Warden v. Hayden, 387 U.S. 294 (1967), overruling Gouled v. United States, 255 U.S. 298 (1921).

12. So long as *Gouled* remained on the books, once electronic surveillance was deemed Fourth Amendment activity, any proposal for law enforcement tapping and bugging, however carefully circumscribed, would have violated the rule articulated in *Gouled*, note 11 supra, that objects of "evidentiary value only" (as opposed to the instrumentalities or the proceeds of crime) are beyond the reach of an otherwise valid warrant.

13. See generally H. Schwartz, "The Legitimation of Electronic Eavesdropping: The Politics of 'Law and Order'," 67 *Mich. L. Rev.* 455 (1969).

14. As Professor Bradley has pointed out, Bradley, supra note 6, at 32, in the final year of Chief Justice Warren's tenure the Court did significantly limit the scope of searches incident to arrest, Chimel v. California, 395 U.S. 752 (1969), and did impose substantial restrictions on the issuance of search warrants, Spinelli v. United States, 395 U.S. 410 (1969).

15. To take one notable example, the Warren Court found no constitutional restrictions on the government's power to utilize spies and undercover agents. It took the position (a viewpoint the Burger Court was to share, United States v. White, 401 U.S. 745 (1971)), that one who speaks to another not only assumes the risk that her listener will later make public what he has heard but also takes the risk that her listener will electronically record or simultaneously transmit what he is hearing. See Lopez v. United States, 373 U.S. 427 (1963); Hoffa v. United States, 385 U.S. 293 (1966).

16. But see Bradley, supra note 6, at 32, maintaining that "despite the existence of powerful societal pressures" to end its reformation of the law of criminal procedure, the Warren Court never lost its zeal to continue the reformation.

17. 392 U.S. 1 (1968). See also the companion cases of Sibron v. New York and Peters v. New York, 392 U.S. 41 (1968).

18. Mapp v. Ohio, 367 U.S. 643 (1961).

19. 392 U.S. at 13.

20. Cf. Dershowitz and Ely, "*Harris v. New York:* Some Anxious Observations on the Candor and Logic of the Emerging Nixon Majority," 80 *Yale L.J.* 1198, 1199 (1971).

21. Miranda v. Arizona, 384 U.S. 436 (1966).

22. See generally LaFave, "'Street Encounters' and the Fourth Amendment: *Terry, Sibron, Peters,* and Beyond," 67 *Mich. L. Rev.* 40 (1968).

23. 392 U.S. at 30. At another point, the Court articulated an even vaguer standard and did so "negatively": "We cannot say [the officer's decision] to seize Terry and pat his clothing for weapons was the product of a volatile or inventive imagination, or was undertaken simply as an act of harassment; the record evidences the tempered act of a policeman who in the course of an investigation had to make a quick decision as to how to protect himself and others from possible danger, and took limited steps to do so." Id. at 28.

24. Pye, "The Warren Court and Criminal Procedure," 67 *Mich. L. Rev.* 249, 256 (1968). See also Allen, supra note 3, at 523, pointing out that although charges of inequality have not been confined to the criminal law, but have encompassed nearly every aspect of society, such charges "possess an even sharper bite when they are hurled at a system that employs as its sanctions the deprivation of property, of liberty, and, on occasion, of life itself."

25. Pye, supra note 24, at 256.

26. Packer, "The Courts, the Police, and the Rest of Us," 57 *J. Crim. L., C. & P.S.* 238, 240 (1966).

27. Gideon v. Wainwright, 372 U.S. 335 (1963) (entitling indigent criminal defendants to free counsel, at least in serious cases). Whether the Burger Court "expanded" or "contracted" Gideon is debatable. Argersinger v. Hamlin, 407 U.S. 25 (1972), applied Gideon to instances where defendant is imprisoned for any offense, but Scott v. Illinois, 440 U.S. 367 (1975), held that the Sixth and Fourteenth Amendments require only that no indigent misdemeanants be incarcerated unless they are afforded the right to counsel. A fairly generous reading of *Gideon*, the day after it was decided, would have been that it applies to all crimes except "petty offenses." The Burger Court went beyond this generous reading of *Gideon* in one respect (*Argersinger*), but fell short in another (*Scott*).

28. 378 U.S. 478 (1964).

29. Id. at 492.

30. For a summary of the wide disagreement over the meaning of *Escobedo*—and over what it ought to mean—see Kamisar, *Police Interrogation and Confessions: Essays in Law and Policy* 161–62 (1980) [hereinafter Kamisar, *Essays*].

31. About half of all felony defendants are indigent; in some urban jurisdictions the indigency rate is in the 70–85% range. See Kamisar, LaFave, and Israel, *Modern Criminal Procedure* 27 (8th ed. 1994).

32. See Kamisar, "Has the Court Left the Attorney General Behind?—The Bazelon-Katzenbach Letters on Poverty, Equality and the Administration of Criminal Justice," 54 *Ky. L.J.* 464, 480–84 (1966) (pre-*Miranda*). See also the response to this paper by Kuh, 54 *Ky. L.J.* at 499, 506–07.

33. Friendly, "The Fifth Amendment Tomorrow: The Case for Constitutional Change," 37 *U. Cin. L. Rev.* 671, 711 (1968). See also Choper, "On the Warren Court and Judicial Review," 17 *Cath. U. L. Rev.* 20, 34–35 (1967).

34. Friendly, supra note 33, at 711.

35. Hearings before Committee on the Judiciary of the U.S. Senate on the Nomination of Ruth Bader Ginsburg to be Associate Justice of the Supreme Court, 103d Cong., 1st Sess. 327 (1993).

36. See Baker, *"Miranda": Crime, Law and Politics* 109 (1983).

37. Id.

38. See Brief for the State Governments, Amici Curiae, 2–3, 16, 21–23, *Gideon v. Wainwright*, 372 U.S. 335 (1963).

39. Id. at 24–25 (emphasis added).

40. *Miranda* "plunge[d] the Court into an ocean of abuse" and made it "one of the leading issues of the 1968 Presidential campaign." Lieberman, *Milestones—200 Years of American Law* 326 (1976).

41. *Miranda*, one commentator has observed, "must rank as the most bitterly criticized, most contentious, and most diversely analyzed criminal procedure decision by the Warren Court." Abraham, *Freedom and the Court* 125 (4th ed. 1982).

42. At one point for example, 384 U.S. at 444, after defining "custodial interrogation"—"questioning initiated by law enforcement officers after a person has been taken into custody or otherwise deprived of his freedom of action in any significant way"—the Court dropped an obfuscating footnote [n.4]: "This is what we meant in *Escobedo* when we spoke of an investigation which has focused on an accused." This footnote suggested that "custody" and "focus" were alternative grounds for requiring the warnings, but these are very different events and they have very different consequences. See Graham, "What Is 'Custodial Interrogation'?," 14 *U.C.L.A. L. Rev.* 59, 114 (1966); Kamisar, "'Custodial Interrogation' Within the Meaning of *Miranda*," in *Criminal Law and the Constitution* 335, 338–51 (1968); Stone, "The *Miranda* Doctrine in the Burger Court," 1977 *Sup. Ct. Rev.* 99, 149. The likely explanation for footnote 4 was the

Miranda Court's effort to maintain some continuity with a much-publicized and much-discussed recent precedent.

43. 384 U.S. at 489 (Goldberg, J.)

44. Id. at 488–89.

45. See Breitel, "Criminal Law and Equal Justice," 1966 *Utah L. Rev.* 1; Friendly, "The Bill of Rights as a Code of Criminal Procedure," 53 *Cal. L. Rev.* 929 (1965); Schaefer, *The Suspect and Society* (1967) (based on lectures delivered two months before *Miranda*); Traynor, "The Devils of Due Process in Criminal Detection, Detention, and Trial," 33 *U. Chi. L. Rev.* 657 (1966). See also the remarks of Judge Friendly at the Forty-Third Annual Meeting of the American Law Institute, 1966 *A.L.I. Proceedings* 250–52.

46. Schaefer, supra note 45, at 9. See also Symposium, 54 *Ky. L.J.* 464, 521, 523 (1966) (pre-*Miranda*), where Justice Schaefer expressed the view that effective enforcement of the criminal law "is not compatible with a prohibition of station house interrogation or with the presence of a lawyer during station house interrogation."

47. 1966 *A.L.I. Proceedings*, supra note 45, at 250 (emphasis added).

48. See Moran v. Burbine, 475 U.S. 412, 426 (1986). "Declining to adopt the more extreme position that the actual presence of a lawyer was necessary to dispel the coercion inherent in custodial interrogation," continued Justice O'Connor, "the [*Miranda*] Court found that the suspect's Fifth Amendment rights could be adequately protected by less intrusive means." Id.

49. See Kamisar, *Essays*, supra note 30 at 88–89.

50. See Ainsworth, "In a Different Register: The Pragmatics of Powerlessness in Police Interrogation," 103 *Yale L.J.* 259, 320–21 (1993); Allen, supra note 3, at 537–38; Ogletree, "Are Confessions Really Good for the Soul?: A Proposal to Mirandize *Miranda*," 100 *Harv. L. Rev.* 1826, 1842–45 (1987); Rosenberg and Rosenberg, "A Modest Proposal for the Abolition of Custodial Confessions," 68 *N.C. L. Rev.* 69, 109–10 (1989); Schulhofer, "Confessions and the Court," 79 *Mich. L. Rev.* 865, 880–82 (1981). But cf. Cassell, "*Miranda*'s Social Costs: An Empirical Reassessment," 90 *Nw. U. L. Rev.* 387 (1996), maintaining that an electronic recording of police interrogation should be regarded as an *alternative* to *Miranda*.

51. At the March 1966 conference on *Miranda* and related cases, Chief Justice Warren emphasized that FBI agents regularly informed suspects of their rights (although the FBI warnings were not as extensive as the *Miranda* warnings) and that the FBI practice had not imposed a substantial burden on law enforcement. See Schwartz, supra note 6, at 589. According to one Justice who attended this conference, "the statement that the FBI did it . . . was a swing factor . . . a tremendously important factor, perhaps the critical factor in the *Miranda* vote." Id.

52. 401 U.S. 222 (1971). The case is severely criticized in Dershowitz and Ely, supra note 20.

53. 420 U.S. 714 (1975).

54. However, as indicated in *Harris* and subsequently made clear in Mincey v. Arizona, 437 U.S. 385 (1978), "involuntary" or "coerced statements," as opposed to those obtained only in violation of *Miranda*, cannot be used for impeachment purposes.

55. The Court subsequently held that a defendant's prearrest silence could be used to impeach him when he testified in his own defense, Jenkins v. Anderson, 447 U.S. 231 (1980), and then, so long as he was not given the *Miranda* warnings, that even a defendant's postarrest silence could be used for impeachment purposes, Fletcher v. Weir, 455 U.S. 603 (1983). Both Jenkins and Weir distinguished Doyle v. Ohio, 426 U.S. 610 (1976), which deemed it a violation of due process to use a defendant's silence for im-

peachment purposes when the defendant remained silent after being given the *Miranda* warnings.

56. See California v. Beheler, 463 U.S. 1121 (1983); Oregon v. Mathiason, 429 U.S. 492 (1977). Cf. Stansbury v. California, 114 S. Ct. 1526 (1994) (per curiam). See also Berkemer v. McCarty, 468 U.S. 420 (1984), explaining at considerable length why the "roadside questioning" of a motorist detained pursuant to a traffic stop is "substantially less 'police dominated'" than station house interrogation and thus should not be considered "custodial interrogation."

57. 446 U.S. 291 (1980). For a close examination of this case see White, "Interrogation Without Questions: *Rhode Island v. Innis* and *United States v. Henry*," 78 *Mich. L. Rev.* 1209 (1980).

58. 446 U.S. at 300–01. Although *Innis* involved police "speech," the Court's definition embraces police interrogation techniques that do not. Thus, the Court seems to have repudiated the position taken by a number of lower courts that confronting a suspect with physical evidence or with an accomplice who has confessed is not interrogation because it does not entail verbal conduct on the part of the police.

59. 496 U.S. 292 (1990).

60. Id. at 294 (emphasis added).

61. See Cohen, "*Miranda* and Police Deception in Interrogation," 26 *Crim. L. Bull.* 534 (1990).

62. One can, however, deliberately elicit incriminating statements from a person without having him realize it—that is what happened in Massiah v. United States, 377 U.S. 201 (1964). The *Massiah* doctrine does prevent the government from "eliciting" or "inducing" incriminating statements from a suspect whether or not he is aware that he is dealing with a government agent (indeed, whether or not he is in custody), but only when "adversary criminal proceedings" have commenced against that person (e.g., he had been indicted or has appeared before a judicial officer). To the surprise of many, the Burger Court invigorated the *Massiah* doctrine in several respects. See Brewer v. Williams, 430 U.S. 387 (1977) (often called the "Christian Burial Speech" case); United States v. Henry, 447 U.S. 264 (1980). But cf. Kuhlmann v. Wilson, 477 U.S. 436 (1986).

63. For a pre-Perkins discussion of "surreptitious interrogation" and the "jail plant" situation, see Kamisar, *Essays*, supra note 30, at 195–96.

64. 451 U.S. 477 (1981).

65. See People v. Grant, 45 N.Y. 2d 366, 371–72 (1978).

66. Six years earlier, the Court held in Michigan v. Mosley, 423 U.S. 96 (1975), that if a suspect asserts his "right to silence" (as opposed to his right to counsel), under certain circumstances the police may, if they cease questioning on the spot, "try again" and succeed at a later interrogation session. Although the *Edwards* Court tried hard to distinguish *Mosley*, I do not think the two cases can be satisfactorily reconciled. See Choper, Kamisar, and Tribe, *The Supreme Court: Trends and Developments* 1982–83 (1984), at 153–58 (remarks of Kamisar). The average person has no idea that different procedural safeguards are triggered by saying "I don't want to say anything until I see a lawyer" rather than "I don't want to say anything" or "I don't want to talk to the police."

67. 451 U.S. at 484–85 (emphasis added).

68. Sonenshein, "*Miranda* and the Burger Court: Trends and Countertrends," 13 *Loyola U. Chi. L.J.* 405, 447 (1982). See also Rosenberg and Rosenberg, "*Miranda*, *Minnick* and the Morality of Confessions," 19 *Am. J. Crim. L.* 1 (1991).

69. Arizona v. Roberson, 486 U.S. 675 (1988).

70. 498 U.S. 146 (1990).

71. The Burger and Rehnquist Courts' reinvigoration of *Miranda*'s right to counsel

element in general and the *Minnick* decision in particular have been explained on the ground that while other features of Miranda "are for the benefit of the social underclass," the right to counsel before and during custodial interrogation is "a safeguard that benefits a far broader segment of society." Rosenberg and Rosenberg, supra note 68, at 33.

72. Oregon v. Bradshaw, 462 U.S. 1039 (1983).

73. 114 S. Ct. 2350 (1994).

74. At this point, I am relying heavily on the federal government's brief in the *Davis* case. See Brief for the United States at 14, 19–20, 32–35. Since the agents of the Naval Investigative Service had asked Mr. Davis, a member of the U.S. Navy, clarifying questions when he made an ambiguous reference to counsel and Davis had then made it plain that he did not want a lawyer, all the government needed to win its case, and all it sought, was for the Court to adopt a middle-of-the road approach, under which the police have to respond to a suspect's ambiguous references to counsel by asking follow-up clarifying questions. One of the most troubling features of the *Davis* case is that the Court reached out to adopt a rule that the government explicitly and forcefully rejected—a police-oriented rule that an interrogator may completely disregard a suspect's ambiguous references to a lawyer.

75. See Ainsworth, supra note 50, at 315–22.

76. 114 S. Ct. at 2364.

77. But see Rosenberg and Rosenberg, supra note 68, at 21–22, 31–34.

78. 417 U.S. 433 (1974).

79. The Court held, a week after *Miranda*, that *Miranda* affected only those cases in which the trial began after that decision. Johnson v. New Jersey, 384 U.S. 719 (1966). The Court probably should have held that *Miranda* affected only those confessions obtained after the date of the decision.

80. See 417 U.S. at 444–46.

81. Miranda v. Arizona, 384 U.S. at 457–58.

82. See 417 U.S. at 444–45.

83. See Stone, "The *Miranda* Doctrine in the Burger Court," 1977 *Sup. Ct. Rev.* 99, 118–19.

84. See 417 U.S. at 444.

85. 384 U.S. at 467 (emphasis added).

86. Id. (emphasis added).

87. Id. at 476 (emphasis added).

88. 467 U.S. 649 (1984).

89. 470 U.S. 298 (1985).

90. See Grano, *Confessions, Truth, and the Law* 174, 185–98 (1993) (drawing upon and elaborating arguments he has made in a number of earlier articles).

91. Id. at 191.

92. Schulhofer, "Reconsidering *Miranda*," 54 *U. Chi. L. Rev.* 435, 453 (1987).

93. Strauss, "The Ubiquity of Prophylactic Rules," 55 *U. Chi. L. Rev.* 190 (1988).

94. Id. at 208.

95. Id.

96. See id. at 194.

97. 113 S.Ct. 1745 (1993).

98. See id. at 1752.

99. Id.

100. Id. at 1753.

101. See the discussion of the case in the text at notes 61–65 supra.

102. See note 69 supra and accompanying text.

103. 486 U.S. at 682.

104. Id. at 681.

105. See the discussion of this case at notes 70–71 supra.

106. 498 U.S. at 151.

107. Id. at 166.

108. Id.

109. 384 U.S. at 541–42 (White, J., joined by Harlan and Stewart, JJ., dissenting). Justice Harlan (joined by Stewart and White, JJ.,) and Justice Clark also wrote separate dissents.

110. See note 79 supra.

111. Graham, *The Self-Inflicted Wound* 184 (1970).

112. See id. at 184–85.

113. Id. at 185. A year later, when the Court applied the right to counsel to lineups and other pretrial identifications, United States v. Wade, 388 U.S. 218 (1967), it did not make the same mistake. It held that the new ruling would apply only to identifications conducted in the absence of counsel after the date of the *Wade* decision.

114. Schulhofer, supra note 92, at 456. See also Stephens, *The Supreme Court and Confessions of Guilt* 168–200 (1973); White, "Defending *Miranda:* A Reply to Professor Caplan," 39 *Vand. L. Rev.* 1, 17–20 (1986). But see Caplan, "Questioning *Miranda,*" 38 *Vand. L. Rev.* 1417, 1464–66 (1985). Many of the empirical studies are summarized and evaluated in A.L.I., *A Model Code of Pre-Arraignment Procedure* 101–49 (study draft no. 1, 1968) and in Stephens, supra.

115. Special Committee on Criminal Justice in a Free Society, Criminal Justice Section, ABA, *Criminal Justice in Crisis* 28 (1988). But see Cassell, "*Miranda*'s Social Costs: An Empirical Reassessment," 90 *Nw. U. L. Rev.* 387 (1996), maintaining that *Miranda* has "significantly harmed law enforcement efforts in this country." Professor Schulhofer has written a response to Professor Cassell, sharply challenging his calculations. See Schulhofer, "*Miranda*'s Practical Effect: Substantial Benefits and Vanishingly Small Social Costs," 90 *Nw. U. L. Rev.* 500 (1996).

116. Withrow v. Williams, 113 S. Ct. at 1755.

117. See Pye, "Interrogation of Criminal Defendants—Some Views on *Miranda v. Arizona,*" 35 *Fordham L. Rev.* 199, 219 (1966); see also Israel, "Criminal Procedure, the Burger Court, and the Legacy of the Warren Court," 75 *Mich. L. Rev.* 1320, 1383 (1977).

118. See Friendly, "The Fifth Amendment Tomorrow: The Case for Constitutional Change," 37 *U. Chi. L. Rev.* 671, 676 n.25 (1968).

119. Id. at 713 (emphasis added).

120. See generally, 1 LaFave and Israel, *Criminal Procedure*, supra note 8, at §§ 6.6(e), (f), and 1991 Supp. See also note 56 supra and accompanying text.

121. Office of Legal Policy, U.S. Dept. of Justice, Truth in Criminal Justice Series, Report No. 1, *Report to the Attorney General of the Law of Pretrial Interrogation* 526 (1986). This report is reprinted in 22 *U. Mich. J.L. Ref.* 437 (1989).

122. Schulhofer, supra note 92, at 460; see also Maclin, "Seeing the Constitution from the Backseat of a Police Squad Car," 70 *B.U. L. Rev.* 543, 588–89 (1990); White, supra note 113, at 21–22.

123. Caplan, supra note 114, at 1471; see also Baker, supra note 36, at 407.

124. 470 U.S. 298 (1985).

125. Id. at 308. As to whether, in considering the admissibility of evidence derived from wrongfully obtained confessions, a bright line should be drawn between *Miranda* violations and coerced or "involuntary" confessions, compare Amar and Lettow, "Fifth Amendment First Principles: The Self-Incrimination Clause," 93 *Mich. L. Rev.* 857

(1995) with Kamisar, "On the 'Fruits' of *Miranda* Violations, Coerced Confessions, and Compelled Testimony," 93 *Mich. L. Rev.* 929 (1995).

126. See Fuller, *The Law in Quest of Itself* 41 (1940).

127. The *Miranda* Court was also trying to provide the police with clear guidelines about lawful interrogation procedures and to reduce the judicial burden of making time-consuming and frequently unreliable determinations about the "voluntariness" of challenged confessions. See Wollin, "Policing the Police: Should *Miranda* Violations Bear Fruit?," 53 *Ohio St. L.J.* 805, 841–43 (1992); "The Supreme Court, 1984 Term," 99 *Harv. L. Rev.* 120, 145–47 (1985). These objectives, too, would seem to require barring the use of the physical fruits of *Miranda* violations.

128. See Brennan, J., joined by Marshall, J., dissenting in *Elstad*, 470 U.S. at 356–59. See also Pitler, "'The Fruit of the Poisonous Tree' Revisited and Shepardized," 56 *Calif. L. Rev.* 579, 611–20 (1968). Cf. Kamisar, "Illegal Searches or Seizures and Contemporaneous Incriminating Statements," 1961 *U. Ill. L.F.* 78, 96–97.

129. Wollin, supra note 127, at 843. See also Brennan, J., joined by Marshall, J., dissenting in *Elstad*, 470 U.S. at 357 and n.39.

130. See Grano et al.: "Do Any Constitutional Safeguards Remain Against the Dangers of Convicting the Innocent?," 72 *Mich. L. Rev.* 719, 723–24 (1974) and authorities discussed therein. See also Allen, "The Judicial Request for Penal Justice: The Warren Court and the Criminal Cases," *U. Ill. L.F.* 518, 541–42.

131. United States v. Wade, 388 U.S. 218 (1967); Gilbert v. California, 388 U.S. 263 (1967); Stovall v. Denno, 388 U.S. 293 (1967).

132. United States v. Wade, 388 U.S. at 235–36.

133. 406 U.S. 682 (1972).

134. 413 U.S. 300 (1973).

135. Neil v. Biggers, 409 U.S. 188, 198–201 (1972). See also Manson v. Brathwaite, 432 U.S. 98, 110–14, 117 (1977).

136. Manson v. Brathwaite, 432 U.S. 98, 110.

137. See Grossman, "Suggestive Identifications: The Due Process Test Fails to Meet Its Own Criteria," 11 *Balt. L. Rev.* 53, 59–60, 96–97 (1981); Jonakait, "Reliable Identification: Could the Supreme Court Tell in *Manson v. Brathwaite?*," 52 *U. Colo. L. Rev.* 511, 515 (1981); Sherwood, "The Erosion of Constitutional Safeguards in the Area of Eyewitness Identification," 30 *How. L.J.* 731, 770 (1987).

138. Whitebread and Slobogin, *Criminal Procedure: An Analysis of Cases and Concepts* 4 (2d ed. 1986). See also Schulhofer, "The Constitution and the Police: Individual Rights and Law Enforcement," 66 *Wash. U. L.Q.* 11, 18 (1988).

139. Alschuler, "Failed Pragmatism: Reflections on the Burger Court," 100 *Harv. L. Rev.* 1436, 1442 (1987).

140. See, e.g., Gerstein v. Pugh, 420 U.S. 103 (1975) (ruling that the Fourth Amendment requires a prompt judicial determination of probable cause as a condition for any significant pretrial restraint on a suspect's liberty); Payton v. New York, 445 U.S. 573 (1980) (holding that the police must be armed with a warrant before entering a suspect's home to make a routine arrest); Tennessee v. Garner, 471 U.S. 1 (1985) (concluding that the police slaying of an unarmed, nondangerous felon to prevent his escape constitutes an "unreasonable seizure" within meaning of Fourth Amendment).

141. Weeks v. United States, 232 U.S. 383 (1914).

142. See the discussion of *Weeks* and other early search-and-seizure cases in Kamisar, supra note 10, at 598–604. See also Schulhofer, supra note 138, at 23–24.

143. See Kamisar, supra note 142, at 621–27.

144. United States v. Calandra, 414 U.S. 338, 348, 354, 349 (1974). *Calandra*, the

most important exclusionary rule case of the 1970s, is extensively discussed and strongly criticized in Schrock and Welsh, "Up from *Calandra:* The Exclusionary Rule as a Constitutional Requirement," 59 *Minn. L. Rev.* 251 (1974).

145. See Calandra, supra note 144 (holding that a grand jury witness may not refuse to answer questions on ground that they are based on fruits of an unlawful search); Stone v. Powell, 428 U.S. 465 (1976) (greatly limiting a state prisoner's ability to obtain federal habeas corpus relief on search-and-seizure grounds); United States v. Janis, 428 U.S. 433 (1976) (concluding that the rule's deterrent purpose would not be furthered by barring evidence obtained illegally by state police from federal civil tax proceedings). An even more important victory was won a decade later in United States v. Leon, 468 U.S. 897 (1984) (adopting a "reasonable, good faith" modification of the exclusionary rule, at least in search warrant cases) (discussed infra).

146. Schulhofer, supra note 138, at 19.

147. *Janis*, 428 U.S. at 452 n. 22, quoted in *Leon*, 468 U.S. at 918. See also *Stone*, 428 U.S. at 492 and n.32.

148. *Leon*, 468 U.S. at 907; 922; *Stone*, 428 U.S. at 490–91.

149. I think it fair to say that the "costs" of the exclusionary rule are "much lower . . . than is commonly assumed." 1 LaFave, supra note 7, at 22. According to probably the most comprehensive study of the available empirical data, the evidence "consistently indicates that the general level of the rule's effects on criminal prosecutions is marginal at most." Davies, "A Hard Look at What We Know (and Still Need to Learn) About the Costs of the Exclusionary Rule," 1983 *Am. B. Found. Res. J.* 611, 622. See also Whitebread and Slobogin, *Criminal Procedure: An Analysis of Cases and Concepts* 45–46 (3d ed. 1993); Dripps, "Beyond the Warren Court and Its Conservative Critics: Toward a Unified Theory of Constitutional Criminal Procedure," 23 *U. Mich. J.L. Ref.* 591, 625, 634 (1990); Nardulli, "The Societal Cost of the Exclusionary Rule: An Empirical Assessment," 1983 *Am. B. Found. Res.* J. 585; Uchida and Bynum, "Search Warrants, Motions to Suppress and 'Lost Cases': The Effects of the Exclusionary Rule in Seven Jurisdictions," 81 *J. Crim. L. & Criminology* 1034 (1991).

150. See Tribe, "Constitutional Calculus: Equal Justice or Economic Efficiency?," 98 *Harv. L. Rev.* 592, 609 (1985).

151. Cf. Stevens, J., dissenting in *Leon*, 468 U.S. at 978.

152. 468 U.S. 897 (1984).

153. Id. at 922.

154. See the cases summarized in note 145 supra.

155. 1 LaFave, supra note 7, at 50–51.

156. See the discussion in LaFave, "The Seductive Call of Expediency: *U.S. v. Leon*, Its Rationale and Ramifications," 1984 *U. Ill. L. Rev.* 895, 927–29 (1984). See also LaFave, supra note 7, at 77–80.

157. See 468 U.S. at 926.

158. 462 U.S. 213 (1983), extensively discussed in Kamisar, "*Gates*, 'Probable Cause,' 'Good Faith,' and Beyond," 69 *Iowa L. Rev.* 557 (1984); LaFave, "Fourth Amendment Vagaries (of Improbable Cause, Imperceptible Plain View, Notorious Privacy, and Balancing Askew)," 74 *J. Crim. L. & Criminology* 1171, 1188–89 (1983); Wasserstrom, "The Incredible Shrinking Fourth Amendment," 21 *Am. Crim. L. Rev.* 257, 274–75, 329–40 (1984). But see Grano, "Probable Cause and Common Sense: A Reply to the Critics of Illinois v. Gates," 17 *Mich. J.L. Ref.* 465 (1984).

159. 462 U.S. at 244, n.13 (emphasis added).

160. United States v. Miller, 425 U.S. 435, 442–43 (1976).

161. Smith v. Maryland, 442 U.S. 735 (1979).

162. Maclin, "Justice Thurgood Marshall: Taking the Fourth Amendment Seriously," 77 *Cornell L. Rev.* 723, 740 (1992).

163. See Schulhofer, supra note 138, at 25–26.

164. Oliver v. United States, 466 U.S. 170 (1984) (expansively reading the "open fields" exception to Fourth Amendment restraints). For strong criticism of this case, see Saltzburg, "Another Victim of Illegal Narcotics: The Fourth Amendment (as Illustrated by the Open Fields Doctrine)," 48 *U. Pitt. L. Rev.* 1 (1986).

165. California v. Ciraolo, 476 U.S. 207 (1986). See also Dow Chemical Co. v. United States, 476 U.S. 227 (1986). For criticism of these cases see LaFave, "The Forgotten Motto of Obsta Principiis in Fourth Amendment Jurisprudence," 28 *Ariz. L. Rev.* 291 (1986).

166. California v. Greenwood, 486 U.S. 35 (1988). According to one federal appellate court, United States v. Scott, 975 F. 2d 927 (1st Cir. 1992), *Greenwood* applies even when individuals shred their papers before putting them in the garbage but IRS agents painstakingly reassemble them.

167. Maclin, supra note 162, at 800.

168. Florida v. Bostick, 501 U.S. 429 (1991). See also California v. Hodari D., 499 U.S. 621 (1991) (ruling that police show of authority directed at a particular individual, such as police pursuit on foot or calling on individual to halt, does not constitute a "seizure" of person unless and until individual submits to authority or is physically restrained by police). For criticism of *Bostick* and *Hodari* and a discussion of earlier cases involving what might be called "close encounters of the non-Fourth Amendment kind," such as United States v. Mendenhall, 446 U.S. 544 (1980) (on confronting a suspected drug courier at an airport), see LaFave, "Pinguitudinous Police, Pachydermatous Prey: Whence Fourth Amendment 'Seizures'?," 1991 *U. Ill. L. Rev.* 729; Maclin, supra note 162, at 745–52, 800–12.

169. 412 U.S. 218 (1973).

170. Foote, "The Fourth Amendment: Obstacle or Necessity in the Law of Arrest?," in *Police Power and Individual Freedom* 29, 30 (Sowle ed., 1962).

171. 412 U.S. at 231.

172. Id. at 227.

173. Cf. Escobedo v. Illinois, 378 U.S. 478, 490 (1964).

174. 497 U.S. 177 (1990). For extensive criticism of this case see Davies, "Denying a Right by Disregarding Doctrine: How *Illinois v. Rodriguez* Demeans Consent, Trivializes Fourth Amendment Reasonableness, and Exaggerates the Excusability of Police Error," 59 *Tenn. L. Rev.* 1 (1991). See also Maclin, supra note 162, at 796–99.

175. 497 U.S. at 193 (Marshall, J., joined by Brennan and Stevens, JJ., dissenting).

176. Id. at 183.

177. Id. at 186.

178. Paulsen, "The Exclusionary Rule and Misconduct by the Police," in *Police Power and Individual Freedom* 87, 88 (Sowle ed., 1992) (emphasis added).

179. People v. Defore, 242 N.Y. 13, 21, 150 N.E. 585, 587 (1926).

180. See, e.g., Black, J. joined by Douglas, J., dissenting in Adamson v. California, 332 U.S. 46, 68 (1947).

181. See Israel, "Selective Incorporation Revisited," 71 *Geo. L.J.* 253, 258 (1992).

182. See id. at 290–98.

183. LaFave and Israel, supra note 8, at 97 (1984).

184. Bradley, *The Failure of the Criminal Procedure Revolution* 18 (1993).

185. 378 U.S. 1 (1964).

186. LaFave and Israel, supra note 8, at 96–97.

187. Id. The quotation from *Duncan*, 391 U.S. 145 (1968) (holding that the Sixth Amendment right to jury trial is fully applicable to the states via the Fourteenth Amendment) appears at 391 U.S. at 149–50 n.14. See also the Court's summary of the "specifics" of the Bill of Rights that it had "selectively incorporated" by the year 1968 in *Duncan*, 391 U.S. at 148.

188. See Harlan, J., dissenting in *Baldwin v. New York* and concurring in Williams v. Florida, 399 U.S. 78, 117 (1970).

189. See the discussion of the *Mapp* opinion in Kamisar, supra note 142, at 621–27.

190. Allen, "Federalism and the Fourth Amendment: A Requiem for Wolf," 1961 *Sup. Ct. Rev.* 1, 26. See also id. at 23–24.

191. The disagreement in *Mapp* was only over the applicability of the search and seizure exclusionary rule to the states: "[T]here is not a word in [Justice Harlan's dissenting opinion] suggesting that the rule is intrinsically bad." Taylor, *Two Studies in Constitutional Interpretation* 20–21 (1969).

192. Concurring in *Mapp*, Justice Douglas observed that *Wolf v. Colorado*, overruled in *Mapp*, had evoked "a storm of constitutional controversy which only today finds its end," 367 U.S. at 670. But the storm of controversy greatly intensified and embraced the 1914 *Weeks* rule as well as *Mapp*.

193. The *Leon* Court, per White, J., quoted with approval (see 468 U.S. at 907 n.6) Justice White's earlier observation (see his concurring opinion in *Gates*, 462 U.S. at 257–58) that the exclusionary rule "must be carefully limited to the circumstances in which it will pay its way by deterring official lawlessness." Because the *Leon* Court concluded that the exclusionary rule can have "no substantial deterrent effect" when the police have acted in reasonable reliance on a search warrant issued by a neutral magistrate that is subsequently found to be invalid, it concluded that the rule "cannot pay its way in those situations" (468 U.S. at 907–08 n.6).

194. See note 147 supra and accompanying text.

195. Gideon v. Wainwright, 372 U.S. 335 (1963).

196. Arnold, *The Symbols of Government* 142 (Harbinger ed., 1962).

197. See text at notes 29–31 and 43–44 supra.

198. See Schulhofer, "Reconsidering *Miranda*," 54 *U. Chi. L. Rev.* 435, 436 (1987).

199. Id.

200. See id. at 454.

201. See id.

202. Graham, supra note 111, at 4.

203. See generally Kamisar, "When the Cops Were Not 'Handcuffed,'" N.Y. *Times* (Magazine), Nov. 7, 1965, reprinted in *Crime and Criminal Justice* 46 (Cressey ed., 1971).

204. 318 U.S. 322 (1943).

205. Hearings on H.R. 3690, Serial No. 12 before Subcommittee No. 2 of the House Committee on the Judiciary, 78th Cong., 1st Sess. 1, 57 (1943) (testimony of Mayor Edward J. Kelly).

206. Hogan and Snee, "The *McNabb-Mallory* Rule: Its Rise, Rationale and Rescue," 47 *Geo. L.J.* 1, 5 (1958).

207. Mitchell v. United States, 321 U.S. 756 (1944).

208. See Inbau, "The Confession Dilemma in the United States Supreme Court," 43 *Ill. L. Rev.* 442, 451–53 (1948).

209. Hogan and Snee, supra note 206, at 8.

210. 335 U.S. 410 (1948).

211. 354 U.S. 449 (1957).

212. Hogan and Snee, supra note 206, at 17. The claim that the *McNabb-Mallory* rule adversely affected law enforcement in the District of Columbia is not supported by the available data. See Kamisar, "On the Tactics of Police-Prosecution Oriented Critics of the Courts," 49 *Cornell L.Q.* 436, 464–71 (1964).

213. See 18 U.S.C. §§ 3501(a) & (c).

214. 322 U.S. 143 (1944).

215. See 322 U.S. at 156 (Jackson, J., joined by Roberts & Frankfurter, JJ., dissenting).

216. 338 U.S. 49, 57, 61 (1949).

217. People v. Cahan, 44 Cal. 2d 434, 282 P 2d 905 (1955). For an explanation by the author of the *Cahan* opinion of why the California Supreme Court adopted the exclusionary rule six years before the U.S. Supreme Court imposed the rule on the states, see Traynor, "*Mapp v. Ohio* at Large in the Fifty States," 1961 *Duke L.J.* 319, 321–22.

218. See the statements of officials quoted in Kamisar, "Public Safety v. Individual Liberties: Some 'Facts' and 'Theories'", 53 *J. Crim. L., C. & P.S.* 171, 188, 190 (1962). The predictions and descriptions of near-disaster that greeted and followed the adoption of the exclusionary rule in California find virtually no support in the available data. See id. at 184–90.

219. Governor's Conference on Crime, the Criminal and Society, *Proceedings* 25–27 (1935). The next day a former governor, Nathan L. Miller, took up the theme. To the accompaniment of applause, he "suggest[ed] that the police ought not to be hampered in dealing with the enemies of society," and he warned that "in a war upon crime, the primary consideration must be not the criminal but the protection of society from the criminal." Id. at 55.

220. See Weschsler, "A Caveat on Crime Control," 27 *J. Crim. L. & Criminology* 629 (1937).

221. See Hearings before Subcommittee of the Senate Committee on Commerce Pursuant to S. Res. 74, 73d Cong., 2d Sess. (1933).

222. See generally Kamisar, supra note 203.

223. Barnes, *Battling the Crime Wave* 87–88 (1931).

224. Id. at 88.

225. Id.

226. Sutherland, "Crime and Confession," 79 *Harv. L. Rev.* 21, 32–33 (1965).

227. Black, "The Death Penalty Now," 51 *Tul. L. Rev.* 429, 455 (1977).

228. Although Title II of the Omnibus Crime Control and Safe Streets Act of 1968 purports to "repeal" *Miranda* in federal prosecutions, 18 USCA § 3501(a), the Department of Justice has studiously avoided the statute. See Friendly, "The Constitution" 24–25 (U.S. Dep't. Justice Bicentennial Lecture Series, 1976). Recently, however, Justice Antonin Scalia announced that he "will no longer be open to the argument that this Court should continue to ignore the commands of § 3501 simply because the Executive declines to insist that we observe them." Davis v. United States, 114 S. Ct. 2350, 2358 (1994) (Scalia, J., concurring).

229. Friendly, supra note 118, at 711–12 (1968).

230. See text at notes 131–32 supra.

231. Allen, "The Judicial Quest for Penal Justice: The Warren Court and the Criminal Cases," 1975 *U. Ill. L.F.* 518, 542.

232. Although Title II of the Omnibus Crime Control and Safe Streets Act of 1968 purports to "repeal" the 1967 lineup decisions, this congressional action has "proved to be meaningless. The inferior federal courts have considered themselves bound by the Su-

preme Court's reading of the Constitution rather than that of the Congress and have appeared to ignore the new statute." McGowan, "Constitutional Interpretation and Criminal Identification," 12 *Wm. and Mary L. Rev.* 235, 249 (1970).

233. Allen, supra note 231, at 542.

234. Stone v. Powell, 428 U.S. 465, 500 (Burger, C.J., concurring).

235. See Elkins v. United States, 364 U.S. 205, 224–25 (1960).

236. Wilkey, "The Exclusionary Rule: Why Suppress Valid Evidence?," 62 *Judicature* 215, 217–18 (1978).

237. See the articles collected in Kamisar, "Remembering the 'Old World' of Criminal Procedure: A Reply to Professor Grano," 23 *U. Mich. J.L. Ref.* 537, 564 n.88 (1990). See also id. at 562 n.82.

238. Bradley, *The Failure of the Criminal Procedure Revolution* 62 (1993). See also Allen, supra note 231, at 540–41 (Despite its "ingenious, persistent, and some may feel, heroic efforts to overcome the inherent limitations of judicial power, the [Warren] Court attempted more than it could possibly achieve."); Amsterdam, "The Supreme Court and the Rights of Suspects in Criminal Cases," 45 *N.Y.U. L. Rev.* 785, 788 (1970) (The U.S. Supreme Court "is uniquely unable to take a comprehensive view of the subject of suspects' rights.").

239. Bradley, supra note 238, at 39, 55, 71.

240. Amsterdam, supra note 238, at 790.

241. Packer, "Policing the Police," *New Republic*, Sept. 4, 1965, at 17, 19.

242. See id.

243. Id. See also Packer, supra note 26, at 240.

244. Allen, supra note 231, at 525.

245. A few state supreme courts, it should be noted, have picked up the torch. See authorities collected and discussed in Kamisar, LaFave, and Israel, supra note 31, at 57–63.

246. Allen, supra note 231, at 539.

• 9 •

THE TAKINGS JURISPRUDENCE OF THE WARREN COURT
A Constitutional Siesta

RICHARD A. EPSTEIN

I. Ebb Tide for Property Rights

During the 1991 Centennial on the Bill of Rights, Justice Stevens visited the University of Chicago Law School to deliver an address on the historical mission of the Supreme Court as a defender of the Bill of Rights.[1] Much of his talk addressed the exploits of the Warren Court and of the major contributions that it made to the law on freedom of speech and religion, on criminal procedure, and on voting rights. As befits a Justice whose own judicial and intellectual work made him sympathetic with the basic orientation of the Warren Court, he spent none of his time talking about the contributions that the Warren Court made in the protection of private property or economic liberties. Nor did he speak of the jurisprudence that explained why these rights might properly be limited under a sound application of the state's admitted police power.

His omissions were not inadvertent. The question of property rights, their status, and protection, was not an issue that much troubled or preoccupied the Warren Court. The Court did not hand down a single decision during the years 1954 to 1969 that ranks in the top dozen of important takings cases under the Constitution. The years before and after the Warren Court, however, saw extensive and difficult litigation under the Takings Clause (not to mention the kindred issues that are raised under the Contracts Clause and the Due Process Clauses). Just to name a few of the great cases, *Mugler v. Kansas*,[2] *Block v. Hirsh*,[3] *Pennsylvania Coal Co. v. Mahon*,[4] *Euclid v. Ambler Realty Co.*,[5] and *Miller v. Schoene*[6] all were decided before the constitutional watershed of 1937, and all sharply expanded the scope of state regulation over private property. Similarly, after the end of the Warren Court, the pace again picks up. There are such important cases as *Penn Central Transportation Co. v. City of New York*,[7] *Agins v. Tiburon*,[8] *Hawaiian Housing Authority v. Midkiff*,[9] *Nollan v. California Coastal Commission*,[10] *Lucas v.*

Coastal Council,[11] and *Dolan v. Tigard.*[12] The closest that one can come to decisive takings cases in the Warren Court are such decisions as *Berman v. Parker,*[13] *United States v. Central Eureka Mining Company,*[14] *Goldblatt v. Hempstead,*[15] and *Armstrong v. United States,*[16] which were either mopping-up operations, or modest extensions of the existing law. Occasionally there are hints of larger problems that have not been fully resolved, but these are mentioned without being fully explored or debated. And some of the most daring innovations in the takings area, such as *Reitman v. Mulkey*[17] and *Jones v. Alfred H. Mayer, Co.*[18] are thought of more as civil rights cases than property cases, which accounts for much of their difficulty. But insofar as the focus of analysis is the protection of property rights and economic liberties, there is little energy, excitement, or sense of intellectual adventure in the Warren Court. If an analysis of any topic of Warren Court jurisprudence could safely be omitted, I suspect takings and economic liberties more generally would be it.

It is instructive to seek some explanations for this high level of Warren Court quiescence on property rights issues when there was such a high degree of tumult in other areas of its work. The best explanations do not reflect ill upon the Warren Court. It is a commonplace observation, easily forgotten, that courts do not generate the controversies that come before them. While the power of certiorari gives the Supreme Court the power to pick its cases and to hone in on its issues, that power does not allow it to enter into areas where there are no existing controversies between litigants. The Court should make sure that important issues stirring below receive its full attention. But it cannot command legislatures and litigants to redirect their independent agendas to suit its own purposes. And for most of the Warren Court, property rights issues of all stripes and decisions were not at the front of the American political consciousness.

There are two explanations for this general trend. The first is historical. The constitutional watershed of the 1937 term[19] had the effect of blocking property-rights-based challenges to the exercise of governmental power on matters of general economic regulation. Questions of economic liberty were also given short shrift, as legislation on these matters was subject to a very low standard of review, largely under the Due Process Clause, where even minimum rationality would suffice.[20] After 1937, *Lochner v. New York*[21] came to symbolize a bygone era in which the Supreme Court abused its constitutional power to protect private property and freedom of contract by falsely elevating common law categories to constitutional levels.[22]

Yet it is important not to overstate the importance of the 1937 revolution on the status of property rights, whose constitutional protection had been in decline for over half a century. Anyone who takes a cool and dispassionate look at the property rights and economic liberties cases between 1880 and 1936 can only reach one conclusion: there was throughout that period a steady expansion in the scope of government power in all areas of economic life: limitations on the power of taxation were rebuffed;[23] state regulation of health and safety were expanded, even in the teeth of private contract;[24] rent control received at least a qualified constitutional blessing;[25] zoning powers received very broad construction on their first go-round;[26] and the common law accounts of nuisance were solemnly adjudged not to place limits on the state's power to protect one neighbor from the harmful activities of another.[27] Only in the area of labor contracts did the pre-1937 court show some genuine constitutional backbone. Mandatory collective bargaining arrangements were wisely struck down at both the federal[28] and the state[29] level. And a minimum wage statute applicable to women only (and thus suspect on two grounds—an infringement of liberty and an explicit sex classification) was similarly derailed.[30] But set against the trends in property law, the view that 1937 represents a sharp break with some laissez-faire past is both an oversimplification of its constitutional sweep and an incorrect denial of the steady enlargement of state power.[31] *Lochner* was a case, not an era.

Substantial limitations commanded broad assent before the 1937 watershed, and continued to command it thereafter. At the onset of the Warren Court, the question was not how the Court should reconsider those limitations on property rights that had uniformly expanded over the past sixty or more years. Rather, the issue was how it could disentangle the question of property rights from the other side of the coin and offer heightened levels of constitutional scrutiny in other areas in order to make good on the "two tiers of justice" that were articulated with such clarity and influence in the famous footnote 4 of the *Carolene Products* case.[32] The first explanation for the passivity of the Warren Court on matters of property rights is that there was no intellectual debate to fuel judicial controversy over the proper size and scope of property rights.

The second explanation is less theoretical and more practical—it involves not history but politics. The contemporary legislative agenda did not force the Court to mediate between aggressive state regulators and beleaguered property owners. It is remarkable to recount the large number of property rights cases in the Warren Court that were concerned with dams and water rights, the precise definition of a flowage easement, the scope of the navigation servitude (largely settled some fifty years before). But these cases doubtless came out of the expansive program for dam construction in an age that was not keen on keeping wilderness pristine. Even five years before, the Court had seen a constant stream of disputes over leasehold property that originated in temporary takings during World War II.[33] Occasionally these cases surfaced in the Warren Court, but in obviously diminishing numbers. Otherwise there were a fair number of cases that dealt with such topics as the priority of government liens, the rules governing the extinction of the equitable rights of redemption in foreclosure (itself a holdover from the questions of the 1930s),[34] and occasionally novel applications of the zoning law. But in truth the early *Euclid* decision[35] was so strongly pro-state that these cases only tested the limits of the basic question, but did nothing to reorder fundamental priorities.

It was only with the rise of far more aggressive legislation in the 1970s and afterward that novel property claims flooded the courts, for by that time there was some effort to attack the existing synthesis (of which my *Takings*[36] book is probably the most prominent, and to many the most misguided). Landmark preservation statutes, wetlands and endangered species, and coastal controls and protection did (and do) represent a new effort of government to go beyond the old powers, one that met with powerful resistance. The holdovers from the Warren Court (e.g., Justices Brennan and White) showed themselves to be generally unsympathetic with these property rights claims,[37] and it seems to be a fair assumption that they would have proved every bit as hostile to similar claims if these had been pressed during the 1950s and 1960s. But far be it from me to condemn the Warren Court for deeds that took place after it passed into the mists of history.

With this said, there is one irony that does deserve a brief mention. The academic scholarship on the Takings Clause has turned out at least in part to be more influential than the decisions of the Court itself. Here, in particular, the work of Joseph Sax,[38] and Frank Michelman[39] were both marked advances over everything in the academic literature that preceded them. Both writers conveyed a clear awareness of the immense difficulty associated with any purported comprehensive solution to the takings problem. This seemingly simple problem requires judgments not only about the status of private property, but the nature of the government institutions that regulate, tax, or take it. Behavioral assumptions about the goodness and badness of government are not simply curiosities that lead nowhere in the debate over constitutional interpretation. Rather, they are an integral part of any analysis, for in dealing with any form of government activity it becomes critical to know the motivations and objectives of the state agencies that initiate the changes, and, of necessity, of the individuals who compose them.[40]

This academic work highlights how difficult it is (pace the current law) to distinguish in principled fashion between regulatory and physical takings. Even with the latter the takings in question must be paid for by someone, and they impose costs above and beyond the raw value of land. Tracking down the distributional consequences of these takings can be quite complex, and the patterns of abuse that can exist with them may be quite large, especially when the "just compensation" measures applied by the courts are systematically below the level necessary to leave individual landowners indifferent between the continued possession of their lands and the compensation that the state offers as a substitute for it. *Berman v. Parker*[41] was a Warren Court decision that implicated a comprehensive use of the takings power, and which anticipated the incidents that took place in Poletown[42] in the 1970s and in Hawaii in the 1980s and 1990s.[43] Efforts to deal with the distinction between arbitral and entrepreneurial government activities, or to find the role of demoralization costs and the like, stem from an awareness that it is not possible to cabin in the eminent domain question by artificial limitation and narrow categorization. The effort to figure out who can take and what can be taken becomes by degrees a blueprint for how good constitutional norms can guard against government disasters.

Oddly enough, there is scant trace of any of this intellectual ferment in the Warren Court decisions. The academic writings did not have time to penetrate into the judicial chambers, so that the two factors identified above—history and politics—continued to hold sway. The absence of any intellectual tension meant that judges had no incentive to probe into these questions. And the absence of bold new government programs kept the judicial doctrine barren of the tough substantive disputes that could have energized a lagging area. The harvest here therefore is far more meager than it is in other areas. Nonetheless, a study of the Warren Court's takings decisions helps set the stage for contemporary understandings of the takings issue.

II. A Critique of the Warren Court Decisions

A regrettable but necessary truth about judicial decisions is that they do not come up in the order in which professors would like to discuss them. Indeed, one of the major function of theorists and editors alike is to come up with some structure that permits unruly cases to be tied into neat bundles. For these purposes, this essay will adopt the structure of argument that flows fairly from the language of the Takings Clause itself, and which in any event is adopted in a mostly post-Warren Court treatment of the subject—my *Takings* book. Thereafter, the loose ends will be picked up with cases outside the takings area that raise similar issues, albeit in very different ways, under both the Contracts and the Equal Protection Clauses.

In *Takings*, two ways of stating the takings problem are distinguished. The first and most common approach asks whether government action amounts to a compensable taking, on the implicit assumption that there is no other kind. The great disadvantage of this view is that it collapses conceptually distinct issues into one undifferentiated mass, and unfortunately confuses the analysis. The analogy, here, is to private tort law. Tort theory does not approach the compensability of injury as a unitary question. Rather, it divides the analysis into at least four elements: (1) the prima facie case (causation and the basis of liability); (2) affirmative defenses, covering the justifications or excuses based on plaintiff's conduct; (3) the choice of remedy (damages, injunctions, or some mix of the two); and (4) the type of compensation or damages that should be provided for the harms so committed. Takings questions are better analyzed by this more nuanced analysis than by merely asking the single question, is the taking compensable?

These tort issues have their concrete parallels in the law of eminent domain. The first task is to set up the prima facie case, and to ask whether property was taken by the government. The second question is to ask whether the taking was justified in virtue of some wrong that the plaintiff committed, or threatened to commit: in constitutional discourse, these are typically questions about the scope of the state's police power to regulate *without compensation*.[44] When such justifications fail, the third question is to ask whether the taking was allowed at all. Stated another way, does the public use requirement in effect limit the power of coercion to certain types of cases and allow the citizen to block the state in at least some cases? The fourth, distinctive question—not commonly found in tort analysis—is the question of whether just compensation has been provided when the taking is done and is for public use, but is not justified under the "police power." These issues are the leitmotifs of any system of takings law, and while the cases themselves do not precisely track the four parts of this analysis, they are best understood if these issues are broken out. Some cases raise two or more of the issues together, and in those cases it is all the more imperative to keep the lines of analysis as clear as possible. Let us consider the four categories in order.

The Prima Facie Case: A Taking of Private Property

WATER The question of what counts as a taking of private property initially depends on the question of what counts as property in the first place. In dealing with land, the question is normally one of metes and bounds and thus is not subject to many definitional inquiries. The fixed nature of the resource creates enormous economic efficiencies from separating land into different plots and policing the boundaries between neighbors by the law of trespass and nuisance. But with water law the position has always (from at least Roman times) been otherwise. The movement of the water means that any attempt to reduce it all to possession destroys the value of the resource so that the idiom of water rights has always been one of limited use, correlative rights and duties, sharing, usufruct, and servitudes. It is therefore jarring, to say the least, that the traditional Supreme Court view of property rights in water says that the federal government, in virtue of its power to regulate under the Commerce Clause, has a "superior navigation easement that sweeps all aside."[45]

That development, however, long predated the Warren Court, having its origin in such cases as *United States v. Chandler-Dunbar,* which attributed to the navigation easement a dominance that it hardly deserves. In *United States v. Twin City Power Co.,*[46] the Warren Court pointedly refused to reexamine these issues. Justice Douglas showed that the dominant approach to the dominant servitude had not lost its teeth. The Twin City Power Company had acquired "fast" or "riparian" lands on both banks of the Savannah River for inclusion in its own Clark Hill project, which had its own hydroelectric component.[47] The issue was stated to be one of valuation, but that was in reality a fig leaf for the antecedent question of the nature of the underlying property rights. The Twin City Power Company had acquired these fast lands because they offered an ideal site for the construction of a dam to meet the growing power demands of the river area, and the market price for the lands in question reflected the value of such a use. But the utilization of the *flow* within the river was precarious, given the dominant nature of the navigation servitude. Justice Douglas took evident delight in pulling the rug out from under the company's plans by holding that the government did not have to compensate the company for the value of the site as a power station, no matter what its own planned use of the land. Under the circumstances of the case, Twin Cities could claim congressional double-cross, for in the period from 1901 and 1919, Congress six times had authorized it to build the dam in question.[48] There is a certain charm in allowing the government to acquire this land for the value of its standing timber only to use it to construct its own dam project. A similar double-cross had been thwarted in *Monongahela Navigation v. United States,*[49] where the private right to charge tolls was treated as a compensable element of damages. But the navigation servitude in *Chandler-Dunbar* swept this precedent away.

Justice Burton, for the four dissenters, insisted that the appropriate measure of compensation was fair market value of the subject property measured by what a third party would pay for the assembled site. But the mistake that Burton makes is that this buyer would be quite happy to pay something for the expectation that the government would not pull the rug on the deal. If, however, the navigation easement is paramount, then the buyer would be subject to the same level of political risk as the seller, and therefore would only pay that reduced sum of money that reflected the risk of the loss, without compensation, of the navigation easement. The government need not pay for that expectation when it is in its own power to dash it. So if the regrettable law on navigation servitudes is correct, then *Twin City* is correct also.

And it is one in a line of cases—the Taylor Act grazing rights are the post-Warren Court example[50]—in which the government's use of its at-will powers has reduced its compensation bill, but left the aspirations of private parties in tatters. The proper cure, though, is not to dispute Douglas's treatment of at-will rights, but to dispute any view that the commerce power has authorized the creation of the paramount navigation servitude in the federal government.

The ability of the government to squeeze the last drop of advantage out of its practical rights was also the theme in *General Box v. United States*,[51] another water rights case involving timber on "batture," a Louisiana institution that gives the state the right to cut down timber that grows on private lands located between the high and low water marks. Since early times, state law has given the state the power to remove this timber, without paying compensation to riparian owners, in order to maintain navigation along the river. As part of the federal program for flood control along the Mississippi River, the state agreed to assign, without cost, its right in batture to the federal government for its part in the project. The United States entered under this servitude, without notice, destroyed the timber, and then was successful in defeating a claim for compensation for the value lost. As assignee of the rights of the state, it had to pay no more compensation than the state did. The question of whether these batture rights were assignable was not discussed in the opinion, and Justice Reed reached the unhappy conclusion that the state's own easement was one that allowed for the bulldozing of the timber without giving the owner the opportunity to harvest it for commercial use.

Once again one is struck by the massive inefficiency in the nature of this operation. If the similar easement of batture had been given to a private party, notice and opportunity to harvest would have reduced the costs of the total operation, since the gains that the government gets from not giving notice (especially when there is no emergency) are small relative to the value of the timber needlessly lost. One could also argue that servitudes of this sort should not be freely assignable—as most riparian rights are not assignable, because of the danger that the assignee will impose far heavier burdens on the servient tenant than would the original owner. But all these points were brushed aside, and the long tradition of construction of easements and contracts in aid of government power carried the day. *General Box* did not establish a power of congressional dominance. But it certainly helped to preserve it.

The third of the Warren Court water cases is in a sense the most difficult to understand. In *United States v. Virginia Electric*[52] the government acquired an interest in some riparian lands by condemnation. Those lands were subject to a flowage easement that the owner had conveyed to the respondent prior to the initiation of the condemnation, and the landowner quite happily agreed to convey to the government a second flowage easement over that same land for one dollar, but "subject to 'such water, flowage, riparian and other rights, if any,' as the respondent owned in the tract."[53] It followed therefore that the government did not have to compensate the riparian owner for the value of the land while flooded, since the owner had ceded that right to a third party. The question is whether it had to compensate the respondent for its loss of the assigned flowage easement (that is, the flow of navigable waters) when the government could keep those waters to itself by exercising the navigation servitude, thus reducing to zero the value of the discrete flowage easement to its purchaser.

If one looks at the two private interests separately, there is a certain logic to the government's case, but this truly looks like a situation in which the sum of the parts should be as great as the whole. If compensation is denied the respondent, then the party that profits from the initial purchase of the flowage easement is not the respondent as purchaser, but the government. The original landowner gets full compensation in two parts, with one part coming from a private party who does not keep the interest so purchased, and the remainder from the government. This divided approach hardly encourages security of exchange, for useful transactions between private parties will not take place if the sum of the values created is necessarily less than the values that existed before the transaction. It will hardly do to promote a sale of an easement if the total value of compensable interests before sale is a thousand dollars, but after the sale of part the total value of the compensable interests is reduced to five hundred dollars. Why enter into any deal that grants a windfall to a stranger? Yet that is one unfortunate development that can occur whenever the government acts like a sleeping giant, armed with the navigation servitude club.

The Supreme Court held that the flowage easement was entitled to some value, but on a very odd theory. It was not that the water itself could be used for power purposes on the riparian lands. Rather the sole source of the value lay in the threat that it gave the holder of the interest over the owner of the land, in its "right to destroy" any uses that might take place on this land—a right so powerful that any prospective buyer of the land would be well-advised to make sure that the easement was purchased as well.[54] The Court thus held that it was a mistake to treat the flowage easement as though it were the "equivalent of the value of the servient lands for agricultural, forestry, or grazing use."[55] The right measure of value under the circumstances was the ability of the holder of the interest to *block* these uses by others. All this is odd if not perverse: the purpose of eminent domain is to overcome holdout problems, a point recognized in the negative in *Twin City Power*, where the claim for value expressly excluded any holdout value. And it makes it utterly unintelligible as to why the holder of the servient land would create the easement in the first place, for the development rights in the land are worth far less split than they are together.

Professor Michelman finds in this case the idea that condemnation is sensible for the outright destruction of a thing, but not for a partial regulation of the thing that leaves the owner with some residual element of value.[56] The problem here is that of the numerator and denominator: does it make a difference if the state takes all of a small thing, or part of a large thing? It is one that has embarrassed the Court in the years since *Virginia Electric*.[57] It might be nice to afford compensation (albeit by the wrong valuation method) because the interest is separate and apart from all others and thus fully wiped out, but it is in my view social folly to have to decide constantly whether a parcel of land that is developed by subdivision over time may be regulated within an inch of its life without compensation.

The overarching theme should be that no division or combination of interests in land should add or detract from the government's obligation to compensate. Private parties should not have an incentive to reconfigure their land to maximize the compensation payable. "Compensation neutrality" should become a mantra of this branch of the law much as "tax neutrality" is a mantra of a sound system of taxation. Justice Stewart, writing in *Virginia Electric*, hinted at just this approach when he noted that "[t]he guiding principle of just compensation is reimbursement to the owner for the property interest taken. He is entitled to be put in as good a position pecuniarily as if his property had not been taken. He must be made whole but is not entitled to more."[58] Just the juxtaposition of these two sentences shows how unsystematically Justice Stewart approached the critical questions. Compensation for the property taken does not include consequential damages; yet these must be included if the property owner is "to be put in as good a position pecuniarily as if his property had not been taken." And any effort to carry this approach over to regulatory takings would lead to a revolution in outcomes, for no longer could the question be whether any viable economic use was retained, but whether that use was equal in value to the property prior to regulation—a rule that makes most zoning restrictions compensable events. But Justice Stewart had no inclination to go beyond the particulars to the larger theory. He thus missed another opportunity to write a far more searching examination of the takings law, and the decision itself is but a small ripple in the general torrent of cases that allow the navigation easement to remain far more dominant than it deserves to be.

OVERFLIGHT EASEMENTS The difficulties that water rights present in the overall scheme of property rights are paralleled in part by overflight rights. Long before the Warren Court, courts and legislatures were forced generally to make peace with the airplane's massive challenge to the *ad coelum* rule, under which, in an incautious moment, the common law gave the surface owner the rights over lands to the heavens, secure in the fact that these rights were of value to no one else. The airplane changed that, and these rights were reduced in size and stature (not withstanding futile eminent domain challenges) to protection of the area of effective occupation, so that a classical holdout problem did not bring air transportation to a halt. The air traffic was regarded as an upper neighbor to the landowner. But the question of trespass in the lower airspace remained, and, in the pre-Warren Court decision in *United States v. Causby*,[59] it was held that airplanes that engage in low overflight have taken a compensable easement in the property for which compensation is required—hardly a threat to the welfare state.

In *Causby* the only party that flew over the lands was the United States, so it was easy to figure out where to point the finger on the question of compensation: by the rules of vicarious liability, the honor fell to the government. With *Griggs v. Allegheny County*,[60] the overflights were by commercial carriers, so that the simple agency model created an incredible problem of apportionment of the harm, with the further embarrassment that the taking of the overflight easement was by a private party. Not to worry. The Court held that the local government that agreed to operate the airport had to pay for the easement it had, de facto, condemned. In essence, the local government was treated as though it stood in the shoes of the United States. Justice Black dissented, saying that the plaintiffs had targeted the wrong defendant, a constant problem in eminent domain cases, for he believed that the federal government that underwrote the program, not the state airport authority, had condemned the easement.[61] The point here is one of little long-term institutional significance, for once the issue is flagged by the courts, any dollars-and-cents financial issues could be decided by contract between the federal government, which supplies funds to local airports, and the airports that receive those funds.

Griggs therefore does little harm, and for that matter, little good. Its moral is that where there is no navigation servitude (in the skies) the compensation model is alive and well. The difficulties surely come with the valuation of the interest in quiet enjoyment that is compromised by the development. The sad point here is that when the nuisance is caused not by an overflight, but by a flight over adjacent properties, that interest became noncompensable, at least by one important circuit court opinion.[62] The whole problem would have been decided far more sensibly if it were understood that nuisance-like activities by the government are compensable wrongs, just as nuisance-like activities by private parties can be suppressed without compensation. Thus the Warren Court had the chance to bring some parity to public takings law and private nuisance law, but, once again, it missed the opportunity.

LIEN RIGHTS In one sense, the most important case decided during the Warren Court years was an obscure dispute over lien rights to unfinished boats. In *Armstrong v. United States*,[63] a shipbuilder in default was forced by the United States to transfer all its interest in the boat and the materials on hand to the United States, free and clear of all mechanics liens on the boat—including that held by Armstrong. No one doubted that the government could call for the unencumbered boat, but it is quite a different question as to whether that option, when exercised, could nullify all state law mechanics liens. In one sense they could, because the government could take free and clear title to the boats, so the lienors' specific security is lost. But in the relevant sense they could not. The Court held that the federal government could take free and clear title only by paying off the liens. Since that option is always open to private parties as well (for the nature of a lien right is for security only), the government in essence was told that it had to respect the existing liens, for which it promptly paid. This result was in the long run a victory for the government, for if the rule had remained otherwise, no one would dare do work without prompt payment on a government vessel. The risk of high-handed government action would lead to more inefficient construction practices that could only increase the government's costs of military procurement. In a sense therefore, *Armstrong* is the flip side of *General Box*.[64] The government as assignee takes subject to liens that bind the assignor.

One may doubt that there is one law professor in a hundred who knows *Armstrong* for its facts. Rather, the case has entered the legal canon solely for one concluding observation, which has become the Bible for all those who wish to limit the scope of government regulation generally (myself included). Its sacred text reads: "The Fifth Amendment's guarantee that private property shall not be taken for public use without just compensation was designed to bar government from forcing some people alone to bear public burdens which, in all fairness and justice, should be borne by the public as a whole."[65]

The sentence is a bolt from the blue that follows an observation that the ability to keep the boat lien-free under its contract with the shipbuilder offers no reason for not compensating the lien holders. Yet in principle the sentence could apply to any form of regulation that imposes heavy burdens on a single individual for the benefit of society at large. Seen in this light, the Eminent Domain Clause is designed to deal with matters of public funding and to counteract the dangers of majority rule. This notion was belittled in the post-Warren Court decision of *Penn Central*,[66] which held that fairness and justice did not apply to mere regulation that prevented the development of valuable land. Intuitive ideas of fairness and justice, though, cannot be so easily expunged from takings jurisprudence. They were appealed to, for example, in dissent by Justice Scalia, who insisted that if San Jose wants to have rent control for the benefit of poor people, it could tax generally and provide specific subsidies.[67] San Jose had no warrant in forcing the costs on the hapless landlords whose units were occupied by indigent tenants.

The efficiency implications of Justice Black's justice claim are also evident. If the state has to pay, it will compare the private costs of development with the state gains, for it has to persuade reluctant taxpayers to foot the bill. But allow these burdens to be imposed on a small minority within the jurisdiction, and socially foolish projects will be fully funded. But of the possible extension of this insight to zoning or rent control—both held clearly constitutional then and now—there was not so much as a glimmer or hint. Another constitutional opportunity missed, by a judge who actually cared something about the larger issues lurking in the case.[68]

GENERAL REGULATIONS *Prohibition on Use.* What is most striking about the Warren Court is that it faced very few cases in which general regulations, short of dispossession, limited the use and development of property. The first case of this sort was *United States v. Central Eureka Mining Co.*,[69] where the government imposed restrictions that prevented mine owners, as owners of nonessential wartime operations, from operating their mines. In these cases the government took nothing, in the sense that it did not seize the mines but only stopped their full economic use, in order to serve the public good in wartime. In order to minimize the scope of the government intrusion, the Court gave this hypothetical: if the order had restricted the use of all equipment needed to operate the mine, there would be no taking; why then complain about the exercise of a larger right that imposes no greater burden?[70] The fallacy in this argument is that it assumes that any ban on equipment use is not a taking of the equipment, with a consequential loss measured by the lost profits from the mine. But that restriction on equipment use appears to constitute a taking as well, for which consequential damages are appropriate. A private party could be held for lost profits whether he barred the mine doors or stole the tools. Why should the government be in a different position? Setting the verbal parry to one side, the hard question is whether this regulation is a taking, and if so, whether that taking is one justified by the exigencies and necessities of war.

At one level this was a straight regulatory takings case, and the decisive precedent is *Mugler v. Kansas*,[71] where the prohibition on liquor manufacture was thought to be less offensive insofar as the government did not take possession of a factory that became a worthless hulk (and potential liability?) for its owner. It came as no surprise that this decision was dutifully cited as a precedent for the outcome in *Central Eureka*, as was *Pennsylvania Coal Co. v. Mahon*[72] whose "too far" test was cited as working on behalf of the government.

Yet the case involves more than a simple taking, for the decision was heavily influenced by an attitude of judicial deference to legislative action in time of war. The decision in *Central Eureka* is a textbook example of how dangerous it is to collapse the questions of takings and justifications into a single undifferentiated mass. If the restriction on use and operations had been treated as a taking, then the government would *clearly* have to pay to effectuate it. The occupation of land for war purposes, even on a temporary basis, resulted in endless lawsuits to calculate the value of taken leasehold interests, a line of cases that had run its course prior to the Warren Court. Those were all actions that triggered obligations for just compensation, and the result here should be the same. But here the Court adopted quite a different standard because a "mere" regulation was involved. "War, particularly in modern times, demands the strict regulation of nearly all resources. It makes demands which otherwise would be insufferable. But wartime economic restrictions, temporary in character, are insignificant when compared to the widespread uncompensated loss of life and freedom of action which war traditionally demands."[73]

There is no awareness that this quotation flies in the teeth of the sentiment expressed some three years later in *Armstrong*, and indeed Justice Black was on the wrong side in *Central Eureka*. Here, for example, the mineowner would surely have no complaint if the government bid up the cost of its mining inputs, even if it were forced to suspend operations or to go out of business altogether. So the question here is not whether there is any special solicitude for established enterprises in time of war, for there is none against competitive injury. But the question does arise, more generally, how the nation should respond to the vicissitudes of war. War places a premium on the efficient use of resources, and it is far from clear that this is done through a command-and-control economy. Surely, if the only question is obtaining sufficient revenues for funding the war effort, those can be obtained by the appropriately high level of taxation. Yet no matter what the tax level, the major fear still remains: the government will not use its tax dollars wisely if it does not have to pay for the substantial dislocation that it forces on this hapless coal miner. But far from facing this problem head on, the Court turned somersaults to avoid the compensation issue.

Oddly enough it is not clear that this case would be decided the same way today, for even this regulation might flunk the "too far" test because the restrictions allowed no viable use of the property, at least for the duration of the war. But again one can never be sure about the legal outcome under current law: with a temporary restriction, as this one surely was, some residual economic value was left for future periods, so it is difficult to know what the reference point should be for deciding whether the rights were fully stripped or not. Temporary occupations of property are surely takings; so why not temporary restrictions on use? In my view, these cases are all part of a seamless web, in which small differences in the magnitude of burdens reflect themselves in small differences in valuation. But the Supreme Court sees, or constructs, a chasm were none exists. *Central Eureka* is thus another wrong decision, and another lost opportunity.

Contract Regulation. The interaction between government regulations and economic liberties is often contested not under the Takings Clause but under the Contracts Clause, and in the Warren Court there was one notable opinion that upheld the right of the state to modify the protection it afforded purchasers of property at foreclosure sales. In *El Paso v. Simmons*,[74] Texas had long allowed the owners of foreclosed property the indefinite right to redeem so long as their redemption rights were not cut off by a sale to a bona fide third party. The effect of this unwise provision was that it made it impossible for title to be quieted so long as property remained in the hands of the state. In this case land was sold in 1910 under a contract that called for a down payment of 2½ percent, with interest due annually on the full amount. The principal on the loan was never paid down. Some thirty-one years after the initial transaction, in 1941, Texas changed the rules of the game so that the right of the defaulting buyer to redeem the property was cut off in five years, whether or not the property was sold. Six years after the passage of this statute, the buyer went into default, and one day after the five year limitation period had expired, the purchaser sought to redeem his land. After the passage of this statute, Simmons took a quitclaim deed from the original purchaser of the property and filed his application for reinstatement of his title, tendering at long last the required payments. That application would have been allowed if the original legal rules were still in place, but was denied on the strength of the 1941 statutory reforms. Thereafter the state conveyed the land to the city of El Paso, which Simmons promptly sued claiming the superiority of his title under the original statute. The Supreme Court,[75] over the lone dissent of Justice Black,[76] upheld the statute on the ground that the state had great latitude in the manipulation of contractual obligations, at least since its critical decision in *Home Building & Loan Association v. Blaisdell.*[77]

All things considered, even a die-hard defender of contract rights has to put in a kind word for the 1941 statutory reform, which goes a long way toward clearing title to lands in the Texas system. Yet this is not to say that the result reached by the Court was correct, for the proper solution is to provide just compensation for the elimination of the original contract rights, a provision to which even *Blaisdell* paid lip service. But what kind of compensation should be paid? In *Blaisdell* the state's argument was that the tenants in possession continued to have to make mortgage payments to the lender for remaining on the property—albeit payments that did not leave the lender indifferent to the loss of his foreclosure rights.

In this case, that compensation theme could have been pursued if the state made a small forgiveness in the total outstanding amount of the loan. But how much? The answer has to be very little indeed. The 1941 statute applied only prospectively, and it allowed any defaulting buyer five years to set matters right from the date of any future breach, a pretty generous forgiveness period. The mortgages carried very low interest rates and the property had appreciated in value, so that the risk of default was quite low. Hence it is quite possible that a one percent downward adjustment in the principal balance would have improved the situation all around, without the need to enter into time consuming negotiation with each purchaser of state lands. The strength of Justice Black's position thus rests on a point that he did not quite make: the ease with which this adjustment can be made, and the importance of making that adjustment for the fidelity of our constitutional tradition. The

Court's eagerness to improve the machinery of conveyance, "to restore confidence in the stability and integrity of land titles," and to avoid the "perpetual reinstatement" of defaulting, led it to read *Blaisdell* as a decision that said that contract rights may be ignored when there is a compelling state interest to do so, a position that is productive of all sorts of mischief when applied generally. That conclusion may well on rare occasions be correct when the public gains from the sacrifice of contract (or property) rights is huge and the possibility of making compensation to the individual losers of the transaction is small. But here an easy mechanism exists, and perhaps it would have been wise to have held Texas's feet to the fire to make sure that it observed the constitutional niceties, not because the 1941 statute was foolish and unwise, but because all its laudable objectives could, and should, have been achieved through payment of just compensation, in the form of a downward debt adjustment.

Once the hard cases go the wrong way, then it is quite easy to allow the state to repudiate obligations—in the public interest, of course—even when one percent adjustments in mortgage balances are wholly inssufficient to carry the day, as happened with the regrettable Supreme Court decisions that allowed the federal government to renege retroactively and with impunity on its promises to firms that joined in its Pension Guaranty Corporation.[78]

Rate-of-Return Regulation. The question of regulation has also arisen in connection with cases dealing with rate-of-return regulation. The rate-of-return formulas were first introduced into the law in order to avoid two horns of a dilemma in dealing with those industries that could be fairly described as natural monopolies, that is, those industries characterized by diminishing marginal costs of production over broad portions of their supply curve. The diminishing marginal return implies that it is more costly for two firms to produce the relevant outcome than one, and hence a cost to competition. The price of judicial and legislative indifference to this prospect is monopoly profits to the producer. The price of excessive legislative regulation, however, is the risk of confiscation of the facilities of the producer, who can craftily be allowed a return sufficient to cover the variable costs of his investment, but not to recover the capital invested within the firm.[79] The "just compensation" solution is one that allows the state to regulate but insists that it allows the regulated firm to recover a risk-adjusted rate of return on its invested capital. The key question is how.

Before the Warren Court, Justice Douglas, in one of his most influential decisions, *Federal Power Commission v. Hope Natural Gas*,[80] held that it was sufficient for the government to give each firm that suitable return on its initial investment without having to determine whether the capital invested was still used in the rate base. The question in the *Permian Basin* cases[81] was whether the investments of separate and distinct companies in a common pool of oil and gas had to have their rates of return under *Hope Natural Gas* calculated on an individual basis, or whether each firm could be required to accept a return based on their pooled investment. "The most fundamental of these [constitutional questions] is whether the Commission may, consistently with the Constitution and the Natural Gas Act, regulate producers' interstate sales by the prescription of maximum area rates, rather than by proceedings conducted on an individual producer basis."[82] The pooling procedure created substantial administrative simplification, and it did not increase the total costs to consumers above and beyond what they would have to pay under *Hope Natural Gas*. But it had the further effect of enriching some members of the pool at the expense of the others. Justice Harlan wrote for eight members of the Court in sustaining the restriction, quoting *Hope* and noting that it applied here. The decision simply followed the general rule that enormous discretion is allowed the government in administrative proceedings, especially on matters of rate regulation that had been "customary since time immemorial"[83] in common law jurisdictions. Once again we have the Supreme Court on cruise control, making not the slightest effort to examine whether the justifications for price regulations in other settings might be exceeded in this particular context, given the equally ancient requirement of a reasonable rate of return on investment. The vast bulk of the opinion was then dutifully devoted to complex administrative law and rate regulation matters.

In something of an irony, Justice Douglas thought that his *Hope Natural Gas* rule still had some teeth, and dissented on the ground that his decision a quarter of a century before required the level of individualized determinations that afforded each party its own just rate of return.[84] Owing to the Court's general lack of interest in the constitutional issues, however, his complaint went largely ignored: but once again the question is why when the issues are so profound and difficult. Could the state condemn a city block of houses and pay each owner the average value of all houses on the block? Or would some individuation be required? The answer is not easy to reach and depends at the least on the interaction of the costs of an individual evaluation relative to the anticipated deviation from the true value that is produced by adopting any short cut. But that relationship was just not probed in a setting that treated judicial deference to administrative decisions as the proper response in all complex administrative settings. Yet the problem is more insistent, and it comes back to haunt us all under the Cable Act of 1992, another price regulation scheme where the costs of individuation are too high, and the dangers of misevaluation too great. But massive impracticality offers no constitutional defense under the Takings Clause against going forward with the regulation, although it should.

Civil Rights Cases. The stakes in the next regulatory takings case of this period are somewhat higher. Most people remember the constitutional battles over civil rights statutes and think of the question of jurisdiction. Is this statute constitutional because it falls under the Commerce Clause or because it falls under the Equal Protection Clause? Yet there was *also* a takings issue raised in *Heart of Atlanta Motel v. United States*,[85] which was dispatched with commendable swiftness by the Court. Once it was decided that the activities in question affected commerce, then the only issue was this: "if it [the statute] had such a basis, whether the means it [Congress] selected to eliminate that evil are reasonable and appropriate. If they are, appellant has no 'right' to select its guests as it sees fit, free from government regulation."[86] Lots of states passed these laws, lots of people thought that they were correct; and the fact that there is an obvious tension between the basic right to exclude and the requirements of the civil rights laws was dismissed by putting the word "right" in quotation marks, as if the scare quotes performed the analysis.

In truth the challenge is far more serious. At one level the argument is that so long as the government does not occupy the land itself, then it is all right to breach the wall of exclusivity. But this means that property ceases to be a way to organize relations among individuals and instead only works as a bulwark against direct government intrusion. The thought that the government has a strong stake in the outcome, given the private constituencies that line up behind or against legislation, was not really addressed in this case. Instead the Court noted that there really was no loss in this case: "It is doubtful if in the long run appellant will suffer economic loss as a result of the Act. Experience is to the contrary where discrimination is obliterated as to all accommodations. But whether this be true or not is of no consequence since this Court has specifically held that the fact that a 'member of the class which is regulated may suffer economic losses not shared by others . . . has never been a barrier' to such legislation."[87]

The impulse is manifestly inconsistent with *Armstrong*, which had been decided only four years before. The question of compensation is a real one, of course, and the possibility that a universal imposition of the prohibition would benefit all such institutions cannot be dismissed out of hand. By the same token, one would hope for more argument about the question. Thus one possible approach asks whether the antidiscrimination norm should apply to firms in competitive industries, where new entry is feasible, or whether it should be confined to monopolistic situations, including protected trade unions, and common carriers and inns that enjoyed a position of that sort in earlier times. Here it could well be that these conditions were no longer satisfied, and the statute could still have been justified as a means to counter the private violence that would have stopped most restaurants from integrating when they wanted to. But no contingent empirical claims were raised in this case. Generalized truths (whose truth is far from self-evident) coupled with statements about irrelevance ruled the day.

For this Court the social issue dominated the narrow legal one. In the light of hindsight one would hope that some people at least would think that a far tighter justification for this restriction on property use is called for. But if so, then we once more have a case of a missed opportunity to strike down a statute that has been extended well beyond its permissible limits under both the commerce and the takings part of the analysis.[88] But for takings law there was no innovation here. And for the Court to innovate on takings in the context of civil rights would have been too suicidal for its political survival. The powerful New Deal conception that property does not include the right to pick one's trading partners was a status quo position that the Warren Court was eager to embrace.

In one sense the challenges to the Civil Rights Act of 1964 broke no constitutional ground, for "all" the Warren Court did was to ratify legislative judgments about the constitutionality of the statute. Its level of judicial innovation, however, became far more pronounced in *Reitman v. Mulkey*[89] where in an ironic sense the tables were turned. In that case, California had passed a statute, the Unruh Act, which prohibited discrimination in private real estate markets, both sale and rental. The statute itself was overturned by a referendum that in effect provided that all private owners had the right to sell or lease their property to whomever they pleased—a restoration of the prior common law position that treats the right to dispose of property to whomever one sees fit as an ordinary property right. The referendum, which was carefully drafted, did not apply to hotels and other forms of public accommodations to which a traditional common carrier duty of universal service attached. And it was not selective in its application: whites and blacks alike each had the same right or power. There is little question that even the Warren Court would have done nothing if the original common law rule had never been disturbed by legislation nor reinstated by referendum. But once the status quo ante was brought about by referendum, then the judicial wheels started to turn. The passage of the statute was clearly motivated to preserve the rights of private individuals to discriminate. From there it was thought to be a short leap to saying that the discrimination was "authorized" by the state, which had returned the power of selection to the individual. From there it was a second short leap to say that a race-blind statute was itself in direct violation of the Equal Protection Clause, whereupon it was struck down.

What is quite remarkable about the case, is that the common law definition of property rights did not suffice to defend a statute against constitutional attack. Thus, once the obvious is established—that real estate rental and sales markets are highly competitive—then the bottom drops out in any case that allows a restriction on the right to choose trading partners. If so, then the proper constitutional fire should be directed not at the referendum that repealed the Unruh Act, but at the act itself. Yet so strong was the Warren Court's commitment on discrimination that it was prepared to strike down the reinstatement of the common law position even though it would not dare to require some antidiscrimination law in private housing. Any conflict between property rights and the modern Civil Rights movement could come out only in one way.[90]

Police Power Justifications

The second of the great eminent domain questions concerns the scope and limits of the police power justification. On this issue the major bone of contention—before, during, and after the Warren Court—has concerned the extent to which the law of nuisance shapes the contours of public law. I have long argued that it does and should, and that the government as agent of successful citizens cannot go beyond their powers, save to condemn upon just compensation.[91] If the boundary lines between neighbors make sense under the law of nuisance, then the government cannot simply inject itself on one side of a private dispute and change the rules of the game. So, in the end, the position here is relatively simple. Where the private party commits the nuisance, then a government injunction, tailored to the situation, can be imposed without paying compensation. Where it has committed no nuisance, there is no wrong to enjoin, and the government must purchase any easement that it desires. There is no right for an individual to pollute; but no right for the government to stop by fiat activities that are short of pollution. In some cases the government stops one nuisance, or tolerates another, but provides compensation under the parallel restrictions imposed on others. These situations raise the question of implicit-in-kind compensation that was not much in evidence during the Warren Court. Here, two police power cases, which are striking not for their differences in outcomes, but for their differences in language and approach, will be discussed.

In *Goldblatt v. Town of Hempstead*,[92] the question before the Court was whether Hempstead was within its rights to stop the appellant from removing all sand and gravel from its mines, an activity that it had undertaken continuously for nearly thirty years. In the first year of the digging, a large crater was made, which was filled with water and thus transformed into a twenty-acre lake with an average depth of twenty-five feet. The question was whether this restriction on the right to remove sand and gravel was so onerous and unreasonable as to constitute a compensable taking.

The first question of course is whether any restriction on the right to mine on one's own land constitutes a prima facie taking by the government. On that issue, the *ad inferos* companion to the *ad coelum* rule indicates that mining sand and gravel is an ordinary incident to property, and one that can be severed and sold as a separate interest. The entire question then is whether the restriction on digging below the water level is necessary to protect from collapse of the homes and structures located in the vicinity. For these purposes the assumption will be that the common law recognizes a right of lateral support, so that if that showing could be made, then the restriction is permissible, unless some lesser restriction yields the same benefit. (The discussion will ignore the question of margins: What happens if a fifty percent relaxation in the restriction increases the chance of subsistence by one percent?)

The Court duly noted that this prohibition wiped out all the economic value from the land but did not think that this itself was sufficient to condemn the ordinance, for *Mugler* and *Central Eureka* were available as precedents, and were duly pressed into service for the propositions for which they so obviously stand.[93] And once again we were assured: "There is no set formula to determine where regulation ends and taking begins."[94] But this basic orientation was strengthened by the "usual presumption of constitutionality" which upheld the restriction as a valid police regulation.[95]

What is most fascinating about the case was the way in which the Court peered into this question. The opinion starts with some promise, when it says that a safety regulation should be evaluated in light of its impact on safety. "To evaluate its reasonableness we therefore need to know such things as the nature of the menace against which it will protect, the availability and effectiveness of other less drastic protective steps, and the loss which the appellants will suffer from the imposition of the ordinance."[96] The Court then notes that there was a "dearth of relevant evidence" on these points, which might lead the uninitiated to think that the state has not carried its burden to show that the regulation is related to safety. But the lack of relevant evidence was turned into a decisive advantage for the state: "Although one could imagine that preventing the further deepening of a pond already 25 feet deep would not have a *de minimis* effect on public safety, we cannot say that such a conclusion is compelled by facts of which we can take notice."[97] The bottom line is a heavy burden of proof on individual owners—"for all we know, the ordinance may have a *de minimis* effect on appellants"[98]—whose productive business has just been wiped out. The question of ends and means is articulated on the one hand, and demolished in application on the other, and the destructive effect of this cavalier opinion on the nature of local politics is a large theme, one that cannot be canvased here. But if *Euclid*[99] set the basic presumption, the Court surely accepted and perhaps expanded it in this case to manifestly unacceptable length. It is as though there were no abuse in local politics that might be sensibly subject to a constitutional counterweight. Whatever one might think of the right of exit as a Tiebout limitation[100] on local government, that sand and gravel could not migrate to the next township to escape the effects of local politics. The expandability of the police power was an important theme, and *Goldblatt* gave the law a solid push in the wrong direction.

The second of the police power cases is much more congenial. In *National Board of Young Men's Christian Associations v. United States*,[101] the question was, was the government responsible for riot damage inflicted on two YMCA buildings in the Panama Canal Zone, close to the Panamanian border? The government moved troops into the area because of rioting and looting, and when the troops took shelter from snipers inside the Y, the buildings were burned down. The action against the rioters was obviously fruitless, so the Y turned to the United States government on the ground that the presence of federal army units inside the building spurred the rioters to take greater destructive steps.

This is one case that the government should win. *Ex ante*, it is far from clear that the Y would prefer to go without protection, and far from clear that if it did, its facilities would escape destruction. So the theory of causation is directed to the wrong target, and it is always a bad argument in tort to say that A should be liable solely because B is not. At one level therefore, the buildings were destroyed by the enemy, not the government. Moreover, even if the government were responsible, its actions were done in good faith for the benefit of the parties harmed, hardly a reason to impose strict liability on the very party who seeks to help you. Indeed the chief contribution of *YMCA* to the takings debate is that it shows how enormous a gulf lies between the justifications that the government asserts when it is in the right, and the mischievous arguments that it makes when, as in *Goldblatt*, as in *Euclid* before it, it is clearly in the wrong. It is not that the Court cannot think of sensible lines of government privilege. It is that they do not think, at least until very recently, that sensible limitations were any part of its supervisory powers over state and local governments, which always received a clean bill of health.

Public Use

The third of our key questions concerns the issue of whether the taking can take place at all. Obviously this issue will not arise if the government restrictions are justified under the police power, for then the public is protected from the aggression of one of its members. But there are many cases where the government offers compensation where this issue is of manifest concern. From the time of *Calder v. Bull*[102] to the present, courts have intoned that it is no part of the proper function of government to take property from A in order to give it to B, even if B is prepared to pay just compensation for it. Bypassing the market in these circumstances is a manifest infringement of individual liberty and an invitation to government abuse, one that undercuts the stability of private ownership that lies at the core of sound constitutional order and a market economy.

The difficulty with this version of the public use test is that few cases of general importance seem to fall within it. In some cases there are lots of people in the position of B, so it looks as though there is some wide-scale public purpose or benefit that justifies the imposition. It becomes somewhat churlish to suggest that if one individual cannot force A off his land, then a conspiracy of many should not have that power. Either can buy in the open market. But with the rise of public housing projects for the poor in the 1930s, this barrier was overrun, for now land could be taken from private owners and rented out to particular tenants, in a taking from A_1 to A_n, with a transfer to B_1 to B_n.[103] Justice Douglas took the basic argument a step further when, in *Berman v. Parker*,[104] he concluded that the state could take over a local department store in a blighted neighborhood, even to sell it off again, as is, to another owner, as part of its neighborhood rehabilitation plan. Underlying his decision was an unqualified deference to Congress and its judgment about the proper determinants for good health and for good community living.[105] Those of us who think that planning is a disease that is best extirpated believe that this presumption is groundless and the exercise of the power is mischievous. But the later cases, most notably *Poletown*[106] at the state level and *Midkiff*[107] at the federal level, have upheld schemes that have allowed the simple transfer of ownership, in one case for the benefit of General Motors and the destruction of an entire neighborhood, and in the other when all that changed was who owned the property.

As indicated, these results are indefensible, and they invite the disruption of a social fabric that falls under the heading (both before and during the Warren years) as noncompensable good will.[108] One reason to insist on a strong reading of the public use limitation is that the just compensation laws are so rigged as to provide landowners little protection against the government bulldozer.[109] Assessor and legal fees, good will, nontransferable goods, are not taken by the government even if they are costs incurred or benefits destroyed by government action. Loss of amenities and neighborhood are treated in the same mechanical fashion. The limitation on public use might be acceptable if the just compensation backstop were firmly in place, but in the absence of robust rules on compensation, there is an open invitation to land-grab policies for the rich and influential that the public use language was designed to deter. Once again the encomium to planning that fell from Justice Douglas's pen reads odd today. One wonders what happened to the blighted area that was targeted for renewal and improvement. It seems all too likely that communities have been savaged by the government that is called upon to protect them. Here is one instance where a stronger protection of property rights goes hand in hand with a stronger protection of community.

Berman aside, there was little that needed to be done or could be done on the public use frontier. The only other case that addresses this question is a deservedly obscure one called *Dugan v. Rank*,[110] which held that if the government diverts water from a private holder for public purposes, the taking cannot be enjoined in district court, but rather by an action under the Tucker Act, which today has to be brought in the federal circuit. This jurisdictional two-step is much more onerous than is usually supposed. Sometimes it is far from clear whether the injunction should be sought in district court, because compensation has not been tendered, or whether damages should be sought in the federal circuit. In *Preseault v. United*

States,[111] for example, the Supreme Court on its own motion dismissed the plaintiff's cause of action for want of jurisdiction on the ground that the Rails-to-Trails Act did not prevent individual holders of reversionary interests from seeking compensation under the Tucker Act against the United States.[112] The Court's unfortunate decision meant that the landowner's petition to regain possession of his property was misguided, and that action had to shift to the federal circuit for compensation. The division of business between the district court and the federal circuit contemplated by *Dugan* is tolerable (if unwise) so long as the government makes it clear that it is committed to the taking. But when the legal situation is murky, the present jurisdictional rules create an unnecessary divide between two different courts, which invites a huge constitutional shell game that should be condemned even by those who think well of vesting the government with major planning powers.

Compensation

The last part of the analysis concerns the nature of the compensation that is offered for a taking. Sometimes it is cash, and in other cases it is in kind. A full analysis of this question is one that requires a close look at the distribution of benefits and burdens of regulations. It is an analysis that looks with presumptive suspicion on selective restrictions on some property owners and presumptive approval on statutes that impose uniform restrictions on the same group that receives a set of uniform benefits. I think that sorting out these relationships is one of the major tasks of a sensible set of constitutional norms of the just compensation issue, but there is little if anything in the Warren Court oeuvre that addresses this question, so the analysis again is focused on decisions before and after it sat.

Conclusion

It should be clear that I am the odd man out from this celebration of the Warren Court. Its work on property was generally perfunctory, occasionally mischievous, and only rarely informative. But lest anyone think that this means I am a strong critic of the Warren Court, I hope that the effort would show that my own positions are decidedly more complex. I am generally supportive of the *Miranda* developments,[113] and of reapportionment. I have no hidden qualms about *Brown v. Board of Education*.[114] While I think that *New York Times v. Sullivan*[115] ventured too far from the safe portals of common law defamation, on its facts the decision was clearly correct, no matter how much I disagree with the *Times*'s editorials on property rights, health care, or affirmative action. Indeed any effort to impose sensible judicial limitations on representative government will have a respectful hearing from me, for mine is not a conservative critique of the position of the Court, but one that accepts its antimajoritarian orientation and wishes that it extended to cover other areas as well. I do not see any opposition between liberty and property but regard them, as the Due Process Clause has them, as linked in a single yoke. My quarrel with the Warren Court is that it fell asleep at a constitutional switch, when it should have been more aware of the major contribution that the strong protection of property rights has for the overall constitutional order.

Notes

1. Stevens, "The Bill of Rights: A Century of Progress," in *The Bill of Rights in the Modern State* 13 (1992). It seems hardly surprising that Justice Stevens issued impassioned dissents in both Lucas v. South Carolina Coastal Council, 112 S.Ct. 2886, 2917 (1992) and Dolan v. City of Tigard, 114 S.Ct. 2309, 2322 (1994).
2. 123 U.S. 623 (1887).
3. 256 U.S. 135 (1921).
4. 260 U.S. 393 (1922).
5. 272 U.S. 365 (1926).
6. 276 U.S. 272 (1926).
7. 438 U.S. 104 (1978).
8. 447 U.S. 255 (1980).
9. 467 U.S. 229 (1984).
10. 483 U.S. 825 (1987).
11. 112 S.Ct. 2886 (1992).
12. 114 S.Ct. 2309 (1994).
13. 348 U.S. 27 (1954).
14. 357 U.S. 155 (1957).
15. 369 U.S. 590 (1962).
16. 364 U.S. 40 (1960).
17. 387 U.S. 369 (1967).
18. 392 U.S. 409 (1968).
19. West Coast Hotel v. Parrish, 300 U.S. 379 (1937).
20. The standard citations are Williamson v. Lee Optical of Oklahoma, 348 U.S. 483 (1955), and Ferguson v. Skrupa, 372 U.S. 726 (1963).
21. 198 U.S. 45 (1905).
22. For a summary of the attack on *Lochner* as falsely constitutionalizing common law norms of property and contact, see Tribe, *American Constitutional Law* § 8.6, 579 (2d ed. 1988). "Just as the *Swift v. Tyson* doctrine that federal judges should apply the 'general common law' in diversity cases could not survive the belief that there just *was* no transcendent body of binding general common law, so too that belief ultimately devastated *Lochner*'s due process doctrine that legislatures may not upset the 'natural' conditions of contract and property enshrined in common law categories and in their logical entailments."

My own views in Epstein, *Takings: Private Property and the Power of Eminent Domain* (1985) are designed to reestablish the broken link between the common law and the constitutional protection of property rights. The book meets with, to say the least, a cool reception from Tribe. See Tribe, at 606 n.6.

23. See, e.g., New York Trust v. Eisner, 256 U.S. 345 (1921).
24. New York Central R. Co. v. White, 243 U.S. 188 (1917).
25. Block v. Hirsh, 256 U.S. 135 (1921).
26. Euclid v. Ambler Realty Co., 272 U.S. 365 (1926).
27. Miller v. Schoene, 276 U.S. 272 (1926).
28. Adair v. United States, 208 U.S. 161 (1908).
29. Coppage v. Kansas, 236 U.S. 1 (1914).
30. Adkins v. Children's Hospital of District of Columbia, 261 U.S. 525 (1923).
31. And on this point at least, Laurence Tribe and I agree. See Tribe, supra note 22, at § 8.5.
32. United States v. Carolene Products Co., 304 U.S. 144, 152 n.4 (1938).

33. See, e.g., United States v. General Motors, 323 U.S. 373 (1945).

34. See El Paso v. Simmons, 379 U.S. 497 (1965).

35. Euclid v. Ambler Realty Co., 272 U.S. 365 (1926).

36. Epstein, supra note 22.

37. See, e.g., Justice Brennan's opinion in Penn Central Co. v. New York, 438 U.S. 104 (1978) and his dissent in Nollan v. California Coastal Commn., 483 U.S. 825 (1987). See also his opinion in Preseault v. United States 494 U.S. 1 (1990).

38. "Takings and the Police Power," 74 *Yale L.J.* 36 (1964).

39. "Property, Utility and Fairness: Comments on the Ethical Foundations of 'Just Compensation Law,'" 80 *Harv. L. Rev.* 1165 (1967).

40. I push this point hard in Epstein, "Property, Speech and the Politics of Distrust," 59 *U. Chi. L. Rev.* 41, 47–55 (1992).

41. 348 U.S. 27 (1954).

42. Poletown Neighborhood Council v. City of Detroit, 304 N.W.2d 455 (Mich. 1981).

43. Hawaii Housing Authority v. Midkiff, 467 U.S. 229 (1984).

44. It is important to recall that in some cases the question is whether it is within the scope of the state's police power to regulate when compensation is required, which raises obviously different questions. Yet even these points are sometimes confused. Compare West River Bridge Co. v. Dix, 6 How. 507 (U.S. 1848), which upheld the power to condemn a bridge that the government had conveyed to a private owner upon just compensation, with Home Building & Loan Association v. Blaisdell, 290 U.S. 398 (1934), where the same police power justification arguably was used to allow a state mortgage moratorium *without* compensation. For a comparison of the two decisions, see Epstein, "Toward a Revitalization of the Contract Clause," 51 *U. Chi. L. Rev.* 703, 735–38,740–43 (1984). For further discussion, see text accompanying notes 74–78.

45. United States v. Chandler-Dunbar Power Co. 229 U.S. 53 (1912). For what it is worth this decision took place during the *Lochner* period.

46. 350 U.S. 222 (1955).

47. Id. at 223.

48. Id. at 231. (Burton, J., dissenting).

49. 148 U.S. 312 (1893).

50. Fuller v. United States, 409 U.S. 488 (1973).

51. 351 U.S. 159 (1956).

52. 365 U.S. 624 (1965).

53. Id. at 625.

54. Id. at 630.

55. Id. at 633.

56. Michelman, supra note 39, at 1232–33.

57. See, e.g., Lucas v. South Carolina Coastal Council, supra note 11.

58. 365 U.S. at 633. The case cited internally is Olson v. United States, 292 U.S. 246 (1934).

59. 328 U.S. 256 (1946).

60. 369 U.S. 84 (1962).

61. Id. at 90.

62. Batten v. United States, 306 F.2d 580 (10th Cir., 1962).

63. 364 U.S. 40 (1964).

64. 351 U.S. 159 (1956).

65. 364 U.S. at 49.

66. The profanation of the sacred text reads as follows: "While this Court has recognized that the 'Fifth Amendment's guarantee . . . [is] designed to bar Government from forcing some people alone to bear public burdens which, in all fairness and justice, should be borne by the public as a whole,' Armstrong v. United States, 364 U.S. 40, 49 (1960), this Court, quite simply, has been unable to develop any 'set formula' for determining when 'justice and fairness' require that economic injuries caused by public action be compensated by the government, rather than remain disproportionately concentrated on a few persons." Penn Central Co. v. New York, 438 U.S. 104, 123–24 (1978). The citation is to Goldblatt v. Hempstead, 369 U. S. 590, 594 (1962), a Warren Court decision, discussed infra in text accompanying note 92.

67. Pennel v. City of San Jose, 485 U.S. 1 (1988), Scalia, J., dissenting.

68. See his lone dissent in El Paso v. Simmons, 379 U.S. 497, 518 (1965).

69. 357 U.S. 155 (1958).

70. Obviously, if the use of equipment were prohibited, the mines would close, and it did not make that order a "taking" merely because the order was, in form, a direction to close down the mines. Id. at 166.

71. 123 U.S. 623 (1887).

72. 260 U.S. 393 (1922).

73. 357 U.S. at 168.

74. 379 U.S. 497 (1965).

75. Id at 517. Compare West River Bridge Co. v. Dix, 6 How. 507 (U.S. 1848), which upheld the power to condemn a bridge that the government had conveyed to a private owner upon just compensation, with Home Building & Loan Association v. Blaisdell, 290 U.S. 398 (1934).

76. 379 U.S. at 517.

77. 290 U.S. 398 (1934).

78. Connolly v. Pension Benefit Guaranty Corp., 475 U.S. 211 (1986).

79. For a discussion of these and kindred difficulties, see Duquesne Light Co. v. Barasch, 488 U.S. 299 (1989).

80. 320 U.S. 591 (1944). That decision rejected the earlier view that the rate of return was calculated only on those assets used and usable in the business. See Smyth v. Ames, 169 U.S. 466 (1898).

81. 390 U.S. 747 (1968).

82. Id. at 768.

83. Id., citing, as one might expect, Munn v. Illinois, 94 U.S. 113, 133 (1876).

84. 390 U.S. at 829.

85. 379 U.S. 241 (1964).

86. Id. at 258.

87. Id. at 260.

88. For this constitutional challenge, see Epstein, *Forbidden Grounds: The Case Against Employment Discrimination Laws*, ch. 7 (1992).

89. 387 U.S. 369 (1967).

90. I use the phrase "modern before civil rights." That commitment was also found in Jones v. Alfred H. Mayer Co., 392 U.S. 409 (1968), which read the 1866 Civil Rights Act to bar private discrimination in housing.

91. Epstein, *Takings*, supra note 22, at chs. 8–9.

92. 369 U.S. 590 (1962).

93. Id. at 593, 594.

94. Id. at 594. It was the words "set formula" that were incorporated into *Penn Central Co. v. New York*, 438 U.S. 104, 124 (1978).

95. Id. at 594–96.

96. 369 U.S. at 595.

97. Id.

98. Id. at 596.

99. 272 U.S. 365 (1926).

100. Tiebout, "A Theory of Local Expenditures," 64 *J. Pol. Econ.* 416 (1956). His theory in effect argued that local governments each provide a mix of goods and services (and the taxes to pay for them) so that the effective constraint against local government abuse is the right to leave the jurisdiction. That might work for families choosing whether to live in an area with good or bad schools, but it hardly protects owners of real estate against local exploitation.

101. 395 U.S. 85 (1969).

102. 3 Dall. 386 (U.S. 1798).

103. See, e.g., Matter of New York City Housing Authority v. Muller, 270 N.Y. 33 (1936).

104. 348 U.S. 27 (1954).

105. Id. at 32.

106. Poletown Neighborhood Council v. City of Detroit, 304 N.W. 2d 455 (Mich. 1981).

107. Hawaii Housing Authority v. Midkiff, 467 U.S. 229 (1984).

108. For my position, see Epstein, "Rights and Rights Talk," 105 *Harv. L. Rev.* 1106, 1114–17 (1992), reviewing Mary Ann Glendon, *Rights Talk: The Impoverishment of Political Discourse* (1991).

109. See, Kanner, "When Is 'Property' Not 'Property Itself': A Critical Examination of the Bases of Denial of Compensation for the Loss of Goodwill in Eminent Domain," 6 *Cal. W. L. Rev.* 57 (1969).

110. 372 U.S. 609 (1963).

111. 494 U.S. 1 (1990).

112. National Trails System Act Amendments of 1983 (Amendments), Pub. L. 98-11, 97 Stat. 48 (codified at 16 U.S.C. § 1247(d)).

113. Miranda v. Arizona, 384 U.S. 436 (1966).

114. 347 U.S. 483 (1954).

115. 376 U.S. 254 (1964). See Epstein, "Was *New York Times v. Sullivan* Wrong?" 53 *U. Chi. L. Rev.* 782 (1986).

• 10 •

THE WARREN COURT AND THE WELCOME STRANGER RULE

RICHARD NEELY

I am a state judge, *not* a federal judge. Nonetheless, every June I attend the Fourth Circuit Judicial Conference where for three hours I listen first to the Chief Justice and then to five law professors summarize what of importance the Supreme Court has done in the past year. For ten years now it has been during these sessions that I have most missed the old Warren Court, because today's Court has reluctance to grapple with urgent social problems that can be addressed by no other institution.

One of the issues today that cries out for attention is national law uniformity. American lawyers are fond of pointing out that the United States is a "common law" country. By that they usually mean that American law, like early English law, relies more on judge-made rules than it does on legislative codes. But to use the term "common law" simply to refer to a malleable, court-dominated legal system misses what was perhaps the most important feature of the original common law—namely, its uniformity.

When William the Conqueror landed in England, he found a country that was governed by a great variety of local customs. Over the next three hundred years the Norman kings succeeded in establishing one uniform system of laws through the use of itinerant royal judges who were professional administrators of the law, all trained in one school. In the context of English law, use of the word "common," then, does not mean "ordinary" or "vulgar" but rather "uniform."

America, however, has turned the common law on its head. When we refer to ourselves as a "common law" country we have slipped behind the looking glass because the United States has very little uniform, national law. Unlike England, with its centralized court system staffed by a cadre of similarly trained judges, the United States today has fifty-three separate court systems. First, there is the nation-wide system of federal courts, which is divided into twelve separate circuits that are only loosely held together by the Supreme Court of the United States. In addition to the federal system, however, there are freestanding court systems in the fifty states, the District of Columbia, and Puerto Rico.

America's diversity of *court systems* leads to a diversity of *law systems*, because American judges, like their English predecessors, have extensive lawmaking powers.

And, because each separate court system is administratively independent of the others, each separate court system can generate eccentric judge-made law at odds with the statutory and judge-made law of other jurisdictions. Whole fields of American law, such as contracts and torts, are creatures of court decisions rather than legislative enactments. Most of the time this system works reasonably well, but there are structural problems today that could probably be solved if we had the national vision of the Warren Court.

As unpopular as what I am about to say next may be in a law school, courts are no place for intellectuals. Historically, the people who became big-time judges were big-time politicians: Earl Warren really wanted to be president; he only settled for being Chief Justice! Hugo Black had been a United States senator, and Thurgood Marshall was a hard-charging civil rights leader. Byron "Whizzer" White was a political operative for President Kennedy, and William O. Douglas (who admittedly had law professor credentials) was also a force in the New Deal.

It was from a politician's understanding of real life, rather than from some pointy-headed intellectual notion of emanations from penumbras inherent in vague clauses or hair-splitting historical discussions of the limitations or lack thereof of federal power that cases like *Gideon v. Wainright*,[1] *Miranda v. Arizona*,[2] and *Escobedo v. Illinois*[3]—in other words the great Warren Court criminal procedure cases—emerged. And, if one reads all of the Warren Court criminal cases together, it is obvious that the Warren Court wanted America to become THE UNITED STATES, instead of *These* United States—a subtle, yet extraordinarily important distinction.

For those of you who are young, the only way to appreciate the triumph of the Warren Court is to delve for a moment into the sociological facts that formed the foundation of that great Court's jurisprudence. In this regard, we must look at what the whole criminal process looked like about 1960.

Violent crime is almost always committed by the poor, the uneducated, and the stupid. Crimes of passion are committed by everyone, of course, but trials involving a middle-class man meticulously planning the murder of his wife, so he can collect the insurance and run off with his secretary, are sensational precisely because they are so rare. Traveling salesmen who spend their off-hours robbing all-night grocery stores, married schoolteachers who take nights off to rape sixteen-year-old girls, and prosperous farmers who routinely eliminate market competition by setting fire to their neighbors' barns are real oddities. Consequently, the entire criminal law system most often boils down to the powerful state with all its weapons—police, prosecutors, courts, prisons, and probation officers—going after poor, uneducated, stupid folks. (That, of course, is not to say that the poor, uneducated, stupid folks did not commit the crimes.) This lower class of criminal suspects is not exactly possessed of enormous political power that it can summon to protect its rights, particularly since when it is not on the receiving end of the whole system geared up to get it, it is the group in society crying most loudly for more law and order.

In the early 1960s, the average criminal defendant was treated like a piece of meat on its way to dressing and processing. A person was arrested, brought in for interrogation (seldom conducted in a gentlemanly manner), threatened with the many dire consequences that awaited him if he did not cooperate (such as a thirty-year sentence for simple burglary), and encouraged to plead guilty. Of course a lawyer could do wonders for him, but ordinarily there was not any lawyer and would not be any lawyer unless he came up with the money to hire one or was accused of a capital crime. For those who knew enough to make a scene and demand to have a court-appointed lawyer, a lawyer might be appointed, but it was frequently the case with overworked courts that the judge indicated either outright, in open court but off the record, or through hints delivered informally by third parties that things would go a lot easier for the defendant if he would plead guilty rather than make a lot of trouble asking for a lawyer and demanding a jury trial. If a person pleaded guilty, that was it—off he went to prison, having waived all grounds for appeal except the jurisdiction of the court, and he just sat in prison until the sentence expired or the parole board released him. Often the process ran an entirely innocent man through its machine, a man so frightened of the circumstantial evidence against him that he would agree to plead guilty to a lesser offense or to confess to a crime he did not commit in the hope of receiving more lenient treatment from a system that was going to get him anyway. This was particularly true of people from out of town who found that in addition to all the disadvantages under which natives were operating, they were subject to the "welcome stranger rule."

It usually happened that in any small town or city where this particular form of expedited due process occurred all the participants were friends, buddies, and colleagues. I grew up in such a system where my grandfather was a United States senator and my uncle was the local criminal judge. We all got driven around by the sheriff's deputies. Typically, indeed, the sheriff, prosecutor, and judge were all members of the same political party who exchanged fishing stories together over lunch down in the jail, while the prisoners served them a subsidized meal, and because each officeholder had power over the others, they had long ago developed the live-and-let-live mentality known in politics as "You've got to go along to get along." Almost everywhere prosecutors, sheriffs, and judges were elected and the staffs were not civil service, so that staff presented no counterbalance to the alliances of party politics. Furthermore, criminal trials have always been both expensive and a lot of work for everyone concerned, and because neither judge, prosecutor, nor sheriff was paid by the case, real due process took money away from payrolls for relatives and a lot of time away from the farm and the trout stream.

The system was not only a fiasco at the interrogation, pretrial confinement, and guilty plea stages; it resembled some of the more unpleasant features of Nazi Germany or modern Iraq in the investigative stages. Men were routinely picked up off the street without a warrant, brought down to the police station, left to sit on hard benches without access to water, food, or sometimes even a clean restroom for hours at a time before "questioning," which frequently involved humiliating insults and a good bit of slapping around. In many cases, the police had nothing more to direct them to their particular suspect than a prior criminal record, the "suspicious behavior" of an arrested person, or personal animosity.

The entire "questioning" process went on without regard for the person's need to be at his job, his school, his wife's side in the hospital, or anywhere else. The convenience of the authorities organized the lives of those without power who came to the authorities' attention. And who was available to give redress? The political process, where most aspirants for office run on a "crack down on crime" platform? The local judge, who would need to dress down the local sheriff or police chief in the morning before they all went out for lunch together? The executive authority, whose very henchmen all these rights violators were? Not very likely.

The criminal procedure cases of the Warren Court did a great deal to ameliorate these problems: obviously, however, the problems were not entirely solved. Unfortunately, the efforts to these ends of the Warren Court are a little like our characterization of the army when I was young: "A system designed by geniuses to be executed by idiots!" Nonetheless, notwithstanding all the problems and imperfections, major progress was made because the Court understood the basic problem and was willing to wrestle with potential solutions.

Today there are similar problems related to the inveterate inclination of courts to apply the "welcome stranger rule," but today's Supreme Court is reluctant to experiment or otherwise wrestle with these problems. The preeminent example of substantive law problems that arise simply from the *structure* of the American legal system is product liability. Typically, in a product liability case, there is an *in-state* plaintiff, an *in-state* judge, an *in-state* jury, *in-state* witnesses, *in-state* spectators, and an *out-of-state* defendant. When states are entirely free to craft the rules of liability any way they want, it takes little imagination to guess that out-of-state defendants as a class will not do very well. All the incentives, at both the trial court level and the policy-making appellate court level, favor the redistribution of wealth from out-of-state defendants to local residents, which is the reason that product liability law becomes more and more oppressive to business as the years go by.

There is no "American" law of product liability in the sense of uniform national standards. Given the profile of product liability suits, where the defendant is almost invariably from out-of-state, there is a "competitive race to the bottom" among state courts to create ever more liberal liability rules. This is not necessarily an intentional antibusiness policy, but simply an exercise in economic self defense: any state court (or state legislature, for that matter) that doesn't keep up with the latest pro-plaintiff rulings is a sucker! This may sound counterintuitive, but it nevertheless follows inevitably from America's uncoordinated federal structure.

Simply put, if you ask the average state judge whether he would like to redistribute some wealth from, say, Ford Motor Company to a local resident who was severely injured in a car crash, the judge will probably answer yes. But if you ask the same judge to make a choice between high local employment in Ford's plants, on the one hand, and redistribution of Ford's money, on the other, he is likely to favor high employment over simple wealth redistribution. The problem is that except for the U.S. Supreme Court, no American judge can effect these trade-offs.

If, for example, as a West Virginia judge I insist that West Virginia have *conservative* product liability rules, then all I do is reduce my friends' and neighbors' claims on the existing pool of product liability insurance paid for by consumers through "premiums" incorporated into the price of everything we buy.

No matter, then, how responsible I want to be as a state court judge, I cannot improve the overall American liability system or reduce the exposure of West Virginia manufacturers to the caprice or malice of out-of-state courts and juries. But by trying to do so unilaterally I can succeed in impoverishing my own state's residents without doing anyone, anywhere, any measurable good. Therefore, unless I want to be a sucker, as a state judge I *must* keep up with the latest pro-plaintiff wealth redistribution theories applied in other states and incorporate them into my own state's decisional law. Furthermore, I can even garner for West Virginia more than our fair share of the national insurance pool if I think up new wealth redistribution theories myself and stick them in the law before any other state.

We cannot expect, then, a rational structure that takes America's competitive position in world markets into account when all decisions about product liability law reform must be made at the state level. Because of the competitive race to the bottom, every jurisdiction will ultimately follow the most irresponsible state. In just the twenty years between 1970 and 1990, product liability went from an "innovative theory" not even recognized by a majority of states to a nationwide business hazard involving billions of dollars annually in judgments. Thus federalism's dynamics have not only created the current monster but they will inevitably create a bigger and more horrible monster in the next decade, and that is the problem that should most concern us now.

Product liability exposure is one of the *most* serious problems facing the American economy, but the full dimensions of the problem are as yet only dimly understood by the general public. In general, most large American companies respond to surveys (such as the 1987 Conference Board survey) by saying that they can live with the current product liability system. But that is because most large American companies manufacture established products with known liability risks and have devised schemes—such as introducing new products off-shore—to keep their product liability exposure in the American market within reasonable limits. Thus, the problem for the American economy is not that product liability will bankrupt otherwise solvent American companies, but rather that the defensive actions that American companies are forced to take to protect themselves from product liability exposure will move American research, development, and jobs off-shore.

Not all segments of American society face the same jeopardy from global competition. Thus, the upper middle class of lawyers, judges, university professors, doctors, and other "professionals" are not subject to having their jobs moved overseas. Skilled and unskilled labor, on the other hand, as well as business managers, face constant competition from low-cost foreign producers. America, then, is divided into two classes—those for whom America's international competitive position is a life-or-death issue, and those who are insulated from international competition.

The strength of the Roosevelt administration's New Deal was the breadth of shared economic concerns. Even those who had secure jobs during the 1930s still had parents, brothers, or friends who were out of work. The same broad unity of interest in economic matters does not exist today. Current social stratification produces a leadership class of professionals, journalists, and academicians who are both psychologically and geographically removed from the lower middle class of blue collar and clerical workers threatened by foreign competition. Were this not the case, far greater attention would be paid in the media to our product liability law.

Draconian product liability rules discourage American companies from introducing new products in the American market until those products have been thoroughly tested abroad. But, if the initial product introduction is to be done, say, in Japan, then it is only intelligent to manufacture the product in Japan initially. And, logically, if the manufacturing is to be done in Japan, then the research, development, and engineering ought to be done in Japan as well. Inevitably, then, the product becomes a Japanese product and not an American product. The company doing the manufacturing may be an American company in the sense that it is owned by American shareholders, but the real wealth—namely the jobs associated with the production of the product and the technical skills acquired by managers and labor force—is owned by the Japanese.

Thus the big loss from runaway product liability law is research and development *not* pursued, new technologies *not* developed, new products *not* introduced, market shares *not dominated*, learning curves *not* exploited, and new jobs *not* created.

All of this is important to the rest of the law uniformity argument because "reforming" irrational civil law, of which product liability law is the preeminent example, is not a matter of reordering our affairs so that wealthy stockholders and managers prosper to the detriment of injured accident victims, consumers, and other "little people." Rather, "reforming" product liability is a matter of realigning our affairs so that the same class of ordinary workers who are usually accident victims have better job opportunities and more secure futures, while at the same time being protected by a reasonable product insurance law administered through the tort system.

Obviously the solution to this "competitive race to the bottom" problem is national product liability law. Business, in fact, has been trying to get bills reforming product liability law through Congress for years, but those bills have gone nowhere. This is because the plaintiffs' lawyers have a lock on the U.S. House of Representatives. Product liability bills do well in the U.S. Senate because senators need big money for statewide media campaigns; the same bills die in the House of Representatives because that's how congressmen pay back their shock troops.

The plaintiffs' lawyers are generally a pretty decent bunch. Their offices are accessible to the little man; they often live in the neighborhoods they serve; and they are active in politics and civic affairs. Business's lawyers, on the other hand, live in upper-middle-class, lily-white suburbs, drive to work in air-conditioned cars, and work on the top floors of fortified skyscrapers. In general, business lawyers socialize with the business clients they represent and are more likely to be able to raise money than they are to put together coffees for candidates in ethnic neighborhoods or organize the vote on election day.

Most congressional districts are small enough that you can walk them in a day. Congressional races, unlike statewide senate races, involve lots of one-on-one flesh pressing. When congressmen need quick help setting up a neighborhood meeting or organizing election day operations, they frequently enlist a plaintiffs' lawyer. For both congressmen and elected state court judges, plaintiffs' lawyers are not a group to trifle with.

The solution to the product liability problem, then, lies in the U.S. Supreme Court and not in Congress. Political gridlock, after all, is the mother of judicial activism, a proposition whose monument is the doctrine of the dormant Commerce

Clause—a proposition whose textual foundation is as small as its beneficent effect is large. The U.S. Supreme Court has the power to make the law on product liability uniform across the United States and to halt or even reverse the competitive race to the bottom among the state courts. Although such sweeping judicial decisions are rare, it was exactly such sweeping decisions that made the Warren Court an institution that justifies volumes like this celebrating its achievements. (After all, *New York Times v. Sullivan*[4] was really a product liability case; the fact that product liability for newspapers is called "libel" does not change the fact that newspapers get sued for libel when they injure someone by producing a defective product.)

The same competitive race to the bottom that we see in product liability would also exist in state taxation of interstate commerce had not the U.S. Supreme Court intervened in the nineteenth century. Left to themselves, all states would tax out-of-state products more heavily than in-state products because the guy everyone wants to tax is the guy who can't vote!

There is little political support for a general rollback of product liability law. What the Supreme Court is likely to be able to do for us is to freeze most parts of the current system and allow some tinkering at the edges to reduce product liability's chilling effect on research, development, and innovation. Business, therefore, must instruct its lawyers to look for good cases that squarely raise issues that will give the U.S. Supreme Court opportunities to make clear, bright-line national rules that bring our liability law more into line with our foreign competitors' law.

This type of litigation, unfortunately, is expensive. "Good" cases (from the defendant's point of view) settle cheaply, so trade associations (like the National Association of Manufacturers) must actively encourage vigorous litigation of the *good* cases and, perhaps, a sharing of legal fees and judgments. Then, of course, the lawyers need to remember to lead with strong social, political, and economic arguments—not legal arguments. In my experience, U.S. Supreme Court justices are politicians, not lawyers: What will impress these high-ranking policy-makers are arguments that link national rules on product liability to a healthy American economy. For example, it has really been the courts, through the expanding law of product liability, who have unintentionally done the most to discourage research and development in contraception in the United States.

The product liability system that works reasonably well to protect people from defective cars and exploding soda bottles does not handle the peculiar problems related to drugs or vaccines well. Genetic diversity ensures that there will always be some people in whom even the safest drug produces adverse effects. If the percentage of such people is substantial, then the adverse effects show up in clinical trials carried out on several hundred people before the drug is released on the market; but if the adverse effects manifest themselves in, say, only one person out of 10,000, then the probability of the adverse effects showing up in clinical trials is negligible. When, however, any new drug is later used by millions, and affected persons sue the manufacturers for negligence, litigation expenses and damages may cost the firm producing a new drug millions of dollars. It is this exposure that makes research in an area like birth control uneconomical.

Perhaps what I say about the U.S. Supreme Court's interest in the macropolitical system is truer of the Warren Court than it is of the Court today; however, I have always thought that we are better off as lawyers and lower court judges if we *pretend* that we are writing for or arguing to the great Warren Court.

Notes

1. 372 U.S. 335 (1963).
2. 384 U.S. 436 (1966).
3. 378 U.S. 478 (1964).
4. 376 U.S. 254 (1964).

· II ·

THE JUSTICES

• 11 •

HUGO L. BLACK

BERNARD SCHWARTZ

During the second third of this century, two members of the Supreme Court were the paradigms of the new judicial approach: Hugo L. Black and Earl Warren. Neither had a defined philosophy of law; neither was a founder, a leader, or even a follower of any school of jurisprudence. Yet each had an influence upon twentieth-century legal thought greater than any writers on jurisprudence. Their forte was one peculiar to the demands of the emerging twentieth-century society—not so much adaptation of the law to deal with changing conditions as a virtual transformation of the law to meet a quantum acceleration in the pace of societal change.

Black himself was the senior Justice of the Warren Court. He had been on the Court sixteen years when Warren became Chief Justice. By then the furor that had surrounded Black's appointment because of the disclosure that he had once been a member of the Ku Klux Klan seemed an echo from another world. "At every session of the Court," a *New York Times* editorial had thundered, after Black's Klan membership had been revealed, "the presence on the bench of a justice who has worn the white robe of the Ku Klux Klan will stand as a living symbol of the fact that here the cause of liberalism was unwittingly betrayed."[1] When Warren took his seat in the Court's center chair, Black himself was the recognized leader of the Court's liberal wing.

Black never forgot his origins in a backward Alabama rural county. Half a century later, he described a new law clerk as "tops in his class though he came from a God-forsaken place—worse than Clay County."[2] His Alabama drawl and his gentle manner masked an inner firmness found in few men. "Many who know him," wrote a reporter when Black turned seventy-five, "would agree with the one-time clerk who called him 'the most powerful man I have ever met.'"[3] Though of only middling height and slight build, Black always amazed people by his physical vitality. He is quoted in the *Dictionary of Biographical Quotation* as saying, "When I was forty my doctor advised me that a man in his forties shouldn't play tennis. I heeded his advice carefully and could hardly wait until I reached fifty to start again."[4]

His competitive devotion to tennis became legend. Until he was eighty-three, he continued to play several sets every day on the private court of his landmark federal house in the Old Town section of the Washington suburb of Alexandria. In envy, retired Justice Sherman Minton, who had been an athlete in his youth, wrote Black in 1964, "The Chief calls me up once in a while and gives me a report on you and your tennis game. What a man! I can barely get around on crutches."[5]

Black brought the same competitive intensity to his judicial work. According to his closest colleague, Justice William O. Douglas, "Hugo Black was fiercely intent on every point of law he presented."[6] Black was as much a compulsive winner in the courtroom as on the tennis court. "You can't just disagree with him," acidly commented Justice Robert H. Jackson to a *New York Times* columnist, "You must go to war with him if you disagree."[7] There was a constant war between Black and Justice Felix Frankfurter, while both sat on the Court.

After Frankfurter had retired, Black wrote him, "Our differences, which have been many, have rarely been over the ultimate end desired, but rather have related to the means that were most likely to achieve the end we both envisioned."[8] An agreeable sentiment, to be sure, but the differences between the two *were* critical and, on Frankfurter's side at least, became increasingly acrimonious as time went on. The year before Warren's appointment, Frankfurter had, for example, written to Justice Jackson, his closest colleague, that Black "represents discontinuity in the law and a stick-in-the-mud like me is concerned with decent continuity."[9]

Frankfurter's papers are replete with indications of the Justice's denigrating attitude toward Black. "'Oh, Democracy,' confided Frankfurter to his diary, 'what flap-doodle is delivered in thy name.' Not the less so because it was all said in Black's irascible and snarling tone of voice."[10] His reaction to a Black opinion, he wrote to Justice John Marshall Harlan, was to refer to a comment by Justice Oliver Wendell Holmes, "On far less provocation, he pithily disposed of writings by colleagues with, 'It makes me puke.'"[11] During World War II, Frankfurter's diary used to call Black and the Justices who voted with him "the Axis."[12]

To Frankfurter, the law was almost an object of religious worship—and the Supreme Court its holy of holies. "Of all earthly institutions," Frankfurter wrote to Justice Frank Murphy, "this Court comes nearest to having, for me, sacred aspects."[13] If Frankfurter saw himself as the priestly keeper of the shrine, he looked on Black as a false prophet defiling hallowed ground.

A recent book about Frankfurter and Black was titled *The Antagonists*.[14] Yet the issue between them was more basic than the differences engendered by personal antipathies. At the core, there was a fundamental disagreement over the proper role of the law in a period of unprecedented acceleration. Frankfurter remained true to the Holmes rule of judicial self-restraint. For him, it was not for the jurist to mold the course of societal change, but only to defer to the course decreed by the political branches, who alone were given the function of deciding these issues in a representative democracy.

By the 1940s, the judicial restraint approach had become established doctrine. By then, too, the issues confronting the law had also begun to change, and judges like Black had come to believe that even the Holmes canon could not suffice as the legal "be-all and end-all." Black was willing to follow the rule of restraint in the economic area. But he believed that the protection of personal liberties imposed more active enforcement obligations. When a law allegedly infringed upon personal rights, Black refused to defer to the legislative judgment that the law was necessary.

Black's view on the matter was well expressed in a 1962 letter. Replying to the question of whether the Court should defer to congressional judgment, Black asserted, "The question just does not make sense to me. This is because if the Court must 'defer' to the legislative judgment . . . , then the Court must yield its responsibility to another body that does not possess that responsibility. If, as I think, the judiciary is vested with the supreme constitutional power and responsibility to pass on the validity of legislation, then I think it cannot 'defer' to the legislative judgment 'without abdicating its own responsibility.'" To Black, decisions should not depend upon any deference doctrine, but only "on the Court's honest judgment." "I think it is the business and the supreme responsibility of the Court to hold a law unconstitutional if it believes that the law is unconstitutional, without 'deference' to anybody or any institution. In short, as to this phase of the discussion, I believe it is the duty of the Court to show 'deference' to the Constitution only."[15]

Black considered the Frankfurter restraint approach a repudiation of the duty delegated to the judge. As Black saw it, abnegation in the end came down to abdication by the Court of its essential role. The Court's decision, he wrote in his 1962 letter, should "not depend at all, however, upon 'deference' to the Congress, but on the Court's honest judgment as to whether the law was within the competence of the Congress."[16] The decision had to be made on the judge's independent judgment; to "defer" to others meant a passing of the buck that had been placed squarely on the judge.

The Black conception of the judge's function meant that the judge was to remain true to his own conception of law however much it differed from that of the legislature or the prior law on the matter. Black's "mental boldness" in this respect, says an admiring commentator, "was illustrated in an early dissent where he argued, brilliantly and alone, that, despite mountains of precedents running the other way, corporations should not be, and should never have been, judicially rated as 'persons' entitled to the protection of the Fourteenth Amendment."[17] The dissent in question was delivered only three months after Black was appointed to the Court. In it, he asserted the view that the Fourteenth Amendment guaranty to all "persons" of due process did not apply to corporations. "I do not believe," Black declared, "the word 'person' in the Fourteenth Amendment includes corporations."[18]

The *New York Times* headlined Black's dissent, "Only Justice Ever to Hold Corporation Is Not a Person under the Due Process Clause."[19] The law on the matter had gone the other way since 1886, when the Court declared its view that legal as well as natural persons were included within the Fourteenth Amendment.[20] Since that time, innumerable cases had been decided on the unquestioned assumption that corporations were entitled to the constitutional protection. The mass of authority in support of the established law did not, however, deter Justice Black. In the Black conception of law, the volume of history was not worth as much as his page of logic, based upon his personal belief that corporations should not be afforded the same constitutional protection as natural persons.

In a 1942 article, Black characterized the changing jurisprudence as one in which "legal realism replaces legal fictionalism."[21] Black himself was the prime example of the new approach in operation. The law, said the Realists, is what the judges do in fact. Black carried this one step further: what the judge does should be based upon his own conception, without deference to the views of others or even to the fact that there is established law going the other way.

The Black approach in this respect was the basis for the two positions that Justice Black most forcefully advocated on the Court: (1) the absolutist view of the First Amendment; and (2) the incorporation of the Bill of Rights in the Due Process Clause of the Fourteenth Amendment.

Without a doubt, in the popular mind Justice Black stands primarily for the absolutist literal interpretation of the First Amendment. Black explained his position in a 1962 interview: "The beginning of the First Amendment is that 'Congress shall make no law.' I understand that it is rather old-fashioned and shows a slight naivete to say that 'no law' means no law. It is one of the most amazing things about the ingeniousness of the times that strong arguments are made, which *almost* convince me, that it is very foolish of me to think 'no law' means no law. . . . But when I get down to the really basic reason why I believe that 'no law' means no law, I presume it could come to this, that I took an obligation to support and defend the Constitution as I understand it. And being a rather backward country fellow, I understand it to mean what the words say."[22]

The Black position on the First Amendment meant "without deviation, without exception, without any ifs, buts, or whereases, that freedom of speech"[23] was protected from *any and all* governmental infringements. When the amendment says that no laws abridging speech or press shall be made, it means flatly that *no* such laws shall, under any circumstances, be made.

Black's absolutist view has never been accepted by the Court. Countless cases hold that the fact that speech is protected by the First Amendment does not necessarily mean that it is wholly immune from governmental regulation. That did not, however, deter Black from following the view of law that he deemed correct. The same was true of the Black assertion that the framers of the Fourteenth Amendment sought to overrule the decision in *Barron v. Mayor of Baltimore*,[24] which limited application of the Federal Bill of Rights to federal action. The Bill of Rights, Black urged, was incorporated in the Due Process Clause of the Fourteenth Amendment. This meant that all the Bill-of-Rights guarantees were binding upon the states as well as the federal government. The Black position was stated in his now-famous dissent in *Adamson v. California*,[25] where he declared, "I would follow what I believe was the original purpose of the Fourteenth Amendment—to extend to all the people of the nation the complete protection of the Bill of Rights."[26]

Once again, the established law was clearly the other way. Since 1884,[27] the Court had rejected the view that the Fourteenth Amendment absorbed all the provisions of the Bill of Rights and hence placed upon the states the limitations that the specific articles of the first eight amendments had theretofore placed upon the federal government. Against the more than half century of uniform precedents, Black set only this: "My study" of the Fourteenth Amendment's legislative history "persuades me" that "one of the chief objects that the provisions of the Amendment's first section . . . [was] intended to accomplish was to make the Bill of

Rights, applicable to the states."[28] It was Black's own view of what the law should be, based upon *his* reading of the relevant provision, that led him to reject all the weighty precedents the other way and take issue with what seemed so settled in Supreme Court doctrine.

As a Justice, Black used the law to reach the results that he believed would best serve the interests of the American society that he saw developing. He had been a populist senator and now he employed judicial power to make social policy that would favor the individual and protect him against the corporate interests that the law had fostered. From this point of view, a Frankfurter satiric portrayal of Justice Black acting as though he were "back in the Senate"[29] contained some truth. Black, however, did not have any overriding social vision. His jurisprudence was instead, like that of many of his judicial confreres, illustrative of the pragmatic instrumentalism that had come to be dominant in American law.

Yet if Black was an instrumentalist in his result-oriented use of the law, he was so in a black-letter sense. He always insisted that his decisions were based upon the literal language of the law. His fundamentalist approach did not permit him to adopt the expansive approach toward individual rights increasingly followed by some of the Justices.

Black stood his ground where the rights asserted rested on specific provisions, such as the First Amendment or the Fifth Amendment privilege against self-incrimination, but when he could not find an express legal base, Black was unwilling to create one to meet a new need. This limited approach would lead Black to his hostility toward school busing in the case where a busing order was challenged. "Where does the word *busing* appear in the Constitution?" Black is said to have asked his law clerks.[30]

The paradigmatic case illustrating Black's literalist approach is *Griswold v. Connecticut.*[31] The Court there struck down a law that prohibited use of contraceptives and the giving of medical advice in their use. Defendants had given advice to married persons on preventing conception and prescribed contraceptive devices for them. The law was ruled violative of the right to privacy—a right protected by the Bill of Rights even though it is nowhere mentioned in the constitutional text.

Black delivered a strong *Griswold* dissent in which he took sharp issue with the majority approach. "The Court," the Black dissent declared, "talks about the constitutional 'right of privacy' as though there is some constitutional provision or provisions forbidding any law ever to be passed which might abridge the 'privacy' of individuals. But there is not." "I like my privacy as well as the next one," Black went on, "but I am nevertheless compelled to admit that government has a right to invade it unless prohibited by some specific constitutional provision"[32]—which was, of course, lacking in *Griswold.*

Perhaps the best expression of Black's objection to protection of rights not based upon a specific text, such as the right of privacy, is contained in a 1966 memorandum that the Justice wrote attacking a draft opinion of the Court, which contained as broad a statement of the right of privacy as any ever made. Black's memo summarized the draft's reliance on the right of privacy as follows: "Describing it as a right 'which the Court derived by implication from the specific guarantees of the Bill of

Rights' yet proclaiming that it 'reaches beyond any of its specifics,' the Court holds that this right is so 'basic to a free society' that its invasion can only be 'justified by the clear needs of community living.'"[33]

Black does not "deny that it is an exquisite thing to be let alone when one wants to be." But, he goes on, "regardless of their value, neither the 'right to be let alone' nor 'the right to privacy,' while appealing phrases, were enshrined in our Constitution as was the right to free speech, press and religion."

Black concedes that certain aspects of privacy are protected by the Third, Fourth, and Fifth Amendments. "But," he asserts, "I think it approaches the fantastic for judges to attempt to create from these a general, all-embracing constitutional provision guaranteeing a general right to privacy. And I think it equally fantastic for judges to use these specific constitutional guarantees as an excuse to arrogate to themselves authority to create new and different alleged constitutional rights to be free from governmental control in all areas where judges believe modern conditions call for new constitutional rights. . . . For judges to have such power would amount to authority on their part to override the people's Constitution."

For the judges to go beyond the constitutional text in protecting rights, Black writes, means that "judges are no longer to be limited to their recognized power to make binding *interpretations* of the Constitution. That power, won after bitter constitutional struggles, has apparently become too prosaic and unexciting. So the judiciary now confers upon this judiciary the more 'elastic' and exciting power to decide . . . just how much freedom the courts will permit. . . . And in making this decision the Court is to have important leeway, it seems, in order to make the Constitution the people adopted more adaptable to what the Court deems to be modern needs. We, the judiciary, are no longer to be crippled and bobbled by the old admonition that 'We must always remember it is a Constitution we are *expounding*,' but we are to work under the exhilarating new slogan that 'We must always remember that it is a Constitution we are *rewriting* to fit the times.' I cannot join nor can I even acquiesce in this doctrine which I firmly believe to be a violation of the Constitution itself."

All that has recently been said against judicial protection of rights not specifically guaranteed was said, and said better, in the 1966 Black memo. To Black, only the black-letter approach was proper. The alternative, in his view, was to accept a "theory . . . that this Court is endowed . . . with boundless power under 'natural law' periodically to expand and contract constitutional standards to conform to the court's conception of what at a particular time constitutes 'civilized decency' and 'fundamental liberty and justice.'"[34]

To many, Justice Black's action in a case like *Griswold* represented "apostasy" from the then-prevailing liberal doctrine. But Black refused to recognize the new right of privacy because he could not find an express textual foundation for it. He also voted to uphold convictions of sit-in demonstrators, stressing the specific guarantees protecting property rights, including the owner's right to limit access to his property.[35] During the conference in the sit-in case, Black emotionally declared that he could not believe that his "Pappy," who ran a general store in Alabama, did not have the right to decide whom he would or would not serve.

In the end, however, it is the "preapostasy" Black, Frankfurter's great rival, who ranks as a prime molder of twentieth-century legal thought. As it turned out, it was Black, rather than Frankfurter, who was more in tune with contemporary constitutional needs. History has vindicated the Black approach, for it has helped protect personal liberties in an era of encroaching public power.

Thus, it cannot be denied that Justice Black's absolutist advocacy was a prime mover in the First Amendment jurisprudence of the past half century. The absolutist view may not have been accepted; but the "firstness" of the First Amendment has been firmly established. In a 1941 dissent, Black declared, "the guaranties of the First Amendment [are] the foundation upon which our governmental structure rests and without which it could not continue to ensure as conceived and planned." If today, as he stated in the same opinion, "Freedom to speak and write about public questions . . . is the heart"[36] of the constitutional scheme, that has in large part been due to Black's consistent evangelism on the matter.

Similarly, Justice Black's *Adamson* position may never have been able to command a Court majority. Under Black's prodding, nevertheless, the Justices increasingly expanded the scope of the Fourteenth Amendment's Due Process Clause. Though the Court continued to hold that only those rights deemed "fundamental" are included in due process, the meaning of "fundamental" became flexible enough to accomplish virtually the result Black had urged in his *Adamson* dissent, absorbing one by one almost all the individual guarantees of the Bill of Rights into the Due Process Clause.[37] By the end of Black's judicial tenure, the rights that had been held binding on the states under the Fourteenth Amendment included all the rights guaranteed by the Bill of Rights except the right to a grand jury indictment and that to a jury trial in civil cases involving over twenty dollars.[38] If Justice Black had appeared to lose the Bill of Rights incorporation battle, did he not really win the due process war?

To be sure, Black as a jurist differed from almost all his colleagues. Even his admirers must admit that Black was no Cardozo-type acolyte of the common law. His contributions were almost entirely in constitutional law. Yet, in that field, he was a catalyst for the most important judicial development since the Marshall Court. Black may not have been a consummate judicial craftsman. His opinions were never noted for their artful expression; they lacked the Holmes aphoristic quality and the Cardozo literary art. Still, if Black's prose does not "skip or dance," it clearly marches.[39] The hallmark of the Black opinion is its simple clarity. As the journalist Heywood Broun once put it, "Black is certainly popular with newsmen, because he recently wrote a dissent in English as plain and simple as a good running story on the first page. Naturally, reporters take to those who speak their own language. And it is a far finer tongue than that invented by Mr. Blackstone."[40]

It was Justice Black as much as anyone who changed the very way Americans think about law. If the focus of juristic inquiry has shifted from duties to rights, if personal rights have been elevated to the preferred plane—that has in large part been the result of the Black jurisprudence. Indeed, if impact on legal thought is a hallmark of the outstanding judge, few occupants of the bench have been more outstanding than Black. It was Black who led the Court to tilt the law in favor of individual rights and liberties and who was, before Chief Justice Warren, the intellectual leader in what Justice Abe Fortas once termed "the most profound and pervasive revolution ever achieved by substantially peaceful means."[41] Even where Black's views have not been adopted literally, they have tended to prevail in a more general, modified form. Nor has his impact been limited to the Black positions that the Court has accepted. It is found in the totality of today's judicial awareness of the Bill of Rights and the law's new-found sensitivity to liberty and equality.

More than anything, Black brought to the law a moral fervor rarely seen on the bench. A famous passage by Holmes has it that the black-letter judge will be replaced by the man of statistics and the master of economics.[42] Black was emphatically a judge who still followed the black-letter approach in dealing with the legal text. "That Constitution," he said, "is my legal bible. . . . I cherish every word of it from the first to the last."[43] The eminent jurist with his dog-eared copy of the Constitution in his right coat pocket became a part of contemporary folklore. In protecting the sanctity of the organic word, Black displayed all the passion of the Old Testament prophet in the face of the graven idols. His ardor may have detracted from the image of the "judicial." But if Black did not bring to constitutional issues that "cold neutrality" of which Edmund Burke speaks,[44] his zeal may have been precisely what was needed in the Supreme Court. Anything less might have been inadequate to make the Bill of Rights the vital center of our law.

Notes

1. Quoted in *The Supreme Court under Earl Warren* 129 (Levy ed., 1972).
2. Dunne, *Hugo Black and the Judicial Revolution* 85 (1977).
3. Levy, supra note 1, at 135.
4. *Dictionary of Biographical Quotation* 79 (Kenin and Winette eds., 1978).
5. Letter from Sherman Minton to Black, September 11, 1964, Black Papers, Library of Congress.
6. Douglas, *Go East Young Man: The Early Years* 450 (1974).
7. Gerhart, *America's Advocate: Robert H. Jackson* 274 (1958).
8. Letter from Black to Frankfurter, December 22, 1964, Black Papers, Library of Congress.
9. Letter from Frankfurter to Robert H. Jackson, January 19, 1952, Frankfurter Papers, Library of Congress.
10. Lash, *From the Diaries of Felix Frankfurter* 283 (1975).
11. Letter from Frankfurter to John M. Harlan, May 19, 1961, Frankfurter Papers, Library of Congress.
12. Lash, supra note 10, at 176.
13. Id. at 264.
14. Simon, *The Antagonists: Hugo Black, Felix Frankfurter and Civil Liberties in Modern America* (1989).
15. Letter from Black to Fred Rodell, September 5, 1962, Black Papers, Library of Congress.
16. Id.
17. Rodell, *Nine Men: A Political History of the Supreme Court from 1790 to 1955*, 265 (1955).
18. Connecticut General Life Ins. Co. v. Johnson, 303 U.S. 77, 85 (1938).
19. Dunne, supra note 2, at 178.
20. Santa Clara County v. Southern Pac. R. Co., 118 U.S. 394 (1886).

21. Dunne, supra note 2, at 184.
22. "Justice Black and First Amendment 'Absolutes': A Public Interview," 37 *N.Y.U. L. Rev.* 549, 553 (1962).
23. Id. at 559.
24. 7 Pet. 243 (U.S. 1833).
25. 332 U.S. 46 (1947).
26. Id. at 89.
27. Hurtado v. California, 110 U.S. 516 (1884).
28. 332 U.S. at 71–72.
29. Schwartz, *Super Chief: Earl Warren and His Supreme Court* 45 (1983).
30. Schwartz, *Swann's Way: The School Busing Case and the Supreme Court* 35 (1986).
31. 381 U.S. 479 (1965).
32. Id. at 508, 510.
33. The Black memo is reprinted in Schwartz, *The Unpublished Opinions of the Warren Court* 272 (1985).
34. Adamson v. California, 332 U.S. at 69.
35. Bell v. Maryland, 378 U.S. 226 (1964).
36. Drivers Union v. Meadowmoor Co., 312 U.S. 287, 301, 302 (1941).
37. Williams v. Florida, 399 U.S. 78, 130–31 (1970).
38. The cases are summarized in Schwartz, *The Great Rights of Mankind* 220–21 (1992 ed.).
39. Frank, *Mr. Justice Black* 136 (1949).
40. Id.
41. *The Fourteenth Amendment Centennial Volume* 34 (Schwartz ed., 1970).
42. Holmes, *Collected Legal Papers* 187 (1920).
43. Dunne, supra note 2, at 414.
44. 5 Burke, *Works* 67 (rev. ed. 1865).

• 12 •

WILLIAM J. BRENNAN, JR.

RICHARD S. ARNOLD

What has come to be called the Warren Court brought a significant, perhaps unprecedented, expansion in the individual rights of citizens of this country, including citizens who previously had not been given their full share in the American dream. All of us owe the Warren Court a great debt of gratitude for that gift to the American people, and I count it a privilege indeed to have been included in this volume. Even more, it is a privilege to write about Justice William J. Brennan, Jr., because serving as his law clerk, for about a year in 1960 and 1961, was probably the best job I ever had. Certainly I learned from the Justice a great deal about law and liberty, about humanity and humility. My feelings for him go beyond affection to reverence.

From time to time I go to Washington, usually to ask Congress for money to run the federal courts, and frequently on those visits I go by and see Justice Brennan for lunch. He is kind enough to keep his door always open to me, and we always have a good time together. Some time ago, I told him I was going to write about his contribution to the law, and his immediate reaction was to say, "Oh, no." For a brief moment I had the sinking feeling that the Justice was voicing the same kind of misgivings that I had been having myself—that I was so clearly an unworthy expositor of his record that I should not have presumed to accept the invitation. Swiftly, though, I realized that this could not be the case: even if the Justice harbored such a view, he was far too much of a gentleman to voice it. What he was really saying, as he explained, was, incredibly, that he did not consider his own life in the law sufficiently noteworthy to justify my time or the space in this volume. I don't usually use the word "ridiculous" to discuss an opinion of Justice Brennan's—in fact, I have never used it before—but perhaps it is appropriate on this occasion. It is really a signal mark of his own humility and self-deprecation that he would have such an inaccurate picture of his own contributions to the liberty of the individual in this country. Probably no Justice in the history of the Supreme Court, certainly none in this century, has done more to strengthen the Bill of Rights, to protect the individual from governmental encroachment, and to bring all Americans into full enjoyment of the blessings of liberty.

So, notwithstanding the Justice's own modest self-assessment, it is altogether fitting and proper that his opinions and achievements should be a focus of this volume. For he was a key part of the Warren Court. As is well known to all students of that era, Justice Brennan and the Chief Justice were particularly close. They were the warmest and most outgoing of people, and their views on most subjects coincided. I remember well the Chief Justice's habit of coming to Justice Brennan's chambers on many Thursdays, the day before the Court's Friday conference. The two Justices would closet themselves in Justice Brennan's private office, sometimes for hours, and we (the law clerks) knew that they were discussing the conference list for the next day. They voted together about ninety percent of the time. Their collaboration was most fruitful. Whatever mark the Warren Court has left on history, a large share of it goes to the credit of Justice Brennan.

My subject here is Justice Brennan's use of history in judicial decision making. I deliberately use the neutral term "history" instead of that dread and charged phrase "original intent," so abused by both (or all) sides. In listening to the debates over original intent, one might suppose that a significant judicial school, including such "liberals" (whatever that means) as Justice Brennan, took the view that history is irrelevant, that judges do not, or at least should not, care about what the Founding Generation thought, and that the Constitution is some sort of disembodied abstraction, taking on content from one generation to the other without regard to what went before. This picture, of course, is a caricature, just as there have been caricatures of the other, so-called originalist point of view. In fact, as I hope to show by some specific examples, Justice Brennan is not the monster of activism that some have pictured. He is by no means irreverent of the past and has taken great pains in a number of opinions to determine the intention of the framers. It is not his position that this intention can always be ascertained accurately, still less that such an intention even exists with respect to many of the precise points that come up for adjudication. He does believe, though, that the Constitution came out of an intellectual context, that its words have to be understood against a historical background, and that determining this background, including whatever evidence there is of the intention of those who wrote the Constitution's broad and grand phrases, can be crucial in deciding lawsuits. In fact, his actions have always been those of a judge, not a legislator: careful, judicious, incremental, and respectful of original intent, to the extent that it can be determined.

Indeed, the Justice was for nine years a member of the National Historical Publications Commission, a body created by act of Congress and charged with the duty of gathering and publishing documentary histories, of the first Congress, of the Supreme Court, of the first federal elections, of the Bill of Rights, and the like. This body, created by Congress in 1934, is now called the National Historical Publications and Records Commission. Since 1950, one member has been a Supreme Court Justice. Those who have served include Felix Frankfurter (1950–1965), William J. Brennan, Jr. (1965–1974), Harry Blackmun (1974–1983), William H. Rehnquist (1983–1986), and Justice Blackmun again (1986 to the present). If history were irrelevant, it would be hard to explain why so much governmental energy, including the energy of Supreme Court Justices, should be spent in its study. The answer of course is that it is not irrelevant; it may not be dispositive, but it is relevant and, in some cases, importantly influential.

Let me give a few examples from the corpus of Justice Brennan's opinions. In *School District of Abington Township v. Schempp,*[1] the Court had before it two cases, one involving a Pennsylvania statute, and the other a Baltimore, Maryland, school rule. The Pennsylvania law in question required that verses be read from the Bible at the beginning of each school day. The Baltimore school rule required that a chapter from the Bible or the Lord's Prayer or both be read at the beginning of each school day. The Court, speaking through Justice Clark, held that both of these requirements violated the Establishment Clause of the First Amendment. (Remarkably, in view of the present political climate, no one dissented from this position: eight Members of the Court agreed that the enactments in question were invalid; Justice Stewart thought the case should be remanded for the taking of additional evidence.) Justice Brennan wrote a separate concurring opinion.

This opinion lays heavy emphasis on the history of the First Amendment. The Justice quotes from the remarks of Representative Daniel Carroll of Maryland during the debate in the House of Representatives on the proposed Bill of Rights. The Justice said that the Constitution "declares as a basic postulate of the relation between the citizen and his government that 'the rights of conscience are, in their nature, of peculiar delicacy, and will little bear the gentlest touch of governmental hand.'"[2] The Justice then invoked the views of "the Framers of the First Amendment." In his view, the Establishment Clause, in the "contemplation of the Framers,"[3] was not limited to any particular form of state-supported theological venture. The Justice then acknowledged that both Jefferson and Madison might have allowed the kind of exercises in question, but warned that "an awareness of history and an appreciation of the aims of the Founding Fathers do not always resolve concrete questions."[4] He went on: "I doubt that their view, even if perfectly clear one way or the other, would supply a dispositive answer to the question presented by these cases. A more fruitful inquiry . . . is whether the practices here challenged threatened those consequences which the Framers deeply feared."[5] History has to be used cautiously in solving contemporary problems. The congressional debate was brief, the framers did not write much on the question, and public education was almost nonexistent in 1789. History is ambiguous, and the particular question presented in these cases was not given any distinct consideration by the framers. In addition, the country is now much more religiously diverse. "[O]ur use of the history of [the Framers'] time must limit itself to broad purposes, not specific practices."[6] Still, the Court must not make up the Constitution as it goes along from case to case. Even though specific original intention cannot be discovered, "the line we must draw between the permissible and the impermissible is one which accords with history and *faithfully reflects the understanding of the Founding Fathers*."[7]

These themes continued in *Walz v. Tax Commission of the City of New York,*[8] in which the Court declined to invalidate the long-standing practice of exempting church-owned property from real-estate taxes. Again, Justice Brennan wrote a separate concurrence, thus underscoring the importance he attached to the subject. The fact that a practice has obtained since the beginning of the country, he said, "is a fact of considerable import in the interpretation of abstract constitutional language."

"[H]istorical support [is] . . . overwhelming," and "'a page of history is worth a volume of logic.'"[9] The real question is whether the exemptions "were . . . among the evils that the Framers and Ratifiers of the Establishment Clause sought to avoid,"[10] and the answer is clearly no. Within ten years of the ratification of the First Amendment, at least four states passed exemption statutes.

The history in Virginia is especially instructive. The movement to disestablish the Episcopal Church culminated in the Act of January 24, 1799, repealing many laws, including those "incorporat[ing] religious sects,"[11] but the very next year, in 1800, a law was passed giving church-owned property an exemption from taxes. There is no record that either Jefferson or Madison objected to this law.[12] Later, it is true, Madison argued against tax exemptions, the incorporation of religious bodies, the employment of chaplains for Congress and the armed forces, and presidential proclamations of days of thanksgiving or prayer, "though he admitted proclaiming several such days at congressional request."[13] These rather uncompromising views expressed by Mr. Madison, however, came after he was no longer in politics, a fact no less relevant in Madison's time than in ours. The fact remains, Justice Brennan concluded, that "'[i]f a thing has been practiced for 200 years by common consent, it will need a strong case for the Fourteenth Amendment to affect it.'"[14] History, to paraphrase the Justice, is important, but the history of the times when the Constitution was written is not the only history that is relevant. A practice existing in those times, and continued ever since, carries with it a presumption of validity.

Another opinion interpreting the Religion Clauses, which seem to have become a special focus of historical debate, was Justice Brennan's dissent in *Lynch v. Donnelly*.[15] The reader will recall that *Lynch* validates the display of a nativity scene in a city park when the display also contains Santa Claus, a Christmas tree, and a banner reading "SEASONS GREETINGS." Justice Brennan, in a powerful dissent joined by Justices Marshall, Blackmun, and Stevens, began by admitting that it is difficult to discern any specific intent on the part of the framers with respect to the particular issue involved in the case. "The intent of the Framers with respect to the public display of nativity scenes is virtually impossible to discern,"[16] not least because Christmas was not widely celebrated in its present form until well into the nineteenth century. Presbyterians, Congregationalists, Baptists, Methodists, and Puritans of all kind took a dim view of Christmas, believing that its celebration gave off too much of a papist aura. On the other hand, Roman Catholics, Episcopalians, and the Dutch and German Reformed churches prominently observed Christmas as a major feast. In the early part of the history of this country, then, whether and how to observe Christmas were matters of denominational dispute among Christians, and "the Religion Clauses were intended to ensure a benign régime of competitive disorder among all denominations."[17] It was not until 1870 that Congress established Christmas as a legal holiday in the District of Columbia,[18] and federal employees didn't get Christmas as a paid holiday until 1885.[19]

The Justice concluded that there was "no evidence whatsoever that the Framers would have expressly approved a federal celebration of the Christmas holiday including public displays of a nativity scene." In addition, "[T]he 'illumination' provided by history must always be focused on the particular practice at issue in a given case."[20] Thus, Justice Brennan's approach to the use of history in judicial decision making is conservative. He is careful not to overstate, and he insists that the intention of the framers be gauged against the background of their own times, times in which Christmas was simply not celebrated or observed in anything approaching the present-day manner.[21]

Another good example of the Justice's historical perspective, this one outside the area of religion, has to do with the death penalty. In *Furman v. Georgia*,[22] the Court held that the death penalty as then administered was a cruel and unusual punishment in violation of the Eighth Amendment. Justice Brennan filed a concurring opinion and took pains to examine the historical case on both sides. In a dissent, Chief Justice Burger (joined by Justices Blackmun, Powell, and Rehnquist) had argued that the death penalty could not possibly be unconstitutional, because it was commonly imposed at the time of the adoption of the Constitution and, indeed, is referred to *eo nomine* in the text of the Fifth Amendment. Justice Brennan responded: "We have very little evidence of the Framers' intent in including the Cruel and Unusual Punishments Clause in the Bill of Rights."[23] In fact, in the debates in the First Congress on the proposed constitutional amendment that became the Eighth Amendment, one member, Representative Livermore, in referring to hanging, whipping, and earcropping, which were common punishments at the time, asked: "Are we in future to be prevented from inflicting these punishments because they are cruel?"[24] Mr. Livermore was an opponent of the clause, and his question, therefore, may not be good evidence of the intention of those who supported the clause, but the fact remains, as Justice Brennan emphasized, that if the death penalty is to be justified on the ground that it was common in 1789, whipping and earcropping would be equally immune from constitutional challenge. As a matter of fact, the First Congress, in which, as has often been remarked, a number of members of the Constitutional Convention sat, prescribed thirty-nine lashes as a punishment for larceny and receiving stolen goods, and one hour in the pillory for perjury.[25]

Justice Brennan's opinion rejects the argument that such historical practices can be conclusive of the constitutional question.[26] In thus rejecting the view that the existence of a specific practice in 1791 meant that it had to be constitutionally permissible, Justice Brennan was not breaking new ground. The Supreme Court had adopted the same position in *Weems v. United States*,[27] and had done so, interestingly, over Justice Holmes's dissent. In *Weems* the Court said that "a principle to be vital must be capable of wider application than the mischief which gave it birth."[28] Yet, Justice Brennan did not claim any judicial right to reinvent the Constitution from one decade to another: "[W]e must avoid the insertion of 'judicial conception[s] of . . . wisdom or propriety,' yet we must not, in the guise of 'judicial restraint,' abdicate our fundamental responsibility to enforce the Bill of Rights."[29]

Perhaps the Justice's most extensive use of history was in a case arising under the Eleventh Amendment, an area controversial enough, but hardly such a political hot button as the death penalty or the Establishment Clause. In *Atascadero State Hospital v. Scanlon*,[30] an action against a California state hospital for violation of Section 504 of the Rehabilitation Act of 1973 was held barred by the Eleventh Amendment. Justice Brennan filed a fifty-five-page dissent joined by Justices Marshall, Blackmun, and Stevens. He took dead aim at the Court's lack of respect for history. The holding, he argued, "rested on a mistaken historical premise."[31] The Justice appealed to "[n]ew evidence concerning the drafting and ratification of the original Constitution"[32] and cited evidence contained in the documentary history of the ratification of the Constitution, one of the publications of the National Historical Publications and Records Commission, which has been referred to above.

This dissenting opinion makes clear that the relevant history goes beyond the specific debates in Congress or in ratifying conventions on the provision in question. It is also important to look at the writings of informed citizens both for and against the provision in question. Especially in interpreting a constitution, or a constitutional amendment, we need to remember that they are organic acts, not mere statutes. They represent the view of an entire society, at least in some indirect sense, and it can therefore be important to understand the climate of informed public opinion among the electorate.

Justice Brennan's dissent in *Atascadero State Hospital* deserves an article of its own. Justice cannot be done to it in this brief paper. Suffice it to say that the analysis is powerful and specific, even pointed. George Mason, James Madison, Patrick Henry, John Marshall, Edmund Randolph, and Richard Henry Lee are all quoted. The history of the drafting of Article III of the original Constitution is extensively discussed, as is that of the drafting of the First Judiciary Act,[33] and the Eleventh Amendment itself. The controversial ground of *Chisholm v. Georgia*,[34] is sensitively replowed. Two of the prominent players in *Chisholm* were members of the Committee on Detail that had drafted Article III. Edmund Randolph (at the time attorney general of the United States) appeared in the Supreme Court for Chisholm, and James Wilson, a member of the Court, delivered an opinion rejecting Georgia's assertion of sovereign immunity. (What better evidence of original intention could there be, than the agreement of two members of the Committee on Detail that an action against a state was not barred? Yet, the present-day Supreme Court reads the Eleventh Amendment as simply a reassertion of the original intent of the drafters of Article III.)

What are we to make of all this? Readers will of course have their own views (as I do) of the merits of each of these cases. That is not the point. What I have tried to show, really, is two simple things. First, Justice Brennan cares about history. He studies it, he knows it, and he refers to it. Second, he uses it with respect and prudence. He is alert to the context in which constitutional provisions were drafted, to the intellectual climate of the times, and to the social and cultural conditions then obtaining. He is wise in his selection of quotations, and he does not overstate. He respects the letter of the law, but he knows that it is the spirit of the law that gives it life, and he delights in appealing to history to discover this spirit.

This is a small aspect of Justice Brennan's legacy to the nation, but nonetheless an interesting and instructive one, adding to our admiration for his spirit and his craft.

Notes

1. 374 U.S. 203 (1963).
2. Id. at 231 (quoting remarks of Mr. Carroll, August 15, 1789, 1 *Annals of Cong.*

730). This speech of Representative Carroll seems to be a favorite of the Justice's. He also quoted it in Braunfeld v. Brown, 366 U.S. 599, 616 (1961) (Brennan, J., concurring in part and dissenting in part). *Braunfeld* was one of the Sunday Law cases.

3. 374 U.S. at 231.
4. Id. at 234.
5. Id. at 236.
6. Id. at 241.
7. Id. at 294 (emphasis added).
8. 397 U.S. 664 (1970).
9. Id. at 681 (quoting New York Trust Co. v. Eisner, 256 U.S. 345, 349 (1921)).
10. 397 U.S. at 682.
11. 2 Va. Statutes at Large of 1792–1806 (Shepherd) 149.
12. 397 U.S. at 684.
13. Id. at n.5.
14. Id. at 686 (quoting Jackman v. Rosenbaum Co., 260 U.S. 22, 31 (1922)).
15. 465 U.S. 668 (1984).
16. Id. at 720.
17. Id. at 723.
18. 18 Stat. 168.
19. 23 Stat. 516.
20. 465 U.S. at 724–25.
21. I have discussed elsewhere Justice Brennan's use of history in another Religion Clause case, Marsh v. Chambers, 463 U.S. 783 (1983), in which the Court, over the Justice's dissent, upheld the practice of paying legislative chaplains from tax money. See Arnold, "Mr. Justice Brennan—An Appreciation," 26 *Harv. C.R.-C.L. L. Rev.* 7 (1991).
22. 408 U.S. 230 (1972).
23. Id. at 258.
24. 1 *Annals of Cong.* 754 (1789).
25. Act of April 30, 1790, §§ 16–18, 1 Stat. 116.
26. Contrast the view of Justice Black, himself of course a leading member of the Warren Court, in McGautha v. California, 402 U.S. 183, 226 (1971) (separate opinion), that the Eighth Amendment cannot be "read to outlaw capital punishment because that penalty was in common use and authorized by law . . . at the time the Clause was adopted. It is inconceivable to me that the framers intended to end capital punishment by the [Clause]."
27. 217 U.S. 349 (1910).
28. Id. at 373.
29. 408 U.S. at 269 (quoting Weems v. United States, 217 U.S. 349, 379 (1910)).
30. 473 U.S. 234 (1985).
31. Id. at 259.
32. Ibid.
33. 1 Stat. 73 (1789).
34. 2 Dall. 419 (U.S. 1793).

• 13 •

WILLIAM O. DOUGLAS

JAMES F. SIMON

One of William O. Douglas's favorite quotations was from the thirteenth-century Persian poet, Jalal ad-Din Rumi who wrote: "All your anxiety is because of your desire for harmony. Seek disharmony; then you will gain peace."[1]

Douglas did his part to create disharmony. Throughout his illustrious career as a law professor, New Deal insider and Justice of the Supreme Court, William O. Douglas teased the establishment with such intuitive skill and timing that he always seemed to advance his professional ambitions as he flouted conventional norms.

As a young Columbia University law professor, Douglas loudly quit the faculty in protest over what he considered a disastrous decanal appointment by the university's imperious president, Nicholas Murray Butler.[2] The day after he submitted his resignation, Douglas formally accepted a pending offer from the president of Yale to teach at the Yale Law School. The timing of Douglas's two decisions made within a two-day period—one a triumphant resignation, the other an equally triumphant acceptance, illustrate a recurring theme in Douglas's phenomenal rise to professional prominence and power: both principle and shrewd pragmatic judgments were critical to his success.

At Yale, Douglas reorganized the courses in his specialty of business law, rejecting the traditional approach which studied what judges wrote in their judicial opinions.[3] Douglas insisted that students learn how corporations worked—how they were formed, financed, managed, merged, organized, and, occasionally, dissolved. Like other legal realists at Yale, he looked at the vital facts and principles that determined what courts did, not just what they said they were doing in judicial opinions.

Yale's Law School Dean, Robert Hutchins, called Douglas "the outstanding professor of law in the nation"[4] and acted upon his high appraisal. After Hutchins left New Haven to become president of the University of Chicago, he offered Douglas the then unheard-of annual professorial salary of $20,000 to join him. Douglas flirted with the Chicago offer long enough to be named Sterling Professor of Law at Yale with a salary of $15,000, a wage significantly below Hutchins offer but still no paltry sum during the Depression.

Douglas, like so many other bright, ambitious young men in the legal academy, was inspired by the promise of Franklin D. Roosevelt's New Deal. In his correspondence with New Deal insiders like Jerome Frank, Douglas made it clear that he wanted to be a part of the national experiment. "The dope is that Judge (Robert) Healy will head up the corporation division of the Federal Trade Commission,"[5] Douglas wrote Frank in 1933, soon after Frank had become general counsel to the Agricultural Adjustment Administration. "I think there is a splendid opportunity for adventurous thinking and planning in that field. I was thinking the other day that it would be a grand thing to go down there for the first year or two of that division's existence and help organize it in an intelligent and efficient way."

His first opportunity was rather more modest than Douglas himself would have wished, but he made the most of it. In 1934 Douglas was asked to direct a study for the newly created Securities and Exchange Commission on the unethical and illegal manipulations of bankruptcies and receiverships by protective and reorganization committees.[6] In his SEC study Douglas discovered a paper trail of deceit, manipulation, and outright illegal conduct.

His investigation resulted in an eight-volume report to Congress, bringing high praise from, among others, Harvard's Professor Felix Frankfurter. "Having a little familiarity with the field," Frankfurter wrote Douglas, "I think I appreciate the thorough preliminary analysis, the indefatigable industry, and resourcefulness in examination and, above all, the fearless clarity that followed trails, wheresoever they led."[7]

Douglas's SEC study, together with his reputation as a pioneering legal realist law professor, led to his appointment as a commissioner of the SEC in 1936. *Time* magazine called him "as brilliant a professor as the New Deal has attracted to Washington."[8] As a commission member, Douglas wasted little time in distancing himself in style and goals from that of the quiet, workmanlike chairman of the SEC, James Landis.[9] Douglas openly challenged the business community and suggested pointedly that the New York Stock Exchange was run more like a private club than a public exchange responsible to individual security holders.

Douglas's public attacks on Wall Street's excesses infuriated the business establishment but delighted the one person who counted most, President Franklin D. Roosevelt. In 1937, FDR appointed Douglas to succeed Landis as SEC chairman. Chairman Douglas continued his fight against the vested interests of Wall Street, holding extensive public hearings and introducing reforms that would, for the first time, make the exchange a public institution, truly responsive to security holders. At the same time, Douglas entered Roosevelt's inner circle of economic advisors.

In 1939, the president appointed Douglas to the Supreme Court, making him, at the age of forty, the third youngest man ever to serve. But even with Douglas's reputation as a brilliant, innovative thinker and administrator, no one expected him to lead the burgeoning group of Roosevelt appointees into the modern judicial era, when civil rights and liberties claims would present the Justices with their greatest constitutional challenges. After all, Douglas's expertise was exclusively in the commercial law field.

When it came to new libertarian leadership on the Court, the name of only one Roosevelt appointee was mentioned: former Harvard professor Felix Frankfurter.

Appointed to the Court three months before Douglas, Frankfurter was the preeminent constitutional law scholar of his generation, as well as a founding member of the American Civil Liberties Union and the celebrated defender of Nicola Sacco and Bartolomeo Vanzetti.

But soon enough, it was clear that Frankfurter's political libertarianism did not easily translate into his judicial opinions. In fact, his philosophy of judicial restraint soon placed him at odds with the three most liberal Roosevelt appointees—Justices Hugo Black, Bill Douglas, and Frank Murphy. The three of them declared their independence from Frankfurter's leadership shortly after Frankfurter had written the Court's opinion in the 1940 case, *Minersville School District v. Gobitis.*[10]

The *Gobitis* case involved two Jehovah's Witnesses students who protested that a public school's requirement that all students salute the American flag violated their religious beliefs, which forbade them to worship false idols. Justice Frankfurter wrote the majority opinion, supported by all of the Roosevelt appointees, which balanced away the children's right to the free exercise of their religion in favor of the government's authority to teach patriotism in the public schools.

Justices Black, Douglas, and Murphy publicly recanted shortly after the *Gobitis* decision, confessing their error in rejecting the Gobitis children's First Amendment claims. The recantation occurred in a second case involving the constitutional rights of Jehovah's Witnesses; in that 1942 decision a Court majority sustained the convictions of Witnesses who had refused to pay a municipal licensing fee required to sell their religious publications. This time, Justices Black, Douglas, and Murphy dissented, and issued a joint statement confessing their error in *Gobitis*:

> The opinion of the Court sanctions a device which in our opinion suppresses or tends to suppress the free exercise of religion practiced by a minority group. This is but another step in the direction which *Minersville School District v. Gobitis* took against the same religious minority and is a logical extension of the principles upon which that decision rested. Since we joined in the opinion in the *Gobitis* case, we think this is an appropriate occasion to state that we now believe it was also wrongly decided.[11]

Hugo Black, not Frankfurter, became the leader of the libertarian wing of the Court in the early 1940s, developing his own insistent and powerful argument that the Supreme Court must play a special role in protecting individual rights and liberties. Frankfurter, on the other hand, became the modern Supreme Court's leading exponent of the philosophy of judicial restraint, contending that the country's best hope for the protection of democratic values, including minority rights, rested primarily with the elected branches of government, not the Court.

Although Douglas's libertarian convictions matched remarkably well with Black's, he was content for most of his years on the Court to follow Black's lead. On more than one occasion, Douglas said that Black should have been the Chief Justice, and he meant it.

"I have only one soul to save," Douglas proudly proclaimed, "and that's my own."[12] He was a loner, happiest working by himself and for himself on the Court. As Justice Potter Stewart once put it, "Bill Douglas seems positively embarrassed if anyone agrees with him."[13] Douglas often ignored the Justices' collective enterprise and, particularly in his later Court years, appeared to have little interest in the craft of judging.

Off the Court, he cultivated the reputation of a "man's man," a tough, rugged outdoorsman who left Washington as quickly as he could (sometimes before the end of the Court's term) to hike, hunt, and fish in his beloved Northwest and in wildernesses in every other part of the world.[14]

He was no ordinary Justice, and his larger-than-life image made him an attractive political candidate throughout the forties.[15] Douglas was mentioned as a possible running mate with both Democratic standard bearers during that decade, Presidents Roosevelt and Truman. Douglas did not encourage his candidacy but he did little to discourage it either and seemed less than pained by all of the national attention.

With his maverick ways on and off the Court, Douglas appeared to colleagues like Felix Frankfurter as, among other things, injudicious.[16] He seemed too rambunctious and free-wheeling for what Frankfurter considered the quiet, isolated life of a Justice of the Supreme Court—for everyone, of course, but Frankfurter himself, who was in constant contact with the White House and State Department after *he* was appointed to the Court.

"Douglas was a westerner," said his close friend Abe Fortas. "He either worked or played. Felix never played and he never understood Douglas who did. It caused him to underestimate Douglas."[17]

Douglas's unorthodox ways tended to make others, in addition to Frankfurter, undervalue his work. Legal scholars, too, often took his work on the Court less seriously than that of Douglas's colleagues, accusing him of shirking his judicial responsibilities by failing to work out his ideas in a reasoned and orderly fashion.[18]

But Bill Douglas did make a unique and enduring contribution to our constitutional law and deserves a revered status among the extraordinary Justices who served on the Warren Court. He made that contribution while assiduously cultivating the image of a free spirit, seemingly oblivious to the consequences of his actions. But he was not indifferent. He advanced his constitutional vision of liberty on the Court with the same extraordinary intelligence, and calculated shrewdness with which he had advanced his professional career before his Court appointment.

Douglas's most important work was his articulation of the constitutional value of liberty, and specifically the right to privacy, that was the product of a lifetime of observation and thought.[19] Douglas proved, moreover, that despite his reputation as the Court's resident curmudgeon, he was capable of working shrewdly, and even collegially, toward a result that he considered important: the establishment of the constitutional right to privacy.

Douglas's belief in the right to be left alone developed during his lifelong love affair with the wilderness, which began when he was a young boy.[20] An early victim of infantile paralysis, Douglas attacked his physical problems as he did all others, with total concentration. He used the foothills outside of his Yakima, Washington, home as others might use barbells in a gymnasium. Soon, his weak legs became stronger and his short hikes extended deep into the beautiful Cascade Mountains.

The wilderness, Douglas wrote, offered man the peace that comes only with solitude, and "in solitude man can come to know both his heart and his mind."[21] If the sanctity of the individual and the right to be left alone formed the core of Douglas's philosophy of liberty, that philosophy also drew heavily on the corollary, that the Constitution was designed, as Douglas observed, "to take the government off the backs of the people."[22] For Douglas, that meant that the Court must be forever vigilant in protecting individual Americans against governmental abuses of power.[23]

When governmental restraints were necessary, Douglas insisted that they be imposed equally—on the rich and poor, the powerful and powerless alike. Douglas's egalitarianism complemented his belief in the right to privacy—for *all* Americans. It was a theme that pervaded his judicial opinions. And it, too, can be traced to his early days growing up in the Northwest, where he remembered watching rich and powerful members of Yakima's establishment take advantage of those, like the Douglases, who were not.[24]

Douglas's first major opportunity to reveal his original and expansive constitutional vision of liberty came in his third term on the Court. The case was *Skinner v. Oklahoma*,[25] a challenge to an Oklahoma law that permitted compulsory sterilization of criminals who had been convicted of three felonies of "moral turpitude." The petitioner in the case had been convicted once for stealing chickens and twice for armed robbery. For these three crimes, a jury concluded that the defendant had satisfied the statutory requirement and, therefore, should be sterilized.

Douglas wrote the majority opinion for the Court, in which he declared that the statute violated the Fourteenth Amendment's Equal Protection Clause, even though he conceded that the clause had been considered by past Courts as "the last resort of constitutional argument" and had rarely been applied by the Justices before *Skinner.* Scribbling his draft opinion on a yellow legal pad, Douglas quickly moved from the original intention of the framers of the Equal Protection Clause, which was to eliminate official discrimination based on race, to the very different issue posed by the Oklahoma law.[26] Under the Oklahoma statute, Douglas noted, certain felonies, such as embezzlement, were not considered crimes of "moral turpitude." A clerk who appropriated over twenty dollars from his employer's till was never in danger of being sterilized, but a stranger who stole the same amount of money was. Both were guilty of a felony. If the robber repeated his act and was convicted three times, he could be sterilized, but the embezzling clerk could not. In *Skinner*, Douglas wrote, "When the law lays an unequal hand on those who have committed substantially the same quality of offense, but sterilizes one and not the other, it has made as invidious a discrimination as if it had selected a particular race or nationality for oppressive treatment." It was no different, Douglas suggested, than if Oklahoma had chosen to draw a line in its treatment between blacks and whites, or between rich and poor.

If Douglas's *Skinner* opinion had stopped there, it would have been recorded as an interesting constitutional curio of the time, since the Court had rarely relied on the Equal Protection Clause to overturn state legislation. But Douglas went further. "We are dealing here with legislation which involves one of the basic civil rights of man," he wrote. "Marriage and procreation are fundamental to the very existence and survival of the race." Since the Oklahoma statute could irrevocably deprive a citizen of one of those basic civil rights, Douglas wrote, the Supreme Court was obligated to apply the highest standard of constitutional analysis, "strict scrutiny."[27]

Douglas's opinion was remarkable on several levels. First, it revealed Douglas's extraordinary ability to cut to the core of an issue. With quick, bold strokes, he had exposed the discrepancy between Oklahoma's treatment of embezzlers and common larcenists. Douglas, moreover, demonstrated his eagerness to extend constitutional principle beyond the intention of the framers. Douglas believed that, as a Justice, he had no other choice unless, as he once wrote, "he let men long dead and unaware of the problems of the age in which he lives do his thinking for him."[28] Finally, and perhaps most importantly, Douglas showed in his *Skinner* opinion his talent for anticipating a critical line of modern Supreme Court decisions. In this instance, Douglas used the phrases "fundamental interests" and "strict scrutiny," the first to describe the rights to marriage and procreation, and the second to refer to the highest standard of constitutional analysis when fundamental interests were at issue. They were phrases, and concepts, that would enter the modern Supreme Court's vocabulary with increasing frequency, most often during the Warren Court years.

Douglas's penchant for constitutional prophecy was demonstrated ten years after *Skinner*, in a dissent in which Douglas provided a partial blueprint for his 1965 Warren Court opinion in *Griswold v. Connecticut*.[29] In the 1952 Court decision, *Public Utilities Commission v. Pollak*,[30] an eight-man Court rejected a constitutional challenge by irate "captive" listeners in District of Columbia buses who protested the transit company's piping in radio broadcasts of music, news, and commercial announcements during their rides.

Douglas's dissent supported the captive listeners, concluding that they had been deprived of their constitutional right to be left alone. "This is a case of first impression," he began. "There are no precedents to construe, no principles previously expounded to apply. We write on a clean slate."[31] This was just fine with Douglas who once said he would rather make a precedent than follow one.

The case, Douglas wrote, came down to the meaning of "liberty" as used in the Fifth Amendment. Liberty in the constitutional sense, he continued, "must mean more than freedom from unlawful governmental restraint; it must include privacy as well, if it is to be a repository of freedom. The right to be let alone is indeed the beginning of all freedom."[32]

Douglas then traced the right to privacy to two other amendments. The First Amendment, he wrote, guarantees more than the freedom of religion and speech. It also guarantees "the freedom not to do nor act as the government chooses. The First Amendment in its respect for the conscience of the individual honors the sanctity of thought and belief."[33]

Douglas also wrote that part of the claim to privacy was found in the Fourth Amendment's prohibition against unreasonable searches and seizures: "It gives the guarantee that a man's house is his castle beyond invasion either by inquisitive or by officious people." And even in activities outside the house—such as riding on a D.C. bus—Douglas wrote that Americans had "immunities from controls bearing on privacy."[34]

Justice Black congratulated Douglas on his *Pollak* dissent, which, Black wrote, was "one of the best pieces of writing you have ever done."[35] He added, "I regret that my own constitutional ideas prevented my agreeing with you." Black could not join Douglas's dissent because he could not find the right to privacy in his literal reading of the Constitution. Black would later express that view vividly in his 1965 *Griswold* dissent.

Douglas's disagreement with Black on the right to privacy suggests one of the reasons that Douglas's opinions are so important: he was willing to probe beneath the words and original intentions of the framers of the Bill of Rights and Fourteenth Amendment to glean their essential meanings for the complex American society of the second half of the twentieth century.

In his official papers on the *Pollak* case, Douglas included, besides his draft dissents and Black's note, a clipping from the *New Yorker*'s "Talk of the Town" column.[36] The magazine reported: "The bus company, by installing a radio and capturing an audience, commits a sly larceny: it steals the time, the attention, the ear of the passenger and sells this commodity to advertisers. Whether this invades privacy, whether it diminishes freedom are subtle and devious questions, but almost always when you find a small, hardy band of protestants who feel in their bones that something has made them less free, it is an even bet that something has."[37] Douglas left no written commentary on the *New Yorker* column, but it is better than an even bet that he approved of it.

Douglas was never discouraged by his minority status on the Court. Five years after his *Pollak* dissent, he again spoke about his theory of a constitutional right to privacy. The occasion was a series of lectures in which he spoke of a right to privacy that was sometimes explicit and sometimes implicit in the Constitution.[38] The "penumbra" of the Bill of Rights—and here Douglas introduced a word and concept that he would later use in his *Griswold* opinion—"reflects human rights which, though not explicit, are implied from the very nature of man as a child of God."[39]

In 1961, Douglas elaborated on his concept of privacy in the case of *Poe v. Ullman*.[40] The Connecticut statute at issue in *Poe* criminalized the use and distribution of contraceptives. The Court refused to decide the case on the merits, concluding that there was a tacit agreement among Connecticut law enforcement officials not to prosecute violators of the law. Writing for a Court plurality, Justice Frankfurter declared that the Court would not "be umpire to debates concerning harmless empty shadows."[41]

Douglas did not see "empty shadows" but rather serious dangers to constitutional liberty posed by the Connecticut law. "If the state can make this law, it can enforce it," he wrote in dissent. "And proof of its violation necessarily involves an inquiry into the relations between man and wife. That is an invasion of the privacy that is implicit in a free society. This notion of privacy is not drawn from the blue. It emanates from the totality of the constitutional scheme under which we live."[42] *Poe* demonstrated the constitutional gulf between Douglas and Frankfurter that had grown ever wider during their more than two decades on the Court together. Douglas found Frankfurter's elaborate justifications for not deciding cases on the merits so much unnecessary judicial needlework. Frankfurter considered Douglas's approach to constitutional law dangerously irresponsible.

On a personal level, Douglas and Frankfurter detested each other. Frankfurter once wrote that Douglas was "one of the two completely evil men" he had ever known.[43] For his part, Douglas owned a sometimes crude and always mischievous sense of humor that he delighted in directing toward a singularly unappreciative Frankfurter. He once told Frankfurter that he and Black viewed him as a nut to be cracked.[44] Frankfurter did not laugh.

Frankfurter retired from the Court in 1962, three years before the Warren Court confronted the same Connecticut statute that had been challenged in *Poe*. But this time the Court, in *Griswold v. Connecticut*,[45] decided the merits of the issue, with seven Justices voting to strike down the statute as unconstitutional.[46] Chief Justice Warren assigned the Court's opinion to Douglas who, given his long, idiosyncratic advocacy of the right to privacy, was a natural, if somewhat risky, choice.

Internal Court documents indicate that while there were seven votes in the majority (only Black and Stewart dissented), there was no consensus among the seven as to the constitutional basis to strike down the statute. At the Justices' *Griswold* conference, Douglas did not make his familiar, broad argument for a right to privacy that he believed was both explicit and implicit in the Bill of Rights guarantees—perhaps sensing that only a narrower position would win a majority of the Justices. Instead, he contended that the Connecticut statute should be struck down on the ground that it violated the First Amendment's right to association.[47]

Douglas's first draft opinion in *Griswold* tracked closely with his conference argument.[48] One day after receiving Douglas's draft, Justice Brennan wrote Douglas a letter suggesting two reasons that Douglas should expand the constitutional grounds of his opinion.[49] First, Brennan warned that pinning the constitutional right to privacy exclusively on the First Amendment's freedom of association provision could create problems, since the Court's right-to-association decisions commonly dealt with the protection of unpopular advocacy within an organization. That focus, Brennan pointed out, was very different from the privacy right of a marital couple in the intimacy of their bedroom that was raised in *Griswold*. Second, Brennan thought that a more expansive draft was justified, because the Court was dealing with fundamental guarantees of the Bill of Rights, an argument certain to appeal to Douglas. Those guarantees, Brennan wrote, "are but examples of those rights and do not preclude applications or extensions of those rights to situations unanticipated by the framers."

Douglas needed no further prodding. Two days after receiving Brennan's letter, he circulated a second draft of his opinion which reflected, not just Brennan's suggestions, but his own broad concept of privacy developed in his earlier opinions and speeches.[50] He wrote that the right to privacy was founded in "emanations" and "penumbras" of the First, Third, Fourth, Fifth, and Ninth Amendments. He also referred to the fundamental interest in marriage, which he had first proclaimed in his 1942 opinion in *Skinner v. Oklahoma*. The Court, Douglas wrote in *Griswold*, was dealing "with the right of privacy older than the Bill of Rights, older than our political parties, older than our school system. Marriage is a coming together for better or for worst, hopefully enduring and intimate to the degree of being sacred."

Douglas's *Griswold* opinion showed, among other things, that Douglas, the proud loner, was perfectly capable of being collegial when it served his purposes. He eagerly accommodated Brennan, who urged him to expand the constitutional base of his opinion, a suggestion that was entirely compatible with his own broad vision of liberty. His final opinion, moreover, lifted—sometimes word for word—his earlier, more fully articulated theory of the constitutional right to privacy. The ample evidence of Douglas's earlier writing undercuts the criticism by Douglas's detractors that he never took the time to work out his ideas.

Griswold also revealed a less admirable Douglas trait. His *Griswold* opinion was no marvel of judicial craftsmanship; indeed, it was not even as carefully reasoned as some of Douglas's earlier writings on the subject had been.

Griswold also demonstrated why Douglas and Black, for all their libertarian battles together, did not always agree on issues of constitutional principle. Douglas's expansive reading of civil rights and liberties during the Warren Court years of the 1960s frequently went beyond Black's. In his *Griswold* dissent, Black wrote the memorable line, "I like my privacy as well as the next one, but I am nevertheless compelled to admit that government has a right to invade it unless prohibited by some specific constitutional provision."[51]

In civil rights cases decided by the Warren Court in the sixties, Douglas's libertarianism proved more adaptable and protective than Black's. Douglas read the First Amendment's protections to cover the full range of civil rights demonstrations; Black did not.

Black wrote the majority opinion in *Adderley v. Florida*[52] in 1966, for example, in which the Court upheld the arrests and convictions under a state trespass law of civil rights protesters who sang hymns and danced in front of a county jail to protest the arrests and incarceration of their fellow students who had demonstrated against segregated public theaters. Black wrote that the protesters had ample opportunity to demonstrate against segregated policies without marching on the county jail; he concluded that the trespass statute had properly been invoked. In his *Adderley* dissent, Douglas wrote: "The jailhouse, like an executive mansion, a legislative chamber, a courthouse, or the statehouse itself, is one of the seats of government. . . . And when it houses political prisoners or those who many think are unjustly held, it is an obvious center for protest. . . . Their [the protesters'] methods should not be condemned as tactics of obstruction and harassment as long as the assembly and petition are peaceable, as these were."[53]

Griswold was not Douglas's final word on the constitutional right to privacy. Six years after *Griswold*, Douglas seized the opportunity to expand on his privacy theory after the two abortion cases, *Roe v. Wade*[54] and *Doe v. Bolton*,[55] were first argued before the Court in December 1971.

At the Justices' first conference in *Roe* that December, Douglas argued that both the Texas and Georgia abortion laws violated a pregnant woman's constitutional right to privacy. In discussing the Georgia case, Douglas also raised another familiar theme: his concern that the effect of the statute was to discriminate against poor women. Douglas was joined in his vote striking down both statutes by Justices Brennan, Marshall, and Stewart. Douglas's notes indicated that Chief Justice Burger and Justices Blackmun and White voted to uphold the statutes (although Blackmun himself and Brennan counted Blackmun's vote as one in favor of striking the statutes).

Since there were two vacancies on the Court at the time, (as a result of the resignations of Justices Black and Harlan), Douglas, as senior Justice in the majority, assumed that he would assign the Court's opinion. Burger, however, sent out his assignment sheet that assigned the abortion cases to Blackmun. Douglas dashed off a brief note of protest to the Chief,[56] but Burger refused to withdraw the assignment. In response to Douglas, Burger said that the Justices' positions at conference were unclear and that he had recorded no formal vote.[57] The Chief added that, in any event, he thought the abortion cases were "probable candidates" for reargument.

Douglas was angry on two counts. First, he suspected that Burger wanted to delay the abortion cases until President Nixon's appointees, Lewis Powell, Jr., and William Rehnquist, could participate and, possibly, change the outcome. Second, he objected to what he considered Burger's manipulation of the majority opinion assignment. Douglas would, in the following months, take dramatic steps to counteract the Chief Justice on both counts.

Douglas did not wait for Blackmun's opinion to circulate. Shortly after receiving Burger's letter rejecting his request to assign the majority opinion, Douglas drafted his own abortion opinion. In his draft, Douglas declared that the right to privacy was a concept that acquired substance from "the emanations" of the various provisions of the Bill of Rights—and included a pregnant woman's freedom to have an abortion.[58] He sent the draft to Brennan who, as he had done in *Griswold*, offered Douglas a perceptive critique.[59]

Brennan agreed with Douglas's broad constitutional theory of privacy but suggested a more precise elaboration of the fundamental freedom that "liberty" encompassed in protecting the pregnant woman's right to an abortion. Douglas again showed a willingness to listen to colleagues, at least to Brennan, and in a revised draft that he sent to Blackmun, he incorporated many of Brennan's suggestions.[60] In fact, many of the concepts expressed by both Douglas and Brennan eventually appeared in Blackmun's 1973 opinion in *Roe v. Wade*.

But there was another significant aspect to Douglas's role in the abortion cases. In May 1972, three months after receiving Douglas's draft, Blackmun circulated his draft in the Texas case striking down the statute as unconstitutionally vague.[61] Both Douglas and Brennan wrote Blackmun, urging him to deal with the "core" constitutional issue of privacy, which he did in his draft in the Georgia case. Still, Blackmun's position was considerably narrower than Douglas's and Brennan's. They, nonetheless, joined both of Blackmun's opinions, rather than encouraging further discussion, delay and, they feared, reargument. Meanwhile, a majority of the Justices—Burger, Blackmun, White, and the new Nixon appointees, Powell and Rehnquist, supported the Chief Justice's proposal to have the abortion cases reargued.

After Burger formally proposed reargument, Douglas exploded with rage. He drafted a dissent to the Court's decision to schedule rearguments, and he did not spare the Chief Justice's feelings or reputation.[62] He accused Burger of an improper manipulation of the opinion assignment in the abortion cases, "an action," Douglas wrote, "no Chief Justice in my time would ever have taken."

As it turned out, Douglas withdrew his angry dissent, but only after he had received Justice Blackmun's assurances that Blackmun would not change his position to strike down the abortion statutes.[63] Blackmun kept his word and wrote the historic *Roe v. Wade* opinion. In his very active role in the abortion cases, Douglas demonstrated that he was both an effective advocate and tough infighter when he saw the opportunity to expand the constitutional right to privacy.

During his thirty-six years on the Supreme Court, Douglas's many publicized outside activities frequently overshadowed his judicial work. He traveled widely and wrote many volumes about his adventures[64] as well as his views on the world and U.S. foreign policy. He served enthusiastically as a rallying figure for environmental causes before ecology issues had captured national attention.[65] And he took four wives, each younger than the last, and this seemed to infuriate or embarrass just about everyone but William O. Douglas.[66]

Conservative members of Congress called for his impeachment more than once. The last and most serious attempt was led by Representative Gerald Ford after Douglas had published his book, *Points of Rebellion*, a thinly veiled attack on the Nixon administration.[67]

But despite the attention given to Douglas's nonjudicial activities, I believe he will be best remembered for his unique contributions to the Court. He was never a leader on the Court, like Black or Frankfurter, or Warren, Harlan and Brennan who followed them. And his opinions were rarely persuasive in the best traditions of legal scholarship. His *Griswold* opinion, surely one of his most important, was no model of judicial scholarship. But Douglas made his mark and found his place in history because his was an original judicial mind, that produced dazzling shafts of constitutional light that have greatly benefited us all.

Notes

1. Douglas, *Go East, Young Man*, i (1974).

2. For the background on Douglas's Columbia protest, see id. at 159–62; Simon, *Independent Journey: The Life of William O. Douglas*, 96–102 (1980); Urofsky, ed., *The Douglas Letters*, 4–7 (1987).

3. For the background on Douglas at Yale, see Simon, supra note 2, at 102–09; Urofsky, supra note 2, at 8–25.

4. Simon, supra note 2, at 109.

5. Id. at 129, 130.

6. Id. at 140–50.

7. Id. at 150.

8. Id. at 153.

9. For background on Douglas at the SEC, see id. at 151–94; Urosky, supra note 2, at 26–38.

10. 310 U.S. 586 (1940). For background on *Gobitis;* see Barth, *Prophets with Honor*, 108–30 (1974); Garraty, ed., *Quarrels That Have Shaped the Constitution*, 222–42 (1964); Simon, supra note 2, at 204–09.

11. Jones v. Opelika, 316 U.S. 584 (1942) at 623. For background on the defection of Black, Douglas, and Murphy from Frankfurter's leadership, see Simon, supra note 2, at 197–215; Simon, *The Antagonists: Hugo Black, Felix Frankfurter and Civil Liberties in Modern America*, 101–29 (1989).

12. Simon, supra note 2, at 250.

13. Author's interview with Justice Stewart, Washington, D.C. (December 7, 1978).

14. For the background on Douglas's reputation as "a man's man," see Simon, supra note 2, at 276–87.

15. For the background on the political interest in Douglas, see id. at 257–75.

16. For Frankfurter's view of Douglas, see id. at 216–19.

17. Id. at 218.

18. For criticism of Douglas's scholarship, see, for example, Kauper, "Penumbras, Peripherics, Emanations, Things Fundamental and Things Forgotten: The Griswold Case," 64 *Mich. L. Rev.* 235 (1965).

19. For more on Douglas's view of liberty, see Reich in *He Shall Not Pass This Way Again: The Legacy of Justice William O. Douglas*, xi–xiii (Wasby, ed., 1990).

20. On Douglas's love of the wilderness, see generally, Douglas, *Of Men and Mountains* (1950); Douglas, supra note 1, at 37–43; Simon, supra note 2, at 37–46.

21. Douglas, supra note 20, at 90.

22. Schneider v. Smith, 390 U.S. 17 (1968) at 25.

23. For Douglas on civil rights and liberties, see generally, Ball and Cooper, *Of Power and Right: Justices Black and Douglas and America's Tumultuous Years, 1937–1975* (1991); Simon, supra note 2; Wasby, supra note 19.

24. On Douglas and the Yakima establishment, see Douglas, supra note 1, at 7, 60, 61; Simon, supra note 2, at 30–33.

25. 316 U.S. 535 (1942).

26. Douglas's drafts in *Skinner* are from William O. Douglas Papers, Library of Congress, Washington, D.C. [hereinafter Douglas Papers].

27. Id.

28. Douglas, "Stare Decisis," 49 *Col. L. Rev.* 735 (1949).

29. 381 U.S. 479 (1965).

30. 343 U.S. 451 (1952).

31. Id. at 467.

32. Id.

33. Id. at 468.

34. Id. at 467.

35. Letter from Black to Douglas (undated) (Douglas Papers, supra note 26).

36. Id.

37. *New Yorker*, June 7, 1952, at 17.

38. Douglas, *The Right of the People* (1958).

39. Id. at 89.

40. 367 U.S. 497 (1961).

41. Id. at 508.

42. Id. at 521.

43. Simon, supra note 2, at 217.

44. Id. at 218.

45. 381 U.S. 479 (1965).

46. For background on *Griswold*, see Garrow, *Liberty and Sexuality: The Right to Privacy and the Making of "Roe v. Wade,"* 131–260 (1994); Schwartz, *Inside the Warren Court*, 229, 230 (1983).

47. Justice William J. Brennan Papers, Library of Congress [hereinafter Brennan Papers]; Douglas Papers, supra note 26.

48. Douglas's *Griswold* drafts are collected in the Douglas Papers, supra note 26.

49. Letter from Brennan to Douglas (Apr. 24, 1965) (Douglas Papers, supra note 26).

50. Douglas Papers, supra note 26.

51. 381 U.S. 497, 510 (1965).

52. 385 U.S. 39 (1966).

53. Id. at 49.

54. 410 U.S. 113 (1973); for background on *Roe v. Wade,* see Garrow, supra note 46; Schwartz, *The Ascent of Pragmatism* (1990) and *The Unpublished Opinions of the Burger Court* (1988). Material from the Justices' *Roe* conference is collected in Brennan Papers, supra note 47 and the Douglas Papers, supra note 26.

55. 410 U.S. 179 (1973).

56. Douglas's note to Burger (Dec. 18, 1971) (Douglas Papers, supra note 26).

57. Burger's response to Douglas (Dec. 20, 1971) (Douglas Papers, supra note 26).

58. Douglas's draft opinion, undated, Douglas Papers, supra note 26.

59. Brennan's critique, Dec. 30, 1971, Douglas Papers, supra note 26.

60. Douglas's revised draft, undated, Douglas Papers, supra note 26.

61. Blackmun's *Roe* draft, May 18, 1972, Douglas Papers, supra note 26.

62. Douglas's draft dissent, June 2, 1972, Douglas Papers, supra note 26.

63. Author's interview with Blackmun, Nov. 16, 1992, Washington, D.C.

64. See, e.g., Douglas, *Strange Lands and Friendly People* (1951), *Beyond the High Himalayas* (1952) and *North from Malaya* (1953).

65. Simon, supra note 2, at 326–33.

66. Id. at 228–40, 366–88.

67. Id. at 391–411; Douglas, *Points, Points of Rebellion* (1970).

· 14 ·

FELIX FRANKFURTER

PHILIP B. KURLAND

Historians tell us that lawyers do not write history, they write polemics. It comes naturally to one trained in legal forensics to martial his evidence in support of a conclusion he chooses to reach. Historians also tell us, or at least each other, that history as compiled is a combination of fact, myth, and personal persuasion. But we all know some historical deconstructions—Washington's cherry tree is an innocent enough example—and since we are talking mostly of biography let me cite a single instance, made popular by that excellent crime novelist Josephine Tey.[1] Richard III of England has come down to us through hundreds of years of history as a miserably deformed and villainous murderer of his two infant nephews in the Tower of London as well as a tyrannical ruler. The portrait has no less a patrimony than Sir Thomas More and William Shakespeare. And those who may have been fortunate enough to have seen Sir Laurence Olivier in the role have never doubted the evil character and physical malformation of Richard. Our schoolbooks continue to republish this version of history as if it were supported by fact. It is not. This is not to say that Richard was the embodiment of good but only that he was—pretty clearly—the victim of defamation, whether intentional or malicious is not relevant here.

The scholar, lawyer, or citizen should maintain a thoroughgoing skepticism whether faced with the claims of a peddler, a politician, or a professor. Truth is a rare and valuable commodity, but not to the publicist. Richard III was an early victim of what has become more recently so dominant a factor of our society. Let me quote the incomparable Learned Hand, speaking in 1942: "[T]he art of publicity is a black art; but it has come to stay; every year adds to its potency and to the finality of its judgments. The hand that rules the press, the radio, the screen and the far-spread magazine, rules the country; whether we like it or not, we must learn to accept it."[2] I do not mean that the "media's" (hateful word) political positions will be necessarily accepted—the 1948 election choice of Truman over Dewey showed that—but only that the alleged factual record is being made at least partially of imagination and not data. The sad part is that even after the spin doctors are long through with their creations, academics still derive their information from what may be called "previously owned" sources rather than proved actualities.

Every time I am asked to participate in commemoration of the Warren Court, I get the feeling that my role is that of Brutus at Caesar's funeral or of the devil's advocate in an old-time sanctification process. (You may take heart from the fact that the devil's advocate seldom if ever succeeded in his advocacy.) In any event I feel a little like the odd man out, a Frankfurter adherent where Frankfurter adherents are at best, tolerated, at worst, disdained. But I have known Professor Schwartz for a very long time—since 1948—which is so long ago that he had by then written barely half a dozen books. He has always been tolerant of heterodoxy, not to speak of heresy. And in his invitation he was kind enough to me—if not to the reader—to say that I could treat my subject, Felix Frankfurter, in any manner I chose and need not be confined to a biographical sketch or a close analysis of his opinions. There are a plethora of both available to you through your PCs, even if you are not so old-fashioned as to believe that learning comes from books, books you can hold in your hands and touch and, if you own them, annotate.

When my colleague Professor Phil Gossett speaks about Verdi or Puccini, he plays piano transcriptions of their music, the better to convey their essence. When our Shakespeare expert, Professor David Bevington, speaks about the Bard, he reads excerpts from the plays or the sonnets, for the same reason. Since I am trying to convey something of the persona of Felix Frankfurter, I thought I would emulate my colleagues by including some extensive readings from some of F.F.'s own heretofore unpublished writings, for they tell you more about him and his thinking than I could hope to convey in my own words. I apologize because I cannot deliver his words with the verve and elan that were so intrinsically a part of him, but I have also included testimony about that quality from his closest friend, Dean Acheson.

Thus, what I have to offer is not a portrait of a jurist, but rather a series of snapshots. Felix Frankfurter took his seat as a Justice of the Supreme Court in January 1939 and retired in August of 1962, physically disabled by a stroke after earlier suffering a heart attack. (Let me say here in order that you may, as Judge Learned Hand mandated, be able to establish your bias against bias, that I am, indeed a stalwart partisan of Frankfurter's; that I consider him, along with Hand, one of the two greatest judicial minds to have served on the bench in my lifetime. Which does not mean that I am not sincere in recounting his faults and failures, for he was very much a human given to error, even as you and I.) If there are ambiguities in my collection of snapshots, remember your own family albums. And it must be added that when I speak of "the Warren Court," I am conscious, as you should be, of the ambiguity of the phrase. Of course, it means the United States Supreme Court over which Earl Warren presided from 1953 to 1969.

Felix Frankfurter served with Warren only from 1953 to 1962. Thus, he was a member of what Professor David Currie called "The First Warren Court." Currie regarded the replacement of Frankfurter by Arthur Goldberg as marking the transfiguration into what he called "The Real Warren Court."[3] Frankfurter had also been a member of the Hughes Court, the Stone Court, and the Vinson Court. The Warren Court consisted of seventeen members, not merely nine, as we think of a Court. For those who lived during the time of the Warren chairmanship, it is often thought of as the nine who unanimously decided *Brown v. Board of Education*,[4] that is, Warren, Black, Reed, Frankfurter, Douglas, Jackson, Burton, Clark, and

Minton; or the Justices at the time of the reapportionment decisions, by which time Harlan, Brennan, Stewart, White, and Goldberg had replaced Reed, Frankfurter, Jackson, Burton, and Minton and made the "real Warren Court." I mention these two sets of cases because Warren regarded them as the two greatest accomplishments of his terms and he gave pride of place to the reapportionment cases.

Frankfurter, as noted, was one of the Justices of the *Brown* Court. One of the myths that has come down to us, thanks largely to "investigative reporters" purporting to write history was that F.F. was one who dragged his feet in getting the Court to outlaw segregation. He did help postpone judgment in the Vinson years, waiting for a Court that might prove amenable to the petitioners' case. It may seem hard to believe that even in 1954 victory for the petitioners was anything but a sure bet until the date of decision. Even then there was some reluctance on the Court, but it tended to be found among those of Southern background and one at least who worried whether the task required action of the elected portions of government rather than the judiciary. The rationale for the use of the Fourteenth Amendment came out of F.F.'s chambers, assuming that the Constitution had anything to do with the decision. Now that all of the Justices of the *Brown* Court are gone, and their papers—to the extent they have been preserved—are open to responsible researchers, maybe we can replace twistory with history.

Frankfurter's relationship with the Warren Court was quite different with regard to the second watershed, the reapportionment cases. He was still a member of the Court and wrote a lengthy disagreement with the notion of judicial interference in electoral districting in *Baker v. Carr*[5] reiterating the position he had stated for the Court in *Colegrove v. Green*.[6] It is to be presumed that he would have dissented from *Reynolds v. Sims*[7] and those that followed, certainly denying that the issue was mete for judicial resolution and unlikely to accept the simplistic formula of "one person, one vote." But this guess is not based on any notion that F.F. was a member of an anti-Warren cabal or a member of any clique within the Court.

Another of the myths that dog Supreme Court history is that differences within the Court resemble the conflicts between the Yorks and the Lancasters in the Wars of the Roses, with no more than an occasional apostasy to keep things interesting. On the first Monday in October, 1993, the *New York Times* page one headline blared—as much as the *New York Times* ever blares: "A YOUNGER COURT FACES OLD SPLITS AS ITS TERM OPENS NEW CONSENSUS MAY EMERGE IN HIGH COURT RESHAPED BY RECENT APPOINTMENTS." To the best of my knowledge, there have been no organized groups within the Court. Certainly there is no hierarchy. There has been a consistency of pairings at times, never absolute. In my day, Justices Black and Douglas were usually—if not always—found together, as were Justices Frankfurter and Jackson. But you must remember in your calculations that the nine members of the Court are usually choosing between two litigants, which will necessarily result in few voting combinations. So far as I know, there is no trading of votes. And the Court issues very little propaganda other than its opinions, which do not seem to me to be self-serving.

Of course there are attempts at persuasion, utilizing various devices that are frequently counterproductive. Indulge me, if you will, in a personal anecdote. When I was about to graduate from law school, I called on my professors to say goodbye. One of them, a Yankee named Warren Seavey, asked what I was going to do and when I told him I would be clerking for Justice Frankfurter, with whom he had served on the Harvard law faculty for many years, he leaned back in his chair and in his best New Hampshire twang said: "Felix is all right. The only real trouble with Felix is that he thinks he can convince someone by calling him a son-of-a-bitch." One may doubt that, if he used it, this rhetorical device carried him very far in the Conference Room at the Supreme Court.

More often Frankfurter's detractors accused him of obsequiousness. There is no sound basis for this criticism. Certainly he lavishly indulged in praise either for the sake of persuasion or merely to afford pleasure to the recipient. He had his heroes, whom he worshipped. And I have no doubt that he fawned over Oliver Wendell Holmes and Henry L. Stimson and, at least after 1932, over Franklin Delano Roosevelt, but like most if not all Supreme Court Justices his vanity made it easy for him to abide by his mother's oft-repeated advice: "Hold yourself dear." I have known no small egos among those who have occupied seats on the Supreme Court. F.F.'s was no exception. And his ego was big enough that he was not bothered by adverse criticism unless it came from someone he deeply respected. As he wrote to Gene Rostow about a vituperative piece by Professor Fred Rodell of Dean Rostow's faculty: "In any event, I was very early in life influenced to try not to have my energy dissipated or deflected by what may be said about me. What Lincoln said on that subject and his own practice deeply entered into my consciousness, and my formative years were, fortunately, spent under Henry L. Stimson. I don't mean to say that I like to have lies or silly things said about me. But through the influences that I have indicated acting on my own temperament, I have disciplined myself to pay practically no attention to scurrility or foolishness about me."[8]

This is not to deny that praise was part of his arsenal of persuasion and critique. To read his letters to Roosevelt makes you wonder how two such sophisticated persons could accept such encomia as sincere. But read F.F.'s letter to Chief Justice Harlan F. Stone's authorized biographer in 1956:

> It will not have escaped you that my letters to Stone indicated that I indulged in the practice of writing him promptly and habitually about opinions of his, more particularly dissenting opinions in which he spoke also for Holmes and Brandeis and, after Holmes's retirement for Brandeis and Cardozo. I need not tell you that I never spoke in approval of his opinions unless I was in agreement with him. But it must have struck you that my appreciation of him was rather regularly in heightened language. There was a reason. I was urged not only to praise him when I saw occasion for praise, but also not to be stinting. Stone had a strong appetite for praise. Like Queen Victoria, he was eager to have it laid on with a trowel.[9]

The letters to Stone were written when F.F. was still a professor and Stone an Associate Justice.

The correspondence showed that even more than Stone's love for praise was his dislike of adverse criticism. It would seem that Stone and his successors, Chief Justices Vinson and Warren, were highly sensitive to criticism, which did not make life with Felix any easier. The reason that a thin skin in a colleague made for difficulties was stated in a letter by F.F. to a very good friend in March of 1957: "I don't like to see manifestations of sensitiveness in you, because sensitiveness leads to unhappiness. Secondly, sensitiveness has its influence on others. It inhibits free interchange and thereby makes inroads on one of the indispensable conditions of critical thinking. I have noticed even in some of the best of men in places of power a sensitiveness that eventually shuts off the kinds of things they ought to hear. Not that I am unaware that this is a natural reaction to what is often ignorant and unjust criticism."[10] There was prescience in this statement, for what started as a warm relationship between F.F. and Warren soon deteriorated. The Chief's geniality wilted under Frankfurter's acerbity, and I cannot tell you that this did not have constitutional consequences.

At the beginning of their relationship on the Court, Frankfurter was ready to give Warren very high marks indeed. He wrote in high dudgeon to his good friend C. C. Burlingham of the delay in confirming Warren's recess appointment: "I know of nothing that has made me more morally outraged . . . than the fact that the confirmation of a man whom the President of the United States has named to be the Chief Justice and who has been discharging that office for four months with true regard to its highest standards and who has thus been entrusted with some of the profoundest issues facing this nation should have to have his confirmation held up until some cops report whether or not he is a security risk or otherwise not qualified for the Chief Justiceship. Will you please tell me why the New York Times and the New York Herald Tribune do not lash out against this fantastic but outrageous nonsense?"[11]

Was Felix Frankfurter one of the great Justices of the Supreme Court? The ratings of jurists is a highly idiosyncratic exercise. It is something like choosing an all-time all-star baseball team. Many baseball experts would probably choose Joe DiMaggio over Ted Williams. None would choose Pete Reiser. Most of today's baseball fans may not know who any of them is. In 1979, Professor Schwartz announced his list of the ten greatest American judges. His list included Warren, but did not include Frankfurter. The only other Warren Court Justice he included was Hugo Black. On the other hand, showing the part that personal predilection plays in such judgments, he also found Arthur T. Vanderbilt among the top ten judges in American history and I dare say that most of you do not know who Arthur T. Vanderbilt was, unless you had a course from Professor Schwartz.[12]

Of course, one's rating of jurists depends on the standards of excellence that one utilizes. Charles Evans Hughes implied his own when he said: "It is safe to say that no member of the Court is under any illusion as to the mental equipment of his brethren. Constant and close association discloses the strength and exposes the weaknesses of each. Courage of conviction, sound learning, familiarity with precedents, exact knowledge due to painstaking study of the cases cannot fail to command that profound respect which is always yielded to intellectual power conscientiously applied."[13] All of these attributes F.F. had in abundance and should have marked him as one of the most influential members of the Court, certainly at least the equal of any other. But there was one factor that disqualified him from great influence within the Court and great popularity outside the Court. His notion of the constitutional role of the judiciary in our democracy often condoned results distasteful to those I would describe for want of a better term—and it certainly is not meant as a pejorative—as adherents to The Liberal Creed. Whereas other judges declared themselves to be followers of Holmes because of the results they thought he would have reached, Frankfurter and Learned Hand were disciples of Holmes's concept of the limitation of the judicial role especially under the Fourteenth Amendment.

It would border on sacrilege for me to attempt to encapsulate what has been described in shorthand as F.F.'s concern with "judicial restraint." The views of both F.F. and Hand are directly descended from James Bradley Thayer's *The Origin and Scope of the American Doctrine of Constitutional Law*[14] and are best set out in Hand's Oliver Wendell Holmes Lectures[15] and in Frankfurter's *John Marshall and the Judicial Function.*[16] The principal difference between F.F. and most of his brethren, not only those of the Warren Court but also those of the Hughes, Stone, and Vinson Courts, was that he was concerned with the proper means for resolving issues in a constitutional democracy, whereas they were primarily concerned with getting the right answers to those issues, however secured. Frankfurter, like Brandeis, thought that the doctrine that the ends justified the means was pernicious. Having served with so many Justices, he had doubts beyond the theoretical that they fulfilled the qualifications for Platonic guardians. Certainly, to me if not to him, their method of selection did not assure that they were so qualified. The history of the chosen did not dispel the doubt.

Frankfurter's concepts of a limited judiciary with reference to constitutional review were not, however, created for purposes of frustrating Earl Warren and his confreres. His notions were long developed before he arrived on the bench, that being an advantage or disadvantage of a professorial background. F.F. was strongly of the view that the best way to express a man's thoughts are in his own words, and so I offer a long quotation from a letter of his to Hugo Black:

> Once you go beyond a procedural content and pour into the generality of the language [of the Fourteenth Amendment] substantive guaranties, it is to me inconceivable that any kind of definition of the substantive rights of the guaranty will not repeat in the future the history of the past, namely will according to the makeup of the Court give varying scope to the substantive rights that are protected—and so I spent practically all my mature lifetime, until I came on the Court, in adding my feeble efforts toward maintaining a conscientious observance by the Court of what I conceive to be the very narrow scope of the Court's power to strike down political action.
>
> My starting point is, of course, the democratic faith on which this country is founded—the right of a democracy to make mistakes and correct its errors by the organs that reflect the popular will—which regards the Court as a qualification of the democratic principle and desires to restrict the play of this undemocratic feature to its narrowest limits. I am aware that men who have power can exercise it—and too often do—to enforce their own will, to make their will, or if you like their notions of policy, the measure of what is right. But I am also aware of the forces of tradition and the habits of discipline whereby men entrusted with power remain within the limited framework of their professed power. More particularly, the history of this Court emboldens me to believe that men need not be supermen to observe the conditions under which judicial review of political authority—that's what judicial review of legislation really amounts to—is ulti-

> mately maintainable in a democratic society. When men who had such background and such relation to so-called property interests as did, for instance, Waite, Bradley, Moody, Holmes, Brandeis and Cardozo, showed how scrupulously they did not write their private notions of policy into the Constitution, then I am not prepared to say that all that a court does when it adjudicates in these constitutional controversies is an elaborate pretense, and that judges do in fact merely translate their private convictions into law.
>
> I appreciate the frailties of men, but the War is for me meaningless and Hitler becomes the true prophet if there is no such thing as Law different from and beyond the individuals who give it expression. And what I am thinking about is that if each temporary majority of this Court—and none is for very long—in fact merely regards its presence on this Court as an opportunity for translating its own private notions of policy into decisions, the sooner an educated public opinion becomes aware of the fact the better not only for truth but also in the true interests of the tribunal for which the wise founders of this country provided, acting however within the very narrow limits within which it was deemed appropriate that it should function.[17]

Holmes was pithier when he wrote in *Truax v. Corrigan*:[18] "There is nothing I more deprecate than the use of the Fourteenth Amendment beyond the absolute compulsion of its words to prevent the making of social experiments that an important part of the community desires, in the insulated chambers afforded by the several States, even though the experiments may seem futile or even noxious to me and to those whose judgment I most respect." Some day, comparison will be made between judgments endorsed by Holmes, those endorsed by Frankfurter, and those of "the real Warren Court." And it may be determined whether the breveted Civil War colonel properly belongs in the pantheon of one or the other. Frankfurter, of course, has no attraction to either "liberals" or "conservatives." The former would have no part of him since his nonactivist stance on the Court. The latter regard him as untrue to the basic creed of Adam Smith and Milton Friedman. Can you imagine the chagrin among my colleagues at the University of Chicago Law School at such statements of Frankfurter's as this in a letter to a close friend: "Was there ever a starting point for a great man's thinking as false as Jeremy Bentham's assumption that a man is governed by enlightened self-interest?"[19]

Over the course of F.F.'s tenure and since, more and more of the Supreme Court's docket has been taken up with constitutional issues, for two reasons. First, more and more cases of constitutional stature have arisen. And second, more and more issues that were once regarded as questions of state law or statutory law were raised to constitutional dignity. Nevertheless, the second most important part of the Supreme Court's docket, however, measured, were issues of statutory interpretation or application. And here Frankfurter, while still affording pride of place to the legislature, was less reticent about judicial participation. He might not have gone so far as John Chipman Gray, who said, "in truth all the Law is judge-made law. The shape in which the statute is imposed on the community as a guide for conduct is that statute as interpreted by the courts."[20] But very early in his tenure on the Court, he made it clear, again in a letter to Hugo Black, that he did not put much regard in charges about judicial legislation:

> Some time ago at the end of a, to me, very stimulating talk between us, I told you that you were a Benthamite. Since I regard Bentham as the most fruitful law reformer of the Nineteenth Century, that was of course fundamentally a term of praise. But as is so often true of a reformer who seeks to get rid of the accumulated abuses of the past, Bentham at times threw out the baby with the bath. In his rigorous and candid desire to rid the law of many far-reaching abuses introduced by judges, he was not unnaturally propelled to the opposite extreme of wishing all law to be formulated by legislation, deeming most [things] that judges do [to be] usurpation by incompetent men as to matters concerning which he believed them [to be] guilty of "judicial legislation."
>
> That phrase "judicial legislation" has become ever since a staple of condemnation. I, too, am opposed to judicial legislation in its invidious sense, but I deem equally mischievous—because founded on an untruth and an impossible aim—the notion that judges merely announce the lawmaking. Here, as elsewhere, the difficulty comes from absolutes when the matter at hand is conditioned by circumstances, is contingent upon the everlasting problem of how far is too far and how much is too much. Judges as you well know, cannot escape the responsibility of filling in gaps which the finitude of even the most imaginative legislation renders inevitable. And so it is that even in the countries governed exclusively by codes and even in the best of codes there are provisions saying in effect that when a controversy arises in court for which the code offers no provision the judges are not relieved of the duty of deciding the case but must themselves fashion the law appropriate to the situation.
>
> So the problem is not whether the judges make law, but when and how much. Holmes put it in his highbrow way, that "they can do so only interstitially; they are confined from molar to molecular motions." I used to say to my students that legislatures make law wholesale, judges retail. In other words they cannot decide things by invoking a new major premise out of whole cloth; they must make the law that they do make out of the existing materials and with due deference to the presuppositions of the legal system of which they have been made a part. Of course I know these are not mechanical devices, and therefore not susceptible of producing automatic results. But they sufficiently indicate the limits within which the judges are to move.[21]

The "new Warren Court" without Frankfurter, indeed began its dedication to a catchword of "equality," much as the "Nine Old Men" whom Roosevelt had sought to stifle used the catchword "liberty."[22] But catchwords are not substitutes for analysis or thought, nor ought they to be. And the serious question that goes unanswered by Supreme Court analysts is not whether Frankfurter's departure from the Court made a difference in the outcome of some cases, but why. Clearly the Goldberg vote was different from what the Frankfurter vote would have been in many cases. But what about the question whether his absence from the Conference had an effect. Remember what Hughes said: "It is safe to say that no member of the Court is under any illusion as to the mental equipment of his brethren. . . . Courage of conviction, sound learning, familiarity with precedents, exact knowledge due to painstaking study of the cases under consideration cannot fail to command that profound respect which is always yielded to intellectual power conscientiously applied."[23] It is easy to say that the post-Frankfurter Court announced judgments that were closer to our personal predilections, which accounts for most of the praise afforded it. Are we equally prepared to say that they were better reasoned? More in keeping with the constitutional plan?

In the space that remains, I should like to write about F.F. the man rather than the judge, for he was a person of many parts. He often complained, and I think sincerely, that he had ever given up the professorial chair for the bench, that life would have been happier for him and for his adored wife Marion had he remained at Harvard. This was not to deny that he had avidly sought the seat on the Court in the first place. It is dubious that anybody was ever compelled against his will to serve as a Supreme Court Justice. But judicial life was too confining for him. Frankfurter's enjoyment of life was not dependent upon office. Some years earlier, even in the immediate aftermath of *Sacco-Vanzetti*, the governor appointed him to the Supreme Judicial Court of Massachusetts, without even asking him. Although this was Holmes's first judicial base, Frankfurter declined it. F.D.R. wanted him to be his solicitor general as a stepping stone to the Court. He declined for a multiplicity of reasons. One should not take one post as a means to another. Second, he would be of more use as an adviser to the president out of office. Third, he wanted to go to Oxford to teach. In assaying Frankfurter, one should never underestimate the importance of his Anglophilia.

During his first years on the bench, he regularly if informally counseled the British government leaders on relations with, at the beginning, a United States committed to neutrality. Thereafter, there was no sphere of legitimate human activity into which he did not stick his nose, except science. He was a self-confessed ignoramus with regard to matters scientific or mechanical, once thinking even of recusing himself in all patent cases until he discovered that most of his brethren were no more enlightened than he. Again, if I may, an anecdote: On his tenth anniversary on the Court, his law clerks over the decade—the Justices had only one each year then—wanted to give him a gift at the annual dinner. We consulted Mrs. F. She graciously said that he would cherish anything he got from us, "so long as it wasn't mechanical—like a fountain pen."

Musicians and playwrights and poets and clowns as well as scholars were numbered among his friends. (I've always been amused by a telegram he received from Groucho Marx on his nomination, which read: "Congratulations. If confirmed please send autographed photo." There was a more poignant note on his resignation from Mrs. Scotty Reston; Scotty was then chief of the *New York Times* Washington Bureau: "We love you on and off.")

He told McGeorge Bundy, the dean of arts and sciences at Harvard, that his hobby was to be president of a university and he frequently proffered advice on how to be one, whether solicited or not. The dean of the Harvard Law School received innumerable comments on the running of that institution. And the publishers and editors of the *Washington Post* and the *New York Times* were also told how to do their jobs. He surveyed the *Congressional Record* and *Hansard* and five or six newspapers every day. His periodical literature was mostly English, but he did see many if not all the law reviews. His personal correspondence was extraordinarily extensive: a small part of it fills numerous files in the Harvard Law School Library. There are so many aspects to him that none of his biographers has yet to encapsulate him.

At heart, I think, he was a conservative, as shown by this quotation from a letter to the poet Archibald MacLeish, who had been one of his law students, and who, like many of them and most of his earlier law clerks, became a devoted friend:

> I was particularly interested, but not surprised, that you put Coleridge at the head of your list of poets who discoursed illuminatingly on the writing of poetry. I was not surprised because my beloved friend, Robert Valentine, instilled in me a sense of the greatness of Coleridge as critic and prose writer. Your reference to Rilke stirs anew in me my ambition to read him one of these days. I have been put off reading him by some of the mystical stuff that I have seen from his admirers, particularly things in *Hounds and Horn* ages ago. I am also aware of the fact that when it comes to the arts I am a stick-in-the-mud. Every time I hear Hindemith and Bartok I find myself longing for Mozart and Beethoven, and occasionally when Rilke crosses my path I revert to Heine. I hope that I am the last person in the world who thinks there are closed categories in the arts. Nobody could be more impatient than I when told that a novel must be thus and so, or that "poetry" must fit some rubrics. It is true that there are only twenty-four hours in the day, all too few of which, alas, are open to a weak character for the delectation of his soul. You remember the saying of Emerson's which I am fond of quoting "Man is as lazy as he dares to be." So it is easier to recall Heine than to explore Rilke. Why Heine? Has not Matthew Arnold given the answer in *Heine's Grave*? Do you remember the stanza that conveys so much of Heine's quality?
>
> The Spirit of the world,
> Beholding the absurdity of man—
> Their vaunts, their fears—let a sardonic smile,
> For one short moment, wander o'er his lips.
> *That smile was Heine*! for its earthly hour
> The strange guest sparkled; now 'tis pass'd away.
>
> And now I must return to the muttons of the law.[24]

The English language was a particular obsession with him. Like the French Academy, he regarded the demeaning of the language as a heinous offense. But he also delighted in its skillful esoteric use and was greatly pleased by Learned Hand's use of the Rabelaisian word "philogrobolized."[25] On March, 25, 1953, he wrote to Hand: "Please recite on 'philogrobolized.' All I can get out of the O.E.D. is the use of the word in a quotation from Rabelais. How did you come to annex it? Not that I have not long been aware of the range and richness of your vocabulary but I am curious about this one." And, on March 31, for their correspondence was full and regular:

> I have had a windfall—your observations on the judgment of Panurge. Patently I misconveyed myself, for all I meant to ask was about the word 'philogrobolized'—*that* I had forgotten, if I ever had taken it in—and I wanted to hear from you whether it was your own private use or whether the word had in fact established itself in the stratospheric flights into the empyrean of the English language, wherein you are such an ace.
>
> Oh, my dear unhumble and disobedient servant, there are things even worse than the judgments of Panurge. I am in the midst of one or two such—not,

> I hasten to add, productions of mine. Yes, the Sherman law leads to much judicial moonshine, but please don't overlook the fruitful provocations of "civil liberties".[26]

In spite of the abundance of diversions that claimed his time, he constantly complained about the overabundance of work assumed by the Court. He did his share of the Court's opinions, but no more. There was too much else to do.

Let me close then with an encomium to Frankfurter by one who knew him well, probably his closest friend, again a former student of his at the Harvard Law School, Dean Acheson. He wrote:

> It has been said of Leslie Stephen, by Maitland, I think that those who did not know him would never understand the source and magnitude of his influence. For that reason, he would be an enigma to future generations. Reading his written words, would give a quite inadequate, often erroneous, impression of the man, and no sense at all of the effect on the hearer of the spoken word. This is preeminently true of Felix Frankfurter. One could read everything he has written—a formidable task from several points of view—and still have little more than an inkling, if that, of why this man has evoked in so many such passionate devotion and exercised for half a century so profound an influence, I can think of no one in our time remotely comparable to him, though it would not surprise me if in another time Dr. Franklin might have had something of the same personal influence.
>
> In the same way, the words, especially the written words of another cannot convey the reality of Felix Frankfurter. . . . Above all one need years of experience to know the depth of his concern about people. He lives in personal relationships as a fish lives in water. This is no secluded scholar immured in library or laboratory, absorbed in intellectual problems, but a man immersed in people.[27]

MacLeish assured us that the "qualities of the man himself . . . must necessarily vanish with him, or, at the latest, with the memories of his friends."[28] If two such wordsmiths as Acheson and MacLeish cannot mold the English language to reveal the mind and spirit of Felix Frankfurter, it is certainly time that I abandoned the attempt. But first I would offer my last Acheson quotation, taken from his letter to the Yale trustees nominating F.F. for an honorary degree. He concluded, as I do: "In these qualities, I think, lie the answer to the puzzle which he has passed to the pundits. How is it that those 'judgments and intuitions more subtle than any articulate major premise' which lie at the roots of the Anglo-Saxon law and institutions form the fabric of the mind of this Jewish immigrant boy from Vienna, who could not speak English until he was twelve?"[29]

Notes

1. Tey, *The Daughter of Time* (1945).
2. Hand, *The Spirit of Liberty* 172 (3d ed. 1960).
3. 2 Currie, *The Constitution in the Supreme Court* 415 (1990).
4. 347 U.S. 483 (1954).
5. 369 U.S. 186 (1962).
6. 328 U.S. 549 (1946).

7. 377 U.S. 533 (1964).
8. Letter to Eugene V. Rostow, August 9, 1957.
9. Letter to Alpheus Thomas Mason, March 1, 1956.
10. Letter to Dean Erwin N. Griswold, March 14, 1957.
11. Letter of February 15, 1954.
12. Peterson and Provizer, *Great Justices of the U.S. Supreme Court* 27 (1993).
13. Hughes, *The Supreme Court* 57 (1928).
14. 7 *Harv. L. Rev.* 129 (1893).
15. Learned Hand, *The Bill of Rights* (1958).
16. Frankfurter, *John Marshall and the Judicial Function: Government Under Law* (Sutherland ed., 1956).
17. Letter to Hugo L. Black, November 13, 1943.
18. 257 U.S. 312, 344 (1921).
19. Letter to Alfred E. Cohen, November 19, 1953.
20. Gray, *The Nature and Sources of the Law* 125 (Beacon Press ed. 1960).
21. Letter to Hugo L. Black, December 15, 1939.
22. See Kurland, Foreword, "Equal in Origin and Equal in Title to the Legislative and Executive Branches of the Government," 78 *Harv. L. Rev.* 143 (1964).
23. Supra note 14.
24. Letter to Archibald MacLeish, May 3, 1954.
25. See Gunther, *Learned Hand*, 626 n. (1994).
26. Letters to Learned Hand, March 25 and 31, 1953.
27. Acheson, *Fragments of My Fleece* 219, 220 (1971).
28. Frankfurter, 1964 *Supreme Court Review* 1, 3.
29. Acheson to Yale University Honorary Degrees Committee, September 6, 1960, in *Among Friends: Personal Letters of Dean Acheson* (McLellan and Acheson eds., 1980).

• 15 •

JOHN MARSHALL HARLAN

NORMAN DORSEN

Justice John Marshall Harlan was an indispensable component of the Warren Court. This is true not only, as a wiseacre might say, because losers are needed if there are to be winners, but because he provided a form of resistance to the Court's dominant motifs that was intelligent, determined, professionally skillful, and above all principled. In a sense he defined the Court by his dissents. For this performance over sixteen years Harlan received extraordinary praise. Earl Warren himself said, "Justice Harlan will always be remembered as a true scholar, a talented lawyer, a generous human being, and a beloved colleague by all who were privileged to sit with him."[1] Judge Henry Friendly, who first worked with Harlan as a young lawyer in the early 1930s, boldly asserted, "There has never been a Justice of the Supreme Court who has so consistently maintained a high quality of performance or, despite differences in views, has enjoyed such nearly uniform respect from his colleagues, the inferior bench, the bar, and the academy."[2] There have been many similar accolades.[3]

This chapter indicates the nature and extent of Harlan's views as a counterpoint to the Warren Court majority and suggests that it would be a mistake to conceive of Harlan solely in this light, as an inveterate reactionary seeking to forestall the brave new world that his brethren sought to welcome or even to create. To a surprising degree Harlan concurred in the liberal activism of the Warren Court, picking his spots carefully and above all seeking (though not always successfully) to be true to his core values of federalism and a limited judicial function. The portrait that emerges, in sum, is not a right-wing Justice, as he is sometimes conceived, but rather that of someone closer to the center, a moderate figure avoiding the extremes.

I

John Marshall Harlan was born in Chicago on May 20, 1899, into a family distinguished in the law. His great-grandfather was a lawyer; his grandfather, for whom he was named, was a Justice of the United States Supreme Court for thirty-four years; his father was a lawyer; and an uncle was a member of the Interstate Commerce Commission.

Harlan studied at Princeton University (A.B. 1920), and was a Rhodes Scholar for three years at Balliol College, Oxford, where he began the study of law and formed personal attachments that he maintained throughout his life. After Oxford, Harlan completed his legal education at New York Law School (LL.B. 1924), and he was admitted to practice in New York in 1925.

Harlan began his career with Root, Clark, Buckner & Howland, a large Wall Street firm that, unlike some of its counterparts, did not discourage its lawyers from engaging in public service. Thus, when a senior member of the firm, Emory R. Buckner, was appointed United States attorney for the Southern District of New York in 1925, Harlan became his assistant. During this period Harlan participated in several noted matters, including the prosecution of Harry M. Daugherty, former United States attorney general, for official misconduct and that of Thomas W. Miller, former alien property custodian, for fraudulent conspiracy.

Harlan was made a partner in the Root, Clark firm in 1931, and, after the death of Buckner in 1941, he became its leading trial lawyer. Harlan's practice had unusual range and complexity. For example, he represented the New York City Board of Higher Education in litigation involving the appointment of Bertrand Russell to teach in City College; he handled the will of Miss Ella Wendel involving an extensive fortune and a host of claimants—at least one of whom was subsequently convicted of fraud; and he represented heavyweight champion Gene Tunney against a claim that Tunney had hired the plaintiff to bring about a Tunney-Dempsey boxing match in 1926.

During World War II Harlan rendered conspicuous service to the country. He became head of the operational analysis section of the Eighth Air Force, which was composed of hand-picked civilians in the fields of mathematics, physics, electronics, architecture, and law, to furnish advice on bombing operations. Harlan was awarded the United States Legion of Merit and the Croix de Guerre of Belgium and France.

On his return to the practice of law in 1945, Harlan was soon recognized as a leader of the New York bar. He participated in a large number of important matters, arguing several appeals before the United States Supreme Court, including one that became a landmark in the fields of corporate law and civil procedure.[4]

Although private practice was his professional love, Harlan soon was again called to public service. From 1951 to 1953, he acted as chief counsel for the New York State Crime Commission, which Governor Thomas Dewey had appointed to investigate the relationship between organized crime and state government. Harlan was also active in professional organizations, serving as a vice president of the Association of the Bar of the City of New York.

In January 1954, Harlan was nominated to the post of United States circuit judge for the Court of Appeals for the Second Circuit. He served for less than a year before President Eisenhower appointed him, at age fifty-five, to the Supreme Court. After some delay in the Judiciary Committee, apparently occasioned by Southern dissatisfaction with the Court because of the recent decision of *Brown v. Board of*

Education,[5] Harlan was confirmed on March 17, 1955, and took his seat on March 28, 1955.

II

Harlan's two principal judicial values were federalism and proceduralism, both directed to keeping the "'delicate balance of federal-state relations' in good working order."[6] On many occasions Harlan in dissent criticized the Court's entry into political matters,[7] or into state procedures,[8] as inconsistent with the demands of the federal structure. His view of federalism is perhaps best summarized by Justice Stephen Field, whom Harlan quoted approvingly: "[T]he Constitution of the United States . . . recognizes and preserves the autonomy and independence of the States. . . . Supervision over either the legislative or the judicial action of the States is in no case permissible except as to matters by the Constitution specifically authorized or delegated to the United States."[9]

Harlan, for example, applied federalism principles to restrict the so-called state action doctrine that permits expansion of federal court authority. He thought that such expansion over activities that are properly the responsibility of state government simultaneously impairs "independence in their legislative and independence in their judicial departments."[10] Thus, despite a strong commitment to racial equality, Harlan did not believe that land bequeathed in trust to a Georgia city as a "park and pleasure ground" for white people was unconstitutionally administered merely because a state court replaced public trustees with private ones and the park was municipally maintained.[11] And in a nonracial context, Harlan dissented from a holding that a privately owned shopping mall was the equivalent of a company town and thus barred from prohibiting peaceful picketing of a supermarket in the mall.[12]

It is of special importance that Harlan saw federalism not only as part of our constitutional design,[13] "born of the necessity of achieving union,"[14] but as "a bulwark of freedom as well."[15] In one of his speeches he declared:

> We are accustomed to speak of the Bill of Rights and the Fourteenth Amendment as the principal guarantees of personal liberty. Yet it would surely be shallow not to recognize that the structure of our political system accounts no less for the free society we have. Indeed, it was upon the structure of government that the founders primarily focused in writing the Constitution. Out of bitter experience they were suspicious of every form of all-powerful central authority and they sought to assure that such a government would never exist in this country by structuring the federal establishment so as to diffuse power between the executive, legislative, and judicial branches.[16]

Harlan also viewed federalism as essential for preserving pluralism and local experimentation. No other political system, he said, "could have afforded so much scope to the varied interests and aspirations of a dynamic people representing such divergences of ethnic and cultural backgrounds, and at the same time unif[y] them into a nation."[17] Addressing government power to regulate obscenity, Harlan said: "One of the great strengths of our federal system is that we have, in the forty-eight States, forty-eight experimental social laboratories."[18]

Harlan's dedication to proceduralism was equally firm. "Proceduralism" refers not only to rules that govern trials and appeals, but also to issues that determine when the judicial power will be exercised. In his dissent, in *Reynolds v. Sims*,[19] from the Court's "one person, one vote" decision, Harlan stated his basic philosophy. He rejected the view "that every major social ill in this country can find its cure in some constitutional 'principle,' and that this Court should 'take the lead' in promoting reform when other branches of government fail to act. The Constitution is not a panacea for every blot on the public welfare, nor should this Court, ordained as a judicial body, be thought of as a general haven for reform movements."[20]

Thus, Harlan urged the Court to steer clear of "political thickets,"[21] lest "the vitality of our political system, on which in the last analysis all else depends, is weakened by reliance on the judiciary for political reform; in time a complacent body politic may result."[22]

Harlan embodied his view of the limited role of courts in a series of doctrines. First, he jealously guarded the Supreme Court's appellate authority, which he believed should be used "for the settlement of [issues] of importance to the public," and "should not be exercised simply 'for the benefit of the particular litigants.'"[23] In addition, he repeatedly called upon the Court to follow a number of practices designed to avoid unnecessary or premature judicial intervention, such as allowing administrative processes to run their course,[24] not passing on the validity of state statutes that have neither been enforced nor interpreted by state courts,[25] avoiding issues not considered below,[26] and refusing to hear appeals of nonfinal orders.[27]

Second, Harlan urged the Court to show deference to other decision-making authorities. For example, perhaps growing out of his experience as a trial lawyer, Harlan believed strongly in deference to the fact-finding of trial courts, saying that "appellate courts have no facilities for the examination of witnesses; nor in the nature of things can they have that intimate knowledge of the evidence and 'feel' of the trial scene."[28]

Finally, Harlan was committed to the stable and predictable development of the law. He protested when the Court resolved important issues hastily. For example, in the *Pentagon Papers* case,[29] Harlan in dissent recounted the "frenzied train of events" whereby, within one week from the date of lower court decisions, the Court heard argument and issued a decision.[30] He identified several difficult issues[31] and noted that the "time which has been available to us, to the lower courts, and to the parties has been wholly inadequate for giving these cases the kind of consideration they deserve."[32]

III

In light of Harlan's commitment to federalism and proceduralism, we may now look more closely at his dissents from the principal civil liberty themes of the Warren Court. Perhaps the most central of these is "equality," an idea that as Archibald Cox put it, "once loosed . . . is not easily cabined."[33] Harlan vigorously opposed egalitarian rulings of many kinds. He was most vehement in condemning the reapportionment decisions, first in *Baker v. Carr*,[34] in which the Court authorized federal jurisdiction to decide the issue whether state legislative districts were malapportioned, then in *Reynolds v. Sims*,[35] in which the Court established the one person–one vote rule, and in the many sequels to these rulings. Harlan never became reconciled to what he regarded as a wholly unjustified encroachment into the political realm, saying in *Reynolds* that "it is difficult to imagine a more intolerable and inappropriate interference by the judiciary with the independent legislatures of the States."[36]

Closely related to the reapportionment cases are those dealing with the right to vote. Harlan dissented from the ruling that invalidated Virginia's poll tax,[37] from a decision that opened school board elections to a man who was neither a parent nor a property-holder in the district,[38] and from the decision upholding Congress's power to extend the franchise in federal elections to eighteen-year-olds.[39]

The poll tax case illustrates an aspect of the Warren Court's egalitarianism to which Harlan especially objected: its idea that government has an obligation to eliminate economic inequalities as a way to permit everyone to exercise human rights. The leading case was *Griffin v. Illinois*,[40] in which a sharply divided bench held that where a stenographic trial transcript is needed for appellate review, a state violates the Fourteenth Amendment by refusing to provide the transcript to an impoverished defendant who alleges reversible errors in his trial. Harlan's dissent maintained that "all that Illinois has done is to fail to alleviate the consequences of differences in economic circumstances that exist wholly apart from any state action."[41] He later dissented in *Douglas v. California*,[42] where the Court held, on a similar theory, that a state had to provide counsel to a convicted indigent seeking to appeal.

Another example of this genre is Harlan's protests at efforts to transform welfare payments into an entitlement. In one such case, Harlan maintained in dissent that states could deny such payments to otherwise eligible welfare applicants who had not resided in the state for a year or more.[43]

Harlan also found himself out of step with the prevailing view on criminal procedure in state trials. The Warren Court rewrote the book in this area,[44] transforming the law relating to confessions and lineups, the privilege against self-incrimination, jury trials, wiretapping and eavesdropping, and the admissibility of illegally obtained evidence. Harlan vigorously dissented from almost all of the key decisions, asserting that a healthy federalism was inconsistent with the assertion of national judicial power over state criminal justice.[45]

Harlan also objected in the interests of federalism to extensions of congressional power. In the two most significant cases, he protested when the Court adopted broad theories in sustaining the authority of Congress to invalidate state English language literacy tests for voting as applied to individuals who completed the sixth grade in Puerto Rican schools[46] and to punish private (as distinguished from state) interference with constitutional rights.[47]

Furthermore, Harlan, contrary to the Warren Court majority, deferred to congressional judgments that resulted in severe and arguably unjustified harm to individuals. For example, he conceded broad authority to Congress over citizenship, rejecting a constitutional right to prevent involuntary denationalization;[48] he protested a benign interpretation of the immigration law that provided for deportation of an alien who had ever been a member of the Communist Party, however nominally;[49] and he rejected a constitutional right to travel abroad.[50]

In addition to these dissents from many of the Warren Court's key decisions, there were many important cases in which Harlan was part of a majority that rejected constitutional theories supported by the liberal Justices. For example, he wrote the prevailing opinions that rejected First Amendment claims by individuals held in contempt by the House Un-American Activities Committee, by individuals denied admission to the practice of law for refusing to respond to questions concerning Communist activities,[51] and by a man sentenced to prison because of membership in the Communist Party.[52] He also agreed with rulings that permitted states to question suspects of crime without regard to the privilege against self-incrimination[53] and that denied women the right to serve on juries equally with men.[54]

The Warren Court ended in mid–1969, but Harlan remained for two more terms, a brief period in which he was the leader of the Court. Possessing seniority and an unmatched professional reputation, he took advantage of the replacement of Earl Warren and Abe Fortas by Warren Burger and Harry Blackmun to regain the position that Felix Frankfurter and he shared until Frankfurter retired in August 1962. Thus, against Harlan's average of 62.6 dissenting votes per term in the period between 1963 and 1967, he cast only 24 such votes in the 1969 term and 18 in the 1970 term.[55]

This new situation meant that Harlan could reassert conservative themes in his own opinions or join such expressions in the opinions of others. For example, during this period he adhered to his long-standing opposition to expansion of the constitutional rights of poor people to public assistance in the leading case rejecting welfare as an entitlement.[56]

Similarly, he prevailed in a series of criminal justice decisions, including those that denied a right to jury trial in juvenile delinquency proceedings, permitted the closing of such hearings to the public, and authorized the death penalty without sentencing guidelines.[57] And Harlan joined Justice Blackmun's opinion sustaining the power of caseworkers to make unannounced visits to their homes that reduced the privacy of welfare recipients in order to check whether they were cohabiting and thus ineligible for assistance.[58]

In the First Amendment area, Harlan also maintained long-standing positions, but here he was more often in dissent. The most notable occasion was *New York Times Co. v. United States*,[59] where he would have permitted the prior restraint of newspaper publication of the Pentagon Papers, an extensive and politically embarrassing history of the Vietnam War.[60] He also dissented in an important libel case[61] and in two decisions restricting the authority of bar examiners to probe into the political associations of applicants.[62] But he prevailed in another bar admission case, recalling issues from earlier days, that upheld questions about Communist associations,[63] and he was part of the majority that sustained an important obscenity prosecution.[64]

IV

But these conservative opinions and votes are far from the whole story. Justice Potter Stewart, one of Harlan's closest colleagues, recognized this when he said at a memorial service for Harlan: "I can assure you that a very interesting law review article could someday be written on 'The Liberal Opinions of Mr. Justice Harlan.'"[65] In virtually every area of the Court's work, there are cases in which Harlan was part of the Warren Court consensus and, indeed, in which he spoke for the Court.

Harlan joined *Brown v. Board of Education II*,[66] and he signed the joint opinion in *Cooper v. Aaron*,[67] a decision instrumental in protecting the principle of school desegregation. He also joined every opinion decided while he was on the Court that rejected other sorts of state-enforced segregation.[68]

He concurred in *Gideon v. Wainwright*,[69] the path-breaking case granting a right to counsel to accused felons, and he wrote the opinion of the Court in *Boddie v. Connecticut*,[70] which held that a state could not deny a divorce to a couple because they lacked the means to pay the judicial filing fee. Although both these cases were decided under the Due Process Clause, they amounted at bottom to judicially mandated equalization of economic circumstance in situations where Harlan concluded that it would be fundamentally unfair to deny poor people legal recourse that others could afford.

In the criminal procedure area, while he opposed the rule that excluded illegally seized evidence in state prosecutions, he nevertheless consistently supported a strong version of the Fourth Amendment protection against unreasonable searches and seizures by federal authorities,[71] including application of the principle to wiretapping and eavesdropping.[72] He also supported the seminal ruling that extended criminal due process protections to juveniles accused of delinquency.[73]

One also finds many important cases in which Harlan supported the right of free expression. For example, he wrote the opinion in *NAACP v. Alabama*,[74] which held that freedom of association protected the right of individuals to join unpopular civil rights groups anonymously. He joined *New York Times Co. v. Sullivan*,[75] which first imposed limits on libel judgments against the media, and some (though not all) of the sequels to that case.[76] He joined opinions that barred states from refusing to seat an elected legislator because of his sharply critical views on the Vietnam War,[77] and from convicting a leader of the Ku Klux Klan for "seditious" speech.[78] And he wrote for the Court to protect the right of a black man, unnerved by the shooting of a civil rights leader, to sharply criticize the country while burning the flag.[79]

In addition, Harlan wrote a number of opinions, all curbing variants of McCarthyism, that were nominally decided on nonconstitutional grounds but rested on First Amendment principles. In the first of these, which invalidated the discharge of a federal food and drug inspector, Harlan interpreted a statute authorizing dismissals of government employees "in the interests of national security" to apply only to jobs directly concerned with internal subversion and foreign aggression.[80] The next year, in what Anthony Lewis has described as a "masterfully subtle opinion,"[81] Harlan construed the Smith Act[82] to permit prosecution of Communist Party leaders only for speech amounting to incitement to action rather than for "abstract doctrine" advocating overthrow.[83] A third instance involved companion cases in which the government had revoked the naturalization of two persons alleged to have obtained their citizenship improperly.[84] The government contended that they were Communists and therefore not "attached to the principles of the Constitution of the United States" as required by the applicable statute.[85] Harlan's opinion found that "clear, unequivocal and convincing evidence"[86] was lacking that the individuals were aware, during the relevant period prior to their becoming citizens, that the Communist Party was engaged in illegal advocacy. During the 1950s these decisions were milestones in lifting the yoke of political repression.

Freedom of religion also showed Harlan as frequently, but not invariably, protective of constitutional guarantees. He joined decisions that prohibited organized prayer in the public schools[87] and invalidated a requirement that state officials declare a belief in a deity.[88] And while approving state loans of textbooks to church schools,[89] he rejected the use of tax-raised funds to reimburse parochial schools for teachers' salaries, textbooks, and instructional materials.[90] Similarly, while unwilling to grant constitutional protection to adherents of Sabbatarian faiths who objected to Sunday closing laws and to unemployment compensation laws that required a willingness of the applicant to work on Saturdays,[91] Harlan wrote a powerful opinion during the Vietnam War declaring that a statute that limited conscientious objection to those who believed in a theistic religion "offended the Establishment Clause" because it "accords a preference to the 'religious' [and] disadvantages adherents of religions that do not worship a Supreme Being."[92]

In all these cases, Harlan emphasized that "[t]he attitude of government towards religion must . . . be one of neutrality."[93] Harlan was sophisticated enough to appreciate that neutrality is "a coat of many colors."[94] Nevertheless, as Kent Greenawalt has observed, "no modern Justice ha[s] striven harder or more successfully than Justice Harlan to perform his responsibilities in [a neutral] manner."[95]

A final area of civil liberties, sexual privacy, is of particular importance because Harlan produced the most influential opinions on this subject written by anyone during his tenure on the Court. In the first case, *Poe v. Ullman*,[96] a thin majority, led by Justice Frankfurter, refused to adjudicate, on the ground that there was no threat of prosecution, the merits of a Connecticut law that criminalized the sale of contraceptives to married and unmarried people alike. Harlan's emotional opinion[97]—a rarity for him—not only differed with this conclusion but extensively defended the proposition that Connecticut's law violated the Due Process Clause of the Fourteenth Amendment. Harlan's position soon prevailed in *Griswold v. Connecticut*,[98] the case that first recognized a right to sexual privacy. It is impossible to know whether Harlan would have extended this reasoning to support the result in *Eisenstadt v. Baird*,[99] which held that a state could not punish the distribution of contraceptives to unmarried persons, or in *Roe v. Wade*,[100] which recognized abortion as a personal right, cases decided soon after he retired. But I am confident that, at a minimum, he would have protected the right of a married woman to proceed with an abortion that was dictated by family considerations.

Harlan's participation in the major thrusts of the Warren Court was not confined to civil liberties and civil rights. In economic cases, too, he sometimes went along with the majority's support of government regulation of business, despite the fact that his private practice had often involved the defense in antitrust cases and other actions involving the government.

While Harlan fortified his formidable conservative record after Warren Burger replaced Earl Warren, he nevertheless provided further evidence of a willingness at times to support liberal activist rulings. Thus, in the equality area, he maintained his support for desegregation rulings,[101] and he joined the new Chief Justice's important opinion that expanded remedies against discriminatory employment tests.[102] And, as noted earlier, his opinion in *Boddie*[103] invalidated a state statute that denied poor couples the right to a divorce because they could not afford court filing fees. Harlan's reliance on the Due Process Clause to reach this result was criticized,[104] and the doctrine has not survived, but the case stands as a rare example of Harlan's reaching out to right an economic imbalance that prejudiced poor people in American society.[105] In another such case involving criminal justice, Harlan joined the Court's opinion prohibiting the incarceration of indigents who were unable to pay criminal fines.[106] Also in the area of criminal justice, he continued his deep concern for Fourth Amendment rights,[107] and he wrote an extensive concurring opinion in support of the strict "beyond reasonable doubt" standard in juvenile delinquency hearings.[108] In the First Amendment field, he wrote a widely cited opinion that protected the display in a state courthouse of a "scurrilous epithet" ("Fuck the draft") in protest against conscription.[109]

V

What should one conclude from the many decisions in which Justice Harlan, a conservative, supported constitutional rights, often in highly controversial cases in which the Court was split? That he was in step with the Warren Court majority? Plainly not—there are too many instances, recounted above, where he marched separately. That he was essentially a civil libertarian? No again—not only are there too many cases to the contrary, but at a basic level that is not the way Harlan reacted to injustice. This is not to say that he was insensitive to human suffering or unmoved by evidence of arbitrariness. It is rather that something else was at the core.

In my opinion, that something was Harlan's deep, almost visceral, desire to keep things in balance, to resist excess in any direction. Many times during my year as his law clerk he said how important it was "to keep things on an even keel." To me, that is the master key to Harlan and his jurisprudence. One recalls Castle, the hero of Graham Greene's novel *The Human Factor*, as he muses on those who are "unable to love success or power or great beauty."[110] Castle concludes that it is not because the people feel unworthy or were "more at home with failure."[111] It is rather that "one wanted the right balance."[112] In reflecting on some of his own perplexing and self-destructive actions, Castle decides that "he was there to right the balance. That was all."[113] Harlan was not a man who avoided success or power or, if one knew Mrs. Harlan, great beauty, but nevertheless in his own eyes "he was there to right the balance." It is significant that he entitled a major speech at the American Bar Association "Thoughts at a Dedication: Keeping the Judicial Function in Balance."[114]

There is evidence of balance not only in the decisions discussed above but in his elaborate views on doctrines of justiciability. These are closely related to his frequent preoccupation with judicial modesty or, put negatively, his opposition to excessive judicial activism, which in turn is related to the central theme of his judicial universe—federalism. Many years ago I suggested, and I still believe, that "his pervasive concern has been over a judiciary that will arrogate power not rightfully belonging to it and impose its views of government from a remote tower, thereby enervating the initiative and independence at the grass roots that are essential to a thriving democracy."[115]

Harlan's thinking on jurisdictional issues was also related to his long period as a practicing lawyer, where he ordinarily represented defendants in litigation. In that role he had to be "constantly aware that it is easier and quicker to achieve victory on grounds such as want of federal jurisdiction, lack of standing or ripeness, of failure to join an indispensable party, than to prevail on the merits of a lawsuit."[116]

This early sensitivity to issues of justiciability carried over to his judicial years, where Harlan often urged jurisdictional rules to avoid deciding controversial cases. Among the most notable are his dissenting opinions in *Baker v. Carr*[117] and *Reynolds v. Sims*,[118] where he concluded that the issue of legislative reapportionment was a political question; in *Dombrowski v. Pfister*,[119] where he objected, on a series of procedural grounds, to the adjudication of the constitutionality of Louisiana's Subversive Activities and Communist Control Act in a federal suit to enjoin a state criminal prosecution under the statute; in *Fay v. Noia*[120] and *Henry v. Mississippi*,[121] where he criticized expansion of federal judicial authority to review state criminal convictions that previously were unreviewable because the convicted person had not complied with state procedural requirements; and in *Flast v. Cohen*,[122] where he dissented from the Court's holding that taxpayers had standing to challenge federal financial aid to religious schools (despite his sympathy with the merits of the plaintiffs' claim).

On the other hand, reflecting his balanced approach, Harlan wrote or joined many opinions that expanded the Court's jurisdiction. Perhaps the most celebrated was *Poe v. Ullman*,[123] where he dissented from the reasoning of Justice Frankfurter in dismissing an early challenge to Connecticut's birth control law on the ground that the statute was not being enforced. Again, in *NAACP v. Alabama*,[124] the first case explicitly recognizing a freedom of association, his opinion for the Court proceeded to its First Amendment conclusion only after overcoming difficult procedural obstacles involving the doctrines of standing and independent state grounds. And in the first school prayer case,[125] and again in the ruling that ordered the House of Representatives to seat Adam Clayton Powell,[126] both decisions of unusual sensitivity, Harlan joined majority opinions that rejected substantial justiciability defenses.[127]

Harlan's often unrecognized willingness to expand judicial authority can be seen in several cases involving the broadening of remedies in individual rights and economic cases alike. In one case, he wrote separately to approve the expansion of federal remedies against municipal officials who violated an individual's civil rights.[128] In a second ruling, involving a provision of the Securities and Exchange Act that prohibited false and misleading proxy statements in respect to mergers, Harlan agreed that a stockholder could sue for rescission and damages even though the statute was silent about private enforcement lawsuits.[129]

Harlan's approach to stare decisis, another area relating to the judge's role, also manifested an activist spirit at times. He recognized that stare decisis "provides the stability and predictability required for the ordering of human affairs over the course of time and a basis of 'public faith in the judiciary as a source of impersonal and reasoned judgments.'"[130] And while the principle should not be "[w]oodenly applied" and "[n]o precedent is sacrosanct, precedent should not be jettisoned when the rule of yesterday remains viable, creates no injustice, and can reasonably be said to be no less sound than the rule sponsored by those who seek change, let alone incapable of being demonstrated wrong."[131] There are therefore many instances where Harlan vigorously protested the jettisoning of precedent.[132]

But there are also many contrary instances which betoken Harlan's flexibility. Thus, Harlan wrote separately in the famous *Gideon* case to give *Betts v. Brady*[133] "a more respectful burial than has been accorded" by the Court.[134] He spoke for the Court in overruling a decision that denied the privilege against self-incrimination to gamblers prosecuted for failing to register and pay taxes.[135] And in *Moragne v. States Marine Line, Inc.*,[136] a celebrated opinion, he overruled a case that "rested on a most dubious foundation when announced, has become an increasingly unjustifiable anomaly as the law over the years has left it behind, and . . . has produced litigation-spawning confusion in an area that should be easily susceptible of more workable solutions."[137]

Finally, one may point to a series of cases in which Harlan exhibited a trait familiar to all of his law clerks—his exceptional open-mindedness and willingness to listen to new arguments. In these cases he dissented from the Court's refusal to hear oral argument on constitutional claims, although in each of them he was unsympathetic to the merits of the appeal. Thus, he joined Justice Douglas's dissent from the refusal to hear a plea that a group was improperly ordered to register as a Communist front organization.[138] And in perhaps the most far-reaching action, he would have set down for oral argument a complaint that challenged the legality of the Vietnam War,[139] although he almost surely would have sustained the decision of the elected branches of government on a great matter of war and peace.[140]

The pattern of decisions provides ample proof that Harlan was not a one-dimensional Justice. What is less obvious is the source of his drive to keep things in balance, to eschew an extreme ideology.

Two possibilities may be suggested. The first is the familiar notion that, in any society, patricians (like Harlan) are concerned less with results in particular controversies, and certainly less about pressing any group against the wall, than with assuring the smooth functioning of institutions without the precipitation of volatility or deep-seated enmities. This means that dissent should be allowed an outlet, that minorities should be able to hope, that political power should not become centralized and therefore dangerous. Thus Harlan's decisions supporting desegregation, a strong federal presence, and law and order. Thus also his fears about court-dominated legislative reapportionment and about the "incorporation" of the Bill of Rights through the Fourteenth Amendment that enhanced judicial authority and represented too dramatic a break with established doctrine. But thus also Harlan's willingness to take reformist steps, to overrule outdated precedent selectively and before a problem worsened, and above all to listen closely to many voices.

These traits are consistent with Harlan's warm embrace of federalism principles. It should be recalled that the idea of federalism itself is a kind of balance—a way of dividing governmental authority to prevent a too-easy dominance of public life by a single institution or faction. The *Federalist Papers* are explicit in extolling, as a "guard against dangerous encroachments," the division of power "between two distinct governments" so that the "different governments will control each other."[141] Years ago I reflected on whether the national government or state and local government is the securer bulwark of—or the greater threat to—civil liberty: "Local units are closer to the people but offer more opportunity for undetected discrimination and repression. The national government acts more visibly and with more formal regard for minority interests, but its vast power is a civil liberties time bomb that in this century has brought us the Palmer Raids, McCarthyism, and Watergate."[142] Whatever the proper resolution of this question, it is clear that Justice Harlan believed, as much as he believed anything, that federalism was "a bulwark of freedom."[143]

The second source of Harlan's overall philosophy is legal process theory, which had its heyday during almost exactly the period that he served on the Supreme Court. In the early 1950s, Henry Hart produced an early draft of the work that he and Albert Sacks published in a "tentative edition" in 1958.[144] The moderate philosophy embodied in these materials was tailor-made to Harlan's personality. It emphasized the central role that procedure plays in assuring judicial and legislative objectivity and argued that "just" policies will result when each branch of government works within its assigned role.[145] In this way courts through "reasoned elaboration" of decisions, and legislatures through the public-seeking interpretation of statutes, will assure maximum fulfillment of society's expectations.[146]

Not surprisingly, Harlan was attracted to this theory, which enabled him to take constitutional steps[147] as long as they were not too long or jarring, while simultaneously offering him ample institutional reasons for resisting excessive judicial authority. This approach often resulted in conclusions, relying in part on Hart and Sacks, that were inhospitable to civil liberties, such as his concurring opinion in cases that limited the rights of nonmarital children[148] and his dissent to the one person–one vote rule of *Reynolds v. Sims*.[149] But Harlan's reliance on legal process also led him at times to the overruling of outmoded precedent[150] and to carefully calibrated exercises of judicial power that advanced civil liberties.

By 1971, when Harlan left the Supreme Court, legal process theory, buffeted by events in society at large, was beginning to lose its hold, even at Harvard,[151] and the more extreme philosophies of law and economics and critical legal studies soon moved to the forefront.[152] The struggle within the Court became ever more polarized as in succeeding years strong civil libertarians, which Harlan was not, waged battle with doctrinaire conservatives, which he also was not.

VI

Looking back over the twenty-four years since Justice Harlan's tenure on the Supreme Court ended, it is striking how his reputation has flourished. Indeed, he has become something of a judicial icon, leading two respected commentators to refer recently to "[t]he near-compulsory admiration of Justice Harlan"[153] by recent and highly diverse nominees to the Court, including Anthony Kennedy, David Souter, Clarence Thomas, and Ruth Bader Ginsburg.

A combination of factors may explain this phenomenon. Not least are Harlan's personal traits—he was calm, fair, and open-minded, and with gentle good humor he resolutely refused to personalize disagreement. Not surprisingly, this led longtime judicial adversaries such as Justice William J. Brennan, Jr., to speak of him with warmth and admiration.

Another element in Harlan's mystique is his acknowledged mastery as a legal craftsman. In an article written while Harlan was still on the bench I said that he "has produced opinions that, in my judgment, have not been exceeded for consistent professional competence by any Supreme Court Justice since Brandeis."[154] It now can be asserted that his opinions have not been exceeded in craft in the years since he retired.

Another reason that Harlan's reputation has risen steadily is that his judicial philosophy is in close tune with the *Zeitgeist*, the temper of the age, as it has evolved since his retirement. Despite the evidence adduced above that shows that Harlan was a multidimensional figure, it is true that for several years he was the most conservative figure on the Warren Court. Succeeding years have seen the steady erosion of the influence of liberal Justices, the arrival of Justices who, by any measure, are more conservative than Harlan, and the apparent ascendancy of a moderate bloc with which Harlan would have found much common ground.

An understanding of Harlan's stature is enhanced if one compares him with two other leading conservatives—Felix Frankfurter, who dominated the nonliberal wing of the Supreme Court during the 1940s and 1950s, and William H. Rehnquist, the most influential conservative voice since 1972.

When Harlan became a Justice in 1955 he looked to Frankfurter as his mentor. He was impressed with Frankfurter's vast knowledge of constitutional law gleaned from his decades as a professor and sixteen years of experience on the Court. They also shared much else, including suspicion of the power of unelected courts, lifelong Anglophilia, and mutual friends such as Emory Buckner, Learned Hand, and Henry Friendly. But Frankfurter's star has dimmed considerably, in part because he "react[ed] to adversaries . . . with heated anger and frustration, with attacks on their integrity and motives."[155] This led to strains with many of his fellow Justices and reduced his influence on the Court. More important, the years have seen the overruling of a remarkable number of Frankfurter's opinions in almost every area of the Court's work. There were flaws in Frankfurter's makeup and judgment that eventually undermined his remarkable gifts and learning. Harlan's opinions, on the other hand, with some notable exceptions have lived on.

Justice Rehnquist, now Chief Justice, shares some of Harlan's collegial qualities. An affable man, he has found it easy, as did Harlan, to become friends with Justices holding very different opinions, and liberal Justices concede that he has presided over conferences of the Court fairly though firmly. He and Harlan shared many ideas, including a reluctance to enforce the Equal Protection Clause in cases not involving racial discrimination, opposition to the Fourth Amendment exclusionary rule, and lack of sympathy for the Court's one person-one vote regime for federal and state elections. But in many other areas Harlan was a far more moderate figure than Rehnquist is, evidenced by Harlan's strong support of remedies to enforce *Brown v. Board of Education*, of Establishment Clause values, and of privacy principles in cases involving government intrusion, private property, and sexual privacy. Above all, Harlan saw himself primarily as a judge deciding cases rather than as an ideological dispenser of general doctrine, as Rehnquist sometimes appears to be.

In summary, it fell to John Marshall Harlan, by nature a patrician traditionalist, to serve on a Supreme Court that, for most of his years, was rapidly revising and liberalizing constitutional law. In these circumstances, it is not surprising that Harlan would protest the direction of the Court and the speed with which it was traveling. He did this in a remarkably forceful and principled manner, thereby providing balance to the institution and the law it generated. Despite this role, Harlan joined civil liberties rulings on the Court during his tenure to the degree that his overall jurisprudence can fairly be characterized as moderate, or conservative primarily in the sense that it evinced caution, a fear of centralized authority, and a respect for process.

Notes

I thank the members of the Legal History Colloquium at New York University Law School, chaired by my colleague William Nelson, for helpful suggestions on how to elaborate my earlier work on Justice Harlan for this essay. Thanks also to Natalia Sorgente for valuable research assistance.

1. Warren, "Mr. Justice Harlan, As Seen by a Colleague," 85 *Harv. L. Rev.* 369, 370–71 (1971).
2. Friendly, "Mr. Justice Harlan, As Seen by a Friend and Judge of an Inferior Court," 85 *Harv. L. Rev.* 382, 384 (1971).
3. See, e.g., Freund, Foreword to *The Evolution of a Judicial Philosophy: Selected Opinions and Papers of Justice John M. Harlan*, xiii (Shapiro ed., 1969); Lewin, "Justice Harlan, 'The Full Measure of the Man,'" 58 *A.B.A. J.* 579 (1972); Powell, Address at the 63rd Annual Meeting of the American Law Institute (May 15, 1986), reprinted in American Law Institute, *Proceedings: 63rd Annual Meeting* 312 (1987); Wright, "Hugo L. Black: A Great Man and a Great American," 50 *Tex. L. Rev.* 1, 3–4 (1971). The first full biography of Justice Harlan is Yarbrough, *John Marshall Harlan: Great Dissenter of the Warren Court* (1992).
4. Cohen v. Beneficial Life Ins. Co., 337 U.S. 541 (1949).
5. 345 U.S. 491 (1954).
6. Harlan, "Thoughts at a Dedication: Keeping the Judicial Function in Balance," 49 *A.B.A. J.* 943, 944 (1963); see also Griswold v. Connecticut, 382 U.S. 479, 501 (1965) (Harlan, J., concurring) ("Judicial self-restraint . . . will be achieved . . . only by . . . wise appreciation of the great roles that the doctrines of federalism and separation of powers have played in establishing and preserving American freedoms.").
7. Reynolds v. Sims, 377 U.S. 533, 624 (1964).
8. Henry v. Mississippi, 379 U.S. 443, 464–65 (1965).
9. Baltimore & Ohio R.R. v. Baugh, 149 U.S. 368, 401 (1893) (Field, J., dissenting), quoted in Fay v. Noia, 372 U.S. 391, 466 (1963) (Harlan, J., dissenting).
10. *Fay*, 372 U.S. at 466 (Harlan, J., dissenting) (quoting Baltimore and Ohio R.R., 149 U.S. 368, 401 (1893) (Field, J., dissenting)).
11. See Evans v. Newton, 382 U.S. 296, 315 (1966) (Harlan, J., dissenting).
12. Amalgamated Food Employees Union 590 v. Logan Valley Plaza, Inc., 391 U.S. 308, 333 (1968).
13. See Pointer v. Texas, 380 U.S. 400, 409 (1965) (Harlan, J., concurring) ("[T]he American federal system itself is constitutionally ordained. . . .").
14. Harlan, supra note 6, at 943.
15. Id.

16. Id. at 943–44.

17. Id. at 944.

18. Roth v. United States, 354 U.S. 476, 505 (1957) (Harlan, J., concurring in part and dissenting in part).

19. 377 U.S. 533 (1964).

20. Id. at 624–25 (Harlan, J., dissenting).

21. Whitcomb v. Chavis, 403 U.S. 124, 170 (1971) (separate opinion of Harlan, J.); Hadley v. Junior College Dist., 397 U.S. 50, 63 (1970) (Harlan, J., dissenting).

22. Reynolds v. Sims, 377 U.S. 533, 624 (1964) (Harlan, J., dissenting).

23. Sullivan v. Little Hunting Park, Inc., 396 U.S. 229, 250 (1969) (Harlan, J., dissenting) (quoting Rice v. Sioux City Memorial Cemetery, Inc., 349 U.S. 70, 74 (1955)).

24. See, e.g., Frozen Food Express v. United States, 351 U.S. 40, 45, 47 (1956) (Harlan, J., dissenting) (stating that the administrative order interpreted by the majority should not have been subjected to judicial scrutiny until all administrative procedures had been exhausted). But cf. Abbott Laboratories v. Gardner, 387 U.S. 136, 153 (1967) (holding that access to the courts under a regulation must be permitted "[w]here the legal issue presented is fit for judicial resolution, and where a regulation requires an immediate and significant change in the plaintiffs' conduct for their affairs with serious penalties attached to noncompliance").

25. See, e.g., Berger v. New York, 388 U.S. 41, 92 (1967) (Harlan, J., dissenting) ("[T]he Court ordinarily awaits a state court's construction before adjudicating the validity of a state statute."); Dombrowski v. Pfister, 380 U.S. 479, 501 (1965) (Harlan, J., dissenting) ("The statute thus *pro tanto* goes to its doom without either state or federal court interpretation, and despite the room which the statute clearly leaves for a narrowing constitutional construction.").

26. See, e.g., Mapp v. Ohio, 367 U.S. 643, 676–77 (1961) (Harlan, J., dissenting) (deciding issues not fully considered below "is not likely to promote respect either for the Court's adjudicatory process or for the stability of its decisions"); NLRB v. Lion Oil Co., 352 U.S. 282, 304–05 (1957) (Harlan, J., concurring in part and dissenting in part) (deciding issues not considered below "depriv[es] this Court . . . of the considered views of the lower courts" and "represents unsound judicial administration"). But cf. Poe v. Ullman, 367 U.S. 497, 522 (1961) (Harlan, J., dissenting) ("While ordinarily I would not deem it appropriate to deal . . . with constitutional issues which the Court [and the court below] ha[ve] not reached, I shall do so here because such issues . . . are entangled with the Court's conclusion.").

27. See, e.g., Organization for a Better Austin v. Keefe, 402 U.S. 415, 420 (1971) (Harlan, J., dissenting) ("In deciding this case on the merits, the Court, in my opinion, disregards the express limitation on our appellate jurisdiction to '[f]inal judgments or decrees.' . . .") (alteration in original) (quoting 28 U.S.C. § 1257 (1988)); Mercantile Nat'l Bank at Dallas v. Langdeau, 371 U.S. 555, 572 (1963) (Harlan, J., dissenting) (asserting that the state court determination related only to venue and thus was "not in itself reviewable as a final judgment"); Parr v. United States, 351 U.D. 513, 518 (1956) ("[R]eview must await the conclusion of the 'whole matter litigated.' . . .").

28. Mesarosh v. United States, 373 U.S. 1, 32 (1963) (Harlan, J., dissenting); see also California v. Lo-Vaca Gathering Co., 379 U.S. 366, 377 (1965) (Harlan, J., dissenting) (concluding that when complex technical matters are involved, "the informed expertise of [an administrative agency] is a necessary adjunct to satisfactory judicial resolution of particular cases"); Hardy v. United States, 375 U.S. 277, 300 (1964) (Harlan, J., dissenting) (stating that decisions that concern the procedures governing *in forma pauperis*

appeals are "best left to the discrete treatment of the Judicial Councils in the various Circuits").

29. New York Times Co. v. United States, 403 U.S. 713 (1971).

30. Id. at 753 (Harlan, J., dissenting).

31. See id. at 753–55.

32. Id. at 755 (footnote omitted); see also United States v. Chicago, 400 U.S. 8, 15 (1970) (Harlan, J., dissenting) ("[W]ithout briefs and oral argument by the parties on the merits of the question, I would refrain from choosing between the conflicting constructions . . . pressed upon the Court by the parties."); Travia v. Lomenzo, 381 U.S. 431, 434–35 (1965) (Harlan, J., dissenting) (opposing the Court's denial of a stay and motion to accelerate an appeal, stating that "these matters bristle with difficult and important questions").

33. Cox, *The Warren Court* 6 (1968).

34. 369 U.S. 186 (1962).

35. 377 U.S. 533 (1964).

36. Id. at 615 (Harlan, J., dissenting).

37. See Harper v. Virginia Bd. of Elections, 383 U.S. 663, 680 (1966) (Harlan, J., dissenting).

38. See Kramer v. Union Free School Dist., 395 U.S. 621, 634 (1969) (Stewart, J., joined by Black and Harlan, JJ., dissenting).

39. See Oregon v. Mitchell, 400 U.S. 112, 152 (1970) (Harlan, J., concurring in part and dissenting in part).

40. 351 U.S. 12 (1956).

41. Id. at 34 (Harlan, J., dissenting).

42. 372 U.S. 353, 360 (1963) (Harlan, J., dissenting).

43. See Shapiro v. Thompson, 394 U.S. 618, 655 (1969)(Harlan, J., dissenting).

44. The Burger and Rehnquist Courts have again rewritten the book on criminal procedure, adopting positions that in general would have been congenial to Justice Harlan. See Coleman v. Thompson, 501 U.S. 722 (1991); Teague v. Lane, 489 U.S. 288 (1989); see also *The Burger Years* 143–88 (H. Schwartz ed., 1987) (discussing the Burger Court's decisions on criminal justice). There is no attempt in this article to trace doctrinal developments in this and other subjects on which Justice Harlan wrote.

45. See Benton v. Maryland, 395 U.S. 784, 801 (1969)(Harlan, J., dissenting); Desist v. United States, 394 U.S. 244, 256 (1969) (Harlan, J., dissenting).

46. Katzenbach v. Morgan, 384 U.S. 641 (1966).

47. United Stated v. Guest, 383 U.S. 745 (1966).

48. See Afroyim v. Rusk, 387 U.S. 253, 268 (1967)(Harlan, J., dissenting); Trop v. Dulles, 356 U.S. 86 (1958) (Frankfurter, J., joined by Burton, Clark, and Harlan, JJ., dissenting); Perez v. Brownell, 356 U.S. 44 (1958).

49. See Rowoldt v. Perfetto, 355 U.S. 115, 121 (1957) (Harlan, J., dissenting).

50. Aptheker v. Secretary of State, 378 U.S. 500 (1964); Kent v. Dulles, 357 U.S. 116 (1958).

51. See Konigsberg v. State Bar, 366 U.S. 36 (1961). See also Barenblatt v. United States, 360 U.S. 109 (1959).

52. See Scales v. United States, 367 U.S. 203 (1961). Another, particularly harsh, decision was Flemming v. Nestor, 363 U.S. 603 (1960), which upheld the denial of social security benefits to an alien who was deported because he had been a member of the Communist Party.

53. See Lerner v. Casey, 357 U.S. 468 (1958), overruled by Malloy v. Hogan, 378 U.S. 1 (1964).

54. See Hoyt v. Florida, 368 U.S. 57 (1961), overruled by Taylor v. Louisiana, 419 U.S. 522 (1975).

55. Friendly, supra note 2, at 388.

56. See Dandridge v. Williams, 397 U.S. 471, 489 (1970) (Harlan, J., concurring).

57. See McKeiver v. Pennsylvania and In re Burrus, 403 U.S. 528, 557 (1971) (Harlan, J., concurring in the judgments); McGautha v. California, 402 U.S. 183 (1971).

58. See Wyman v. James, 400 U.S. 309 (1971).

59. 403 U.S. 713 (1971).

60. Id. at 752.

61. See Rosenbloom v. Metromedia, Inc., 403 U.S. 29, 62 (1971) (Harlan, J., dissenting).

62. See *In re* Stolar, 401 U.S. 23, 34 (1971) (Harlan, J., dissenting); Baird v. State Bar, 401 U.S. 1, 8 (1971) (Harlan, J., dissenting).

63. See Law Students Civil Rights Research Council v. Wadmond, 401 U.S. 154 (1971). Harlan consistently upheld regulation of the bar in the face of claims under the First Amendment. See, e.g., NAACP v. Button, 371 U.S. 415, 448 (1963) (Harlan, J., dissenting); Konigsberg v. State Bar of California, 366 U.S. 36 (1961).

64. See United States v. Reidel, 402 U.S. 351, 357 (1971) (Harlan, J., concurring).

65. See "John Marshall Harlan, 1899–1971," Memorial Addresses Delivered at a Special Meeting of the Association of the Bar of the City of New York by Justice Stewart, former Attorney General Brownell, and Professor Bator (Apr. 5, 1972), cited in Gunther, "In Search of Judicial Quality on a Changing Court: The Case of Justice Powell," 24 *Stan. L. Rev.* 1000, 1004 n.23 (1972).

66. 349 U.S. 294 (1955).

67. 358 U.S. 1 (1958).

68. See, e.g., Heart of Atlanta Motel v. United States, 379 U.S. 241 (1964) (public accommodations); Griffin v. County School Board, 377 U.S. 218 (1964) (public schools); Goss v. Board of Education, 373 U.S. 683 (1963) (public schools); Watson v. City of Memphis, 373 U.S. 526 (1963) (recreational facilities); Peterson v. City of Greenville, 373 U.S. 244 (1963) (public accommodations).

69. 372 U.S. 335, 349 (1963) (Harlan, J., concurring).

70. 401 U.S. 371 (1971).

71. See, e.g., Jones v. United States, 357 U.S. 493 (1958) (no probable cause to search); Giordenello v. United States, 357 U.S. 480 (1958) (defective search warrant).

72. See Katz v. United States, 389 U.S. 347, 360 (1967) (Harlan, J., concurring). But cf. Berger v. New York, 388 U.S. 41, 89 (1967) (Harlan J., dissenting) (opposing application of exclusionary rule where the state is engaged in electronic eavesdropping).

73. See *In re* Gault, 387 U.S. 1, 65 (1967) (Harlan, J., concurring in part and dissenting in part).

74. 357 U.S. 449 (1958); see also Talley v. California, 362 U.S. 60 (1960) (Harlan, J., concurring) (invalidating a Los Angeles ordinance prohibiting the circulation of anonymous handbills as a violation of free speech and association).

75. 376 U.S. 254 (1964).

76. See, e.g., St. Amant v. Thompson, 390 U.S. 727 (1968) (holding that sufficient evidence is required to show that the defendant had serious doubts as to the truth of the alleged defamatory statement to invoke actual malice standard); Garrison v. Louisiana, 379 U.S. 64 (1964) (holding that the *New York Times* case limits state power to impose sanctions for criticism of public officials in criminal cases as well as civil cases). Cf.

Rosenblatt v. Baer, 383 U.S. 75, 96 (1966) (Harlan, J., concurring in part and dissenting in part) (stating that an impersonal attack on government operations will not constitute defamation unless it is specifically directed at the plaintiff).

77. See Bond v. Floyd, 385 U.S. 116 (1966).

78. See Brandenburg v. Ohio, 395 U.S. 444 (1964) (per curiam).

79. See Street v. New York, 394 U.S. 576 (1969).

80. Cole v. Young, 351 U.S. 536 (1956); see also Vitarelli v. Seaton, 359 U.S. 535 (1959) and Service v. Dulles, 354 U.S. 363 (1957) (holding security discharges in both cases invalid because the agency failed to follow prescribed procedures).

81. Lewis, "Earl Warren," in *The Warren Court: A Critical Analysis* 1, 15 (Sayler et al. eds., 1968).

82. 18 U.S.C. § 2385 (1988).

83. See Yates v. United States, 354 U.S. 298, 318–27 (1957).

84. See Maisenberg v. United States, 356 U.S. 670 (1958); Nowak v. United States, 356 U.S. 660 (1958).

85. *Nowak*, 356 U.S. at 662 (quoting the Nationality Act of 1906, ch. 3592, § 4, 34 Stat. 596, 598, repealed by Act of Oct. 14, 1940, ch. 876, § 504, 54 Stat. 1172).

86. Id. at 663 (quoting Schneiderman v. United States, 320 U.S. 118, 158 (1943)).

87. Abington School Dist. v. Schempp, 374 U.S. 203 (1963); Engel v. Vitale, 370 U.S. 421 (1962).

88. See Torcaso v. Watkins, 367 U.S. 488 (1961).

89. See Board of Education v. Allen, 392 U.S. 236 (1968).

90. See Lemon v. Kurtzman, 403 U.S. 602 (1971).

91. See Sherbert v. Verner, 374 U.S. 398, 418 (1963) (Harlan, J., dissenting).

92. Welsh v. United States, 398 U.S. 333, 357 (1970) (Harlan, J., concurring).

93. *Allen*, 392 U.S. at 249.

94. Id.

95. Greenawalt, "The Enduring Significance of Neutral Principles," 78 *Colum. L. Rev*. 982, 984 (1978).

96. 367 U.S. 497 (1961).

97. See id. at 522 (Harlan, J., dissenting).

98. 381 U.S. 479 (1965); see also id. at 499 (Harlan, J., dissenting).

99. 405 U.S. 438 (1972).

100. 410 U.S. 113 (1973).

101. See Adickes v. Kress & Co., 398 U.S. 144 (1970); Northcross v. Board of Education, 397 U.S. 232 (1970).

102. See Griggs v. Duke Power Co., 401 U.S. 424 (1971).

103. Boddie v. Connecticut, see supra note 70 and accompanying text.

104. See, e.g., "The Supreme Court, 1970 Term," 85 *Harv. L. Rev*. 3, 104–13 (1971) (arguing that Harlan was mistaken in his view that the rationale for procedural due process was that commencement of a lawsuit effectively forecloses the opportunity for extrajudicial settlement and that the actual rationale for procedural due process springs from the Court's power to settle conclusively legal relations by final judgment). But see Tribe, *American Constitutional Law* 1462–63, 1639–40 (2d ed. 1988) (citing with approval Harlan's belief that constitutional protection for the poor rests better in the Due Process Clause because it contains a "natural limiting principle" and arguing that the Court has not subsequently drawn valid distinctions between the application of the Due Process Clause to a divorce case as opposed to bankruptcy, contract, or "any case").

105. For another example, see Goldberg v. Kelly, 397 U.S. 254 (1970), in which

Harlan joined Justice Brennan's path-breaking opinion granting welfare recipients pretermination procedural rights.

106. See Williams v. Illinois, 399 U.S. 235 (1970); see also Tate v. Short, 401 U.S. 395, 401 (1971) (Harlan, J., concurring) (joining the majority's holding for reasons set forth in *Williams*).

107. See Coolidge v. New Hampshire, 403 U.S. 443, 490 (1971) (Harlan, J., concurring).

108. *In re Winship*, 397 U.S. 358, 368 (1970) (Harlan, J., concurring).

109. Cohen v. California, 403 U.S. 15 (1971). This is the leading opinion of the Court recognizing "the communicative power of speech's emotive content." Karst, "Boundaries and Reasons: Freedom of Expression and the Subordination of Groups," 1990 *Ill. L. Rev.* 95, 101; see also Farber, "Civilizing Public Discourse: An Essay on Professor Bickel, Justice Harlan, and the Enduring Significance of *Cohen v. California*," 1980 *Duke L.J.* 283 (contrasting Harlan's *Cohen* opinion with Professor Bickel's belief that obscenities erode social values and create "pollution of our common moral environment").

110. Greene, *The Human Factor* 148 (Vintage ed. 1978).

111. Id. at 149.

112. Id.

113. Id.

114. See Harlan, supra note 6.

115. Dorsen, "The Second Mr. Justice Harlan: A Constitutional Conservative," 44 *N.Y.U. L. Rev.* 249, 271 (1969).

116. Id. at 254.

117. 369 U.S. 186, 330 (1962) (Harlan, J., dissenting).

118. 377 U.S. 533, 589 (1964) (Harlan, J., dissenting). See also Wesberry v. Sanders, 376 U.S. 1, 20 (1964), in which Harlan dissented at length from a ruling that in congressional elections "as nearly as is practicable one man's vote . . . is to be worth as much as another's." Id. at 7–8.

119. 380 U.S. 479, 498 (1965) (Harlan, J., dissenting).

120. 372 U.S. 391, 448 (1963) (Harlan, J., dissenting).

121. 379 U.S. 443, 457 (1965) (Harlan, J., dissenting).

122. 392 U.S. 83, 116 (1968) (Harlan, J., dissenting).

123. 367 U.S. 497, 522 (1961) (Harlan, J., dissenting).

124. 357 U.S. 449 (1958).

125. See Engel v. Vitale, 370 U.S. 421 (1962).

126. See Powell v. McCormack, 395 U.S. 486 (1969).

127. For another Harlan opinion that adopted a broad view of standing, see Parmelee Transp. Co. v. Atchison, Topeka & Santa Fe R. Co., 357 U.S. 77 (1958).

128. See Monroe v. Pape, 365 U.S. 167, 192 (1961) (Harlan, J., concurring).

129. See J. I. Case Co. v. Borak, 377 U.S. 426 (1964).

130. Williams v. Florida, 399 U.S. 78, 127 (1970) (Harlan, J., concurring in part and dissenting in part) (quoting Moragne v. State Marine Lines, Inc., 398 U.S. 375, 403 (1970)).

131. Id. at 128–29. See also Afroyim v. Rusk, 387 U.S. 253, 268 (1967) (Harlan, J., dissenting); Mapp v. Ohio, 367 U.S. 643, 676 (1961) (Harlan, J., dissenting).

132. See, e.g., Afroyim, 387 U.S. 253, 268 (1967) (Harlan J., dissenting) (opposing the overruling of Perez v. Brownell, 356 U.S. 44 (1958)); Mapp v. Ohio, 367 U.S. 643, 672 (1961) (Harlan J., dissenting) (opposing the overruling of Wolf v. Colorado, 338 U.S. 25 (1949)). See generally Dorsen, supra note 115 at 257.

133. 316 U.S. 455 (1942).

134. Gideon v. Wainwright, 372 U.S. 335, 349 (1963) (Harlan, J., concurring).

135. Marchetti v. United States, 390 U.S. 39 (1968).

136. 398 U.S. 375 (1970).

137. Id. at 404. Harlan overruled obsolete precedents in other cases, too, with "particularly acute analyses," Eskridge, "Overruling Statutory Precedents," 76 *Geo. L.J.* 1361, 1390 (1988). These included Lear, Inc. v. Adkins, 395 U.S. 653 (1969) and Walker v. Southern Ry., 385 U.S. 196, 199 (1966) (Harlan, J. dissenting).

138. See Veterans of the Abraham Lincoln Brigade v. Subversive Activities Control Board, 380 U.S. 513 (1965) (Douglas, J., joined by Black and Harlan, JJ., dissenting).

139. See Massachusetts v. Laird, 400 U.S. 886 (1970).

140. See, e.g., New York Times Co. v. United States, 403 U.S. 713, 752 (1971) (Harlan, J., dissenting).

141. *The Federalist* No. 51, at 322, 323 (James Madison) (Rossiter ed., 1961); see also *The Federalist* No. 28 (Alexander Hamilton) (discussing the manner in which state governments would protect their citizens against encroachments by the national government, and vice versa).

142. Dorsen, Preface to *The Future of Our Liberties* ix, xi (Halpern ed., 1982); cf. Dorsen, "Separation of Powers and Federalism," 41 *Alb. L. Rev.* 53, 69 (1977) (proposing that local government units have historically been less responsive to minority concerns within their jurisdictions and that progress for minorities has come at the hands of the federal government).

143. See supra notes 13–16 and accompanying text.

144. See Hart and Sacks, *The Legal Process: Basic Problems in the Making and Application of Law* (tentative ed. 1958); the work was recently published in hard cover, edited by W. Eskridge and P. Frickey (1994).

145. See id. at 715–16.

146. Id. at 4–5.

147. The Hart and Sacks materials did not address constitutional problems, and it is doubtful whether the authors intended their work to apply to such issues. See Dorsen, "In Memoriam: Albert M. Sacks," 105 *Harv. L. Rev.* 11, 13 n.12 (1991). But see also Eskridge and Frickey, "The Making of the Legal Process," 107 *Harv. L. Rev.* 2031, 2049 n.113 (1994). Nevertheless, many judges and scholars have applied legal process themes to constitutional cases. See, e.g., Ely, *Democracy and Distrust* (1980).

148. See Labine v. Vincent, 401 U.S. 532, 540 (1971) (Harlan, J., concurring).

149. See Avery v. Midland County, 390 U.S. 474, 494 (1968) (Harlan, J., dissenting).

150. See Moragne v. States Marine Line, Inc., 398 U.S. 375 (1970).

151. Harlan's sympathy with legal process may be traced in part to the fact that about two-thirds of his law clerks were graduates of Harvard Law School and students of Henry Hart or Albert Sacks.

152. For a recent learned discussion of the evolution of legal process and its successor theories, see Eskridge and Frickey, "An Historical and Critical Introduction to the Legal Process," in Hart and Sacks, *The Legal Process: Basic Problems in the Making and Application of Law* (W. Eskridge and P. Frickey eds., 1994). See also Eskridge and Peller, "The New Public Law Movement: Moderation as a Postmodern Cultural Form," 89 *Mich. L. Rev.* 707 (1991).

153. Strauss and Sunstein, "The Senate, the Constitution, and the Confirmation Process," 101 *Yale L.J.* 1491, 1493 (1992).

154. Dorsen, supra note 115, at 250.

155. Hirsch, *The Enigma of Felix Frankfurter* 177 (1981). See also the discussion in Dorsen, Book Review, 95 *Harv. L. Rev.* 367, 384–86 (1981).

· 16 ·

EARL WARREN

BERNARD SCHWARTZ

There have been two great creative periods in American public law. The first was the formative era, when the Marshall Court laid down the foundations of our constitutional law, giving specific content to the broad general terms in which the Constitution is written. The judicial task at that time was to work out from the constitutional text a body of legal doctrines adapted to the needs of the new nation and the new era into which it was entering. The second great creative period was the Warren Court era. The judicial task then was to keep step with the twentieth century's frenetic pace of societal change. To do this, the Warren Court had to perform a transforming role, usually thought of as more appropriate to the legislator than the judge. In the process it rewrote the corpus of American constitutional law. Earl Warren, in the judicial pantheon, can only be compared to John Marshall.

Warren himself was extremely proud of his reputation in this respect. Once, after he had delivered a talk to hundreds of students in the basement lounge of Notre Dame Law School, he was responding to questions. A student in the back of the packed lounge began a question, "Some people have suggested that you'll go down in history with Marshall as one of the two greatest Chief Justices." Warren smiled broadly and interrupted, "Could you say that again—a little louder please? I'm having a little trouble hearing."[1]

Warren and His Background

As is well known, the Supreme Court is a collegiate institution whose collegiate nature is underscored by the custom the Justices have had of calling themselves "brethren." But each of the brethren could only be guided, not directed. As Justice Felix Frankfurter once stated in a letter to Chief Justice Vinson, "[G]ood feeling in the court, as in a family, is produced by accommodation, not by authority—whether the authority of a parent or a vote."[2]

The Court "family" is composed of nine individuals, who have borne out James Bryce's truism that "judges are only men."[3] "To be sure," Frankfurter once wrote to Justice Stanley Reed, "the Court is an institution, but individuals, with all their diversities of endowment, experience and outlook determine its actions. The history of the Supreme Court is not the history of an abstraction, but the analysis of individuals acting as a Court who make decisions and lay down doctrines."[4]

Foremost among the individuals who made up the Warren Court was, of course, the Chief Justice. In many respects Earl Warren could have been a character out of Sinclair Lewis. Except for his unique leadership abilities, he was a rather typical representative of the Middle America of his day, with his bluff masculine bonhomie, his love of sports and the outdoors, and his lack of intellectual interests or pretensions.

The early Warren was a direct product of his upbringing and surroundings. Born and raised in California, he grew up in a small town that was a microcosm of the burgeoning West. From a last vestige of the American frontier—with cowboys on horses, saloons, and gunfights—the town and state quickly came to be the paradigm of twentieth-century America. "All changed, changed utterly,"[5] as growth became the prime element of California life.

Like his state, Warren displayed a capacity for growth throughout his career. The popular conception of Warren's judicial career has, indeed, been one of a virtual metamorphosis—with the political grub suddenly transformed into the judicial lepidopteran. Certainly, Warren as Chief Justice appeared an entirely different person than he had been before his elevation to the Court. As his state's leading law-enforcement officer, Warren had been perhaps the foremost advocate of the forced evacuation of persons of Japanese ancestry from the West Coast after the Japanese attack on Pearl Harbor in December 1941. As Chief Justice, Warren was the foremost proponent of racial equality. From his crucial role in the *Brown* segregation case[6] to the end of his Court tenure, he did more than any other judge in American history to ensure that equality would become a basic theme in our public law.

As governor, Warren strongly opposed reapportionment of the California legislature, even though, as he later conceded, "[m]y own state was one of the most malapportioned in the nation." As Chief Justice, Warren led the movement to bring the apportionment process within the equal protection guaranty, a movement that culminated in the Chief Justice's own opinion laying down the "one person, one vote" principle.[7]

Like John Marshall, Earl Warren had a political background. Soon after he had obtained his law degree from the University of California, Warren worked in the office of the district attorney of Alameda County, across the bay from San Francisco. Five years later, in 1925, he was elected district attorney, serving in that position until 1938. A 1931 survey of American district attorneys by Raymond Moley (later famous as a member of President Franklin D. Roosevelt's so-called Brain Trust) "declared without hesitation that Warren was the best district attorney in the United States."[8]

In 1938 Warren was elected attorney general of California and became governor in 1942. He was a most effective chief executive; he reorganized the state government and secured major reforming legislation—notably measures for a modern hospital system, improving the state's prisons and its correction system, providing an extensive highway program, and improving old-age and unemployment benefits.

Warren proved an able administrator and was the only governor in his state to be elected to three terms.

On September 8, 1953, Chief Justice Vinson suddenly died. President Eisenhower appointed Warren to the seat. The California governor resigned his position and took up his new duties as Chief Justice at the beginning of the 1953 term.

Leadership Not Scholarship

According to a famous Macaulay statement, "There were gentlemen and there were seamen in the navy of Charles II. But the seamen were not gentlemen, and the gentlemen were not seamen." There have been scholars and there have been great Justices on the Supreme Court. But the scholars have not always been great Justices, and the great Justices have not always been scholars.

To be sure, outstanding scholars did sit on the Warren Court; among them, Felix Frankfurter stands out. Frankfurter was as learned a Justice as ever sat on the bench. Unlike so many juristic scholars, his scholarship far exceeded the bounds of legal arcana. The range of the Justice's scholarly interests is illustrated not only in his opinions and published writings, but also in his amazingly varied correspondence with the leading intellectual figures of the day—ranging from Alfred North Whitehead to John Dewey to Albert Einstein. Publication of Frankfurter's best letters would serve not only law, but scholarship and literature as well.

Yet Frankfurter may have been a better letter writer than he was a judge. With all his intellect and scholarly talents, Frankfurter's judicial career remained essentially a lost opportunity. As far as public law was concerned, he may well have had more influence as a law professor than as a Supreme Court Justice. Although Frankfurter expected to be the intellectual leader of the Court, as he had been of the Harvard law faculty, the Chief Justice himself performed the true leadership role in the Warren Court.

But Warren was never a legal scholar in the Frankfurter sense. "I wish that I could speak to you in the words of a scholar," the Chief Justice once told an audience, "but it has not fallen to my lot to be a scholar in life."[9] The Justices who sat with him all stressed that Warren may not have been an intellectual like Frankfurter, but then, as Justice Stewart once observed to me, "he never pretended to be one."

In assessing the importance of scholarship as a judicial attribute, one should distinguish sharply between a member of the Supreme Court and its Chief Justice. Without a doubt, Justice Joseph Story was the greatest legal scholar ever to sit on the Court. His scholarship enabled him to make his outstanding judicial record, and his legal expertise supplied the one thing that Chief Justice Marshall lacked. Indeed, Marshall is reputed to have once said: "Brother Story here . . . can give us the cases from the Twelve Tables down to the latest reports."[10] It is safe to assume that Story's learning often fleshed out the Chief Justice's reasoning with the scholarly foundation needed to support some Marshall opinions.

Still, no one conversant with American law will conclude that Story was a greater judge than Marshall. Story's scholarship could scarcely have produced the constitutional landmarks of the Marshall Court. When Marshall died, Story's admirers hoped that he would become the new Chief Justice. "The Supreme Court," Harvard President Josiah Quincy toasted, "may it be raised one Story higher."[11] But Story's appointment could have been a disaster; the scholar on the bench would have been a misfit in the Court's center chair.

This hypothesis is not mere conjecture. It is supported by the Court's experience under Chief Justice Harlan F. Stone, who, like Frankfurter, had been a noted law professor. From an intellectual viewpoint, Stone was an outstanding judge. Yet he failed as Chief Justice; his lack of administrative ability nearly destroyed the Court's effectiveness. The Stone Court presented a spectacle of unedifying atomization wholly at variance with its functioning as a collegiate tribunal.

Warren clearly did not equal Stone as a legal scholar. But his leadership abilities and skill as a statesman enabled him to be the most effective Chief Justice since Charles Evans Hughes. Those Justices who served with him stressed Warren's leadership abilities, particularly his skill in conducting the conference. "It was incredible," said Justice William J. Brennan just after Warren's death, "how efficiently the Chief would conduct the Friday conferences, leading the discussion of every case on the agenda, with a knowledge of each case at his fingertips."[12]

A legal scholar such as Stone treated the conference as a law school seminar, "carrying on a running debate with any justice who expresse[d] views different from his."[13] At conference, Chief Justice Warren rarely contradicted the others and made sure that each of them had his full say. Above all, he stated the issues in a deceptively simple way, reaching the heart of the matter while stripping it of legal technicalities. As the *Washington Post* noted, "Warren helped steer cases from the moment they were first discussed simply by the way he framed the issues."[14]

In his first conference on *Brown v. Board of Education*,[15] Warren presented the question before the Court in terms of racial inferiority. He told the Justices that segregation could be justified only by belief in the inherent inferiority of blacks and, if *Plessy v. Ferguson*[16] was followed, it had to be upon that basis. A scholar such as Frankfurter certainly would not have presented the case that way. But Warren's "simplistic" words went straight to the ultimate human values involved. In the face of such an approach, arguments based on legal scholarship would have seemed inappropriate, almost pettifoggery.

The work of a Chief Justice differs greatly from that of other members of the Court as far as legal scholarship is concerned. A person without scholarly interest would find the work of an Associate Justice most unrewarding, since an Associate Justice spends time in Court only hearing and voting on cases and writing opinions. Thus, while considering the appointment of a successor to Chief Justice Fred M. Vinson, President Eisenhower asked a member of Governor Warren's staff whether Warren would really want to be on the Court after his years in high political office: "Wouldn't it be pretty rarified for him?" "Yes," came back the answer, "I frankly think he'd be very likely to be bored to death [as an Associate Justice]." But, the response went on: "My answer would be emphatically different if we were talking about the Chief Justiceship. He could run the place."[17]

The staff member's answer gets to the heart of the matter. The essential attribute of a Chief Justice is not scholarship but leadership. One who can "run the place" and induce the Justices to follow will effectively head the Court.

The Chief Justice must still write opinions backed by the traditional indicia of legal scholarship: discussion of complicated technical issues, citation and consideration of precedents, and learned-looking footnotes. But a lack of scholarly attainments does not necessarily preclude the production of learned opinions. The necessary scholarship can be supplied by the bright, young, former law review editors who serve as the Justices' law clerks. It did not take *The Brethren*[18] to make students of the Court aware of how much of the opinion-writing process has been delegated to the clerks. "As the years passed," wrote Justice Douglas of his own Court years, "it became more and more evident that the law clerks were drafting opinions."[19] The first drafts of the opinions that Chief Justice Warren assigned to himself were almost all prepared by his law clerks.

The Chief Justice would outline the way he wanted the opinion drafted, leaving the clerk with a great deal of discretion to flesh out the details of the opinion. Warren never pretended to be a scholar interested in research and legal minutiae. He left the reasoning and research supporting the decision to his clerks, as well as the task of compiling extensive footnotes, an indispensable component of the well-crafted judicial opinion.

Perhaps the most famous footnote in any Supreme Court opinion appeared in *Brown v. Board of Education.*[20] Noted footnote 11 listed seven works by social scientists to support the statement that segregation meant black inferiority. Yet one of Warren's law clerks inserted the footnote into the opinion, and neither the Chief Justice nor the Associate Justices paid much attention to it at the time.

It Was the *Warren* Court

There are those who claim that although Chief Justice Warren may have been the nominal head of the Court that bears his name, the actual leadership was furnished by other Justices. Thus Professor Dunne's biography of Justice Hugo L. Black is based on the proposition that the Alabaman was responsible for the "judicial revolution" that occurred during the Warren years.[21] More recently, one review of my Warren biography asserts that, more than anything, it shows that the proper title of the Court while Chief Justice Warren sat in its center chair would be the *Brennan* Court.[22]

Justice Black himself always believed that he had led the judicial revolution that rewrote so much of our constitutional law. Black resented the acclaim that the Chief Justice received for leading what everyone looked on as the Warren Court. As Justice Black saw it, the Court under Chief Justice Warren had only written into law the constitutional principles that Justice Black had been advocating for so many years. When Warren retired as Chief Justice, the Justices prepared the traditional letter of farewell. The draft letter read, "For us it is a source of pride that we have had the opportunity to be members of the Warren Court." Justice Black changed this to "the Court over which you have presided."[23]

Nevertheless, the other Justices who served with Chief Justice Warren all recognized his leadership role. Justice William O. Douglas, closest to Justice Black in his views, ranks Warren with Marshall and Hughes "as our three greatest Chief Justices."[24] Another member of the Warren Court told me that it was the Chief Justice who was personally responsible for the key decisions during his tenure. The Justices who sat with him have all stressed to me that Chief Justice Warren may not have been an intellectual like Justice Frankfurter, but then, to quote Justice Stewart again, "he never pretended to be one." More important, says Stewart, he possessed "instinctive qualities of leadership." When I asked Stewart about claims that Justice Black was the intellectual leader of the Court, he replied, "If Black was the intellectual leader, Warren was the *leader* leader."

Chief Justice Warren brought more authority to the Chief Justiceship than had been the case for years. The most important work of the Supreme Court, of course, occurs behind the scenes, particularly at the conferences where the Justices discuss and vote on cases. The Chief Justice controls the conference discussion; his is the prerogative to call and discuss cases before the other Justices speak. All those who served with him stressed Chief Justice Warren's ability to lead the conference.

Justice Stewart told me that at the conferences, "after stating the case, [Warren] would very clearly and unambiguously state his position." The Chief Justice rarely had difficulty in reaching a decision, and once his mind was made up, he would stick tenaciously to his decision. As Justice Byron R. White expressed it to me in an interview, Warren "was quite willing to listen to people at length . . . but, when he made up his mind, it was like the sun went down, and he was very firm, very firm about it." The others never had any doubt about who was the head of the Warren Court.

A reading of the conference notes of Justices on the Warren Court reveals that the Chief Justice was as strong a leader as the Court has ever had. As the *Washington Post* summarized my Warren biography, it "shows Warren as even more a guiding force in the landmark opinions of his court than some have previously believed. Chief Justice Warren helped steer cases from the moment they were first discussed simply by the way he framed the issues."[25] In almost all the important cases, the Chief Justice led the discussion toward the decision he favored. If any Court can properly be identified by the name of one of its members, this Court was emphatically the *Warren* Court and, without arrogance, he, as well as the country, knew it. After an inevitable initial period of feeling his way, Chief Justice Warren led the Supreme Court as effectively as any Chief Justice in our history. When we consider the work of the Warren Court, we are considering a constitutional corpus that was directly a product of the Chief Justice's leadership.

Activism versus Judicial Restraint

There is an antinomy inherent in every system of law; the law must be stable and yet it cannot stand still.[26] It is the task of the judge to reconcile these two conflicting elements. In doing so, jurists tend to stress one principle or the other. Indeed, few judges can keep an equipoise between stability and change.

Chief Justice Warren never pretended to try to maintain the balance. As soon as he had become established on the Court, he came down firmly on the side of change, leading the Supreme Court's effort to enable our public law to cope with rapid societal transformation. Warren strongly believed that the law must draw its vitality from life rather than precedent. What Justice Oliver Wendell Holmes termed "intuitions" of what best served the public interest[27] played the major part in Warren's jurisprudence. He did not sacrifice good sense for the syllogism. Nor was he one of "those who think more of symmetry and logic in the development of legal rules than of practical adaptation to the attainment of a just result."[28] When symmetry and logic were balanced against considerations of equity and fairness, he normally found the latter to be weightier.[29] In the Warren hierarchy of social values, the moral outweighed the material.[30]

Throughout his tenure on the Court, the Chief Justice tended to use "fairness" as the polestar of his judicial approach. Every so often in criminal cases, when counsel defending a conviction would cite legal precedents, Warren would bend his bulk over the bench to ask, "Yes, yes—but were you fair?"[31] The fairness to which the Chief Justice referred was no jurisprudential abstraction. It related to such things as methods of arrest, questioning of suspects, and police conduct—matters that Warren understood well from his earlier years as district attorney in Alameda County, California. Decisions like *Miranda v. Arizona*[32] were based directly upon the Warren fairness approach.

The Chief Justice's emphasis upon fairness and just results led him to join hands with Justices Black and Douglas and their activist approach to constitutional law. Their activism led to Warren's break with Justice Frankfurter—the foremost advocate on the Court of the Holmes doctrine of judicial restraint. To Justice Holmes, the legislator was to have the primary say on the considerations behind laws; the judge's duty was to enforce "even laws that I believe to embody economic mistakes."[33] Justice Frankfurter remained true to the Holmes approach, insisting that self-restraint was the proper posture of a nonrepresentative judiciary, regardless of the nature of the asserted interests in particular cases. Warren followed the canon of judicial restraint in the economic area, but he felt that the Bill of Rights provisions protecting personal liberties imposed more active enforcement obligations on judges. When a law allegedly infringed upon personal rights guaranteed by the Bill of Rights, the Chief Justice refused to defer to the legislative judgment that had considered the law necessary.

Warren rejected the Frankfurter philosophy of judicial restraint because he believed that it thwarted effective performance of the Court's constitutional role. Judicial restraint, in the Chief Justice's view, all too often meant judicial abdication of the duty to enforce constitutional guarantees. "I believe," Warren declared in an interview on his retirement, "that this Court or any court should exercise the functions of the office to the limit of its responsibilities." Judicial restraint meant that "for a long, long time we have been sweeping under the rug a great many problems basic to American life. We have failed to face up to them, and they have piled up on us, and now they are causing a great deal of dissension and controversy of all kinds." To Warren, it was the Court's job "to remedy those things eventually," regardless of the controversy involved.[34]

The Warren approach in this respect left little room for deference to the legislature, the core of the restraint canon. Warren never considered constitutional issues in the light of any desired deference to the legislature. Instead, he decided those issues based on his own independent judgment, normally giving little weight to the fact that a reasonable legislator might have voted for the challenged law.

For Chief Justice Warren, the issue on judicial review was not *reasonableness* but *rightness*. If the law was contrary to his own conception of what the Constitution demanded, it did not matter that a reasonable legislator might reach the opposite conclusion. When Warren decided that the Constitution required an equal population apportionment standard for all legislative chambers except the United States Senate, the fact that no American legislature had followed the new requirement did not deter him from uniformly applying the standard.[35] Justice John M. Harlan's dissent may have demonstrated that the consistent state practice was, at the least, reasonable. For the Chief Justice, however, legislative reasonableness was irrelevant when the practice conflicted with his own interpretation of the Constitution.

Fountain of Justice

A much quoted statement by Anthony Lewis asserts that "Earl Warren was the closest thing the United States has had to a Platonic Guardian, dispensing law from a throne without any sensed limits of power except what was seen as the good of society."[36] But Warren was more than the judicial counterpart of the Platonic philosopher-king. He consciously conceived of the Supreme Court as a virtual modern Court of Chancery—a residual "fountain of justice" to rectify individual instances of injustice, particularly where the victims suffered from racial, economic, or similar disabilities. He saw himself as a present-day Chancellor, who secured fairness and equity in individual cases, particularly where they involved his "constituency" of the poor or underprivileged.

"If the Chief Justice," Justice Stewart once commented to me, "can see some issue that involves widows or orphans or the underprivileged, then he's going to come down on that side."

Justice Frankfurter strongly disagreed with the Warren conception of the Court. The disagreement emerged when the Court agreed to reconsider the merits of cases involving employment injury under workers' compensation laws or the Federal Employers Liability Act (FELA). Based on the facts, the Chief Justice's very first opinion reversed a lower court injunction against enforcing a workers' compensation award. The decision emphasized that "[t]his Act must be liberally construed in conformance with its purpose."[37] During the Warren years, the Chief Justice led the Court in reversing a large number of employment injury cases on their merits. In fact, Supreme Court "decisions relating to the sufficiency of the evidence under the FELA" increased fourfold during Warren's first three terms, compared with the three terms before he became Chief Justice.[38]

Justice Frankfurter believed that the Supreme Court should never have taken these cases. "I do not think," he wrote to the Chief Justice, "the correction of an erroneous decision, after two courts have dealt with the matter . . . is the proper business of this Court."[39] In the Frankfurter view, the Supreme Court was not "a court for the correction of errors."[40] In a number of these cases, Frankfurter dissented[41] and "read his colleagues a lecture on the need to conserve the Court's time and energy, by avoiding trivial cases."[42]

The Chief Justice felt just as strongly that the job of the Supreme Court was to ensure a just result in these cases. Warren looked upon the Court as the last resort of the employees and their widows and orphans who had lost under the FELA and in other employment injury cases. The Chief Justice used to stress to his law clerks how important it was that the Court take some FELA cases each year to make sure that the lower courts understood that the statute was intended to protect the employee's right to recover.

Yet Warren's conception of the Supreme Court as the residual "fountain of justice" went far beyond instances where recovery had been denied in employment injury cases. To the Chief Justice, the Court functioned to ensure fairness and equity in all cases where they had not been secured by other governmental processes. In Warren's view, the political branches of government had defaulted in such cases. Where a constitutional requirement remained unenforced due to governmental failure to compel obedience to it, the Court had to act. The alternative as Warren saw it was an empty Constitution, the essential provisions of which were rendered nugatory because they could not be enforced.

For example, the Chief Justice explained the Warren Court decisions requiring legislative reapportionment on the following basis: "Most of these problems," he declared some years after those decisions, "could have been solved through the political processes rather than through the courts. But as it was, the Court had to decide."[43]

This same legislative inaction influenced the most important cases decided by the Warren Court. The Chief Justice and his colleagues felt that they had to step in because the political branches had not acted to vindicate certain constitutional rights, and the government could not or would not act in the future to correct the situation. From this point of view, the Warren Court acted not so much out of an activist desire to remake the law and society, but rather out of the need to remedy the constitutional effects of governmental paralysis. Analyzing the principal decisions of the Warren Court sustains this thesis.

Political Default and Warren Court Decisions

Brown v. Board of Education

Any analysis of the Warren Court's principal decisions should begin with *Brown v. Board of Education*,[44] in many ways the watershed constitutional case of the century. When the *Brown* decision struck down school segregation as violative of the Equal Protection Clause, it signaled the beginning of effective civil rights enforcement in American law.

The *Brown* decision was a direct consequence of the political process's failure to enforce the Fourteenth Amendment's guarantee of racial equality. Before *Brown*, it had become a constitutional cliché that the amendment had not succeeded in securing equality for blacks; that failure largely resulted from governmental default. Government had not acted to eliminate the almost patent violation of equal protection; instead, both state and federal laws perpetuated the segregation that existed in much of the country, including the nation's capital.

It was utterly unrealistic to expect state governmental action to end segregation in those states where Jim Crow had become the norm. But Congress also failed to take action. Not only had Congress failed to outlaw segregation in the states, it had affirmatively provided for segregation in Washington, D.C. Chief Justice Vinson emphasized this point in his presentation to the Justices while presiding at the first conference held on the *Brown* case. Vinson stressed that segregation had never been questioned by Congress. "However [we] construe it," he said, "Congress did not pass a statute deterring and ordering no segregation." On the contrary, Congress itself had commanded segregation in the nation's capitol. "I don't see," Vinson affirmed, "how we can get away from the long-established acceptance in the District [of Columbia]. For 90 years, there have been segregated schools in this city." Vinson did admit that "it would be better if [Congress] would act."[45] But Congress had not done so and there was no indication that it would in the foreseeable future.

Chief Justice Warren approached the *Brown* issue from an entirely different point of view. Unlike his predecessor, Warren began his first *Brown* conference with a ringing declaration that segregation was unconstitutional. He stated the issue in moral terms: "[T]he more I've read and heard and thought, the more I've come to conclude that the basis of segregation and 'separate but equal' rests upon a concept of the inherent inferiority of the colored race."[46]

To one who felt this way, the claim of congressional acquiescence through inaction could scarcely justify the imprimatur of legality upon a patently immoral and unconstitutional practice. On the contrary, the years of legislative inaction coupled with the unlikelihood that Congress would attempt to correct the situation in the foreseeable future made it imperative for the Court to intervene. The alternative would leave untouched a practice that flagrantly violated both the Constitution and the ultimate human values involved. The Chief Justice found such an alternative unpalatable. Since the other branches had defaulted in their responsibility, the courts had to ensure enforcement of the constitutional prohibition against racial discrimination.

Baker v. Carr

Next to *Brown v. Board of Education*, the most significant case decided by the Warren Court was *Baker v. Carr*.[47] According to the Chief Justice, *Baker v. Carr* "was the most important case of my tenure on the Court."[48] The Court's decision in the case led to a drastic shift in political power throughout the nation. Through *Baker v. Carr* and its progeny, the Warren Court ultimately worked an electoral reform comparable to that achieved by the British Parliament when it incorporated the program of the English Reform movement into the statute book.

Even more than *Brown*, *Baker v. Carr* may be explained as a judicial response to the default of the political branches. The 1901 Tennessee statute at issue in the case, which apportioned seats in the state legislature, apparently was a fair law when enacted. As time went on, however, population shifts increasingly altered the picture. By the time Baker brought his lawsuit, the 1901 law no longer reflected the state's population distribution. Baker's complaint claimed that voters from urban areas had been denied equal protection "by virtue of the debasement of their votes," since a vote from the most populous county had only a fraction of the weight of one from the least populous county. The population ratio for the most and least populous districts by then was over nineteen to one.

To correct this situation by a nonjudicial remedy, the very legislature whose existence depended upon the malapportionment under the 1901 statute would have had to pass a new reapportionment law. That would have been tantamount to the rural legislators who profited from the situation voting many of their seats out of existence. It would have been quixotic to expect them to do so. Political paralysis resulted, with an inevitable increase in the gross disparities as time brought further demographic changes.

To remedy this problem, the Supreme Court finally had "to enter this political thicket."[49] No other feasible way existed to correct the patent violation of the constitutional command of voting equality. This lack of any other remedy strongly influenced at least one member of the *Baker v. Carr* majority, Justice Tom C. Clark. He had originally voted not to hear Baker's suit and had agreed to join the Frankfurter dissent in the case. Justice Frankfurter had tried to firm up Clark's vote by suggesting that he write separately to describe the other remedies open to Tennessee's voters.[50] Clark soon found that no other remedies existed. His discovery led him to write to Frankfurter: "Preparatory to writing my dissent in this case, along the line you suggested of pointing out the avenues that were open for the voters of Tennessee to bring about reapportionment despite its Assembly, I have carefully checked into the record. I am sorry to say that I cannot find any practical course that the people could take in bringing this about except through the Federal courts."[51] Clark, therefore, decided to switch his vote and join the *Baker v. Carr* majority.

While considering the matter, Justice Clark jotted down a note: "Here a minority by representatives ignores the needs and desires of the majority—and for their own selfish purpose hamper and oppress them—debar them from equal privileges and equal rights—that means the failure of our constitutional system."[52] The Justice had decided that only a judicial remedy could redress that failure.

There is little doubt that the Chief Justice had come to the same conclusion. Warren's statement on the basis of his Court's reapportionment decisions bears requoting: "Most of the problems could have been solved through the political processes rather than through the courts. But as it was, the Court had to decide."[53] The decision in *Baker v. Carr* came down because "the political process" had failed to remedy the constitutional violation that deprived Baker of an equal vote.

Mapp v. Ohio

The government's failure to remedy another constitutional violation formed the foundation for the opinion in *Mapp v. Ohio*,[54] a decision that Justice Fortas characterized to me as "the most radical decision in recent times." The *Mapp* decision held that the exclusionary rule, which bars evidence obtained in violation of the Fourth Amendment's ban against unreasonable searches and seizures, applies in state as well as federal cases.

The *Mapp* majority was strongly influenced by Ohio's failure to take action against Fourth Amendment violations by state police officers. *Wolf v. Colorado*,[55] the leading case prior to *Mapp*, noted that the Fourth Amendment was "basic to a free society. It is therefore implicit in 'the concept of ordered liberty' and as such enforceable against the States through the Due Process Clause."[56] Nevertheless, *Wolf* refused to hold that the federal Constitution required application of the exclusionary rule in state criminal cases. The result was, in the words of the *Wolf* opinion, "that in a prosecution in a State court for a State crime the Fourteenth Amendment does not forbid the admission of evidence obtained by an unreasonable search and seizure."[57]

Wolf refused to extend the exclusionary rule to state cases because that rule was not, "in the face of prospectively available alternative remedies such as private damage suits, the pressure of an informed public opinion and internal police disciplinary measures, so clearly the only safeguard against invasion of privacy by *local* officers." In *Mapp,* however, the Court found "the claimed alternative safeguards . . . unsatisfactory in their deterrence of police invasions of privacy."[58]

Though the *Mapp* opinion made this point, it was spelled out more fully in the draft opinion that Justice Clark circulated two months before he delivered the opinion of the Court. Like the final opinion, Clark declared in his draft that "other means of protection" to safeguard the Fourth Amendment right, other than the exclusionary rule itself, were "worthless and futile."[59] The draft, however, more specifically addressed what it termed the "obvious futility of any longer seeking to relegate the Fourth Amendment to the protection of other remedies."[60]

Concerning "private damage remedies," Justice Clark's draft asked, "how can we expect to defend 'the indefeasible right of personal security' by telling him who suffers its invasion to seek damages for 'the breaking of doors?'" In addition, he asserted that "[a]n aroused public opinion and internal police discipline are equally without the deterrent value."[61] According to Clark's draft, "[I]t appears hopelessly impractical to consider formulation of an effective body of public opinion as a remedy practicably available to those who suffer unconstitutional invasions of their privacy. They are in large measure criminal defendants, and more unlikely organizers of an effective and respectable public opinion would be difficult to find."[62]

The default of other remedies led directly to the *Mapp* decision. As Justice Clark noted in his draft, "The question is whether there presently exists available to citizens of the non-exclusionary states any remedy which can be said to meet 'the minimal standards of Due Process.' One fails of discovery, and we are bound to require adherence to the constitutionally mandated rule of *Weeks*"[63]—namely, the exclusionary rule.

Once again, the Warren Court made a far-reaching decision because it concluded that there was no other way to effectuate a constitutional right. The remedies suggested by the *Wolf* Court had proved to be futile, and the Court could not depend on the political branches to implement the Fourth Amendment safeguard. On the contrary, government failure to take any enforcement action led to the *Mapp* situation. If the Court did not act, the constitutional safeguard would remain nugatory.

Though Chief Justice Warren did not play a leading role in the *Mapp* decision, he concurred in the approach just stated. One case referred to in *Mapp* was *Irvine v. California,*[64] in which Warren joined a majority decision affirming a conviction based on evidence obtained in violation of the Fourth Amendment. Although Warren followed the *Wolf* approach in *Irvine,* he joined Justice Robert H. Jackson in going out of the way to state that, if the police in *Irvine* had willfully violated the Fourth Amendment, their conduct constituted a federal crime. Warren and Jackson directed the clerk of the Court "to forward a copy of the record in this case, together with a copy of this opinion, for attention of the Attorney General of the United States."[65]

Warren later informed his law clerks that nothing ever came of forwarding the record and opinion to the attorney general. The failure of the Department of Justice to investigate the situation showed Warren that the judicial abnegation in *Irvine* had been misguided. If constitutional rights would remain unenforced in practice, the Chief Justice had to consider a more activist judicial role. As Warren put it in an interview just after he retired, either the Court would act to enforce the constitutional guarantees involved in these cases, "or we let them go and sweep them under the rug, only to leave them for future generations."[66]

Miranda v. Arizona

Next to *Mapp v. Ohio*, the Warren Court rendered its most important criminal law decision in *Miranda v. Arizona*.[67] It was also the most controversial. *Miranda* gave rise to complaints from law enforcement officers throughout the country, who denounced the Court for putting "another set of handcuffs on the police department."[68]

"The *Miranda* decision," the Court stated a decade ago, "was based in large part on this Court's view that the warnings which it required police to give to suspects in custody would reduce the likelihood that the suspects would fall victim to constitutionally impermissible practices of police interrogation in the presumptively coercive environment of the station house."[69] From this viewpoint, *Miranda* was a direct consequence of Chief Justice Warren's own experience as a district attorney. Justice Fortas, a member of the *Miranda* Court, told me that the decision "was entirely [Warren's]." The Chief Justice's conference presentation led the way to the majority decision that he himself delivered.

In *Miranda*, as in the other cases discussed, Warren was influenced most by the fact that the required warnings were the only effective way to protect Fifth Amendment rights during police interrogation. The *Miranda* majority was as aware as the dissenters in the case that the Court's requirement "would have the effect of decreasing the number of suspects who respond to police questioning."[70] But the need to prevent unconstitutional police practices outweighed that factor. "The *Miranda* majority . . . apparently felt that whatever the cost to society in terms of fewer convictions of guilty suspects, that cost would simply have to be borne in the interest of enlarged protection for the Fifth Amendment privilege."[71]

Warren's own experience as a former district attorney played a crucial role in his thinking. Methods of arrest, questioning of suspects, and police conduct in the station house were matters that the Chief Justice intimately understood from his years as prosecutor in Alameda County, California. Above all, he recognized the problem of police abuses and the lack of effective methods to deal with them. All that had been said in *Mapp* about the lack of remedies against Fourth Amendment violations applied with even greater force to practices in police interrogation rooms.

Here, as with the other cases previously discussed, there was little likelihood of effective action by the other branches of government to rectify the problem. Political default again made judicial action imperative. Once more, if the Court did not step in, there was no way to "reduce the likelihood that suspects would fall victim to constitutionally impermissible practices of police interrogation."[72]

Warren's Jurisprudence

Chief Justice Warren may have led a legal revolution, but he did not have any defined program to be accomplished by the far-reaching legal changes for which he was responsible. Nor did he have an overriding philosophical theory that molded his jurisprudence. Instead, he was the model of the pragmatic instrumentalist—using the law to reach the result he favored in the given case, without fitting the decision into any master plan designed to remake the society or even the law itself.

Of course, Warren had overriding values which were reflected in his jurisprudence. First was his adherence to traditional American values. As Justice Stewart put it to me in an interview, "Warren's great strength was his simple belief in the things which we now laugh at—motherhood, marriage, family, flag, and the like." If, as Stewart pointed out, Warren looked at cases in terms of "those eternal, rather bromidic, platitudes," such as home, family, and country, it was only that they were "platitudes in which he sincerely believed." Warren's own home and family life furnished the foundation for his scale of values throughout his professional life. If there was something of the Babbitt in this, it was also, as Stewart said to me, "a great source of strength, that he did have these foundations on which his thinking rested, regardless of whether you agreed with him."

Near the top in the Warren hierarchy of values was the family. In a case where the majority came close to upholding consensual divorces, Warren wrote a strong draft dissent, urging that the majority was threatening the very place of "marriage . . . our basic social institution," as well as "the very conception of the place of the family in our civilization."[73]

Warren's adherence to traditional values may also be seen in his reaction to obscenity cases, where, observers have noted, the Chief Justice departed from his normal approach in favor of free expression. Despite that approach in most First Amendment cases, Warren could never overcome his personal abhorrence of pornography and what he called smut-peddlers. His law clerks constantly disagreed with the Chief Justice on what they deemed his puritanism in obscenity cases. Once, when they were pressing Warren on his view about pornography, his answer was, "You boys don't have any daughters yet." Warren found the sexual material that had become so widely available "unspeakable."[74] A magazine quoted him telling a colleague, when he was shown a pornographic work, "If anyone showed that book to my daughters, I'd have strangled him with my own hands."[75]

It was not, however, only the traditional values of family and morality that influenced the Warren jurisprudence. Even more important, for they formed the basis of Warren's major decisions, were fairness and equality. Fairness as a Warren fundamental has already been stressed. For the Chief Justice, the technical issues traditionally fought over in constitutional cases always seemed to merge into larger questions of fairness.[76] His great concern was expressed in the question he so often asked at argument: "But was it fair?"[77] His conception of fairness was the key to most of the Warren criminal-law decisions. When government lawyers tried to justify decisions of lower courts by traditional legal arguments, Warren would interject, "Why did you treat him this way?"[78] When the Chief Justice concluded that an individual had been treated in an unfair manner, he would not let legal rules or precedents stand in the way in his effort to remedy the situation.

Even more important than fairness was the notion of equality in the Warren jurisprudence. The Warren concept of law was one that applied equally to all the components of an increasingly pluralistic society. It is true that, ever since de Tocqueville, observers have emphasized equality as the overriding American "passion."[79] But it was not until the decisions of the Warren Court that our law, in W. H. Auden's phrase, really "found the notion of equality." If one great theme recurred in the Warren jurisprudence, it was that of equality before the law—equality of races, of citizens, of rich and poor, of prosecutor and defendant. Without the Warren Court decisions giving ever-wider effect to the right to equality before the law, most of the movements for equality that have permeated American society might never have gotten started.

Equality was the great Warren theme in the *Brown* school segregation case[80]—as well as the decisions enshrining the "one person, one vote" principle in the law. In addition to racial and political equality, Warren moved to ensure equality in criminal justice. The landmark case was *Griffin v. Illinois*.[81] Griffin had been convicted of armed robbery in a state court. He filed a motion for a free transcript of the trial record, alleging that he was indigent and could not get adequate appellate review without the transcript. The motion was denied. In the conference on the case, Warren pointed out that the state had provided for full appellate review in such a case. A defendant who could pay for a transcript should not be given an advantage over one who could not. "We cannot," declared the Chief Justice, "have one rule for the rich and one for the poor." Hence, he would require the state to furnish the transcript. The Court followed the Warren lead and held that it violates the Constitution for a state to deny free transcripts of trial proceedings to defendants alleging poverty.

As it turned out, *Griffin* was a watershed in the Warren jurisprudence. In it the Court made its first broad pronouncement of equality in the criminal process. After *Griffin* Warren and his colleagues appeared to agree with Bernard Shaw that "the worst of crimes is poverty," as they tried to equalize criminal law between those possessed of means and the less affluent.

To Warren, the law was the instrument to give effect to his scale of values—particularly the notions of fairness and equality. Yet he did so pragmatically—moved not by an overriding vision of the law and the society, but by his conception of what would further fairness and equality in the case before him.

Hence, in Warren's opinions, one does not find doctrinal threads of the kind that run through the works of a Frankfurter or even a Black, arguing a juristic theory decade after decade. "A Warren opinion," says one commentator, "is a morn made new—a bland, square presentation of the particular problem in that case almost as if it were unencumbered by precedents or conflicting theories."[82]

To Warren, the law was an instrument to produce the "right" result in the particular case. When he had determined what that result was, the Chief Justice was prepared to reach it regardless of how many legal rules and precedents there were to the contrary. In *Reynolds v. Sims*,[83] where the proper standard of legislative apportionment was the issue, Warren had originally led the conference to a requirement of equality of population in only one house of the legislature. That was the rule generally followed until then by all the states, including California where a 1948 speech by Governor Warren had effectively killed an effort to reapportion the state senate on a population basis.[84]

Reynolds laid down its categorical equal-population standard because Warren changed his mind while working on the opinion. Justice Brennan told me how the Chief Justice had burst without ceremony into his chambers, declaring, "It can't be. It can't be." Warren proceeded to tell Brennan that the equal-population standard must apply to both houses of a state legislature. He persuaded a majority of the correctness of his new position and that became the *Reynolds* rule. So contrary to all the precedents was the new rule, that an observer who was in the pillared courtroom when Warren read his opinion wrote, "[L]isteners, as he spoke, felt as if they were present at a second American Constitutional Convention."[85] And what of the contrary view expressed by Governor Warren? "I was just wrong as Governor," Warren later told a law clerk.[86]

Warren's approach to law was more ethical than analytical. Justice, to him, was not a process of decision but of seeing that the right side prevailed in the given case. The dominant consideration was his conception of social good—not the good of society under a defined philosophy, but what would favor the "good" side in the case before him. If Warren was the outstanding example of twentieth-century instrumentalism in action, he used the law to achieve the right result in particular cases, without any overriding philosophy and too often without even reliance upon law in the traditional sense. That is what led Judge Learned Hand to write deprecatingly about the Chief Justice, "It is all very well to have a man at the top who is keenly aware of the dominant trends; but isn't it desirable to add a pinch or two of what we used to call 'law'[?]"[87]

In many ways, Warren the judge was the paradigm of the realist school of jurisprudence. To him clearly, the life of the law was not logic, but the experience of the given case. What he considered the "felt necessities" of the case were the motivating factors in his decision process. The realists had asserted that neither rules nor logic produced court decisions. That was certainly true of the Warren jurisprudence, based as it was upon his personal view of what the "right" decision should be.

Warren in the Pantheon

How then can Earl Warren's work as a judge be summarized?

Chief Justice Warren will never rank with the consummate legal craftsmen who have fashioned the structure of Anglo-American law over the generations—each professing to be a pupil, yet each a builder who added his few bricks.[88] But Warren was never content to deem himself a mere vicar of the common law tradition. Instead he was the paradigm of the "result-oriented" judge, who used his power to secure the result he deemed right in the cases that came before his Court. Employing the authority of the ermine to the utmost, he never hesitated to do whatever he thought necessary to translate his own conceptions of fairness and justice into the law of the land.

In reaching what he considered the just result, the Chief Justice was not deterred by the demands of stare decisis. For Warren, principle was more compelling than precedent. The key decisions of the Warren Court overruled decisions of earlier Courts. Those precedents had left the enforcement of constitutional rights to the political branches. Yet, the latter had failed to act. In Warren's view, this situation left the Court with the choice either to follow the precedent or to vindicate the right. For the Chief Justice, there was never any question as to which was the correct alternative.

Warren cannot be deemed a great juristic technician, noted for his mastery of the common law. But he never pretended to be a legal scholar or to profess interest in legal philosophy or reasoning. To him, the outcome of a case mattered more than the reasoning behind the decision. He took full responsibility for the former and delegated the latter, in large part, to his law clerks.

The result may have been a deficiency in judicial craftsmanship that subjected Warren to constant academic criticism, both during and after his tenure on the bench. Without a doubt, Warren does not rank with Holmes or Cardozo as a master of the opinion, but his opinions have a mark of their own. Warren would go over the drafts prepared by his clerks and make changes, usually adding or substituting straightforward language typical of his manner of presentation. As one of his law clerks told me, "He had a penchant for Anglo-Saxon words over Latin words and he didn't like foreign phrases thrown in if there was a good American word that would do."

As a consequence, the important Warren opinions have a simple power of their own; if they do not resound with the cathedral tones of a Marshall,[89] they speak with the moral decency of a modern Micah. Perhaps the *Brown* opinion did not articulate the juristic bases of its decision in as erudite a manner as it could have, but as the Chief Justice wrote in his memorandum transmitting the *Brown* draft, the opinion was "prepared on the theory that [it] should be short, readable by the lay public, non-rhetorical, unemotional and, above all, non-accusatory."[90] The decision in *Brown* emerged from a typical Warren moral judgment, with which few today would disagree. The Warren opinion was so *right* in that judgment that one wonders whether additional learned labor in spelling out the obvious was really necessary.

When all is said and done, Warren's place in the judicial pantheon rests, not upon his opinions, but upon his decisions. If impact on the law is the hallmark of the outstanding judge, few occupants of the bench have been more outstanding than Chief Justice Warren. The decisions under his leadership made the greatest contribution to our law since the days of John Marshall. The impact on a whole society's way of life can be compared only with that caused by political revolution or military conflict.

Justice Fortas once said to me that in his conference presentations, Chief Justice Warren normally went straight to the ultimate moral values involved—just as he did in his first *Brown* conference. Faced with that approach, traditional legal arguments seemed out of place. As Fortas put it, "[O]pposition based on the hemstitching and embroidery of the law appeared petty in terms of Warren's basic value approach."

The same appears to be true when we consider Earl Warren's judicial performance. To criticize him for his lack of scholarship or judicial craftsmanship seems petty when we weigh these deficiencies against the contributions he made as leader in the greatest judicial transformation of the law since the days of John Marshall.

Notes

1. Schwartz, *Super Chief: Earl Warren and His Supreme Court—A Judicial Biography* 766 (1983).
2. Letter from Frankfurter to Fred Vinson (n.d.), Frankfurter Papers, Library of Congress.
3. 1 Bryce, *The American Commonwealth* 274 (1917).
4. Letter from Frankfurter to Stanley Reed (April 13, 1939), Frankfurter Papers, Library of Congress.
5. Yeats, "Easter 1916."
6. Brown v. Board of Education, 347 U.S. 483 (1954).
7. Reynolds v. Sims, 377 U.S. 533 (1964).
8. Weaver, *Warren: The Man, the Court, the Era* 44 (1967).
9. Pollack, *Earl Warren: The Judge Who Changed America* 193 (1979).
10. Dunne, *Justice Joseph Story and the Rise of the Supreme Court* 91 (1970).
11. Id. at 307–08.
12. N.Y. *Times*, July 10, 1974, at 24.
13. Lash, *From the Diaries of Felix Frankfurter* 152 (1975).
14. June 15, 1983, at A16.
15. 347 U.S. 483 (1954).
16. 163 U.S. 537 (1896).
17. Schwartz, supra note 1, at 4.
18. Woodward and Armstrong, *The Brethren: Inside the Supreme Court* (1979).
19. Douglas, *The Court Years, 1939–1975*, 173 (1980).
20. 347 U.S. 483, 494, n.11 (1954).
21. Dunne, *Hugo Black and the Judicial Revolution* (1977).
22. Hutchinson, "Hail to the Chief: Earl Warren and the Supreme Court," 81 *Mich. L. Rev.* 922, 923 (1983).
23. "Dear Chief," June 23, 1969. Black Papers, Library of Congress.
24. Douglas, supra note 19, at 240.
25. June 15, 1983, at A16.
26. Pound, *Interpretations of Legal History* 1 (1923).
27. Holmes, *The Common Law* (1881).
28. Id. at 1, 35–36.
29. Compare Cardozo, J., in Jacob and Youngs v. Kent, 230 N.Y. 239, 242–43 (1921).
30. Compare Cardozo, *Paradoxes of Legal Science* 57 (1927).
31. Lewis, *Portrait of a Decade: The Second American Revolution* 139 (1964).
32. 384 U.S. 436 (1966).
33. 1 *Holmes-Pollock Letters* 167 (Howe ed., 1961).
34. *U.S. News & World Report*, July 15, 1968, at 64.

35. Reynolds v. Sims, 377 U.S. 533 (1964).
36. Schwartz, supra note 1, at 2726.
37. Voris v. Eikel, 346 U.S. 328, 333 (1953).
38. Ferguson v. Moore-McCormack Lines, 352 U.S. 521, 548 app. A (1957) (Frankfurter, J., dissenting).
39. Letter from Frankfurter to Warren (Jan. 26, 1956), Felix Frankfurter Papers, Library of Congress.
40. Id.
41. The cases are cited in Ferguson v. Moore-McCormack Lines, 352 U.S. at 526 n.3.
42. N.Y. *Times*, May 19, 1959, § 1, at 1.
43. Pollack, supra note 9, at 209.
44. 347 U.S. 483 (1954).
45. Schwartz, supra note 1, at 74.
46. Id. at 86.
47. 369 U.S. 186 (1962).
48. Warren, *The Memoirs of Earl Warren* 306 (1977).
49. Colegrove v. Green, 328 U.S. 549, 556 (1946).
50. Letter from Tom C. Clark to Frankfurter (Feb. 3, 1962), Frankfurter Papers, Harvard Law School.
51. Letter from Tom C. Clark to Frankfurter (Mar. 7, 1962), Frankfurter Papers, Harvard Law School.
52. Note of Tom C. Clark, Clark Papers, Tarlton Law Library, University of Texas.
53. Pollack, supra note 9, at 209.
54. 367 U.S. 643 (1961).
55. 338 U.S. 25 (1949).
56. Id. at 27–28.
57. Id. at 33.
58. Clark, Draft opinion in *Mapp v. Ohio*, at 5–6. Tom C. Clark Papers, Tarlton Law Library, University of Texas.
59. 367 U.S. at 651–52.
60. Clark, supra note 58, at 11.
61. Id. at 11, 12.
62. Id. at 12.
63. Id. at 13, referring to Weeks v. United States, 232 U.S. 383 (1914).
64. 347 U.S. 128 (1954).
65. Id. at 138.
66. "The Law: The Legacy of the Warren Court," *Time*, July 4, 1969, at 63.
67. 384 U.S. 436 (1966).
68. Weaver, supra note 8, at 234, quoting Los Angeles Mayor Sam Yorty.
69. New York v. Quarles, 467 U.S. 649, 656 (1984).
70. Id.
71. Id. at 656–57.
72. Id. at 656.
73. Schwartz, *The Unpublished Opinions of the Warren Court* 26 (1985). The Warren draft was never published, as the case became moot before the Court could decide it. Id. at 39–40.
74. Pollack, supra note 9, at 355.
75. Weaver, supra note 8, at 273.

76. Compare Lewis, in 4 *Justices of the United States Supreme Court* 1789–1969, 2725 (Friedman and Israel eds., 1969).

77. Id.

78. Id.

79. 2 de Tocqueville, *Democracy in America* 102 (Bradley ed., 1954).

80. 347 U.S. 483 (1954).

81. 351 U.S. 12 (1956).

82. Lewis, supra note 76, at 2724.

83. 377 U.S. 533 (1964).

84. See Schwartz, supra note 1, at 503.

85. Lewis, supra note 76, at 2745.

86. Schwartz, supra note 1, at 504.

87. Letter from Learned Hand to Frankfurter (Oct. 25, 1956), Frankfurter Papers, Library of Congress.

88. Compare Hand, "Mr. Justice Cardozo," 52 *Harv. L. Rev.* 361 (1939).

89. Compare Cardozo, "Law and Literature," in *Selected Writings of Benjamin Nathan Cardozo* 342 (Hall ed., 1947).

90. Memorandum from Warren to Members of Supreme Court (May 7, 1954), Clark Papers, Tarlton Law Library, University of Texas.

• 17 •

CLERKING FOR THE CHIEF JUSTICE

TYRONE BROWN

When I was asked to write a paper for this volume, I was somewhat reluctant to accept. Ever since my year as a law clerk at the Supreme Court, I have had very mixed feelings about the experience, not unaffected by sad recollections that sometimes I would just as soon forget. It was the end of the 1967 term, in June 1968, when Chief Justice Warren announced his resignation after fifteen years at the head of the Court.

That year, 1968, I submit, was a bad one for our country. Protests by the draft-age generation, *my* peers, over our involvement in the civil war in Vietnam had become an open rebellion and had laid low an otherwise effective president in March. Martin Luther King, Jr., fell to an assassin's bullet in Memphis a few days before Easter. In outrage, black sections of our major cities went up in flames. Later that spring, while campaigning for president in Los Angeles, Robert F. Kennedy also died at the hands of an assassin.

I have two very poignant images from that time. In the first, with my co-clerks, I am sitting in the Chief's clerks' offices upstairs from the main floor of the Supreme Court building, watching the smoke and flames rise from downtown Washington on the Friday after Martin Luther King's death. In the second image, I am waiting, part of a crowd of thousands, along Constitution Avenue north of Union Station, waiting in the growing dusk for Robert Kennedy's body to pass on its way home from the funeral services in New York.

The week after Senator Kennedy's death, Earl Warren told his law clerks—Wilson, Simon, and me, and Dudley and Nichols who were on semipermanent loan from retired Justices—that he would resign once the Court completed its business for the term. However, President Johnson's failed attempt to appoint Justice Abe Fortas as Chief Justice and the election of Richard Nixon that November kept *our* Chief on the bench for another term.

But that Saturday afternoon (it must have been in May) at the University Club, which he had so happily desegregated with my presence at the regular Saturday luncheon with his clerks—on that occasion when he told us of his intention to resign, I felt that I was bearing witness to the end of an era, not only in the life of the Supreme Court, but in the life of the country as well.

I never have come fully to terms with the peculiarity of fate that made me part of that intimate company on that bittersweet Saturday afternoon. Nor, for that matter, have I ever fully comprehended the fateful twists that brought me—a passive beneficiary, at best, of the social revolution that Earl Warren rode so well for so long—to Washington to be his law clerk in the first place.

Perhaps it simply comes down to this: The man was my hero. Perhaps it is my lot, finally and simply, to say why. In any event, that is what I shall try to do.

In 1952, when Linda Brown, age nine, was denied enrollment at the Sumner School in Topeka, Kansas, I at the same age, along with two of my brothers and my sister, attended an integrated elementary school in a working-class community in Newark, New Jersey. We were not as poor as I sometimes suggest we were. My father was the best ditch-digger in Essex County, New Jersey, and my mother worked nights as a nurse's aide. My mother, in particular, had admired Earl Warren from the time that he was a presidential candidate in 1952, in part, I believe, because like my parents, then-Governor and Mrs. Warren had a brood of children.

Because of the importance that she attached to education, my mother elevated Chief Justice Warren and NAACP advocate Thurgood Marshall to the status of personal heroes in our household when, on May 17, 1954, the Court ruled that "separate educational facilities" maintained by the state were "inherently unequal" and, therefore, were violative of the Equal Protection Clause. Since my mother drummed this lesson into us, Warren and Marshall became my heroes, too, though on a tier somewhat below that of Willie Mays.

The *Brown* decision[1] had no direct impact on me in that little integrated school in Newark, New Jersey. But in the fall of 1954, my mother having prevailed on my father to move us back to their original "home" in the Tidewater area of Virginia, my oldest brother and I were enrolled in a spanking new, segregated high school near Portsmouth. I do not recall being troubled by segregation at Crestwood High, though my brother was. Certainly, the facilities were more modern, more spacious than anything we had experienced before.

But in the event, my father could not support us in Virginia, and he detested a job where he was referred to as "Boy" but had to address the boss as "Captain." So before the end of the 1954–1955 school year, my parents moved their seven children back to New Jersey. There I completed high school, untouched by the *Brown* decision as far as I knew.

From that time onward, however, *Brown* and its progeny, judicial and legislative, had a direct impact on my life: on the fact, for example, that I ever went to college at all, and to law school, in the first years when the principles enunciated in *Brown* prompted colleges and universities to open their doors, and their purses to poor bright black students; on the fact, for example, that President Carter chose me in the late 1970s to fill the "minority" seat at the Federal Communications Commission; on the fact, for example, that I was chosen from among many-score eligible law review editors to serve as a clerk to Chief Justice Warren.

By the time that I took that post in 1967, Earl Warren had finally overshadowed even Willie Mays in my constellation of personal heroes. I recall coming to the job with three very strong impressions about the Chief Justice and his Court.

First, the treatise, to use the term loosely, that had most captured my attention during my first year at the Cornell Law School had to do, not with contracts or torts, but rather with criminal procedure. Authored by the *New York Times* Supreme Court reporter Anthony Lewis, it was entitled *Gideon's Trumpet*. The book recounted how Gideon, an indigent prisoner, with the help of then-practicing attorney Abe Fortas as appointed counsel, had prevailed upon the Supreme Court to extend a constitutional right to counsel to criminal defendants in the state courts. *Gideon v. Wainwright*[2] was authored by Justice Black. Still, for me, it was representative of the insistent drive by the Warren Court to particularize and enforce basic principles of procedural fairness in criminal proceedings.

My constitutional law professor at Cornell, a Southern gentleman who had taught at Tulane for many years, condemned *Gideon* and the other Bill of Rights "incorporation" decisions as usurpations by the Court. Mindful of the Scottsboro boys, however, I considered those decisions to embody a command that the state must play fair with even the least of its citizens whom it would deprive of personal liberty.

My admiration for the principal architect of this not-so-startling concept only grew when, on taking up my duties as law clerk, I realized what a great interest the Chief took in the *in forma pauperis*, or miscellaneous, docket from which many of the landmark criminal procedure rulings came. Based on his long experience in law enforcement in California, as he so often told us, Chief Justice Warren was convinced that the authorities could be *both* effective and fair in enforcing the law. His clerks, among our other duties, would have the important assignment of briefing the miscellaneous docket cases for the entire Court.

The second strong impression that I brought to my clerkship was how simple and direct the Chief Justice could be in conveying an irresistible moral conviction. I had in mind, in particular, the Chief's opinion for the Court in *Sweezy v. New Hampshire*,[3] which I had found to be both irresistible and very moving when I read it in law school.

What is so irresistible about that decision is Mr. Sweezy's statement, set forth verbatim in the margin of the opinion, as to why he could not conscientiously cooperate with an unbridled state-conducted loyalty investigation. Mr. Sweezy's statement, an eloquent peroration on the values underlying the First Amendment, takes up four or five pages, single-spaced, in the Supreme Court's opinion.

A decade later, watching Chief Justice Warren at close quarters, I did not doubt that including Mr. Sweezy's statement of deep moral conviction as an underpinning of *Sweezy v. New Hampshire* was as important to the Chief as the legal analysis contained in the body of the opinion.

But Chief Justice Warren needed no Sweezy to impel him to irresistible moral hyperbole. His decisions rang with imperative declarations:

> Legislators represent people, not trees or acres. Legislators are elected by voters, not farms or cities or economic interests.[4]

> Separate educational facilities are inherently unequal.[5]

My law school professor had contrasted the Court's bold pronouncement in *Brown* with the "fine" opinion of Warren's predecessor, Chief Justice Vinson, for the Court in *Sweatt v. Painter*,[6] describing the earlier decision as appropriately judicious and *Brown* lacking in judicial self restraint.

I believed, and this was my third strong impression, that the Chief had demonstrated great courage in undertaking to move the court the few inches from *Sweatt v. Painter* to *Brown v. Board of Education*. And, I thought, he demonstrated great skill in persuading all the other Justices to join in his opinion for the Court.

So, the man for whom I clerked in 1967–1968 was virtually obsessed by an abiding conviction of the government's obligation to be fair to all of its citizens. He was quick to take the moral high ground, which at times must have been exasperating to his colleagues; once there, he would not be budged. He was also very courageous.

As I saw him, Earl Warren wore these qualities with an ease, an air of modesty and tolerance, that suggested that he had long since found his guiding star in public life and was well satisfied with his place in history.

I embarked on the year as his law clerk feeling woefully unprepared, having taken only the basic constitutional law course at Cornell. Moreover, at twenty-four, I was nearly struck dumb by the awe in which I held the Chief. I mean that quite literally.

One day, after the Chief had returned from his summer travels, his long-time assistant, Mrs. Margaret McHugh, telephoned me to come to his chambers to meet Mrs. Warren. I dutifully went, and nervously mumbled my way through the interview as Mrs. Warren and the Chief tried to put me at ease. And happily did I escape from their presence. Only I had gone through the wrong door and into the Chief's private restroom.

Knowing that if I paused, things could only get worse, I got out of there instantaneously. As I passed through the chambers and fled from their presence again, the Chief holding the *correct* door open, Mrs. Warren gave me a grandmotherly "It's okay" and a pat on the back.

My co-clerks worked on some major opinions that year: *United States v. Robel*,[7] *Terry v. Ohio*,[8] *Flast v. Cohen*.[9] My most difficult assignment was doing the spadework for the Court's attempt—the last one I believe—to rationalize the provisions of the Robinson-Patman Act.[10] Perhaps the most significant item that I worked on was a decision that overruled *McNally v. Hill*,[11] and extended federal habeas corpus review to consecutive criminal sentences to be served in the future.[12]

But the research assignment that received more of my emotional energy, and brought me the most attention from the Chief, was never even argued before the Court. Professor Schwartz alluded to it in his book on the Warren Court.[13]

At Raiford State Prison in Florida, there had been a riot by prisoners. After the authorities regained control, they corralled at least thirteen of the alleged culprits, stripped them naked, and placed them, three to a cell, in seven-foot-by-six-foot holding tanks that were unfurnished except for one hole in the floor that served as a latrine. After two weeks of this treatment, subsisting on "four ounces of soup three times a day and eight ounces of water," each of the alleged rioters was brought, still naked, into an adjoining room, where they each were prevailed upon to sign a written confession to felonious riot. These confessions were used to convict the prisoners in a Florida court, for which convictions they were sentenced to additional time to be served after their prior sentences were completed.

These cases were particularly troubling to Chief Justice Warren. For him, the additional jail time, based upon convictions tainted by coerced confessions, should not have been permitted to stand. For most of the Justices, however, the cases involved internal prison discipline, an area that the Court traditionally shied away from.

The Chief decided to dissent from the Court's refusal to review the cases, and he directed me to draft a short statement. I did a learned research job, I thought, on why internal prison discipline was not at the heart of these cases. But I did not say much about the sordid facts.

The Chief called me to his office and observed that he wanted less analysis and more emphasis on the facts. I tried to comply but I was, frankly, too squeamish. So he called me to his office a third time.

Rising from his chair, he said, "Let's tell them what really happened. Tell them that the authorities placed these men in threes in tiny sweat boxes for two weeks, naked and on a starvation diet with just a hole in the floor to defecate in! Tell them that they brought these men out, still naked, and forced written confessions from them! Tell them that these confessions were used to convict these men of new crimes, that many years were added to the terms they already were serving. Tell them what really happened," said the Chief, "in plain language. Put it in those books," said he, pointing to the bound volumes of *United States Reports* on the shelves in his office, "and let *posterity* decide who was right!"

So that was what we did. After the Chief circulated his dissent from the denial of review, I began to receive reports that other Justices were joining his dissent. Within a week, after the Raiford Prison cases next came up for discussion at the Justices' weekly conference, the Chief told us that *all* the Justices had joined his dissent. It had become a per curiam opinion of the Court, ordering summary reversal, without oral argument, of the tainted convictions.[14]

Within the context of this minor group of cases, I felt that I saw Chief Justice Warren at his most effective—impelled by an offended sense of fairness; unafraid to call a duck a duck, or a coerced confession, in any context, a coerced confession; quick to seize the high moral ground, and to dare his brethren *not* to join him there.

That was the Chief.

Later that year, in a less public context, I obtained another revealing view of him. At one meeting in his office—in the early spring of the year—I told him how much my mother admired him. "Bring her in," he said, "I'd love to meet her." It was a nice gesture, I thought, but there was no way that I would take up his time for a nostalgic meeting, even for my mother.

Well, during the last week of the Term, I received a telephone call from the indomitable Mrs. McHugh. "The Chief says you never brought your mother in. Can you get her here tomorrow?" Certainly I could, and certainly she came, taking the train down from New Jersey, and spending the better part of an hour closeted with the Chief Justice.

I later asked my mother what she and the Chief talked about. "That's between him and me," she said. Their meeting took place in that hectic last week of the term, a few days before Chief Justice Warren announced his resignation.

So, who was Earl Warren? I do not know. I believe he was a man of good cheer and good will all his life.

I agree with those who believe that he was greatly affected by the role that he played, as attorney general and as governor of California, in the sorry affair of the removal of Japanese Americans from the Pacific coast in the early months of World War II.

I believe that he came greatly to regret that role and to regret the part he played in the racial hysteria of that time and place. In my year at the Court, he seemed to have embarked on a course to distinguish out of existence the *Hirabayashi* decision[15] in which the Court had validated the Japanese exclusions.[16]

Earl Warren, I believe, experienced a transformation when, during World War II, he realized how mistaken he had been—that instead of leading the effort to deny Japanese Americans their rights as citizens, he should have been defending those rights. As a result, I believe, Warren experienced a deep personal awakening that was not unlike that experienced nearly two hundred years earlier by a man named John Newton, who became so revolted by his life as a slave ship's captain, that he repented, became a minister in the Church of England, and authored the great Protestant hymn "Amazing Grace."

After the experience with Japanese exclusion, I believe that Earl Warren vowed never again to neglect to consult the compass inside him, his conscience, before playing God with other's lives. He became, I believe, a priest at the altar of equal justice. That became the central core of his jurisprudence. That is why he is my hero.

Certainly, sitting at our luncheon that Saturday after Robert Kennedy died, Chief Justice Warren was devastated by the epidemic of divisiveness and violence that seemed to be on the verge of overwhelming our society. Certainly he was disappointed that his day had come to an end. And he did know, he *told* us, that his era had come to an end. But he was not shattered; he was not demoralized.

When you came by the chambers he occupied as retired Chief Justice in later years, he was as cheerful and sparkle-eyed as ever, surrounded by his beloved *United States Reports*. You could almost hear him saying, "Tell them the truth; tell them what really happened, in plain language. Put it in those books and let *posterity* decide who was right."

Notes

1. Brown v. Board of Education, 347 U.S. 483 (1954).
2. 372 U.S. 335 (1963).
3. 354 U.S. 234 (1957).
4. Reynolds v. Sims, 377 U.S. 533, 562 (1964).
5. Brown v. Board of Education, 347 U.S. at 495.
6. 339 U.S. 629 (1950).
7. 389 U.S. 258 (1967).
8. 392 U.S. 1 (1968).
9. 392 U.S. 83 (1968).
10. FTC v. Fred Meyer, Inc., 390 U.S. 341 (1968).
11. 293 U.S. 121 (1934).
12. Peyton v. Rowe, 391 U.S. 54 (1968)

13. Schwartz, *Super Chief: Earl Warren and His Supreme Court* 719 (1983).

14. Brooks v. Florida, 389 U.S. 413 (1967).

15. Hirabayashi v. United States, 320 U.S. 81 (1943).

16. See, for example, United States v. Robel, 389 U.S. 258 (1967), and Loving v. Virginia, 388 U.S. 1 (1967).

· III ·

A BROADER PERSPECTIVE

· 18 ·

THE WARREN COURT AND THE LEGAL PROFESSION

Shouldering the Responsibility of a Common Law Legal System

GEORGE E. BUSHNELL, JR.

It is both a pleasure and an honor to write this essay on the legacy of what was the most dynamic Court since Chief Justice Marshall's.[1] My role in this volume is to represent the practicing bar and, thus, provide a bit of leavening to this rich mix of academicians, jurists, and skilled observers. Since I do not qualify in any of these categories, I would note, therefore, that for most of us in active practice, the day-to-day impact of the United States Supreme Court—no matter who occupies the Chief Justice's chair—is somewhat less than overwhelming. There are, of course, the exceptions when a particular decision is relevant to the matter or case at hand.

However, even for us "on the street," the Court—each Court—creates a legal environment in which the practicing lawyer functions and which affects our representation of our clients and their causes.

And it is in that context that the practicing bar views the Warren Court. For, as we all recognize, the influence of that Court continues to be profound.

Having said all that, let me dare to sound a somewhat discordant note. The fact of the matter is that the Warren Court's legacy—or to put it more accurately, our misuse of that rich legacy—has a dark side. It is one little recognized. But it is one that I submit presents American society with an imposing challenge as the twentieth century approaches its close.

The ability of the Warren Court, through its employment of a common law approach to constitutional analysis, to resolve certain seemingly unresolvable social problems confronting America gave us great hope. But at the same time, that heritage has tempted us into shirking our responsibility as a society to resolve matters through other means and in other nonjudicial arenas. The Warren Court's record of accomplishment has lulled us into an unrealistic view of the efficacy of our justice system to treat, and in fact to cure, any societal ill. Indeed, Americans now consider our justice system to be a black box into which *any* social problem can be placed and, by the mere act of placing, be resolved.

The result? Our legal system, which should properly be viewed as the last resort in the affairs of this nation, has instead increasingly become the first resort. Because of that phenomenon all of us have a duty to rethink and reshape our approach to the myriad perplexing problems that confront us as a nation.

How then do we meet our responsibility to use wisely the common law legal system that the Warren Court bequeathed to us? Having put the question, this effort does not presume to answer it. In part because a full answer to the question could easily itself occupy a volume. In part, it is because I simply do not have a complete answer. (But I do take comfort in the fact that no one does.) However, to obtain any worthwhile answer, one must first pose the right question. Therefore, I trust that the posing of this question is in itself worthwhile to do. And I am prepared to offer a methodology by which to determine an answer. To wit: The Bar, organized and individually, must shoulder a large share of responsibility by assuming a leadership role in the debate that must ensue.

Before going further, having posited a dark side to the Warren Court's achievements, I feel obliged to emphasize that I am by no means a complete apostate. To the contrary, I consider myself a true believer in the legal revolution wrought by Warren and his colleagues. When *Brown v. Board of Education*[2] was decided, I had been called to the bar but three years. Like most of my contemporaries who lived through the Warren revolution, I could not help but be inspired by the Court's ability to cut a swath through the strangling undergrowth of constitutional jurisprudence—making straight, if you will, a highway from where America, as a practical reality, stood to where America, as a political ideal, should be. I was in equal parts astonished, heartened, and energized.

Indeed, the peculiar genius of the Warren Court lay in its ability to solve intractable social and political problems—problems that seemed to have no legal solution either, by virtue of stultifying precedent or by our reluctance to face reality. As commentators have noted, Warren and the Court did so through the rejection of traditional Frankfurtian jurisprudence, which valued strict analytical reasoning from precedent and other accepted sources above all else,[3] and which needlessly hamstrung the Court in the face of manifest and palpable injustice. Instead, Warren and a majority of his Court embraced a common law approach to deciding cases, one that emphasized experience,[4] fairness, and equality.[5]

Such an approach did more than merely shape the resolution of issues that heretofore had defied all attempts to impose political or legal solutions; it enabled the Court to resolve—and to resolve justly—such issues in the first instance.[6] A review of what one commentator[7] has termed the Court's three most important decisions[8]—*Miranda*,[9] *Reynolds*,[10] and *Brown*[11]—demonstrates this point.

In *Miranda*, Warren's experience as a former prosecutor as well as the record before him established that, in the 1960s, police officers routinely used psychological, if not physical, coercion to secure statements from suspects.[12] It was no doubt beyond the reach of the political system in 1966[13]—as, for that matter, it would be today—to end such unfair practices.[14] The Chief Justice ignored traditional reasoning and sources in *Miranda* to remedy this manifest injustice, finding that the general language of the Fifth and Sixth Amendments required an unprecedented series of warnings.[15]

In *Reynolds v. Sims*,[16] in which the Court required the reapportionment of a state legislature, Warren was clearly motivated by common law concerns centering on the unfairness and inequality created by a system that gave more weight to the votes of rural citizens than to urban and suburban residents.[17] Reapportionment was not achievable by those same legislatures for the obvious reason that a vote for reform was, for many legislators, a vote for political suicide.[18] Ignoring precedent, legislative history, and indeed the literal language of the Constitution, Warren did justice through the principle of one person, one vote.[19]

Finally, in *Brown v. Board of Education*,[20] the Court, of course, did away with that particular institution's peculiar legacy, segregation. This result, while morally imperative, was, obviously, politically impossible in the white legislatures of the South. The Court was greatly influenced by the sociological effects of the segregation of Negro school children, which it found rendered a separate but "equal" school system inherently unequal. Ignoring the stuff of traditional jurisprudence—precedent, legislative history, and the will of the state and local legislative bodies—the Court found the Equal Protection Clause to have been violated.[21]

Again and again, the Warren Court boldly settled issues that had found their way to the Court because of the failure of the political process to provide a just resolution. These were issues that impacted the life of the entire nation.[22] The Warren Court's record marks the first time in our history that the Court assumed such a role in such a complete way. Granted, certain past cases had had a similar impact—cases like *Plessy v. Ferguson*,[23] the *Dred Scott* decision,[24] *Marbury v. Madison*,[25] and so on. But these decisions were merely isolated events in the life of the Court over the preceding century and a half. Under Warren, such sweeping decisions became almost a commonplace.

Beyond question, the Warren Court's dynamic approach and dramatic results forever changed America's view of the role of the courts in particular and the legal system in general.[26] Where previously courts were perceived primarily as fora for the adjudication of rights between private parties, they now routinely came to be seen as the engine of change for all manner of social problems affecting not simply individual persons and entities, but entire segments of society: for example, African Americans, urban populations, and criminal suspects.

Much of what resulted was unmitigated good. For example, if Americans as a people were ever to be fully roused from the lingering nightmare of slavery, *Brown v. Board of Education* was imperative. In addition, besides the substance of the Court's rulings, the mere fact that our legal system provided a broad, new avenue of progress on so many issues was profoundly energizing. A generation of Americans, especially women and minorities, were inspired to embark on a great rush to the nation's law schools. They sought, by becoming lawyers, to themselves become instruments of hope.

Unfortunately—and this is the point—we have allowed the Warren Court's legacy to become tarnished. Indeed, we have allowed it to be tarnished in a manner that the Warren Court certainly never desired and likely never even contemplated. The simple truth is that the common law approach that the Warren Court championed is a powerful and efficacious tool used correctly. But that very power and efficacy tempts misuse as well.

We, as a people, have been tempted. And we, as a people, have succumbed. We have begun to expect our justice system to resolve every troublesome issue, every nettlesome question that we, as a society, confront. As a result, we have unthinkingly bound over to the courts an ever-growing number of social problems, restyled as legal issues. We do so with a naive belief that the courts, as a sort of magic box for social problems, can solve these issues.[27] We do so with relief that, at a minimum, recasting a problem as a legal issue ostensibly frees us from any responsibility toward resolving it. Indeed, I do not think it an exaggeration to say that Americans now routinely commend to the courts the thorniest social problems of our times. In so doing, we declare them, if not solved, at least adequately addressed.

Let me be clear about what I am and am not saying. I have not written this essay to tell you that the Warren Court's jurisprudence and practical results were not correct and were not morally imperative. On the contrary, I believe—fervently—that they were. Moreover, the perversion of what should be the rightful legacy of that Court is certainly not one that can be laid at the feet of the Chief Justice whom we both honor and analyze in this volume. Rather, those who have broken faith are our politicians, our society, and, indeed, ourselves.

Whether the issue be social, economic, criminal, family, or health, Americans and America's leaders now routinely seek to shirk our responsibility to attempt to resolve America's problems by legislative and executive means; rather, we pass them off to the judiciary. And we—all of us—are parties to this abdication of responsibility.

To illustrate this point, consider the issues with which we now grapple. Many of us perceive the level of violence in our nation to be one of the greatest problems our society faces. The response of most of our political leaders is not to address and treat the root causes of violence through social service and other agencies. The response has not been to consider what makes eleven-year-olds capable of murder. Rather, the response has been to divert the problem of violence to the courts through so-called tough, antiviolence crime legislation that judicially processes and locks up those who act violently, but does not seek ways to prevent the violence in the first place.

Many Americans remain greatly concerned about the scourge of drugs in America. Our greatest efforts on that score have been on the law enforcement front—interdiction, mandatory sentencing for offenders, the death penalty for drug kingpins, and so on. The prospect of legalization of drugs so that our efforts can be focused on treatment and prevention is rarely mentioned and nowhere practiced. Law enforcement and referral to the courts are easier than attempting to understand and eradicate the causes of drug abuse. Tough talk on crime attracts more votes than proposing that we create enough hospital beds to treat what is in large measure a medical issue.

With respect to health issues, many of those problems are turned into legal matters. To give one example, the issue of what sort of experimental medical treatments[28] should be available to our citizens is not determined by legislative or executive actions. Instead, to date we have been content to let those matters be resolved by lawsuits brought by individuals against their health care insurers.

Complicated issues of family life such as difficult custody questions are today within the exclusive purview of the courts. We might well ask ourselves whether the adversarial court system is in fact the best way to resolve the already traumatic problems facing so many families in our family courts. But we do not even seriously consider nonjudicial approaches to this problem.

While I could go on at length, I trust my point is clear. We have turned over to the courts many, many other issues. We have done so in the belief—or at least the hope—that the courts will be able to solve what society cannot because society lacks the necessary solution, resolution, or consensus to act. And that, I put to you, is the "dark side" of the Warren Court.

I submit that much of what I have cited in the preceding categories is not what courts are for. The underlying causes of these problems are often complicated, nuance-laden tangles that require patience, trial and error, and a long-term approach to resolve. Even with respect to the issues I have just addressed that are appropriately matters for the court—for example, family matters—certainly the legal system was never meant to resolve these issues in the first instance.

Rather, courts should not be the first resort. They must be the last resort. The justice system should be turned to only when nonlegal approaches have been tried and found wanting.

This is where we find ourselves twenty-five years after Chief Justice Warren left the bench. When we look back at that Court from a vantage point of a quarter-century, we look back at a Court that fashioned and bequeathed to us a common law legal system carried to perhaps its farthest boundaries. I submit to you that it is a potent legal system that we have not yet learned how to use. Perhaps more to the point, it is a legal system that we must learn how not to abuse.

As I have argued, the legacy of the Warren Court today is twofold: hope and responsibility. The Warren Court's record of doing justice continues to inspire. Its legacy, secured by a common law approach that, above all else, values and advances notions of fairness and equality is an abiding trust that our justice system stands ready, as a *last resort*, to protect and vindicate rights.

But we must not forget that we have an obligation to use this common law system responsibly. We must not misuse the system by employing it to resolve every problem that we face. We must not. For the simple reason that the justice system is an inappropriate repository for these matters. Nor may we allow our elected leaders to misuse the legal system in the hopes that the consignment of an issue thereto absolves them of the failure to resolve it themselves.

To date, we have roundly failed in this responsibility. Time does not permit a thorough discussion of the possible solutions to this problem. I am compelled to confess, as I did at the beginning, that I do not know what the proper solutions are.

But let me identify one segment of our society that, by its silence, is conspicuously absent in this struggle. As President of the American Bar Association, I must ask, where has the Bar been? Our profession should be the first on the barricades defending our justice system from those politicians and demagogues who would abuse it—from those who would use it to shield their own inability to address the most pressing problems of our time. There have been a few lonely voices among us raised: for example, the various senior federal judges who have refused to hear drug cases because of the unconscionable mandatory sentences required.[29] But by and large, lawyers have abandoned the field and have allowed society and our political leadership to misuse the justice system as they see fit.

Our voice in this debate has been stilled. Worse, we are the ones who have stilled it. If America's lawyers are to play a role in ensuring that our society forges real answers—not mere political solutions—to the social problems that plague us, we as a profession must find our voice again. Indeed, it is not hyperbolic to say that, if we are to save our justice system from the disaster toward which, overburdened and underfunded, it is slowly but surely slouching, we must resume our place in the debate.

It is therefore incumbent upon the legal profession to return to leadership in the field it has abandoned.

It is incumbent upon the legal profession to defend the justice system against those who would abuse it.

It is incumbent upon the legal profession to educate the public as to the use and misuse of our justice system.

In short, it is incumbent upon the legal profession to impress upon America that, despite the sweeping achievements of the Warren Court, our legal system is not omnipotent, nor was it meant to be.

Twenty-five years later, then, the challenge posed by the Warren Court to the legal profession is the same challenge that it poses to America in general: use the common law system the Warren Court forged with wisdom, with restraint, and without illusion.

Notes

1. Lewis, "Earl Warren," in *The Warren Court: A Critical Analysis* vii (Sayler, Boyer, and Gooding eds., 1969). Another commentator has more sweepingly opined that it was "[u]nquestionably the most activist, law-changing Court in the nation's history. . . ." Rice, *The Warren Court* x (1986).

2. 347 U.S. 483 (1954).

3. White, "Earl Warren's Influence on the Warren Court," in *The Warren Court in Historical and Political Perspective* 39 (Tushnet ed., 1993).

4. As Holmes put it in his famous aphorism, "the life of the law has not been logic, it has been experience." Holmes, *The Common Law* 1 (1881). Soon-to-be Justice Abe Fortas, arguing for the petitioner in *Gideon v. Wainwright*, described it more colorfully as "the realities of what happens downstairs," i.e., in the trenches of state criminal courts. See oral argument in Gideon, 372 U.S. 335 (1963) in *May It Please the Court* 188 (Irons and Guitton eds., 1993).

5. See, e.g., Lewis, supra note 1, at 6–7 (observing that Warren "seemed often in his opinions to merge technical issues that had traditionally been fought over in civil liberties cases into larger questions of fairness"). To Warren's mind, no other approach discharged the Court's highest duty: to vindicate constitutional rights. As he put it in *Miranda*, "As courts have been presented with the need to enforce constitutional rights, they have found the means of doing so." Miranda v. Arizona, 384 U.S. 436, 490 (1966). The common law approach similarly was compatible with Warren's view of the Constitution as an evolving document. In his words, "[O]ur contemplation cannot be only of what has been but of what may be. Under any other rule a constitution['s] general principles would have little value and be converted by precedent into impotent and lifeless formulas." *Miranda*, 384 U.S. at 443 (quoting Weems v. United States, 217 U.S. 349, 373 (1910)).

6. See Tushnet, "The Warren Court as History" in Tushnet, supra note 3; White, supra note 3.

7. White, supra note 3, at 40.

8. Interestingly, Warren himself identified *Brown*, Baker v. Carr, 369 U.S. 186 (1962) and Gideon v. Wainwright, 372 U.S. 335 (1963) as the three most important opinions of his Court during his tenure. Friedman, "The Warren Court: An Editorial Preface," in Sayler, Boyer, and Gooding eds., supra note 1, at vii.

9. Miranda v. Arizona, 384 U.S. 436 (1966).

10. Reynolds v. Sims, 377 U.S. 533 (1964).

11. 347 U.S. 483 (1954).

12. E.g., *Miranda*, 384 U.S. at 444–56. That Warren was mindful of his past experience and concerned about the realities of state criminal practice was evident at oral argument in criminal cases as well. See oral argument in Gideon v. Wainwright, 372 U.S. 335 (1963) in Irons and Guitton eds., supra note 4, at 191. The judging of Justice Hugo Black, also a former state prosecutor, was similarly informed. Id. at 193. The experience of other law enforcement agencies with the use of warnings was also important to the justices. See Schwartz, *Super Chief: Earl Warren and His Supreme Court—A Judicial Biography* 589 (1983).

13. The Warren Court apparently had little faith in the legislatures' ability to resolve this matter. Indeed, the Court declined the suggestion raised by certain respondents in *Miranda* to withhold decision on the issues presented until state legislatures could address them, 384 U.S. at 490.

14. Little has changed. Just imagine if you will the political debate that would take place in 1995 over *Miranda* if such warnings were not constitutionally mandated. Can anyone doubt that our political leaders, in a race to prove themselves the toughest on crime, would attempt to one-up each other by depriving suspects of their rights not only to *Miranda* warnings, but to the underlying rights *Miranda* protects by permitting unlimited questioning without counsel? Indeed, polls of Americans themselves reveal that they are willing to surrender numerous constitutional rights to fight crime.

15. White, supra note 3, at 40–41.

16. 377 U.S. 533 (1964).

17. E.g., *Reynolds*, 377 U.S. at 561–71, 576, 580.

18. Chief Justice Warren acknowledged the impossibility of a political solution in *Reynolds*, observing the inactivity with respect to reapportionment in Alabama over the preceding sixty years and the rural "minority strangle hold on the State Legislature." 377 U.S. at 569–70. See also oral argument in Baker v. Carr, 369 U.S. 186 (1962) in Irons and Guitton eds., supra note 4, at 10, 14. See also Lewis, supra note 1, at 10–11.

19. White, supra note 3, at 40–41.

20. 347 U.S. 483 (1954).

21. White, supra note 3, at 40–41. See Schwartz, supra note 12, at 87.

22. Warren was by no means oblivious to the political difficulties of the Court's action under his leadership. As he observed in Reynolds, "We are cautioned about the dangers of entering into political thickets and mathematical quagmires. Our answer is this: a denial of constitutionally protected rights demands judicial protection; our oath and our office require no less of us." 377 U.S. at 566.

23. 163 U.S. 537 (1896).

24. Scott v. Sandford, 19 How. 393 (U.S. 1857).

25. 1 Cranch 137 (U.S. 1803).

26. Keeva, "Demanding More Justice," 80 *A.B.A. J.* 46, 48–49 (1994) ("I think

that in *Brown v. Board of Education* you have *the* turning point in terms of people's conception of what the law can do. . . . Where medieval societies had morality plays, we have *Brown*.") (quoting University of Virginia law professor A. E. Dick Howard).

27. As Leah Sears-Collins, an associate justice of the Georgia Supreme Court, has put it, Americans view "[t]he law [as] a great panacea, it opens things up and cures all social evil. . . . But not everything can be done in the courts." Quoted in Keeva, supra note 26, at 49.

28. E.g., bone marrow transplants to treat breast cancer patients.

29. E.g., Senior United States District Judge Jack B. Weinstein of the Eastern District of New York. See Reske, "Senior Judge Declines Drug Cases," 79 *A.B.A. J.* 22 (1993).

19

THE WARREN COURT IN HISTORICAL PERSPECTIVE

KERMIT L. HALL

The Revisionists' Attack on Liberal Instrumentalism

Woody Allen once observed that "relationships are like sharks: they either move forward or they die."[1] Much the same can be said about scholars of the Supreme Court: they either revise received wisdom or they perish. There are no good insights, only new insights. The passage of time usually exacerbates this phenomenon, often to the point of making well-intentioned prevaricators out of even the most skilled revisionist scholars. As the past recedes, we too often begin to believe that what was really was not, only to discover, upon reflection at anniversaries such as this one marking the quarter-century since Earl Warren's retirement, that it really was.

This practice of creative interpretation has become pronounced in the scholarship treating the Warren Court. President Richard Nixon understood the Court and the political stakes created by its work better than many scholars do today. Nixon exclaimed repeatedly in the course of the 1968 campaign that the Court's decisions had, in his words, "gone too far in weakening the peace forces as against the criminal forces of this country."[2] Nixon promised to select only strict constructionists, Justices who would stop the coddling of criminals, restore the proper place of the states in the federal system, and promote respect for family values. Yet today we seem to have forgotten Nixon's simple lesson. We have so disentangled the Warren Court and its jurisprudence from their historical contexts that we fail to appreciate that Court's singular place in the American constitutional experience.

The traditional, consensus approach to the Warren Court, like Nixon, took the Justices' liberalism seriously. Scholars such as Martin Shapiro, Robert Dahl, Anthony Lewis, Archibald Cox, Bernard Schwartz, and G. Edward White, while addressing the Warren Court in somewhat different ways, nonetheless concluded that it was instrumental in its aims, policy-making in its decisions, and committed to enhancing the rights of historically underepresented groups.[3] This liberal, instrumental interpretation held that the Warren Court shared a general commitment to social ends such as efficiency, humanitarianism, equality of economic opportunity, and equal treatment before the law. According to this interpretation, the Warren Court was an engine of modern liberal reform powered by a substantive jurisprudence that stressed results and gave only modest attention to *polity* principles.

Three schools of revisionist scholarship have sharply challenged this liberal-instrumentalist view. Conservatives argue that political bias and problematic scholarship characterized the Warren Court. Garry McDowell and Raoul Berger, among others, condemn Warren and his colleagues for faulty constitutional reasoning, a muddled reading of the founding generation and its fidelity to the Constitution, and usurpation of legislative authority.[4] The conservatives agree with the liberals that the Warren Court was instrumental, but they insist that this instrumentalism had ruinous results, both in terms of public policy and the authority of the Court. The Justices, according to these scholars, ran amuck in their own liberalism and welfare-statism.

A second body of scholars, the so-called civic republicans, view the Warren Court from a perspective at once sympathetic with yet critical of the Justices. Michael Perry, Mark Tushnet, and Sanford Levinson, for example, while differing on the particulars, agree that there is no necessary connection between constitutional choices and good moral values, and that each choice, therefore, must be analyzed with regard to moral theory and outcomes.[5] This view holds that politics and law should not be based on raw power and preferential self-interest; instead, it posits that both should respond to and protect the public good.

The civic republicans take exception to the level of success achieved by the Court and to the grounds upon which the liberal majority rested its position. If anything, the Warren Court acted *too* instrumentally, failing to anchor its policy positions in concern about the common good and in exalting individual rights at the expense of community interests. The Warren Court erred because it presumed to do those things in politics that its power, and the power of any judicial body, could never reach legitimately. According to the civic republicans, the appropriate means of social transformation resides in the political branches, not in the courts.

A third revisionist interpretation not only blends elements of the other two, but succeeds in standing the Warren Court on its head in doing so. This "constitutive" interpretation asserts, with a remarkable historical flourish all too familiar in much of the scholarship dealing with modern constitutional jurisprudence, that "[i]t is important to note that the Warren Court's genius was not of its own making."[6] Ronald Kahn, for example, argues that the Warren Court was neither concerned with rights nor due process; instead, its approach was "constitutive," not "instrumental." The Justices of the Warren Court well understood the limits of their powers and realized that their most important task was to find the best way to constitute the political and legal communities, to take doctrinal debates seriously, and to disregard the pressure of the ballot box for such change. The Warren Court, it turns out, really was not politically motivated; instead, it was overwhelmingly a legal institution, one in which the rule of law—the Constitution, precedents, and fundamental rights and legal principles—influenced judicial decision making. The Warren Court fashioned only modest adjustments in the constitutional landscape and its most important contributions were only fully realized under the leadership of Warren's successor, Warren Burger. The constitutive interpretation, by focusing so fully on constitutional theory and jurisprudence, drains the Warren Court of life.

These revisionist interpretations tend to diminish the Warren Court's stature and to deny the singular nature of social and political change in the 1950s and sixties. They rob the Warren Court of either its legitimacy or its energy, and in some cases both. Kahn, for example, tells us that in the past quarter-century life has become more complex, leaving a sense that the Warren Court in some ways faced a challenge less daunting than does our own time. The conservatives crudely argue bad faith and a lack of principle on the part of the Justices. The civic republicans admire the Warren Court's efforts but find it unable to offer a coherent theory of constitutional politics.

No doubt each of these views has some merit, yet each of them makes the Warren Court something less than the major historical force it was. On this twenty-fifth anniversary of Earl Warren's retirement, it seems appropriate to shift our attention from matters of theory and jurisprudence and recall what the Warren Court did—to put it in historical perspective. One of the best ways to do so is by listening to the times *and* heeding what contemporary critics of the Justices, like Richard Nixon, had to say.

The Warren Court in the History of the Court

Perhaps nowhere is such an approach more important than on the simple question of whether the Warren Court really existed. A good number of revisionist scholars apparently have doubts. Some scholars have not only questioned the proposition that there was, but concluded that naming Supreme Court epochs after Chief Justices is problematic at best and misleading at worst. There has often been considerable overlap in the Associate Justices on the Court even after the Chief leaves the bench. More than seventy percent of all Associate Justices appointed to the High Court outlast the Chief Justice serving at the time of their appointment. That was certainly the case with the Warren Court; of the eight Associates appointed during Warren's term, only one, Charles Whittaker, left before Warren's retirement. Two leading scholars take the position that the Warren Court should be called the Brennan Court. Dennis Hutchinson argues that "to the extent that the Court over which Warren presided has any intellectual legacy that is accessible to those trained in doctrine and not in ethics, it is Brennan who is responsible." Robert Post has proposed that the Warren years really should be called the "Brennan Court" era, since Associate Justice William Brennan, who only missed participating in one landmark decision (*Brown v. Board of Education* (1954)), outlived Warren and was the most effective banner carrier for liberal jurisprudence from the 1960s to the early 1990s.[7]

Some Chief Justices have not stayed long enough to have much of an impact on the Court. Such was certainly the case with John Jay, John Rutlege, and Oliver Ellsworth early in the history of the Court; the same was true with Harlan Fiske Stone and Fred Vinson. Chief Justices can also stay too long; their influence becomes diminished when transformations in the political culture bring appointees to the Court either not of the same political generation nor of the same ideological views as the chief. Both John Marshall and his successor, Roger B. Taney, faced similar fates, as Andrew Jackson in the case of the former and Abraham Lincoln in the case of the latter placed members on the High Court whose views were radically at odds with the Chief's. At the time of their deaths, both Marshall and Taney had essentially lost control of their respective Courts.[8] Both of these Chief Justices served more than double Warren's sixteen years on the bench.

Warren's term as Chief Justice was about average and, even more important, he had enormous good luck in the way that appointments fell during his time on the bench. Within three years of taking on the position of Chief Justice, the composition of the Court had undergone radical change. Four of the Associate Justices (Stanley Reed, Robert H. Jackson, Harold H. Burton, and Sherman Minton) left. Either President Franklin D. Roosevelt or President Harry Truman appointed all of these Justices. None of them, with the exception of Jackson, was much of a force on the Court. Their replacements were not only more talented jurists but political moderates of a comparable if not quite similar ideological stripe to Warren.[9]

This ideological continuity was a central feature of the Warren Court, and its presence, along with Warren's leadership, helped to define the era. Republican President Dwight Eisenhower made four appointments to the bench in addition to Warren. He selected John Marshall Harlan III in 1955, William J. Brennan, Jr., in 1956, Charles Whittaker in 1957, and Potter Stewart in 1958. Only Harlan and Stewart emerged as anything like the representative voice of the constituency that elected Ike. Brennan became an important liberal voice on the Court; Whittaker served only four years. His replacement was Byron White, one of President Kennedy's two appointments to the High Court. Eisenhower concluded that in the cases of Warren and Brennan he had made his two biggest political mistakes. Even Harlan was a moderate conservative. The other appointees were all selected by Democratic presidents and the major holdovers—Hugo Black, William O. Douglas, and Felix Frankfurter—were selected by Democratic President Franklin D. Roosevelt. In short, there was a strong ideological predisposition in favor of liberal instrumentalism that came to typify the Warren Court.[10]

Warren's contribution to the Court was his ability to lead this liberal majority toward important changes in public policy. If he had not done so, then the case for the Warren Court would be less persuasive. His biographer, G. Edward White, has explained that Warren succeeded through his leadership in investing "his Court with a discernible character, if not necessarily a coherent jurisprudence."[11]

Scholars today disagree about what attributes contribute to the success of a Chief Justice.[12] Some argue that technical proficiency in the law is more important than a result orientation. For example, many students of the high Court believe Charles Evans Hughes was the greatest Chief Justice of the twentieth century because he commanded his colleagues by force of intellect and technical legal ability. Justice William O. Douglas concluded that in sheer legal talent "Warren was closer to Hughes than any others. Burger was closer to Vinson. Stone was somewhere in between."[13] Hughes, however, exercised that leadership through a photographic memory, authoritative demeanor, and personal charisma. Hughes, according to Stone, conducted conferences "much like a drill sergeant."[14]

Warren shaped and defined his Court in an entirely different way. His style was reminiscent of John Marshall, who depended on charm, an even temperament, an ability to have others warm to him, and on a vision of the Court's role.[15]

Warren, however, was not a legal scholar; he was a former governor and district attorney. He was a politician, a big bear of man with great personal charm. Justice Potter Stewart once commented, "We all loved him."[16]

Warren also possessed great self-confidence. Initially, he relied on this quality to compensate for his lack of experience with the High Court and it served him well throughout his tenure, especially in dealing with Felix Frankfurter who tried and ultimately failed to bring Warren under his influence. Warren turned Frankfurter's imperious style to his advantage by successfully building strong personal relations with the other Justices, most notably William J. Brennan.[17] Warren was smart enough to understand that he and Brennan shared similar views on important matters; that together they were likely to build the level of support necessary to reach those goals on the High Court. Commentators today, who concentrate on Brennan's twenty-year career after Warren retired, tend to read too much into the relationship when the two of them were on the Court together.[18] Like Brennan, Warren shared a result-oriented view of the Court's business.

Warren left his mark on the Court in other ways. In managing the case load, for example, he concentrated on forging majorities, and to do that he successfully directed the energy that came from the clash of competing jurisprudential attitudes wrapped up in strong personalities such as Felix Frankfurter, Douglas, and Hugo Black.

Because the Court had a liberal majority, it did not follow that the Justices readily agreed with one another. To the contrary, dissent rates continued the steady rise that had begun during the Chief Justiceship of Harlan Fiske Stone.[19] There was no intellectual leader on the Warren Court, we should remember; instead, several strong figures (Black, Douglas, Frankfurter, Harlan, and Goldberg) stood in uneasy coexistence. Warren's challenge was to mold this talented but frequently quarrelsome group.

Warren did so through his power to assign opinions. "During all the years," Warren observed in retirement, "I never had any of the Justices urge me to give them opinions to write, nor did I have anyone object to any opinions that I assigned to him or anyone else."[20]

Warren made his Court work through consultation and an even-handed distribution of opinion writing. Unlike John Marshall, who dominated his brethren through force of opinions, Warren led through collaboration.[21] Nowhere was the success of this approach more apparent than in *Baker v. Carr* (1962), a decision that Warren believed to be more important than any other taken during his time on the Court. The opinion was written by Justice Brennan, but had Warren's influence stamped all over it. Moreover, Warren assigned the opinion to Brennan because he was urged to do so by Black and Douglas, both of whom believed that Brennan's views were closer to those of Potter Stewart, the necessary fifth vote for a majority.[22]

When placed in historical perspective, Warren emerges as perhaps the most persuasive and persistent Chief Justice the Court has ever had. Warren was not a great lawyer in the mold of Taney or Hughes, not a great legal scholar like Brandeis or Frankfurter, not a supreme stylist like Cardozo or Jackson, not a judicial philosopher like Holmes or Black, not a resourceful, efficient administrator like Taft or Burger. Nonetheless, he was the most important presence on the Court from 1953 to 1969; that is why it is fair to call the Court of this period after him. He was second in institutional leadership only to Marshall, at least as measured by impartial critics of the Court.[23] As Henry Abraham has written, Warren "was his court, *the* judicial activist court."[24]

If it is fair to claim the existence of the Warren Court, then it is also appropriate to note that, like other eras of the Court's history, the Warren period had its own phases. There were, in fact, two Warren Courts. During the first, from 1953 and 1962, the Court did not have a major public presence, with the notable exception of *Brown v. Board of Education* (1954, 1955). In those years an imperfect match existed between the public perception of the Warren Court as liberal, largely because of its decisions in race-related cases, and the day-to-day reality. The Court Warren inherited from Fred Vinson at the beginning of the 1953 term was not liberal in the realm of civil liberties. The early Warren Court was indifferent to the rights of the accused in state courts and inconsistent in its protection of First Amendment rights.[25] Moreover, not until the 1961 term did the Court begin to take such matters seriously.[26] From 1953 to 1961 the Court's percentage of liberal civil rights and liberties decisions ranged from a low of forty-seven (1953) to a high of sixty-two (1954). Following the 1960 term, in which fifty-four percent of these cases were decided liberally, the proportion jumped to eighty percent in the 1961 term and remained in the seventies or above for six of the remaining seven years of the Warren Court.

This dramatic shift in the early 1960s is almost universally recognized, but explanations vary about why it occurred. The conventional wisdom ascribes the shift to the appointment of Goldberg at the beginning of the 1962 term.[27] The major changes in the Court's direction came because of the incapacity suffered by Justice Frankfurter as a result of a stroke and the mid-term retirement of Justice Whittaker, both developments that shifted influence to Justice Stewart.[28]

After the 1962 term, the Warren Court emerged as the powerful institution of liberal change against which Nixon and others railed. The Court routinely took a strong liberal position in eighty percent of civil liberties cases.[29]

The Warren Court was distinctive in another way. The majority of its Justices invariably adopted innovative approaches to major constitutional controversies. Warren and at least four other of his colleagues, Douglas, Brennan, Fortas, and Thurgood Marshall, had little sustained interest in general matters of constitutional theory. Such behavior, while not unique, certainly stood out from the practices of the nineteenth century, when Justices such as Joseph Story, Joseph Bradley, and Stephen J. Field persisted in a long-standing quest to rationalize the Court's actions with those of acceptable constitutional theory. The Warren Court Justices were remarkable for their lack of concern about the era's main currents of constitutional thought. Warren did not agree, he wrote in his memoirs, "with the so-called doctrine of 'neutral principles.' It . . . is a fantasy," he continued, "and is used more to avoid responsibilities than to meet them. As the defender of the Constitution, the Court cannot be neutral."[30] The great controversy over incorporation, which brewed throughout the Warren Court era, was evidence enough of precisely that lack of concern.[31] In this setting, the role of a Justice was to figure out the right answer, as a matter of public necessity and not some abstract theory of justice. Underlying this approach was the belief that the Constitution was a living document, and that the Justices had a responsibility to facilitate its evolution and development.[32] Such a view set the Warren majority in sharp contrast with its predecessors, especially those eras of the Court's history that had stressed their formalist role. At the same time, the Warren Court was also notable because it managed to shift the emphasis in the developmental character of the Constitution to one that stressed individual rights.

Like Courts of other eras, the Warren Court had a reciprocal and reinforcing relationship with its own times. It reflected much of the sympathies of the New Dealers; and its liberal policies extended beyond the period of Earl Warren's Chief Justiceship. Still, there was without a doubt a Warren Court, an identifiable judicial entity of which we can make sense and which was distinctive in the overall history of the Supreme Court.

The Warren Court and Its Times

Throughout American history, constitutional law has developed in constantly changing dialogue between the Court and the country, and the Warren Court was no exception. For example, the Warren Court did not discover the issue of race and its pernicious effects on American life. That matter had been part of the original constitutional understanding, an understanding that earlier Justices had enforced by countenancing first slavery and then, following the Civil War, a system of de jure segregation. By the 1930s, however, the Court had begun the tortured process of reexamining its previous decisions in this area, not so much because it wished to do so but because the newly created National Association for the Advancement of Colored People pressed it to do so. To that extent, the Warren Court's great decision in *Brown v. Board of Education* (1954, 1955) built upon and expanded a line of constitutional development begun much earlier.[33] At the same time, it contributed to the constitutional elaboration of race issues during the remainder of the Warren Court and beyond. Much the same can be said in other areas of constitutional law, notably the rights of the accused, First Amendment free expression and religion cases, and the development of the idea that the political thicket was, in the end, not nearly as thorny as previous Courts had believed. Each of these areas of major Warren Court constitutional development had been cultivated by earlier Courts and, once treated by Warren and his colleagues, contributed to developments in American society.

To recognize that the Warren Court built on the work of its predecessors merely underscores that it is in such ways that the Court works. The Warren Court stood out, however, because in each of these areas it brought about a resolution of existing law that was at once transformative and liberating.

In an era in which political outsiders pressed their case with more energy than ever before, the Warren Court responded. Doing so made it distinctive in the history of the Court and for the first and only time the Justices empathized with the social and political outsiders. The Court, of course, has had a long history of protecting minority rights, but in most instances that protection has been aimed at property rather than human rights. In this way, the Warren Court was notable, because it concluded that discrimination was not a random, individualized act but a governmentally supported set of social preferences structured along cultural lines. Warren and his liberal colleagues were eager to attack the concept of state action through the incorporation doctrine because they realized that by doing so they held the power to redefine political and social relationships in favor of those who had previously been disadvantaged.

The Warren Court was very much *in*, not outside the stream of history, as some revisionist scholars are prone to argue. The Justices operated in a political culture in which big government had been accepted, indeed embraced. To suggest that this environment was in any meaningful way less complex and demanding than our own so woefully misses the point as to trivialize much contemporary history. The rise of legislative and executive power over economic matters was one of the enduring legacies of the New Deal, a legacy that remains firmly in place today and that shaped the actions of not only Warren but those of his colleagues and the litigants that appeared before them. It is also the source of much that is perplexing in modern economic life.

President Franklin Roosevelt's shock treatment in the Court-packing plan left little doubt that the Justices no longer had broad support to intervene in economic matters. It was a lesson learned by successor Courts, especially that over which Warren presided. Between 1953 and 1969 the Court did not declare a single piece of federal legislation regulating property unconstitutional and it invalidated only a few state laws regulating industry and providing welfare programs as interferences with contract or property rights. While revisionists such as Kahn have made it fashionable to believe that the High Court does not read the election returns, there is ample evidence that the post–New Deal Courts, including that of Earl Warren, had no interest in refighting the battle of property rights, since that battle had been conceded to the legislative branch and the administrative state.[34]

The Warren Court, however, was a product of its time, just as were previous Courts. What was embarrassingly obvious was that economic security, at least the level of security envisioned by the New Deal, was overoptimistic. The problem of raising the level of political and social rights, however, required an effort similar to that made by the federal government in securing economic rights. It also presented an entirely different and in many ways more complicated problem than revisionists admit, given the nation's prevailing class and race relations. Where government had exercised its authority in the past, it had done so in a way to promote differences and discrimination, whether through segregation, the poll tax, state-sanctioned religious practices, or limits on speech and press. At the time of the Warren Court, these practices were deeply embedded and entirely supportive of the existing political and social order. The quest to enhance social and political rights was a uniquely judicial and legal task, since the existing centers of political and social power were unlikely, without some pressure, to change their behavior. The Warren Court responded to this challenge by clearing out a legal thicket of archaic interpretations that were simply not going to be swept away through elected democratic practices.

In retrospect, conservative critics of the Warren Court argue that it should not have done what it did because it usurped power either from the other branches or from state and local governments.[35] Yet here again the Warren Court Justices inherited an institutional legacy that encouraged them to embrace controversial issues that could not find resolution elsewhere in the governmental structure.[36] Previous Courts had been disposed more often than not to resolve such matters in favor of property rights and community rather than individual interests. For example, meaningful racial integration of public schools and other public facilities could not be achieved without removing the standing gloss of "separate but equal" on the Equal Protection Clause of the Fourteenth Amendment.[37] Congress had great difficulty accepting the limited civil rights measures proposed by the Truman administration, none of which even came close to addressing the issue of segregation. Neither was Congress likely to strike down local laws designed to muzzle protestors seeking a new level of individual rights nor address, under the First Amendment, protection for religious minorities. The literal wording of the First Amendment made clear that Congress was explicitly prohibited from doing so. There was no way under existing political arrangements that Congress was going to break the long-standing practice of rural domination of state legislatures. As a matter of constitutional law and practice, crime control and policing had historically been left to state and especially local officials. Practices varied widely from state to state, and more often than not varied in quality within these areas based on the races of the victims and the accused.

Perhaps as important, the Court was operating within the structure of its own constitutional purposes. Revisionists have fastened on the Warren era as the most blatant example of runaway judicial activism. The result, they insist, was the rise of an imperial judiciary.

Yet the Court had historically performed the role of construing established statutes and legal language in the context of both initial meaning, or what's called today original intent, and current societal demands. The results were simply different in the Warren era. When, for example, Chief Justice Roger B. Taney and his colleagues decided in *Dred Scott* that no person of African American heritage could be a citizen of the United States, they were greeted with a uniform chorus of condemnation by Abraham Lincoln and the Republican party for usurping power through judicial lawmaking.[38] Many more Democrats, however, applauded Taney's boldness. Hence, the Warren Court was able to move legitimately toward assuring the values of equality, fairness, natural justice, and morality in individual and public relationships because the history of the Court had long since established that it could do so.

Warren and the majority of the Court also took seriously the duty imposed on them by their oath of office to "administer justice without respect to persons, and do equal right to the poor and to the rich."[39] Such a position, however, stirred one or another group to condemn most of the Court's landmark decisions. These changes in the direction of the Warren Court were important, and they belie the notions put forth by some that, on balance, the Warren Court was not really liberal at all or, at the same time, that it had, to use the phrase of Senator Harry Byrd of Virginia "usurped authority to which it is not entitled and is not serving the best interests of our nation."[40] First its critics and then many scholars have made a caricature of the High Court.

In the wake of *Engle v. Vitale* (1962), for example, Representative George W. Andrews of Alabama asserted: "They put the Negroes in the schools and now they have driven God out."[41] Representative L. Mendell Rivers of South Carolina asserted that as a result of *Engle* the Court "had now officially declared its disbelief in God."[42]

These protests seem not to have fazed Warren and his colleagues. Legal scholars particularly have given so much attention to the jurisprudential workings of the Warren Court that they have often missed the obvious literal-mindedness and courage of the liberal majority and especially of its Chief Justice. America had historically professed ideals of equality, fairness, and justice. Why shouldn't such ideals be supported in constitutional law and through the actions of the Supreme Court? "So many times in life," Warren wrote, "the only permanent satisfaction one can find comes from bucking an adverse tide or swimming upstream to reach a goal."[43] While some scholars have perhaps gone too far in arguing that the Warren Court was committed to a scheme of equitable jurisprudence, there is little doubt that the Warren Court majority believed that early generations of Americans had, at best, given lip service to these concepts and that it was appropriate, at this juncture in the nation's history, for the Justices to end the process by which such ideals had been compromised, qualified, and even destroyed.[44] In many ways, this strain of Warren Court commitment—to the reconciliation of professed values with behavior—did more than anything else to stir the ire of its critics, many of whom believed that they were being blamed for having benefited from such hypocrisy. The Court's actions placed it squarely at odds with one of the central contradictions of the American experience, one too often ignored.[45] The majority of Americans had come to embrace the contradiction between theory and practice in many areas of life. In responding to this contradiction the High Court initiated an extended educational dialogue with the American public about the extent of Justices' responsibility to first recognize and then resolve this tension.

The Warren Court's revolution in public law promoted acrimony and bitterness precisely because it empowered those who had previously not had the opportunity to exercise power. Whether we approve of their behavior or not, there is little doubt that these new groups added dramatically and often disturbingly to the contours of American society. Much of what the Warren Court did was to release dissident minorities from long-standing legal and social strictures. Critics complained that the Court was the root of the problem; it was fostering subversive action by civil rights advocates, Communist agitators, criminals, smut peddlers, and racketeers who hid behind the Fifth Amendment when called to account.

One of the more interesting yet unexplored issues involving the Warren Court was the extent to which the Justices themselves appreciated the consequences of their actions. While we can dress up the Court's actions by analyzing the Justices as either interpretivists or nonintepretivists, as originalists or nonoriginalists, or as advocates of constitutive or polity theories of governance, the inescapable fact is that they knew what they wanted and, often times, if they did not exactly achieve it they came very close. In the case of *New York Times v. Sullivan* (1964), Hugo Black asked the counsel for three white city commissioners from Montgomery, Alabama, if he could seriously argue that a newspaper advertisement by the supporters of Martin Luther King, Jr., that called into question Lester B. Sullivan's public conduct would actually hurt him with his all-white political supporters.[46]

Nor was Warren so naive as to believe that what he and his colleagues wanted could be accomplished without controversy. "Every man who has sat on the Court," Warren wrote in retirement, "must have known at the time he took office that there always has been and in all probability always will be controversy surrounding that body." "Accordingly," Warren continued, "I venture to express the hope that the Court's decisions always will be controversial, because it is human nature for the dominant group in a nation to keep pressing for further domination, and unless the Court has the fiber to accord justice to the weakest member of society, regardless of the pressure brought upon it, we never can achieve our goal of 'life, liberty and the pursuit of happiness' for everyone."[47] A goal, of course, articulated in the Declaration of Independence and not the Constitution.

The constitutional revolution unleashed by the Court created serious problems, ones echoed in today's debates about the High Court. The exercise of judicial power to achieve social goals opened the Court to charges that it departed from its traditional role and became primarily a legislative body. In essence, so the charge went, the unelected Justices substituted their views for those of elected and therefore properly representative legislators. Such an argument misses the point that all of these issues were quite beyond the grasp, either by law or by force of will, of the political branches of government.

Yet the Warren Court *was* often on shaky ground when it attempted to justify what it was doing. The great English legal historian Sir William Holdsworth once wrote that "for certainty in the law, a little bad history is not too high a price to pay."[48] Warren and his colleagues perhaps too frequently followed Holdsworth's advice. The Justices were wildly bad historians, so misreading the historical record on such matters as freedom of conscience and race relations as to call into question the very soundness of their approach to these matters. Even worse, the Justices frequently ended up arguing the fine points of history with one another and, in the process, adding to the sense of illegitimacy that accompanied several of their boldest pronouncements.[49] They were no worse than their predecessors in using history, just more persistently bad at doing so.

The arguments among the Justices about history easily spilled over into serious disagreements about the nature of the judicial process and the scope of judicial review. We are prone today to minimize the sharp debates between Black and Frankfurter over judicial activism and judicial restraint, doing so in favor of seemingly more sophisticated ideas such as originalism, noninterpretivisim, and constitutive jurisprudence.[50] Throughout the 1960s a majority of the Warren Court supported judicial activism, even to the point that the activists had themselves come to disagree about what it was they could and could not do. The decision of President Lyndon Johnson to replace retiring Chief Justice Warren with Abe Fortas only underscored the extent to which the Court had moved toward an activist role that included direct involvement by Fortas in the day-to-day business of the White House while he was a sitting Justice.[51]

Still, a critical minority on the bench, led by Justice Harlan, complained repeatedly that his brethren acted far beyond the traditional and understood boundaries set for Justices in our constitutional system. Harlan was explicit in warning that recent history demonstrated the virtues of judicial restraint. The Supreme Court before 1937, Harlan and others argued, demonstrated repeatedly what the Justices should not do: interfere in areas that were properly not theirs to begin with.

Even more fundamental to this critique was the view that such interference actually sapped the democratic process of its vitality. It bred a sense of distrust in popular elected forms of government while placing too much trust in a judiciary that lacked the means even to command obedience to its decisions and that made its decisions in secret.[52] Felix Frankfurter explained in his dissent in *Baker v. Carr* (1962) that "[d]isregard of inherent limits in the effective exercise of the Court's 'judicial power' may well impair the Court's position as the ultimate organ of 'the supreme Law of the land' in that vast range of legal problems, often strongly entangled in popular feeling, on which this Court must pronounce."[53] Justice Harlan added a note in taking exception to the Court's later decision in *Reynolds v. Sims* that introduced the concept of "one person, one vote." "These decisions," Harlan wrote, "give support to a current mistaken view of the Constitution and the constitutional function of this Court. This view, in a nutshell, is that every major social ill in this country can find its cure in some constitutional 'principle,' and that this Court should 'take the lead' in promoting reform when other branches of government fail to act."[54] Earlier Chief Justice Harlan Fiske Stone and Justice Robert H. Jackson had warned against the Court taking on too great a role. Jackson summed the matter up neatly by observing that a "4,000 word eighteenth-century document or its nineteenth-century amendments" could not provide "some clear bulwark against all dangers and evils that today beset us internally."[55]

Faced with this attack, the majority on the Warren Court found it necessary to offer a different explanation of its actions. Chief Justice Warren, for example, insisted that the Court merely acted at the call of those parties bringing cases before it. "There are many people, and I fear some lawyers, who believe that whenever the Court disapproves of some facets of American life, it reaches out and decides the question in accordance with its desires. We can reach for no cases. They come to us in the normal course of events or we have no jurisdiction."[56] Justices Black and Douglas made clear, as well, that they were not going to be bound by precedent, and their attitude toward it fostered even more contention. In the case of *Gideon v. Wainwright* (1963), for example, Harlan pleaded with the majority, which included Black and Frankfurter, that by refusing to abide by precedent the Court refused to recognize that in most matters it was more important that the applicable rule of law be settled than that it be settled right.[57]

The Warren Court had little difficulty finding new areas to explore. To many of Warren's critics, his belief that the Court merely waited for cases to come to it was disingenuous. After all, the Warren Court revolution was not just substantive; it was procedural as well. The Justices loosened significantly such historical limitations on access to it as standing to sue, and, perhaps most dramatically in *Baker v. Carr* (1962), political questions.[58] Placed against this background, the Warren Court majority went well beyond simply responding to the wishes of the litigants.

Warren's argument nonetheless fitted the new reality of the 1950s and sixties. The Warren Court benefited from a long-term development in which it emerged as the agency most likely to afford protection to minorities that could find no other avenue. Special-interest group litigation predated the Warren Court by at least fifty years, but it matured during the 1950s and 1960s. One of the important historical developments of the first half of the twentieth century was the rise of so-called special-interest litigation groups that expected through the judicial process to accomplish goals that were otherwise out of reach to them through the political process, susceptible as it was to prevailing shifts in public sentiment. The American Civil Liberties Union, the NAACP, the National Lawyers Guild, the National Organization of Women, and various left-wing religious, labor, and ethnic organizations brought test cases designed purposefully to challenge what they believed were impediments to certain individual freedoms and civil rights.[59] Even the Department of Justice, which had pursued civil rights issues infrequently since Reconstruction, began during the Kennedy and especially the Johnson administrations to press these matters before the federal courts. Moreover, these groups gathered additional incentives with the passage of major legislation, much of it prompted by the actions of the Court itself in the area of civil rights and voting rights in particular. As judicial activism triumphed on the Court in the 1960s, more and more groups turned to the Justices for solutions. In the area of criminal justice the Warren Court's decisions extending the right to counsel and providing greater scrutiny of the major elements of criminal justice practice resulted in additional litigation before the Court, litigation that forced the Justices to further explain and expand the rationale for controversial landmark decisions.[60]

The Court's activism was both grist for the growing media and a pressure on the Court itself. The Warren Court, we should recall, was the first modern Court in the sense of having its work broadly evaluated for the public and, at the same time, in bringing a sense of humanity and approachability to the institution. Press coverage of the Court soared in the wake of *Brown* and it never came down. The Court became headline news; it was a subject for nightly reporting on recently created television evening news. Even Justices Black and Douglas agreed to be interviewed at length about their views on the Constitution. Through books, magazines, newspapers, radio, and television the Warren Court was presented to the world for evaluation and, depending on where one sat on the issue, either praise or condemnation in a way that no previous Court had experienced. The new light of publicity only amplified the already controversial nature of the Court's work.

Measuring public reaction to the Court during these years is difficult. Yet certain themes do emerge. First, over time the American public has held the institution of the Court in generally high regard, embracing the need for the Justices at a level of unvarnished understanding that accepts their role without necessarily being able to explain it. The Warren Court inherited a public attitude toward the Court that was framed, at least in part, by the notion that the Justices in the 1920s and 1930s had been biased toward special privilege and vested interests and unwilling to cooperate with Congress during the New Deal to restore economic prosperity. The Court's "switch in time that saved nine" in 1937 began a long-term process of changing such attitudes among the citizenry that the Court could be helpful in providing relief from the pressing problems of modern society. Significant parts of the Court's behavior received strong, but not necessarily uniform, support. The decisions involving equal justice for African Americans in *Brown* and the sit-in decisions received popular responses, and there was support for the extension of counsel to indigents, the curtailment of excessive search and seizure and the invasion of privacy, and for the end of rural domination of state legislatures.[61]

Perhaps as much as any time in the nation's history, however, controversy and not consensus usually characterized reaction to the Warren Court. In 1968, as the stewardship of Warren drew to a close, the Gallup Poll asked Americans to rate the Supreme Court. The response indicated considerable skepticism: eight percent responded excellent; twenty-eight percent, good; thirty-two percent, fair; and twenty-one percent, poor.[62] The Court was most strongly supported among the young and the well educated; it was most opposed in the South, where its decisions, from race relations to free press to reapportionment, had the greatest impact.[63]

These numbers testify to the continuing suspicion on the part of many Americans about the proper functioning of the Court. Rather than being a force of stability, the Court had become such a powerful instrument of change that it threatened the social fabric.[64] While some of the Warren Court's holdings did receive support, many more of its landmark rulings produced real hostility, disobedience, and even calls for the impeachment of some of the Justices, including Warren. Particularly controversial were the Court's holdings in school prayer cases, pro-Communist speech and protest decisions, its obscenity rulings, and many of its criminal procedure rulings, particularly those that granted new protections to the accused and were, as a result, portrayed as coddling the criminal element. To many Americans, the nation seemed to be unraveling, and the Court seemingly contributed to that process.[65] While the Justices crafted constitutional decisions that opened the political and social systems, protest over civil rights, major urban rioting, and, by the end of Warren's tenure, dissent against the Vietnam War contributed to the unsettling of American society. The marketplace of ideas, some thought, had become a free-for-all in which obscene and libelous statements had crowded out civility, decency, and respect for authority.[66]

Moreover, liberal goals came to be mixed with notions of moral corruption, even depravity. Hence, war protestors and pornographers were lumped together as part of the problem of modern American culture, a problem seemingly sponsored by a latitudinarian Supreme Court.

Mobilization against the Warren Court was quite impressive, especially since Americans have repeatedly accorded the Court great respect even as they have taken often bitter exception to decisions that affect their lives. The Warren Court was no exception.[67]

Criticism of the Justices reached its crescendo in the nomination hearings of Associate Justice Abe Fortas to replace Warren. Senator Strom Thurmond of South Carolina asked Fortas in the course of the hearings to justify more than fifty cases decided by the Court involving the rights of the accused and obscenity that covered the entire course of the Warren Court era.[68] Fortas ultimately withdrew from consideration amid disclosures of conflict of interest. Fortas's life seemed to the

Court's critics an affirmation of the inherent corruption associated with liberal instrumental activism.

Similar resistance came from many state and local officials. Especially in the area of criminal justice procedure, the Warren Court's seemingly radical pronouncements often elevated into national constitutional protections practices that were already well established in the states.[69] In other instances, however, the innovation by the Justices stirred protest from below. Many state political leaders, and not all of them in the South, believed that the Court had become too involved in monitoring their historic functions in areas including voting practices, apportionment, racial segregation, education, censorship, loyalty, and welfare programs. State judicial leaders also expressed their dismay at the Court's criminal justice rulings. The Conference of State Chief Justices in 1958 passed a resolution blasting the Warren Court's "policy making" and proclaiming that "strong state and local governments are essential to the effective function of the American system of federal government."[70] Four years later the annual meeting of the Council of State Governments adopted a proposal for "returning the Constitution to the states and the people."[71] That proposal included a plan for the creation through a constitutional amendment of a "Court of the Union," comprised of the fifty state chief justices, to review the work of the Supreme Court.

Even the American Bar Association, itself an aggregation of local and state bars, contributed to the attack on the High Court. The ABA's house of delegates refused to endorse the active support given by the Warren Court to sustaining the Bill of Rights, an action that prompted Warren's quiet resignation from that organization.[72]

The political right wing took aim at the Chief Justice and his brethren. The John Birch Society in the late 1950s launched a nationwide campaign to stir popular support for the impeachment of the Chief Justice, a campaign that included billboards sprinkled across the American countryside that simply proclaimed: "Impeach Earl Warren." The Society even sponsored a high school essay contest with an award to the best paper on the subject: "Grounds for the Impeachment of Earl Warren."[73] The Texas millionaire H. L. Hunt used his fortune to sponsor radio and televisions programs that attacked the Chief Justice and Associate Justice William O. Douglas. The most extreme demands were registered by Fulton Lewis, Jr., and retired Marine Colonel Mitchell Paige, both of whom proposed before public audiences that Warren should be hanged.[74]

In Historical Perspective

Current fashion among many Warren Court scholars holds that its Justices did less than we would have supposed, that in the end it was little different from either its successors or predecessors, and that what achievements it did earn turn out not to have been as significant as once believed. Hence, it is now stylish to think of the Burger Court as an extension of the Warren Court and in so doing to denigrate the achievements of the latter. Other commentators have suggested that, in the end, the Court was hypocritical; it did not go as far as it could have in such crucial areas as race relations and gender discrimination. In the former it accepted only "all deliberate speed" and in the latter it simply ignored obvious discrimination against women. Indeed, there is now an effort to demonstrate that Warren and his colleagues really were not politically motivated, that they did not take big risks, and that they were confused in their agenda. There are no *good* insights, we are once again reminded, only *new* insights.

Sometimes simple lessons are the most difficult to grasp. The current wave of revisionism surrounding the Warren Court has missed the essential historical point that its liberal majority was important because it had the courage to be in tension with the dominant political culture. The Warren Court was historically significant not just for what it did, which was substantial, but for reaffirming that the Justices could help to shape public policy and that their role in doing so was appropriate and constitutionally defensible, even if it was not popular. At the same time, the approach to judging adopted by the majority of the Justices did break historically from the pretense that judges merely judge and the associated idea that law is an autonomous profession. The Warren Court disrupted the prevailing consensus that the goals of law were to train professionals in analytical reasoning that was to be applied in narrow ways to appellate opinions. The Court, according to the older view, was important, not because it made policy, but because it imposed certain institutional and doctrinal restraints on the political branches through precedent and a close reading of the Constitution. The Warren Court Justices had another goal. They were willing to turn to extralegal materials, as was the case in footnote 11 of *Brown*, to usher in, according to G. Edward White, the first stirring of the "law and" movement.[75]

The High Court became a place where practical politics, social scientific learning, and morality were viewed as quite comfortably fused in Supreme Court decisions as never before.

What the Warren Court did was to reintroduce political culture into mainstream constitutional discourse, something that had not been present so significantly since the debate over slavery in the Taney Court of the mid-nineteenth century. Since the Warren Court it has been impossible to separate social domination from political domination in matters of constitutional debate.[76] Warren and his colleagues brought a pragmatic focus to American constitutional law, one that has surely altered it for years to come.

With the retirement of Warren an era certainly did come to an end, in large measure because the Chief Justice, in his unassuming but persistent ways, had managed to become the symbol of it. Much like the period following the death of John Marshall, an era of unprecedented general judicial assertion of power came to an end. That is not to say, of course, that the jurisprudence of the Warren era ended, which is an entirely different manner. Chief Justice Warren Burger was, in this regard, something of a disappointment to those conservatives who expected a sharp turn to the jurisprudential right. The Warren Court holdovers, most notably Douglas, Brennan, and Marshall, were usually able to get the fourth, fifth, and often sixth vote to maintain and, in some instances, actually expand liberal decisions of the Warren era.

We should in all matters of historical interpretation respect the obvious at the same time we doubt it. To borrow a phrase from the current student vernacular, all of the heavy lifting was done in the Warren era. One of the Warren Court's most important achievements was the acknowledgment of concrete human realities and the qualities of empathy, compassion, and justice as central to constitutional decision making. That was new in the American constitutional tradition. The legacy of the Warren Court, therefore, was not simply in the case law that it propounded, some of which has been narrowed although none of it abandoned, but in the general approach that it took toward judging, the judicial process, and the role of the Court in opening to many new groups the promise of American life.

Like sharks, scholars have no choice but to move forward. Hegel was right; there is a scholarly dialectic. But in pursuing that dialectic, we should at least honor the past on its own terms. If we do so, then we will appreciate that the Warren Court, when placed in historical perspective, is and will continue to be, the ghost present at the constitutional banquet served each year beginning on the first Monday in October.

Notes

1. *Annie Hall* (United Artists 1977).
2. As quoted in Dunne, *Hugo Black and the Judicial Revolution* 409 (1977).
3. Shapiro, *Law and Politics in the Supreme Court* (1964); Shapiro, "The Supreme Court and Economic Rights," in *Essays on the Constitution of the United States* (Harmon ed., 1977); Shapiro, *Judicial Activism, in America in the Twenty-First Century* (Lipset ed., 1979); Shapiro, "The Supreme Court from Warren to Burger" in *The New American Political System* (King ed., 1978); Shapiro, "Fathers and Sons: The Court, the Commentators and the Search for Values," in *The Burger Court: The Counter-Revolution That Wasn't* (Blasi ed., 1983); Dahl, "Decision Making in a Democracy: The Supreme Court as a National Policy-Maker," 6 *J. Pub. L.* 279 (1957); Lewis, "Earl Warren," in 4 Friedman and Israel, *The Justices of the United States Supreme Court* (1969); Lewis, *Gideon's Trumpet* (1964); Lewis, *Make No Law* (1991); Cox, *The Warren Court* (1968); Cox, *The Role of the Supreme Court in American Government* (1976); Schwartz, *Super Chief Earl Warren and His Supreme Court—A Judicial Biography* (1983); White, *Earl Warren: A Public Life* (1982).
4. McDowell, *The Constitution and Contemporary Constitutional Theory* (1985); Berger, *Government by Judiciary* (1977).
5. Perry, *Morality, Politics and Law* (1988); Tushnet, *Red, White and Blue: A Critical Analysis of Constitutional Law* (1988); Levinson, *Constitutional Faith* (1988).
6. Kahn, *The Supreme Court and Constitutional Theory* (1994).
7. Hutchinson, "Hail to the Chief: Earl Warren and the Supreme Court," 81 *Mich. L. Rev.* 922, 924 (1983); Post, "Justice William J. Brennan and the Warren Court," 8 *Const. Commentary* 11 (1991), republished in *The Warren Court in Historical and Political Perspective* 123 (Tushnet ed., 1993).
8. The best historical discussion of the office of Chief Justice is contained in Steamer, *Chief Justice* 219–57 (1986). Concerning the effect of a too-long tenure on Marshall and Taney see Newmyer, *The Supreme Court under Marshall and Taney* 26, 89 (1968) and Schwartz, supra note 3, at 68, 149.
9. Abraham, *Justices and Presidents* 251–95 (3d ed. 1992).
10. Id. There was greater ideological continuity on the Warren Court than under Burger, although they shared many of the same values. Schwartz, *A History of the*

Supreme Court 331 (1993); Blasi, "The Rootless Activism of the Burger Court," in *The Burger Court* (Blasi ed., 1983).

11. White, *The American Judicial Tradition* 318 (1976).

12. O'Brien, *Storm Center: The Supreme Court in American Politics* 186–89 (1986).

13. Id. at 186.

14. Id. at 187.

15. White, *The Marshall Court and Cultural Change* 365–75 (1988).

16. As quoted in O'Brien, supra note 12, at 188.

17. Warren took to the practice of consulting with Brennan on the Thursday preceding the Friday conference. Id.

18. White, "Earl Warren's Influence on the Supreme Court," in Tushnet ed., supra note 7, at 37, 46. The case for Brennan's role is made most forcefully by Hutchinson and Post, supra note 7.

19. Dixon, "On the Mysterious Decline of Consensual Norms in the United States Supreme Court," 50 *J. Pol.* 361 (1988).

20. O'Brien, supra note 12, at 247.

21. Newmyer, supra note 8, at 24.

22. O'Brien, supra note 12, at 247.

23. Blaustein and Mersky, *The First One Hundred Justices* (1978); Abraham, supra note 9, at 259.

24. Abraham, supra note 9, at 259.

25. See, for example, the Court's decisions in Breithaupt v. Abram, 352 U.S. 432 (1957); Watkins v. United States, 354 U.S. 178 (1957) and Barenblatt v. United States, 360 U.S. 109 (1959).

26. Segal and Spaeth, "Decisional Trends on the Warren and Burger Courts: Results from the Supreme Court Data Base Project," 73 *Judicature* 103, 104 (1989).

27. Id. at 104 n.6.

28. Id. at 104.

29. Id.

30. Warren, *The Memoirs of Earl Warren* 332–33 (1977).

31. Tushnet, "The Warren Court as History," in Tushnet ed., supra note 7, at 18.

32. Horwitz, "The Warren Court and the Pursuit of Justice," 50 *Wash. and Lee L. Rev.* 5 (1993).

33. Missouri *ex rel* Gaines v. Canada, 305 U.S. 337 (1938) (denial of admission to law school); Mitchell v. United States, 313 U.S. 80 (1941) (exclusion from pullman berth); Shelley v. Kraemer, 334 U.S. 1 (1948) (restrictive covenant); Henderson v. United States 339 U.S. 816 (1950) (exclusion from railroad dining car); Sweatt v. Painter, 339 U.S. 629 (1950) (segregated law school); McLaurin v. Oklahoma State Regents, 339 U.S. 637 (1950) (segregated graduate school); Brown v. Board of Education, 347 U.S. 483 (1954) and 349 U.S. 294 (1955).

34. Murphy, *The Constitution in Crisis Times, 1918–1969*, at 459 (1972).

36. Supra note 4. Warren was quick to dump cold water on the notion that the Justices did the bidding of the public. "Every man on the Court must choose for himself which course he should take. . . . To habitually ride the crests of the waves through the constantly recurring storms that arise in a free government, always agreeing with the dominant interests, would be a serene way of life. As tempting as that might be, I could not go that way." Warren, supra note 30, at 332.

36. Funston, "The Supreme Court and Critical Elections," 69 *Am. Pol. Sci. Rev.* 795 (1975); and Lasser, The *Limits of Judicial Powers* (1988).

37. Plessy v. Ferguson, 163 U.S. 537 (1896).

39. Scott v. Sandford, 60 U.S. 393 (1857); Fehrenbacher, *The* Dred Scott *Case: Its Significance in American Law and Politics* (1978) and Hyman and Weicek, *Equal Justice Under Law: Constitutional Development, 1835–1875,* at 190–92, 196–97 (1982).

39. Warren, supra note 30, at 332.

40. "Southern Declaration on Integration," March 12, 1956, reprinted in *American Legal History: Cases and Materials* 514–15 (Hall et al. eds., 1991).

41. Quoted in Pfeffer, *This Honorable Court* 421 (1965).

42. Id. at 422.

43. Warren, supra note 30, at 332.

44. Hoffer, *The Law's Conscience* 2–6 (1990).

45. Murphy, supra note 34, at 462–63.

46. Lewis, *Make No Law*, supra note 3, at 151.

47. Warren, supra note 30, at 334–35.

48. Holdsworth, *Essays in Law and History* 24 (1946).

49. See, for example, the debate between Justices Frankfurter and Black over religion in Engel v. Vitale, 370 U.S. 421 (1962); and Miller, *The Supreme Court and the Uses of History* 100–48 (1969).

50. Supra notes 3, 4, 5, and 6.

51. O'Brien, supra note 12, at 125–33; Kalman, *Abe Fortas* 310–18 (1991); *The Oxford Companion to the Supreme Court of the United States* 270–73 (Hall ed., 1992.)

52. Yarbrough, *John Marshall Harlan* 149–53 (1992).

53. Baker v. Carr, 369 U.S. 186, 267 (1962).

54. Reynolds v. Sims, 377 U.S. 533, 620 (1964).

55. Jackson, *The Supreme Court in the American System of Government* 57–58 (1955).

56. As quoted in Katcher, *Earl Warren: A Political Biography* 452 (1967).

57. While Harlan was willing to overrule precedent, he believed it deserved at least a decent burial especially from members of the Court who were not present when it had been established. Gideon v. Wainwright, 372 U.S. 335, 349 (1963).

58. Flast v. Cohen, 392 U.S. 83 (1968) (standing); Baker v. Carr, 369 U.S. 186 (1962).

59. Cortner, *The Supreme Court and the Second Bill of Rights* 282 (1981).

60. Escobedo v. Illinois, 378 U.S. 478 (1964); Miranda v. Arizona, 387 U.S. 486 (1966); *In Re* Gault, 387 U.S. 1 (1967).

61. See Mitau, *Decade of Decision: The Supreme Court and the Constitutional Revolution, 1954–1964* (1967).

62. *New York Times,* July 10, 1968, at A19.

63. Id.

64. Supra note 4.

65. Matusow, *The Unraveling of America: A History of Liberalism in the 1960s* (1984).

66. New York Times v. Sullivan, 376 U.S. 254 (1964); Hall, "Justice Brennan and Cultural History: *New York Times v. Sullivan* and Its Times," 27 *Cal. W. L. Rev.* 339 (1990–91).

67. For example, following the Court's decision in *Brown,* most of the Southern members of Congress issued a "manifesto" denouncing the decision and the Court. The remedy, according to Southerners, was to limit the jurisdiction of the Court, an old chestnut regularly wheeled out against the Justices. In 1957 Senator William Jenner of Indiana introduced during the later stages of the debate over the 1957 Civil Rights Act an omnibus anti-Court bill "to limit the appellate jurisdiction of the Supreme Court in

certain cases." Jenner claimed that "by a process of attrition and accession, the extreme liberal wing of the Court has become a majority; and we witness today the spectacle of a Court constantly changing the law, and even changing the meaning of the Constitution, in an apparent determination to make the law of the land what the Court thinks it should be." So serious was the threat to the Court, that Senator Jacob Javits of New York, a liberal, proposed a law to prevent Congress from interfering with the Court's appellate jurisdiction. Neither measure passed; nor did other efforts by Congressman Howard Smith of Virginia and Senator John M. Butler of South Carolina to limit other parts of the Court's jurisdiction with regard to criminal justice procedures and the ability of the Court to review state legislation, including segregation measures. 103 *Cong. Rec.* 12,806 (1957); 105 *Cong. Rec.* 2996–97 (1958); Murphy, supra note 34, at 332–33.

68. 24 *Cong. Q. Almanac* 531 (1968).

69. Mapp v. Ohio, 367 U.S. 643 (1961); Miranda v. Arizona, 387 U.S. 83 (1966); Gideon v. Wainwright, 372 U.S. 335 (1972).

70. As quoted in Murphy, supra note 34, at 477.

71. Id. at 478.

72. Warren, supra note 30, at 321–31.

73. Murphy, supra note 34, at 482.

74. Katcher, supra note 56, at 3.

75. White, supra note 18, at 49.

76. Horwitz, "The Warren Court: Rediscovering the Link Between Law and Culture," 55 *U. Chi. L. Rev.* 450, 455 (1988).

• 20 •

THE WARREN COURT AND STATE CONSTITUTIONAL LAW

JAMES G. EXUM, JR.
LOUIS D. BILIONIS

I

It has been said that the Supreme Court does best when it remembers that encouraging other institutions to reform is preferable to commanding them to do so. Indeed, the most formidable critics of the Court under Earl Warren—represented by jurists like Felix Frankfurter, John Marshall Harlan, and Henry Friendly,[1] and scholars like Herbert Wechsler,[2] Henry Hart,[3] Alexander Bickel,[4] and Philip Kurland—questioned whether the Court failed to heed that admonition. Professor Kurland summarized the objection succinctly in his Cooley Lectures delivered at the University of Michigan in 1969, just as the curtain was going down on the Warren era. (In a fashion characteristic of the objectors, he would enlist one of the patron saints of judicial self-restraint for support.) "Most important of the Court's major failings," Professor Kurland said, "has been its unwillingness to accommodate to Mr. Justice Brandeis's wisdom uttered in another context: A judge 'may advise; he may persuade; but he may not command or coerce. He does coerce when without convincing the judgment he overcomes the will by the weight of authority.' The Supreme Court, too, cannot compel; it must convince. For its strength ultimately depends on the support of public opinion. . . ."[5] All too often, Professor Kurland concluded, the Warren Court's opinions "tended toward fiat rather than reason."[6] "From now on," he advised, "it must seek to persuade rather than coerce."[7]

Twenty-five years have passed since Earl Warren's retirement. Two decades have passed since the consolidation of the Burger Court and the last of the epic Warren-style decisions, *Roe v. Wade*[8] and *Furman v. Georgia*.[9] Events have unfolded, developments have ensued, and threads that link our present to our past have begun to emerge. While it may be premature to claim a historian's ideal perspective on the Warren Court,[10] the passage of time has left us today with matters to ponder that were unknown a quarter-century ago and with enough detachment to consider them with some dispassion. It thus seems profitable to ask whether the Warren Court was a better persuader than its contemporaries could have realized at the time.

In the celebrated resurgence of state constitutional law that our nation is now witnessing—a development no observer was anticipating during the Warren Court years—there is reason to think the answer is yes.

II

To be sure, state constitutional law existed long before the Warren Court. Written state constitutions predated the federal Constitution, the earliest of them having been ratified by citizens of the original colonies just before and immediately after the signing of the Declaration of Independence.[11] The early state constitutions heavily influenced the framers of the federal Constitution who convened in Philadelphia,[12] and public satisfaction with the protection that state constitutions afforded civil liberties proved instrumental in the adoption of the Bill of Rights.[13] Before the Constitutional Convention of 1787, state constitutions also had provided the stage for judicial review's debut in America, establishing precedent for the judicial invalidation of a legislative act that would shape Chief Justice Marshall's thinking in *Marbury v. Madison*[14] nearly sixteen years later. From then on, throughout the nineteenth and early twentieth centuries, many interesting examples of constitutional adjudication arose under those state charters.[15]

State constitutional law continued to advance in important ways even as the Warren Court went about the innovational work that some feared would quell any urges to develop the law at the state level.[16] The American people were rather busily engaging their state constitutions during Earl Warren's tenure, approving literally hundreds of amendments to them[17]—carrying on the long (and to this day continued) American tradition of state constitutional amendment and revision. (It is a tradition, some suggest, which casts doubt on the claims of state constitutions as enduring sources of fundamental values.)[18] During the Warren years, there also were significant judicial decisions based upon state constitutions, not all of them dealing with the details of state and local government that are unique to those state charters. In several cases, for instance, state courts employed their constitutions to maintain a vigorous judicial scrutiny over governmental acts that unduly hindered the economic liberty of the citizenry,[19] thereby filling a void created by the United States Supreme Court's wholesale retreat from the field in 1937.

Nonetheless, state constitutional law is now burgeoning in a way wholly unforeseen during the Warren Court years. Today, state courts are identifying dimensions of liberty under their state constitutions which, twenty-five years ago, no one would have thought to lie within the purview of these documents. More remarkable still, state courts today are frequently interpreting their constitutions to extend protections to individual liberties that exceed those afforded by the post-Warren Court's decisions under the federal constitution. One scholar's count, as of 1988, reported more than four hundred such cases.[20]

This renaissance of state constitutional law has generated an extensive literature.[21] To fully appreciate the phenomenon, however—and to explore its relationship to the Warren Court—it is helpful to focus briefly on the wide range of activity that is taking place.

Recall the late 1950s and the turbulent days following *Brown v. Board of*

Education[22] and *Cooper v. Aaron*[23]—days when it was fair to wonder whether state officials would meet the Warren Court's call for an end to racial segregation in public education with anything other than massive resistance. Who then would have had the prescience to predict that state courts in Texas and elsewhere would one day surpass the United States Supreme Court in their efforts to address the troublesome problem of inequitable school funding? Yet state courts have done so, invoking their own constitutions to strike down school financing schemes that disadvantage poor (and all too frequently minority) schoolchildren—schemes that the United States Supreme Court has refused to invalidate under the federal constitution.[24]

Recall the early 1960s, when the Warren Court searched the penumbras and emanations of the Bill of Rights for a right to privacy nowhere specifically enumerated therein.[25] Who then would have foreseen that state courts in Florida and elsewhere would one day locate privacy rights in their state constitutions broad enough to invalidate legislative restrictions on the availability of an abortion—restrictions, no less, that the United States Supreme Court had upheld under the federal constitution?[26] Would anyone then have anticipated that the Kentucky Supreme Court eventually would discern in its state constitution an implicit right to engage in private, consensual homosexual activity[27]—and that the court would do so despite a United States Supreme Court ruling denying the existence of such a right under the federal constitution?[28] Could anyone then have imagined that in so ruling, the Kentucky court would follow the lead of judges in the Lone Star State?[29]

Recall the clamor that followed the Warren Court's 1961 decision in *Mapp v. Ohio.*[30] Who then would have supposed a day would come when several state courts, including the supreme courts of Georgia and North Carolina, would recognize exclusionary rules under their state constitutions that are broader than the one applicable to federal trials under prevailing United States Supreme Court decisions interpreting the federal charter?[31] Recall, too, the hue and cry raised in response to Chief Justice Warren's opinion in *Miranda v. Arizona*[32] in 1966. It is hard to imagine anyone then suggesting that, before too long, state courts would be interpreting their state constitutions to afford suspects more expansive rights in the interrogation setting than the United States Supreme Court would require. Yet today, they regularly do.[33]

Recall, finally, those days in the 1960s when it appeared that the Warren Court was heading toward a declaration of the death penalty's constitutional invalidity (a declaration which, as it turned out, would not ultimately come until the early Burger years and, even then, would come only provisionally). It is doubtful that many then expected that courts in Tennessee, Louisiana, Georgia, Indiana, and elsewhere one day would find state constitutional restrictions on the death penalty that substantially exceed those imposed by the United States Supreme Court under the Eighth Amendment.[34]

These are but a few of the impressive accomplishments that have prompted one observer to conclude that "[r]ediscovery by state supreme courts of the broader protections afforded their own citizens by their state constitutions . . . is probably the most important development in constitutional jurisprudence of our times."[35] Were these the words of a state court justice, they might be discounted as forgivable exaggeration—the product of someone understandably proud of his work, but unduly forgetful of the Warren Court's unparalleled groundbreaking achievements. They are the words, however, of Justice William J. Brennan—for many, the personification of the jurisprudential revolution perfected by the Warren Court.[36]

III

Invoking Justice Brennan's name leads us directly to at least one of the connections between the Warren Court and today's state constitutional law—the leadership of Justice Brennan himself.

State court justices and constitutional litigators alike point to his 1977 article in the *Harvard Law Review*, entitled "State Constitutions and the Protection of Individual Rights,"[37] as the Magna Carta of the modern state constitutional law movement.[38] As Justice Brennan is quick to note, his call for the revitalization of state constitutional law was by no means the first.[39] Several state jurists, Justice Hans Linde of Oregon notable among them, already had begun to observe that state constitutions could serve as complements to the federal constitution in the protection of individual rights. State courts already had begun to discuss their obligation to construe their constitutions with critical independent judgment. And civil liberties advocates already were beginning to see the strategic advantages in channeling litigation away from an increasingly conservative federal judiciary and redirecting it toward potentially more hospitable state courts. We will never know whether these realizations alone would have triggered a nationwide rediscovery of state constitutions. But when brought together by Justice Brennan, the acknowledged keeper of the Warren Court's constitutional faith, these concepts were galvanized into an attractive new declaration of constitutional mission tailored for the post-Warren years.

Federal constitutional adjudication in the Warren Court tradition remains essential, Justice Brennan insisted. But its salutary goals can be neither persistently pursued nor secured without a correspondingly vital and vibrant body of state constitutional law. "State constitutions, too," Justice Brennan wrote, "are a font of individual liberties, their protections often extending beyond those required by the Supreme Court's interpretation of federal law. The legal revolution which has brought federal law to the fore must not be allowed to inhibit the independent protective force of state law—for without it, the full realization of our liberties cannot be guaranteed."[40]

If this was true when the federal Constitution was being given a charitable construction in favor of individual rights and liberties, it is all the more so today. "Unfortunately," Justice Brennan lamented,

> federalism has taken on a new meaning of late. . . . Under the banner of vague, undefined notions of equity, comity and federalism the Court has condoned both isolated and systemic violations of civil liberties. Such decisions hardly bespeak a true concern for equity. Nor do they properly understand the nature of our federalism. Adopting the premise that state courts can be trusted to safeguard individual rights, the Supreme Court has gone on to limit the protec-

> tive role of the federal judiciary. But in so doing, it has forgotten that one of the strengths of our federal system is that is provides a double source of protection for the rights of our citizens. Federalism is not served when the federal half of that protection is crippled.[41]

"With federal scrutiny diminished," Justice Brennan concluded, "state courts must respond by increasing their own."[42]

What Justice Brennan did, of course, was conscript state constitutional law into the Warren Court cause, outlining the integral role that it can play in perpetuating and perfecting the constitutional revolution begun in the 1950s. For dyed-in-the-wool Warren Court loyalists, no more needed to be said; their call to arms had been issued, and their task was clear.

But given the relatively few identifiable Warrenesque liberals in state judiciaries, to say nothing of the strong conservative strains that made their way into law and politics during the 1970s and 1980s, it would seem that there must be more to the story behind state constitutional law's phenomenal growth. Indeed, there is. Increased professionalization at the state court level and the welcome addition of growing numbers of women and minority jurists to the bench appear to have made state courts more sensitive to the independent possibilities and potentials of their own constitutions.[43] Simple reacquaintance with the constitutional texts themselves—the unique provisions that they frequently contain, provisions which either have no counterpart in the federal document or speak with an emphasis or clarity that comparable federal clauses lack—also accounts for some of the new decisional law.[44]

Probably the greatest influence has been nothing less than the extremely attractive vision of constitutional adjudication impressed upon the current generation of state court judges by the Warren Court. By its words and deeds, the Warren Court proved to a generation of rising lawyers that constitutional adjudication has a noble and critical function to perform in the American polity. It demonstrated that the processes of constitutional adjudication can successfully identify and rearticulate our most fundamental values in order to make them continually relevant in a world beset by rapid and profound changes—even when (or particularly when) our cherished democratic political institutions are disagreeable to such changes. Through its own masterful use of the processes of constitutional adjudication, the Court introduced principles of equality, human dignity, fairness, and individual autonomy to succeed the exhausted doctrines of property and contract. The Court thus transformed the content of American constitutional liberty, giving it a substance with meaning for our times.

The young lawyers who came of age when the Warren Court's vision of constitutional adjudication was being developed are now the judges who comprise the state judiciaries. When they decide cases raising state constitutional questions, that vision inevitably bears on their work. The distinctive conception of constitutional adjudication forged by the Warren Court is, quite simply, too well grounded and appealing to ignore, and it is the vision that animates state constitutional law today. This constitutes the deepest and strongest connection between the Warren Court and today's resurgent state constitutionalism.

What is it about the Warren Court's conception of constitutional adjudication that makes it so attractive to state judges who decide today's state constitutional questions? Perhaps the heroic role the conception reserves for judges has something to do with its allure, especially insofar as the judges themselves are concerned. Most probably, however, the strong attraction of the conception comes from its fundamental integrity and the dramatically successful way that it came together. Volumes, of course, have been devoted to that subject. For our purposes, it suffices to highlight three key ingredients that seem to have contributed most to the Court's success.

First, the Court accurately discerned that new values of fundamental dimension were emerging in post–World War II America, values quite different from those that dominated constitutional and political discourse in the era of *Lochner v. New York*.[45] As Archibald Cox noted, "libertarian, egalitarian, and humanitarian impulses" had arisen in response to the major changes that had buffeted the nation since the 1930s:

> Among those concerned for civil liberties, the multiplication and magnification of government activities and bureaucracy raised fears of disregard for fair procedure and individual justice. Humanitarianism, aided by the prevailing teaching of the psychological and social science, cast doubt on the sterner aspects of the criminal law. A wave of egalitarianism stirred by war against Hitler's theories of a master race and by the rise of the peoples of Asia and Africa gave support to the civil rights movement.[46]

The Court correctly recognized that these libertarian, egalitarian, and humanitarian values commanded constitutional attention. Although these values ran deep, although they resonated at the moral and ethical level, several factors were conspiring to render the political departments insensitive, and sometimes even hostile, to their force.[47]

Second, the Court successfully located these emerging values in the constitution. Discerning egalitarianism in the Equal Protection Clause of the Fourteenth Amendment was easy enough, but finding convincing textual roots for the kind of humanitarian and libertarian impulses that were surfacing in America took more work. The Court was not always sure-footed; it suffered a fair bit of chiding for its practice of "law office history,"[48] and the creative indulgences of *Griswold v. Connecticut*[49] may never be forgiven by some sticklers. But in the end, the Court's efforts to generalize principles underlying and uniting the Bill of Rights—reminiscent of the approach taken nearly a century before in the great case of *Boyd v. United States*[50]—proved persuasive. As Robert Post has observed, constitutional law was "reconstruct[ed] . . . on individualistic principles" and "the vigorous articulation and revivification of egalitarian values."[51]

Finally, the Court committed itself to the protection of those individualistic and egalitarian values with unprecedented zeal. In doing so, the Court certainly cut through legal technicalities too quickly to suit all tastes. As Alexander Bickel remarked:

> More than once, and in some of its most important actions, the Warren Court got over doctrinal difficulties of issues of the allocation of competences among

> various institutions by asking what it viewed as a decisive practical question: If the Court did not take a certain action which was right and good, would other institutions do so, given political realities? The Warren Court took the greatest pride in cutting through legal technicalities, in piercing through procedure to substance. But legal technicalities are the stuff of the law, and piercing through a particular substance to get to procedures suitable to many substances is in fact what the task of law most often is.[52]

On the whole, though, the Court successfully justified its activism on behalf of individual liberty in terms that have withstood scrutiny and the test of time. By blending the philosophy of heightened scrutiny suggested by then-Justice Stone in his legendary *Carolene Products* footnote,[53] the less categorical and more functional approach to federalism invited by Justice Brandeis's famous dissent in the *New State Ice Co.* case,[54] and a determinedly pragmatic approach to the formation of legal doctrine made possible by legal realism,[55] the Warren Court crafted a powerful new conception of the judicial role.

A large number of state judges came of age professionally during the years when the Warren Court was expounding its vision of constitutional adjudication. They tended to like *Griswold*. If the Constitution did not protect us from that kind of governmental intrusion, they asked, then what's a constitution for? Justice Brandeis's memorable admonition in *Olmstead*[56] that our government is an omnipresent teacher for good or ill, which foreshadowed the Warren Court vision, had a profound influence on many of these judges.

The Warren Court's unwavering concern for the rights of disfavored minorities seemed to these judges to be an attractive vision of the role of the judiciary. It was a vision in which they believed and which, to them, made sense. Democracies must find a way to give effect to this concern if they are to endure. That is why the emerging democracies in Eastern Europe are so much more interested in our legal and judicial system than in other aspects of our government, and rightly so.

The most disfavored minority in the country today are the criminally accused. Yet they have rights that the law affords and that judges are sworn to protect. Although we know these rights can be protected without diminishing the effectiveness of law enforcement and its daunting fight against crime, it is a task as unpopular as it is essential. The Warren Court taught us these things. The Court was right. Its vision still makes sense.

IV

With time's passage, the precise details of the Warren Court's cases fade from memory. Arguable missteps that once seemed so important have receded to the background. We have tended to suppress, for example, the sweeping arguments, but not the holding, of *Griswold*. The outcries of the disgruntled have trailed off. What remains fixed in memory is nothing less than a constitutional *tour de force*: the successful redefinition of constitutional adjudication to serve the needs of a changing America. It is quite a performance to recount, let alone to have watched as it unfolded. It made a lasting impression, convincing a generation or two of state judges that vigorous commitment to individual liberty and the pursuit of equality is fundamental to the judicial mission.

To the extent that there is a direct reflection of the Warren Court's vision in the many progressive state constitutional law decisions being handed down today, then it seems time is serving the Court well. In the rebirth of state constitutional law, there is telling new evidence of the Warren Court's considerable powers of persuasion.

Notes

1. Friendly, "The Bill of Rights as a Code of Criminal Procedure," 53 *Cal. L. Rev.* 929 (1965).

2. Wechsler, "Toward Neutral Principles of Constitutional Law," 73 *Harv. L. Rev.* 1 (1959).

3. Hart, "The Supreme Court, 1958 Term—Foreword: The Time Chart of the Justices," 73 *Harv. L. Rev.* 84 (1959).

4. Bickel, *The Morality of Consent* 120–21 (1975).

5. Kurland, *Politics, the Constitution, and the Warren Court* xx–xxii (1970) (quoting Horning v. District of Columbia, 254 U.S. 135, 139 (1920)).

6. Id. at xxii.

7. Id. at xxv.

8. 410 U.S. 113 (1973).

9. 408 U.S. 238 (1972).

10. See Tushnet, "The Warren Court as History: An Interpretation," in *The Warren Court in Historical and Political Perspective* 1, 1–2 (Tushnet ed., 1993) [hereinafter *Perspective*].

11. See, e.g., Exum, "Rediscovering State Constitutions," 70 *N.C. L. Rev.* 1741, 1741 (1992).

12. See, e.g., id. at 1741–42 (1992); Williams, "'Experience Must Be Our Only Guide': The State Constitutional Experience of the Framers of the Federal Constitution," 15 *Hastings Cont. L.Q.* 403, 404 (1988).

13. See, e.g., Exum, supra note 11, at 1742; Williams, supra note 12, at 422–23.

14. 1 Cranch 137 (U.S. 1803). A leading precedent establishing the propriety of judicial review was Bayard v. Singleton, 1 N.C. (Mart.) 5 (1787). For a discussion of the influence of *Bayard* on Chief Justice Marshall's opinion in *Marbury*, see Exum, supra note 11, at 1742–45, and Orth, "Fundamental Principles" in "North Carolina Constitutional History," 69 *N.C. L. Rev.* 1357, 1357–58, 1363–64 (1991).

15. See, e.g., Trustees of the Univ. of N.C. v. Foy, 5 N.C. (1 Mur.) 58 (1805) (invalidating legislation that repealed a grant to trustees of the university of "all the property that had theretofore or should thereafter escheat to the State"); State v. Biggs, 46 S.E. 401 (N.C. 1903) (prohibiting the criminalization, as unauthorized practice of medicine, of provision of nonmedical natural healing methods, such as massage); Commissioners of Union Drainage Dist. No. 1 v. Smith, 84 N.E. 376 (Ill. 1908) (invalidating legislation that denies individual judicial determination by an impartial tribunal); State v. Strasburg, 110 P. 1020 (Wash. 1910) (invalidating legislative abrogation of insanity defense).

16. E.g., Mapp v. Ohio, 367 U.S. 643, 680–81 (1961) (Harlan, J., dissenting) (expressing concerns that expansive federal constitutional interpretations would impede development of state law).

17. The amendments are noted in the various editions of the *Book of the States* (Smothers ed., 1954–65) (Weber ed., 1970).

18. See, e.g., Gardner, "The Failed Discourse of State Constitutional Law," 90 *Mich. L. Rev.* 761, 819–21 (1992).

19. E.g., Ackerman v. Port of Seattle, 348 P.2d 664 (Wash. 1960) (holding that low airplane flights constitute taking of property); Remington Arms. Co. v. G.E.M. of St. Louis, Inc., 102 N.W.2d 528 (Minn. 1960) (invalidating state Fair Trade Act); Roller v. Allen, 96 S.E.2d 851 (N.C. 1957) (invalidating legislation requiring licensing of tile layers); Cox v. General Electric Co., 85 S.E.2d 514 (Ga. 1955) (invalidating state Fair Trade Act); Chapel v. Commonwealth, 89 S.E.2d 337 (Va. 1955) (invalidating statute regulating dry cleaning); State v. Gleason, 277 P.2d 530 (Mont. 1954) (invalidating statute requiring examination and licensing of photographers). For contemporaneous discussions of the economic due process jurisprudence conducted under state constitutions during the 1950s and early 1960s, see Hoskins and Katz, Comment, "Substantive Due Process in the States Revisited," 18 *Ohio St. L.J.* 384 (1957), and Note, "Counter-revolution in State Constitutional Law," 15 *Stan. L. Rev.* 309 (1963).

20. Schuman, "The Right to 'Equal Privileges and Immunities': A State's Version of 'Equal Protection,'" 13 *Vt. L. Rev.* 221, 221 (1988).

21. See, e.g., Symposium, "Emerging Issues in State Constitutional Law," 65 *Temp. L. Rev.* 1119 (1992); Symposium, "'The Law of the Land': The North Carolina Constitution and State Constitutional Law," 70 *N.C. L. Rev.* 1701 (1992); "The 1970 Illinois Constitution in Review: A Symposium on Issues for Change," 8 *N. Ill. U. L. Rev.* 565 (1988); Symposium, "The Emergence of State Constitutional Law," 63 *Texas L. Rev.* 959 (1985); "Developments in the Law—The Interpretation of State Constitutional Rights," 95 *Harv. L. Rev.* 1324 (1982). See also Watts, *State Constitutional Law Development: A Bibliography* (1991) (assembling extensive bibliography).

22. 347 U.S. 483 (1954).

23. 358 U.S. 1 (1958).

24. Compare San Antonio Independent School Dist. v. Rodriguez, 411 U.S. 1 (1973) (upholding Texas school financing system against federal equal protection challenge) with Edgewood Independent School Dist. v. Kirby, 777 S.W.2d 391 (Tex. 1989) (invalidating Texas scheme under state constitution). See also Rose v. Council for Better Education, Inc., 790 S.W.2d 186 (Ky. 1989) (requiring equitable school financing system under state constitution); Helena Elementary School Dist. No. 1 v. State, 769 P.2d 684 (Mont. 1989) (same); Abbott v. Burke, 575 A.2d 359 (N.J. 1990) (same).

25. See Griswold v. Connecticut, 381 U.S. 479 (1965); Poe v. Ullman, 367 U.S. 497 (1961); Kauper, "Penumbras, Peripheries, Emanations, Things Fundamental and Things Forgotten: The *Griswold* Case," 64 *Mich. L. Rev.* 235 (1965).

26. Compare Harris v. McRae, 448 U.S. 297 (1980) (upholding restrictions on public funding of abortion) and Maher v. Roe, 432 U.S. 464 (1977) with Doe v. Maher, 515 A.2d 134 (Conn. Super. Ct. 1986) (invoking state constitution to invalidate limits on state funding of abortion to cases involving danger to the life of the mother), Moe v. Secretary of Admin. & Fin., 417 N.E.2d 387 (Mass. 1981) (same), Right to Choose v. Byrne, 450 A.2d 925 (N.J. 1982) (same), and Hope v. Perales, 571 N.Y.S.2d 972 (N.Y. Sup. Ct. 1991) (same).

27. Commonwealth v. Wasson, 842 S.W.2d 487, 491–93 (Ky. 1992).

28. Bowers v. Hardwick, 478 U.S. 186 (1986).

29. State v. Morales, 826 S.W.2d 201 (Tex. App. 1992), *rev'd on other grounds*, 869 S.W.2d 941 (Tex. 1994).

30. 367 U.S. 643 (1961).

31. Gary v. State, 422 S.E.2d 426 (Ga. 1992) (refusing to adopt "good faith" exception of United States v. Leon, 468 U.S. 897 (1984), to exclusionary rule under state constitution); State v. Carter, 370 S.E.2d 553 (N.C. 1988) (same); State v. Oakes, 598 A.2d 119 (Vt. 1991) (same); Commonwealth v. Edmunds, 586 A.2d 887 (Pa. 1991) (same); State v. Marsala, 579 A.2d 58 (Conn. 1990) (same); State v. Novembrino, 519 A.2d 820 N.J. 1987) (same); People v. Sundling, 395 N.W.2d 308 (Mich. Ct. App. 1986) (same); People v. Bigelow, 488 N.E.2d 451 (N.Y. 1985) (same).

32. 384 U.S. 436 (1966).

33. See, e.g., State v. Gravel, 601 A.2d 678 (N.H. 1991) (invoking state constitution to exclude physical evidence discovered due to custodial interrogation unaccompanied by warnings; decision questionable under federal Constitution in light of Oregon v. Elstad, 470 U.S. 298 (1985)); People v. Bethea, 493 N.E.2d 937 (N.Y. 1986) (rejecting *Elstad* and suppressing a second, warned statement that was obtained after initial unwarned statement). See Crossley, "*Miranda* and the State Constitution: State Courts Take a Stand," 39 *Vand. L. Rev.* 1693 (1986) (gathering instances of broader state constitutional protections).

34. See, e.g., State v. Middlebrooks, 840 S.W.2d 317 (Tenn. 1992) (holding that use of underlying felony as aggravating circumstance in felony murder case fails to adequately narrow class of death-eligible offenders), *cert. dismissed as improvidently granted,* 114 S. Ct. 651 (1993); State v. Black, 815 S.W.2d 166 (Tenn. 1991) (invalidating "especially heinous" aggravating circumstance for failure to channel sentencer's discretion adequately); State v. Jones, 639 So.2d 1144 (La. 1994) (invalidating statutory requirement that capital sentencing jury be instructed on governor's power to grant reprieve, pardon, or commutation); Fleming v. Zant, 386 S.E.2d 339 (Ga. 1989) (forbidding death penalty for mentally retarded offenders); Cooper v. State, 540 N.E.2d 1216 (Ind. 1989) (forbidding death penalty for defendant who was fifteen years of age at the time of the offense); State v. Koedatich, 548 A.2d 939 (N.J. 1988) (holding that constitutional and statutory interests in safeguarding reliability of death-sentencing decisions dictate the rule that a defendant may not waive the right to present mitigating evidence); State v. Smith, 392 S.E.2d 362 (N.C. 1990) (finding broad and unwaivable right of capital defendant to be present at critical stages of prosecution). See Bilionis, "Legitimating Death," 91 *Mich. L. Rev.* 1643, 1682–90 (1993) (analyzing state constitutional developments in capital punishment).

35. Special Section, "State Constitutional Law," *Nat'l L.J.*, Sept. 29, 1986, at S–1.

36. In Professor Post's words: "Brennan, more than any other single justice, most fully assimilated the full jurisprudential consequences of the Warren Court's revolutionary new vision of the American polity. He grasped, with comprehensive clarity and coherence, the relationship between individualism and equality, the bureaucratization of government, and the correspondingly augmented functions of the federal judiciary. He fully discerned that individualism required opposition both to the communitarianism of traditional federalism and to the statism that has since come to dominate the Court. . . ." Post, "William J. Brennan and the Court," in *Perspective*, supra note 10, at 123, 129–30.

37. Brennan, "State Constitutions and the Protection of Individual Rights," 90 *Harv. L. Rev.* 489 (1977). It has proved to be one of the "most frequently cited law review articles of modern times." Lousin, "Justice Brennan: A Tribute to a Federal Judge Who Believes in State's Rights," 20 *J. Marshall L. Rev.* 1, 2 n.3 (1986).

38. See Pollock, "State Constitutions as Separate Sources of Fundamental Rights," 35 *Rutgers L. Rev.* 707, 716 (1983) (referring to Brennan's article as the "Magna Carta of state constitutional law").

39. Brennan, Foreword to "'The Law of the Land': The North Carolina Constitu-

tion and State Constitutional Law," 70 *N.C. L. Rev.* 1701, 1701 (1992) ("I was hardly the first to recommend that state constitutional law be revitalized," citing Linde, "Without 'Due Process': Unconstitutional Law in Oregon," 40 *Or. L. Rev.* 125, 133–35, 181–87 (1970)).

40. Brennan, supra note 37, at 491.

41. Id. at 502–03.

42. Id. at 503.

43. See Curriden, "The Changing Faces of Southern Courts," *A.B.A. J.*, June 1993, 68.

44. See, e.g., Bilionis, "On the Significance of Constitutional Spirit," 70 *N.C. L. Rev.* 1803, 1806–07 (1992) (presenting examples of distinctive state constitutional texts).

45. 198 U.S. 45 (1905).

46. Cox, *The Court and the Constitution* 179–80 (1987).

47. "In the 1950s, because of the Cold War, increased crime, fear of social disorder, and perhaps entrenched economic and political power, the political process had become resistant to libertarian, humanitarian, and egalitarian impulses." Id. at 179.

48. Kelly, "Clio and the Court: An Illicit Love Affair," 1965 *Sup. Ct. Rev.* 119; Kurland, supra note 5, at 100.

49. 381 U.S. 479 (1965).

50. 116 U.S. 616 (1886).

51. Post, supra note 36, at 123.

52. Bickel, supra note 4, at 120–21; Cox, supra note 46, at 181–82.

53. United States v. Carolene Prods. Co., 304 U.S. 144, 152 n.4 (1938).

54. New State Ice Co. v. Liebmann, 285 U.S. 262, 311 (1932) (Brandeis, J., dissenting).

55. See, e.g., Cox, supra note 46, at 180–81; Post, supra note 36, at 123.

56. Olmstead v. United States, 277 U.S. 438, 485 (1928) (Brandeis, J., dissenting).

• 21 •

FROM MODERNISM TO POSTMODERNISM IN AMERICAN LEGAL THOUGHT

The Significance of the Warren Court

STEPHEN M. FELDMAN

American legal thought has crossed a shadowy border separating two eras: moving from modernism to postmodernism.[1] For more than a century, modernist legal scholars have sought to ground knowledge of our legal system on some firm foundation. Frequently, they have attempted to explain how the rule of law both mandates and facilitates objective judicial decision making. Moreover, they have assumed that legal actors—judges, legislators, and even scholars—are empowered to confront legal, social, and political problems by considering an array of options, choosing the best one, and then effectively implementing it. Over the past two decades, though, more and more legal scholars have emerged as postmodernists.[2] These postmodernists are antifoundationalists and antiessentialists: they insist that the meaning or truth of a text is never grounded or stable, and that therefore one can always find multiple meanings or truths. Furthermore, postmodern legal scholars do not assume that individuals are independent and autonomous subjects who possess the ability to make and implement substantive value choices. Rather, social and discursive practices construct the subject or self.

My purpose in this essay is to interpret (or explain) the importance of the Warren Court in this movement from American legal modernism to postmodernism. I do so by sketching a narrative of the development of legal thought that accords the Warren Court a prominent role. From one perspective, the significant role played by the Warren Court in this narrative is unremarkable: a common observation is that, over the past forty years, many scholars have devoted their careers to either defending, attacking, or chronicling the Warren Court. Indeed, the entire field of constitutional theory can reasonably be understood as developing around scholarly efforts to denounce or justify the Warren Court's judicial activism. My thesis, though, differs from this commonplace, albeit reasonable, observation. I argue that, by provoking these extensive scholarly efforts within a distinct intellectual and social context, the Warren Court helped terminate one era of American legal scholarship while ushering in another. In short, the Warren Court precipitated a crisis in American legal scholarship that spurred the movement from modernism to postmodernism.

Section I of this essay focuses on the development of American legal thought during its modernist era. I begin by dividing modernism into four successive stages, and then I trace the passage of American jurisprudence through the first three stages. Section II turns to the intervention of the Warren Court in the further evolution of legal thought. In particular, I focus on two definitive Warren Court decisions, *Brown v. Board of Education*[3] and *Griswold v. Connecticut*.[4] Section II first explores how *Brown* helped catapult legal scholarship into the fourth and final stage of legal modernism. Section II then discusses the significance of *Griswold* in pushing legal thought toward postmodernism. The essay concludes by describing the main differences between postmodernism and modernism.

I. Modernism and American Legal Scholarship

The Four Stages of Modernism

This section presents a narrative of modernism that revolves around the gradual and simultaneous development of two related metaphysical premises: first, modernists are committed foundationalists, and second, modernists believe in an independent and autonomous subject or self. These two metaphysical premises do *not* define modernism; indeed, modernism cannot be reduced to any determinative set of tenets or practices. Nonetheless, most modernists commit to these premises by tacitly assuming them—though an occasional modernist acknowledges and even defends them. These two metaphysical premises or commitments unfold through four specified stages of modernism.[5] To be clear, these four stages are *not* presented as facts: they are neither distinct events that occurred at precise times in history nor structural necessities that must eventually occur. Rather, the stages are heuristic devices somewhat akin to Weberian "ideal types."[6] They are interpretive constructs designed by highlighting certain recurrent and prominent (though contingent) historical features of modernism, and, as such, the stages can facilitate the narrative analysis of the development of modernism in different fields. I draw heavily upon examples from philosophy and social theory to articulate the four stages. I do so not because the constitutive elements of the stages were fully realized in the actual historical events of those fields (they were not), but because the theorists in those fields tended, more so than in other disciplines, to focus self-consciously on the two metaphysical premises. Although I believe that these stages of modernism could facilitate the interpretive analysis of many different academic fields, my ultimate aim is to develop a coherent narrative of the development of American legal thought that will appropriately feature the Warren Court.

The first metaphysical (and epistemological) commitment is foundationalism: modernists believe that knowledge ought to (and indeed must) be firmly grounded on some objective foundation. Unlike premodernists, though, modernists claim to reject traditional, mythological, and religious footings and thus search for some alternative foundation or Archimedean point.[7] A corollary of foundationalism is essentialism: a belief in the existence of universal and eternal truths that emanate from stable and fixed cores or essences. Thus, for the modernist, the subject or self somehow is able to access or know essentialist truths, yet truth does not emerge as immediate or transparent because culturally produced traditions obscure one's view of the eternal and universal. Traditional beliefs or prejudices act as layers of film covered with cloudy and misleading illusions; these layers of film must be peeled away to uncover the truth.

During the first stage of modernism—which I call rationalism—pure abstract reason seems capable of uncovering or disclosing the truth. According to the Cartesian method in philosophy, the thinking subject or self turns inward to question or doubt all beliefs, and through this reasoning process, clear and distinct ideas emerge as foundational knowledge.[8] Thus, when purified of historical and traditional prejudices, reason itself seems to yield certainty—that is, the truth. This Cartesian turn inward, to a reasoning self, however, rips asunder the metaphysical unity that had characterized the premodern world. Contrary to the premodern belief that humanity exists as an integral part of a unified natural world, the modernist self or subject rather suddenly stands divided from an external and objective world. This acute division between subject and object stands as a preeminent development of modernism. Not only does it spawn the emergence of the independent and autonomous subject or self, but it also generates further epistemological problems characteristic of modernism. In particular, the modernist eventually wonders whether truth arises from the objects of the external world. And if it does, then how can the subject bridge the (modernist) gap that exists between itself and that world?[9]

During the second stage of modernism—which I call empiricism—the focus shifts from the reasoning subject to the external world as the exclusive source of truth. In this stage, the objects of the external world seem to shape human experience, so the subject therefore can secure foundational knowledge empirically, through the direct sense experience and understanding of that world.[10] To be sure, reason, while no longer the source of first premises and foundational knowledge, still performs significant functions. Reason can provide valuable insights about the world and can facilitate the performance of certain tasks, but only if empiricism first provides the foundational premises—the knowledge—that can adequately ground the subsequent rational processes. Reason becomes instrumental: it is a vessel emptied of content, and only empirical observation can fill the void with the necessary substance about the world.

The significance of instrumental reason corresponds with the further elaboration and development of the independent and autonomous subject. For example, in philosophy, the empiricist John Locke was perhaps the first theorist to focus on a concept of personal identity.[11] At this stage, then, we begin to see the autonomous self more distinctly, as it asserts an ostensible power to control the external world and social organization. As modernism already has stripped the authority from historical and traditional beliefs, traditional societal organization no longer seems necessary or legitimate. The self, though, can use instrumental reason to help achieve certain goals, such as promoting peace or protecting property. In short, the self can use instrumental reason to reorder or reorganize society. As Zygmunt Bauman observes, modernist society is like a garden: humans rationally design and cultivate it, nurturing some plants while eliminating others, which are derisively called weeds.[12] Modernism, perhaps presumptuously, "boasts the unprecedented ability to improve human conditions by reorganizing human affairs on a rational basis."[13]

Like the first stage, the second stage of modernism also eventually encounters further epistemological problems. To access the truth, the subject or self must somehow know the objective and external world, but Cartesian rationalism sharply divided the subject from the world. Thus, the second stage leads to a crisis when modernists realize that, despite the pretensions of rationalism and empiricism, the subject might never bridge the chasm between itself and the external world. If so, modernists might then never achieve their self-imposed goal—foundational knowledge. Moreover, if neither reason nor experience can ground knowledge, then modernism appears to have rushed down a dead end, yet there is no turning back. Because modernism already has revealed the irreparable metaphysical failings of the premodern world, a return to the now exposed illegitimate traditions of that earlier era is impossible. In short, the modernist crisis threatens to become modernist despair. Modernism continues unceasingly to demand foundational knowledge, even as modernism itself reveals that the tools or techniques of modernism as well those of premodernism are inadequate for this task.

In a sense, the third stage of modernism—which I call transcendentalism (or idealism)—tries to pull the rabbit out of the hat: "Nothing up this sleeve (rationalism). Nothing up this sleeve (empiricism). But, abracadabra—and after a pass of my magic wand—I can still pull the rabbit (knowledge) out of the hat!" Just when modernism seems to have exhausted its possible routes to knowledge, third-stage modernists desperately yet ingeniously attempt to turn back to the thinking subject and reason in order to resurrect the possibility of foundational knowledge. Second-stage modernist philosophers had argued that, for knowledge to be possible, the objects of an external world must shape human experience. But the transcendental reasoning of the third stage reverses this schema: the foremost transcendental philosopher, Kant, argued that humans impose form and structure on the objects or phenomena of experience. Certain structures or categories, in other words, are inherent to and therefore shape all human experience and thought. Knowledge is possible, according to Kant, exactly because the categories are necessary preconditions of human experience. Kant's epistemological project then was to identify the precise categories that are a priori conditions of experience:[14] the categories specify how humans must process their experiences of the external world. Transcendental reason, in short, provides synthetic a priori knowledge—knowledge that is prior to experience but that is nonetheless informative about the objective world. Moreover, during this third stage, the independent and autonomous self continues, as in the second stage, to use instrumental reason to perform activities and achieve certain goals. Modernist rationality allows society constantly to progress, to improve.

Transcendentalism, while unmistakably brilliant, does not eradicate the modernist crisis. To many theorists—call them critics—the transcendental solution eventually seems suspect, and thus modernism enters a fourth and final stage, which I call late crisis. Critics cynically doubt the transcendentalists: it is as if modernism looked despair in the face, and frightened by its countenance, declared instantly that there just *has* to be a solution to these epistemological problems. Thus, the transcendental modernist, anxiously struggling to find a last-gasp answer, urgently thinks, "We *must* have knowledge, but what conditions are necessary in order to have knowledge?" Then, presto! The modernist concludes, "We must already have satisfied those prerequisite conditions of knowledge because, after all, we so clearly have knowledge (since, of course, we *must* have knowledge)."[15] To the critic, though, transcendentalism seems to be an empty speciosity, born from desperation. In a sense, the transcendental modernist merely has described what conditions *would* exist *if* we had foundational knowledge. But describing these conditions does not make them a reality; the transcendental argument for foundational knowledge means only that the modernist can imagine what such knowledge might be if it were a reality.

Significantly, even the critic of the transcendental solution remains a modernist. She cannot envision any alternatives to modernism, and indeed, she cannot transcend the modernist desire for foundational knowledge and essentialist truth. Thus, for lack of options, the critic continues to use the tools of modernism: rationalism and empiricism. She even uses these modernist tools to demonstrate the inherent limits of modernism, to show the utter impossibility of achieving modernist goals.[16] Consequently, the critic plunges modernism into despair because, while the desire for truth and knowledge remains, the hope for fulfillment has vanished. Other modernists, though, still hopeful for success, react to the critics in one of two ways. First, some of them peremptorily declare, in effect, "If you don't have anything better to offer, just shut up!" These loyal reactionaries typically condemn the despairing critics as nihilists. Second, other more receptive yet still sanguine modernists listen to the critical arguments, are indeed troubled, and thus respond by trying to save the modernist project with some new wrinkle, some further complication.

Fourth-stage modernism thus is marked by swirling and inconsistent attitudes and projects: deep despair, anxiety, anger, accusatory denunciations, and increasingly intricate modernist "solutions" that pick and choose elements from rationalism, empiricism, and transcendentalism, all the while adding layers of complexity. For example, some fourth-stage modernists might acknowledge that tradition or culture has proven unexpectedly persistent and thus difficult to overcome or peel away. Consequently, foundational knowledge is even more difficult to access than previously imagined. Yet, some inventive strategy—structuralism, phenomenology, Freudian psychology—is imagined nonetheless to penetrate into the deep regions of reality. The persistence of tradition or culture might also affect the modernist conception of the subject or self: some fourth-stage modernists admit that traditional or cultural constraints limit the options or choices for the self. The self seems, after all, not quite as independent and autonomous as originally formulated. Ultimately, however, these modernists retain an image of the self that somehow remains in control, remains able to choose, remains an origin of power. Modernism, at this stage, might no longer boast of a totally independent and autonomous self, but in Pierre Schlag's terminology, a "relatively autonomous self" nonetheless endures.[17]

Significantly, this relatively autonomous self continues to assert its power to use instrumental reason to organize society. Meanwhile, critics, while often acknowledging the effectiveness of instrumental reason, fearfully wonder about the legitimacy of the normative values issuing from the supposedly autonomous selves. For it is these normative values that generate the substantive goals which propel instrumental reason, which aim it toward some target. Indeed, in some modernist visions, the self becomes the sole legitimate source of normative values, so the self, through sheer force of will, generates substantive goals and, with instrumental reasoning, manipulates the world (including other selves) to attain its purposes. For some critics, their despair fuses with terror when they consider the prospect of instrumental reason running wild, untethered by any legitimate normative values, or at best, tied to the purely personal preferences of isolated individuals.[18]

The Development of Modernist American Legal Thought

I shall place the beginning of American legal modernism at 1870, when Christopher Columbus Langdell was appointed as the first dean of Harvard Law School.[19] I do not mean to suggest that before this time, American legal thought was clearly premodern. It was not; rather the early and middle parts of the nineteenth-century were characterized by an uncertain mix of premodern and modern elements. For example, early nineteenth century conceptions of the common law manifested the metaphysical unity present in premodernity: the common law was understood to reflect acceptable social customs and simultaneously to impose social obligations dependent upon one's status within society. And many individuals believed that legal obligations and rights were self-evident to ordinary intuition—no special method of reasoning was necessary to strip away traditional beliefs and prejudices to reveal the truth, for the truth itself resided in the natural development of custom and tradition.[20] At the same time, the more modernist notion of a legal science was already emerging; some members of the legal elite insisted that only their "highly educated reason" could discover the obligations and rights inherent in American customs and traditions.[21]

Langdell's appointment as dean at Harvard was significant because, in effect, he invented the academic lawyer—a full-time law teacher and scholar.[22] This university-affiliated and professional legal scholar ushered in the era of classical orthodoxy and precipitated the clear ascension of legal modernism. More particularly, classical orthodoxy represents first-stage modernism, when pure abstract reason seems capable of uncovering or disclosing truth. To Langdell and other believers of classical orthodoxy, the study of law should be a "science" that culminates in the discovery of objective legal truths.[23] Since the academic lawyer's position within the university provided the time necessary for this scientific study of law, Langdell and his colleagues bore the task of discovering the legal truths—the indubitable and absolute principles of law. Most important, the primary tool of discovery was formal and abstract reason—that is, logic. A good scholar was a dispassionate logician, who carefully parsed through the decided cases in an inexorable quest for authentic knowledge. But not all cases contributed to knowledge—to the discovery of truth—in Langdell's words, many cases were "useless, and worse than useless."[24] With abstract legal reasoning, though, the scholar could strip away the misleading cases that skewed the common law tradition and, ultimately, could specify a small number of legal principles. Legal principles, thus, were analogous to the axioms of Euclidian geometry:[25] they were few in number, they could be "classified and arranged"[26] into a formal framework so that each was in its "proper place,"[27] and they served as the fountainhead for the logical derivation of all other legal rules. Classical orthodoxy neatly and rationally ordered the entire legal system into a conceptual framework resembling a pyramid, with the few axiomatic and abstract principles at the apex of the pyramid and more precise and numerous rules at the base. These lower-level rules were derived from the top-level principles through a process of noncontroversial deductive reasoning.

Thus, classical orthodoxy starkly illustrates first-stage modernism: scholars supposedly discovered objective legal truths by turning inward and using abstract reason, not by relying on sensory experience. To be sure, Langdellians did insist upon the study of appellate cases, but the cases were not empirical data that could be used to test the verity of hypothesized principles and rules. Rather, the cases provided, in effect, ready manifestations of the principles and rules, thus facilitating the scholar's isolated and lonely quest for truth in the comfort of the library and office. And as already mentioned, cases that did not fit the specified principles were simply dismissed as useless and wrong. With regard to the possible consideration of social experiences or consequences beyond the cases, Langdell emphasized that he was pointedly uninterested in such experiences. In his discussion of the mailbox rule—which specifies whether a posted acceptance of an offer to contract is effective upon dispatch or receipt—Langdell argued that logic and axiomatic contract principles mandated one conclusion: an acceptance was effective only upon receipt. Langdell acknowledged that other commentators had argued that this rule led to unjust social results. His response to this problem was striking: "The true answer to this argument is that it is irrelevant."[28]

In perhaps an odd manner, this sharp separation between the legal system and the remainder of social reality significantly fortified the legal science of classical orthodoxy. Classical orthodoxy emphasized two methodological features: a tenacious reliance on formal logic and a disregard for social consequences. As the basis for a legal system, either of these features, standing alone, would be troubling (or repugnant). When combined together, though, they at least strengthened each other (but to me, they remain dubious). Langdellians implicitly realized that the relation between abstract propositions (rules and principles) and social reality is problematic: to talk of a purely logical relationship between rules and principles, on the one hand, and social reality, on the other, does not necessarily make sense. Yet, it does make sense to talk of a logical relationship between different abstract propositions—that is, between different rules and principles. Therefore, when Langdellians insisted that social experiences and consequences should be irrelevant to the law, their claim that logical order provides the key to understanding the legal system at least becomes plausible. At a minimum, we can imagine a legal system based purely on abstract reason *if* it is unconnected to social reality.[29]

Classical orthodoxy manifests first-stage modernism not only by emphasizing abstract reason but also by facilitating the emergence of the autonomous and independent subject or self. First, classical orthodoxy implicitly presents the legal scholar as the authoritative pronouncer of legal truth. That is, classical orthodoxy tacitly assumes that the legal scholar is the autonomous and independent self qualified to proclaim legal principles and rules and to instruct judges about the content and application of those legal truths.[30] Second, classical orthodoxy helped develop legal principles and rules that gradually drew boundaries around a field or sphere of private, self-interested action. Within that field, the independent and autonomous self supposedly could pursue the satisfaction of its economic and social desires free of governmental interference.[31]

One politically significant manifestation of classical orthodoxy was the Supreme Court's protection of liberty of contract during the *Lochner* era of the late nineteenth and early twentieth centuries.[32] In *Lochner v. New York*,[33] decided in 1905, the Court held unconstitutional a state law that restricted the number of hours which employees could work in bakeries. The Court concluded that the law violated the Due Process Clause of the Fourteenth Amendment because it infringed on liberty of contract: employees might wish to work more than sixty hours per week or ten hours per day, and the government should not stop them from doing so. The Court's reasoning reflected classical orthodoxy in at least two related ways. First, the Court used formalist reasoning of the Langdellian variety by assuming that there was a preexisting field or sphere of private activity and that any conduct that fell within that sphere was categorically protected from governmental interference. In other words, the case turned on the Court's supposedly logical deduction of whether the prohibited activities fell within a predefined conceptual category of protected private conduct. Second, the Court's formalist conclusion itself then reinforced the ostensible boundary around the sphere of private action, where independent and autonomous selves supposedly entered freely into contractual agreements.

Rudimentary elements of the second stage of legal modernism initially surfaced around the turn from the nineteenth to the twentieth century in the writings of Oliver Wendell Holmes, Jr.,[34] and the sociological jurisprudes, such as Roscoe Pound and Benjamin Cardozo.[35] By the end of World War I, at least three factors combined to prompt the further growth of the incipient second-stage movement. First, the work of classical orthodoxy seemed nearly exhausted: Langdellian legal scholars, for the most part, had readily mastered and even completed their task, the abstract rationalization and conceptual ordering of the legal system. Many young legal scholars therefore faced the frustrating prospect of mundanely repeating the past, rationalizing and rerationalizing the law over and over again.[36] Second, some of these young legal scholars recognized the significance and the potential of the burgeoning social sciences, which were rapidly developing in other parts of the universities.[37] Third, political pressure began to mount (especially with the coming of the New Deal in the 1930s) to reject the formalist reasoning of the *Lochner*-era Supreme Court in order to clear a path for progressive social legislation. Partly because of these factors, then, second-stage legal modernism fully bloomed in the 1920s and 1930s with the advent of American legal realism. In terms of the transition from first-stage to second-stage modernism, two components of the realist movement bear emphasis: first, the rejection of the abstract rationalism of classical orthodoxy, which manifested first-stage modernism, and second, the turn to empiricism as a source of foundational knowledge.

Realists denounced the abstract and decontextualized rationalism of classical orthodoxy as unrelated to meaningful social reality, unrelated to human experiences of the external world. Whereas Langdellian scholars claimed that their abstract reasoning enabled them to discover objective legal truths—the rules and principles of the common law—realists such as Felix Cohen denounced the Langdellian rationalism and the resultant rules and principles as "transcendental nonsense."[38]

Karl Llewellyn, writing in *The Bramble Bush*, trumpeted the realists' iconoclastic stance toward classical orthodoxy: "[G]eneral propositions are empty. . . . [R]ules alone . . . are worthless. [The] doing of something about disputes, [the] doing of it reasonably, is the business of law. And the people who have the doing in charge, whether they be judges or sheriffs or clerks or jailers or lawyers, are officials of the law. What these officials do about disputes is, to my mind, the law itself."[39]

According to the most radical realists, the rationalism of classical orthodoxy was irrelevant to the law. Abstract rules and principles had little or nothing to do with judicial decision making. The Langdellian image of the legal system as a conceptually ordered framework of absolute and certain legal principles and rules was a dangerous and misleading myth. In a remarkable confession, a realist federal district court judge, Joseph Hutcheson, claimed to decide cases based on intuitive hunches. Rules and principles served at most as post hoc rationalizations, cleverly constructed to obscure while appearing to justify the judge's intuitive conclusions.[40]

Most realists, however, did not reject the modernist commitment to foundational knowledge; they merely denied that abstract reason could disclose legal truths.[41] To the realists, the rationalism of classical orthodoxy had proven inadequate to strip away culturally produced traditions and prejudices, so in a move typical of second-stage modernism, realists turned to experience as the source of objectivity. Perhaps, abstract legal rules and principles did not constrain judicial decisions, but concrete facts of the external (and social) world did influence or even determine such decisions. Furthermore, consistent with the development of second-stage modernism, the relevant facts increasingly seemed to revolve around the actions of individuals. The facts that might sway a particular judge could be as seemingly idiosyncratic and arbitrary as the hair color of a witness, the nasal twang of an attorney, or the breakfast the judge happened to eat that morning.[42] Consequently, realists argued that only empirical studies carefully attending to the observable behavior of legal actors could reveal the stimuli that caused predictable judicial responses. In short, for these realists, the methods of the emerging social sciences promised to produce objective knowledge of the legal system.

Realism also manifested the emphasis of second-stage modernism on the independent and autonomous individual who asserts the power to use instrumental reason to reorder society. Although all realists rejected the abstract and formal rules of classical orthodoxy, some realists suggested that a new type of legal rule could be formulated based on the realist/empirical approach to the law. According to this view, judges and scholars should shape the law based on the real-world consequences of legal rules and judicial decisions. Felix Cohen called this method the functional approach: judges should *make* the law to function in a way that it would promote certain ethical values and substantive goals. In short, judges should perform "social engineering."[43] For example, Cohen argued that in answering the question "Is there a contract?" a judge should not focus on abstract and formal legal principles such as consideration. Instead, the judge should concentrate on whether one party or the other should be liable for certain actions. What real-world consequences would follow, what values and goals would be promoted, by the various possible decisions?[44]

The realists' politically motivated attack on the *Lochner*-era Supreme Court further illustrates elements of second-stage modernism. Basically, the realists attacked with two types of argument. The first originated with Holmes's dissent in the *Lochner* case itself.[45] Holmes strongly argued that the Court should have deferred to the legislative decision to restrict the hours of employees. The Court, failing to exercise the appropriate degree of judicial restraint, intruded into the institutional role of the legislature.[46] As developed by realists who eventually became New Dealers, this call for judicial restraint in constitutional cases emphasized the ability of individual governmental experts other than judges—that is, experts in *legislatures* and *administrative agencies*—to use instrumental reason to reorder society for the promotion of the economic and social well-being of a broad spectrum of citizens. Of course, this criticism of judicial activism in *Lochner* was somewhat in tension with the realist argument that judges should do social engineering. For the most part, though, this tension was avoided by emphasizing judicial social engineering in the common law fields, such as contracts and property, and insisting upon judicial restraint in constitutional law.

The second type of realist criticism of *Lochner* focused on the Court's use of abstract formalist reasoning. The case had turned on the Court's supposedly logical deduction that the legislatively prohibited employment activities fell within a predefined conceptual category or sphere of private conduct, purified of governmental interference. The realists asserted that this abstract rationalism not only failed to peel away traditional cultural prejudices, but that it actually reflected and reinforced those prejudices, thus further obscuring the truth. In other words, the *Lochner* Court relied upon the assumed existence of a preexisting sphere of private conduct that protected individual freedom, but that reliance was not grounded on the experience of social reality. Rather, the assumed sphere of private conduct was an illusion generated by cultural prejudices. Individuals could enter into employment contracts, which were supposedly within the private sphere, only because the government already had created and continued to sanction the body of contract law. The so-called private sphere could not exist purified of governmental action: to the contrary, the private sphere existed only *because* of governmental action. Moreover, despite the Court's assumptions, individuals within the private sphere were not necessarily free: the absence of governmental interference was not equivalent to freedom since various individuals and groups within the private sphere constantly coerced each other. Indeed, in many instances, governmental action could increase individual freedom.[47]

Realism eventually encountered a form of the epistemological crisis that typifies the conclusion of second-stage modernism: the recognition that foundational knowledge might be unattainable because, regardless of the pretensions of rationalism and empiricism, the subject might never bridge the chasm between itself and the external world. More specifically, realism encountered this crisis in the area of substantive or ethical values. The realist critique of first-stage rationalism meant that values could no longer be derived from abstract reasoning, and of course, the earlier rejection of premodernism meant that realists could not locate values in some preexisting natural order. Consequently, a mounting ethical and cultural relativism accompanied the rise of realism and the related empirical social sciences. To the realists and other intellectuals of this time, values appeared to arise out of the concrete and particular vagaries of human experiences. By the 1930s, intellectuals found it difficult to justify any set of moral values or cultural tenets over any others.[48] All values and cultures had equal claims to validity (and invalidity).

This rise of ethical and cultural relativism presented a serious challenge to legal and democratic theorists in the 1930s. How could political decision makers—judges, legislators, and administrators—legitimately determine substantive values and goals? Even more broadly, how could citizens in a democracy rationally discuss and decide political issues if they were swayed by cultural prejudices and demagogic symbols? To many theorists, politics seemed to be no more than a matter of raw power with political decisions spewing irrationally from the interplay of interests in each particular and concrete circumstance.[49] In fact, by 1940, most realists had abandoned empirical research. Such research might uncover value-free truths for social scientists, but for legal and political theorists who hoped to articulate and justify substantive values and goals, empirical research simply could not provide the necessary foundational knowledge.[50] Finally, political events toward the end of the decade intensified this challenge to legal and democratic theory. Specifically, for many American intellectuals, the international ascent of totalitarianism rendered a firm belief in democracy and the rule of law a necessity, yet the rise of ethical and cultural relativism severely weakened the theoretical supports of free government. Intellectuals were forced to ask a definitive question: If all values are relative, then why is American government better than totalitarianism?

Theorists responded to this crisis by taking the transcendental (or idealist) turn to third-stage modernism. Quite simply, American government was better than totalitarianism just because it was democratic: the commitment to democracy was unshakable. So, just as Kant had asked what conditions are necessary to explain human experience, political theorists now asked what conditions are necessary for democracy. For example, in 1939, John Dewey asked what type of culture promotes the political freedoms of democracy.[51] To Dewey, democracy had flourished in America because the culture had produced "a basic consensus and community of beliefs"[52]—that is, a commitment to democracy. Yet, Dewey queried, how can we insure that democracy would not degenerate into totalitarianism, as it had in other parts of the world? He concluded that the political methods of democracy—such as consultation, persuasion, negotiation, and communication—need to be extended into the cultural realm in order to assure the development and preservation of a culture that would, in turn, promote political democracy. In short, for Dewey, the key to democracy lay in democratic procedures: "[D]emocratic ends demand democratic methods for their realization."[53]

Two of Dewey's themes—the commitment to procedures or processes and the belief in an American social consensus—became central components in the development after World War II of a relativist theory of democracy.[54] While only a few years earlier, the relativity of values threatened to disarm democracy, the same relativism now became the theoretical foundation for free government. According to relativist democratic theory, a society must constantly choose what substantive values to endorse and thus what ends to pursue, but since values are relative, the only legitimate means for choosing among disparate values is the democratic process. In other words, the democratic process itself provides the only criterion for validating normative choices; there is no standard of validity higher than acceptance by the people in the political arena.

The most important formulation of this relativist theory of democracy was called pluralism, which viewed the political process as a legitimate battle among competing interest groups, all of whom bring preexisting and largely irrational (or arational) values to the political arena. Interest groups attempt to form coalitions, to compromise, and otherwise to gather political support in an unprincipled struggle to satisfy their own desires by influencing or controlling legislators.[55] Individuals, interest groups, and legislators never consider a community interest or common good. Robert Dahl typified this perspective when he wrote, "If unrestrained by external checks, any given individual or group of individuals will tyrannize over others."[56] The results of political battles therefore matter less than the process itself: the process legitimates the results. Values are relative, but democracy must continue.

Moreover, many political theorists believed that American culture produced a needed consensus regarding democratic processes. Although various individuals and interest groups might clash in political struggles, they shared certain elementary cultural norms that prevented the society from splintering into embittered fragments. Thus, these theorists, including many pluralists, saw an American society fundamentally and harmoniously joined in a cultural consensus celebrating the processes of democracy: individuals freely express diverse viewpoints, they negotiate, they disagree, and they compromise.[57] As Edward Purcell has noted, postwar theorists saw Americans as committed to a process of "unreflective practicality."[58]

Legal theorists, for the most part, accepted the relativist theory of democracy, but they still needed to address specific questions concerning the rule of law in a democracy. If judicial decision making were merely a matter of fiat, of kadi justice, then the rule of law was no more than a myth, and the balloon of democratic government would rapidly deflate. Since the political commitment to democracy was steadfast,[59] so too was the legal commitment to the rule of law. The legal realists were now condemned as nihilists because they had rejected legal rules and rationality as significant determinants in judicial decision making.[60] Legal reasoning and the rule of law must be an undeniable given. Thus, like the political theorists, legal theorists took a transcendental turn. Just as the political theorists had asked what conditions are necessary for democracy, legal theorists asked what conditions are necessary for the rule of law. If these conditions for the rule of law could be specified, they would provide the desired foundational source for objective judicial decision making. In their quest for these essential conditions, the legal theorists, again like the political theorists, focused primarily on process, supported by an assumed social consensus about the acceptability of the American legal system.

Although this "legal process" school of thought blossomed after World War II, its roots are evident in contemporaneous prewar criticisms of the realists. For example, Lon Fuller argued that the realists focused too heavily on the observable behavior of judges and other legal officials. Consequently, the realists undermined democracy by assuming that the law is simply what judges do and that legal rules and judicial reasoning are meaningless.[61] Further, to Fuller, the realists' haste to reject legal reasoning prompted them to make a positivist error by impugning a necessary connection between fact and value—between the law as it is and the law as it ought to be. As Fuller eventually elaborated his theory, this connection between fact and value becomes manifest in an inner morality of law. Fuller specified the components of this inner morality of law by asking the transcendental question characteristic of third-stage modernism: What are the conditions that make law possible? He concluded that these conditions consist of eight *procedural* desiderata, such as the requirements that laws should be clear, well publicized, and prospective.[62] In short, according to Fuller, the processes of the inner morality of law constitute "an essential condition" for the presence and power of law.[63]

Hence, third-stage legal modernism, in the form of the legal process school of thought, had emerged clearly by the 1950s. Legal process theorists were thoroughly committed to explaining the rule of law and justifying judicial decision making in the American democracy.[64] As early as 1951, Henry M. Hart already had articulated the central theme of legal process: the "principle of institutional settlement."[65] As restated by Hart and Albert Sacks in their well-known though unpublished course materials, "The Legal Process: Basic Problems in the Making and Application of Law," "The principle of institutional settlement expresses the judgment that decisions which are the duly arrived at result of duly established procedures . . . ought to be accepted as binding upon the whole society unless and until they are duly changed."[66] The legal process principle of institutional settlement developed the realists' institutional critique of *Lochner*: according to the realists (following Holmes), the Court had been guilty of judicial activism because it had intruded into the institutional role of the legislature. Legal process theorists, though, pushed this institutional critique to its extreme limit: the concept of the institution becomes paramount. According to legal process, society creates and designates different legal institutions to resolve different kinds of societal problems. Courts are, quite simply, different from legislatures: judges are not free to make law in the same way that legislators are free to do so. Most important, the various governmental institutions are largely defined by the different procedures or processes that are integral to them, and individuals working within different governmental institutions are therefore constrained by the respective processes.[67] In effect, the legal process theorists took the realists' institutional critique of *Lochner* and elaborated it through transcendental analysis: if courts, legislatures, and other governmental entities have different institutional roles, what are the processes that define those roles or make them possible?

According to legal process theory, the process that defines judicial decision making is called "reasoned elaboration."[68] Reasoned elaboration requires a judge always to give reasons for a decision, to articulate those reasons in a detailed and coherent manner, and to assume that "like cases should be treated alike."[69] The judge must relate the decision to the relevant rule of law, and must apply the rule of law in a manner logically consistent with precedent. Furthermore, in the context of common law cases and statutory interpretation, reasoned elaboration requires the judge to apply the law "in the way which best serves the principles and policies it expresses."[70] In a sense, then, the process of reasoned elaboration acknowledges a limited amount of judicial activism in certain specified contexts. Nevertheless, the central message of legal process theory is opposed to legal realism: legal rules and judicial opinions matter. According to legal process, the requirements of reasoned elaboration meaningfully constrain judges in ways that executive officers, legislators, and administrators are not constrained. Reasoned elaboration specifies the conditions or processes that engender the rule of law in a democracy, and those processes provide an objective foundation for neutral and apolitical judicial decision making.

In addition, during this third stage of legal modernism, the commitment to the independent and autonomous self who uses instrumental reason to control and reorder society continued unabated. This commitment was evident in at least three ways. First, political and legal theorists typically claimed that the relativist theory of democracy was rooted in Lockean individualism, which supposedly supported the American constitutional framework. For example, Louis Hartz argued that the shared fundamental assumption of both Lockean theory and American constitutional thought is that free and atomistic individuals existing in a state of nature join together to form a political community for the protection of their preexisting rights, especially liberty.[71] Second, in legal process theory, the principle of institutional settlement asked the fundamental question: Who decides?[72] That is, what governmental institution or actor should appropriately decide specific issues (and then, of course, what processes should guide or constrain those decisions)? Quite clearly, experts within certain governmental institutions—legislatures and administrative agencies—were deemed qualified to use instrumental reason to direct society. Indeed, as already discussed, even judges occasionally could make law to help achieve the principles and policies of statutes and the common law. Third, the legal process scholars firmly believed that they themselves were important actors in the legal system. They were convinced that they should instruct Supreme Court Justices about the law, that the Justices would listen, and that the Court's decisions (and hence the scholars' instructions) changed American society.[73]

From one perspective, legal process theorists merely identified, albeit carefully and precisely, the craft norms for legal institutions, particularly judicial decision making.[74] If a judge wants to be good, the theorists insisted, then he or she should just do what we say. Indeed, looking backward at legal process scholars, they often seem so arrogant, yet prosaic, as to be puzzling: Why would intelligent scholars devote their careers to articulating such trite maxims as "Treat like cases alike"? But when legal process is viewed as third-stage modernism, the dedication and even zeal of its devotees become understandable. After World War II, legal foundationalism seemed endangered: the rule of law and the objectivity of judicial decision making were under intellectual siege. The realists had irremediably discredited the abstract rationalism of classical orthodoxy, and now the realists' own empiricism was likewise disparaged. And in the midst of this intellectual crisis and impending despair, the legal process theorists believed that they had discovered the solution. They somehow had pulled the rabbit out of the hat! With transcendental reasoning, they explained how America had democracy and the rule of law. They justified America during the Cold War. They described the structures, the conditions, the *processes* of the American legal system that produced the objective foundations necessary for judicial decision making.

II. The Warren Court Intervenes

Brown v. Board of Education

Political and intellectual pressure led to the transformation of the Supreme Court in 1937: a commitment to judicial restraint replaced the *Lochner* Court's activism in cases involving economic regulations.[75] For the most part, the Court accepted the realists' institutional critique of *Lochner*, and at least temporarily, a majority of Justices consistently deferred to Congress and the state legislatures. Nonetheless, a crack in this judicial consensus quickly appeared with Justice Stone's footnote 4 in *United States v. Carolene Products*,[76] decided in 1938. Stone suggested that although judicial restraint was appropriate in cases involving economic regulations, some degree of judicial activism might be appropriate in cases involving certain personal rights and liberties. Soon, the previously aligned Progressives and New Deal liberals on the Court divided into two groups.[77] One group of Justices, led by Black and Douglas, seized upon Stone's insight and declared that there were "preferred freedoms," such as freedom of speech and freedom of religion, which merited special judicial protection. The second group of Justices, led by Frankfurter and Jackson, insisted on (almost) strict adherence to a philosophy of judicial restraint. According to this latter group, if the Court were to pick and choose among various rights, designating some as preferred and others as not, then it would be as guilty as the *Lochner* Court of unconstrained activism. This dispute was never merely a matter of constitutional theory; political and social pressures also bore on the Justices. For example, in 1940, the Court upheld the expulsion of two public school students, who were Jehovah's Witnesses, for their religiously motivated refusal to salute the flag.[78] Subsequently, religious bigotry surged across the nation, sometimes erupting in violence.[79] Hence, in an abrupt about-face, the Court overruled itself, holding in 1943 that compulsory flag-salutes were unconstitutional.[80]

In this context, with a divided and volatile set of Justices, *Brown v. Board of Education*[81] arrived at the Supreme Court in 1952, challenging the constitutionality of racial segregation in public schools. Unsurprisingly, after the Justices' post-oral argument conference in December 1952, the result in the case was unclear.[82] Most important, though, Justice Frankfurter already had decided to vote that racial segregation should be held unconstitutional, regardless of his otherwise staunch advocacy of judicial deference to legislative actions.[83] At the conference, Frankfurter convinced the Justices to order reargument for the next Court term, supposedly to answer specific questions drafted by him and his clerk, Alexander Bickel. The questions focused on the history of the Fourteenth Amendment and the problems related to a decree if segregation were held unconstitutional. But Frankfurter's primary purpose in seeking reargument was simply to delay: after the 1952 oral argument, he believed that, at best, the Justices would hold segregation unconstitutional by only a five-to-four vote. With the decision delayed until the following term, Frankfurter hoped he might generate a stronger majority.[84] In a remarkable turn of events, Chief Justice Vinson died in September 1953. By the time that *Brown* was reargued in December 1953, Earl Warren was the new Chief Justice.

Ultimately, an uncertain mix of factors led to the final unanimous decision in

Brown. Chief Justice Warren, even more than Frankfurter, played a crucial role in securing unanimity. Among other strategic maneuverings, Warren facilitated unity by convincing the Justices to split the case into two parts, treating the question of the decree (*Brown II*) separately from the merits of the constitutional claim (*Brown I*).[85] With regard to the individual Justices, a desire to do the right thing, morally and constitutionally, surely motivated some of them,[86] but a variety of other factors were at least equally important. For example, the NAACP had orchestrated a sustained (though often unsystematic) campaign that built slowly but steadily on the already existing tradition of equal protection until the "separate but equal" doctrine of *Plessy v. Ferguson*[87] appeared facially indefensible.[88] Furthermore, domestically, racial segregation hampered the economic development of the nation, especially the South, and overt racism suddenly seemed embarrassing and uncomfortable after the Holocaust. Internationally, Jim Crow laws severely disadvantaged the nation in its Cold War battle for the allegiance of emerging Third World nations.[89]

In any event, *Brown* of course held that racial segregation of public school children violated the Equal Protection Clause of the Fourteenth Amendment.[90] Warren's opinion was uncommonly brief. He began by stating that the history of the adoption of the Fourteenth Amendment did not provide any clear guidance to the Court, and hence, he reasoned, the Constitution must be interpreted in light of the current social context surrounding racially segregated public education.[91] Warren then emphasized two points. First, segregation had detrimental psychological effects on African American children.[92] Second, public education was immensely important in America:

> Today, education is perhaps the most important function of state and local governments. Compulsory school attendance laws and the great expenditures for education both demonstrate our recognition of the importance of education to our democratic society. It is required in the performance of our most basic public responsibilities, even service in the armed forces. It is the very foundation of good citizenship. Today it is a principal instrument in awakening the child to cultural values, in preparing him for later professional training, and in helping him to adjust normally to his environment. In these days, it is doubtful that any child may reasonably be expected to succeed in life if he is denied the opportunity of an education. Such an opportunity, where the state has undertaken to provide it, is a right which must be made available to all on equal terms.[93]

Therefore, Warren concluded, "Separate educational facilities are inherently unequal."[94]

Fourth-Stage Legal Modernism

The decision and opinion in *Brown* helped catapult American legal thought into the fourth stage of modernism, late crisis, with its deeply inconsistent attitudes and projects—anxiety, despair, anger, denunciations, and increasingly complex modernist solutions that pick and choose elements from rationalism, empiricism, and transcendentalism. *Brown* not only generated social furor, it also engendered academic uproar. The early legal process materials had not focused on the question of judicial review in the context of constitutional decision making. *Brown* brought this problem to the forefront, and in so doing, *Brown* almost immediately uncovered the inherent weaknesses within the transcendental reasoning of legal process theory.

Interestingly, in the first Harvard Law Review Foreword after *Brown*, Albert Sacks effusively praised the decision and the Court.[95] He wrote that *Brown* "illustrates the functioning of the judicial process at its best,"[96] and that Warren's brief opinion represented "judicial statesmanship"[97] because, in part, of "[i]ts style of straightforward simplicity."[98] Nonetheless, Sacks initiated the legal process assault on the Warren Court by criticizing its excessive use of per curiam summary opinions.[99] Here, then, a basic tension between legal process and the Warren Court immediately crystallized. Legal process theorists emphasized the importance of rules and legal reasoning in judicial opinions, but the Warren Court was deciding cases without adequately explaining its reasoning process. By the next Foreword, the relationship between the legal process scholars and the Court already had deteriorated. In a rebuke partially aimed at Sacks, Robert Braucher caustically noted that he would *not* be praising the Warren Court's "judicial statesmanship."[100]

The tension between the legal process scholars and the Warren Court continued to simmer over the next few years. The legal process theorists, consequently, elaborated their basic theoretical points in the course of criticizing the Court. For example, Alexander Bickel and Harry Wellington condemned not only the Warren Court's excessive use of unexplained per curiam decisions (as Sacks had done), but also the Court's issuance of vacuous opinions, resembling negotiated agreements, instead of "rationally articulated grounds of decision."[101] Ernest Brown criticized the Court for summarily disposing of too many cases without the benefit of full briefing and oral argument. The Court, in other words, was failing to follow the procedures that were necessary for reaching properly reasoned conclusions.[102] Henry Hart argued that the mounting case load of the Court prevented it from fulfilling its institutional role—to write opinions with clearly articulated reasons and principles.[103] The Court must exemplify the rule of law: "Only opinions which are grounded in reason and not on mere fiat or precedent can do the job which the Supreme Court of the United States has to do."[104] In presenting this argument, Hart elucidated the process of reasoned elaboration at the appellate level. According to Hart, a group of judges who reason together through a case should experience a "maturing of collective thought,"[105] a rationalizing process that allows the tribunal to transcend the idiosyncrasies of the individual judges.

The heated dispute between legal process theory and the Warren Court finally boiled over in 1958, when Herbert Wechsler issued the ultimate challenge to the Warren Court and its defenders. In his article, "Toward Neutral Principles of Constitutional Law,"[106] Wechsler argued that because of institutional demands, courts (but not legislatures and executives) must give reasoned explanations for their decisions. These explanations must not be ad hoc, instrumental, or unprincipled. To the contrary, a court must justify each decision with a "neutral principle":[107] a ground or reason that attains "adequate neutrality and generality"[108] by transcending the immediate result of the particular case. Most important, Wechsler then tested *Brown*, the Warren Court's flagship decision, against this standard of neutral principles. His effort to identify a neutral principle to support the decision led to the conclusion that freedom of association was the only possibility. Wechsler acknowledged that segregation contravenes the freedom of association of those who want to integrate (the plaintiffs in *Brown*), but he questioned whether the use of this principle in *Brown* was truly a neutral or reasoned application. Wechsler strikingly concluded that forced integration also *contravenes* the freedom of association—the freedom of association of those who wish to remain segregated. Consequently, Wechsler charged that the principle or rule of *Brown* was not neutral, and therefore the decision was objectively wrong.[109]

Wechsler's attack on *Brown* sparked an immediate flurry of scholarship, marked by an emerging sense of fourth-stage modernist anxiety and despair, as the third-stage transcendental solution threatened to collapse. On the one hand, Wechsler's attack on *Brown* seemed almost inevitable. After Sacks's initial praise of *Brown*, legal process scholars had become increasingly hostile toward the Warren Court. Their primary complaint revolved around the Court's supposedly inadequate opinions, which repeatedly failed to satisfy the requirements of reasoned elaboration. Thus, if not Wechsler, some other legal process theorist was sure to return eventually to *Brown* as the Warren Court's preeminent decision. Moreover, such a reexamination of the remarkably brief *Brown* opinion was likely to conclude that it had not satisfied the demands of legal process (since Warren apparently made no effort to do so). As Wechsler had resolved, "The problem [in *Brown*] inheres strictly in the reasoning of the opinion."[110] Yet, on the other hand, many scholars saw Wechsler's attack and conclusion as categorically unacceptable. If nothing more, *Brown* symbolized American equality and thus stood invulnerable, even if its acceptance somehow undermined the legal process defense of the rule of law.

Consequently, many scholars struggled to vindicate the decision in *Brown*, though often without offering any broader defense of the Warren Court. Louis Pollak offered an alternative opinion for the *Brown* decision that, he claimed, satisfied Wechsler's demand for a neutral principle.[111] Charles Black likewise offered a neutral principle in defense of *Brown*, but more important, he also angrily denounced Wechsler and legal process. To Black, racial segregation was a tragic social relationship in a concrete historical reality, and the demand for a neutral principle tended to dangerously abstract the human pain of this calamity. Thus, according to Black, the substantive result in *Brown* was so compelling that it should endure regardless of whether it could be justified with a neutral principle.[112] If legal process could not defend *Brown*, then by necessity, legal process must be wrong. *Brown* must stand.

By around 1960, then, *Brown* and the Warren Court had helped precipitate the late crisis of fourth-stage legal modernism. During the third stage, legal process theorists had used transcendental reasoning to describe the conditions needed for the rule of law and objective judicial decision making in a democracy. But the Warren Court, and *Brown* in particular, presented an intransigent reality. Warren Court opinions suggested that, at best, legal process theory described an imaginary world, not reality. Thus, the anxiety of legal process scholars intensified as they saw the Warren Court undermine their defense of the rule of law. For example, Moses Lasky lamented that the concepts of reasoned elaboration and neutral principles were merely theoretical, unrelated to the actuality of judicial decision making.[113] Despite this despair, though, legal process theory did not immediately collapse.

Some loyal legal process scholars pressed on, battling against the Warren Court; cries of nihilism once again were heard.[114] Meanwhile, other still-hopeful scholars struggled to defend *both* legal process and the Warren Court by developing increasingly complex theories. Indeed, over time, Wechsler's challenge to *Brown* generated some of the best legal process writing.

To the most loyal and rigid legal process theorists, the Warren Court seemed to be little more than a wayward realist, refusing to recognize the importance of the rule of law as expressed in well-reasoned judicial opinions. Perhaps more so than anyone else, Richard Wasserstrom eloquently articulated the legal process response to the realists' rule-skepticism and ostensible irrationalism, which seemed to characterize so many Warren Court opinions.[115] According to Wasserstrom, the realists had confused two distinct processes: the process of discovery and the process of justification. The process of discovery describes how a court reaches a conclusion in a case, while the process of justification describes how the court justifies or legitimates its conclusion. As applied to the process of discovery, the realist critique of legal reasoning and judicial opinions is correct: judicial opinions often do not accurately describe how judges reach their conclusions. As applied to the process of justification, however, the realists were mistaken: judicial opinions accurately describe (or *should* accurately describe) how judges justify their conclusions. That is, the realists failed to recognize that the purpose of the judicial opinion should be to describe the justification and not the discovery of the conclusion. Whereas the process of discovery might not be rational, the process of justification can and should be strictly rational. For ultimately, according to legal process, this requirement of strict rationality in the process of justification meaningfully (and objectively) constrains judicial decision making.[116] Hence, the Warren Court's consistent failure to adequately justify its decisions improperly and dangerously freed the Justices from the institutional restraints of reasoned elaboration.

If Wasserstrom most eloquently articulated the legal process argument for well-reasoned judicial opinions, then Alexander Bickel most eloquently stated the institutional critique of judicial activism in constitutional decision making. Bickel, echoing pluralistic political theory, argued that the legislative process is (or should be) a wide-open clash of interests, accessible to everyone and controlled by shifting majorities. Legislative actions are largely unprincipled and, at best, reflect the most expedient means for solving problems and attaining goals.[117] Nonetheless, to Bickel, the central commitment of our constitutional government is the democratic process, and legislative actions are therefore legitimate exactly because they are democratic—they supposedly represent the will of the majority of the people. Thus, when the Supreme Court strikes down a legislative act as unconstitutional, the Court supposedly defeats the democratic will. If the institutional role of the legislature is to allow the free play of democracy, then the institutional role of the Court in judicial review forces it to act contrary to the spirit of democracy. The Court's role, in short, creates a "counter-majoritarian difficulty."[118]

Bickel himself presented one possible solution to this countermajoritarian difficulty. According to Bickel, judicial review can be justified only if it adds something significant to government that is otherwise lacking. Because Bickel believed that the legislative process allows an unprincipled clash of interests, he argued that judicial review should inject principles or ethical values into our governmental system. Since, consistent with pluralistic political theory, Bickel saw an American society agreeing on basic cultural norms, he concluded that the Supreme Court's institutional function must be to enunciate and to apply those "enduring values of our society"[119]—Wechsler's neutral principles. Even so, Bickel insisted, the Court should act prudently, exercising self-restraint, so as to minimize its conflicts with the democratic process of the legislature. The "passive virtues"—doctrines such as standing, mootness, and ripeness—allow the Court carefully to bide its time. By relying on these passive virtues, the Court can avoid deciding on the merits many constitutional cases, thus deferring to the legislative judgments, but the Court can still seize those rare cases where a decision on the merits fosters the articulation of enduring values. The Court thus maintains its precarious yet crucial countermajoritarian function in our democratic system.[120]

As American legal thought already was entrenched in fourth-stage modernism, Bickel's solution to the countermajoritarian difficulty was immediately suspect, despite its sophistication and ingenuity. Gerald Gunther accused Bickel of undermining the rule of law because his passive virtues did not provide objective foundations for judicial decision making. To Gunther, the passive virtues were a "hollow formula"[121] that provided "virtually unlimited choice [to the Court] in deciding whether to decide."[122] As such, they were "law-debasing"[123] and ultimately inconsistent with legal process theory. More significant, Bickel himself eventually questioned whether the Court could ever articulate truly neutral principles. If all substantive values were relative—as the relativist theory of democracy suggested—then the Court could articulate neither neutral nor objective values. To the later Bickel, the modernist quest for foundations purified of cultural traditions was tragically absurd: reason (standing alone) was empty of content, and values necessarily arose from tradition itself.[124] Consequently, the entire legal process defense of the rule of law in the American democracy seemed doomed. Legal scholars had tumbled into the deep despair of fourth-stage modernism.

This despair, however, drove some legal process scholars to even higher levels of sophistication. Indeed, legal process theory may have reached its apex with John Hart Ely's constitutional theory of representation reinforcement, which attempted to harmonize legal process and *Brown*.[125] Accepting Bickel's skeptical conclusion about neutral principles, Ely vowed to intensify the commitment to process. The only solution to the problem of value relativism, according to Ely, was to develop a pure process-based approach to constitutional adjudication. The Court should never even attempt to articulate substantive values or goals, neutral or otherwise; all substantive value decisions must issue from the democratic process.[126] Yet, Ely realized, the democratic process is not always fair and open, so the Court should not automatically defer to legislative judgments. Instead, the Court should police the processes of democratic representation: a legislative action should be overturned as unconstitutional if and only if it resulted from a malfunctioning or defective democratic process. In Ely's view, process alone provides the foundation for objective judicial decision making. Furthermore, representation reinforcement actually dissolves the countermajoritarian difficulty because judicial review supports and promotes the democratic process.[127]

Ely elaborated his theory by arguing that the Court can police the democratic process in two ways. First, the Court should clear the channels of political change. To do so, the Court prevents the political "ins" from insuring their continued political power by choking the channels of political change and permanently excluding the political "outs."[128] For example, denying or diluting the right to vote through legislative malapportionment is a "quintessential stoppage" in the democratic process and therefore must be prevented by the Court.[129] Second, and most important for the defense of *Brown*, the Court should facilitate the representation of minorities. That is, the Court must prevent representatives from systematically disadvantaging minorities because of hostility or prejudice. The democratic process is malfunctioning if everyone is not "actually or virtually represented."[130] Minorities that technically participate in the democratic process by voting are nonetheless excluded if their elected representatives ignore their interests merely because they are minorities. Hence, for example, when a legislature intentionally discriminates against a minority for an improper motive, such as racial hostility, the Court should find the legislative action unconstitutional. For this reason, then, representation-reinforcement theory supposedly justified *Brown* and its condemnation of racial segregation in the public schools. Legislatures that had mandated racial segregation had not adequately represented the interests of African American constituents. Moreover, the segregated education of African American children eventually inhibited their ability as adults to fully participate in the democratic process.[131]

Griswold v. Connecticut

The decision in *Griswold v. Connecticut*[132] arose after a prolonged political and legal battle over the anticontraception statute of Connecticut.[133] The statute already had been challenged in a declaratory judgment action before the Supreme Court four years earlier. In *Poe v. Ullman*,[134] the Court held, by a slim five-to-four majority, that the case was not ripe for adjudication. Justice Frankfurter, one of the strongest advocates of judicial restraint on the Court, wrote a plurality opinion celebrating the passive virtues.[135] By the time that *Griswold* reached the Court, however, Frankfurter and another member of the *Poe* majority had retired.[136] Thus, Estelle Griswold, the director of the Planned Parenthood League of Connecticut, and most of her colleagues were confident of finally achieving victory.[137]

In *Griswold*, Justice Douglas wrote a rather disjointed majority opinion holding that the anticontraception statute unconstitutionally violated a right of privacy. Douglas seldom revised his opinions extensively, but in this case, he substantially modified his first draft in reaction to a letter from Justice Brennan. Douglas's first draft relied primarily on the First Amendment right of association, but Brennan's letter, drafted largely by one of his clerks, suggested that even though Douglas did not rely on substantive due process, his reasoning "may come back to haunt us just as *Lochner* did."[138] In the revised opinion, Douglas took two steps to deflect the likely accusation that the Warren Court was, in effect, reenacting *Lochner*. First, after briefly addressing the question of standing, Douglas claimed that, contrary to *Lochner*, the Court in *Griswold* would not move beyond the bounds of its institutional role: "We do not sit as a super-legislature to determine the wisdom, need, and propriety of laws that touch economic problems, business affairs, or social conditions. This law, however, operates directly on an intimate relation of husband and wife and their physician's role in one aspect of that relation."[139]

Second, Douglas significantly modified his line of reasoning. Although he began his analysis of the merits by retaining his original emphasis on the right of association, in the midst of this discussion, Douglas abruptly declared that the First Amendment has a penumbra that protects privacy.[140] He then shifted his focus from the right of association to several other guarantees in the Bill of Rights. Each of these guarantees, he reasoned, produces or emanates penumbras of privacy. Douglas then recast his initial discussion of the right of association as merely illustrative:

> [S]pecific guarantees in the Bill of Rights have penumbras, formed by emanations from those guarantees that help give them life and substance. Various guarantees create zones of privacy. The right of association contained in the penumbra of the First Amendment is one, as we have seen. The Third Amendment in its prohibition against the quartering of soldiers "in any house" in time of peace without the consent of the owner is another facet of that privacy. The Fourth Amendment explicitly affirms the "right of the people to be secure in their persons, houses, papers, and effects, against unreasonable searches and seizures." The Fifth Amendment in its Self-Incrimination Clause enables the citizen to create a zone of privacy which government may not force him to surrender to his detriment. The Ninth Amendment provides: "The enumeration in the Constitution, of certain rights, shall not be construed to deny or disparage others retained by the people."[141]

Then, after briefly discussing some specific protections of privacy, Douglas found that these various penumbras combine to generate a *zone* of privacy—a whole greater than the sum of its parts (the respective penumbras).[142] Rather abruptly again, though, Douglas shifted his focus, now to the marital relationship,[143] and then he quickly concluded that the anticontraception law infringed the protected zone of privacy.

> The present case, then, concerns a relationship lying within the zone of privacy created by several fundamental constitutional guarantees. And it concerns a law which, in forbidding the use of contraceptives rather than regulating their manufacture or sale, seeks to achieve its goals by means having a maximum destructive impact upon that relationship. . . . Would we allow the police to search the sacred precincts of marital bedrooms for telltale signs of the use of contraceptives? The very idea is repulsive to the notions of privacy surrounding the marriage relationship.[144]

Douglas finished the majority opinion by suggesting that the right of privacy was natural law: "We deal with a right of privacy older than the Bill of Rights—older than our political parties, older than our school system."[145]

The Justices themselves blatantly revealed their considerable concern about the reasoning in *Griswold*. During oral argument and at the post-argument conference, Chief Justice Warren and Justices Black and White were troubled by the possible justifications for overturning the statute and the potential reach of those justifications. In particular, they wondered about the implications for abortion.[146] Furthermore, although the vote to hold the statute unconstitutional was seven to two, only four other Justices joined Justice Douglas's opinion. Justices Harlan and White each concurred only in the judgment and wrote his own opinion. Even Justice Goldberg, who joined Douglas's opinion, nonetheless wrote a separate concurrence, and Chief Justice Warren and Justice Brennan joined Goldberg's concurrence as well as Douglas's majority opinion. Justices Black and Stewart wrote dissents.[147]

As was true of Douglas, all of the other Justices wrote their concurring and dissenting opinions in the shadow of *Lochner.* All of the Justices, except for White, revealed an anxious awareness of the institutional critique of *Lochner.* Goldberg, emphasizing the relevance of the Ninth Amendment to the Court's holding, reasoned that the Fourteenth Amendment protects fundamental personal rights. But he wrote circumspectly: "In determining which rights are fundamental, judges are not left at large to decide cases in light of their personal and private notions. Rather, they must look to the 'traditions and (collective) conscience of our people' to determine whether a principle is 'so rooted (there) . . . as to be ranked as fundamental.'"[148]

Justice Harlan most clearly accepted a substantive due process approach, closely resembling *Lochner*, but he stressed that the Court was nonetheless constrained in constitutional adjudication: "Judicial self-restraint . . . will be achieved in this area, as in other constitutional areas, only by continual insistence upon respect for the teachings of history, solid recognition of the basic values that underlie our society, and wise appreciation of the great roles that the doctrines of federalism and separation of powers have played in establishing and preserving American freedoms."[149]

Of course, the dissents of both Black and Stewart expressly accused the Court of overstepping its institutional constraints and of therefore acting like the *Lochner* Court.[150] At times, Black sounded remarkably similar to a legal process theorist:

> My point is that there is no provision of the Constitution which either expressly or impliedly vests power in this Court to sit as a supervisory agency over acts of duly constituted legislative bodies and set aside their laws because of the Court's belief that the legislative policies adopted are unreasonable, unwise, arbitrary, capricious or irrational. The adoption of such a loose, flexible, uncontrolled standard for holding laws unconstitutional, if ever it is finally achieved, will amount to a great unconstitutional shift of power to the courts which I believe and am constrained to say will be bad for the courts and worse for the country.[151]

From Modernism to Postmodernism

Unsurprisingly, the Justices were not alone in voicing their concerns about the reasoning in *Griswold.* Legal process theorists, joined by other scholars, continued their assault on the Warren Court with two typical and related criticisms: first, the legal reasoning in the opinion was inadequate, and second, the Court had moved beyond its proper institutional role (it was *Lochner* all over again). Paul Kauper, for instance, castigated Douglas's opinion as a lame attempt to appear objective when it was truly based on substantive due process.[152] Hyman Gross maintained that Douglas had distorted the meaning of "privacy,"[153] while Alfred Kelly criticized Goldberg's use of constitutional history, suggesting that it obscured the Court's return to "an open-ended concept of substantive due process after *Lochner*."[154] Raoul Berger insisted that *Griswold* "exemplifies the readiness of the Justices to act as a 'super-legislature' when their own emotions are engaged."[155] Even Thomas Emerson, who had represented Griswold before the Supreme Court, acknowledged that scholars could easily criticize the opinion.[156]

Robert Bork was perhaps the most outspoken critic of *Griswold*.[157] Bork agreed with Wechsler that all constitutional decisions must be based on neutral principles, but Bork then argued that the *Court* cannot legitimately *choose* any fundamental values for judicial protection. Any such choice by the Court would not be neutral—the value would not be a neutral principle.[158] To Bork, the Court should decide constitutional issues based on values chosen solely by "the Founding Fathers."[159] The Court can identify these values through only two methods: first, by finding rights "specified" in the constitutional text or intent of the framers, or second, by recognizing rights, such as in the free speech area, that are necessary to preserve our governmental processes.[160] Otherwise, the Justices necessarily impose their own values on the rest of American society: "When the Constitution has not spoken, the Court will be able to find no scale, other than its own value preferences, upon which to weigh the respective claims. . . ."[161] Finally, Bork concluded that *Griswold* was "a typical decision of the Warren Court":[162] it perfectly illustrated how unprincipled judicial decision making can undermine the democratic process.

At a minimum, Bork was wrong on one important point: *Griswold* was not a typical Warren Court decision. Most of the earlier significant Warren Court cases, including *Brown*, could reasonably be explained as promoting or protecting the democratic political process. Regardless of the actual reasoning in the opinions, representation-reinforcement theory could at least plausibly justify most of the decisions. Representation reinforcement, though, could not adequately justify *Griswold*.[163] Consequently, this consummate legal process theory came under a two-pronged attack. First, many scholars cared more about maintaining the Warren Court decisions, including *Griswold*, than they cared about defending representation reinforcement or any other type of legal process theory. These scholars willingly sacrificed legal process as they searched for some alternative theory that might better justify the Warren Court.[164] Typically, these alternative theories, such as natural law,[165] were throwbacks to earlier modernist and even premodernist eras, and consequently, they were patently inadequate within the parameters of third- and fourth-stage modernism.[166] Second (and related to the first prong), many scholars not only abandoned legal process in their quest for a better defense of the Warren Court, they also directly attacked representation-reinforcement theory. For example, Ely had argued that the Court should police the democratic process by facilitating the representation of minorities. Critics stressed, however, that the *Court* had to differentiate among the various societal groups who lost in the unprincipled battles of pluralistic democracy. Some such groups were designated as (discrete and insular) minorities deserving special judicial protection, while other groups were deemed mere losers in the democratic process. From the perspective of legal process theory, though, this necessary differentiation between societal groups was problematic: it required the Court to engage in exactly those unconstrained substantive value choices that representation-reinforcement theory was supposed to forbid.[167] Thus, *Griswold* and its progeny, especially *Roe v. Wade*,[168] helped reveal that representation-reinforcement theory had failed in its mission: to harmonize legal process with *Brown*. At best, representation reinforcement offered a defense of *Brown*, but it did so (if at all) only by sacrificing the central goal of legal process, neutral and objective judicial decision making.

Legal thought thus swirled into a maelstrom of despair. Legal modernism demanded that judicial decision making—including constitutional adjudication—be based on some objective foundation. Yet, despite yeoman (and sometimes even heroic) efforts for over one hundred years—despite sundry attempts at rationalism, empiricism, and transcendentalism—legal theorists were unable to discover any such ground for the rule of law. The Warren Court's overt disregard for the tenets of legal process highlighted this failure and magnified the scholarly desperation. Quite simply, the key Warren Court decisions, such as *Brown* and *Griswold*, could not be defended within the parameters of modernist legal thought, yet those same decisions often seemed substantively right—almost too right to dispute.

If, as I have argued, the early Warren Court helped catapult legal thought into the anxiety, despair, and creative complexity of fourth-stage (late crisis) modernism, then the later Warren Court forced modernism to confront the possibility of its own demise because its self-imposed demands now seemed plainly unachievable. Archibald Cox's 1966 Foreword to the *Harvard Law Review* epitomized the dilemma that the Warren Court engendered for legal scholars. Cox unabashedly praised "the magnificent accomplishments of the Warren Court,"[169] yet simultaneously, he lamented that "when all this is said, ability to rationalize a constitutional judgment in terms of principles referable to accepted sources of law is an essential, major element of constitutional adjudication."[170]

Other factors—both social and intellectual—then rushed into this intellectual vortex. Legal process scholars, like most 1950s political theorists, believed that Americans were joined in a consensus celebrating American democracy and the rule of law. But during the 1950s and 1960s, the Civil Rights movement, the Vietnam War protests, and then later, the women's movement, belied any such consensus. If anything, American society seemed to be splintering irreparably into diverse and opposed groups (or perhaps, more precisely, many Americans were first becoming aware of certain societal divisions that had long existed). And the legal system, in reality, did not appear to deal equally with these different groups; the neutral application of some objective rule of law was uncovered as a myth.[171] When some former Vietnam War student-protesters became law professors in the early 1970s, they founded the critical legal studies movement, which focused on economic divisions and inequities in American society. These "crits," disenchanted with mainstream liberalism and the American legal system, completely rejected the predominant forms of legal thought, especially legal process theory, and thus they searched for some alternative methods or frameworks for approaching the law. Their frequent turns to Marxist, Weberian, and structuralist social theories helped introduce new vocabularies and techniques to legal thought.[172] While Marx, Weber, and the structuralists were themselves modernists, as were most of the crits, the mere use of continental theory and terminology opened a path for other legal theorists to follow.

And following immediately behind the crits were scholars who took the "interpretive turn" in jurisprudence, especially in constitutional theory.[173] As already discussed, constitutional scholars, at least since *Griswold*, had been searching for some theory that could justify the key Warren Court decisions without sacrificing the rule of law, but all of these proffered theories were patently inadequate. By the 1970s and early 1980s, constitutional theorists in fourth-stage modernism were suffocating in despair; in fact, crits insisted that the entire enterprise of constitutional theory was futile (and worthless).[174] Then, influenced by a wide range of scholars from outside the legal academy—such as Thomas Kuhn, a historian of science,[175] Stanley Fish, a literary critic,[176] and Hans-Georg Gadamer, a continental philosopher,[177] some constitutional theorists finally stopped asking the inveterate modernist question: What foundations can objectively constrain constitutional interpretation and adjudication? Instead, these constitutional scholars began asking a *postmodern* question: How does (constitutional) interpretation occur? Eventually, this question led legal scholars to other late-twentieth century postmodern thinkers, such as Michel Foucault, Jacques Derrida, Richard Rorty, and Jean-François Lyotard.

Meanwhile, the Civil Rights and the women's movements helped transform legal education, as more and more racial minorities and women became law professors and scholars. The writings of these "outgroup" scholars often revealed a vision of the legal system that differed radically from that of the legal process (and other mainstream) scholars.[178] Whereas the mainstream modernist scholar typically sought to ground knowledge on some essential or core truth, the outgroup scholar was more likely to recognize the existence of multiple truths. An African American constitutional scholar, for instance, might recognize more readily than a white scholar that the Constitution is a tool of both oppression and liberation: the Constitution legitimated slavery and Jim Crow as legal institutions, yet supported the Civil Rights movement and desegregation.[179]

Hence, because of a combination of diverse factors, legal thought began to twist over a shadowy border from modernism to postmodernism.[180] I have mentioned several dialectically related factors: the intervention of the Warren Court in third- and fourth-stage modernism (which I have emphasized), certain broad societal changes in America, and the influence of continental and then postmodern philosophy and social theory. The degree and way in which these factors combined is anything but clear. For example, most scholars have assumed that *Brown* and the Warren Court significantly aided the Civil Rights movement, but some now argue to the contrary, that *Brown* actually impeded the movement by inflaming Southern white resistance to political change (no one suggests that *Brown* was irrelevant to the societal changes that eventually spread through the nation).[181] Despite this uncertainty, it is clear that no single factor was alone sufficient or even necessary to cause the transition from modernism to postmodernism; rather, this transition represents a broad cultural transformation that transcends disciplinary boundaries, and hence, all academic fields will eventually be touched. Yet, within the particular historical context of American legal thought, these specific factors all played significant roles.

What is postmodernism? I will not attempt to categorically define it (since it cannot be defined in a modernist sense), but rather I will accentuate certain themes that distinguish postmodernism from modernism.[182] In particular, postmodernism rejects the two metaphysical premises that supported modernism: epistemological foundationalism, and a belief in an independent and autonomous self. Postmodernism is antifoundationalist because it accentuates that meaning and knowledge always remain ungrounded.[183] Unlike modernists, postmodernists do not attempt to strip away cultural traditions and prejudices to reveal a firm foundation for knowledge. In fact, for postmodernists, traditions and prejudices cannot be entirely stripped away, and even more important, our participation in communal traditions *enables* us to understand and communicate in the first place.[184]

Postmodernism also is antiessentialist because ungrounded meanings are always unstable and shifting: meaning (and truth) cannot be reduced to a static core or essence.[185] In Derridean terms, meaning is never grounded on a stable signified, rather there always is a play of signifiers.[186] Hence, postmodernists easily recognize that any text or event has many potential meanings, many possible truths. As Joel Weinsheimer tersely declares: "[T]ruth keeps happening."[187] Thus, the postmodernist often invites the reader to perform gestalt flips or paradigm moves. Just when the reader seems to have settled on an essential meaning for the text, the postmodernist insists that the reader should flip, and the reader suddenly sees a totally different meaning. For example, the postmodernist says, "It may look like a duck now, but look again, and it's a rabbit!"[188] Hence, one can now see how postmodernism and outgroup scholarship are intimately and dialectically related. Outgroup scholarship generates legal postmodernism by recognizing or uncovering multiple truths where before but one appeared, yet simultaneously, postmodernism supports outgroup scholarship by explaining the existence of multiple truths and meanings.

Postmodernism not only rejects modernist foundationalism, it also rejects the modernist belief in an independent and autonomous self. Postmodernists do not envision a self who uses instrumental reason to control and improve society; instead, the self is socially constructed. For instance, Pierre Schlag emphasizes that the discourse of modernist legal scholars helps to construct the modernist (relatively autonomous) self. That is, modernist scholars always implicitly assume that they address a reader—another self, who is typically a Supreme Court Justice—who uses reason to exercise control over others and over the external world. Moreover, these scholars assume that they too are able to exercise control over the world—what the scholars write presumably changes or is likely to change the world consistently with their own desires.[189] Postmodern scholars, on the other hand, no longer assume (or pretend) that they are talking to the Supreme Court Justices or to any other judges. Instead, postmodernists explicitly detach themselves from the judiciary and dissociate themselves from the practical concerns of attorneys.[190] Moreover, this postmodern attitude seems justified. Few judges read and care about legal scholarship, especially postmodern scholarship. A busy judge does not have time to plod through reams of scholarship that appear to say so little about judicial practice. Besides, judges are unconcerned whether scholars approve or disapprove of their decisions and opinions.[191] Postmodern legal scholars thus are free to discuss Derrida and deconstruction,[192] Foucault and poststructuralism,[193] and Gadamer and philosophical hermeneutics.[194] It doesn't matter. Once legal scholars renounce any pretense of practically aiding lawyers and judges, they no longer seem bound to the discursive modes ordinarily used in those legal discourses.

At most, postmodern legal scholars are interpreters: they offer narrative interpretations of legal and other social developments.[195] As interpreters, though, postmodern scholars are not politically neutered: their narratives display their political commitments, and they often write critically of the current structures or arrangements of power within society.[196] Nonetheless, unlike modernist scholars, postmodern scholars are not compelled to finish every critical work by *recommending* some alternative social arrangement; such a recommendation necessarily reinscribes the relatively autonomous self by assuming that the reader (as well as the author) is empowered to intentionally transform society.

Interestingly, despite their different intentions or attitudes, postmodern legal scholars largely maintain the same social role or position as modernist scholars. All legal scholars, whether modern or postmodern, teach students and try to write and publish articles and books. Put differently, postmodern legal scholars are enmeshed largely in the same structures of social relationships as modernist legal scholars, or in other words, power frequently is structural. Power "exists in relationships—it has a primary location in the ongoing, habitual ways in which human beings relate to one another."[197] Individuals often exercise power (or perform certain activities) not because of expertise or knowledge but rather because they occupy certain relatively embedded though contingent social positions or institutional roles that endure within complex social practices. Thus, unless and until the practice of legal scholarship changes, legal scholars will remain legal scholars, regardless of whether they write about modernist or postmodernist themes.

Although power is structural insofar as social roles and practices are ongoing and embedded, those roles and practices—whether modern or postmodern—always remain inherently contingent. Social practices, such as the practice of legal scholarship, must be continually reconstructed, or they will cease to exist. And within this process of reconstruction, the possibility of transformation always pulses; practices can and do change. Moreover, while all enduring social practices—whether modern or postmodern—tend to reconstruct and transform themselves, a distinctive aspect of many *postmodern* practices is their reflexive (or reflective) self-production.[198] That is, postmodernists realize that their (our) social practices are historically and culturally contingent and that those practices constantly reconstruct themselves through their (our) own words, thoughts, and actions. Postmodernists turn toward their own social practices and make the cultural and theoretical awareness of those practices part of the practices themselves. In a sense, then, postmodernism transforms practices to include self-reflexive or self-referential awareness. Postmodern legal scholars reveal this self-reflexivity in their somewhat narcissistic tendency to focus on the practice of legal scholarship itself (as in this very essay).[199]

To a great extent, then, the transition from modernism to postmodernism in legal scholarship amounts to a change in attitude.[200] Despite continuing in the social role of the legal scholar, the postmodernist sheds the dual metaphysical commitments of modernism—foundationalism and the relatively autonomous self. Moreover, postmodernists are no longer committed to the argumentative modes or tools of modernism: rationalism, empiricism, and transcendentalism. Nevertheless, postmodernists often continue to use these modernist tools *as if* they led to foundational knowledge. In so doing, though, postmodernists act self-reflexively, always understanding the inherent limits of the tools. To avoid being or appearing merely modernist, then, postmodernists must somehow connote the irony of this self-reflective use of modernist techniques—thus, the metaphorical raised eyebrow, wink, or grin.

Once again, Schlag illustrates this postmodern approach. In an article entitled "The Problem of the Subject," Schlag largely follows the strict decorum of formal legal writing (that is, modernist legal thought), yet in the midst of underscoring the link between the form and content of modernist discourse, Schlag manages to poke fun at the vapid rigidity of formal writing by referring to Langdell as "Chris."[201] This playful mix of styles marks the metaphorical arched eyebrow, suggesting Schlag's self-reflexive and ironic use of the more formal style. Thus, even in the midst of writing in the fashion of modernism, Schlag manages to disclose his self-reflexive postmodern attitude.

Conclusion

This narrative has sketched the development of American legal thought through four stages of modernism and a transition to postmodernism. Legal modernism is characterized by two metaphysical commitments: epistemological foundationalism and the belief in the relatively autonomous self. The first stage of legal modernism, represented by classical orthodoxy, focused on abstract rationalism as a means to foundational knowledge. The second stage, most fully developed in legal realism, turned to empiricism as a source of objectivity. During the third stage, legal process theorists largely used transcendental reasoning to theoretically secure the objectivity and neutrality supposedly needed to justify and explain the rule of law. But the early Warren Court, and *Brown* in particular, quickly revealed the failings of legal process. Consequently, American jurisprudence rushed into the fourth stage, which was marked by confusion, despair, and creative complexity. The later Warren Court decisions, including *Griswold*, then forced modernism to confront its own demise because its self-imposed demands now seemed patently unachievable. Through a combination of factors, including the Warren Court decisions, legal thought began to edge toward postmodernism. Most simply, postmodernism rejects the metaphysical premises of modernism; postmodern legal scholars are antifoundationalists and insist that the self is socially constructed. Consequently, although postmodernists still perform as legal scholars, they write with an attitude (and often in a style) that radically differs from that of the modernists.

Finally, at this point in American legal thought, two concluding remarks are in order. First, postmodernism has not yet completely replaced modernism in jurisprudence (or for that matter, in other fields). Clearly, many current legal scholars remain modernists, and indeed, a postmodernist might insist that vestiges of modernism will always remain visible within postmodernism.[202] Second, to modernists, postmodernism often appears nihilistic, irresponsible, and indeed, without any redeeming social value. Modernists therefore often recommend that we should choose to stave off postmodernism and to remain modernists. To the postmodernist, however, we do not have a choice between modernism and postmodernism. The very notion of a choice illustrates and reinscribes the modernist (relatively autonomous) self. From a postmodern perspective, the movement from modernism to postmodernism is a contingent cultural transformation. Individuals and societal groups might influence this transition, but they do not control it. Only in a modernist dream can we consider the options, choose the best one, and then effectively implement it. Postmodern legal scholars might be dreamers, but they are no longer having this particular dream.

Notes

I thank Stanley Fish, Laura Kalman, Gary Minda, Mark Tushnet, Larry Catá Backer, Linda Lacey, Johnny Parker, Nick Rostow, Bernard Schwartz, and the participants in the University of Tulsa College of Law Colloquy Series for their helpful comments on earlier drafts. I also thank the Faculty Summer Research Grant Program of the University of Tulsa College of Law for its financial support.

1. I previously have discussed postmodernism in Feldman, "Diagnosing Power: Postmodernism in Legal Scholarship and Judicial Practice (With an Emphasis on the *Teague* Rule Against New Rules in Habeas Corpus Cases)," 88 *Nw. U. L. Rev.* 1046 (1994) [hereinafter Feldman, "Diagnosing Power"]; Feldman, "The Persistence of Power and the Struggle for Dialogic Standards in Postmodern Constitutional Jurisprudence: Michelman, Habermas, and Civic Republicanism," 81 *Geo. L.J.* 2243 (1993) [hereinafter Feldman, "The Persistence of Power"]; see also Feldman, "The Politics of Postmodern Jurisprudence," 95 *Mich. L. Rev.* (forthcoming 1996).

I rely heavily on the following books and essays that focus on postmodernism. Bauman, *Intimations of Postmodernity* (1992); Connor, *Postmodernist Culture* (1989); Harvey, *The Condition of Postmodernity* (1989); Jameson, *Postmodernism, or The Cultural Logic of Late Capitalism* (1991); Lyotard, *The Postmodern Condition: A Report on Knowledge* (Bennington and Massumi trans., 1984); *Feminism/Postmodernism* (Nicholson ed., 1990); Boyne and Rattansi, "The Theory and Politics of Postmodernism: By Way of an Introduction," in *Postmodernism and Society* 1 (Boyne and Rattansi eds., 1990); Crook, "The End of Radical Social Theory? Notes on Radicalism, Modernism and Postmodernism," in *Postmodernism and Society* 46 (Boyne and Rattansi eds., 1990).

2. Some books and essays by legal scholars who either arguably are postmodern or at least write about postmodernism include the following: Cornell, *Beyond Accommodation* (1991) [hereinafter Cornell, *Beyond*]; Cornell, *The Philosophy of the Limit* (1992) [hereinafter Cornell, *Limit*]; Fish, *Doing What Comes Naturally* (1989); Minda, *Postmodern Legal Movements: Law and Jurisprudence at Century's End* (1995); Backer, "Raping Sodomy and Sodomizing Rape: A Morality Tale About the Transformation of Modern Sodomy Jurisprudence," 21 *Am. J. Crim. L.* 37 (1993); Backer, "Of Handouts and Worthless Promises: Understanding the Conceptual Limitations of American Systems of Poor Relief," 34 *B.C. L. Rev.* 997 (1993); Balkin, "Transcendental Deconstruction, Transcendent Justice," 92 *Mich. L. Rev.* 1131 (1994) [hereinafter Balkin, "Transcendental Deconstruction"]; Balkin, "What is a Postmodern Constitutionalism?," 90 *Mich. L. Rev.* 1966 (1992) [hereinafter Balkin, "Postmodern Constitutionalism"]; Balkin, "Ideology as Constraint," 43 *Stan. L. Rev.* 1133 (1991) [Balkin, "Ideology"]; Boyle, "Is Subjectivity Possible? The Post-Modern Subject in Legal Theory," 62 *U. Colo. L. Rev.* 489 (1991); Delgado, "Storytelling for Oppositionists and Others: A Plea for Narrative," 87 *Mich. L. Rev.* 2411 (1989); Delgado and Stefancic, "Why Do We Tell the Same Stories?: Law Reform, Critical Librarianship, and the Triple Helix Dilemma," 42 *Stan. L. Rev.* 207 (1989); Harris, "Race and Essentialism in Feminist Legal Theory," 42 *Stan. L. Rev.* 581 (1990); Levinson and Balkin, "Law, Music, and Other Performing Arts," 139 *U. Pa. L. Rev.* 1597 (1991); Michelman, "Law's Republic," 97 *Yale L.J.* 1493 (1988);

Mootz, "Postmodern Constitutionalism as Materialism," 91 *Mich. L. Rev.* 515 (1992); Mootz, "Is the Rule of Law Possible in a Postmodern World?," 68 *Wash. L. Rev.* 249 (1993) [hereinafter Mootz, "Rule of Law"]; Patterson, "Postmodernism/Feminism/Law," 77 *Cornell L. Rev.* 254 (1992); Radin and Michelman, "Pragmatist and Poststructuralist Critical Legal Practice," 139 *U. Pa. L. Rev.* 1019 (1991); Schanck, "Understanding Postmodern Thought and Its Implications for Statutory Interpretation," 65 *S. Cal. L. Rev.* 2505 (1992); Schlag, "The Problem of the Subject," 69 *Tex. L. Rev.* 1627 (1991) [hereinafter Schlag, "The Problem"]; Schlag, "Normativity and the Politics of Form," 139 *U. Pa. L. Rev.* 801 (1991) [hereinafter Schlag, "Normativity"]; Tushnet, "The Left Critique of Normativity: A Comment," 90 *Mich. L. Rev.* 2325 (1992); Williams, "Rorty, Radicalism, Romanticism: The Politics of the Gaze," 1992 *Wis. L. Rev.* 131; Winter, "Indeterminacy and Incommensurability in Constitutional Law," 78 *Calif. L. Rev.* 1441 (1990).

3. 347 U.S. 483 (1954).

4. 381 U.S. 479 (1965).

5. Three books that were especially helpful in generating the ideas in this section were the following: Bernstein, *Beyond Objectivism and Relativism: Science, Hermeneutics, and Praxis* (1983); Rorty, *Philosophy and the Mirror of Nature* (1979); Tarnas, *The Passion of the Western Mind* (1991).

6. See Weber, *Economy and Society* 20–22 (Roth and Wittich eds., 1978); Weber, *The Methodology of the Social Sciences* 90, 100 (Shils and Finch eds., 1949); Feldman, "An Interpretation of Max Weber's Theory of Law: Metaphysics, Economics, and the Iron Cage of Constitutional Law," 16 *L. & Soc. Inquiry* 205, 212 n.31 (1991).

7. Nonetheless, some early modernists, such as Descartes, Francis Bacon, and Newton, still saw their insights as related to religion. See Tarnas, supra note 5, at 269–90. Indeed, the complex relation between religion and the development of modernism underscores that insofar as the four stages of modernism have crystallized during history, they are often due as much to political, cultural, and religious developments as to purely intellectual concepts. For example, the Reformation helped generate the modernist view that tradition can and should be questioned since the reformers attacked the traditional authority of the Roman Catholic Church. See Feldman, *Please Don't Wish Me a Merry Christmas: A Critical History of the Separation of Church and State* (N.Y.U. Press forthcoming 1997); Tarnas, supra note 5, at 233–47. See generally Cotterrell, *The Politics of Jurisprudence* (1989) (jurisprudential theory should be understood within its historical, political, and social contexts).

8. See, e.g, Descartes, *Meditations* (1641) (Veitch trans., Anchor Books ed. 1974), reprinted in *The Rationalists* 97, 112–27 (1974) (Descartes's cogito).

9. The second metaphysical commitment of modernism and its implications are crucial for distinguishing modernism from premodernism. Premodernism, like modernism, was committed to foundational knowledge, but that knowledge usually inhered in nature or God. The individual therefore did not need to bridge any gaps to the external world or mirror the external world in consciousness in order to have knowledge.

10. Locke argued that we gain knowledge from both our sensations of the external world and our perceptions of the operations of our own minds. See Locke, *An Essay Concerning Human Understanding*, reprinted in *The English Philosophers from Bacon to Mill* 238, 248–49 (Burtt ed., 1939). One can reasonably argue that, in the history of modernist philosophy, empiricism preceded rationalism since Francis Bacon (1561–1626) preceded Descartes (1596–1650). Bacon was undoubtedly important to the development of modernism as he encouraged both the questioning of tradition and the domination of nature through science. See Tarnas, supra note 5, at 272–75; see, e.g., Bacon, *Novum*

Organum, reprinted in Burtt, ed., supra, at 24–123. Nonetheless, most historians of philosophy focus on Locke as the progenitor of modernist empiricism. See, e.g., Hamlyn, *A History of Western Philosophy* 123–33, 168–78 (1987) (classifying Bacon as Renaissance philosopher and Locke as empiricist); Wedberg, 2 *A History of Philosophy: The Modern Age to Romanticism* 74 (1982) (acknowledging Bacon as reviving empiricist approach, but saying nonetheless that Locke "inaugurated an empiricist tradition which has since been in continuous existence up to our own time").

11. See Hamlyn, supra note 10, at 174; cf. Borgmann, *Crossing the Postmodern Divide* 37–47 (1992) (on Locke's emphasis on the individual).

12. Bauman, *Modernity and the Holocaust* 65, 70, 73, 91–92, 113–14 (1989).

13. Id. at 65.

14. See Kant, *Critique of Pure Reason*, reprinted in *Kant Selections* 3–5, 14–27, 43–66 (Greene ed., 1929).

15. Nietzsche wrote: "Kant wanted to prove in a way that would dumbfound the common man that the common man was right." Nietzsche, *The Gay Science* 193, reprinted in *The Portable Nietzsche* 93, 96 (Kaufmann ed., 1982).

16. Indeed, David Luban argues that a central component of modernism is the use of the "methods of a discipline to criticize the discipline itself." Luban, "Legal Modernism," 84 *Mich. L. Rev.* 1656, 1660 (1986).

17. See Schlag, "Fish v. Zapp: The Case of the Relatively Autonomous Self," 76 *Geo. L.J.* 37 (1987). Schlag writes that the relatively autonomous self is "a constructed self that concedes that it is socially and rhetorically constituted yet maintains its own autonomy to decide just how autonomous it may or may not be." Schlag, "Normativity," supra note 2, at 895 n.248.

18. See Bauman, *Modernity*, supra note 12, at 98, 138, 143 (arguing that modernist instrumental rationality is separate from moral evaluation). For a discussion of Weber's distinction between formal and substantive rationality, see Feldman, *Weber's Theory of Law*, supra note 6, at 213–29.

19. The following sources provide helpful accounts of the transitions in American jurisprudence, the legal profession, and legal education: Auerbach, *Unequal Justice: Lawyers and Social Change in Modern America* (1976); Friedman, *A History of American Law* (2d ed. 1985); Gilmore, *The Ages of American Law* (1977); Hall, *The Magic Mirror* (1989); Horwitz, *The Transformation of American Law, 1870–1960* (1992); Kalman, *Legal Realism at Yale, 1927–1960* (1986); LaPiana, *Logic and Experience: The Origin of Modern American Legal Education* (1994); McCloskey, *The American Supreme Court* (1960); Purcell, *The Crisis of Democratic Theory* (1973); Schwartz, *A History of the Supreme Court* (1993); Stevens, *Law School: Legal Education in America from the 1850s to the 1980s* (1983) [hereinafter Stevens, *Law School*]; Gordon, "Legal Thought and Legal Practice in the Age of American Enterprise, 1870–1920," in *Professions and Professional Ideologies in America* 70 (1983); Stevens, "Two Cheers for 1870: The American Law School," 5 *Persp. Am. Hist.* 405 (1971).

20. See Gordon, supra note 19, at 83–89; Singer, "Legal Realism Now," 76 *Cal. L. Rev.* 465, 477 (1988) (reviewing Kalman, *Legal Realism at Yale, 1927–1960* (1986)).

21. Gordon, supra note 19, at 84; see LaPiana, supra note 19, at 29–38 (stating that antebellum legal science understood legal principles as universal truths emanating from God).

22. See Gilmore, supra note 19, at 42–48; Warren, 2 *History of the Harvard Law School* 372–74 (1970) (reprint of 1908 ed.); Feldman, "Diagnosing Power," supra note 1, at 1090. The president of Harvard, Charles Eliot, who appointed Langdell, was perhaps even more responsible than Langdell for many of the changes in legal

education. See LaPiana, supra note 19, at 7–28; Stevens, *Law School*, supra note 19, at 36.

23. See Langdell, *Cases on Contracts* vii–ix (2d ed. 1879) (preface to 1st ed.). An excellent discussion of classical orthodoxy is Grey, "Langdell's Orthodoxy," 45 *U. Pitt. L. Rev.* 1, 16–20 (1983).

24. Langdell, supra note 23, at viii.

25. See Friedman, supra note 19, at 617–18; Grey, supra note 23, at 16–20.

26. Langdell, supra note 23, at ix.

27. Id.

28. Langdell, *Summary of the Law of Contracts* 21 (2d ed. 1880).

29. Cf. Marmor, "No Easy Cases?," in *Wittgenstein and Legal Theory* 189, 193 (Patterson ed., 1992) (noting that rule-rule relations can be logical, but rule-world relations cannot be).

30. See Schlag, "The Problem," supra note 2, at 1633–62 (on Langdell and the social construction of the self).

31. See Gordon, supra note 19, at 88–89; Peller, "Neutral Principles in the 1950s," 21 *U. Mich. J.L. Ref.* 561, 576 (1988).

32. See, e.g., Bailey v. Drexel Furniture Co. (Child Labor Tax Case), 259 U.S. 20 (1922); Hammer v. Dagenhart (Child Labor Case), 247 U.S. 251 (1918); Lochner v. New York, 198 U.S. 45 (1905); Allgeyer v. Louisiana, 165 U.S. 578 (1897); Chicago, Milwaukee & St. Paul Railway v. Minnesota (Minnesota Rate Case), 134 U.S. 418 (1890).

33. 198 U.S. 45 (1905).

34. At least as early as 1880, Holmes questioned Langdell's focus on logic as the key to understanding law: "The life of the law has not been logic: it has been experience." Holmes, Book Review, 14 *Am. L. Rev.* 233, 233 (1880) (reviewing Langdell, *Summary of Contracts* (1880)); see Holmes, *The Common Law* 5 (1881). In *The Common Law*, however, Holmes ultimately offered a highly formalistic framework for the common law.

35. See, e.g., Cardozo, *The Nature of the Judicial Process* (1921); Pound, "Mechanical Jurisprudence," 8 *Colum. L. Rev.* 605 (1908) [hereinafter Pound, "Mechanical Jurisprudence"]; Pound, "The Scope and Purpose of Sociological Jurisprudence," 25 *Harv. L. Rev.* 489 (1912); Pound, "The Theory of Judicial Decision," 36 *Harv. L. Rev.* 940 (1923) [hereinafter Pound, "The Theory"]. For an excellent discussion of sociological jurisprudence, see White, "From Sociological Jurisprudence to Realism: Jurisprudence and Social Change in Early Twentieth-Century America," in *Patterns of American Legal Thought* 99 (1978).

36. See Feldman, "Diagnosing Power," supra note 1, at 1090–91; Schlegel, "Langdell's Legacy, or The Case of the Empty Envelope," 36 *Stan. L. Rev.* 1517, 1529–30 (1984) (reviewing Stevens, *Law School: Legal Education in America From the 1850s to the 1980s* (1983)).

37. Cf. Purcell, supra note 19, at 3–73 (on the emergence of scientific naturalism).

38. Cohen, "Transcendental Nonsense and the Functional Approach," 35 *Colum. L. Rev.* 809 (1935). Cohen, here, was using the term "transcendental" in a manner only loosely related to my notion of transcendental reason in what I have called third-stage modernism. Cohen meant to suggest that classical orthodoxy was ridiculous because it was unconnected to experience or reality. For a discussion of Cohen's realist jurisprudence and its influence on American Indian law, see Feldman, "Felix S. Cohen and His Jurisprudence: Reflections on Federal Indian Law," 35 *Buffalo L. Rev.* 479 (1986).

39. Llewellyn, *The Bramble Bush* 12 (1930) (emphasis omitted). The final sentence in the quoted passage eventually became the center of controversy, and Llewellyn

retracted it in a subsequent edition of the book. See Llewellyn, *The Bramble Bush* 8–9 (1951 ed.).

40. See Hutcheson, "The Judgment Intuitive: The Function of the 'Hunch' in Judicial Decision," 14 *Cornell L.Q.* 274, 278, 286–87 (1929); Llewellyn, "Some Realism About Realism—Responding to Dean Pound," 44 *Harv. L. Rev.* 1222, 1238–41 (1931); Radin, "The Theory of Judicial Decision, Or: How Judges Think," 11 *A.B.A. J.* 357 (1925).

41. Insofar as I consider most American legal realists to be just as modernist as were the Langdellians, I agree with Gary Peller's conclusion that the transition from classical orthodoxy to realism was not a radical shift. See Peller, "The Metaphysics of American Law," 73 *Calif. L. Rev.* 1151, 1154 (1985).

42. See Frank, *Law and the Modern Mind* (1930).

43. The sociological jurisprudes first began using this term. See Pound, "Mechanical Jurisprudence," supra note 35, at 609; Pound, "The Theory," supra note 35, at 954.

44. Cohen, supra note 38, at 839–40; see Cohen, *Ethical Systems and Legal Ideals* (1933); Feldman, supra note 38, at 487–92. For an excellent discussion of functionalism and the many realists who followed it, see Kalman, supra note 19, at 3–10.

45. Lochner v. New York, 198 U.S. 45, 74–76 (1905) (Holmes, J., dissenting).

46. See, e.g., Boudin, *Government by Judiciary* (1932).

47. See, e.g., Cohen, "The Basis of Contract," 46 *Harv. L. Rev.* 553, 585–87 (1933); Hale, "Force and the State: A Comparison of 'Political' and 'Economic' Compulsion," 35 *Colum. L. Rev.* 149, 149, 168, 198–201 (1935).

48. See Purcell, supra note 19, at 40–42, 69–73.

49. See id. at 96, 112–14.

50. See White, "From Realism to Critical Legal Studies: A Truncated Intellectual History," reprinted in *Intervention and Detachment* 274, 278 (1994); Schlegel, "American Legal Realism and Empirical Social Science: From the Yale Experience," 28 *Buff. L. Rev.* 459, 579–83 (1979).

51. Dewey, *Freedom and Culture* (1939). Dewey used the term *culture* in a broad sense so that it would include economic and other social institutions. See id. at 6–12.

52. Id. at 134.

53. Id. at 175.

54. See Purcell, supra note 19, at 235–66; "Mansbridge, The Rise and Fall of Self-Interest in the Explanation of Political Life," in *Beyond Self-Interest* 8–9 (Mansbridge ed., 1990).

55. See, e.g., Key, *Politics, Parties, and Pressure Groups* (4th ed. 1958) (first published in 1942) (emphasizing politics as the exercise of power, and discussing the role played by pressure groups in that exercise of power); Truman, *The Governmental Process* (1951) (extensive study of the functioning and influence of political interest groups).

56. Dahl, *A Preface to Democratic Theory* 6 (1956).

57. See Purcell, supra note 19, at 235–66. Robert Dahl wrote: "To assume that this country has remained democratic because of its Constitution seems to me an obvious reversal of the relation; it is much more plausible to suppose that the Constitution has remained because our society is essentially democratic." Dahl, supra note 56, at 143. Likewise, Louis Hartz argued that America was marked by a moral unanimity that simultaneously allowed or included conflict. Hartz, *The Liberal Tradition in America* 14–20 (1955).

58. Purcell, supra note 19, at 253.

59. See, e.g., Lasswell and McDougal, "Legal Education and Public Policy: Profes-

sional Training in the Public Interest," 52 *Yale L.J.* 203, 206, 217 (1943) (arguing that legal education should be training for policy-making to help achieve democratic values). Lon Fuller emphasized a "spirit of compromise and tolerance without which democratic society is impossible." Fuller, "Reason and Fiat in Case Law," 59 *Harv. L. Rev.* 376, 395 (1946).

60. See, e.g., Lucey, "Natural Law and American Legal Realism," 30 *Geo. L.J.* 493 (1942). I do not mean to suggest, however, that realism was dead. Laura Kalman argues that Yale remained a hotbed of realism in the years after World War II. See Kalman, supra note 19, at 145–87.

61. Fuller, *The Law in Quest of Itself* 45–59, 109–10, 122–23 (1940); see Dickinson, "Legal Rules: Their Place in the Process of Decision," 79 *U. Pa. L. Rev.* 833 (1931); Fuller, supra note 59, at 378–79, 395. For a discussion of Fuller's importance to legal process, see White, supra note 50, at 280; see also Duxbury, "Faith in Reason: The Process Tradition in American Jurisprudence," 15 *Cardozo L. Rev.* 601, 622–32 (1993).

62. See Fuller, *The Morality of Law* (rev. ed. 1969) [hereinafter Fuller, *Morality*]. Fuller elaborated his early ideas in the context of a dispute with H. L. A. Hart. See Hart, *The Concept of Law* (1961); Hart, "Positivism and the Separation of Law and Morals," 71 *Harv. L. Rev.* 593 (1958); Fuller, "Positivism and Fidelity to Law—A Reply to Professor Hart," 71 *Harv. L. Rev.* 630 (1958).

63. Fuller, *Morality*, supra note 62, at 155.

64. See, e.g., Hart, "Holmes' Positivism—An Addendum," 64 *Harv. L. Rev.* 929, 934 (1951) (criticizing the behaviorism and positivism of Holmes and the legal realists for rejecting the power of ideas or reason to change conduct); Jaffe, "Foreword: The Supreme Court, 1950 Term," 65 *Harv. L. Rev.* 107 (1951) (criticizing realists for believing that the Supreme Court's work focused on politics and not law).

65. Hart, supra note 64, at 936 n.21. Hart wrote: "Has not the law which has been duly settled, by the judgment of a court, or by the enactment of a statute, or by administrative decision, a moral claim to acceptance, at least until it is duly changed?" Id. at 936.

66. Hart and Sacks, "The Legal Process: Basic Problems in the Making and Application of Law" 4 (unpublished, tentative ed. 1958). Hart and Sacks were already working on these course materials by 1954. In addition, they and other professors had been developing related courses (for example, courses on legislation) for more than a decade, and Hart and Sacks drew upon those related course materials. See Eskridge and Frickey, "The Making of the Legal Process," 107 *Harv. L. Rev.* 2031, 2033–45 (1994).

67. See Eskridge and Frickey, supra note 66, at iii, 3, 366–68, 662; Hart, "The Power of Congress to Limit the Jurisdiction of Federal Courts: An Exercise in Dialectic," 66 *Harv. L. Rev.* 1362 (1953) (emphasizing the institutional roles of different governmental entities). Many of these legal process themes were featured in the casebook that has (for evermore) defined the subject matter of federal courts courses, Hart and Wechsler, *The Federal Courts and the Federal System* (1953).

68. Hart and Sacks, supra note 66, at 164–67.

69. Id. at 166.

70. Id. at 165; see id. at 166–67.

71. Hartz, supra note 57, at 59–62; see Feldman, "Republican Revival/Interpretive Turn," 1992 *Wis. L. Rev.* 679, 687–88.

72. See Fallon, "Reflections on the Hart and Wechsler Paradigm," 47 *Vand. L. Rev.* 953, 962 (1994); Peller, supra note 31, at 568–72.

73. For many years, the Harvard Forewords, which began in 1951, see Jaffe, supra

note 64, were the special preserve of legal process scholars as they tried to talk to the Supreme Court. As late as 1968, a somewhat pessimistic Foreword writer still assumed that scholarship seriously affected the Court: "Even in a day when the law reviews are much cited but not often heeded, it may still serve a purpose to hold up to the Court a mirror that emphasizes its warts." Henkin, "Foreword: On Drawing Lines," 82 *Harv. L. Rev.* 63, 63 (1968).

74. See White, "Judicial Activism and the Identity of the Legal Profession," reprinted in *Intervention and Detachment* 222, 234 (1994).

75. See, e.g., West Coast Hotel Co. v. Parrish, 300 U.S. 379 (1937).

76. 304 U.S. 144, 152 n.4 (1938).

77. For discussions of this split on the Court, see Horwitz, supra note 19, at 252; Kluger, *Simple Justice* 240–41, 582–84 (1975); Schwartz, supra note 19, at 253–55, 269–76; Schwartz, *Super Chief: Earl Warren and His Supreme Court–A Judicial Biograhy* 32, 40–48 (1983).

78. Minersville v. Gobitis, 310 U.S. 586 (1940).

79. See Mason, "The Core of Free Government, 1938–1940: Mr. Justice Stone and 'Preferred Freedoms,'" 65 *Yale L.J.* 597, 622 (1956). I do not mean to suggest that the Court's decision alone caused these outbreaks of bigotry and violence.

80. West Virginia State Board of Education v. Barnette, 319 U.S. 624 (1943), overruling Minersville v. Gobitis, 310 U.S. 586 (1940).

81. 347 U.S. 483 (1954).

82. See Schwartz, supra note 19, at 286–88.

83. Schwartz, supra note 77, at 76–77.

84. See Kluger, supra note 77, at 599; Schwartz, supra note 77, at 78–81.

85. See *Brown*, 347 U.S. at 495–96; Brown v. Board of Education, 349 U.S. 294 (1955) (*Brown II*); Schwartz, supra note 77, at 88–93. The Court ordered another reargument on the issue of the decree.

86. Cf. Kluger, supra note 77, at 710 (concluding that the Supreme Court acted as the conscience of the nation by enforcing American principles, by granting "simple justice").

87. 163 U.S. 537 (1896).

88. See Tushnet, *Segregated Schools and Legal Strategy: The NAACP's Campaign Against Segregated Education*, 1925–1950 (1987); Culp, "Toward a Black Legal Scholarship: Race and Original Understandings," 1991 *Duke L.J.* 39, 55 and n.42 (arguing that the NAACP had a more consistent legal strategy than acknowledged by Tushnet).

89. See Bell, "*Brown v. Board of Education* and the Interest-Convergence Dilemma," 93 *Harv. L. Rev.* 518 (1980); Dudziak, "Desegregation as a Cold War Imperative," 41 *Stan. L. Rev.* 61 (1988).

90. *Brown*, 347 U.S. at 495.

91. Id. at 492–93.

92. See id. at 493–95.

93. Id. at 493.

94. Id. at 495.

95. Sacks, "Foreword: The Supreme Court, 1953 Term," 68 *Harv. L. Rev.* 96 (1954).

96. Id. at 96.

97. Id. at 98.

98. Id.

99. Id. at 99.

100. Braucher, "Foreword: The Supreme Court, 1954 Term," 69 *Harv. L. Rev.* 120, 120 (1955). Braucher proceeded to emphasize the institutional roles of the Court, Congress, and the president.

101. Bickel and Wellington, "Legislative Purpose and the Judicial Process: The *Lincoln Mills* Case," 71 *Harv. L. Rev.* 1, 6 (1957).

102. See Brown, "Foreword: Process of Law," 72 *Harv. L. Rev.* 77 (1958).

103. Hart, "Foreword: The Time Chart of the Justices," 73 *Harv. L. Rev.* 84, 94–101 (1959). This article and several other important legal process pieces were developed during a faculty seminar at Harvard during the 1956–1957 academic year. See Eskridge and Frickey, supra note 66, at 2047–48.

104. Hart, supra note 103, at 99.

105. Id.

106. Wechsler, "Toward Neutral Principles of Constitutional Law," 73 *Harv. L. Rev.* 1 (1959).

107. Id. at 16.

108. Id. at 15.

109. See id. at 31–34.

110. Id. at 32. Other prominent criticisms of *Brown* included the following: Berger, *Government by Judiciary* 243–45 (1977) (claiming that Warren ignored the true history of the adoption of the Fourteenth Amendment); Bickel, *The Supreme Court and the Idea of Progress* 37 and n.* (1978 ed.) (1st ed. 1970) (arguing that *Brown* was headed toward historical obsolescence); Hand, *The Bill of Rights* 54–55 (1958) (criticizing the *Brown* Court for acting like the *Lochner* Court).

111. Pollak, "Racial Discrimination and Judicial Integrity: A Reply to Professor Wechsler," 108 *U. Pa. L. Rev.* 1 (1959).

112. Black, "The Lawfulness of the Segregation Decisions," 69 *Yale L.J.* 421 (1960).

113. See Lasky, "Observing Appellate Opinions from Below the Bench," 49 *Cal. L. Rev.* 831, 832–34 (1961).

114. See, e.g., Bickel, *The Least Dangerous Branch* 82–83 (2d ed. 1986) (1st ed. in 1962); Gunther, "The Subtle Vices of the 'Passive Virtues'—A Comment on Principle and Expediency in Judicial Review," 64 *Colum. L. Rev.* 1, 4–5 (1964) (applauding Bickel's condemnation of supporters of the Warren Court).

115. Wasserstrom, *The Judicial Decision* (1961).

116. See id. at 25–28. The early roots of this legal process argument can be traced back to John Dewey, who argued that the logic of reaching judicial decisions differs from the logic of justifying them. See Dewey, "Logical Method and Law," 10 *Cornell L.Q.* 17, 24 (1924).

117. See Bickel, supra note 114, at 24–25, 225–26; Bickel, supra note 110, at 37 and n.*.

118. Bickel, supra note 114, at 16.

119. Id. at 58.

120. See Bickel, supra note 114, at 111–98; Bickel, Foreword, "The Passive Virtues," 75 *Harv. L. Rev.* 40 (1961).

121. Gunther, supra note 114, at 15.

122. Id. at 17.

123. Id. at 13.

124. See Bickel, supra note 110, at 99, 165; Bickel, *The Morality of Consent* 24–25 (1975); cf. Wright, "Professor Bickel, The Scholarly Tradition, and the Supreme Court," 84 *Harv. L. Rev.* 769 (1971) (criticizing Bickel's transition).

125. See Ely, *Democracy and Distrust* (1980).

126. See id. at 1–73.

127. Id. at 73–104; see Choper, *Judicial Review and the National Political Process* 2, 127–28 (1980).

128. See Ely, supra note 125, at 105–34.

129. Id. at 117.

130. Id. at 101.

131. See id. at 150–70.

132. 381 U.S. 479 (1965).

133. See Garrow, *Liberty and Sexuality: The Right to Privacy and the Making of "Roe v. Wade"* 1–269 (1994).

134. 367 U.S. 497 (1961).

135. See id. at 508.

136. In 1962, Justices White and Goldberg had replaced Frankfurter and Whittaker. See Garrow, supra note 133, at 224. Mark Tushnet suggests that the true Warren Court existed only after this transition in personnel. Tushnet, "The Warren Court as History: An Interpretation," in *The Warren Court in Historical and Political Perspective* 1, 4–6 (Tushnet ed., 1993).

137. See Garrow, supra note 133, at 196–269.

138. Id. at 246; see id. at 245–48.

139. *Griswold*, 381 U.S. at 482.

140. See id. at 482–83.

141. Id. at 484 (citations omitted).

142. See id. at 485.

143. See id. at 485–86.

144. Id.

145. Id. at 486.

146. See Garrow, supra note 133, at 240–41.

147. Hence, Justices Clark, Goldberg, Brennan, and Chief Justice Warren joined Douglas to create the majority opinion. See *Griswold*, 381 U.S. at 479–531; Garrow, supra note 133, at 248–52 (discussing the accumulation of five votes to create a majority opinion).

148. *Griswold*, 381 U.S. at 493 (Goldberg, J., concurring) (quoting Snyder v. Massachusetts, 291 U.S. 97, 105 (1934)).

149. *Griswold*, 381 U.S. at 501 (Harlan, J., concurring).

150. See id. at 511–18 (Black, J., dissenting); id. at 527–31 (Stewart, J., dissenting).

151. Id. at 520–21 (Black, J., dissenting).

152. In fact, Kauper supported the conclusion in *Griswold*, and suggested that the Court should have more openly admitted that it was a substantive due process/fundamental rights case. Kauper, "Penumbras, Peripheries, Emanations, Things Fundamental and Things Forgotten: The *Griswold* Case," 64 *Mich. L. Rev.* 235, 253–54 (1965); see also Dixon, "The *Griswold* Penumbra: Constitutional Charter for an Expanded Law of Privacy?," 64 *Mich. L. Rev.* 197 (1965) (supporting the result but criticizing the reasoning in *Griswold*).

153. See Gross, "The Concept of Privacy," 42 *N.Y.U. L. Rev.* 34, 40–46 (1967).

154. Kelly, "Clio and the Court: An Illicit Love Affair," 1965 *S. Ct. Rev.* 119, 155; see Kelley, Note, "The Uncertain Renaissance of the Ninth Amendment," 33 *U. Chi. L. Rev.* 814, 832 (1966) (criticizing Goldberg's Ninth Amendment reasoning in the *Griswold* concurrence).

155. Berger, supra note 110, at 265.

156. Emerson, "Nine Justices in Search of a Doctrine," 64 *Mich. L. Rev.* 219, 234 (1965).

157. See Garrow, supra note 133, at 263–65.

158. Bork, "Neutral Principles and Some First Amendment Problems," 47 *Ind. L.J.* 1, 1, 7–8 (1971).

159. Id. at 4.

160. See id. at 17, 22–23.

161. Id. at 9.

162. Id. at 7.

163. See Tushnet, supra note 136, at 16–17. In an article attacking *Roe v. Wade,* the most important offspring of *Griswold,* John Ely offered tepid support for *Griswold.* See Ely, "The Wages of Crying Wolf: A Comment on *Roe v. Wade,*" 82 *Yale L.J.* 920, 928–30 (1973). This support was perhaps due more to Ely's loyalty to Warren, for whom Ely had clerked, than out of true respect for the opinion and decision. In fact, the Court decided *Griswold* during Ely's clerkship, and Ely had advised Warren not to join Douglas's opinion and not to find a right of privacy. See Garrow, supra note 133, at 248.

164. See, e.g., Perry, *The Constitution, the Courts, and Human Rights* (1982) (emphasizing moral philosophy and seeing judicial review as an opportunity for the moral development of the nation); Grey, "Eros, Civilization and the Burger Court," 43 *Law & Contemp. Probs.* 83, 84–85 (1980) (claiming that the best defense of *Griswold* was based on tradition); Michelman, "Foreword: On Protecting the Poor Through the Fourteenth Amendment," 83 *Harv. L. Rev.* 7 (1969) (arguing that the Warren Court's decisions on equality could best be defended by a purpose to vindicate a state duty to protect against hazards endemic to an unequal society).

165. See, e.g., Grey, "Origins of the Unwritten Constitution: Revolutionary Thought," 30 *Stan. L. Rev.* 843 (1978).

166. For example, Bork relied heavily on originalism as a method leading to objective constitutional decision making. But many other constitutional theorists had underscored the considerable difficulties and the indeterminacies arising from a reliance on the text and intent of the framers. See, e.g., Ely, supra note 125, at 11–41.

167. See, e.g., Brest, "The Substance of Process," 42 *Ohio St. L.J.* 131, 140 (1981); Tushnet, "Darkness on the Edge of Town: The Contributions of John Hart Ely to Constitutional Theory," 89 *Yale L.J.* 1037 (1980).

168. 410 U.S. 113 (1973).

169. Cox, "Foreword: Constitutional Adjudication and the Promotion of Human Rights," 80 *Harv. L. Rev.* 91, 94 (1966).

170. Id. at 98.

171. See Auerbach, supra note 19, at 263–306; Minda, "Jurisprudence at Century's End," 43 *J. Legal Educ.* 27, 35 (1993).

172. See Gordon, "New Developments in Legal Theory," in *The Politics of Law* 281 (Kairys ed., 1982); see, e.g., Kennedy, "The Structure of Blackstone's Commentaries," 28 *Buff. L. Rev.* 205 (1979) (using structuralist techniques). For a summary of critical legal studies, see Kelman, *A Guide to Critical Legal Studies* (1987).

173. See Feldman, supra note 71, at 701–14; Feldman, "The New Metaphysics: The Interpretive Turn in Jurisprudence," 76 *Iowa L. Rev.* 661 (1991).

174. See Brest, "The Misconceived Quest for the Original Understanding," 60 *B.U. L. Rev.* 204 (1980); Tushnet, "Following the Rules Laid Down: A Critique of Interpretivism and Neutral Principles," 96 *Harv. L. Rev.* 781 (1983).

175. See Kuhn, *The Structure of Scientific Revolutions* (2d ed. 1970).

176. See Fish, *Is There a Text in This Class?* (1980); see, e.g., Fiss, "Objectivity and

Interpretation," 34 *Stan. L. Rev.* 739 (1982) (relying on Fish to develop views on law and interpretation); Levinson, "Law as Literature," 60 *Tex. L. Rev.* 373 (1982) (same). But see Fish, "Fish v. Fiss," 36 *Stan. L. Rev.* 1325 (1984) (criticizing how Fiss had interpreted Fish's works); Fish, "Interpretation and the Pluralist Vision," 60 *Tex. L. Rev.* 495 (1982) (criticizing how Levinson had interpreted Fish's works).

177. See Gadamer, *Truth and Method* (Weinsheimer and Marshall trans., 2d rev. ed. 1989) (originally published in German in 1960; first English translation in 1975); Gadamer, "The Universality of the Hermeneutical Problem," in Bleicher, *Contemporary Hermeneutics* 128 (1980) [hereinafter Gadamer, "The Universality"]. For discussions of Gadamer's philosophical hermeneutics and its relation to law, see Feldman, "Diagnosing Power," supra note 1, at 1059–74; Feldman, "New Metaphysics," supra note 173, at 681–98.

178. Delgado, "Shadowboxing: An Essay on Power," 77 *Cornell L. Rev.* 813, 818 (1992) (using the term "outsider jurisprudence").

179. See, e.g., Bell, *And We Are Not Saved* 251–54 (1987) (suggesting the possibility that the Constitution and American society can be transformed to eliminate economic oppression); Cook, "Beyond Critical Legal Studies: The Reconstructive Theology of Dr. Martin Luther King, Jr.," 103 *Harv. L. Rev.* 985, 1015–21 (1990) (arguing that religion both legitimated and delegitimated authority for African American slaves). But cf. Bell, supra, at 22 (noting that guarantees of racial equality get transformed into devices to perpetuate the racial status quo).

180. See Feldman, "Diagnosing Power," supra note 1, at 1084–1104 (on postmodern legal scholarship); Minda, supra note 171, at 58 (observing the growing sentiment that we are at the end of an era in jurisprudence); Schlegel, supra note 50, at 462 ("[P]ost-Realist legal theory has about run its course headlong into a dead end.").

181. Compare Rosenberg, *The Hollow Hope: Can Courts Bring About Social Change?* 110–56 (1991) (claiming that *Brown* impeded the Civil Rights movement by inflaming Southern racists, who were able to delay political changes) and Klarman," *Brown*, Racial Change, and the Civil Rights Movement," 80 *Va. L. Rev.* 7 (1994) (claiming that *Brown* indirectly aided the Civil Rights movement by generating violent Southern resistance, which in turn aroused apathetic Northern whites to support political change) with Kluger, supra note 77, at 758–61 (claiming that although *Brown* alone did not change America, it was central element in social change).

Mark Tushnet argues that the Warren Court itself contributed to the dissolution of the Great Society agenda and thus undermined the Court's own legacy. For example, the Court's reapportionment decisions shifted political power from conservative rural areas to cities, where the larger populations initially resided. But population growth then shifted to the more conservative and Republican suburbs. See Tushnet, supra note 136, at 19–21.

182. See Feldman, "Diagnosing Power," supra note 1, at 1046–48, 1052–1104 (extensive discussion of the themes of postmodernism). Zygmunt Bauman suggests that one cannot completely or consistently narrate postmodernity because one of its attributes is incoherence. See Bauman, supra note 1, at xxiv.

183. Peter Schanck writes: "There are no foundational principles from which other assertions can be derived; hence, certainty as the result of either empirical verification or deductive reasoning is impossible." Schanck, supra note 2, at 2508–09.

184. See Gadamer, "The Universality," supra note 177, at 133; Balkin, "Ideology," supra note 2, at 1138 (arguing that ideology constrains yet makes legal doctrine intelligible); Boyle, supra note 2, at 522 (arguing that we are always limited and empowered by our traditions).

185. See, e.g., Cornell, *Beyond,* supra note 2, at 3–4, 150 (claiming that feminists can talk about women without being essentialist).

186. See Derrida, *Of Grammatology* 50, 73 (Spivak trans., 1976); Derrida, *Positions* 20 (Bass trans., 1981). The play of signifiers relates to Derrida's concept of differance. See Derrida, "Differance," in *Margins of Philosophy* 3, 11 (Bass trans., 1982).

187. Weinsheimer, *Gadamer's Hermeneutics: A Reading of Truth and Method* 9 (1985); see id. at 200 (arguing that the truth of a text exceeds each understanding).

188. See Wittgenstein, *Philosphical Investigations* 193–94 (Anscombe trans., 3d ed. 1958).

189. See Schlag, "The Problem," supra note 2, at 1700–01; Schlag, "Normative," supra note 2, at 185–86; see also Boyle, supra note 2; Winter, supra note 2, at 54 (writing on the politics of the relatively autonomous self).

190. Jack Balkin writes, "[The legal academy] has become increasingly distanced from the work of actual lawyers and judges." Balkin, "Postmodern Constitutionalism," supra note 2, at 1985; cf. Cotterrell, supra note 7, at 223–28 (writing on factors contributing to the disjunction between legal theory and legal practice).

191. See Sirico and Drew, "The Citing of Law Reviews by the United States Courts of Appeals: An Empirical Analysis," 45 *U. Miami L. Rev.* 1051 (1991) (noting that federal courts of appeals rarely cite law reviews); Stier et al., "Law Review Usage and Suggestions for Improvement: A Survey of Attorneys, Professors, and Judges," 44 *Stan. L. Rev.* 1467, 1485 (1992) (noting that attorneys rarely use law reviews, and when used, law reviews are used for overviews of the law and citation finding, not for theory). Sanford Levinson notes that an empirical study shows that the Supreme Court was less likely to cite law review articles in 1986 than twenty years earlier. Levinson, "The Audience for Constitutional Meta-Theory (Or, Why, and To Whom, Do I Write the Things I Do?)," 63 *U. Colo. L. Rev.* 389, 405 n.28 (1992). Nonetheless, Harry Edwards, a federal circuit court judge, laments that judges and attorneys have little use for most current legal scholarship. They want more prescriptive and doctrinal writing. Edwards, "The Growing Disjunction Between Legal Education and the Legal Profession," 91 *Mich. L. Rev.* 34, 35, 42–43 (1992); see Symposium, "Legal Education," 91 *Mich. L. Rev.* 1921 (1993) (presenting reactions to Judge Edwards's article). See generally Bauman, *Intimations,* supra note 1, at 95 (stating that in postmodernity, there is no longer a demand for the traditional services provided by intellectuals).

192. See, e.g., Cornell, *Limit,* supra note 2; Balkin, "Transcendental Deconstruction," supra note 2.

193. See, e.g., Feldman, "Diagnosing Power," supra note 1.

194. See, e.g., Feldman, "New Metaphysics," supra note 173; Feldman, "Diagnosing Power," supra note 1, at 1060–74; Mootz, "Rule of Law," supra note 2.

195. See Bauman, *Intimations,* supra note 1, at 21–23 (noting that postmodern intellectuals become interpreters).

196. See, e.g., Cornell, *Limit,* supra note 2; Balkin, "Transcendental Deconstruction," supra note 2; Feldman, "The Persistence of Power," supra note 1, at 2276–88 (discussing possibility of postmodern critical theory); Winter, supra note 2, at 77 (on critical theory).

197. Wartenberg, *The Forms of Power* 165 (1990) (emphasis omitted).

198. See Bauman, *Intimations,* supra note 1, at vii, 204 (noting that postmodernism is marked by self-reflexive reinterpretation); Connor, supra note 1, at 5 (noting that self-reflexivity is key to postmodernism); Levinson and Balkin, supra note 2, at 1639 (noting that postmodernism is self-referential insofar as the focus or subject of culture becomes the culture itself); cf. Connor, supra note 1, at 119 ("[T]he purpose of formal self-reflexivity in

postmodern writing [is] to dislodge the reader."); Crook, supra note 1, at 66–68 (writing on reflexivity as a necessary feature of postfoundational radicalism).

199. See, e.g., Balkin, "Postmodern Constitutionalism," supra note 2; Feldman, "Diagnosing Power," supra note 1, at 1084–1104; Schlag, "The Problem," supra note 2.

200. Gary Minda writes of "an emerging postmodern aesthetic or temperament in legal scholarship." Minda, supra note 171, at 30.

201. See, e.g., Schlag, "The Problem," supra note 2, at 1649.

202. See Feldman, "Diagnosing Power," supra note 1, at 1083; cf. Duxbury, supra note 61, at 668–69 (writing on the continuing importance of legal process theory). Anthony Giddens prefers to talk of the radicalizing of modernity instead of a transition to postmodernity. See Giddens, *The Consequences of Modernity* 45–53 (1990).

• 22 •

THE INTERNATIONAL IMPACT OF THE WARREN COURT

THE RIGHT HONORABLE THE LORD WOOLF

At the same time as we in England viewed with amazement the embarrassing and painful experience that Justice Thomas had to undergo in order to become an Associate Justice of your Supreme Court, it happened that three new members of the Judicial Committee of the House of Lords were appointed.[1] They were appointed by the Queen in theory but in practice by the prime minister. Unusually, they were appointed well before they were due to take up their appointment, at a time when a general election could well take place, resulting in a change of government prior to their appointments taking effect. They were young by the standards of appointments to the judicial committee and likely to constitute almost a third of its then membership of ten[2] for a great many years. Yet their appointment was hardly noticed by the media, and it caused not a ripple of controversy.

I draw attention to this contrast in the treatment of what I appreciate was a particularly controversial appointment of yours because I think it highlights the difference in the public's perception in the two countries as to the importance of the two institutions—our respective supreme courts. I do not envisage that a volume comparable to this would be likely to be published in England. In England it is unlikely that any court would ever be identified with one of its members, even a chief judge, so that it became known as his court.

However, as it happens, at the time when Chief Justice Warren retired, a number of exceptionally distinguished judges happened to be on the English bench at the same time. They included Lords Reid, Diplock, and Wilberforce, and the Master of the Rolls, Lord Denning. Their individual influence on the development of our law has been considerable, but it was not a collective but a several contribution, and any assessment of their contributions would probably recognize this. Part of the explanation for this is that no English appellate court is collegiate to the same extent as the U.S. Supreme Court. English appellate courts are not regularly constituted by the same members. The House of Lords, for example, sits in two committees of five, whose membership regularly revolves. The position is the same in relation to the various three-member divisions of the Court of Appeal. This means that even the most distinguished judge is unable to impose his personality on a court to the extent that it becomes associated with his name. No doubt the absence of a written constitution and the overwhelming sovereignty of Parliament also contributes to this limited personalization of our courts.

In this situation it was not to be expected that the English courts would rush to emulate the innovativeness of the Warren Court, and they did not do so. The immediate direct impact of the example of the Warren Court was limited. However, given the necessary support, individual judges can be readily identified who would have been extremely sympathetic to the dramatic reforms with which the Warren Court is associated. In particular, Lord Denning throughout his long judicial career, stretching from 1944 to 1982, virtually single-handedly strove to bring about a similar "revolution" within the English legal system, a revolution that Professor Schwartz has described as involving the Warren Court in "[e]xpanding civil liberties, broadening political freedom, extending the franchise, reinforcing freedoms of speech, assembly and religion, limiting the powers of the politicians . . . and defining limits of police power. . . ."[3] Nevertheless, for the major part of his judicial career, Lord Denning was engaged in a mainly personal crusade. The majority of the House of Lords, of which he was a member from 1957 to 1962, had no stomach for his approach. Their approach was reflected in the judgment of Lord Simonds, delivered just days before he became lord chancellor. He described the "Denning approach" as involving the courts in "writing into legislation what the legislature had failed to include." It was "a naked usurpation of the legislative function under the thin disguise of interpretation. And it is the less justifiable when it is guess-work with what material the legislature would, if it had discovered the gap, have filled it in. If a gap is disclosed, the remedy lies in an amending Act."[4]

At that time, unlike Chief Justice Warren, Lord Denning was unable to carry his colleagues with him. Therefore when, after a spell as a law lord, he was offered the solution of stepping down a tier and becoming the Master of the Rolls, who presides over the civil division of the Court of Appeal, he accepted. In that capacity, notwithstanding setbacks when there were appeals to the House of Lords, usually he was able sufficiently to influence the two other judges with whom he sat to progress a limited way down the path blazoned by the Warren Court and increase to an extent the protection of the individual against the activities of government. This was despite the fact that Lord Simonds made his remarks in a period that has been aptly described as one in which "English judges grew to love their constitutional chains too well. So keen were they to avoid judicial law-making that they shackled themselves in heavier chains of their own making; and by their omissions as well as their actions, they made or refused to unmake what would now be regarded as thoroughly bad law."[5]

Thus, the early years of the Warren Court was a period in England that, for the control of government and other public bodies, has been described as a "great depression." In the words of perhaps our most distinguished academic administrative lawyer, it was a period in which "deep gloom" settled upon our administrative law, reducing it

> to the lowest ebb at which it had stood for centuries. The courts and the legal professions seemed to have forgotten the achievements of their predecessors and

> they showed little stomach for continuing the centuries-old work of imposing law upon government. . . . [I]nstead the subject relapsed into an impotent condition marked by neglect of principles and literal verbal interpretation of the blank-check powers which Parliament showered upon ministers. Leading cases made a dreary catalogue of abdication and error. Eminent judges said that the common law must be given a death certificate, having lost the power to control the executive.[6]

A situation in stark contrast to that which existed in the United States. As you know, the approach of Chief Justice Warren to the Bill of Rights was to regard it as reflecting the "natural rights of Man" or, ironically, "the common law rights of Englishmen."[7] Common law rights to which, to contemporary eyes, the courts of England were then astonishingly inattentive. In this situation it was Parliament and not the courts that had to give effect in England to the principles of equality and nondiscrimination that were reflected in the landmark decisions of the Warren Court during its early years, such as *Brown v. Board of Education.*[8] This occurred because what the English courts failed to do for themselves the European Court of Justice and the European Court of Human Rights did for them by adopting the Warren approach as a result of cases that were brought before them.[9] It was not until 1975 that Parliament enacted the Sex Discrimination Act and in 1976 the Race Relations Act. These acts, which contain our current law, brought our domestic law into conformity with European law. It is generally acknowledged that they were inspired by the experience of the United States in dealing with sex and race discrimination, which had its roots in the *Brown* case. Indeed, before the form of the legislation was settled the then home secretary consulted American experts including Dean (now Judge) Louis Pollak who had participated in Thurgood Marshall's team to argue *Brown v. Board of Education.* As a result, the legislation covered both direct and what we call indirect discrimination, which is your discrimination in effect. Hence, as the successor court to the Warren Court was, in the view of some observers, going into reverse, English law was firmly embracing the pure Warren approach to gender and race equality.[10]

Before the end of the Warren Court era, a wind of change began to revive English judicial activity. The wind came not only from Washington but also from other parts of the common law world where judicial thinking had been inspired by the Warren Court. Lord Reid reflected the new approach to judicial interpretation when he said in 1972:

> There was a time when it was thought almost indecent to suggest that judges made law—they only declare it. Those with a taste for fairy tales seem to have thought that in some Aladdin's Cave there is hidden the common law in all its splendor. That on a judge's appointment there descends on him knowledge of the magic words "Open Sesame!" Bad decisions are given when the judge muddles the password and the wrong door opens. But we do not believe in fairy tales anymore."[11]

In 1969, at the beginning of the era of change in England, an Anglo-American legal exchange took place where the leader of the English delegation was Lord Diplock, whose judgments in later years were going to play such a dramatic role in the development of English administrative law. He was undoubtedly influenced by what he learned in consequence of that exchange. Fortunately, in that exchange were both Professor Schwartz and his nearest counterpart in the English scene, Professor William, now Sir William, Wade, to whom I have referred earlier. They made a contemporary record of the results of their exchange in *Legal Control of Government.*[12] The professors noted the contrast that still existed at that time between the British approach and the American approach in these terms:

> No observer of the American scene is likely to doubt that the courts under the vigorous leadership of the Supreme Court have recently come to regard themselves as an agency for supplying legal reforms which are demanded by public opinion but not affected by Congress. The American system of checks and balances makes controversial legislation difficult to enact, . . . [so] if the Constitution will not meet the needs of the times, some safety valve must be found. If Congress will not legislate for the desegregation of schools, then the reapportionment of unfairly divided voting districts, or the rejection of evidence obtained by legal police methods, it is tempting for the Courts to do so taking advantage of their sacrosanct position as expounders of the Constitution. However much they may seem to stretch the meaning of "the equal protection of the laws," there is no power in the Constitution, short of drastic amendment, which can invalidate their decision.

There were no fairy tales in the United States. By contrast:

> The British attitude . . . is that legislation by the Courts of an advertently political character is a usurpation, justifiable only in case of constitutional emergency. Most British lawyers feel that any such activity must in the long run be damaging to the whole status of judges and to the trust reposed in them.

They gave this warning, which may reflect the motivation of the Supreme Court for subsequently changing direction:

> Is not the Supreme Court already reaping where it has sown? Having embroiled itself deeply in politics, and invaded the province of Congress, it has provoked a determined counter-attack by Congress which in 1969 and 1970 defeated two presidential nominations to the Court. No judiciary could long survive a series of such attacks, and it already seems that the court may have to return to a policy of restraint. But the dilemma will remain: does the malfunction of the legislature justify legislation by the judiciary?

This assessment of the contrasting approaches concludes by pointing out that one of the faintly endearing characteristics of the British judiciary is that while they do their share of "less spectacular legislation," they are fond of denying the fact.

It is interesting to contrast those comments with what Sir William Wade had to say when he came to write the sixth edition of his book *Administrative Law* in 1988. He referred to the "seismic disturbance" that Lord Diplock had brought about in his landmark judgment in *O'Reilly v. Mackman,*[13] which drew a rigid dichotomy between public and private law of which Sir William disapproved. Having pointed out that English judges in defiance of theoretical obstacles had extended their empire by reviewing the exercise of the royal prerogative, the rulings of non-legal bodies, decisions that conflict with published policies or undertakings, discretionary decisions that an earlier generation of lawyers would have considered impregnable, he went on to say:

> Every admirer of the late Lord Diplock would agree that his speech in that case was a brilliant virtuoso performance but . . . a solitary judgment in a single case is not an ideal instrument for proclaiming radical and sweeping changes. In his later years Lord Diplock was inclined to yield to the temptation to restate whole branches of the law in his own terms. His mastery of administrative law and his outstanding contributions to it entitled these ex cathedra statements to great respect; but it may not be, I hope, impertinent to point out their drawbacks as a technique either of codification or of law reform. A feat of Lord Diplock's, however, as a mere academic, I can only envy in his ability to put forward a novel theory in a lecture and then enshrine it canonically in a speech in the House of Lords.[14]

That comment was made of a House of Lords of which Lord Diplock was only one of a number of jurists of the highest caliber. That generation made a huge contribution to the development of our law. They have however been superseded by a new generation, the appointment of three of whom I have already mentioned. And now they have been joined in turn by four more. Seven out of ten new members have attracted, after the event, some media attention. In particular, attention has been drawn to the contrast between the opinions expressed by this new generation of the judiciary and the approach of the government of the day to the same issue. Some of the issues are highly sensitive, but what is being said by the judiciary is redolent of the values of the Warren Court—of equality, due process, and freedom of speech.

The sometimes confrontational image that is being created is perhaps being given undue prominence because in keeping with the new ethos, the English judiciary express views extrajudicially more commonly, I believe, than in the United States. English judges are required to head inquiries that, like the commission Chief Justice Warren found himself compelled to head, excite considerable public interest. It also arises because of the peculiarity of the English constitution, as a result of which law lords can take part in the legislative processes of the House of Lords. Here they express views that usually command considerable attention, on subjects that are confined by convention to ones on which they are particularly qualified to speak. Another explanation suggested is that judges have been motivated by the fact that for a period it seemed that the government was lacking any sufficiently powerful political opposition because of the dominance of the Conservative Party in the House of Commons. Like the Warren Court, the English judiciary may have been drawn into a semivacuum where they were required, perhaps reluctantly to take action to protect, as was pointed out by a distinguished advocate, "ethical and social values" by "standing as an impartial arbiter between government and the governed."[15]

> No Government—whether Conservative or Labour—has sought to strengthen civil rights and freedoms by making the European Convention of Human Rights directly enforceable in our courts, or by enacting a British Bill of Rights, or by codifying and extending the principles of administrative law, or by adding new

legal remedies—notably compensation for maladministration and injunctions against the Crown.[16]

So if the judges had not used their lawmaking powers to develop greater judicial protection of the individual against the misuse of public powers, we can be certain that no government would have sought to persuade Parliament to do so. If the judges had not led the way, an uncontrolled discretion would have remained the distinctive hallmark of public administration in Britain.

This new ethos was receptive to the principles that the Warren Court had propounded. It was an ethos in which the fundamental freedoms that Earl Warren had associated forty years earlier with the common law of Englishmen could be developed. One of the most important of those freedoms is freedom of speech. In the *Spycatcher* litigation[17] some of the decisions can be criticized for not showing sufficient respect for this most important freedom. However, when the various judgments in that ongoing saga of litigation are examined, encouraging pointers to a more enlightened approach can be found. For this, in addition to the decisions of the United States Supreme Court in the Warren era, the influence of the decisions of the European Court of Human Rights, which were in turn nurtured in that source, can be traced. The House of Lords had found it impossible themselves to take the initiative of treating the European Convention to which the United Kingdom subscribed as part of our domestic law. The constitutional position was clear that this required an act of Parliament.[18] But this inhibition has been undermined, not of course by rubbing an Aladdin's lamp, but by the judiciary discovering that the fundamental freedoms enshrined in the European Convention were no more extensive than the common law.

In the *Spycatcher* litigation Lord Goff of Chieveley, now the senior English law lord, stated in *Attorney General v. The Guardian Newspaper Limited*[19] that in the field of freedom of speech there was no difference in principle between English common law on the subject and the European Convention of Human Rights. In 1993 the same issue again came before the House of Lords in a case where the House had to determine whether a local government body could sue for libel. The House of Lords[20] was unanimously of the opinion that it could not. Lord Keith in giving a speech that was endorsed by the other members of the House, basing himself upon *Chicago v. Tribune Company*[21] and, more importantly for the present purposes, on *New York Times Company v. Sullivan*,[22] decided it could not. In addition, Lord Keith founded his reasoning on the common law of England. He apparently accepted that there was no material distinction between the position of the U.S. Supreme Court in those cases and the common law. Significantly, he also referred to a speech of Lord Bridge in the Privy Council (*R. v. The Attorney General of Antigua and Barbuda*)[23] where Lord Bridge, using language worthy of the Warren Court had said that "[i]n a free democratic society it is almost too obvious to need stating that those who hold office in government and who are responsible for public administration must always be open to criticism. Any attempt to stifle or fetter such criticism amounts to political censorship of the most insidious and objectionable kind."

Statements of this sort demonstrate that there has been a dramatic change in the approach of the British judiciary, a change that enables them to rely upon the well-established democratic values when developing the law. In doing so now, they are still seeking to give effect to Parliament's intention. However, they do so by being more ready to assume that Parliament should be presumed not to have intended to act inconsistently with those values. In seeking to perform the latter task they have removed the shackles to which reference was made earlier. They look at the principles that have been developed in other jurisdictions. They are even now, as a result of a landmark decision in *Pepper v. Hart*,[24] prepared to take into account, in appropriate circumstances, what was stated in Parliament when the legislation was being promoted.

Where no legislation bars progress, considerable initiatives are permissible. For 250 years in the United Kingdom, a husband could not be guilty of raping his wife. However, as Lord Keith recognized, not only are these principles that the common law enshrines, they are also principles that are "capable of evolving in the light of changing social, economic and cultural developments." So a husband was held to have been guilty of committing rape on his wife.[25] The way in which the common law evolved has to be assessed against a broad international background—an international background that takes into account the developments across the common law world: New Zealand, Australia, India, South Africa, and North America—to which there has, as we have seen, to be added now the developments in Europe.

There are of course still areas where the growth is stunted. This is particularly true of the civil right of privacy. There is no such right in English law at the present time.[26] This is so notwithstanding that the latest decision in England recognizes that such a right had been developed on a case-by-case basis in the American courts and those cases were in turn inspired by a number of English nineteenth-century decisions.[27]

The position is that judges on my side of the Atlantic are still not comfortable in their lawmaking, especially if they perceive that it involves legislating. This was very apparent from the decision of the House in the very difficult and worrying case involving Anthony Bland,[28] who was reduced to a persistent vegetative state for three and a half years after suffering severe injuries in a football disaster. He continued to breathe unaided and his digestion continued to function, but he could not see, hear, taste, smell, speak, or communicate and was incapable even of involuntary movement. He could not feel pain and had no cognitive functions. In these circumstances, the doctors who had devotedly treated him wanted to know whether it would be appropriate to cease further treatment. This would involve withdrawing the artificial feeding and declining antibiotic treatment when infection appeared. It would involve his being deprived of sustenance, which would bring to an end the physical functioning of his body. The doctors were concerned over the legality of this course. The courts could only help by providing a remedy when in the past no remedy would have been thought possible. They came to the conclusion that a declaration as to the legality of what was proposed should be granted. They did, however, also lay down suitable safeguards. The development of the law in this manner caused profound concern for two members of the House in particular. Lord Browne-Wilkinson said:

> If the judges seek to develop new law to regulate the new circumstances, the law so laid down will of necessity reflect judges' views on the underlying ethical questions, questions on which there is a legitimate division of opinion. . . . Where a case raises wholly new moral and social issues, in my judgment it is not for the judges to seek to develop new, all-embracing, principles of law in a way which reflects the individual judges' moral stance when society as a whole is substantially divided on the relevant moral issues. . . . It seems to me imperative that the moral, social and legal issues raised by this case should be considered by Parliament. The judges' function in this area of the law should be to apply the principles which society, through the democratic process, adopts, not to impose their standards on society. If Parliament fails to act, then judge-made law will of necessity through a gradual and uncertain process provide a legal answer to each new question as it arises. But in my judgment that is not the best way to proceed.[29]

Lord Mustill was equally worried. Having referred to the combination of sympathy and respect that motivated an urgent desire to take up the burden and reach a conclusion and put that conclusion into effect as speedily and humanely as possible, he added that

> [t]his task does, however, have its own risks for it leads to an assumption that the central question of ethics is the only question and that anything which stands in the way of a solution should be brushed aside as an empty technicality. However natural this impulse may be, I believe it must be resisted for the authority of the state, through the medium of the court, is being invoked by one group of citizens to terminate the life of another. . . . The Court must therefore be concerned not only to find a humane and morally justified solution to the problem of those directly involved but also to examine rigorously both the process by which the solution is reached and the legal foundation on which it rests. Otherwise the pressure created by this extreme case may distort the law in a way which leads to false conclusions in situations where the issues are similar but more finely balanced and may, in addition, create unforeseen anomalies in criminal cases far removed from the present.[30]

He then went on to say that "it was on the legal rather than the ethical aspects of the appeal that he would dwell."

There is, indeed, a very careful distinction to be drawn, a distinction that can perhaps be said to involve the uncertain line between lawmaking and legislating. In making rape between husband and wife into a crime, as they did recently, has the House of Lords overstepped the line? In *R. v. Brown*,[31] the House of Lords had to decide whether sadomasochistic practices that resulted in actual bodily harm and unlawful wounding when done between consenting adults in private was criminal. The majority of three thought it was, but the minority thought this decision constituted unwarranted judicial lawmaking. There are bound to be cases in which it is debatable as to which side of the line the case falls. Though it is essential to be conscious of the dangers and therefore to move forward cautiously, I have no doubt that progress by the judiciary is justified, as long as that progress is based on principle. Indeed if those principles are as fundamental as those identified by Chief Justice Warren, not to progress would be to abrogate judicial responsibility.

There are, therefore, situations where significant developments can take place without giving rise to the same degree of hesitancy on the part of the judiciary. One such case was *R. v. The Horseferry Magistrates Court Ex parte Bennett.*[32] The question for determination was whether the concept of abuse of process (due process), which would justify a trial being stopped, was confined to what happened during the course of the trial itself or extended to an unlawful extradition. Here, Bennett was being extradited from South Africa to New Zealand, by a journey that involved a surprising stop at London. A gratifying route for the British police, who were waiting to greet him! Attention was paid to the decisions of American courts accepting jurisdiction in criminal cases regardless of the circumstances in which the accused was brought within the jurisdiction. Lord Griffiths identified the scope of the issue when he said:

> If the court is to have the power to interfere with the prosecution in the present circumstances it must be because the judiciary accept the responsibility for the maintenance of the rule of law that embraces a willingness to oversee executive action and to refuse to countenance behaviour which threatens either basic human rights or the rule of law. . . . I am in no doubt that the judiciary should accept this responsibility in the field of criminal law. The great growth of administrative law during the latter half of this century has occurred because of the recognition by the judiciary and Parliament alike that it is the function of the High Court to ensure that executive action is exercised responsibly and as Parliament intended.

Subsequently, this principle of abuse of process was taken further in two cases in the Privy Council. (The law lords sitting in the Privy Council still act as final court of appeal for some, but not all, [as you will be aware] former colonies.) Both involved Caribbean jurisdictions. In Jamaica, as in other Caribbean countries, there have been particular problems in relation to the death row phenomenon, which is partly brought about by the time that it takes to go through the processes of exercising a defendant's constitutional rights, including the right to apply to international bodies. In 1994 the Privy Council held[33] that a long delay in carrying out a sentence of death after that sentence had been passed could amount to inhuman punishment, or other treatment contrary to the Jamaican constitution, and also to an abuse of process. "Process" did not terminate with the passing of sentence but continued to cover the execution of sentence. The Privy Council made it clear that if capital punishment is to exist in a country, it must be carried with all possible expedition. If an execution is to take place more than five years after sentence there will be strong grounds for believing that delay of this length is unconstitutional. In coming to this conclusion, the Privy Council departed from its own previous decisions in 1979 and 1982 and of course took a different view from those that had been adopted in cases decided in the United States. The council was also influenced by the decision of the European Court in *Soering v. The United Kingdom*,[34] where it was considered that the decision of the U.K. home secretary to extradite someone to the United States to face a charge of capital murder would involve a breach of the European Convention of Human Rights. This was because of the delays that can exist in carrying out an execution in the United States.

The second case[35] involved an appeal to the Privy Council from the Caribbean, this time from Trinidad. The question at issue was the validity of a pardon that had been granted by a head of state in order to secure the end of the insurrection where, prior to the grant of the pardon, the parliament building had been seized, Ministers and others were being held hostage and the prime minister and another minister had been deliberately shot and wounded to further the ends of the insurrection. We found guidance in that case from the approach adopted in the United States authorities to a pardon given in the wake of the Civil War. The pardon was upheld, but the Privy Council came to the conclusion that nonetheless, because the condition to which the pardon was subject had not been complied with, it could not be relied on. It would be an abuse of process to prosecute the insurgents again. The relevance of the American authorities was heightened by the fact that apparently at that time the United States courts felt that they were giving a decision that reflected the approach of the English common law. This is an example of the way in which the two great common law jurisdictions sustain each other. Decisions in one jurisdiction cross the seas and fertilize the decision-making process in another jurisdiction. I believe this is what happened as a result of the immense energy and initiative of the Warren Court. I suspect that in developing the principles of abuse of process we were following the spirit of the inheritance that that Court left. In turn, in doing so, are the English Courts now taking forward further than the American Court the concepts of equality and due process and the protection of individual rights that the Warren Court propounded? If so, is it possible that in time your courts may build on European developments? Speculating in this way I do not ignore the fact that in 1994 there was another Anglo-American forum, and we had the pleasure of welcoming to our shores the American delegation, which included no fewer than three of your Supreme Court Justices, and, in addition, a fourth (to my knowledge) who visited our shores.[36] In any developed legal system there are periods when the flames of judicial creativity burn brightly. There are other periods when the fire appears almost to have been extinguished. Fortunately, however, there are usually embers that, as the result of a fresh wind, can be turned first into a strong glow and then a blaze. In my country, we are fortunate that the prevailing wind is normally one which blows easterly from the United States to our shores.

Notes

1. The Judicial Committee is the British equivalent of the U.S. Supreme Court.
2. Increased to twelve in 1995.
3. Schwartz, *The Unpublished Opinions of the Warren Court* 17 (1985).
4. Magor and St. Mellons Rural District Council v. Newport Corp., A.C. 189, 191 (1952).
5. Lester, "English Judges as Lawmakers," *Public Law* 271 (1993).
6. Wade, *Administrative Law* (6th ed. 1988).
7. Warren, "The Law and the Future," *Fortune*, November, 1955, at 107, and White, *Earl Warren: A Public Life* 223 (1982).
8. 347 U.S. 483 (1954).
9. See for example East African Asians Case, 3 Eur. H.R. 76 (1973).

10. See the admirable article of Lester, "The Overseas Trade in the American Bill of Rights," 88 *Colum. L. R.* 550 (1988).

11. "The Judge is Lawmaker," *J. Pub. Teachers of L.* 22 (1972).

12. Clarendon Press Oxford (1972). The passages quoted are from pp. 15 and 16.

13. 2 A.C. 237 (1983).

14. Wade, *Administrative Law* vii (6th ed. 1988).

15. Lester, supra note 5, at 279.

16. Id. at 279.

17. Attorney General v. Guardian Newspapers Ltd., 1 W.L.R. 1248 (1987).

18. See Brind v. Secretary of State for the Home Department, 1 A.P. 696 (1991).

19. No. 2 1 A.C. 109, 283–84 (1990).

20. Derbyshire County Council v. Times Newspapers Ltd., A.C. 534 (1993).

21. 307 Ill. 595 (1923).

22. 376 U.S. 254 (1964).

23. A.C. 312 (1992). Lord Bridge's quotation appears on p. 318.

24. 3 W.L.R. 1032 (1992).

25. R. v. R., 4 E.R. 481 (1991).

26. K. v. Robertson, R.S.R. 62 (1991).

27. See Lester, supra note 5, at 282 and the dissenting judgment of Justice Brennan and Justice Stephens in Cruzan v. Director, Missouri Department of Health, 497 U.S. 261 (1990).

28. Airedale National Health Service Trust v. Bland, A.C. 789 (1993).

29. Id. at 879–80.

30. Id. at 886.

31. 1 A.C. 212 (1994).

32. 1 A.C. 42 (1994). Lord Griffiths's quotation appears on pp. 61–62.

33. Pratt v. Attorney General of Jamaica, 2 A.C. 1, (1994).

34. 11 E.H.R.R. 439 (1989).

35. Attorney General of Trinidad & Tobago v. Phillip, 3 W.L.R. 1134 (1994).

36. A return visit by a British delegation was made in 1995.

· 23 ·

SPOOK OF EARL
The Spirit and Specter of the Warren Court

ALEX KOZINSKI

I have been assigned the task of criticizing the Warren Court, which, in the context of this love-fest, is rather like being asked to disclose embarrassing things about Santa Claus at a Christmas Party, or perhaps like being the master of ceremonies at a Mother Teresa roast. On the other hand, for a conservative like myself, what could be a more tantalizing target? After all, I have actually been hired to take potshots at the very embodiment of judicial activism, the antithesis of judicial restraint, the big, bad Warren Court. Where, oh where, does one begin?

Any criticism of the Warren Court—at least any honest and fair criticism—must start with the acknowledgment that this was a truly great Court, that many of its members were giants of our modern jurisprudence. It was a Court imbued with vision and courage at a time in our nation's history when vision and courage were scarce commodities. I am referring in particular to the Court's desegregation cases, starting with *Brown v. Board of Education*[1] and, perhaps more importantly, following through with the later cases[2] in the face of fierce political opposition and popular defiance.[3] Had the Warren Court done nothing else of substance, it would surely rank among the greatest of Supreme Courts.

Good as it was for the country that the Warren Court confronted the desegregation cases so early in its tenure, it may not have been the best thing for the Court itself. Let us face it: Effectively overruling a fifty-eight-year-old precedent,[4] staring down angry Southern politicians, precipitating a constitutional crisis when the president was required to call out federal troops to force Arkansas to integrate its schools,[5] suffering the vilification of so many citizens and ultimately coming out triumphant—all that is pretty heady stuff, even for the likes of Supreme Court Justices. The experience must have taught the Justices, and Earl Warren in particular, a thing or two: the importance of sticking to principle, the need for persistence, the absolute necessity of ignoring popular discontent with constitutionally based decisions.[6] Earl Warren himself learned of the influence a Chief Justice could have on his colleagues and the crucial importance of leadership within the Court.[7]

But there were some other lessons the Court no doubt learned from the desegregation cases, lessons that may have contributed to some of its more dubious later actions. The first concerned power: by precipitating a sea change in the area of race relations, the Court sensed the full sweep of its authority. If it could force the integration of schools and colleges, bus terminals[8] and other public facilities in states where many still thought about the days of slavery with nostalgia, what was there the Court could *not* do? The second lesson, more subtle but perhaps more important, had to do with justice. As Richard Kluger's book about the *Brown* decision proclaims,[9] what was at stake there was not merely an abstract constitutional principle, but also a matter of "simple justice." Now it is certainly a happy coincidence when the constitutional result is also the morally just result. But the two do not inevitably go together: For example, it may be constitutional to impose an income tax,[10] but few taxpayers think their taxes are just. The Constitution says aliens are entitled to less solicitude than American citizens,[11] but some argue that justice requires equal treatment for *all* people. And in what is perhaps the most egregious example of constitutional injustice, Article Two, Section One, requires that a candidate for president be a natural-born citizen and, alas, although I am a citizen and was born quite naturally, . . . well, you understand.

It is, of course, impossible to know for sure, but I suggest that the struggle and eventual triumph of the Court in the desegregation cases may have imbued some of its members—and Chief Justice Warren in particular—with the notion that the Court can serve as a powerful force for good, and that it should use its enormous power to make society more just—or at least to bring society into line with the Court's vision of justice. Chief Justice Warren wrote in 1955 that "it is the spirit and not the form of law that keeps justice alive."[12] But if doing justice, rather than following the Constitution, becomes the prime objective, the constitutional lever for achieving that just result becomes a secondary consideration; means to the end are mined from the crevices between the lines of constitutional text, or fabricated by stretching constitutional language beyond recognition. But focus on righting wrongs the Court did, seemingly pursuing a manifesto like that admirably expressed on Earl Warren's gravestone:

> Where there is injustice, we should correct it;
> where there is poverty, we should eliminate it;
> where there is corruption, we should stamp it out;
> where there is violence, we should punish it;
> where there is neglect, we should provide care;
> where there is war, we should restore peace;
> and wherever corrections are achieved we should add them
> permanently to our storehouse of treasures.[13]

Perhaps the best example of the Warren Court's penchant for tackling major social problems is the redistricting cases of the early and mid-1960's.[14] The central claim in these cases was relatively straightforward, and like the desegregation cases, these inspired an appeal to simple justice: The fellow down the road casts a vote that is twenty times more powerful—sometimes a hundred times more powerful—than mine. That is just as if I get to vote once while he votes twenty times. Now is that fair?

Claims of such inequity grew out of the failure of many states to reapportion political districts to keep pace with growing and shifting population patterns. In the nation as a whole in 1961, counties with a population under 25,000 had more than twice as many representatives as counties of over 100,000.[15] In thirteen states, districts encompassing less than a third of the population could elect solid majorities in both houses of the legislature.[16] The Tennessee legislative districts challenged in *Baker* had population disparities exceeding 22 to 1. In 1960, one California state senator represented 14,000 constituents, while another—the one from Los Angeles—represented six million.[17] The Court had last confronted malapportionment in 1946 in *Colegrove v. Green*,[18] when it held the issue nonjusticiable under the political question doctrine. By 1962, however, the Court was ready to deal with the issue and overruled *Colegrove*, much to the dismay of Justice Frankfurter, the author of the famous plurality opinion in that case.

Reversal of precedent is nothing new, and recent precedents are more easily overruled than ancient ones.[19] But what the Court did in *Baker v. Carr*, *Reynolds v. Sims*, and the other reapportionment cases was not merely to reconsider a judgment made just sixteen years earlier. By everyone's acknowledgment, what the Court did was to defy a century of constitutional history,[20] not to mention the language of the Fourteenth Amendment.[21]

The problem, as the Court saw it, was this: Although the system in many states had fallen badly out of kilter, apportionment decisions were the province of state legislatures, which had every incentive to maintain the status quo. As the Court well understood, all legislators, regardless of political persuasion and party affiliation, put one interest above all others: their own reelection. Legislators from low-population rural areas, who had lost voters to higher-density urban areas, would never vote for a plan that exported their jobs to a bunch of lucky city boys. In many states there was no other mechanism for achieving the redistricting that the legislature refused to perform. Consequently Tennessee had not been reapportioned since 1901,[22] even though state law called for reapportionment every ten years.[23] The political system, then, was sort of like a large turtle that had fallen on its back and could not right itself without help from an outside force, and the Court saw itself as that force.[24]

The reapportionment cases thus had two of three key ingredients in common with the desegregation cases: an apparent injustice and the power to do something about it. More tenuous was the third ingredient, the one the Court needed to legitimate its actions: a constitutional basis for its decision. Many years earlier, in *Luther v. Borden*,[25] the Court had rejected the Constitution's Guaranty Clause—which purports to ensure a republican form of government—as a source of judicial authority to second-guess the legitimacy of state governments.[26] The Court might have reconsidered or narrowed *Luther*, but instead it reached into the magic hat of equal protection, which had served so well in the desegregation cases, and pulled out the novel doctrine of "one man, one vote."

"One man, one vote" ranks right up there with "a chicken in every pot" and "two cars in every garage" as one of the all-time great political slogans, but it leaves a lot to be desired as a constitutional doctrine. To begin with, using the Equal Protection Clause, which concerns individual rights, to resolve structural questions of governance is itself a bit of a stretch. By and large, individual rights and government structure are covered by separate provisions in the Constitution;

equal protection seems eminently better suited to the former type of issue than to the latter.

More important, however, applying equal protection principles to questions of governance raises exotic questions about just exactly what equality means in that context. In the Court's view, equality is achieved by giving every voter not only a single vote, but also an equally weighted vote. According to the Court, in one of its most celebrated phrases, "Legislators represent people, not trees or acres."[27] Well, that's certainly a constitutional conversation-stopper; the only thing one can say in response is "So what?" To derive the principle that everyone's vote must have an equal weight, regardless of other circumstances, takes more than this colorful rhetorical flourish. In its struggle to find a constitutional rationale for its decision, the Court suggested that to give someone a vote that is weighted less than someone else's diminishes the first person's rights of citizenship. But this is a circular argument, for there is nothing about the right of citizenship per se that calls for an equally weighted vote—unless the Court says it does.

In fact, as is pointed out by Justice Frankfurter's dissent in *Baker*,[28] and Justice Harlan's in *Reynolds*,[29] it is perfectly plausible and rational to give votes different weights depending on other circumstances; indeed, to do so may serve the purpose of equality. The classic example, of course, is the U.S. Senate, where voters in Nevada and Rhode Island get to cast votes twenty-eight times more powerful than voters in California.[30] Does this make the voters of California second-class citizens? Would true equality be better served if both houses of Congress were elected based on population alone, and the interests of such people-poor states as Nevada and Alaska were overlooked?

The fact is, legislators *are* elected by people but, in a very real sense, they also represent the nonhuman resources in their districts, such as forests and acres of arable land. At least one of the members of the *Reynolds* majority, Justice Douglas, seemed to recognize this idea later in *Sierra Club v. Morton*,[31] where he argued that trees and other inanimate objects should be given standing for purposes of environmental litigation. One might have asked Justice Douglas, if trees should be entitled to sue in court, why shouldn't they also be represented in the legislature?

A plausible argument can also be made that strict equality of numbers does not accurately measure true equality of participation in government: The remoteness of rural voters from government services, and the difficulty rural voters have in gaining access to their representatives, might justify burdening these representatives with smaller constituencies.

At bottom, what the Warren Court did in the reapportionment cases was to rely on a particular political theory—the theory of strict voter equality—rather than a constitutional principle. In the years that followed, the country's political structure has been recast in the Court's image, as exact population equality became the hallmark of subsequent reapportionments.[32]

Whether this is a good thing or not is difficult to say. The tendency, of course, is to believe we live in the best of all worlds and to consider alternative realities as necessarily inferior. But let me try to conjecture at least some possible ill effects of totemistic adherence to population equality as the hallmark of reapportionment. The major effect of apportionment based on population to the exclusion of other criteria is that political power follows the voters the way water flows downhill. And a good thing, too, you might say. But perhaps, as the song goes, it ain't necessarily so.[33]

The tendency for votes to ebb and flow with demographics has meant that political power has shifted from rural areas to urban ones, and then from the inner cities to the suburbs.[34] Is it really wise, is it prudent, to have political power readily mimic, and thus reinforce, demographic changes? We are indeed a society of voters, but we are also a society of land and forests, of governments and institutions. There is something to be said for the view that voters should not be able to take their political power with them quite as easily as they root up their possessions, leaving those who stay behind—those on the farm, those in the inner city—with a decaying infrastructure and no political base to sustain it.

A system, such as existed in many states before *Baker* and *Reynolds*, where shifts in political power lag substantially behind shifts in population density, tends to discourage the easy decision to abandon one place for another, which we in America have come to take for granted. Are you unhappy with local schools? Don't like the traffic? Not enough police protection? Find yourself greeting new neighbors with "There goes the neighborhood"? Don't bother sticking around and trying to make it work. The cheap and easy answer is to pick up your marbles and move elsewhere, exacerbating the problems in the place you are leaving, and adding new problems to the one you are going to.

The strict population-based model may also have had some deleterious effects on racial and ethnic reapportionment. When it comes to providing remedies for such things as minority vote dilution, strict adherence to "one person, one vote" is usually a hindrance, not a help.[35] As Professor Lani Guinier observes, "The upshot of absolute population equality as the basis for representation is that equipopulous districts are more important than districts that preserve communities of interests or leave neighborhoods intact."[36] There's something to be said for a regime that allocates greater political power to a neighborhood ravaged by white flight—based precisely on the notion that schoolhouses, parks, libraries, and public swimming pools don't vote, but do require a political base for their continued upkeep. Such a regime might provide a far more honest and satisfying solution to the practical political problems of minorities than do endless quibbles about whether a district's lines are sufficiently straight or encompass precisely the right number and ethnic mix of voters.[37]

Whether or not you are persuaded that the one person–one vote system of governance is worse than the alternatives, it is nevertheless troubling that such a profound, such a pervasive and permanent change in the way we operate as a society, was effected by the judgment—the *political* judgment—of nine government officials who themselves are insulated from the political process.

Nor was reapportionment the only area where the Warren Court saw its mission as righting serious injustice with relatively little guidance from the constitutional text. Another area is criminal procedure, where the Court erected a number of rules governing the admissibility of evidence against defendants in criminal cases. That there was a need for restraining unfair and often unlawful police tactics is pretty clear, so it is difficult to take issue with the Court's objectives. Yet one cannot but marvel at the *deus ex machina* boldness of, for example, the *Miranda* litany[38] or the "reasonable expectation of privacy" standard derived from *Katz v. United States.*[39]

Nevertheless, you say, we ought not to quibble too much with the Court's methods: After all, it did manage to curb widespread police misconduct. Well, I was asked to contribute to this volume precisely to quibble, so I had better quibble with gusto. To begin with, there may well be more police misconduct still going on out there than we like to believe; it is hard to know, but some clues suggest that the rules adopted by the Supreme Court may only have driven the problem underground. The recent report of New York's Mollen Commission, for example, faces up to the open secret, long shared by prosecutors, defense lawyers and judges, that perjury is widespread among law enforcement officers.[40] As Alan Dershowitz has written,[41] new rules about what goes in the courtroom haven't changed the conduct of the police so much as encouraged them to perfect the fine art of "testilying." The advent of the home video camera has also started to offer us a glimpse of how police sometimes act when they don't think their conduct will be revealed in court.[42]

If these indications are typical, it may well be that we have only marginally dealt with the misconduct problem, but have added to it another, more serious problem. We may have engendered among law enforcement officials the Dirty Harry ethic—that constitutional rules are obstacles, placed in their path by criminal-coddling, pointy-headed, liberal judges, and that conscientious police officers must lie in court and otherwise cover up for each other. Perhaps it would have been wiser to leave the problem of police misconduct to the political branches of government, rather than fostering the complacent faith that there is no need to do anything because the courts—under the banner of the Constitution—have solved the problem.

And, while I'm quibbling, let me point out how very little is left of the Warren Court legacy in this area. The exclusionary rule is now so riddled with exceptions that it is the rare case indeed when evidence seized in a questionable manner is actually thrown out. The "reasonable expectation of privacy" standard, having had no constitutional mooring to begin with, and being devoid of objective meaning in any event, has become a means more of validating dubious searches than of throwing out unlawful ones.[43] And the expansion of federal habeas supervision over state convictions, itself a bold Warren Court departure from almost two centuries of precedent, alas is still with us, particularly in death penalty cases. But it is now so mired in the procedural quicksand of exhaustion, deliberate bypass, adequate and independent state grounds, abuse of the writ, and retroactivity, that the question of whether the defendant had a fair trial often gets lost in the process.[44] Nor, on the other side, should we overlook that the availability of federal habeas review—and the stay of execution that often comes with it—has turned the great writ into a procedural endgame that many death row petitioners use to postpone the inevitable, sometimes for years or decades.[45]

Perhaps as troubling as the areas where the Warren Court chose to mold society in its own image are the areas it ignored. As Professor Richard Epstein has pointed out, this was a quiescent time for Takings Clause jurisprudence. In the same vein, between 1953 and 1969, there were only four copyright cases before the Court. Only three cases even mention the Contract Clause;[46] the majority actually addressed (but of course rejected) the Contract Clause claim in only one of the three,[47] while in the other two cases the Contract Clause claim merited mention, and rejection, only in the dissent.[48] There were a mere three trademark cases, only one of which even discussed a substantive aspect of trademark law.[49] The Court just was not much interested in the problems of the business and property owner. The Court did take a variety of cases involving labor law and antitrust, but the results were overwhelmingly against business and property interests.[50]

Every Court, of course, reflects the philosophy and interests of its members, but evenhandedness is particularly important for an activist Court, as the Warren Court surely was. The Constitution features a variety of clauses protecting property and contracts no less prominently than those protecting speech, religion, and the other rights the Warren Court was so fond of enforcing. When a Court is activist—that is, when it reads constitutional protections broadly—it easily becomes subject to the charge that it is not following the Constitution but rather pursuing its own judgment of good and bad. The charge is less likely to stick if the Court adopts an activist stance toward all constitutional claims, not merely those the judges happen to favor as a matter of policy.

It is impossible, alas, to accuse the Warren Court of an overwhelming degree of evenhandedness when it comes to constitutional claims. Contrast, for instance, the following two Warren Court cases: *New York Times v. Sullivan*[51] and *Williamson v. Lee Optical.*[52] What can I possibly say about *Sullivan* that has not already been said? You could, of course, read the opinion again, or, better yet, read Anthony Lewis's excellent book, *Make No Law: The* Sullivan *Case and the First Amendment*. Or, best of all, read the brilliant review of Tony's book in the *Columbia Journalism Review*, authored by a certain Ninth Circuit Judge whose name modesty forbids me to mention.[53] Suffice to say that Justice Brennan, speaking for a unanimous Court, gave the First Amendment a broad and generous reading. Never mind that the constitutional text only prohibits laws abridging freedom of speech and freedom of the press, and here the Court was dealing with a libel lawsuit. The *effect* of such a lawsuit would be no different than a law prohibiting publication outright, Justice Brennan said, because the crushing liability from a verdict would effectively stifle free expression.[54]

Now, I have no trouble at all with *Sullivan*. In fact, I think it's an excellent example of the vigor with which judges and Justices should approach constitutional provisions that protect individuals from government oppression.

Contrast this, however, with the other case I mentioned, *Williamson*. There the Court considered an Oklahoma law that forbade opticians from grinding lenses, or even fitting a customer's own lenses to a new set of frames, without a prescription from an opthalmologist or an optometrist.[55] The district court had found that an optician could, with the simplest measurement, determine the power of a lens, even a broken one, and grind a new one of equivalent power.[56] And making a new frame for existing lenses certainly seems not to require a vast amount of medical expertise. Plainly what had happened was that the opthalmologists and optometrists had simply out-lobbied the opticians: They had convinced the Oklahoma legislature to give them a monopoly at the expense of both the consumer and the opticians.

How did the Supreme Court react? It struggled mightily to stay awake. Extremely uninterested in interfering with legislative judgements in the economic sphere, the Court bent over backwards to validate the entirely irrational and inefficient legislative judgment.

To be sure, *Sullivan* and *Williamson* are different in many ways and one cannot fault the Court merely for upholding a novel constitutional claim in one but not in the other. There is, however, a contrast in the zeal with which the two opinions go about their constitutional task. In *Sullivan*, Justice Brennan literally breathes life into the terse words of the First Amendment. He considers carefully not only what the language says, but what it *means*, what its purpose is. The amendment embodies "a profound national commitment to the principle that debate on public issues should be uninhibited, robust, and wide open."[57] Justice Black's concurrence characterizes the libel suit against the *New York Times* as not merely a private dispute between private parties—as it easily and fairly *could* have been characterized—but as a "technique for harassing and punishing a free press"[58] for supporting civil rights activities within the state of Alabama. "To punish the exercise of [the] right to discuss public affairs or to penalize it through libel judgments," Black argues, "is to abridge or shut off discussion of the very kind most needed."[59]

Contrast the ringing declarations of constitutional principle in *Sullivan* with this memorable prose from *Williamson*: "An eyeglass frame, considered in isolation, is only a piece of merchandise. But an eyeglass frame is not used in isolation . . . it is used with lenses; and lenses, pertaining as they do to the human eye, enter the field of health."[60] So it makes perfect sense to regulate the sale of frames because frames are connected to lenses and lenses pertain to eyes, and the eyebone's connected to the thighbone, and the thighbone's connected to the trombone. Even if you don't find this as silly as I do, you do have to wonder what *Williamson* would have looked like if the underlying claim there—namely that opticians and consumers were being sold down the river so that optometrists and opthalmologists could get rich—had been treated with as much respect and empathy as the *New York Times*'s claim in *Sullivan*.

And herein lies my final quibble with the Warren Court—and a fairly major quibble it is. By staking out certain constitutional areas in which it took an intense interest, and giving short shrift to others, the Warren Court contributed to the now widespread perception that there really *is* no such thing as constitutional law, that it's all a matter of the philosophy of the particular judges who are making the decision. This is a view that has come to dominate the thinking in our law schools and in the profession. It is certainly the view held firmly by those who pick judges and Justices in Washington, regardless of political party. The effort to create constitutional law by picking just the right individual (or by blocking the wrong individual) is the name of the game for both Democrats and Republicans. This attitude, if it persists, will mean that the Warren Court has essentially made itself obsolete. Who, after all, in the current climate would dare nominate, much less confirm, a former member of the Ku Klux Klan?[61] A politically active and highly outspoken law school professor?[62] A politician who was responsible for the wartime internment of Japanese Americans, and who then opposed their return saying, "If the Japs are released, no one will be able to tell a saboteur from any other Jap"?[63]

The Warren Court is often compared to a bevy of Platonic Guardians.[64] But to my mind there's a better Greek analogue for the Court: Icarus, whose flight toward the sun was noble, daring, dazzling, and set air travel back years. The Court at times shook the surly bonds of precedent and text, and struck out for the sun of Justice itself. In doing so, it may have clipped the wings of future Courts. But it has also forever changed the way we look at the sun.

Notes

I thank Mark Ouweleen, my law clerk, for his valuable assistance with this article.

1. 347 U.S. 483 (1954).

2. See, e.g., Alexander v. Holmes County Bd. of Educ., 396 U.S. 19 (1969) (compelling integration of schools and other facilities); Green v. County School Bd. 391 U.S. 430 (1968); Evans v. Newton, 382 U.S. 296 (1966); Heart of Atlanta Motel, Inc. v. United States 379 U.S. 241 (1964) (Civil Rights Act of 1964 prevents hotels and restaurants from refusing service to blacks); Katzenbach v. McClung, 379 U.S. 294 (1964); Goss v. Board of Education 373 U.S. 683 (1963) (invalidating transfer plans that allowed students to attend schools outside their districts in which their race was in the majority); Burton v. Wilmington Parking Authority 365 U.S. 715 (1961) (using doctrine of state action to compel private establishments to admit blacks); Cooper v. Aaron, 358 U.S. 1 (1958) (reaffirming Brown).

3. See Cooper v. Aaron, 358 U.S. at 15–16 (criticizing violent resistance to Brown); Freyer, "Hugo L. Black and the Warren Court in Retrospect," in *The Warren Court in Historical and Political Perspective* 86, 94 (Tushnet ed., 1993); Tushnet, *The Warren Court as History*, in id. at 1, 25–26.

4. Plessy v. Ferguson, 163 U.S. 537 (1896).

5. President Eisenhower sent federal troops to protect nine black high school students entering Little Rock's Central High School from crowds encouraged by Governor Orval Faubus. See Spritzer, "Thurgood Marshall: A Dedicated Career," 26 *Ariz. L.J.* 353, 364 (1994).

6. See Bork, *The Tempting of America* 77 (1990) ("Much of the rest of the Warren Court's history may be explained by the lesson it learned from its success in *Brown*.").

7. See Schwartz, *Super Chief: Earl Warren and His Supreme Court* 204 (1983) ("As [Justice Potter] Stewart sees it, Warren may not have been an intellectual, but 'he had instinctive qualities of leadership.'").

8. Pierson v. Ray, 386 U.S. 547 (1967).

9. Kluger, *Simple Justice: The History of* Brown v. Board of Education *and Black America's Struggle for Equality* (1975).

10. U.S. Const. Amend. XVI.

11. See, e.g., Mathews v. Diaz, 426 U.S. 67, 77–80 (1976) (conditioning alien eligibility for federal medical assistance benefits on five-year residency and application for permanent residence; classification based on alienage need only be reasonable under the Fifth Amendment).

12. Warren, "The Law and the Future," *Forbes*, Nov. 1955, 106, 224.

13. White, "Warren Court," in *Encyclopedia of the American Constitution* 2023, 2031 (Levy et al., eds. 1986).

14. Baker v. Carr, 369 U.S. 186 (1962) (ruling that political question doctrine does not bar Court from considering reapportionment cases); Gray v. Sanders, 372 U.S. 368 (1963) ("The conception of political equality from the Declaration of Independence, to Lincoln's Gettysburg Address, to the Fifteenth, Seventeenth, and Nineteenth Amend-

ments can mean only one thing—one person, one vote."); Reynolds v. Sims, 377 U.S. 533 (1964) (one man, one vote); Lucas v. Forty-Fourth Gen. Ass'y, 377 U.S. 713 (1964) (invalidating Colorado's districting plan which apportioned only one house of the state legislature on population basis).

15. Anderson, Note, "When Restraint Requires Activism: Partisan Gerrymandering and the Status Quo Ante," 42 *Stan. L. Rev.* 1549, 1555 (1990) (citing David and Eisenberg, *Devaluation of the Urban and Suburban Vote* 64 (1961)).

16. Ibid. (citing National Municipal League, *Compendium on Legislative Apportionment* 45 (1961)).

17. Weaver, *Warren: The Man, The Court, the Era* 238 (1967).

18. 328 U.S. 549 (1946).

19. See, e.g., Garcia v. San Antonio Metro. Transit Auth., 469 U.S. 528 (1985) (reversing National League of Cities v. Usery, 426 U.S. 833 (1976)); see also Payne v. Tennessee, 501 U.S. 808 (1991) (overruling cases that only four and two years earlier had held victim impact evidence inadmissible during the penalty phase of a capital trial); id. at 853–54 (Marshall, J., dissenting) (arguing that the majority's willingness to reconsider an opinion merely because it was narrowly decided over strong dissents undermines the rule of law and invites open defiance of precedents).

20. See Reynolds v. Sims, 377 U.S. at 590–91, 595–608 (Harlan, J., dissenting) (arguing that history shows the Fourteenth Amendment was intended to be inapplicable to state legislative apportionment, as courts recognized until 1962); Bork, *The Tempting of America* 85 (1990); Berger, "Robert Bork's Contribution to Original Intention," 84 *Nw. U. L. Rev.* 1167, 1183–85.

21. Reynolds, 377 U.S. at 593 (Harlan, J., dissenting) (claiming that Section 2 of the Fourteenth Amendment recognizes that states may abridge the right to vote).

22. See Baker v. Carr, 369 U.S. at 191.

23. Id. at 188.

24. In Colorado, however, there was a provision for a referendum, through which the electorate could resolve problems in apportionment. Nevertheless, in *Lucas*, the Court invalidated an apportionment scheme for violating "one man, one vote" even though the electorate had just approved that scheme. Go figure.

25. 48 U.S. 1 (1849).

26. For a perspicuous examination of the history and meaning of the Guaranty Clause, see generally Amar, "The Central Meaning of Republican Government: Popular Sovereignty, Majority Rule, and the Denominator Problem," 65 *U. Colo. L. Rev.* 749 (1994).

27. Reynolds v. Sims, 377 U.S. at 562.

28. 369 U.S. at 301–24.

29. 377 U.S. at 608–10.

30. Calculated using the following highly scientific method: Since all states have the same number of senators, simply divide California's population (about 26 to 27 million) by that of Nevada or Rhode Island (each about 970,000), and then do a lot of rounding off.

31. 405 U.S. 727, 741–43 (1972) (Douglas, J., dissenting).

32. See Issacharoff, "Judging Politics," 71 *Tex. L. Rev.* 1643, 1647–48 (1993) ("In the great reapportionment cases of the 1960's . . . the Supreme Court placed its decisive mark on the political institutions of this country more formidably than at any other point save perhaps the initial establishment of the power of judicial review in *Marbury v. Madison*"). Equipopulous apportionment became the sole measure of the fairness of the electoral process, reaching the point of absurdity in Karcher v. Daggett, 462 U.S. 725

(1983), where the Court invalidated New Jersey's congressional districting scheme not so much because of the manifest partisan gerrymandering, but because of a statistically insignificant deviation from the equipopulation principle. See Issacharoff, supra at 1650–56.

33. Gershwin, "It Ain't Necessarily So," in *Porgy and Bess*.

34. For a general discussion of such population shifts, see Jackson, *Crabgrass Frontier: The Suburbanization of the United States* (1985).

35. Computer technology has made it easy to design districts that are reasonably compact, perfectly equipopulous, and terribly gerrymandered. Minority voting strength can be diluted by "packing" minority voters to limit their influence to one or a few districts, and by "spreading" voters so that they constitute a small and powerless minority in a number of districts. See Guinier, "Groups, Representation, and Race-Conscious Districting: A Case of the Emperor's Clothes," 71 *Tex. L. Rev.* 1589, 1615 (1993). The focus on "one man, one vote" cannot eliminate these practices.

36. Id. at 1607.

37. In *Lucas*, Justice Stewart criticized the Court for privileging the personal right to vote over the efforts of local government to represent regional needs, communities of interest, or political subunits. 377 U.S. at 750 (Stewart, J., dissenting). See also Guinier, supra note 35, at 1607.

38. Miranda v. Arizona, 384 U.S. 436 (1966).

39. 389 U.S. 347, 360 (1967) (Harlan, J., concurring).

40. Mollen, et al., "Report of the Commission to Investigate Allegations of Police Corruption and the Anti-Corruption Procedures of the Police Department" 36–43 (1994) ("Our investigation indicated . . . that [perjury] is probably the most common form of police corruption facing the criminal justice system . . . .").

41. See Dershowitz, "Controlling the Cops: Accomplices to Perjury," *N.Y. Times*, May 2, 1994, at A17.

42. Of course the videotape of Los Angeles police beating Rodney King is the most famous example, but there are others. In May of 1994, police on Staten Island were videotaped beating a young handcuffed prisoner. See "Tape May Lead to Cops in Beating," *Record*, May 4, 1994, at A4. In July of 1994, an officer in the Los Angeles suburb of Compton repeatedly beat prone seventeen-year-old Felipe Saltero under the watchful eye of a neighbor's videocamera. See "Facts on File," *World News Digest*, Dec. 22, 1994, at 960 G1. In November of 1994, two Buffalo police officers were filmed in an exchange with two young men that sparked allegations of police brutality. Gryta, "Dillon Weighing Appeal in Zenner St. Incident," *Buffalo News*, Nov. 4, 1994, at 4.

43. See, e.g., California v. Greenwood, 486 U.S. 35 (1988) (ruling that there can be no reasonable expectation of privacy in discarded garbage left for collection outside home); Dow Chemical Co. v. United States, 476 U.S. 227 (1986) (ruling that the taking of precision aerial photographs from navigable airspace is not a search prohibited by Fourth Amendment); Oliver v. United States, 466 U.S. 170 (1984) (ruling that the Fourth Amendment protection does not extend to areas or activities conducted in "open fields"); United States v. Place, 462 U.S. 696 (1983) (ruling that a canine sniff of luggage is not a search under Fourth Amendment); see also United States v. Pinson, 24 F.3d 1056 (8th Cir. 1994) (ruling that the use of a thermal imager is not a search because there is no reasonable expectation of privacy in heat emissions).

44. "What matters to the overwhelming majority of this Court is not whether an individual was convicted in an unconstitutional manner . . . but rather, (a) when did we, the Supreme Court, first make it absolutely clear that the rights which were admittedly

violated were protected by the Constitution? (b) when did the unlawfully incarcerated . . . defendant file his claim, and did he successfully wend his way through every possible procedural obstacle erected by the state? and (c) did the state consider the question fully and fairly, even if erroneously? But not, I repeat, whether the constitutional rights of the defendant were violated." Reinhardt, "The Supreme Court, the Death Penalty, and the *Harris* Case," 102 *Yale L.J.* 205, 206–07 (1992).

45. See, e.g., United States v. Frady, 456 U.S. 152 (1982) (Frady, originally sentenced to death for first-degree murder in 1963, filed at least nine collateral attacks over twenty years.).

46. City of El Paso v. Simmons, 379 U.S. 497 (1965); Louisiana Power & Light Co. v. City of Thibodaux, 360 U.S. 25 (1959); Maryland Cas. Co. v. Cushing, 347 U.S. 409 (1954).

47. *El Paso,* 379 U.S. at 509.

48. See Louisiana Power & Light, 360 U.S. at 34 (Brennan, J., dissenting); *Cushing,* 347 U.S. at 428 (Black, J., dissenting).

49. That one is Fleischmann Corp. v. Maier Brewing, 386 U.S. 714 (1967), which held that attorneys' fees are not available in trademark infringement cases under the Lanham Act. The other two are Hudson Distributors v. Eli Lilly, 377 U.S. 386 (1964) (McGuire Act exempts from the prohibitions of the Sherman Act price schemes authorized by state statute permitting trademark owner to set minimum retail prices for his products), and Switzerland Cheese Ass'n v. E. Horne's Market, Inc., 385 U.S. 23 (1966) (ruling that denial of summary judgment is not an interlocutory order because does not reach the merits).

50. See Spaeth, *The Warren Court: Cases and Commentary* 34–35 (1966).

51. 376 U.S. 254 (1964).

52. 348 U.S. 483 (1955).

53. A Certain Ninth Circuit Judge, "The Bulwark Brennan Built," *Columbia Journalism Review* 85 (Nov.–Dec. 1991).

54. *Sullivan,* 376 U.S. at 277–78.

55. 348 U.S. at 485.

56. Id. at 486.

57. 376 U.S. at 270.

58. Id. at 295 (Black, J., concurring).

59. Id. at 297 (Black, J., concurring).

60. 348 U.S. at 490.

61. There was talk during Justice Black's confirmation hearings that he might have been a member of the Klan. Black said nothing. After his confirmation, the *Pittsburgh Post Gazette* presented proof that Black had been in the Klan from 1923 to 1925. Lewis, "Justice Black at 75: Still the Dissenter," in *The Supreme Court Under Earl Warren* 128, 128–29, 133 (Levy ed., 1972).

62. Many considered Harvard law professor Frankfurter a left-wing radical, in part because of his role in publicizing and criticizing the murder convictions of anarchists Sacco and Vanzetti. See Lewis, "An Appreciation of Justice Frankfurter," in Levy ed., supra note 61, at 122–23.

63. Lewis, "Earl Warren," in *Encyclopedia of the American Constitution* 2019, 2020 (Levy et al. eds., 1986).

64. "For myself, it would be most irksome to be ruled by a bevy of Platonic Guardians, even if I knew how to choose them, which I assuredly do not." Hand, *The Bill of Rights* 73 (The Oliver Wendell Holmes Lectures, 1958). See Lewis, 4 *Justices of the*

United States Supreme Court 1789–1969, at 2726 (1969) (stating that Warren was the "closest thing the United States has had to a Platonic Guardian, dispensing law from a throne without any sensed limits of power except what was seen as the good of society. Fortunately he was a decent, humane, honorable, democratic Guardian."), quoted in Berger, "Insulation of Judicial Usurpation," 44 *Ohio St. L.J.* 611, 638 (1983); White, "Earl Warren as Jurist," 67 *Va. L. Rev.* 461, 542 (1981).

• 24 •

WHAT THE WARREN COURT HAS MEANT TO AMERICA

DAVID J. GARROW

This chapter's title succinctly states the question that I have been asked to address. To answer it most directly and most specifically, I can say that the most appropriate response comes in four parts, three of which are readily visible and apparent. First, the Warren Court meant racial equality. Second, as Judge Kozinski has already discussed in the context of *Baker v. Carr*,[1] the Warren Court also meant political equality in the form of "one person, one vote." Third, and somewhat more prospectively, vis-à-vis *Griswold v. Connecticut*,[2] the Warren Court additionally meant sexual liberty and gender equality. And then, fourth and finally, in a point that other essays in this volume have not touched upon as much as they might, the Warren Court also, especially in the context of *Cooper v. Aaron*,[3] meant judicial courage and judicial authority.

The United States of today is to a very significant extent the product of what are perhaps the three most notable and justly famous Warren Court decisions: *Brown v. Board of Education*,[4] *Baker*, and *Griswold*. However, it is also incumbent upon us to turn the assigned question around a bit, and, in addition to asking "What did the Warren Court do for America?" to inquire as well as to "What did America do for the Warren Court?" for the important changes that the Warren Court helped produce in American life between 1954 and 1969 were of course not produced solely by the Court. To this equally crucial query I believe the answer comes in three parts—one which is readily apparent, a second which is both significantly ironic and somewhat obscure, and the third which I believe—at least within our context here—is potentially at least somewhat controversial.

Whether we look at *Brown*, or at *Baker*, or at *Griswold*, or at all three cases in tandem, we must of course first remember that judges and Justices played at most only one-third of the roles that helped produce those landmark decisions. All of us who write about the Court (whether historians or journalists or law professors) need to regularly remind ourselves that we are always in danger of saying too little about the litigants and the lawyers who bring their cases before the Court and too much about the nine individuals who sit on the high bench. Thanks particularly to Richard Kluger's invaluable book on *Brown*,[5] we all know that not only did

Thurgood Marshall and his fellow NAACP Legal Defense and Educational Fund attorneys play major roles in helping to produce *Brown*, but that other, far less heralded activists, such as Clarendon County's Reverend Joseph A. DeLaine, a major initiator of the *Brown* partner case of *Briggs v. Elliott*,[6] likewise were essential—and necessary—to the cases' origination and development.[7]

The role of Reverend DeLaine, and others like him, highlights how important ordinary citizens (without law degrees) were to the process that took *Briggs* and the other cases that comprised *Brown* up to the Supreme Court. But, second, if we ask the question "Who created the constitutional revolutions represented by *Brown*, and by *Baker*, and by *Griswold*?" the answer is not simply Thurgood Marshall and Reverend DeLaine in *Brown* and *Briggs*, or political reformers in *Baker*, or Planned Parenthood activists in *Griswold*, for the other people who also contributed significantly to creating those three substantive revolutions were the opposition. In the *Brown* case, of course, those roles were played by the raft of segregation-minded public officials who had failed to make good even on the legal protection that the Court had offered them in *Plessy v. Ferguson*[8] and its less well-remembered progeny.[9] In *Baker*, and in its even better-known progeny, *Reynolds v. Sims*,[10] the political revolution that was heralded by "one man, one vote" reapportionment was tremendously *assisted* by the forces of political reaction whose officeholders had refused to redistrict so many state legislatures, and not just those in Tennessee and Alabama.[11] And crucial to *Griswold*, of course, was the Roman Catholic church hierarchy, in Connecticut and in other northeastern states such as Massachusetts, which for upwards of fifty years had refused to in any way accept or tolerate reform or repeal of the nineteenth-century statutes that criminalized any use or distribution of contraceptives.

Too often when we speak of *Brown*, of *Baker*, or of *Griswold*, we think of these cases simply as decisions written and handed down by the Supreme Court without fully appreciating or acknowledging the historical and political contexts from which those cases emerged or sprang. But, thirdly and additionally—and this is the point that I identified somewhat earlier as being potentially controversial—with regard to the internal life of the Supreme Court itself, I believe that all of us who are historians are obligated to deal very straightforwardly and very forthrightly with the fact that Supreme Court clerks, not only today but also in the "glory years" of the Warren Court, often played a very major role in the construction and crafting of the Court's opinions.

For example, especially since the Bush administration's 1989 request, in the person of outgoing solicitor general Charles Fried, that the Court in *Webster v. Reproductive Health Services*[12] jettison and reverse *Roe v. Wade*,[13] it has been especially ironic that Fried—best known to most people for his Reagan administration service—played a predominant role, as Justice John M. Harlan's clerk in the 1960 term, in crafting Harlan's exceptionally influential and now justly famous dissent in *Poe v. Ullman*.[14] The Harlan dissent in *Poe* powerfully prepared the way for the outcome four years later in *Griswold*, and undeniably opened the doctrinal door—even Professor Fried acknowledged to the *Webster* Court that Harlan's dissent was "in some sense, the root of this area of law"[15]—to the ruling in *Roe v. Wade*. Likewise, another very well-known present-day law professor, Anthony Amsterdam, as Justice Frankfurter's clerk during that same term of Court, played a very major role in preparing both the majority opinion in *Poe* and the oft-quoted Frankfurter dissent in *Baker v. Carr* that came down nine months later.[16]

Previous papers have asserted that the Supreme Court today is both a less remarkable and decidedly less gifted body than was the Court of thirty or thirty-five years ago. With all due respect, I have to dissent from that generalization, first and foremost because the present Court has at least three members—the "three S's," one might say—who by any scholarly standard, irrespective of whether one heartily agrees or heartily disagrees with one or another Justice's jurisprudence, are intellectually the equal of any of the Justices that sat on the Warren Court. Indeed, we very much need to be critical rather than romantic when we look back at the "great Justices" of the Warren era, particularly at individual Justices such as Frankfurter, Douglas, and Black, whose doctrinal and analytical legacies have shrunk rather than grown with the passage of time. As we ought increasingly to realize and accept, the full light of history shows how some of these excessively celebrated jurists of the Warren era do not in actuality loom larger or look better than some of today's less-heralded Justices.[17]

Now, to turn, in order, to each of the three substantive areas that I highlighted at the outset—racial equality, political equality, and sexual liberty/gender equality. With regard to the landmark decision in *Brown v. Board of Education*, we nonetheless first and foremost have to acknowledge how the actual opinion in that case—just as in *Baker* and *Griswold*—is rightfully open to very significant criticism. First, and most starkly, the *Brown* opinion failed to offer as much legal ballast as it might have, particularly in failing to make use of good, existing Supreme Court precedents from the nineteenth century such as *Strauder v. West Virginia*.[18] Second, as many commentators from the black community have emphasized over the course of this past generation, the *Brown* Court—and the *Brown* opinion—also failed to appreciate or manifest any awareness of how Black America could experience—and generate—top-quality education apart from and independent of any cheek-by-jowl classroom exposure to white folks.[19]

Additionally, we often are too rosy-eyed with regard to how we speak of the Warren Court's behavior in race cases more generally. We justly celebrate *Brown*, and we correctly celebrate *Cooper v. Aaron*, but we usually fail to highlight how badly and ham-handedly the Court behaved in its two "successful" attempts to dodge *Naim v. Naim*[20] and we often fail to acknowledge how uncertain and muddled the Court was in its efforts to deal with a significant number of early 1960s Civil Rights movement protest cases.[21] We need to remember that, prior to the landmark Civil Rights Act of 1964, the Warren Court had been unable to produce five votes to affirm the principle that racial discrimination in public accommodations was constitutionally unacceptable. Likewise, we sometimes fail to point out how in its most crucial 1964 and 1966 civil rights rulings, upholding the constitutionality of first the Civil Rights Act of 1964[22] and then the Voting Rights Act of 1965,[23] the Warren Court was simply in the position of ratifying decidedly more dramatic and far-reaching legislative actions that had been initiated by successive presidents and approved by successive Congresses. Only in 1968, in a case that unfortunately is not well remembered or much cited any more, *Jones v. Alfred H. Mayer Co.*,[24] did the

Court by virtue of the Thirteenth Amendment finally voice a clear constitutional declaration that racial discrimination as a badge or incident of slavery was utterly unacceptable in twentieth-century America.

When one turns from racial equality to political equality, what one sees, beginning with *Baker* to *Gray*[25] and *Wesberry*[26] and then to the entire family of cases headed by *Reynolds*,[27] is once again—just as in the *Brown* and *Briggs* set of cases—very powerful evidence of how local activists and local attorneys all across the country forced this legal agenda of revolutionary redistricting and dramatic political change upon the Supreme Court. I am reminded of a story, a story that is very nicely told in Professor Schwartz's *Super Chief*,[28] that is perhaps the most memorable aspect of *Baker*'s consideration by the Court first during the 1960 term and then again in the 1961 term. In the 1960 term, the Court, wrestling with the question of whether *Baker* would lead them to essentially reverse *Colegrove v. Green*[29] on equal protection rather then "Republican Form of Government" grounds,[30] found itself split four to four, with Justice Potter Stewart uncertain and undecided. At Stewart's initiative, *Baker* was carried over into the 1961 term for reargument, but by the beginning of that next term, Stewart had made up his mind and knew that he was going to side with Chief Justice Warren and Justices Black, Brennan, and Douglas to hold that the scale of malapportionment that existed in Tennessee presented a justiciable case under the Fourteenth Amendment's Equal Protection Clause.[31]

Following Stewart's determination, *Baker* appeared to be headed toward formal announcement as a five-to-four decision. Among the Justices who intended to dissent was Tom C. Clark. With hearty encouragement from Justices Frankfurter and Harlan, who were each also preparing dissenting opinions, Justice Clark set to work on a dissent aimed at highlighting what other alternative avenues for representational reform and remedy the Tennessee plaintiffs and other underrepresented urban voters could pursue instead of seeking a far-reaching constitutional declaration from the Supreme Court.

Much to Justice Clark's surprise, and perhaps even more so to Justice Frankfurter's deep dismay and painful embarrassment, Justice Clark, after being encouraged to pursue this mission, came to the rather quick and highly ironic conclusion that actually there were not any alternative avenues of recourse for Tennessee's urban voters.[32] And, as students of the Court and of America's phenomenally far-reaching but now somewhat forgotten reapportionment revolution may well remember, Justice Clark instead authored a quite wonderful concurrence in *Baker v. Carr* that resulted in a six- rather than five-vote majority.[33] Since I for one have grown up without the benefit of a rural upbringing or childhood work on a family farm, there are a number of phrases in Justice Clark's concurrence which I am unable to fully appreciate (or explain to puzzled, city-bred students),[34] but I nonetheless would most heartily recommend Justice Clark's concurrence to anyone who is even the least bit tempted to accept or agree with any part of Judge Kozinski's critique of *Baker* and of the constitutional necessity of the one person–one vote reapportionment revolution. Clark's twelve-page concurrence demonstrates, perhaps more persuasively than any other *Baker* opinion, how that revolution, just like the one heralded by *Brown*, was in equal protection terms nothing more or less than a matter of simple justice; his *Baker* concurrence ought also to demonstrate to most anyone's satisfaction that Justice Clark has been an underrated Justice.

With regard to sexual liberty and gender equality, earlier chapters have made repeated reference to *Griswold v. Connecticut*. It is important to remember that *Griswold* involved the appeal from Connecticut state courts of two criminal convictions that the defendants, Estelle Griswold and Dr. C. Lee Buxton, had sustained for the crime of aiding and abetting married couples in the *use* of contraceptive devices and materials. Here again, as in *Brown*, *Briggs*, and *Baker*, the full story of the parties—both the litigants and the litigators—is a wonderfully rich history that conclusively and utterly disproves the dismissive characterizations of the *Griswold* decision that have often been offered by such commentators as former Judge Robert H. Bork.[35] But, here again, in what is perhaps the most dramatic example of the irony of which I spoke earlier concerning how crucial the opponents of change have been in post–World War II America, *Griswold* comes to pass as one of the major constitutional holdings of the Warren Court only because of the utter stubbornness with which the Roman Catholic hierarchy in Connecticut exercised its dominant political influence in the state legislature to block any liberalization of Connecticut's 1879 criminalization of birth control from 1923 right up until 1965.

Like *Brown*, *Griswold* too is, as Professor Feldman discusses in his chapter, unfortunately another good example of how the Warren Court, while rendering landmark decisions, often did not manage to propound or advance them in landmark opinions. And that is not only true of Justice Douglas's overly brief and far too hasty majority opinion in *Griswold*; it is also quite dramatically true of Justice Black's very simplistic and very unpersuasive dissent.[36] Although it is an argument that I am either hesitant and/or ambivalent about making, I am afraid that on all counts *Griswold* is a case that has to be cited against or in contradiction of anyone who seeks to contend that the "great Justices" of the 1960s were somehow intellectually superior to the Justices who sat on the Court either before their time or since.

Griswold's importance and the reason why it belongs in the same constitutional pantheon as *Brown* and *Baker*, of course, has relatively little to do with how it finally decriminalized the marital usage of birth control in Connecticut. Instead it has to do with the way in which *Griswold* opened the constitutional door to a "rights" conception that really no one in this country had ever envisioned or articulated prior to 1965: namely whether abortion, or more precisely a woman's desire to choose to have an abortion early in pregnancy, could imaginably merit constitutional protection as a constitutional "right." *Griswold*, by opening up the conceptual or intellectual space that led directly toward *Roe v. Wade* (and its equally important but often forgotten partner case of *Doe v. Bolton*,)[37] I think rather unarguably echoes forward into our time as just as significant and influential a Warren Court decision as *Brown* and *Baker*.

It bears some emphasis (although perhaps this slips beyond our 1969 Warren Court endpoint) that within the judicial context of 1970–1972, the constitutional argument that *Griswold*'s fundamental right to privacy ought to be extended to apply to the question of abortion was neither particularly controversial as a matter of doctrine (especially when one keeps in mind all of the lower court decisions in which this analysis was advanced and most oftentimes accepted, in advance of

Roe,)[38] nor—when one carefully absorbs that judicial context of 1970–1972—was the High Court's extension of *Griswold*'s privacy right to abortion in *Roe* really at all surprising.

All in all, it is very difficult to imagine the America of today without highlighting *Brown*, *Baker*, and *Griswold* as the three foremost judicial influences from the Warren Court era upon what our daily and public lives are now like. But, as mentioned at the outset, there is also a fourth utterly crucial and fundamental Warren Court legacy, one which in a certain fashion, particularly in the judicial context of this volume, is perhaps even more centrally important than *Brown*, *Baker*, and *Griswold*. That fourth legacy revolves around *Cooper v. Aaron*. *Cooper*, as many people will recall, was the 1958 resolution of the Little Rock school controversy that had been provoked exactly twelve months earlier by then Arkansas governor Orval Faubus. *Cooper*, especially when one looks at some of the latter passages in the Court's opinion,[39] is the most important and most intimate link between the Warren Court and the other great, formative Court—the Court of John Marshall.

The Warren Court in *Cooper*, in reaffirming the constitutional stature and status of *Brown*, really "pulled out all the stops" in reminding Americans, and particularly Southern segregationists like Governor Faubus, that *Marbury v. Madison*[40] was indeed the formative building block of American constitutional law and judicial authority. It is important to emphasize that *Cooper* was not just about Little Rock, or Orval Faubus, or even just simply about racial discrimination and school desegregation. *Cooper* at bottom was fundamentally about the institutional role and judicial supremacy of the Supreme Court in constitutional cases involving even intense political controversy and turmoil. In *Cooper*, it is important to remember, the Supreme Court "pulled out all the stops" not just substantively but also symbolically, for the *Cooper* opinion was presented to the American people in an utterly unique format, as jointly authored by all nine members of the Court, rather than—as is usually the case—as having been written by one Justice on behalf of his or her majority colleagues.

Cooper should be remembered as a crucial—and perhaps the utmost—legacy of the Warren Court. And, if anyone in the present day is inclined to doubt the importance of *Cooper* and what it represents, we need only refer to what a five-Justice majority did four years ago in *Planned Parenthood of Southeastern Pennsylvania v. Casey*,[41] the case in which the Court—and particularly the controlling trio of Justices O'Connor, Kennedy, and Souter—reaffirmed in a very clear and ringing manner the constitutional essence of *Roe v. Wade*. *Casey*, and *Casey*'s very intimate linkage to *Cooper*, merits mention because in the same way in which *Cooper* was not simply about race, *Casey* was not simply about abortion.

Casey, as perhaps anyone might agree after having the opportunity to carefully study the "trio" opinion, was, like *Cooper*, first and foremost about the institutional status and role and responsibility of the Supreme Court, especially in those instances where—like *Brown* and like *Roe*—constitutional precedent encounters intense and prolonged political opposition and turmoil. *Casey* not only acknowledges that substantive due process liberty is a central and inescapable part of America's constitutional guarantees of individual rights; the *Casey* majority also recognized that *Roe v.*

Wade has stood not just for Due Process Clause protection of a woman's right to choose abortion, but that *Roe* has also been absolutely essential to the realization or advancement of gender equality in the United States over the past twenty-odd years. Most particularly, *Casey* in terms of how the "trio" opinion acknowledges and articulates the importance of equal protection perspectives with regard to gender is in many ways a decided step forward from *Roe*.

But *Casey* is most important because it more than any other single recent decision is powerful present-day evidence of just how influential and significant the real legacy of the Warren Court is. Furthermore, *Casey* is also impressive evidence of how that legacy is very much a living legacy, because beyond *Brown*, beyond *Baker*, and beyond *Griswold*, what is most central to our constitutional history of the last forty-odd years is the acknowledgment—and I think it is the almost universal acknowledgment—that the Justices of the Supreme Court bear preeminent responsibility for applying and extending the fundamental constitutional guarantees of individual rights in (and into) contexts that were not fully appreciated or understood or even imagined, whether in the late eighteenth century or in the mid-nineteenth century.

Thus *Planned Parenthood v. Casey*, more than any other Supreme Court decision of the last two and one-half decades, signals and symbolizes how for us the Warren Court should not be "just" a question or topic of history, but how the Warren Court's legacy is indeed a very powerful and very real *living* presence both with the Supreme Court of today and with the Court that we will have in the future.

Notes

1. 369 U.S. 186 (1962).
2. 381 U.S. 479 (1965).
3. 358 U.S. 1 (1958).
4. 347 U.S. 483 (1954). See also Bolling v. Sharpe, 347 U.S. 497 (1954), and Brown v. Board of Education, 349 U.S. 294 (1955) ["*Brown II*"].
5. Kluger, *Simple Justice* (1976).
6. 98 F.Supp. 529, (E.D.S.C., 1951), *vacated and remanded*, 342 U.S. 350 (1952), 103 F.Supp. 920 (E.D.S.C., 1952).
7. See especially Kluger, supra note 5, at 3–26.
8. 163 U.S. 537 (1896).
9. See especially Cumming v. Richmond County Board of Education, 175 U.S. 528 (1899), and Gong Lum v. Rice, 275 U.S. 78 (1927).
10. 377 U.S. 533 (1964).
11. See also WMCA, Inc. v. Lomenzo, 377 U.S. 633 (1964) [New York], Maryland Committee for Fair Representation v. Tawes, 377 U.S. 656 (1964), Davis v. Mann, 377 U.S. 678 (1964) [Virginia], Roman v. Sincock, 377 U.S. 695 (1964) [Delaware], and Lucas v. Forty-Fourth General Assembly of Colorado, 377 U.S. 713 (1964).
12. 492 U.S. 490 (1989).
13. 410 U.S. 113 (1973).
14. 367 U.S. 497, 522 (1961). See also Garrow, *Liberty and Sexuality: The Right to Privacy and the Making of* Roe v. Wade, 174–75, 190–91 (1994).
15. Transcript of Oral Argument, *Webster v. Reproductive Health Services*, 26 April 1989, as quoted in Garrow, id. at 675.

16. Regarding Amsterdam and Poe, see Garrow, id. at 186, 190.

17. See, e.g., Gerhardt, "A Tale of Two Textualists: A Critical Comparison of Justices Black and Scalia," 74 *B. U. L. Rev.* 25–66 (1994).

18. 100 U.S. 303 (1879).

19. See Cruse, *Plural but Equal* (1987); cf. Garrow, "A Contrary View of Integration," *Boston Globe*, May 31, 1987, at B14–B16.

20. 350 U.S. 891 (1955), 350 U.S. 985 (1956).

21. See, e.g., Griffin v. Maryland, 373 U.S. 920 (1963), and Bell v. Maryland, 378 U.S. 226 (1964); see also Schwartz, *Super Chief: Earl Warren and His Supreme Court—A Judicial Biography*, 479–86, 508–25 (1983).

22. See Heart of Atlanta Motel v. U.S., 379 U.S. 241 (1964), and Katzenbach v. McClung, 379 U.S. 294 (1964).

23. See South Carolina v. Katzenbach, 383 U.S. 301 (1966).

24. 392 U.S. 409 (1968).

25. Gray v. Sanders, 372 U.S. 368 (1963).

26. Wesberry v. Sanders, 376 U.S. 1 (1964).

27. See note 11 supra.

28. See Schwartz, supra note 21, at 422–24.

29. 328 U.S. 549 (1946).

30. See U.S. Const. art. IV, § 4.

31. Schwartz, supra note 21, at 412–18.

32. Id. at 420–21, 422–24.

33. 369 U.S. 186, 251 (1962).

34. See, e.g., "the backlash of his own bull whip" (id. at 255), and "Instead of chasing those rabbits" (id. at 258).

35. See generally Garrow, supra note 14, at 196–255, especially at 264–68; cf. Kalman, "The Promise and Peril of Privacy," 22 *Rev. in Am. Hist.* 725–31, at 727–28 (1994) (*Liberty and Sexuality* "conclusively proves the stupidity of . . . Robert Bork's characterization of *Griswold* as 'practically an academic exercise'").

36. 381 U.S. 479, 507 (1965).

37. 410 U.S. 179 (1973).

38. See generally Garrow, supra note 14, at 389–472.

39. See 358 U.S. 1, 18.

40. 1 Cranch 137 (U.S. 1803).

41. 112 S.Ct. 2791 (1992).

• 25 •

THE LEGACY OF THE WARREN COURT

ANTHONY LEWIS

It is a great privilege for me to take part in this important volume, one with so many luminous contributors. I reported on the Warren Court for the *New York Times*, and I want to begin with a journalist's reminiscence of that time.

On the morning of June 15, 1964, a Monday and hence a decision day, the first decision to be announced was in *Reynolds v. Sims*,[1] the most important of the reapportionment cases. As Chief Justice Warren began reading portions of his opinion of the Court, pages passed copies to the solicitor general and to six reporters who in those days sat at small desks between counsel tables and the bench. As I listened and skimmed the printed opinion, I realized the momentous character of what was being announced: a judgment that would require the redistricting of virtually all the state legislative houses in this country. I scribbled a note to a friend sitting at the counsel table nearby, asking him how it felt to be present at the second American Constitutional Convention. It was perhaps a somewhat disrespectful quip, but it reflected the awe that all of us in that courtroom felt at what was happening.

That scene came back to me when I read my colleague Linda Greenhouse's report on the opening day of the Supreme Court's 1993 term. The Court dealt with more than 1,600 petitions for certiorari, she reported, and granted not a single one. She wrote: "The names and docket numbers of the rejected appeals marched across sixty-eight typewritten pages, comprising a kind of legal salon de refusés of dashed hopes and failed expectations."

A Court that acted like a second constitutional convention and one that is a salon de refusés: of course neither of those phrases really gives an accurate picture of the institution then and now. Life is more complicated. But those descriptions do convey a mood, a sense of what we came to expect from the Supreme Court in the Warren years and what we expect today. Then, it was a Court that undertook to grapple with fundamental problems of American governance and society, and solve them. Now, it is a Court that takes a more traditional—which is to say a more limited—view of the role of judges.

Rather than characterizing the attitude of Earl Warren and the Court that took his name, I should give you the words that the Chief Justice himself used in performing the Court's high function as he and his colleagues saw it. Here is a passage from his opinion in that same case, *Reynolds v. Sims*.

"We are told," Chief Justice Warren wrote,

> that the matter of apportioning representation in a state legislature is a complex and many-faceted one. We are advised that States can rationally consider factors other than population in apportioning legislative representation. We are admonished not to restrict the power of the States to impose differing views as to political philosophy on their citizens. We are cautioned about the dangers of entering into political thickets and mathematical quagmires. Our answer is this: a denial of constitutionally protected rights demands judicial protection; our oath and our office require no less of us. . . .
>
> To the extent that a citizen's right to vote is debased, he is that much less a citizen. The fact that an individual lives here or there is not a legitimate reason for overweighting or diluting the efficacy of his vote. . . . A citizen, a qualified voter, is no more nor no less so because he lives in the city or on the farm. This is the clear and strong command of our Constitution's Equal Protection Clause. This is an essential part of the concept of a government of laws and not men. This is at the heart of Lincoln's vision of "government of the people, by the people, [and] for the people." The Equal Protection Clause demands no less than substantially equal state legislative representation for all citizens, of all places as well as of all races."[2]

In that passage you can see the distinguishing marks of the Warren Court. It determined to resolve a fundamental question of American political organization: a question, moreover, that earlier Supreme Courts had said was unfit for judicial decision because it would lead judges, as Justice Frankfurter said, into a political thicket.[3] The problem was long-standing. Legislatures had had districts of unequal population, often grotesquely unequal, for decades. The Warren Court cut through those obstacles of precedent and history. It faced the substantive issue and laid down a sweeping new rule: one that would upset political patterns fixed for many years. And it did so without embarrassment, without agonizing over the proper role of the judges.

As was often the case with the transforming judgments of the Warren Court, the germ of the reapportionment decision came from Justice Hugo L. Black. He dissented when the Supreme Court first dismissed an attempt to litigate the constitutionality of unequal districts, in 1946.[4] He told me years later that when he circulated that dissenting opinion, his colleagues thought that he had gone over the edge. The argument of that dissent became the law in *Reynolds v. Sims.* But the opinion in that reapportionment case was a characteristic Earl Warren opinion: straightforward, unconcerned with nice questions of doctrine, dealing with the problem as a question of right and wrong.

The way the Chief Justice put the question really determined the answer. He did not ask whether the Constitution applied to the whole issue of legislative apportionment. He did not canvas the history of the Equal Protection Clause. He began with the premise that the democratic norm was equal treatment of individual voters and that the Equal Protection Clause embraced that norm, and then asked what departures from absolute numerical equality the Constitution would countenance.

He considered the idea of representation for geographical areas, one with a long history of approval in many states including his own, California, and dismissed it with disarming simplicity: "Legislators represent people, not trees or acres."[5]

When Chief Justice Warren was asked at the end of his life to name the most important decisions of his years on the Supreme Court, he put the reapportionment cases at the head of the list. In terms of the break with past legal doctrine, they were surely the most striking, the most daring. But for most Americans the landmark of those judicial years was *Brown v. Board of Education.*[6] And in terms of public and political reaction it was by far the more controversial of the two. After a brief flurry of outrage from the Senate Republican leader, Everett Dirksen, and threats to legislate the courts out of the field of political districting, the principle that state legislative districts must be based on population passed into the country's legal and political bloodstream. Courts deal regularly now with apportionment problems, and no one thinks that unusual or forbiddingly difficult.

But the problem of race remains a tormenting one for judges and for all of us. The school segregation case was a beginning, not an end. Affirmative action cases are among the more important on the Supreme Court's current docket. So are cases challenging the design of congressional districts so that members of a minority population have a good chance to elect one of theirs as a representative.

If we reflect on May 17, 1954, and the years since, I think we can see a paradox in *Brown v. Board of Education.* It did not lead to a stable set of rules in the law of race relations. It certainly did not solve the social problem, the racism and angry race-consciousness that continue to mar our society. Yet the decision was inescapably right. And courageous.

Think what it would have been like if the Supreme Court in 1954 had come out the other way: if it had upheld the constitutionality of racial segregation in public schools. It is hard to think that because it is almost unthinkable. America and the world had just seen the result of Nazi racism that began with making Jews wear yellow stars and ended in the Holocaust. For the Supreme Court to have held, in the context of that reality, that segregating children because of their skin color did not deny those segregated the equal protection of the laws would have been a legal and a moral travesty.

The school segregation decision was not a sudden break with precedent like the reapportionment cases. For fifteen years the Supreme Court had been whittling away at the unpleasant realities of the Southern claim that "separate but equal" public education was provided for blacks. The reality was that black colleges and schools, and for that matter black hospitals and other public facilities, were separate and grossly unequal. The Court first held that a Southern state had to provide the higher education desired by a black student within its own borders, not farm the student out to some other state.[7] Then it held that a separate law school set up by Texas for black students was not equal because, among other things, it lacked the alumni network and other intangible qualities that make for greatness in a law school.[8] The decision came to the verge of saying that separate could never be equal. But that was about graduate education.

To order an end to segregation in public schools remained a daunting decision for the Court. There, unlike higher education, children were compelled to attend.

And the scale of the problem was enormous: seventeen Southern and border states, with forty percent of the country's enrollment, required segregation in public schools. Moreover, as President Eisenhower reminded us in his calls for understanding of Southern attitudes, the states had created their school systems and built their school buildings in reliance on the Supreme Court's decision in *Plessy v. Ferguson*,[9] approving the "separate but equal" doctrine.

The difficulty of reordering public education in forty percent of the nation's schools made the Court approach the issue with exceptional care. A school segregation case reached the docket in 1951; the Justices sent it back to a lower court for further findings. *Brown* and its associated cases were argued in 1953 but then set down for reargument the next term. We know from various historical studies, notably Richard Kluger's *Simple Justice*,[10] that more than one member of the Court was reluctant to declare public school segregation unconstitutional. Justice Jackson proposed that the Court decline to decide the question, instead referring it to Congress for action under the clause of the Fourteenth Amendment authorizing Congress to enforce its terms. If that prescription had been followed, we can well imagine the political warfare that would have ensued, in Congress and the states. The effort to end racial segregation in schools and other public facilities would have been even more arduous and politically distorting than it was after *Brown*.

The segregation cases have been discussed by others in this volume, and I should not dwell on them. But I do want to recall another scene that I witnessed as a Supreme Court reporter. It was in the Little Rock school case, *Cooper v. Aaron*.[11] Counsel for the school board suggested that Governor Orval Faubus's opposition to segregation was a reason for delay. From the bench Chief Justice Warren said: "I have never heard such an argument in a court of justice before, and I have tried many a case through many a year. I never heard a lawyer say that the statement of a Governor as to what was legal or illegal should control the action of any court."

The sense of outrage expressed by Earl Warren in those unusually personal terms eventually stiffened the Court's resolve and ended what Southern politicians called "massive resistance" to desegregation. Events stiffened the country's resolve, too. Before the *Brown* decision, most Americans had really been unaware of the true nature of what was called the Southern way of life, its cruelty and brutality. They did not know that blacks were prevented from voting by trick and threat in large parts of the Deep South. They did not know that in a city like Birmingham, Alabama, taxicabs were segregated, and department store restrooms; that blacks could not sit at lunch counters or use most hotels. The *Brown* decision encouraged black people in the South to resist those indignities. To put it another way, *Brown v. Board of Education* made possible Rosa Parks and Martin Luther King, Jr. As Dr. King's Civil Rights movement exposed the true nature of racism, Congress responded with the first serious civil rights legislation in a century. Blacks could vote, and they did. Southern politics was transformed.

A third great area of the law in which the Warren Court confronted history and made a liberating change in our society was freedom of speech. We think of this country as one dedicated to openness, to freedom even for the thought that we hate. But that phrase was used by Justice Holmes in dissent. And through most of its history the Supreme Court had not been a brave defender of unpopular speech.

Here again others have addressed the subject in this volume, but I cannot omit some mention of one of the most important legacies of the Warren Court.

The decision in *New York Times v. Sullivan*[12] is treated by my profession, the press, as *its* great victory. It was that: the imposition of constitutional restraints on libel actions for the first time. But Justice Brennan's opinion was not in fact an essay on freedom of the press. It was about the freedom of all Americans to criticize their rulers, government and government officials. "The citizen-critics of government," Justice Brennan called them. Gathering together the threads of free speech doctrine, often laid down in dissent, he said that we live in a society committed to robust, uninhibited speech about public matters. He found the old English crime of seditious libel, punishment for criticism of the state, inconsistent with the First Amendment. James Madison's view of American freedom, argued 166 years earlier, became constitutional law.

The Warren Court liberated American society in another aspect of speech and press: the law of obscenity. That may seem a strange thing to say, given the tortuous trail of decisions in this field, but I have no doubt that we have ended up a much less puritanical country than we were as recently as the early postwar years, when the Watch and Ward Society of Boston was still bringing about the banning of serious literary works.

The change began with Justice Brennan's opinion of the Court in *Roth v. United States*[13] How odd, you may think: for Justice Brennan said in that opinion that obscene matter was outside the protection of the First Amendment. But the importance of the case lay in its definition of obscenity. As explained in later cases, nothing could be obscene unless it was utterly without redeeming social value, and it was up to judges to see that the censorious did not go beyond that strict boundary. The efforts of the Supreme Court to apply that liberating rule produced a certain amount of hilarity, with the Justices watching dubious movies—except for Justice Black, who in principle thought nothing could be banned although he warned his wife against possibly racy films—and the Court often reversing censorship actions without opinion. But even with later modifications of the *Roth* definition, allowing localities to differ in their judgments of what is socially acceptable, we are less plagued by blue-nosed censors than we were. It was also highly significant when the Warren Court forbade the banning of films that were thought to have an improper theme: a sympathetic view of adultery in the case at hand in 1959.[14]

The record of the Warren Court was less happy, and less courageous, when it came to another test of First Amendment freedoms: the rights of Americans accused of association with Communism. It was a crucial test at the time, the time of Senator Joe McCarthy and the Red Scare. Congress was busy investigating alleged Communists and passing all kinds of legislation described as protecting us from Communist influence. The executive was prosecuting Communists, deporting them and removing federal employees as supposed security risks.

In 1954, the same year as *Brown v. Board of Education*, the Court decided *Galvan v. Press.*[15] Galvan was a resident alien who had come to the United States at the age of seven in 1918, lived here ever since, and had an American wife and four children. From 1944 to 1946 or 1947, he had been a member of the Communist Party, which was a legal party at the time. But the McCarran-Walter Immigration

Act of 1950 retrospectively made membership in the party at any time after entry ground for deportation. The government moved to deport Galvan, and the Supreme Court upheld a deportation order. Only Justice Black, joined by Justice Douglas, argued in dissent that the freedoms of speech and association guaranteed by the First Amendment protected aliens as they did citizens from subsequent penalties for exercising those rights. Chief Justice Warren was with the majority.

That same year there was *Barsky v. Board of Regents.*[16] Edward K. Barsky, a distinguished New York doctor, had been called before the House Committee on Un-American Activities and directed to produce the records of the Joint Anti-Fascist Refugee Committee. When he refused, he was convicted for contempt of Congress. Then the New York Board of Regents suspended his license to practice medicine. He argued that the weighing of political matters unrelated to his fitness to practice medicine was unconstitutional. The Supreme Court rejected his claim, Justices Frankfurter, Black, and Douglas dissenting.

The two cases indicate the mood of those years on anything to do with Communism: a mood that today seems paranoid. The cases also show, in my view, that in his first term on the Court, Chief Justice Warren had not yet found his way to his own deepest beliefs. After that term I know of no case in which he was unresponsive to a claim by someone suffering for his beliefs or associations. It is impossible to imagine the later Earl Warren, the one we remember, voting as he did in the *Barsky* case.

Barsky was not the only decision in which the Court found First Amendment interests outweighed by the claims of a congressional investigating committee. In *Watkins v. United States,*[17] an opinion by the Chief Justice reversed a contempt conviction on the ground that the committee had not adequately defined the "question under inquiry" or the pertinence to it of what the witness was asked. But it was a narrow victory for the witness, and a rare one in those years.

The worst of the congressional investigation cases, in my judgment—indeed the low point of the First Amendment after the Court sustained the conviction of Communist Party leaders in 1951[18]—was the *Barenblatt* decision of 1959.[19] A former instructor at Vassar College had refused to answer questions by the Un-American Activities Committee about alleged Communist associations. It would be hard to imagine a more dangerous area for a congressional committee to probe than the mind and associations of a college teacher, or one more remote from any serious security interest of the United States. But the Supreme Court affirmed the conviction. Justices Black and Douglas were now joined in dissent by the Chief Justice and by Justice Brennan, who had joined the Court since the *Barsky* decision. The same five-to-four majority sustained, in 1961, the constitutionality of a clause in the Smith Act making criminal mere membership in a party advocating the government's overthrow.[20] The same year the Court rejected First Amendment objections to an order by the Subversive Activities Control Board requiring the Communist Party to register.[21]

How long ago and far away those decisions seem now. The very idea of having a "Subversive Activities Control Board" or an "Un-American Activities Committee" is embarrassing. And within a few years the Supreme Court turned away from the premises of those decisions.

In 1964 the Court struck down, as a violation of the liberty to travel embraced in the Fifth Amendment, a provision of the Subversive Activities Control Act making it a crime for a member of any organization required to register to apply for or use a passport.[22] A year later the Court held that individuals could counter registration orders by invoking the Fifth Amendment privilege against compelled self-incrimination.[23] And the same year a federal statute requiring the Post Office to detain "Communist political propaganda" mailed from abroad unless and until the addressee requested its delivery was found to violate the First Amendment.[24] It was the first time a federal law had been held to conflict with the First Amendment: the first after 174 years of the Bill of Rights.

Some of these later cases involving Communism, and others that there is no space to mention, came out as they did because the membership of the Supreme Court had changed: a reminder that the phrase "the Warren Court" is not some absolute term. But occasionally the Court was unanimous. It had found the courage to confront government arguments that any suspicion of a Communist connection was enough to trump the First Amendment.

The fourth large area of constitutional law on which the Warren Court left a deep imprint was of course the criminal law. After what has been written earlier in this volume, I need do no more than sketch what amounted to a revolution.

Over many decades the Supreme Court had refused to read into the Fourteenth Amendment, and thereby apply to the states in the same terms, the specific protections afforded by the Bill of Rights against abuses by the federal government in criminal matters. The Warren Court overturned that historic reluctance and, one after another, applied the criminal law restraints to state proceedings. It did so unanimously, and to general approval, in 1963 in the *Gideon* case,[25] applying to the states the rule derived from the Sixth Amendment's guarantee of the right to counsel that lawyers must be provided by the state to defendants too poor to hire their own. There was more controversy when the Warren Court, again overruling earlier decisions, read into the Fourteenth Amendment the Fourth Amendment's protection against unreasonable searches and seizures,[26] the Fifth Amendment's privilege against self-incrimination,[27] the Eighth Amendment's prohibition of cruel and unusual punishments[28] and other provisions of the Bill of Rights.

The greatest controversy in this field was stirred by Chief Justice Warren's opinion in the *Miranda* case in 1966,[29] holding that the police must warn every arrested person before questioning that he has a right to counsel and a right to remain silent. Police and prosecutors called the decision a devastating blow to law enforcement.

The years since *Miranda* have demonstrated that the cries of havoc were foolish. The "Miranda warning" has become institutionalized, as familiar to television viewers as to the police, and there is no indication that it has had any noticeable effect on the difficult task of fighting crime.

But public concern about crime, and the easy political tactic of blaming it on soft-headed judges, have had significant effects on the law. The applications of the Bill of Rights to the states remain a lasting landmark of the Warren Court. But the content of some of those protections has been weakened by a changed Supreme Court. Today's Justices are less ready to find that a search was unreasonable. They are much less ready to let a state prisoner challenge his conviction, or in capital cases his death sentence, by federal habeas corpus; the Court has erected a series of technical barriers to habeas corpus relief that would win Yossarian's admiration. We have to conclude that the Warren Court's bold efforts in the criminal law field were less successful, less lasting, than in reapportionment or race or freedom of expression.

The *Miranda* decision was criticized for a reason other than its putative effect on law enforcement. The Chief Justice's opinion, laying out what amounted to a code of police procedure after arrest, seemed to some more legislative than judicial in character. That leads to a more general criticism of the Warren Court.

Justice John Marshall Harlan expressed it eloquently in his dissent in the reapportionment cases. "These decisions," he wrote, "give support to a current mistaken view of the Constitution and the constitutional function of this Court. This view, in a nutshell, is that every major social ill in this country can find its cure in some constitutional 'principle,' and that this Court should 'take the lead' in promoting reform when other branches of government fail to act. The Constitution is not a panacea for every blot upon the public welfare, nor should this Court, ordained as a judicial body, be thought of as a general haven for reform movements."[30]

The question is whether a body of judges, appointed for life and subject to no direct popular control, should be so assertive, so free-wheeling, in applying the law of the Constitution to profound problems of American society. Should it read the Constitution so expansively? Some critics of the Warren Court were aggrieved partisans of defeated causes: Southern racists, for example. But others, even while agreeing with the results of the Court's bold ventures, questioned whether the Court should have undertaken the role it did. They remembered when earlier Justices, equally confident of right and wrong, ruled that a state could not limit the work of bakers to ten hours a day[31] and held unconstitutional a federal law against interstate shipment of goods made by child labor.[32]

Undoubtedly there were examples of overreaching; there were mistakes. But three decades later the major decisions of the Warren Court seem to me to stand up well on the whole. In particular, I think time has proved quite wrong the complaint that the Court's activist role was inconsistent with democracy. The reality is to the contrary.

The rotten boroughs that existed in many state legislatures before *Reynolds v. Sims*—the gross malapportionments—were by definition not curable by ordinary political means. The politicians who benefited from the inequality would not vote themselves out of office. By deciding the question as it did, the Warren Court made this a far more democratic society, our legislatures more representative. Similarly on the racial issue, the Court's willingness to deal with a social ill that Congress had ignored for nearly a century awoke the country's conscience and, in the end, forced politicians to act. Of the First Amendment decisions, the ones that seem wrong now—indeed shameful—are those like *Galvan v. Press* and *Barenblatt* that yielded to anti-Communist hysteria. The dominant thrust of the cases on freedom of expression and association made this a more open society than it has ever been, more tolerant of thoughts that we hate. Today few conservatives *or* liberals would want to go back to a time when Americans were imprisoned for their opinions.

Ronald Dworkin has lately made an important counterargument to the contention, often heard, that the constitutional role of the Supreme Court is undemocratic. Political institutions, he said, devoted as they are to the art of compromise, seldom consider issues in terms of moral principles. But when the Supreme Court makes a great decision of principle, it starts a debate in political forums and among the public—a debate, Dworkin suggests, closer to the ideal of republican government than what the legislative process on its own is likely to produce. That certainly was true on the issue of race.

Looking at the United States today, with its high level of public cynicism and political frustration, I sometimes long for a new era of judicial leadership. We cannot expect that from our more cautious contemporary Justices. The age of judicial heroism is past. But I think we are a better country, more free and more just, because of the legacy of the Warren Court.

Notes

1. 377 U.S. 533 (1964).
2. Id. at 566–67.
3. Colegrove v. Green, 328 U.S. 549, 556 (1946).
4. Id. at 566.
5. 377 U.S. 533, 562.
6. 347 U.S. 483 (1954).
7. Missouri *ex rel.* Gaines v. Canada, 305 U.S. 337 (1938).
8. Sweatt v. Painter, 339 U.S. 629 (1950).
9. 163 U.S. 537 (1896).
10. Kluger, *Simple Justice* (1975).
11. 358 U.S. 1 (1958).
12. 376 U.S. 254 (1964).
13. 354 U.S. 476 (1957).
14. Kingsley International Pictures v. Regents, 360 U.S. 684 (1959).
15. 347 U.S. 522 (1954).
16. 347 U.S. 442 (1954).
17. 354 U.S. 178 (1957).
18. Dennis v. United States, 341 U.S. 494 (1951).
19. Barenblatt v. United States, 360 U.S. 109 (1959).
20. Scales v. United States, 367 U.S. 203 (1961).
21. Communist Party v. Subversive Activities Control Bd., 367 U.S. 1 (1961).
22. Aptheker v. Secretary of State, 378 U.S. 500 (1964).
23. Albertson v. Subversive Activities Control Bd., 382 U.S. 70 (1965).
24. Lamont v. Postmaster General, 381 U.S. 301 (1965).
25. Gideon v. Wainright, 372 U.S. 335 (1963).
26. Mapp v. Ohio, 367 U.S. 643 (1961).
27. Malloy v. Hogan, 378 U.S. 1 (1964).
28. Robinson v. California, 370 U.S. 660 (1962).
29. Miranda v. Arizona, 384 U.S. 436 (1966).
30. Reynolds v. Sims, 377 U.S. 533, 624–25.
31. Lochner v. New York, 198 U.S. 45 (1905).
32. Hammer v. Dagenhart, 247 U.S. 251 (1918).